Media Law, Ethics, and Policy in the Digital Age

Nhamo A. Mhiripiri
Midlands State University, Zimbabwe & St. Augustine University, Tanzania

Tendai Chari
University of Venda, South Africa

A volume in the Advances in Media, Entertainment, and the Arts (AMEA) Book Series

IGI GLOBAL
DISSEMINATOR OF KNOWLEDGE

www.igi-global.com

Published in the United States of America by
IGI Global
Information Science Reference (an imprint of IGI Global)
701 E. Chocolate Avenue
Hershey PA, USA 17033
Tel: 717-533-8845
Fax: 717-533-8661
E-mail: cust@igi-global.com
Web site: http://www.igi-global.com

Library of Congress Cataloging-in-Publication Data

Names: Mhiripiri, Nhamo A., editor. | Chari, Tendai, editor.
Title: Media law, ethics, and policy in the digital age / Nhamo A. Mhiripiri, Midlands State University, Zimbabwe & St. Augustine University, Tanzania, Tendai Chari, Univesity of Venda, South Africa, editors.
Description: Hershey PA : IGI Global, [2017] | Series: Advances in media, entertainment, and the arts (AMEA) book series | "Premier Reference Source"--Cover. | Includes bibliographical references and index.
Identifiers: LCCN 2016054401| ISBN 9781522520955 (hardcover) | ISBN 9781522520962 (ebook)
Subjects: LCSH: Mass media--Law and legislation. | Digital media--Law and legislation. | Mass media--Law and legislation--Africa, Sub-Saharan.
Classification: LCC K4240 .M434 2017 | DDC 302.23/1--dc23 LC record available at https://lccn.loc.gov/2016054401

This book is published in the IGI Global book series Advances in Media, Entertainment, and the Arts (AMEA) (ISSN: Pending; eISSN: pending)

British Cataloguing in Publication Data
A Cataloguing in Publication record for this book is available from the British Library.

For electronic access to this publication, please contact: eresources@igi-global.com.

Advances in Media, Entertainment, and the Arts (AMEA) Book Series

Giuseppe Amoruso
Politecnico di Milano, Italy

ISSN:Pending
EISSN:pending

MISSION

Throughout time, technical and artistic cultures have integrated creative expression and innovation into industrial and craft processes. Art, entertainment and the media have provided means for societal self-expression and for economic and technical growth through creative processes.

The **Advances in Media, Entertainment, and the Arts (AMEA)** book series aims to explore current academic research in the field of artistic and design methodologies, applied arts, music, film, television, and news industries, as well as popular culture. Encompassing titles which focus on the latest research surrounding different design areas, services and strategies for communication and social innovation, cultural heritage, digital and print media, journalism, data visualization, gaming, design representation, television and film, as well as both the fine applied and performing arts, the AMEA book series is ideally suited for researchers, students, cultural theorists, and media professionals.

COVERAGE

- Visual Computing
- Drawing
- Print Media
- Blogging & Journalism
- Traditional Arts
- Fabrication and prototyping
- Digital Heritage
- Digital Media
- Gaming
- Color Studies

IGI Global is currently accepting manuscripts for publication within this series. To submit a proposal for a volume in this series, please contact our Acquisition Editors at Acquisitions@igi-global.com or visit: http://www.igi-global.com/publish/.

The Advances in Media, Entertainment, and the Arts (AMEA) Book Series (ISSN Pending) is published by IGI Global, 701 E. Chocolate Avenue, Hershey, PA 17033-1240, USA, www.igi-global.com. This series is composed of titles available for purchase individually; each title is edited to be contextually exclusive from any other title within the series. For pricing and ordering information please visit http://www.igi-global.com/book-series/advances-media-entertainment-arts/102257. Postmaster: Send all address changes to above address.

Titles in this Series

For a list of additional titles in this series, please visit: www.igi-global.com

Handbook of Research on the Facilitation of Civic Engagement through Community Art
Leigh Nanney Hersey (University of Louisiana Monroe, USA) and Bryna Bobick (University of Memphis, USA)
Information Science Reference • copyright 2017 • 672pp • H/C (ISBN: 9781522517276) • US $275.00 (our price)

Convergence of Contemporary Art, Visual Culture, and Global Civic Engagement
Ryan Shin (University of Arizona, USA)
Information Science Reference • copyright 2017 • 390pp • H/C (ISBN: 9781522516651) • US $195.00 (our price)

Cultural Influences on Architecture
Gülşah Koç (Yıldız Technical University, Turkey) Marie-Therese Claes (Louvain School of Management, Belgium) and Bryan Christiansen (PryMarke, LLC, USA)
Information Science Reference • copyright 2017 • 352pp • H/C (ISBN: 9781522517443) • US $180.00 (our price)

Design Innovations for Contemporary Interiors and Civic Art
Luciano Crespi (Politecnico di Milano, Scuola del Design, Italy)
Information Science Reference • copyright 2017 • 427pp • H/C (ISBN: 9781522506669) • US $205.00 (our price)

Applying the Actor-Network Theory in Media Studies
Markus Spöhrer (University of Konstanz, Germany) and Beate Ochsner (University of Konstanz, Germany)
Information Science Reference • copyright 2017 • 315pp • H/C (ISBN: 9781522506164) • US $175.00 (our price)

Projective Processes and Neuroscience in Art and Design
Rachel Zuanon (Anhembi Morumbi University, Brazil)
Information Science Reference • copyright 2017 • 290pp • H/C (ISBN: 9781522505105) • US $185.00 (our price)

Exploring the Benefits of Creativity in Education, Media, and the Arts
Nava R. Silton (Marymount Manhattan College, USA)
Information Science Reference • copyright 2017 • 458pp • H/C (ISBN: 9781522505044) • US $210.00 (our price)

Handbook of Research on Visual Computing and Emerging Geometrical Design Tools
Giuseppe Amoruso (Politecnico di Milano, Italy)
Information Science Reference • copyright 2016 • 924pp • H/C (ISBN: 9781522500292) • US $450.00 (our price)

Creative Technologies for Multidisciplinary Applications
Andy M. Connor (Auckland University of Technology, New Zealand) and Stefan Marks (Auckland University of Technology, New Zealand)
Information Science Reference • copyright 2016 • 467pp • H/C (ISBN: 9781522500162) • US $205.00 (our price)

Table of Contents

Detailed Table of Contents

New digital technologies have radically transformed the face of journalism in general and photo journalism in particular. These new technologies have not only made it easy for photo journalists to obtain images and to transmit them quickly to newsrooms and consumers across the globe, but they have also provided limitless opportunities for photo manipulation to take place, thus raising questions about the authenticity of those images. This has led to some scholars calling for the rethinking of media ethics to address these ethical dilemmas. This chapter, therefore, examines the codes of conduct for journalists in ten southern African countries to ascertain whether they have responded to this ethical dilemma brought in by the new digital technologies and if so, whether these responses give adequate guidance to journalists when called upon to make ethical decisions while processing photographs. The concepts of truth, reality and accuracy are also interrogated in the chapter. Findings revealed that most of the codes which do not make reference to photo manipulation are outdated and that those which do, are not comprehensive enough to give guidance to photo journalists.

Several authors have researched on diverse challenges affecting media practice in different parts of the world: the growing influence of bribery, one-sided and distorted reporting, pornographic and oversexed content, an inclination to acceptance of the brown envelope, and the disconnect between media training and practice. But with ICT, contemporary challenges include sources of news. With the aid of modern technology, a story that has appeared in one media house or platform can be reproduce in another without the reproducing journalist citing the previous source, and without disclosing to audiences that the story being presented is not original. Further, some journalists have presented stories that only exist in their fantasy. All these are cases of media lies. This chapter examines select cases of media lies and the ethical and credibility threat they pose to journalism.

The probing thesis in this study is premised on investigating why the mass media which are globally regarded as the playing field of politics as well as the road upon which presidential campaign travels every four years could suddenly develop contours, leading to the game of politics being devoid of convivial and smooth playing in Nigeria, especially between 1999 and 2011. The study observes that hardly was there any election in the post-independent era in Nigeria that did not end in serious disputations, crisis, violence and bloodletting such that academics across disciplines declared that since independence on

October 1, 1960, the electioneering process in Nigeria has been an experience of tears, blood and sorrow. The study evaluates media compliance to reportorial code which demands factual, accurate, balanced and fair reportage of electioneering stories. Using historical research method which relies on primary and secondary data collected from 150 media professionals consisting of 44 political editors, 10 line editors and 96 political reporters, the study, using power and conflict theories found out that non-compliance to ethical code of conduct for media professionals as well as legal rules governing the practice of journalism as one of the major factors responsible for publication or airing of provocative stories capable of engendering violence during elections. The study therefore suggested how the existing plural media system could be exploited to grow democracy, engender peace and promote national development as it's done in South Africa and other countries of the world.

Laws and regulations are important instruments for governing the relationships between people. In recent years, however, scholars have noted a growing judicialization, which concerns particularly immaterial cultural goods that are turned into intellectual and cultural properties. This chapter explores the implications of these regulations for the different actors involved, their moral responsibility and economic practices in the domains of branding and copying with examples of immaterial cultural goods from different African countries and from Austria. It argues that legal regulations that govern the use of immaterial cultural goods form part of the capitalist system. These regulations may be good for some and a hindrance for others. Piracy might damage the investments of an entrepreneur or artist in a brand or art work but might also help to secure the livelihood of other people and enhance the renown of products. Hence, it is important to analyze the perspectives and interests of individuals that are related to these economically important and ethically relevant activities.

This chapter examines the media, intellectual property rights and the protection of Africa's traditional knowledge in the digital age. It reviews literature on intellectual property, intellectual property rights, the various forms of intellectual property rights and the misappropriation and infringement on intellectual property rights, traditional knowledge, and media in digital age. The chapter provides perspectives on the issues and controversies on the non-protection of traditional knowledge within the existing frameworks of IP system and rules. It points out that the products of Africa's traditional knowledge are in dire need of protection against global competitors and therefore urges African governments to take advantage of the IP rules to negotiate with industrialized countries for the protection of their products. The chapter called for the enactment of tougher legislations to halt the menace of counterfeiting and digital piracy and deliberate use of the media to promote the products. It also made some recommendations that would help Africa defend its IP.

When one thinks of barriers to setting up a news corporation, one might think in terms of the costs of machinery and staffing. This case study of a start-up news corporation called Crocels News shows that the biggest cost can be in resolving legal disputes, most significantly from news articles scrutinising public bodies and their staff. This chapter investigates the difficulties faced by Crocels News in providing news content. By considering the legal correspondence received, the chapter provides insights into some of the problems all news services are likely to experience if they do not have access to the huge legal budgets of the established news corporations. The findings are particularly worrying for emerging forms of news reporting, such as citizen journalism. The chapter therefore proposes changes in statute so that case law that protects free speech is more easily enforced.

Opinion polling during elections plays a pivotal role in influencing the political and media agenda, and can potentially affect voting behaviour. However, evidence from various countries indicates that electoral polls have been characterised by contradictions and contentious debates which undermine their usefulness in democratic processes. The digital age has also led to a mushrooming of online polls, but some of them are of dubious quality. Thus, the chapter questions the continued use of electoral polls in multiparty politics in Africa. It argues that as a result of the inherent political and electoral volatility in many African countries, the utility of opinion polls need to be reconsidered. The paper recommends strategies for addressing the identified pitfalls, including increased professionalization of opinion polling, voter education on the limitations of pre-election polls and stronger appreciation of data journalism for media professionals. Stricter regulations, such as the embargo of election opinion polling may also be considered in different contexts.

This chapter is an analysis of the law in the face of the growing digital media in Uganda. It begins with a summary of Uganda's digital media terrain which helps the chapter to raise an argument of numbers in relation to relevance and external pressure, as forces behind digital media regulation. The background introduces the gist of the chapter, which is the regulation of Uganda's media in the digital age. A recent court case in Uganda, in which a local singer was sentenced to one year in jail along with her video producer, who was convicted for producing a pornographic music video that was distributed online, inspires this chapter. Didi Mugisha pleaded guilty and became the first victim of the Anti-Pornography

Preface

Are new media technologies enablers or banes of the mass media? Do they empower or disempower the media and the public? *Media, Law, Policy, and Ethics in the Digital Age* guides readers through a labyrinth of literature on ethical, legal and policy implications of the digital media on the mass media and society. It examines the opportunities, dialectics, ironies and complications, ironies and conundrums brought to bear on the mass media by digital technologies. That new media technologies such as the Internet have reconfigured the mass media in a fundamental way has been common cause. However, very little academic effort had been devoted (particularly in the Global South) in unpacking exactly how the proliferating technologies are altering the media. However, this book has a global appeal beyond Africa and the Global South because of the mix of authors and the drawing of empirical materials and examples on ethics, law and policy from countries such as the USA, UK, Austria and so forth. Authors such as Jonathan Bishop, Robin Blom based in the USA and Ute Röschenthaler from Germany definitely give such necessary diversity to the remarkable list of contributors. *Media Law, Ethics and Policy in the Digital Age* deals with related issues focusing on both traditional media and new media, professional journalists and non-professional communicators such as citizen journalists. The book draws on case studies and examples from throughout the world and compliments other books and journals that are systematically addressing the paradoxes, challenges, complexities and opportunities of media and communications in the contemporary new information age.

The idea of this book was born out of the realization that new issues and questions were emerging during our Media, Law, Policy and Ethics university classes (Nhamo in Zimbabwe and Tendai in South Africa) and yet there were hardly any current academic sources apart from a miniscule of newspaper articles and blogs (such as Stephen Ward's 'Digital Media Ethics' at the Centre for Journalism Ethics, University of Wisconsin Madison and the Journalist's Resource by the Harvard Shorenstein Center Project). Cecilia Friend and Jane Singer (2007), John Pavlik (2008), and Charles Ess (2009) and Packard (2010) had published engaging materials and formed part of the reading lists for our undergraduate courses but there remained a glaring lacunae occasioned by spatial and temporal and methodological exigencies. We noticed that digital technologies were disrupting existing media practices and brought about new challenges and opportunities to the communicative actions and to the media industry in particular, yet there was very little scholarly engagement with these changes and emerging media and communication practices.

The contributors in this volume, who are high profile academics in different parts of the world explore the interface between the digital technologies and the mass media, and are based on original empirical research, primarily from the historically marginalized regions in the Global South.

The book is largely designed as a primary reference text on undergraduate and post-graduate courses on Media Studies, Communication, Information Technology, Social and Cultural Anthropology, Law, Journalism and Mass Communication. It will also appeal to government bureaucrats, executives in the communications industry, non-governmental workers and the ordinary reader who wants to keep abreast of the ever-changing media, communication and journalism landscape. The lucid manner in which the various authors engage with these issues makes it easy for the reader to comprehend.

The topics addressed in the book are diverse but all have a deliberate focus on addressing fundamental questions on the curious nexus between digital media and mass media, particularly the way in which digital technologies are implicated in contemporary media and journalistic practices. The majority of contributors have vast experience in academia and command expertise in diverse fields as media studies, law, social and cultural anthropology, political science and journalism. Many of the contributors have also worked in the media industry, government, non-governmental, research institutions and their chapters combine insights gleaned from both practical as well as theoretical engagements with the subject.

The fifteen chapters selected for this volume were authored by seventeen seasoned and internationally recognised scholars tackling an equally diverse range of topics revolving around the legal, ethical, and regulatory implications of digital technologies on the mass media and society. Unlike single-authored books, the volume combines the insights of scholars from a diverse range of academic environments who approach the issue of digital technologies and the mass media from different theoretical and methodological perspectives and disciplinary approaches. Topics covered include criminal defamation and freedom of expression in the context of the digital era, ethical dilemmas and practices, emerging issues in relation to journalism and media professional codes of ethics, copying, branding and ethical implications, election reporting, electoral polling, conflict management and privacy issues. In Chapter 1, Nhamo Mhiripiri and Jacqueline Chikakano critically examine criminal defamation and criminalisation of expression using material gleaned from the courts. They argue that the proliferation of digital technologies and their use by ordinary citizens has brought about new legal and ethical conundrums in criminal defamation. This argument is taken up by Tendai Chari, in Chapter 2, where he argues he uses two illustrative cases to explore the plethora of ethical pitfalls confronting the media in the Internet era. Chari posits that the Internet's architecture predisposes journalists to unethical practices that were uncommon to the legacy media environment. In Chapter 3, Bevelyn Dube interrogates journalism ethical codes of conduct in ten Southern African countries in order to ascertain whether they are adequately responding to the unethical dilemmas attendant to the digital media environment. Her observations are that most of the ethical codes of conduct are antiquated as they fall short in terms of providing journalists with guidance on emerging ethical problems such as photographic manipulation. In Chapter 4, Agnes Lucy Lando picks up the issues of journalistic malpractices introduced by Tendai Chari in Chapter 2. She examines the preponderance of "media-invented reality" or "media lies" in both the electronic and print media, drawing her examples from the media in Kenya, Nigeria, Austria, Syria, Malaysia, Argentina and the United States of America, thereby demonstrating that the media have become more amenable to unethical practices in the digital media environment, hence adversely impacting on the credibility of the media and undermining their ability to influence society. Like Chari, Lando's work demonstrates that the unethical practices are not a preserve of the small or local media, but the 'disease' has also afflicted the big global media giants who were once regarded as "newspapers of record". In Chapter 5, Ibitayo Popoola takes up the issue of unethical reporting raised by Lando and Chari, through an examination of ethical and legal challenges faced by the media in Nigeria in reporting elections, using the historical research approach. He observes that the media in Nigeria have consistently failed to adhere to journalistic ethical and legal codes of conduct governing the media in reporting elections, thereby fostering election violence. Popoola proposes a number of interventions for the existing plural media environment epitomised by digital technologies in order to harness the media for the deepening of democracy and promotion of peace and national development. Copying, branding and ethical implications of rights in immaterial cultural goods is the focus of Chapter 6 by Frankfurt based and Goethe University social and cultural anthropologist, Ute, Röschenthaler. She examines the implications of the judicialization of immaterial cultural that are turned into intellectual properties in Africa and Austria. Her argument is that the legal frameworks that govern the use of immaterial cultural goods disadvantage some individuals while advantaging others, hence the need to balance the conflicting economic and moral interests of different communities. The debate is picked up in Chapter 7 by Benjamin Enahoro Assay, who examines the media, intellectual rights and the protection of African traditional knowledge systems in the digital era. Assay maintains that both traditional and online media could be harnessed for the promotion and preservation of African traditional knowledge and African governments stand to benefit by leveraging these media, particularly the online media, to publicize traditional knowledge systems locally and internationally because of their global reach. In Chapter 8, Jonathan Bishop investigates the legal challenges faced by a small start-up news outfit that is critical of authorities and public office bearers in the United Kingdom. His chapter provides insights into how small-size news outfits without huge legal budgets to fight lawsuits associated with their critical content and how such news organizations circumvent legal obstacles in order to continue existing. Electoral polling and reporting and policy implications for media practitioners is the focus of Adebayo Fayonin's chapter (Chapter 9). Fayonin questions the relevance of electoral polls in multi-party politics in Africa. He posits that the use of social media platforms in conducting electoral opinion polls bodes ill in the dissemination of information as it has brought about dubious polls. Fayonin advocates stricter regulations for opinion polling in the context of the digital era. In Chapter 10, Brian Semujju analyses the conflict between law and morality in Uganda. Using a pornographic video that was published online by a Ugandan musician and a video producer as a case study, Semujju demonstrates how the Anti-Pornography Act was interfering with the right to free expression by and by in the broader Ugandan society in the context of growing digitization. Semujju argues that the law was inconsistent with the legitimate right of free expression enshrined in the Ugandan constitution. How digital technologies, particularly citizen journalism is transforming media regulatory systems of states is the focus of Collen Sabao and Vimbai Chingwaramusee's chapter (Chapter 11). Using the case of a shadowy Zimbabwean Facebook character called "Baba Jukwa" (Father of Jukwa), Sabao and Chingwaramusee examine how citizen journalism is circumventing strict media regulations through publication of anti-establishment language and images. They argue that the digital environment in which citizen journalists operate presents serious regulatory headaches for an authoritarian state as well as ethical challenges for the journalists themselves. Chapter 12 by Robin Blom echoes the concerns raised by Sabao and Chingwaramusee in Chapter 11. Blom examines the dilemmas faced by journalists in reporting crime in the digital age. Whether news outlets should or should not name crime suspects is the question. While naming crime suspects is done in the interests of exposing the truth, naming crime suspects who may later be declared innocent causes irreparable harm to individuals because digital records are often not deleted and assume a ubiquitous presence. Such records can be easily retrieved years later and those who access them later can misread them and might fail to find the ones that exonorate the accused. It is not unusual for innocent people to get accused of certain criminal acts or misdemeanours. The media often report on the allegations made against those accused of all forms of crimes. Some of the crimes are proven and irrefutable but yet others remain unsubstantiated accusations and allegations that might even be dismissed in courts of law. The traditional media such as radio and newspapers could write about the accusations and allegations, but if a case was dismissed the very form of the media platform was somewhat equally mitigating to the unfortunate accused. The physical form of the materials was not always 'instantly' retrievable hence a wrongly accused person would not suffer perpetual stigmatisation. However, at literally the 'click of a button' nowadays digital content is easily retrievable due to its electronic digital archival form and persons suffer irreparable damage to their reputations as others nearly instantaneously search and access the offensive material. It is this dilemma that Blom addresses in his chapter. In the circumstances, journalists often find themselves at the cross-roads of whether to publish the names of accused or not and there is no simple rule for them in charting the way forward. Blom counsels that journalists need to weigh whether they would like to seek the truth or minimize harm. It is a difficult choice. In Chapter 13, Afu Isaiah Kunock examines the role of the Cameroonian media in the Boko Haram insurgency. He challenges the Cameroonian media to report the crisis in a manner that may result in conflict management rather than escalation. In this regard, framing and censorship, according to Kunock, will ensure that the Boko Haram terrorists are denied publicity which has been essential for their survival. In Chapter 14 William Heuva examines the reluctance by the Namibian government to adopt an Access to Information Act. He sees a chasm between the government's paternalistic conception of 'provision of information' to citizens vis a vis the constitutional tenets of the right to information. Heuva calls for the country's 'organic intellectuals' to take the lead in the fight for genuine access to information by rallying the citizens, civil society organizations and public representatives and the government in an authentic public social intercourse as part of a social contract that may ensure that the citizens' right to know may not be deferred any longer. Chapter 15, which is the last chapter, by Ufuoma Akpojivi interrogates the adequacy or lack of the application of the concept of privacy in South Africa and Nigeria in the context of connectivity. He observes that, conceptions and applications of the concept differ between the two countries, with South Africa providing a more comprehensive application of the concept as it covers the online media environment. Akpojivi argues that the Nigerian legal framework on privacy is inadequate as her legislative frameworks do not cater for the online media. Akpojivi argues that the boundaries of normativity in relation to the concept of privacy in the context of connectivity are shifting.

It is our conviction that the contributions in this volume will expand knowledge on the influence of digital technologies in the legal, ethical and policy aspects of the media, particularly in relation to world regions that have been historically marginalised in scholarly discourse. Arguably Media Law, Ethics and Policy have not been popular areas for media studies and there are relatively few books or special journal issues that have paid attention to these as compared to areas such as political economy of the media and media and cultural studies. There are barely any texts that have comprehensive or all encompassing approaches to the legislative aspects of the media and how these are defined, executed or negotiated in different countries. The situation is even worse with the inception of ICTs and social media and how these are/can be regulated. The adoption of new ICTs by media practitioners (journalists, filmmakers, and musicians, amongst other sectors) and ordinary citizens is posing new challenges and problems that require immediate attention. The use of blogging, social media and small-message-sending (smses) has been generally adopted by media practitioners, but the legal, ethical and policy implications of these is not always satisfactorily or comprehensively studied and explained for. This edited book intended to make students and researchers conversant with the general and specific laws and ethics that regulate the media industry. The media operate as industries governed and regulated by laws and ethical codes, and the same media industries and related enterprises are situated in statutory contexts. Laws and ethics often are formulated and legitimized by specific socio-political institutions. Laws can be specific to a media type such as Radio and TV broadcasting, print, and others relate to media technology and infrastructure. Our intention is to broaden and complement the existing body of scholarship on the digital technology- mass media nexus through fresh theoretical and empirical perspectives. We believe that the contributions in this volume go a great length in doing that.

We must confess that the scope and robust manner in which these issues are tackled by the various authors in this volume surpassed what we anticipated in our initial call for book chapters in 2015. Our anonymous reviewers helped a great deal in ensuring that we ended up with the best papers and remained focused rather than an 'omnibus' compendium. We would like to thank them sincerely for helping us prune the contributions to ensure that we end up with the best papers. Their selflessness and dedication to duty is in fact unparalleled and priceless. A lot of other people also contributed in various ways. We owe profound gratitude to IGI Global for having faith in our proposal and for the very insightful comments which helped in shaping it. In particular, we would like to express our gratitude to Jan Travers, Director of Intellectual Property and Contracts, Courtney Tychinski, the Assistant Managing Editor – Book Development, and Taylor Chernisky, Marketing Assistant, all at IGI Global. We owe profound gratitude to various colleagues who contributed through ideas and suggestions and advice on abstracts and chapters submitted for the volume. Our students contributed in a big way through their insightful and probing questions which prodded us to conceptualise this book. We are particularly indebted to them. Our families also contributed in various ways and the book could not have seen the light of day. Without their love, encouragement, material, and moral support we would not have been able to maintain our sanity during the project. We are deeply indebted to them.

Nhamo A. Mhiripiri
Midlands State University, Zimbabwe

Tendai Chari
University of Venda, South Africa
November 2016

Introduction

RETHINKING MEDIA LAW AND ETHICS IN THE DIGITAL AGE: ISSUES, CHALLENGES, AND CONTROVERSIES

The digital explosion at the turn of the century portends numerous challenges as well as opportunities for ordinary citizens who interface with digital communication technologies as either users, recipients or producers of content, professional journalists and other media practitioners as well as communication regulators. The Internet, for instance, has been dubbed a boon as well as a bane for media practitioners. As much as it is an enabler of journalism practice, it also brings in its wake a plethora of ethical and legal challenges which do not only undermine media credibility, but also make it easy for the media and non-professional communicators alike to commit legal and ethical 'sins' such as criminal defamation, plagiarism, publishing stories without verifying facts, falsehoods, lies, fabrications, photo- manipulation, a penchant for sensationalizing stories in order to improve ratings, and so forth.

Media Law, Ethics and Policy in the Digital Age reaffirms what Ashley Packard earlier observed in his single authored book *Digital Media Law* exhorting that observation of media laws is no longer the prerogative of traditional media organisations and professional journalists alone. According to Packard (2010):

It is time to stop thinking about media law as though it were the exclusive domain of traditional media organizations. Our global shift to digital media has precipitated a shift in information control. Meanwhile the affordability of digital media and their ease of use has democratized media production. With the right equipment, anyone can produce a website, listserv, blog or video with the potential to reach a mass audience. When anyone *can become a media producer,* everyone *should know something about media law – both to protect their own rights and to avoid violating the rights of others. (p. vii; emphasis as in original)*

It is arguable that the ordinary members of the public and professional communicators alike might also need to be conversant with the basic ethical standards associated with digital communications as well as respective regulatory and policy environments in order for them to cope with minimal problems as national or global citizens.

Digital technologies have been the epicentre of several high profile legal and ethical controversies that have attracted global attention. Julius Assange's WikiLeaks, Edward Snowden's exposure of invasion of privacy by the US government, disgraced former IMF boss Dominique Strauss-Khan's alleged sexual scandals, South African Paralympic Oscar Pistorius's hyper-mediated court trial in 2014, Charlie

Hebdo's controversial cartoons, to mention but a few. Social media platforms such as Twitter, Facebook, blogging, Whatsapp have become key platforms of the architecture for producing and disseminating information about global events, thereby undercutting traditional media's monopoly in breaking news. The use of new information and communication technologies by all and sundry has the capacity to subvert the old regulatory regimes with telling consequences. Oscar Pistorius's murder trial was broadcast in real-time globally on Twitter thereby raising concerns about the legality and ethicality of a 'trial by the media' which flies in the face of the *sub-judice rule*. The digital production, dissemination, appropriation and regulation of immaterial products have also invited both challenges and controversies, thereby bringing to the fore the complexities and contradictions attendant to the digital revolution conundrum. As a consequence of the transformative nature of digital technologies, there are new and different ways of conceptualizations of piracy, privacy, morality, communal knowledge, and private ownership of intellectual property. As the use of digital technologies disrupt old narratives, practices and conceptualizations in the media it is imperative to rethink conventional media practices and modes of disseminating and regulating information. Some institutions of higher learning such as Harvard University's Kennedy School of Shorenstein Centre on Media, Politics and Public Policy, and the University of South Carolina, St Petersburg's College of Arts and Sciences have designed 'model' syllabi on 'Journalism Ethics in the Digital Age' and 'Digital Media Ethics and Law' respectively, to help learners to 'think digitally' about media, law and ethics in the new online environment. Further, issues linked with media, ethics and law in the digital age are also increasingly taking centre stage in the scholarly agendas of peer reviewed international journals such as the *Journal of Media Law and Ethics* published by the school of law at the University of Baltimore. Across the world more and more professional organisations are coming up with digital media codes of ethics too. While these developments are commendable, it is troubling to note that very little academic attention has been given to the way in which the digital age complicates the dynamics of the media in the global South, where questions of freedom of speech, journalism ethics and media regulation have been particularly contentious. As noted by Dube (in this volume), it is also worrying that professional codes of most media organizations in Africa are silent on ethics on vexatious ethical issues occasioned by the digital environment, such as photographic manipulation, and yet there is a general impression that journalistic standards globally, not least in Africa, are being eroded and the new digital environment has complicated this conundrum.

This book grapples with the foregoing and related issues through insightful and theoretically and methodologically innovative scholarly contributions. The fifteen chapters in the book examine various aspects on the interface between the digital media, ethics, law and policy. It examines challenges, opportunities, issues, controversies and contradictions of digital technologies in relation to media law and ethics and how they play out in different socio-political and economic realities. Its aim is to critically interrogate issues, controversies, challenges and opportunities that digital technologies bring to bear on media and communications. We intended to come up with a compendium with a comparative global focus which would become a key reference on media, law, policy and their interface with new communication technologies.

The initial idea of the book sprang from the realization that digital technologies spawned phenomenal changes in media practice and brought about new challenges and opportunities to the communicative actions and to the media industry in particular, yet there was very little scholarly engagement with these changes and emerging media and communication practices. As a consequence, there was very little literature, if any on the way in which media practitioners and ordinary communicators were interacting with new communication technologies. We were subtly seeking attention to policy-makers, media regulators, corporates, and professional bodies to rethink their practices, ethics and values in the new technological dispensation. As editors, we were concerned that existing literature on media law, ethics and policy was dated as it did not sufficiently address vexing questions relating to how digital technologies were transforming media practices. We noted that most current books on media law and ethics (see Spilsbury, 2000; Crone, 2002; Feltoe, 2002; Bloy, 2007) were primarily crafted with the traditional media in mind, meaning that there is a dearth of literature in relation to law and ethics with regards to the new media, including social media and mobile communication.

The digital explosion has spawned new journalistic practices which have rendered the old laws and ethics redundant, thus rendering media regulatory authorities sitting ducks as they watch laws and ethics being flouted by bloggers and citizen journalists who, seemingly have become law unto themselves. As pointed out by the Bureau of International Information Program (2010), in some cases bloggers and citizen journalists, "unlike mainstream journalists publish anonymously or use pseudonyms. In some societies, those holding controversial or dissenting views withhold their identity as a matter of personal security. But those who speak anonymously still have an ethical obligation to be truthful, accurate and as transparent as possible about conflicts of interest" (p. 50). There are competing views regarding whether, bloggers, ordinary citizens (citizen journalists) and amateur journalists who publish on the Internet should be subjected to similar legal and ethical standards as professional journalists (see Mhiripiri and Chikakano, in this volume). But as has been observed by the Bureau of International Information Program (2010) "…Many of the intensely personal and highly opinionated weblogs proliferating on the Internet inhabit a world apart from the sometimes-dreary, realm of meticulously sourced and fact-checked traditional journalism" (p. 50). However, as has been demonstrated in this volume, the false dichotomy between traditional media and amateur journalism is fast disappearing as the mainstream media is increasingly becoming amenable to sloppy journalism epitomised by the increasing instances of "media invented stories" (see Lando in this volume) and numerous other ethical pitfalls (see Chari in this volume), the consequence being that the mainstream's credibility and its capacity to engender democratic politics is increasingly coming under the spotlight. As Wilson (2016) argues, if the media are perceived not to be credible they cannot be of much service to the public because the public relies on them for information to facilitate informed decision-making and political choices.

The fifteen chapters in this volume tackle a host of thorny issues around media, law, ethics and regulation in the digital age using a variety of methodological and theoretical approaches. Themes range from criminal defamation and the digital age, ethical practices and malpractices in the Internet era, journalistic professional codes of conduct, legal and ethical challenges in election reporting, controversies around the regulation of immaterial cultural goods in the context of the digital age, digital technologies and intellectual property rights, legal challenges faced by start-up news organizations, reporting suspects of crime and the dilemma of naming or not naming them in the media when online publications gives those 'named' a semblance of permanent condemnation regardless of at times favourable court verdicts, electoral polling and reporting in the digital media, media regulation and citizen journalism, emerging practices in crime reporting, and information piracy. Contributors spotlight the various emerging practices, controversies and challenges confronting the media in the digital age.

A key observation made in most of the contributions is that of the contradictory impact of new communication technologies, whereby, the digital technologies democratize communication while at the same time make it easy to violate the rights of others or those of the state. Digital technologies are hailed for promoting free speech in the sense that citizens no longer need a lot of money or sophisticated equipment to communicate among themselves or give feedback to the authorities. Anyone with a computer and a modem "and a little software can share their thoughts with the world through weblog or blog" (Bureau of International Information Program (2010, p. 52). Whereas in the 'old' media consumers used to give feedback to media organisations through letters to the editors or through telephone calls, in the digital age, news consumers can instantly give feedback through User Generated Content (UGC), social media networks such as Twitter, Facebook or MySpace, thus empowering citizens to participate in the democratic polity. However, the unfettered freedom enjoyed by bloggers, citizen journalists, netzens, and amateur journalists often encroach on the fine line separating freedom of speech and the tyranny of free speech as they are not always protected by the shelter of anonymity which the digital media platforms can provide. Unlike in the traditional media where only media practitioners were amenable to media law and ethics, any individual who communicates via these online platforms is liable for legal offences such as defamation. Against this backdrop, media training institutions, media professional bodies and regulators need to re-examine their approaches by among other things updating their curricular and ethical codes of ethics in tandem with the changing online communication environment, an argument convincingly canvassed respectively by Ashley Packard in his *Digital Media Law* and Dube (in this volume). However, there is no rule of thumb here, for there is no consensus as to whether traditional media ethics should be applied to bloggers, citizen journalists and other amateur communicators since they are not professional journalists. Scholars like Lasica (1997) argue that new technology does not make ethics old fashioned, implying that core values of media ethics such as integrity, balance, truth-telling, accuracy and balance should endure in the new media environment. This, however, does not resolve questions on how untrained people who disseminate messages online for nothing else, other than fulfilling their constitutional right to free speech should also be bound by the same ethics and laws that govern the mainstream media. Similar contradictions play out in the regulation of cultural products whereby file sharing could be viewed as a form of democratization of immaterial goods by easily making them available to everybody at no cost and yet patenting and copyright protection laws privatize them. The moral and legal considerations for and against appropriation and protection and copyrighting of goods formerly available for use by communities is a conundrum that is not easy to resolve, and as argued by Röschenthaler's and Assay's chapters (both in this volume) is an issue that is made more complex by the digital technologies. While the contributors in this book have managed to open debate on these issues, they do not prescribe a silver bullet for resolving these controversies. As editors, we are pleased and convinced that the book has started a conversation which can be broadened through further engagement in journals, academic conferences and other academic interventions. Although, our ambition was to have continentally more comparative cases as indicated in our original call for book chapters, the contributions straddle diverse topics on the thorny issues on media, law ethics and the digital era by a majority of authors who hail from a historically marginalised region in terms of scholarly texts.

The authors are seasoned scholars in media, communication, law, sociology, cultural studies and information technology and the case studies are drawn from Southern, East and West Africa, the UK and the United States of America. The quality of scholarly engagement in these chapters attests to the fact that the authors are well positioned to critically engage on the link between media law, ethics and policy in the digital age. While the book's primary market is students and academics in tertiary institutions and media practitioners, we are convinced that the debates raised in this book will also appeal to communication policy-makers, researchers, government officials, Non-Governmental Organizations and other stakeholders who have an interest in the implications of digital technologies on media law, ethics and regulation in contemporary times.

Tendai Chari
University of Venda, South Africa

Nhamo A. Mhiripiri
Midlands State University, Zimbabwe

REFERENCES

Bloy, D. (2007). *Media Law*. London: Sage.

Bureau of International Information Program. (2010). *Media Law: Handbook Series*. New York: United States Department of State.

Crone, T. (2002). *Law and the Media*. Oxford, UK: Focal Press.

Feltoe, G. (2002). *A Guide to Press Law in Zimbabwe*. Harare: Legal Resources Foundation.

Fletcher, J. F. (1966). *Situation Ethics: the New Morality*. Philadelphia: Westminster Press.

Lasica, J. D. (1997) Preserving Old Ethics in a New Medium. *American Journalism Review*. Retrieved from http://ajrarchive.org/article_printable.asp?id=1787

Packard, A. (2010). *Digital Media Law*. Oxford, UK: Wiley-Blackwell. doi:10.1002/9781444318197

Spilbury, S. (2000). *Media Law*. London: Taylor & Francis.

Chapter 1
Criminal Defamation, the Criminalisation of Expression, Media and Information Dissemination in the Digital Age:
A Legal and Ethical Perspective

Nhamo A. Mhiripiri
Midlands State University, Zimbabwe

Jacqueline Chikakano
Media Institute of Southern Africa, Zimbabwe

ABSTRACT

Criminal defamation and the criminalisation of communication in general often result in severe punishment for the media and other content producers accused and prosecuted for committing such 'crimes'. There are severe financial penalties involved and /or the incarceration of those who are convicted of breaking the law. This chapter studies the existence and feasibility of criminal defamation in largely contemporary Africa, but also making references to 'older' democracies in the Western hemisphere. In short, the chapter critiques criminal defamation and the criminalisation of expression, making a strong legal and ethical perspective quite often using empirical materials from the courts. The inception and proliferation of new digital technologies amongst ordinary citizens also means that besides the traditional media or fourth estate, ordinary non-professional communicators are also highly likely to get into trouble over defamation, criminal defamation and other forms of crimes associated with the criminalisation of communication.

DOI: 10.4018/978-1-5225-2095-5.ch001

INTRODUCTION

Criminal defamation and the criminalisation of communication in general often result in severe punishment for the media and other content producers accused and prosecuted for committing such 'crimes'. There are severe financial penalties involved and/or the incarceration of those who are convicted of breaking the law. This chapter studies the existence and feasibility of criminal defamation selected contemporary African countries, but also making references to the USA as an 'older' democracy. The chapter critiques criminal defamation and the criminalisation of expression, making a strong legal and ethical perspective quite often using empirical materials from the courts. The inception and proliferation of new digital technologies amongst ordinary citizens also means that besides the traditional media or fourth estate, ordinary non-professional communicators are also highly likely to get into trouble over defamation, criminal defamation and other forms of crimes associated with the criminalisation of communication. Firstly, in a criminal case a prosecutor on behalf of the state brings charges against a defendant, whereas in a civil suit the plaintiff brings suit (Creech, 2007). Secondly, the chargeable offense is considered grave or serious that it can result in the imprisonment of the defendant (Feltoe, 2002, p 12). Criminal defamation and other criminal offences that are linked to utterances and or publication of information is a common and long standing feature of most legal systems. Their existence is justified on the basis that freedom of expression as with other rights, is not absolute and has to be exercised in cognisance of other rights and as such, it can be limited. Even in one of the oldest democracies - the USA - there are debates on whether or not America's First Amendment confers absolute rights of the media and expression, or there are specific justifiable limitations (Packard, 2010).

Criminal charges can be invoked for disturbing public peace through publications in the conventional media (fourth estate) or in the new media (fifth estate). The internet is a fairly easy and accessible medium for committing the publications or communication related crimes, in the same way conventional defamation can be committed against individuals and organisations there. There is need to trace how libel or criminal defamation charges have been instituted in countries of the North and South such as Zimbabwe and Tanzania, and the USA against communicators that use internet and other channels of public communication. When assertions are made that criminal defamation is undemocratic, archaic and backward, is this a statement to dissuade and censure countries of the South that are often viewed as lagging behind in adherence to ideals and tenets of modern democracy? These countries seem to have a higher prevalence of such type of litigation. Are criminal defamation and the criminalisation of expression, including sedition and criminal insults of powerful politicians, a universal phenomenon found even in so-called developed and progressive nations? When a country such as the USA arrests and gives a lengthy sentence to Chelsea Manning for leaking sensitive materials in the so-called Cablegate case, or when it demands the arrest of activists such as Edward Snowden or investigates a man like Julian Assange, what are the ethical and legal implications given that some sections of global society view these accused as iconic proponents of freedom of information? Again are states justified in intruding into the personal communications of all citizens, and alternatively, do 'whistleblowers' such as WikiLeaks have a right to publish personal information which is not of 'public' importance? All these questions have a bearing on criminal libel.

METHODOLOGY

This chapter uses the words 'defamation' and 'libel' interchangeably. This chapter purposively selects archival materials on publication on criminal defamation and other criminal charges pertaining to utterances and publications both in the traditional media and in new internet based media in Africa and the rest of the world. The literature review seeks to establish what has been prevailing especially in older democracies such as the United State of America. Materials are then presented on recent cases where utterances or publications were criminalized with or without successful prosecution in selected African countries such as Zimbabwe, Tanzania, Mozambique and South Africa. The focus is also important especially in instances where criminal defamation arose out of publications on new internet based media platforms such as blogsites and Facebook. The researchers used both published books and the internet to establish conveniently selected cases that were brought before the courts of law in the twenty-first century and what verdicts were passed on criminal defamation and general criminal offenses pertaining to utterances and publications, in digital media of whatever form. The methodology is particularly aware of the nebulous area of criminal defamation and its intersection with other criminal charges like sedition, where 'whistleblowing' and disclosure of state secrets raised controversies on the public's right to know and states inclination to keep 'secrets' or protect the public peace and order. Packard notes that 'defamation … has always been the bane of traditional media, but is now increasingly applied to 'average people' who post damaging accusations on websites, blogs and listservs." (pviii)

Again the methodology of selection of cases might appear 'over-stretched' because there are various technologies used for the different digital media platforms that make communicative action possible. For instance, Packard (2010) outlines the ubiquity of 'digital media' and its equally wide-ranging relationship and implications for media law. Digital media law, just like digital media, "is characterized by it general applicability". Alongside the conventional or traditional media such as newspapers, books, television and radio there is now the electronic forms of the very same 'traditional/conventional' media channels, as well as digital media channels such as websites, web logs, pod casts, vod casts, videos on U-tube, and social networking sites. While the wide-rangingness of media and digital media are openly both beguiling and intimidating from a conceptual point of view, escaping neat definition and demarcation in most cases, the same applies to the possibility of cases or law suits that can arise from the use and infringements of communication on these platforms or channels. For instance, Packard's ambitious book reflexively entitled *Digital Media Law* claims that within the orbit and confines it seeks to address a plethora of media law and digital media law issues and concerns. Packard (2010, p. vii) argues knowledge about media law should not be confined to traditional media organisations since the revolution in the production and access to information through digital media means "(w)ith the right equipment, anyone can produce a website, listserv, blog or video with the potential to reach a mass audience. When *anyone* can become a media producer, *everyone* should know something about media law – both to protect their own rights and to avoid violating the rights of others".

Cases cited in this chapter range from threats of arrests, arrests with or without prosecutions in courts of law, and those that have been tried in courts of law leading to final verdicts. The 'legal' process is intricate and problematic with citable cases wielding different 'legal' status hence the need to cite these diverse cases in their diverse stages of occurrence. What is important is that they appeared in the public domain through publication in the mass media. Zimbabwean cases dominate due to the availability of these to the authors and researchers, but also because Zimbabwe has received incessant media coverage in the last two decades and the Zimbabwe state is also often accused of blatant disregard for media freedom, much as section 61 and 62 of the new Zimbabwe constitution categorically extend to citizens freedom of information and freedom of expression and freedom of the media (Mhiripiri, 2015). A case is also cited from the African Court on People's and Human Rights in order to ascertain what the overall projection of perception on the issue of freedom of the media and expression is in a court that adjudicates over a continent which is generally viewed as lagging in development and adherents to modern principles of human and media rights. The chapter is also cognizant of the existence of legislation on cyber-crime such as Tanzania's Cyber-Crime Act of 2015.

THEORISING CRIMINAL DEFAMATION AND CRIMINALISATION OF EXPRESSION

According to Steve Forster (2003, p. 436-437) "(a) defamatory remark is one that causes a person to be shunned or avoided, or subjected to ridicule, hatred or contempt. Alternatively, the statement must lower the person's reputation in the eyes of right-thinking members of society". Zimbabwean lawyer Jeff Feltoe (2002) notes that criminal defamation, is qualified from civil defamation on the basis of the gravity or seriousness of the former. However, several other scholars make a distinction on the fact that criminal defamation involves state prosecution of the offending party on behalf of the party whose reputation has been injured, and there is the possibility of imprisonment of the guilty party (Beyene, 2011; Creech, 2007; Crone, 2002: Pember & Calvert, 2005/6). In some instances, state institutions can file criminal defamation suits to protect their own image or reputation in the public perception as was the case in Zimbabwe where some laws prohibited the media and individuals from bringing state institutions into public "disaffection" (Mhiripiri, 2013).

Underlining defamation and criminal defamation is the need to protect reputation. Invariably, it can be protection of reputation and dignity of an individual, an organisation or even state institutions and public officials from reckless or malicious injury to their character and self-esteem in the eyes or regard of other people in society. Criminal defamation, according to Zimbabwean media law scholar Geoff Feltoe, is of 'a serious nature and courts consider factors such as extravagance of the allegation, the extent of the publication and whether the words are likely to have results that may detrimentally affect interests of the state and community' (2002: 12). Kenneth Creech (2007, p. 348) makes a distinction between civil and criminal defamation cases as follows situating the definitions in the US context:

Civil law provides monetary awards for successful plaintiffs. On the other hand, jail sentences are part of the punishment for those who violate criminal law. Many states have criminal libel laws on the books. These laws were designed to punish those who might utter words that provoke riots or otherwise threaten the public order and are rarely enforced today.

The area of defamation, criminal defamation and the criminalisation of media and communication in general are slippery and tricky terrain as it is contextual and situational. For instance, the US government entities do not sue for defamation although public officials and bureaucratic can sue in their own personal capacity. Packard (2010, p. 180) clarifies on the same US system:

Government entities may not sue for defamation under the theory that the government should not be permitted to use public funds to prevent the public from criticizing it. But government officials are en-

titled to sue on their own behalf. By necessity, public officials are subject to greater scrutiny than private citizens, so courts require them to meet a higher standard of proof in defamation cases.

Where the American state permits an individual to sue for criminal defamation the theoretical understanding is that there are critical instances when it is proper for the state to act on behalf of the party harmed by the libel and bring criminal charges against the defendant (Pember & Calvert, 2005/6). The state takes responsibility due to the perceived gravity of the matter and in order to eliminate the possibility of citizens taking the law into their own hands and eventually provoking anarchy.

The Zimbabwe government on the other hand has used legislation to protect the state President and institutions, to such an extent where a public official may claim that their reputation has been injured beyond a personal level, but to extend the injury to the very status of the public office they occupy.

Zimbabwe's Criminal Law [Codification Reform] Act's (Chapter 9:23)(No 23 Of 2004) Chapter 111 on "Crimes against the State") states that speakers, authors and publishers can attract criminal charges if they are deemed guilty of:

30. *Causing disaffection among Police force or Defense forces.*
31. *Publishing or communicating false statements prejudicial to the state.*
33. *Undermining authority of or insulting the President.*

Again, the country's Access to Information and Protection of Privacy Act's Section 80 on Abuse of Journalistic Privilege criminalizes publication of information, which (a journalist) intentionally and recklessly falsified or fabricated in a manner that:

1. *Threatens the interests of defence, public safety, public order, the economic interests of the state, public morality or public health; or*
2. *Is injurious to the reputations, rights and freedoms of other persons.*

These acts explain why several politicians and government officials have sued the media for criminal defamation, although fortunately there have never been successful convictions. The insult laws which protect the image and reputation of the state President have also caused many people to stand trial.

Don Pember and Clay Calvert's book *Mass Media Law* has provided comprehensive material on how libel can be committed on Internet. Indeed scholarly publications that draw empirical examples from the countries of the North still cite criminal charges against both media and individual communicators. In the US nowadays more criminal libel charges are often made against individuals operating websites than journalists. In worse situations, naïve students who use the Internet to criticise their schools have also fallen foul to the law (Packard 2010, p. 193).

Several countries still have criminal defamation statutes which continue to be evoked to control both unprofessional media practices or just to stifle genuine critical media. Yes, indeed, the media are not all saints and can be operated by unscrupulous persons without regard for other people's rights and dignity. For instance, in Kenya there is a 'gutter' press that appears and disappears unceremoniously, and quite often blatantly scandalizes politicians and public figures without respecting the best norms and practices of media. The state has been forced to use criminal defamation and other restraining measures to bring order amongst these. Some of Kenya's fly-by-night publications have been described thus:

Kenya's gutter or alternative press would best be described as "now-you-see-them-now-you-don't" after their nature of appearing only when there is a major scandal involving the nation's politicians or socialites. These papers range from a single A4 sheet to as many as 12 pages. It may be sold on news-stands, but more often on street corners for less than half the price of the daily newspapers. Most are technically and editorially mediocre with occasional but unpredictable flashes of brilliance. Generally, these publications have no fixed address, no known publisher, and tend to focus on rumor and sometimes make very spectacular claims. These papers often draw the ire of the Kenyan government. Three are worth mentioning: The Weekly Citizen, Kenya Confidential, *and* Independent. *The later was recently shut down after the publisher-editor was arrested and jailed for criminal libel. He has since been released on presidential clemency. (Fackler et al, 2011, pp. 632-33)*

In another East African country, Ethiopia, media scholar Zenebe Beyene (2011) notes that "many press defendants were accused of criminal defamation laws and were charged by prosecutors" (p. 724) and actually served time in prison (pp.717- 724). Unlike in the U.S where precedence was set in the *New York Times vs Sullivan* case, in Ethiopia public officials are not open to scrutiny and often win the criminal libel suits. Beyene contrasts Ethiopia with the U.S:

In the United States it is nearly impossible for a public official to win a libel suit. "Public officials and public figures have to prove a higher level of fault than do private individuals." *Government or public officials must prove actual malice to win libel lawsuits. Cases such as* New York Times *vs. Sullivan are evidence of this. Public officials should be open to public scrutiny. (Beyene 2011, p. 721, emphasis as in original)*

While law might be used to restrict speech and expression, it is still prudent to "minimally" use regulatory powers of the state to curtail excesses of expression or the media. Freedom cannot be absolute. Some scholars prefer restrictions confined within the precincts of civil defamation to protect individuals from unreasonable injuries to their reputations (Adam, 2009; Mill, 1967). Seditious libel or expression or media crimes committed directly against the state should also be "legitimately… used to protect democratic institutions from disruptions that would prevent them from operating." In his widely celebrated thesis, *On Liberty*, John Stuart Mill justifies limits on speech where speech, the press, or what we commonly refer to as the media today, might incite rioting or subject an individual or group to risk (Adam, 2009, p.325). These *justifiable* restrictions to speech and expression, must on the whole promote a higher humanism, justice, peace and stability, and they are applicable to both traditional media (the fourth estate) and non-professional mass communicators who constitute what is now known as the fifth estate most of whom operate digital media platforms (Chiumbu, 2010; Mhiripiri & Mutsvairo, 2013).

It is now possible to abuse journalistic ethics and professionalism through social media and citizen journalism, in the same way it is possible to publish litigious materials that constitute all forms of defamation or are just potentially criminal. Social media and citizen journalism are part of what is now defined as the Fifth Estate. This is that emergent space where ordinary people who are not necessarily media professionals who neither work for specific media institutions publish their stories (Hyde-Clarke, 2010). While features of the regular 'Fourth Estate' include institutionalization through bureaucratic media organisations, capitalization, regulation and professionalism, the emergent Fifth Estate is largely a de-institutionalized, de-capitalized and de-professionalized space. There are also erroneous assumptions that the latter is also de-regulated although cases involving the arrest and prosecution of those who have published supposedly offensive materials on social media shows evidence to the contrary. The Fifth Estate is quite often on the Internet appearing as blog sites or social media networks such as *Facebook*, *Twitter*, *Badoro*, and *Linkedin,* or it is the publications on smartphones using Whatsapp, twitter, etc. In short, professional and non-professional users of the World Wide Web and other digital media must realise that courts regard communications and publications here similarly to what is published or disseminated through so-called traditional media such as books, newspapers and magazines (Pember & Calvert, 2005/6, p. 146). While whistleblowing is traditionally considered a normative role of the media, evidence below shows that courts and the state can be harsh and intolerant to whistleblowers who are not 'journalists' in the conventional sense, but leak sensitive information online or via the media.

ETHICS, CRIMINAL DEFAMATION, AND THE CRIMINALISATION OF MEDIA AND COMMUNICATIONS IN THE DIGITAL AGE

Media ethics are usually compatible with legal expectations except in a few instances. Ethical standards are supposed to bring creditability and respect to the media profession. Professional standards of communication are outlined by most media organisations and civil society. Nonetheless, private citizens who participate in both interpersonal and mass communications are generally expected to respect the best communicative norms and values, notwithstanding that there have been a laxness with regards to how they are penalized if they breach ethical codes. For instance, it is not unusual to find private non-professional communicators publishing certain materials recklessly, even when such materials have no legal repercussions. A good example is how some individuals insensitively publish horrific scenes of violent accidents without giving consideration to how this can be distressing to their 'audiences'. Just because non-professionals are capable of being mass communicators using digital technologies the same ethical expectations that govern the mass media (see Wilkins & Christians, 2008) must be applicable to this new breed of 'mass communicators'. Some countries now have codes of standards for digital media. Voluntary Media Council of Zimbabwe (VMCZ) in 2015 crafted a code of ethics that is applicable to all media houses and those individuals involved in mass communication. This Digital Media Code of Ethics which is widely distributed, including on the VMCZ's website[1]. While there are no remarkable or exceptional characteristics of the code that differ from the best practices expected of traditional media, it is notable that digital media is receiving timely attention and consideration. The emphasis on the technical qualities of the mode of publication seems not to demand any really new ethical consideration worth underscoring due to the very nature of the technology used. The same old ethical requirements for traditional media remain relevant, although there is a renewed emphasis on digital media. It is commendable that ethics and digital media are beginning to receive the attention that they deserve as shown from scholarship from developing countries such as Zimbabwe where media and public communication are often presented as under siege from an over-bearing state system (Chari, 2013; Moyo, 2015.)

Whereas Codes of Ethics for traditional media appear to be targeted at professional journalists and media practitioners, the VMCZ code has a wider application. It is expected to apply over "groups and individuals, traditional media practitioners (print and broadcast), registered and unregistered organizations/companies that share information using digital media and have agreed to be bound by this Code and have to submit to the disciplinary jurisdiction of the Voluntary Media Council of Zimbabwe (VMCZ)".

This new digital media code does not directly refer to 'protection of reputation' or libel or defamation, although it is inferable that these critical issues subsist within the conceptual framework of various ethical clauses.

THE PUBLIC INTEREST AS DEFENSE FOR FORMS OF DEFAMATION

There are several recognised defenses for defamation and criminalisation of the media, paramount of which is the public interest. While countries such as Zimbabwe have declared criminal defamation is unconstitutional and unacceptable in a democratic society, the citizens' right to know crucial information remains pertinent and over-riding. Citizens have to make important decisions in the general conduct of their lives, from making business choices as well as making decisions on the election of political leadership. The Press Complaints Commission Code of Practice of the UK, whilst it has no legal standing, defines 'public interest' from the perspective of the journalist. Public interest includes but is not limited to, amongst other crucial components:

1. Identifying or revealing crime or serious impropriety,
2. Protecting public health, peace and safety,
3. Protecting the public from misleading statements or action by an organisation or organisations,
4. Protecting freedom of expression (Bloy, 2007: 59-60).

The media have however the responsibility to prove that they are serving the public interest when publishing any contentious materials. When the media seem to contradict ethical requirement such as the reporting of sensitive materials leading to the disclosure of identities of minors or victims of sexual assault, the editors must demonstrate that public interest 'overrides the normal standards of journalistic practice such as protecting the interest of the child or of victims of sexual assault. Some information might 'interest the public' but do not carry convincing justification of public interest. It is therefore arguable, in the public interest, to show that a government such as that of the US is becoming too intrusive and overbearing over citizens' right to privacy if that government snoops into the private details or communication of private citizens who do not pose a danger to other citizens or society in general. Therein lie the major controversies of exposures made by people such as Chelsea Manning, Julian Assange and Edward Snowden.

CASES OF CIVIL DEFAMATION OR CRIMINALISATION OF COMMUNICATION AND INFORMATION DISSEMINATION

Chelsea Manning, Julian Assange, and Edward Snowden and the Public Interest

Three computer and internet linked people are remarkable icons of the debate on media law, ethics and social justice in the digital age. These are Chelsea Manning, Edward Joseph Snowden and Julian Assange. Manning, who worked in the US army, leaked information to WikiLeaks about US war crimes and other major revelations of public interest. Considered by many as a hero, Manning was apprehended and is serving 35 years in prison for leaking sensitive information. Snowden, an American computer professional and former Central Intelligence Agency employee, also leaked to the mass media classified and highly confidential information from the US's National Security Agency in 2013; and Julian Assange an Australian born computer hacker published the WikiLeaks. Snowden leaked information to *The Guardian* and *The Washington Post*, before the same material was published in *Der Spiegel* and *The New York Times*, following which it was picked up by all sorts of global media. His disclosures made known to the world how NSA with the cooperation of telecommunications companies and European governments willfully subjected world citizens to global surveillance disregarding their privacy. The fight against global terrorism makes governments such as that of the US codify anti-terrorism statutes that empower them to snoop into private citizens communications as a preemptive measure to stop mindless terrorism especially in the wake of the 9/11 attacks. However, this 'noble' action means a majority of innocent law abiding citizens are subjected to constant monitoring thereby compromising their privacy and dignity. The powers of states and companies are therefore questioned when counterposed to the rights and privacy of such innocent citizens. Due to Snowden's disclosures the US Department of Justice charged him for violating the Espionage Act of 1917 for theft of state property. Snowden is currently a refugee in Russia, but his actions triggered a debate on whether he is a hero and whistleblower working in the global public's interest, or a dissident and traitor. Mass surveillance, government secrecy, national security and information privacy became poignant moral, ethical and legal subjects, especially when viewed within the context of anti-terror statutes such as the Patriots Act and cyber-crime acts enacted in various countries.

Besides Snowden, Australian citizen Julian Assange is another controversial notable 'media' figure in the digital era. Assange who describes himself as Editor-in-Chief of WikiLeaks, in 2006 founded with his colleagues the secret information and news leaks site. The site specialised in publishing thousands of protected documents of public interests, documents which Assange described as "a giant library of the world's most persecuted documents"[2]. Again Assange has elicited different responses and attitudes from world leaders and governments, celebrated by some and vilified by others. In Australia his work was considered 'illegal' by the Prime Minister although Australian police noted that Assange had broken no Australian law.[3] The US government purportedly investigated Assange and WikiLeaks with the intention of prosecuting him under the Espionage Act of 1917. When someone engages in hacking and publishing the secret information online, it is possible for complainants – organizations, states and individuals – to sue the perpetrator wherever they are. Writing specifically on defamation Bloy (2007, 17) notes that the internet transcends jurisdictional boundaries because literally anyone throughout the world can access the websites in question; hence the person allegedly defamed can logically sue wherever they believe their reputation has been damaged. The claimant only needs to show that the tort (wrong) was committed in that specific area, and that he or she has a reputation of a sufficient magnitude to protect or uphold within that jurisdiction or area. Both the Snowden and Assange cases definitely pose the problematique of whether global citizens are willing to forego their individual rights in preference over global security, but immediately critiquing the possibilities of states and companies abusing the private information their acquire from 'unknowing' innocent citizens.

Traditional media that have relied on informants who request confidentiality in exchange for vital information leaks also now largely using computers and internet in their news gathering, production and dissemination. This has forced to them to find ingenuous means of concealing certain information from state surveillances. Some of the efforts are to protect whistleblowers such as Manning and Snowden, but others are merely to protect the media in the digital age when storage of sources and sensitive information is in computer files prone to state surveillance or direct seizure (Lowenthal, 2015).

NEW WIKILEAKS AND EMERGING ETHICAL COMPLEXITIES

Whistleblowing is not always steeped in the values of presenting accurate information to the public in the most responsible manner as Sandra Upson (2016) has divulged in the article "WikiLeaks has morphed from journalism hotshot to malware hub". Since investigative whistleblowing is also bedeviled with the vagaries of personality and state politics, paranoia, fear and other challenges which make online activists vulnerable and frail, such activists can easily degenerate into non-admirable psycho-political states of existence. Assange's case is remarkable. He no longer has an amicable relationship with the public media which partly publicised his radical efforts. He is holed up as a refugee in the Ecuadorian embassy and threatened with a sexual harassment case. The US government's arrest and sentencing of Manning to 35 years in prison unnerved Assange and Snowden. The relationship between Assange and newspapers such as *Guardian* and *Times* soured. WikiLeaks became more critical of conventional journalists. The new WikiLeaks releases are criticised for "wanton release of personal data", disclosing personal details of private citizens who remotely have links with public administration or corruption. WikiLeaks' stance in the US 2016 Presidential run-up is also viewed with suspicion as there seems vindictiveness in bringing down Hillary Clinton at all costs. The sites' discretion and competence in judging what type of content ought to be disclosed has been questioned. Information mismanagement is another indiscretion. Casual visitors to the WikiLeaks sites are also endangered as hackers can install a bot that enables hackers to take over computer files of unsuspecting readers. Some visitors have been forced to pay "ransom" when their files are encrypted and a payment is demanded. Files are infected and WikiLeaks does little to warn its visitors who visit thinking they are going to read 'public truth'. Besides carelessly disclosing the names of Afghans that collaborated with the US military, thereby putting these Afghans lives to imminent danger, the journalists and the public seeking 'truth' from the WikiLeaks files risk emerging infected. Writes Upson; "WikiLeaks has degraded into a malware snakepit".

ZIMBABWEAN CASES

In Zimbabwe limitation of the right to freedom of expression was provided for under the Lancaster house constitution that was adopted at the time of independence from colonial rule in 1980, and is similarly encompassed in the current constitution of Zimbabwe Amendment Act no. 20 of 2013 as is the case with other national constitutions albeit to differing degrees. According to Mhiripiri (2013) in Zimbabwe there were lots of court actions for criminal defamation prior to the rendering of the crime as unconstitutional in 2014. The Zimbabwean Supreme Court ruled in a case in 2014 that the charge is undemocratic, archaic and a disproportionate punishment for any form of defamation. Then, Criminal defamation cases were frequently instituted by public officials and politicians who argued that their reputations were not only injured in their personal capacity, but that there was adverse harm on the integrity of the very offices they occupied.

Despite the 2014 ruling there continued a tense debate with government insisting on the relevance of criminal defamation and the need to retain the offense on the statures. Pro-criminal defamation exponents argued it provided a deterrent to media excess and maliciously reckless communication. Freedom of the media activists argued that criminal defamation is often used in Zimbabwe and other developing nations as an instrument of press censorship in order to brow-beat the media into submission and compliance. Politicians and the public officials holding state position use criminal defamation as a convenient arsenal against pertinent media scrutiny.

There followed an increasing number of cases referred to the constitutional court challenging the constitutionality of various laws that criminalise expression including criminal defamation. Most of these referrals have been in respect of provisions of the Criminal Law (Codification and Reform) Act, [Chapter 9:23] such as section 31 which criminalises the *publication or communication false statements prejudicial to the State*, section 33, which provides for the offence of *undermining authority of or insulting President* and section 96 which provides for the offence of *criminal defamation* among others.

What has been particularly common in the determination of recent cases particularly by the current constitutional court of Zimbabwe, is the fact that while freedom of expression and media freedom are not absolute rights, their limitation has to be carefully balanced to avoid a situation whereby they are severely limited to the extent of eroding the constitutional guarantee altogether. The constitutional court has also emphasized the need to employ the most appropriate and proportionate measures in limiting freedom of expression. Both the old Lancaster House Constitution and the new constitution adopted in 2013 provide that freedom of expression can be limited by a law in the interests of defence, public safety, public order, the economic interests of the State, public morality or public health besides the protection of reputations of other citizens.

Three recent cases in particular, have had extensive effect on the criminalization of expression that is, Constantine Munyaradzi Chimakure, Vincent Kahiya & Zimbabwe Independent Publishers v The Attorney General [Constitutional Application No. SC 247/09], Nevanji Madanhire & Nqaba Matshazi v Attorney General [Judgment No. CCZ 78/12] and recently that of MISA-Zimbabwe & 4 others v Minister of Justice, Legal and Parliamentary Affairs & 2 others [CCZ7/15].

Aside from the MISA-Zimbabwe case, the judgments in these earlier cited cases elicited increased national discourse on the validity of criminalising people's expression such that in 2015 alone, more than three cases were filed or referred to the constitutional court seeking declarations of invalidity of criminal defamation in terms of the obtaining constitution.[4] [5]This was amidst growing confusion of the fate of these laws in light of the fact that on one hand judgments in the aforementioned cases had indicated that the declarations of invalidity of these two cases had been in terms of the former constitution. On the other hand, the state including the minister responsible for Justice legal and Parliamentary Affairs, insisted that the laws remained in force[6].

Despite the uncertainty that lingered on whether the false news and criminal defamation laws survived the declaration of constitutional invalidity, the Zimbabwean constitutional court in aforementioned cases made a number of insightful and key pronunciations regarding the balancing of freedom of expression on one hand and state and public interests on the other and to what extent and by what means the right to freedom of expression can be justifiably limited. The two cases are discussed below briefly. A few other Zimbabwean cases will also be discussed that bring different dimensions to criminalization of other forms of expression, specifically, online expression.

We acknowledge this chapter ought to focus more on the digital media and their interaction with the criminal law or criminal libel, rather than traditional media. However, the cases involving traditional media can provide a solid background of what has been prevalent before and allude to the implications for social or digital media in some African context. Admittedly, most African journalists have been prosecuted for their publications in traditional media as compared to new media, probably because the latter are a relatively new phenomenon.

Constantine Munyaradzi Chimakure, Vincent Kahiya, and Zimlnd Publishers (Pvt) Ltd v Attorney General of Zimbabwe [Judgment No. SC 14/2013]

The two appellants, a journalist and editor of "*The Independent*" a privately owned Zimbabwean newspaper, and the third applicant a representative of their publishing company, were in 2009 arrested and charged for the *publication or communication of a false statement which harms or is likely to harm the interests of the State in the performance of its functions*. The offence is provided for under section 31(a)(iii) of the Criminal Law (Codification and Reform) Act [*Cap. 9:23*] ("the Criminal Code"). This followed two newspaper stories that they had written and published collectively.

After the initial court appearances at the Magistrates court, the trio applied for referral of their case to the Supreme Court claiming that the provision under which they were charged was in contravention of the right to freedom of expression as provided under section 20(1) of the Lancaster House constitution. In trying to determine whether or not there was any infringement of the applicants' constitutional right to freedom of expression, the Constitutional court looked at a number of key aspects relating to the nature and scope of freedom of expression including what follows below.

Scope of Freedom of Expression

The court outlined that the right to freedom of expression as guaranteed in section 20(1) had three dimensions that are intertwined and which should be respected equally[7]. The three were described as;

1. An internal dimension (the formation and holding of opinion, ideas and information);
2. A communicative dimension (the expression of opinion, imparting of ideas and information); and
3. An external dimension (the effect of opinions, ideas and information on the addressee or the audience i.e. on the rights of others or public interests listed in s 20(2) (a) of the Constitution.

It was further clarified that the right to freedom of expression guarantees protection to the communicative process as well as the effect on the audience that is caused by a particular dissemination of ideas or information. Nevertheless, the state may interfere only when the activity or expression poses danger of direct, obvious and serious harm to the rights of others or the public interests listed in s 20(2) of the Constitution.[8]

Protection of Freedom of Expression and Truth

The court also emphasised that limitation of freedom of expression is not per se, derived from the falsity of a statement or publication but more on the actual or potential harm caused. In emphasis of this point, the court pointed that;

What is protected is really the indivisible freedom of everyone to speak even when they may after they have done so be called liars. Anyone has a right to impart or receive ideas and information about the activities of security service institutions regardless of the falsity or truth of the message conveyed, provided no harm or real likelihood of harm to the rights of others or public interest results in breach of law[9].

Permissible Legislative Limitation of the Exercise of Freedom of Expression

The court also noted that any kind of freedom can be abused and thus harm others or the public interest and as such its exercise has to be limited but the measures to limit this right must conform to the principle of proportionality.[10]

The interference imposed in terms of the impugned law must be limited to being a restriction or hindrance of the enjoyment of the exercise of the right to freedom of expression and it must be exclusively directed towards the pursued legitimate aim.

Proportionality of Measures Employed to Limit Freedom of Expression

The applicable penalty was also analysed to see if it was a proportional to the legitimate aim being pursued and the seriousness of the offence and the court went on to hold that the twenty year imprisonment term impossible for this offences was "draconian" and that the only inference that could be drawn from such a lengthy maximum penalty of imprisonment was that it was intended to have a chilling effect on the exercise of the right to freedom of expression by all citizens rather than to simply deter persons from the prohibited acts. Having determined thus, the court went on to hold that;

- The chilling effect of the disproportionate threat of the period of the maximum penalty of imprisonment to which a person convicted of the offence is liable harms operations of a free media.
- By authorising the discretionary imposition of a maximum punishment of twenty years imprisonment for offences amounting to attempts, s 31(a) (iii) of the Criminal Code has a serious inhibiting effect on the exercise of the right to freely criticise public institutions in the performance of their functions.
- A strong constitutional protection of freedom of expression cannot tolerate the imposition of self censorship on free speech and press through fear of lengthy sentences of imprisonment for offences of publishing or communicating false news.
- Taking into account the fact that freedom of expression is peculiarly more vulnerable to the "chilling effects" of criminal sanctions than any other fundamental right as stated by the UN Special Rapporteur on freedom of opinion and expression, penal sanctions particularly imprisonment, should never be applied to offences of publishing false news.
- The higher the level of the maximum penalty of imprisonment the greater the chilling effect on freedom of expression.

With this, the court declared that section 31(a) (iii) of the Criminal Law (Codification and Reform) Act [*Cap. 9:23*) ("the Criminal Code") was in contravention of the right to freedom of expression as provided for in section 20 (1) of the Lancaster house constitution in operation at the time and therefore void.

Nevanji Madanhire and Nqaba Matshazi v Attorney-General [Judgment No CCZ 2/14]

The two an Editor and journalist at "*The Standard* " newspaper at the time, were in 2011, arrested and charged with criminal defamation as defined in section 96 of the Criminal Law Codification and Reform Act following a story written and published by the two Applicants collectively. The offence of criminal defamation criminalises the intentional publication of false material which causes serious harm to another person's reputation. If found guilty of this offence one faces a fine or imprisonment of up to two years or both. Following their arrest and appearance at the Magistrates court, the two applied for the offence of criminal defamation as defined in s 96 of the Criminal Law Code to be declared unconstitutional and struck down and ultimately for the perpetual stay of their prosecution for this offence. The determining the constitutionality or lack thereof of criminal defamation, the court analysed a number of key aspects including the following.

Whether or Not Criminal Defamation Is a Justifiable Limitation of the Right to Freedom of Expression

The court conceded that criminal defamation is one of the permissible derogations or limitations of the right to freedom of expression but aimed at the protection of the rights and reputations of other persons. However while this objective was so observed and well accepted, the limitation of this right to this and such means was questionable in as far as its proportionality to the harm likely to be caused and to the interests as stake. The court thus considered at length whether it was necessary to criminalise defamatory statements in order to protect the said interests. In considering thus, the court made a number of observations including that criminal defamation has a stifling or chilling effect on the right to speak and to know by its very existence. This Judge Patel noted was:

... the more deleterious consequence of its retention in the Criminal Law Code, particularly in the present context of newspaper reportage.... This, in turn, may result in the citizenry remaining uninformed about matters of public significance and the unquestioned and unchecked continuation of unconscionable malpractices.[11]

The court also went on to observe that it is impossible to expect the media to perform its investigative and informative functions without defaming one person or the other

Proportionality of the Penalty

Also scrutinized, was the effect and proportionality of the maximum two year imprisonment sentence. On this, the court noted that the sentence only serves to exacerbate the chilling effect caused by criminalising defamation and further stressed that the sentence was "excessive and patently disproportionate" to the intended purpose of prohibiting the publication of statements that injure the rights and reputations of others.

Adequacy of Civil Remedies

Having declared that criminal measures and the accompanying term of imprisonment were excessive and disproportionate to the objective of protecting the rights and reputations of other persons, the court went on to hold that the offence is not reasonably justifiable in a democratic society and was inconsistent with the freedom of expression guaranteed by section 20(1) of the constitution at the time and therefore void. The court further noted that the country has in place "an appropriate and satisfactory alternative civil remedy ....to combat the mischief of defamation[12]." The essence, the constitutional court in this case emphasized and based its decision on a number of issues similarly observed in the aforementioned case of Chimakure and Kahiya which include that;

- Criminalising defamation results in harmful consequences such as the chilling possibility of arrest, detention as well as imprisonment and that these are excessive in effect.
- While the objective of the criminal defamation offence is to protect the reputations, rights and freedoms of other persons, criminalising defamation is a disproportionate remedy to the objective being pursued.
- The harmful and undesirable consequences of criminalising defamation such as the chilling possibilities of arrest, detention and two years imprisonment, are manifestly excessive in their effect
- The effect of criminal defamation extends to the public as well as it stifles and silences free-flow of information in the public domain resulting in an uninformed citizenry on matters of public significance.
- It is unnecessary to criminalise defamatory statements as the country's civil remedies for defamation afford ample compensatory redress for injury to one's reputation or dignity.

2016: Criminal Defamation Put to Rest

Media Institute of Southern Africa (Zimbabwe Chapter) and 4 Others v Minister of Justice, Legal and Parliamentary Affairs and 2 others CCZ07/15

In February 2015, MISA-Zimbabwe together with three journalists (2nd to 4th Applicants) and one citizen and independent publisher filed a constitutional court application seeking clarity on the status of the criminal defamation offence under the new Zimbabwe Constitution following the Madanhire judgement (CCZ 2/14).

The application was necessitated by the fact that the 2014 Madanhire v Attorney General Judgment indicated that the declaration of invalidity of criminal defamation was in respect of the right to freedom of expression under the previous Constitution of Zimbabwe. Further in that judgment, PATEL J had included a passage that suggested that as the formulation of the right to expression in the new Constitution was different, it was possible that the offence of criminal defamation would be constitutional in terms of the new constitution, thus creating uncertainty on whether the law was still alive or not under the current constitutional dispensation.

At the 3rd of February 2016 hearing MISA-Zimbabwe advanced the argument that by virtue of the declaration that criminal defamation was void, the Madanhire judgment had in effect removed the offence from Zimbabwean law. The State representatives eventually conceded this argument and an order to this effect was granted confirming that criminal defamation is no longer a part of Zimbabwean law.

Online Expression: State v Vikazi Mavhudzi

In 2011, Mavhudzi was charged with contravening section 22(2) of the Criminal Law (Codification and Reform) Act [Chapter 9:23] i.e. "subverting a constitutional government" for allegedly suggesting to the then Prime Minister Mr Morgan Tsvangirai to take over or attempt to take over the government by unconstitutional through a facebook post on the Prime Minister's facebook page. The facebook post in question allegedly read; "I am overwhelmed don't know what to say PM, what happened in Egypt is sending shock waves to all dictators around the world. Worth emulating hey." The charges against Mavhudzi were later discharged the same year for lack of evidence

State v Matsapa

Zimbabwean police arrested Ernest Matsapa in 2016 for circulating a video on social media to a Whatsapp group called Nyanga Free Range. The audio-visual clip was considered as "denigrating the person of" President Robert Mugabe hence Matsapa appeared in the Nyanga Magistrates court facing charges of criminal nuisance for alleging the president was too old and a burden to all Zimbabweans."The audio and video clip has the impression that the President Cde Robert Mugabe is incapacitated and has become a burden to the majority including his family due to diminishing responsibility." Matsapa could be jailed for potentially attempting to destabilize the country through publication of utterances that could cause Zimbabweans to lose trust and confidence in the presidency. Such criminal cases have inherent potential to cause riots, violence and instability.

THE SOUTH AFRICAN APPROACH

Hoho v The State [2008] ZASCA 98 -

In this case which involved a non-media person charged with criminal defamation, the South Africa's Supreme Court of Appeal held that the crime of defamation was consistent with the constitution of South Africa. The Court held that the crime of defamation still exists. In arriving at this decision, the court pointed presented several arguments, amongst which was the drawing of similarities between civil and criminal cases of physical assault before the courts, and that of defamation. The court pointed out that

... there is also a civil remedy available for common assault, yet nobody would suggest that there is for that reason no need for the crime of common assault. There is in my view no reason why the state should oblige and prosecute in the case of a complaint in respect of an injury to a person's physical integrity but not in the case of a complaint in respect of an injury to reputation, which may have more serious and lasting effects than a physical assault.[13]

Motsepe Ntele Cecil v the State [Case No: A816/2013]

In 2014, the South African High Court (Pretoria) delivered judgment in the case of the *Sowetan* journalist Motsepe who had been convicted for criminal defamation relating to a series of articles that he had published in the paper. Upon his conviction, Motsepe had been fined and in lieu of that fine he would face a ten-month imprisonment term wholly suspended on specified conditions. Motsepe then challenged both the conviction and sentence and the appeal was joined by fifteen *amici curiae* that specifically appealed to the court on the negative effects of criminal defamation on the freedom of the media and on this basis challenged the constitutionality of criminal defamation laws.

From the inception, the court concluded that on analysis, the articles in question were defamatory and that what only needed to be determined was whether or not the requisite intention to defame was present and the unlawfulness of the action by the appellant. After analyzing the facts further, the court concluded that while the appellant may have been reckless in not verifying the facts as much as he should have, recklessness still does not equate to intention and as such, his conviction could not stand. In arriving at this conclusion, the court stressed that; "Once a person thinks that the published words are covered by one of the recognised defences to a claim for defamation, such person lacks the necessary intention required for a conviction on criminal".[14]

AMICI CURIAE APPLICATION

On the other hand, the Amici Curiae's application was to the effect that the common-law crime of defamation is inconsistent with the constitution of South Africa in that it is an unjustifiable limitation to the right to freedom of the media. The application was further to the effect that the crime should be limited to the publication of defamatory statements by other persons who are not members of the media as previous decisions in cases such as Hoho, had not dealt with the impact of criminal defamation on the media and that the impact of the law on the media and on non-media persons differed.

The Amici further contended that the civil remedy for defamation provides adequate means to cure and deter defamation by the media. The application was opposed by the state on the basis that a ruling to that effect would have adverse consequences

The Effect of Criminal Defamation on Freedom of the Media

After considering regional and international standards and case law on freedom of expression, the high court held that;

- The right to freedom of expression is not unrestrained and that it must yield to the individual's right not to be unlawfully defamed and to the individual's right to dignity.[15]
- The request to have criminal defamation declared unconstitutional "undermines the constitution and the promotion of Equality and Prevention of Unfair Discrimination Act.
- The court further noted that the case for repealing of criminal defamation laws at international level was in respect of "extreme" cases of governmental abuse of journalists which in the court's view did not apply in South Africa. Instead, the court relied on the founding of the South African Constitutional Court in Dikoko v Mokhatla 2007 (1) BCLR 1 (CC) at para 141-142 where the court held that the right to freedom of expression must at times be relegated in favour of the right to dignity.

The Need to Balance Freedom of Expression and Other Competing Interests

On this aspect, the court observed that the law of defamation still requires that a balance be struck between freedom of expression and the protection of reputations and while further conceding that criminal sanctions were a drastic remedy to the intended objective that civil remedies, the high court maintained that this was cured by the fact that criminal defamation came with an extensive burden of proof to which the court attributed the low number of prosecutions under that law.[16] Having considered thus the court held that;

- Criminal prosecution of the media for defamation in not inconsistent with the constitution of South Africa.
- Even though criminal defamation limits the right to freedom of expression, such limitation was justifiable in an open and democratic society.[17]

THE MOZAMBIQUE RULING

The ruling in a Mozambique Court is remarkably significant in that it involved publication of material alleged libelous material against a state President. The alleged offending material was originally published on a blogsite then found its way into mainstream newspapers. Prominent Mozambican economist Carlos Nuno Castel-Branco and journalist, Fernando Mbanze, editor of the independent newssheet "Mediafax", were in September 2015 acquitted by a Maputo court acquitted of libeling former President Armando Guebuza. The court action had emanated from a post Castel-Branco published on his Facebook page in November 2013, lambasting then President Guebuza's governance and calling on him to resign. Two papers, *Mediafax* and the weekly *Canal de Mocambique* republished Carlos-Branco's text. Libeling the head of state and other senior political figures is considered a security offence in Mozambique; hence the Public Prosecutor instituted charges against Castel-Branco under the law on crimes against state security. For republishing the article, Mbanze was charged under the vague offence of "abuse of press freedom" under the 1991 Press Law. Initially, the director of *Canal de Mocambique*, Fernando Veloso, was also accused, but since he was in Portugal for medical treatment he was not in the dock, nor was he tried in absentia.

Delivering the verdict a panel of three judges, Presiding Judge Joao Almeida Guilherme, observed that the court analysed in detail Castel-Branco's Facebook post and found nothing libelous in it. Judge Gulherme protected Castel-Branco's freedom of opinion in view of the latter's criticism of Guebuza's governance of the country. Other people could find such criticisms unpalatable, but that did not make them a crime. On the whole, according to the court, Castel-Branco's words fell within the confines of freedom of expression, and were protected by the Constitution. Some words were considered as just criticism notwithstanding that they could be exaggerated. The court was averse to thrust itself on the unsavory "list of the most undemocratic organizations", through convicting the accused, especially when some of the accusations made by Castel-Branco were factually true, such as reference to the appointment of a convicted criminal "to command one of the main police units in the centre of the country". This was a matter in the public domain, Guilherme noted, and Castel-Branco had made "a legitimate criticism and it's reasonable to expect the government to clarify this". The court acknowledged the language used by

Castel-Branco might be regarded as "impertinent and vulgar", but the law did not deal with mere impertinence and vulgarity. Since Castel-Branco was ultimately found not guilty, other parties involved in the republication of his text were similarly acquitted. Judge Guilherme concluded that, however tough some people might find the language used in the article, "it is perfectly acceptable in a democracy.... People have the right to give their opinions on how the President is governing the country". The prosecution did not appeal against the ruling. If found guilty Castel-Branco could have faced a jail sentence of up to two years, although international pressure groups such as Amnesty International were already lobbying that he be regarded "a prisoner of conscience". This case is significant because it heralded the first time in Mozambican history that anyone has been prosecuted for alleged libel published on Facebook.[18]

TANZANIAN CASES AND THE ILLUSION OF NORMALCY

Tanzania is typical of countries where the criminalisation of the use of new ICTs seems to have affected ordinary people and citizen journalists more than professional journalists. By professional journalists here, we refer to those persons working in conventional media houses and are recognised news reporters fitting the old definitions and identity of newspersons (Tuchman). A recent doctoral thesis from Tanzania observes that professional journalists work easily within a legislative context where there is a Cyber-Crime Act amongst other pieces of legislation that criminalise certain forms of expression (Hassani 2016). Tanzanian journalists revealed that the Cyber Crime Act has not directly affected them in the immediate present. It is arguable that professional journalists are general conscious and sensitive and cautious about all forms of defamation hence they conduct themselves with either due diligence or they self-censor. The editorial chain of news production can also ensure that potentially litigious publications are eliminated before they attract adverse responses from those who think their reputations have been unduly or maliciously harmed.

Previously Tanzania has used older laws to prosecute for alleged social media transgressions but recently they have on the statutes the Cyber Crime Act of 2015. This act criminalises certain forms of expression as it states,

Any person who publishes information or data presented in a picture, text, symbol or any other form in a computer system knowing that such information or data is false, deceptive, misleading or inaccurate, and *with intent to defame*, threaten, abuse, *insult*, or otherwise deceive or mislead the public or concealing commission of an offence, commits an offence, and shall on conviction be liable to a fine of not less than five million shillings or to imprisonment for a term of not less than three years or to both.

Tanzanian doctoral candidate Abbasi Hassani (2016) has listed social media and defamation related cases in his recent thesis. In spite of some cases having been filed before the enactment of the Cyber Crime Act, there are several recent cases that show that there are levels of criminalisation of publication of materials regarded as offensive in that country. The first case involved a university student and the state, and is referred to as "Mwamunyage case." Benedict Angelo Ngonyani was charged for publishing on 25 September 2016 on social media that Tanzanian Chief of Defence Forces (CDF), General Davis Mwamunyange had died from poisoning. If found guilty Ngonyani is liable to serve three years imprisonment or payment of a fine of TSh5 million or both sentences.

Another notable case with a verdict is that of Isaac Emery Hubakuki, a resident of Arusha in Tanzania. He was charged for insulting President of the United Republic of Tanzania, Dr. John Pombe Magufuli.

Hubakuki was arrested and charged at the Arusha Magistrate Court for publishing defamatory materials contrary to section 16 of the Cybercrimes Act. He pleaded guilty as charged. The court sentenced him to either pay a fine of TSh 7 million or to be imprisoned for three years. Hubakuku paid the fine. Several more young and naïve people have been arrested for insulting the President or spreading false and malicious statement either on internet or Whatsapp.

Some Tanzanian civil society groups have protested about the criminalisation of communications through the Cyber Crimes Act. They a allege the law is overly harsh and potentially incriminates well-intentioned whistle blowers who possess credible information that can be used to prosecute government officials involved in crime or corruption. However, journalists interviewed by Habassi seemed to be comfortable to work in a legal environment where the new act exists (Habbasi 2016). The cosy view Tanzanian journalists present is contradicted by harsh empirical realities presented elsewhere on the continent and throughout the world about how professional journalists using digital media are surviving. We have already noted how Tom Lowenthal (2015) has observed how journalists the world over are under siege and operate under constant surveillance forcing them to "to think and act like spies" especially when practicing investigative journalism using new ICTs. Another report shows the distressing fatality figures of journalists especially those using new media technologies. Writes Catherine Guchera (2016);

According to the Committee to Protect Journalists (CPJ), over the past two decades 780 journalists worldwide were murdered while reporting or investigating stories. Many used digital tools in their daily work, which exposed them to cyber threats as well. This trend is reflected in a recent CPJ report indicating that 109 out of the 199 journalists jailed (in 2015) worked online. Article 19 has also increasingly documented attacks against journalists who work online. In many African countries as elsewhere in the world, laws have been enacted to allow security agencies to intercept communications... The ubiquitous mobile phone with built-in geolocation software makes the user traceable anywhere and at all times. Merely making an appointment can expose both the journalist and his or her source to unwanted surveillance. What is disconcerting is that while state actors and corporate entities have become more and more adept at using surveillance tools, many journalists have yet to learn how to protect themselves online.

Such details are shocking when journalists are made to pay the ultimate prize when criminalisation alone is not deterrent enough.

CRIMINAL DEFAMATION FROM THE PERSPECTIVE OF THE AFRICAN COURT ON HUMAN AND PEOPL'S RIGHTS

Lohé Issa Konaté v Burkina Faso- Application No. 004/2013

The applicant a Burkinabe citizen was charged with defamation, public insult and contempt of court arising from an article he wrote and published in one of the country's newspapers relating to one of the country's prosecutors. He was subsequently convicted and sentenced to twelve (12) months imprisonment and also ordered to pay various amounts in fines and damages including an order suspending the operation of the publishing newspaper for six (6) months.

Konate appealed against both conviction and sentence at the African court on human and people's rights (the African Court) on the grounds that the jail term, huge fine, damages and costs of suit ordered against him violated his right to freedom of expression as protected under article 9 the African Charter on Human and People's Rights (the Charter) and under Article 19 of the Covenant on Civil and Political Rights (the Covenant). It was further argued on Konate's behalf that criminalising the tarnishing of the image of a public figure was a disproportionate sanction which brought about a chilling effect to the public when discussing public interest issues.

Konate therefore sought the following relief from the African Court among other aspects;

1. A declaration that his conviction and sentence were in violation of the right to freedom of expression.
2. A declaration that Burkina Faso's laws on defamation and insult are in contravention of the right to freedom of expression OR ALTERNATIVELY that the jail term for defamation is a violation of the right to freedom of expression and that Burkina Faso be should amend its laws accordingly.

In arriving at its decision, the court considered a number of key issues including the following;

Justifiable Limitations to Freedom of Expression

The court stressed that while the right to freedom of expression can be limited, it must still be subjected to a lesser degree of interference and that a limitation to this right is not acceptable simply because it is provided by law but rather, reasons for limiting this right must be based on legitimate public interest and the limitation must be *proportionate* to and *necessary* for the intended objective. To this end, any criminal sentence must conform to the criteria of necessity and proportionality and any that do not conform are not in sync with the dictates of the Charter. Having considered all the facts at hand, the African Court held that;

1. Custodial sentences should not be used to remedy violations of the right to freedom of expression and of the media except in "serious and very exceptional circumstances" such as in international crimes among others.
2. All sentences that were imposed on Konate were disproportionate to the pursued aim in the law and were thus in contravention of article 9 and 19 of the Charter and of the Covenant respectively and of the revised ECOWAS treaty.
3. Particularly because of the existence of custodial sentences for defamation in the law.

CONCLUSION

Criminal libel is viewed as archaic and undemocratic but it still subsists even in countries that claim to be leading in espousing principles of democracy. The criminalisation of freedom of expression or freedom to disseminate information is also an ongoing challenge apparent in the US and other states that claim to be 'civilised' and tolerant. In the US it is still possible in a number of states for individuals to institute criminal libel charges. In the digital era both media houses and individuals who have the capacity to communicate on a mass scale ought to be wary of the possibilities of getting sued and prosecuted for different forms of libel or defamation, even in those countries that might claim to have dumped criminal defamation. The criminalisation of communication and publication remain, and at stake is the reputation of individuals or organisations or the state who claim their rights and interests have been injured. Whether verdicts which correspond with the plaintiff or complainants' alleged injury are issued in any courts of law or not is a matter of the jurisdictional decision and justification of such verdict. It is not always certain that courts will reject to hear and accept the prosecution of parties accused of criminal defamation/libel or any other communication that attracts the criminalisation of communication or publication. Internet users must also remain wary of the possibilities of litigation, and offenses rooted in publications and utterances as 'criminal' can be defined or classified variously in order to charge and penalize originators and distributors of such communication. The several examples cited in this chapter show that defamation and criminal defamation, and alternatively the criminalisation of communication in the public sphere are no longer exclusive to the traditional media, the so-called fourth estate. Individuals who now operate in the emergent 'fifth estate' and with the capacity to communicate and distribute messages and information at a mass scale due to the ubiquity of digital technologies are also prone to getting arrested and prosecuted for defamation and 'criminal defamation' or other criminalizing charges. New ICTs and their uses by both the fourth and fifth estate confirm that "When *anyone* can become a media producer, *everyone* should know something about media law – both to protect their own rights and to avoid violating the rights of others" (Packard, 2010). It remains the states prerogative to use terms such as 'criminal defamation' or "criminal nuisance" to conveniently reject them as archaic, but if the latter is the case, there is never outright assurance that freedom of expression and freedom of the media are not bludgeoned and compromised through other 'criminalising' torts or terminology that can be attended to in courts of law. Precedence might guide the determination of current and future cases on criminal defamation and the criminalisation of communication and publication, but it still remain the prerogative of each individual court attending to a particular case to determine whether defamation or any other offensive publication or utterance can be classified to be a crime.

Theoretical and political correctness posits that criminal defamation is archaic, undemocratic and unjustifiable in the contemporary world. However, in numerous countries practical exigencies make the 'crime' persist at best as a 'theoretical' possibility, and in extreme scenarios as a real punitive instrument or deterrent for possible excesses of the media against either private citizens or public officials. There are instances such as in Zimbabwe where criminal defamation has been categorically struck off the statutes. It remains to be seen if it will not be invoked for blatant and extreme cases of defamination that threaten public peace and stability, or those that 'serious' damage the reputation of complainants or public officials. South Africa, for instance, observes that while it is the standard and norm to repeal extreme cases of governments abusing criminal defamation laws against journalists throughout the world, it did not apply in the country. It is however reassuring those courts even in nation-states generally considered being strict and intolerant such as Zimbabwe criminal defamation has been struck of the statutes. Where it has possibility of reappearing as a suit other considerations also apply in mitigation for the journalists and non-professional communicators. For instance, a reckless journalist will not be heavily penalized if there is no proof of malice or intention in committing the crime, and punishments need also not be disproportionate in the severity to the offense committed. All this is in apparent consideration that communicators are not saints and may flout some legal and ethical tenets of communication even when they purport to serve the best interests of humanity through such actions as raising alarm of transgressions as has been shown in the considerable deterioration in the standards and performance of the new WikiLeaks exposures.

REFERENCES

Adam, G. S. (2009). Freedom of Expression and the democratic liberal tradition. In *The Handbook of Mass Media Ethics*. New York: Routledge.

Beyene, Z. (2011). Media use and abuse in Ethiopia. In R. S. Fortner & P. M. Fackler (Eds.), *The Handbook of Global Communications and Media Ethics*. Oxford, UK: Wiley-Blackwell.

Bloy, D. (2007). *Media Law*. London: Sage.

Chari, T. (2013). How new media technologies are impacting ethical practices: Perceptions of Zimbabwean journalists. *International Journal on Media and Communications*, *1*(1), 66-74.

Chiumbu, S. (2010). Media, alternativism and power: The political economy of community media in South Africa. In N. Hyde-Clarke (Ed.), *The Citizen in Communication* (pp. 115–137). Claremont, South Africa: Juta.

Creech, K. (2007). *Electronic media law and regulation*. London: Focal Press.

Crone, T. (2002). *Law and the Media*. Oxford, UK: Focal Press.

Fackler, P. M., Obonyo, L., Terpstra, M., & Okaalet, E. (2011). Media and post election violence in Kenya. In R. S. Fortner & P. M. Fackler (Eds.),*The Handbook of Global Communications and Media Ethics*. Oxford, UK: Wiley-Blackwell.

Feltoe, G. (2002). *A Guide to Media Law in Zimbabwe*. Harare: Legal Resources Foundation. Retrieved from http://www.kubatana.net/docs/resour/021101mediaguide_ gf.pdf

Foster, S. (2003). *Human Rights & Civil Liberties*. London: Pearson.

Guchera, C. (2016). African journalists must do more to protect themselves online. *International Journalists' Network*. Retrieved from http://ijnet.org/en/blog/african-journalists-must-do-more-protect-themselves-online

Habassi, H. (2016). *New Media, New Rules: The impact of internet defamation and Press freedom in Tanzania* (Doctoral thesis). St Augustine University of Tanzania.

Hyde-Clarke, N. (2010). *The Citizen in Communication*. Claremont, CA: Juta.

Lowenthal, T. (2015). Surveillance forces journalists to think and act like spies. *Committee to Protect Journalists*. Retrieved from https://cpj.org/2015/04/attacks-on-the-press-surveillance-forces-journalists-to-think-act-like-spies.php

Mhiripiri, N. A. (2013). Alternative Dispute Resolution (ADR) Systems in the Zimbabwean Media Industry and the Debate On Self-regulation. *Journal of African Media Studies*, *5*(3), 313–336. doi:10.1386/jams.5.3.313_1

Mhiripiri, N. A. (2015). Narratives of the Zimbabwe Crisis, National Sovereignty and Human and Media Rights Violations. In S. Adejumobi (Ed.), *National Democratic Reforms in Africa: Changes and Challenges*. New York: Palgrave MacMillan. doi:10.1057/9781137518828_6

Mhiripiri, N. A., & Mutsvairo, B. (2013). Social Media, New ICTs and the Challenges Facing the Zimbabwe Democratic Process. In *New Media Influence on Social and Political Change in Africa* (pp. 402-421). IGI Global.

Mill, J. S. (2006). *On Liberty and the Subjection of Women* (A. Ryan, Ed.). London: Academic Press. (Original work published 1859)

Mill, J. S. (1967). *Essays on Government, Jurisprudence, Liberty of the Press, and the Law of Nations*. New York: Academic Press. (Original work published 1825)

Moyo, L. (2015). Digital age as ethical maze: Citizen journalism ethics during crises in Zimbabwe and South Africa. *African. Journalism Studies*, *36*(4), 125–144. doi:10.1080/23743670.2015.1119494

Packard, A. (2010). *Digital Media Law*. New York: McGraw-Hill. doi:10.1002/9781444318197

Upson, S. (2016). WikiLeaks has morphed from journalism hotshot to malware hub. *BackChannel*. Retrieved from https://backchannel.com/wikileaks-has-morphed-from-journalism-hotshot-to-malware-hub-1bdd68cc560#.fz4qcvnk6

Wilkins, L., & Christians, C. (Eds.). (2008). *The Handbook of Mass Media Ethics*. New York: Routledge.

ENDNOTES

1 Voluntary Media Council of Zimbabwe Digital Code of Ethics http://www.vmcz.co.zw/index.php/news/387-vmcz-digital-code-of-conduct)

2 Der Spiegel - Interview with Julian Assange: 'We Are Drowning in Material', 20 July 2015

3 "WikiLeaks acting illegally, says Gillard," *Sydney Morning Herald*, 2 December 2010. Retrieved 25July 2016.

4 http://www.herald.co.zw/zimpapers-contests-defamation-law/

5 http://www.herald.co.zw/criminal-defamation-state-gets-ultimatum/

6 http://www.herald.co.zw/vp-mnangagwa-defends-criminal-defamation/
https://www.dailynews.co.zw/articles/2014/04/10/mnangagwa-defends-criminal-defamation-law

7 Page 9-10- SC14/2013

8 Page 10...judgement No......

9 Page 14 of the judgement

10 Page 16-17

11 Page 10-11

12 Page 16 of CCZ2/14

13 Hobo v State, https://globalfreedomofexpression.columbia.edu/cases/hoho-v-state/

14 Page 6

15 Page 15 of the judgement

16 Page 18 of the judgment

17 Page 19 of the judgment

18 See Mozambique: Guebuza Libel Trial Postponed, http://allafrica.com/stories/201507250043.html.

Chapter 2
Ethical Pitfalls in the Digital Age:
When the Desire to "Serve Hot" Gets in the Way of Verification

Tendai Chari
University of Venda, South Africa

ABSTRACT

Using the case study approach, this chapter examines ethical shortfalls confronting the media in the Internet era. The one case is drawn from a story published in The New York Times in 2015, while the other is a story published in a Zimbabwean newspaper, the Daily News. The objective was to broaden knowledge on how the Internet is impacting ethical practices in local and global political environments. The chapter argues that the Internet's architecture predisposes journalists to a host of unethical practices that were uncommon to the legacy media environment. Its immediacy exerts pressure on journalists to publish stories without adequate verification out of the fear of being "scooped" by competitors and citizen journalists who are less constrained to adhere to old-age journalistic ethics such as factual reporting and verification.

INTRODUCTION

There is no technological innovation that has had a contradictory impact on journalism practice more than the Internet. On the one hand, the medium has been an enabler of journalism practice, unlocking new opportunities for practitioners. On the other hand, it is viewed as a bane for journalism, inviting in its wake a plethora of ethical pitfalls linked to its ability to 'instantly distribute highly searchable information without space restrictions..." (Mendoza, 2012). This chapter examines the impact of the Internet on journalism ethics in order gain deeper insights on the transformative impacts of new communication technologies on journalism practice. Empirical data were drawn from two review cases illustrative of the adverse impact of the Internet on journalism ethics in local and global environments.

DOI: 10.4018/978-1-5225-2095-5.ch002

Previous studies tend to romanticise the role of the Internet on journalism practice, foregrounding the Internet as an enabler of journalism (Berger, 1996, 2005; Moyo, 2007, 2009; Mudhai et al, 2009; Lee, 2012), while overlooking its negative impacts. This has tended to mask the Internet's negative impact on ethical practices. Klein and Kleinman (2002, 38) rightly assert that that different social groups interpret technologies differently and seek to shape them differently as well. Mabweazara (2010, 1) concurs when he states that new media technologies should be viewed as "embedded in in existing social, cultural and political and economic networks in which journalism is entrenched".

Although the social constructivist perspective accentuates social agency in the use of new communication technologies (see Mabweazara, 2010, 2011; Lee, 2015) debates have not broadened to encompass the negative effects of the Internet on journalism practice. As a result, there is a lacuna on threats posed by the Internet on journalism practice. This chapter fills this gap through an exploration of two review cases in which the Internet's architecture, could be directly or indirectly implicated in aiding unethical practices. The first case is the *Daily News* (Zimbabwe)'s publication of a fictitious story claiming that a woman had been beheaded by ruling Zanu PF supporters in front of her daughters. The second is a story published by the *New York Times's* East African Bureau Chief, Jeffrey Gentleman in December 2015, alleging that Zimbabwean President, Robert Mugabe had called Kenyans "thieves". These two stories, about separate incidents separated by more than a decade are illustrative of the Internet's negative impact on ethical journalism. The two case studies mentioned above are used as illuminating rods to shed light on how the Internet is negatively impacting on journalism ethics.

The rest of the chapter is divided into five parts. The first part is a discussion of the theoretical framework which underpins this article, namely the concept of global media ethics. It critically reviews the debate on global media ethics in order to situate the present study in a context. The second part discusses the methodological design and outlines the research questions. The third part gives a synopsis of the two 'case reports' (Zucker, 2009) which are the focus of this article, namely the *Daily News* (Zimbabwe) and *the New York Times* story referred to above. In the fourth part the two case reports are discussed through the prism of the global media theoretical framework. Part five, which is the final part of the paper is the conclusion and is a critical reflection of the chapter's findings and their implications on journalism practice in local and global political environments.

GLOBAL MEDIA ETHICS AND EMERGING NORMATIVE ETHICS: A CONCEPTUAL FRAMEWORK

"Ethics" is a slippery term which suffers from semantic entropy. However, the term generally relates to whether actions are either right or wrong. "Media ethics", thus, connotes wrong or right in media practice. Ward (2008, 139) defines media ethics as a type of applied ethics which entail the analysis of media practice and "the application of its principles to situations and issues". Since what is right or wrong depends on the cultural and political context in which journalism is practiced, it is difficult to pin down what is ethical or unethical behaviour by the media. Media ethics are not static but forever evolving, implying that they are bound to be change as contextual factors change.In the Internet age journalism ethics are being redefined in an irrevocable way (Ward, n.d.; Lasica, 1997; Arant, 2000; 2003; Friend, and Singer, 2007; Ess, 2009; Ward, 2010; Berman and Shumway, 2003). How journalists should navigate the rugged ethical terrain in the digital age is a more of a conundrum. It is however incontrovertible that the Internet has enabled the media to have a global reach, thereby rendering geographical boundaries superfluous. With this global reach,the power of the media has increased tremendously. In addition, different media now co-exist in different platforms, thus rendering the 'Berlin' wall that used to separate print and broadcast media invisible. News stories can now be distributed instantaneously to a mixed audience globally via different platforms, thereby exerting pressure on news organisations to publish before verification of facts. Some news organisations have fallen prey to rumours published online withequally telling consequences on their credibility. The internal logic of the Internet lends itself to anonymity, meaning that it is difficult, if not near impossible to verify information published online. Ward (2013) argues that there is need to reconstruct media ethics to suit the changed physical and cultural context of the new media because of the increased power of the media. Similarly,Arant (2000) arguesthat the myriad of ethical challenges occasioned by the online media require that journalists "formulate, utilize and regularly update ethics methodologies".

The process of transforming traditional journalism ethics into global ethics should of necessity entail adapting journalistic norms that are in tandem with the changing media scene in a globalising world, while at the same time ensuring that the core principles that have guided journalism remain. It is within this spirit that scholars like Ward (2013) advocate that journalism should be guided by global media ethics because technological changes and new ownership patterns in geographic regions where journalism practice is now characterised by plurality of traditions, cultures and values. Ward (2010) further asserts that "current media practices are narrowly based within the borders of a single country and thus unable to inform the public about a globalised world". As a framework for guiding journalistic behaviour in the digital age, global media ethics is still underdeveloped and there is no consensus what it is, what it should be or how it can be developed. Ward (2010, p.2) defines global media ethics as "an evolving field that motivates a loosely connected set of activities and studies united by the belief that ethics must go global...". Thus,journalists should go through some form of "global revolution" in their self-consciousness and in the manner in which they practice their profession Ward (2010, p.2). In this vein journalists should view their responsibilities from a cosmopolitan perspective by resisting parochialism, narrow patriotism and extreme nationalism (Ward, 2010, p.2).

Journalists practice their profession in different spatial, political and cultural contexts and their consciousness is shaped by the local environment in which they operate, even though their work has a global impact. It is not clear how journalists may bridge the gulf between their local socialization and their new status as cosmopolitan citizens whose work has impact beyond the confines of their geographical boundaries. Questions have been raised about the fact that global media ethics is characterised by different approaches and a "plurality of types of theorizing" and "a plurality of contending views"on global media ethics, thus making it difficult to concretise global media ethics. Ward (2010, p.2) as much acknowledges this conundrum when he describes global media ethics as an "evolving" or "emerging" project. Ethical values contemplated in global media ethics are therefore, work in progress and there is no agreement on a single global media ethics. Hence, the core values embedded in global media ethics are underdeveloped and there islittle or no empirical data about the ethical challenges confronting the media in the new media dispensation.

The development of a global media ethics framework must therefore, be informed by a deeper understanding of the new ethical challenges facing the media of the digital context. As Wasserman (2010) rightly asserts, the role of the media is not similar globally, implying that there should be contestations about the normative role of the media in such non Western contexts, such as post-apartheid South Africa where journalists are torn between "the democratic value of individual responsibility" and the group loyalty required to build a fractured nation. Wasserman's argument that such "one size fits all" approaches to global media ethics and freedom of speech may not work is plausible. A relativist approach to ethics calls for journalists to be sensitive to the cultural peculiarities so as not to cause unnecessary harm. Wasserman (2011, p.86) argues that if "human dignity is to serve as a universal value strived for globally, it would have to be interpreted and applied within local contexts, but in relation to a global set of power relations within which media producers, audiences and participants are mutually interdependent". Given the lopsided global power relations whereby normative ethical values tilt more in favour of the global North's universal morality, understanding of global media ethics appears to be influenced by the Western epistemologies at the expense of other world regions. Christians (2010,p.6) argues that global media ethics should be guided by universal principles – in particular a "universal ethic of humanity, dignity and truth", three ethical principles that bind humanity, while Shakuntala (2010, p.103) proposes an "epistemic syncretism", where media personnel can adopt both Western theories of ethics as well as local traditions and practices. To this end, "the local should be borne upon the Universal in a non-coercive way" (Shakuntala 2010, p.103). For Shakuntala, both the Western and the local ethical theories should be acknowledged and appreciated (Shakuntala 2010, p.103) but, again it is not clear how such a syncretism can be achieved given the global hegemonic order whereby journalistic practices in the global South are dominated by the journalistic ethos of the North. Against this backdrop, one may argue that even Banda's (2010) claim that journalistic practices in Zambia are a product of the fusion of Western and local practices (glocalisation) sounds too optimistic in so far as it portrays a false sense of equality between global and local cultures, when indications are that local cultures are suffocated by Western cultures in the new global order. Gebremedhum (2010, p.169) notes that local realities have a strong bearing on how media ethics are manifested in a local context, adding that there is "need for further investigation in the areas of culture-specific codes which are at work in determining the perceptions of the journalists and their professional ideology".

Using the neo-Aristotelean virtue of ethics Couldry (2010) proposes a framework of global media ethics which integrates media producers and consumers. He argues that because media production and consumption have become part of the same continuum, it is no longer necessary to separate media ethics from the citizens. In this spirit, the construction of a global media ethics framework entails the reformulation of the scope and fundamentals of media ethics in order to cater for the exigencies of the digital era. The construction of such an ethical global media framework should begin with the accumulation of knowledge on emerging ethical practices in the digital age. This chapter makes an attempt at gaining deeper insights on these emerging journalistic experiences through an examination of the ethical pitfalls that confront journalists in the Internet age.

Methodological Discussion

This article sought to examine the nature of ethical pitfallsconfronting journalists in the context of the Internet. How ethical pitfalls directly and indirectly induced by the Internet manifest themselves and their broader implications to journalism practice are questions that are germane to this study.

Following Newman and Benz's assertion that the choice of a research method is dictated by the research questions,this study adopted the qualitative case study method (Newman and Menz, 1998). Yin (cited in Zainal, 2007, p.2) defines a case study as "an empirical inquiry that investigates a contemporary phenomenon within its real – life context; when boundaries between phenomenon and context are not clearly evident; and in which multiple sources of evidence are used". Bromely (1990,p.302) conceives a case study as a "systematic inquiry into an event or set of related events which aims to describe and explain the phenomenon of interest". Zucker (2009, p.2) notes that the value of the case study research strategy lies in its "scientific credentials and evidence base". This clearly distinguishes the other loose applications of the term such as the "case review" or the "case report" (Zucker, 2009), terms which are more applicable to the present study.

The choice of the case review was influenced by Yin's (2004) recommendation that when the focus of a study is a descriptive question (what?) or an explanatory question (why?) a case study becomes the most appropriate strategy. This study sought to examine the nature of ethical pitfalls that journalists when practising journalism in the digital environment. The case study strategy was therefore, found suitable to explore ethical pitfalls in the media through an in-depth explanation of the phenomenon in question (Yin, 2004). Baxter and Jack (2008, p.544) note that when the case study approach is used appropriately, it can be a valuable tool for developing theory, evaluate programs and developing interventions.

The process of formulating the case study followed the method recommended by Yin (2004) namely, design, selection, analysis, and reporting. Since the main purposive was to give a description and an explanation of the ethical pitfalls in the context of the Internet, the case review was descriptive cum- explanatory. The two cases were selectedbecause they were considered revealing in relation to the contradictory impact of new the digital media in the practice of journalism, and were also typical in that they they represent the real-life ethical challenges in the Internet era. Although there could possibly be numerous cases of newspapers and journalists falling prey to fake online stories, the two cases were chosen because they were widely publicised in the Zimbabwean and other media. Because of this publicity, the author figured out that sufficient data could be obtained to enable meaningful analysis. Yin (2004, p.7) asserts that cases studies do not necessarily have to "represent a "formal" sample from some larger universe, instead generalizing from case studies reflects substantive topics or issues of interest". Thus, the value of case studies lies in their ability to make logical inferences that can contribute to theory building. Using two cases was imperative in order to demonstrate how journalists, regardless of their geography, social or economic status could become amenable to unethical journalistic practices in the Internet era. As will be demonstrated in the next section, although the two stories and their newspapers differ in terms of context, geography and global status, they share a number of similarities in relation to how the Internet predisposes journalists to unethical actions.

The Unit of Analysis

In this study, the unit of analysis is the whole story. Empirical data were thus derived from a corpus of archival material published invarious local and international newspapers. The first story was published in the *Daily News* (Zimbabwe) on 23 April 2002. The story claimed that ruling Zanu PF supporters had beheaded a woman, Blandina Tadyanemhandu in front of her daughters, allegedly because "she was an opposition supporter". The second one is a story published by the *New York Times's* East African Bureau Chief, Jeffrey Gentleman claiming that Zimbabwean President, Robert Mugabe had called Kenyans "thieves". In both cases the stories turned out to be fictitious. The stories were retrieved from online archives of various newspapers. The stories were content analysed with a specific focus on key phrases, words, and sources used. Additional insights were drawn from various newspaper reports and commentaries on the ethical content of the stories, their implications, the reactions of various parties and actions taken after the stories had been published. The analysis also focused on similarity/difference of circumstances of the two cases with a view to map out discernible patterns in the manner in which ethical lapses manifest themselves in papers operating in different environments. The data from the different newspaper stories were synthesised thematically, interpreted using the hermeneutic method, and presented in the form of a narrative report.

The study sought to examine the nature of ethical pitfalls confronted by journalism in the Internet age, but did not seek to understand these ethical challenges from the perspective of the journalists who experience them. As a result, analysed data was limited to textual and archival sources. The study could therefore not shed light on what measures were being taken to prevent a recurrence of such ethical pitfalls or how journalists negotiated these ethical decisions in their day- to- day operations. In addition, the fact that only two cases were selected limits the scope and potential for generalising findings from the study. Zainal (2007, 5) rightly notes that the dependency on the exploration of one or few cases or samples makes it difficult arrive at a generalised conclusion.

In spite of these limitations, the case study strategy enabled the researcher to describe actual real-life ethical experiences in journalism practice in the Internet era, which might not have been possible if say an experimental or survey research design had been utilised.

The Selected Newspapers

The New York Times is an influential global newspaper published in New York City (United States of America) founded as a penny paper in 1851 by Henry Jarvis Raymond and George Jones. It ispublished by *The New York Times* company and commands a circulation of 1.865,827, ranking second in the US, after the *Wall Street Journal* and 39th in the world (Wikipedia, https://en.wikipedia.org/wiki/List_of_newspapers_in_the_United_States). *The New York Times* has long been regarded as a "newspaper of record" (EncyclopaediaBritannica 2015) on account of its compelling journalism which rests on three ethical pillars, namely fairness, integrity and truth (*The New York Times,* 2004). Going by the motto "All News Fit to Print", the newspaper's commitment to objective and restrained reporting of news is flagged in its ethical charter which puts premium on "creating, collecting and distributing high quality news and information", impartiality, treating news readers and sources with respect, practising journalism that is beyond reproach as well as a commitment to "checking facts, the exactness of quotations, the integrity of photographs" and distaste for "anonymous sourcing" (*The New York Times,* 2004). The newspaper is well aware of its global status and commits itself to correcting all errors great and small. It states thus:

Because our voice is loud and far reaching, The Times recognizes an ethical responsibility to correct all its errors, large and small. The paper regrets every error, but it applauds the integrity of a writer who volunteers a correcting of his or her own published story. (The New York Times, 2004)

The Daily News is a tabloid size mass market privately-owned, daily newspaper published in Zimbabwe by the Associated Newspapers Zimbabwe (ANZ), a company founded by a consortium of local and foreign businessmen in 1999. The Newspaper was shut down in 2003 after failing to comply with the requirements of a new media law, the Access to Information and Protection of Privacy Act (2002) but was relaunched in March 2011 after a protracted legal battle. As was before its closure, the paper remains pro-capital, pro-opposition and highly critical of the ruling ZANU PF party and government led by President Robert Mugabe. According to a Zimbabwe All Media Products Survey,(ZAMPS) (2014) first half results the *Daily News* had a readership of 15% of the print media market share (IMPI Report, 2015). Moyo notes that the *Daily News* assumed the role of the opposition, becoming President Mugabe's government's most strident and 'fearless' critic of President Mugabe's government and its print run rose from 60 000 to 120 000, torpedoing the state-run daily, *The Herald* whose circulation stood at 90 000. Flagging the tag line "Telling it like it is", the *Daily News* was viewed by some as being able to provide a "counter-narrative" to the state media but Zanu PF officials labelled it an "enemy of the state" (Dombo, 2014), thus setting it on a collision course with the government of the day.

The Daily News 'Beheading' Story

On 23 April 2002, a privately-owned Zimbabwean newspaper, and a staunch critic of the ruling party and government published a story claiming that one Brandina Tadyanemhandu, an opposition party supporter in Magunje, a district of Mashonaland West province had been decapitated by alleged Zanu PF supporters while her two daughters watched (see Excerpt 1). The story ran under the headline 'Young Girls see their Mother's head being cut off'. The newspaper reported that Tadyanenemhandu, aged 53 had been "butchered" by about 20 Zanu Pf youths for being an opposition party supporter (the *Daily News*, 23 April 2002). It however, turned out that the story was false as the newspaper had fallen prey to the antics of a confidence trickster, one George Nyadzayo, alias Enos Tadyanemhandu, who was husband to the deceased. The paper later claimed that Nyadzayo had approached an opposition Movement for Democratic Change (MDC) Member of Parliament for Seke, in the dormitory town of Chitungwiza, one Bennie Tumbare-Mutasa for financial assistance after his home had been burnt by Zanu PF supporters. This also turned out to be a lie. After the newspaper discovered that the story was false, it retracted the story and apologised to both government and Zanu PF. In a comment published in the paper's 27 April 2002 edition, the paper stated that:

It appears we were misled. It is difficult to believe Mr Tadyanemhandu could have made up such a story. What remains more of a mystery is why he took such a pain to create a story that has potential to undermine the credibility of The Daily News. (Daily News, 27 April 2002)

The paper added that:

A Daily News team has failed over the past two days to locate the grave of Brandina Tadyanemhandu, whose husband, Enos, claimed this week that she had been murdered by having her head chopped off by assailants alleged to be Zanu PF youths as her two daughters watched....Until (Brandina) Tadyanemhandu's grave is located and positively identified, we were left with no option but to...tender our most profound apologies to Zanu PF, whose image was tarnished by the report in question. (The Daily News,27 April 2002)

Although the newspaper retracted the story and apologised to the affected parties it had been reproduced by various media outlets worldwide, including *Guardian* (UK) whose correspondent, Andrew Meldrum then based in Zimbabwe could not authenticate its veracity. The story still exists online and can be accessed via the link http://www.freerepublic.com/focus/news/671152/posts. This means that, although the story might have been removed from the *Daily News* website, it is still available to a global public on different online platforms and continues to attract comments from the public as if it were a true story. It worth noting that apart from its ethical dimension, the story also had a legal dimension as its publication resulted in the arraignment of the reporters who wrote the story, Collin Chimwanza and Lloyd Mudiwa, then editor of the newspaper, Geoff Nyarota and the *Guardian* (UK) correspondent,

Excerpt 1. Part of the story from the Daily News

April 23, 2002 | Lloyd Mudiwa
Posted on 2002/04/23 12:36:09 PM by Clive
TWO young girls aged 10 and 17 watched in horror as their mother was brutally murdered by having her head chopped off at the neck.
Brandina Tadyanemhandu, 53, was butchered inside her hut by about 20 youths, suspected to be Zanu PF supporters, in Magunje on Sunday.
The reason for Tadyanemhandu's grisly murder was the accusation by the youths that the deceased was a supporter of the opposition Movement for Democratic Change (MDC). Tadyanemhandu will be buried today at Magororo village in Magunje, Hurungwe East.
She was the mother of MDC youth activist Tichaona Tadyanemhandu, 20, who went missing in Hurungwe in June 2000. His body was found six months later in the mortuary at Harare Central Hospital.
Brandina Tadyanemhandu's attackers, who were allegedly led by a war veteran known as Cde Chifamba, also burnt the family's main house, destroying property worth thousands of dollars.
Tadyanemhandu's husband, Enos, 63, yesterday said: "They killed my only son in a family of eight children and now they have killed my wife. Why are they fighting us after they won the election? I will not be silenced. I will speak out against this evil."
A distraught Tadyanemhandu said it seemed like a normal day when he drove his herd of cattle to the dip tank at Magororo township at about 6am on the fateful day. On his way back, at about 10am, he said he was surprised when his 17-year-old daughter, Chipo, weeping, approached him.
"She was crying," he said. "My first thought was that she had been assaulted by a friend. She struggled to tell me that her mother's head had been cut off by Zanu PF supporters." Tadyanemhandu said……..

Source: Free Republic http://www.freerepublic.com/focus/news/671152/posts.

Andrew Meldrum, who was later deported after his acquittal by a Harare court. Meldrum was acquitted on the grounds that he had taken reasonable steps to contact the police who could not confirm the story to him (even if he went ahead and published it) (International Freedom of Expression Exchange, 2002; Gaingons, 2008).

The New York Times Story on Mugabe

On November 4, 2015, *The New York Times* published a feature story with fabricated quotes attributable to Zimbabwean president, Robert Mugabe. Headlined, 'An Anti-Corruption Plea in Kenya: Please Just Steal Less', the story, authored by the newspaper's East African Bureau Chief, Jeffrey Gentleman used fabricated quotes from a Kenyan satirical news magazine, Spectator C.O.K.E claiming that Mugabe had called Kenyans 'thieves'. Mugabe is alleged to have said:

Those people of East Africa shock me with their wizardry in stealing sometimes. I tend to believe that stealing is in every Kenyan's blood. These people go their schools and read good courses but they qualify as the best thieves. You can even think that there is a subject in their universities called Bachelor of Stealing. Whenever they get an opportunity as employees, they never disappoint. They steal enough money to buy their freedom because even the judges who listen to their cases are financially powerless. I urge my people to be on high alert in case you by bad luck happen to visit that East African nation. They might infect you with that disease and we don't want it here. Zimbabweans are honest people who love their country and don't want such stealing tendencies. (iMediaEthics, 8 November 2015)

It however, turned out that the fake quotations attributable to Mugabe had been fabricated by The Spectator C.O.K.E, a Kenya satirical online which later explained that it was using 'satire to fight corruption in Kenya' (iMediaEthics, 8 November 2015). *The New York* Times removed the fake quotations from the story and in its 12 November edition and explained that:

An article last Thursday about extraordinary rise in public corruption in Kenya, no stranger to graft, erroneously included remarks attributed to Robert Mugabe, the Zimbabwean president, saying that Kenyans were thieves and telling his countrymen to be on alert when visiting Kenya so as not to "catch that disease". The Spectator, a Kenyan newsmagazine that published the remarks, said last week that they had been fabricated, and were intended as satire. (The New York Times, 12 November 2015)

The Zimbabwean government, through the presidential spokesperson accused Gentleman of being a "blunderous, if not outright racist" bent on "contriving a conflict between Zimbabwe and Kenya" (*The Chronicle*, 13 November, 2015). Gentleman admitted to have made an 'error' and said he took "full responsibility for the mistake" (*The Chronicle 12* November 2015). Responding to a barrage of harsh Tweets by Kenyans and Zimbabweans who took umbrage with his 'unprofessionalism', Gentleman tweeted that "Guilty as charged. The Mugabe quote was fake. I deeply regret the way we presented it" (*The Southern Daily*, 13 November 2015). He also gave a background about how the story had been originated (see Excerpt 2).

Gentleman further claimed that, in trying to verify the story he had contacted a Zimbabwean journalist in Harare whom he sent a copy of the story before it was published to check with the President's Office if Mugabe had indeed made the statement attributed to him. According to Gentleman the journalist he requested to verify the quotes came back to him 'several hours later; before the story was published confirming that Mugabe had made 'appeared' to have uttered the statement. According to Gentleman, this was his "own attempt to verify the story and it was only after the story was published" that it dawned on him that the journalist in Harare had not checked with the president's office or "other appropriate sources" (*The Southern Daily*, 13 November 2015). It was later reported that police in Zimbabwe had launched a 'witch-hunt' on the journalist who had corroborated Gentleman's fake story, and would be prosecuted under the law of the country (*The Standard*, 15 November, 2015).

Excerpt 2. The New York gentleman's response to the fake Mugabe quotations

Corruption in Kenya is real but that Mugabe quote was fake.
I want to explain what happened. A source sent me an article from the Spectator magazine that included harsh quotes from Mugabe criticizing Kenya's corruption, which many people in Kenya and beyond say has reached an outrageous level.
The article: http://www.spectator.co.ke/…/robert-mugabe-god-should-neve…/
I emailed it to a Zimbabwean journalist in Harare to check if Mugabe had actually said those things. The Zimbabwean journalist told me that it appeared he had.
Many Kenyans, too, believed Mugabe had said those things.See this link: http://www.bbc.com/news/blogs-trending-34735212
After my article was published, I started receiving messages that the Mugabe quote was fake. I looked into it immediately and contacted the Spectator and an official in the Zimbabwean government. The Spectator admitted to fabricating the story, saying that it was using satire to fight corruption.
We have amended our article, which can be found here:nytimes.com
I deeply regret the way I presented that part of the story and I've learned from this mistake. Unfortunately it has drawn attention away from what many believe is an alarming problem in Kenya: runaway graft. As that story revealed, Kenyan officials are believed to have stolen millions of dollars in public money through a scheme of wild purchases, like buying simple ballpoint pens for $85 each.
The Kenyatta government's response is that it is investigating these allegations seriously.
Many Kenyans have told me that corruption is the single greatest problem in their country.

Source: Watiri Sue: New York Times Journalist Forced to Apologise for Publishing Part of the Fake Mugabe story That Triggered KOT's War Against Mugabe', GHAFLA, 10 November 2015.

The Internet, Misinformation and the Erosion of the Verification Ethic

Although the contextand circumstances in which the two stories differ considerably, there are a number of similarities that underscore the tensions between traditional and global journalism ethics (Price, 2015). The two stories underline the fact as journalism gets into the supersonic mode, aided by new communication technologies such as the Internet,the core values of traditional journalism such as verification are shunted to the backburner. Both the *Daily News* and the *New York Times* story illustrate how journalism ethics take a back stage when journalists succumb to the desire to publish at the first instance. According to the Verification Hand Book (2013), verificationhas come back to the fore of journalismbecause of the digital explosion.Both the *Daily News* and the *New York Times* reporterpublished their stories without adequately verifying their stories.The fast pace of journalism in the digital age leaves journalists without enough time to verify their stories while the imperative to publish instantly has become more compelling. Brandtzaeg, Luders, Spangeberg, Ruth-Wiggins and Folstad (2016, p.323) conceives verification as a critical element of the newsgathering and dissemination process which requires skilled determination of the accuracy or validity of the content in question. In the age of the digital era, print publications operate under perpetual fear of being scooped by online newspapers and social media and the trade-off between verification and supersonic speed journalism often plays itself out in an unpleasant manner. The Verification Handbook published by the European Journalism Centre (Silverman & Perlman, 2013, p.1) notes that "The abundance of content from disparate sources spread all the world, make the application of verification more essential than ever before", while Buttry (2013, p.16) asserts that "verification is the essence of journalism". Both the *Daily News* and the *New York Times* highlight the risk of misinformation and the declining importance attached to verification and fact checking in the Internet age.

As will be demonstrated below, both journalists did not exercise rigour in verifying the authenticity and validity of their information or stories before publication. This shows that regardless of their political and social context the mainstream press is becoming more amenable to factual inaccuracies because fear of losing stories to competitors in the context of citizen journalism. Buttry (2013, p.17) argues that the 24/7 news cycle and the rise of the social media and user generated content requires journalists to "gather and report as events unfold, making swift decisions about whether information has been sufficiently verified…". This means that journalists must be more committed to question their sources and the material they use in developing their stories and to resist the temptation to be presumptuous about bother their sources and the events and people they report on.

The desire to undercut competitors and the obsession with speedy publication means that journalists are increasingly less worried about the accuracy of their stories as their attention is fixated on scooping competitors. It could be argued that the Internet has somewhat exacerbated this cut throat competition in the sense that mainstream publications are not just competing amongst themselves, but also with online publications and websites which leverage their digital presence for instantaneous publication. Wood (2013) rightly asserts that "If speed is the currency of the modern information era, misinformation is the increasingly high cost…We have more information, but it's a morass of the truths, and what we used to call libel. Its fast, but it's bad. And bad information is a cancer that just keeps growing…". This shows that the desire to publish instantly has resulted in core journalism principles like fact checking and verification being downplayed in the digital context. As demonstrated in the two cases reviewed in this chapter, verification is no longer as rigorous as it was in traditional journalism as journalists devote less time towards verifying stories as the determination of the credibility of news sources is sometimes "outsourced" to third parties, who might even an interest in the story being investigated (Godler & Reich, 2015). In the two cases outlined above, both *The Daily* News and the *New York Times* became victims of 'spooky' sources because they outsourced the credibility of their sources to second hand sources, who possibly might have an interest in the stories under investigation. In the case of the *Daily News*, Geoff Nyarota, the then editor of the newspaper admitted that his paper had been misled by a source "who had not been sincere" (Afrol, 2002). However, using the insincerity of a source is an unacceptable alibi for not getting facts right. Given the sensitivity of the story the *Daily News* was supposed to cross-check the story until it found irrefutable evidence that indeed the alleged murder of Brandina Tadyanemhandu had happened. In both the *Daily News* and the *New York Times*case story verification was done after publication rather than in the pre-publication stage. Whenthe *Daily News* was challenged about the authenticity of its story it dispatched a team of reporters to look for the grave of the alleged murdered woman but did not find it. Geoff Nyarota later stated that:

A Daily News team has failed over the past two days to locate the grave of Brandina Tadyanemhandu whose husband Enos, claimed this week that she had been murdered by having her head chopped off by assailants alleged to be Zanu-PF youth as her two daughters watched. (Daily News, 27 April 2002)

The *Daily News* was supposed to do this kind of verification before it published the story, but the newspaper chose to do so after the truthfulness of the story was questioned. The newspaper became a victim of the "publish first, verify later" syndrome, which afflicts mainstream publications against the backdrop of intense competition in the digital age.Similarly, the *New York Times* sought to verify the false quotes attributed toMugabe afterthe newspaper was exposed by President Mugabe's office, thus demonstrating a case of "closing the stable after the horse had bolted out'. In addition, both papers ignored the 'Two Reliable Sources Rule' (Brewer, 2011) which requires journalists all facts about sensitive stories be confirmed by at least two sources. The failure by the two newspapers to triangulate their sources clearly shows that in the Internet age, verification is no longer accorded a higher priority as the veracity of stories can now be outsourced to second hand and third hand sources.

Outsourcing Credibility: The Emergency of Second and Third Hand Sources

It is worth noting that although the original source of the *Daily News* was an offline source, (while that of the *New York Times* was an online source (the Kenyan Online Satirical Online Magazine) in both cases, the laxity of verification was manifested through the reliance on second hand/third hand sources.

As was noted above, the *Daily News* relied on the supposed husband of the deceased (who was introduced to the newspaper by an opposition, MDC Member of Parliament) while the *New York Times'* lifted the fake quotes from the Spectator C.O.K.E). While 'trust' could have played a role in the publication of the fake story, in the case of the *Daily News*, and to some extent the *New York Times* (in the sense that Gentleman trusted the unnamed Zimbabwean journalist who reportedly confirmed the fake quotes), it would appear that the anonymity of the Internet was more influential in the publication of the fake quotes by the *New York Times*. Given the millions information sources on the Internet, it is difficult for journalists to verify the authenticity of every story, hence they become prone to hoaxes, rumours and fabrications. Schifferes and Newman (2013, p.876) rightly point out that most of the challenges faced by journalists in the Internet age are not entirely new, but the Internet has made them more complex in a world "where the volume and speed of information is growing exponentially". Whereas the *Daily News* journalists fell prey to the shenanigans of an "insincere" off-line source, the *New York Times* was a victim of an online source that looked too authentic not to be doubted in a context where, to quote Godler and Reich (2015, p.9) "journalistic practices of fact-finding are merely rituals brought about source-characteristics and journalistic –source exchanges and negotiations". Against this backdrop "journalists are not to believe anything on the basis of evidence, but rather choose or decide to believe due to the specific interactions with sources (including sympathies, negotiations, trust)". The ritualistic way in which news is verified makes journalists amenable to second hand and third hand sources who are equally detached from the situation under investigation, thus compromising the credibility of news stories. That *New York Times* journalists relied on another journalists based in Zimbabwe to verify President Mugabe's remarks on his behalf suggests that in the age of the Internet, second hand news sources are gaining currency and 'lazy journalism' is taking root. It is now generally acknowledged that the Internet promotes 'lazy journalism' because journalists rely on Internet based tools such as email and Facebook to interact with their news sources rather than themselves venturing outside the newsroom where they have personal contacts with news sources (Chari, 2013).

Pavlik, (cited in Mabweazara 2010, p.183) observes that using email to interview news sources is increasingly becoming a viable option especially for interviewing sources in distant locations. Mabweazara (2010) points out that using email as an interviewing tool is largely predicated on "prior relationships cultivated over time between the reporters and sources" as is the case with the *New York Times's* Jeffrey Gentleman who 'interviewed' a fellow journalist based in Zimbabwe. Although their prior relationship helped to build trust, it must be remembered that, in the specific case of the *New York Times* the 'interview' was between a journalist and a fellow journalist, which brings another ethical dimension in relation to whether a journalists should rely on another journalist to ascertain the authenticity of a story. *The NewYork Times's* Jeffrey Gentleman stated that he emailed the Zimbabwean journalist in Harare to check if Mugabe had uttered the disputed statements and the journalist confirmed that Mugabe had made the statements. By not contacting Mugabe's office before the publication of the story, the *New York Times*, like the *Daily News* over-relied on a second hand source. Like the *Daily* News, the *New York Times* only contacted President Mugabe's office and the Spectator C.O.K.E, the originator of the quotes after the story had been published and disputed, thus underscoring the tendency of "publish and verify later" syndrome. It is evident that in both cases the normative requirement for verification and fact-checking did not go beyond the threshold permitted when dealing with sensitive stories because the authenticity of the story (in the case of the *Daily News*) and quotes (in the case of The *New York Times*) was not established with certainty as if to suggest that what certain individuals say or do (in this case Mugabe and his government) scepticism can be suspended and treat whatever allegations levelled against the personality as common cause. Gentleman's statement that the Zimbabwean journalist said Mugabe "appeared" have uttered the fake statements, and that "Many Kenyans, too, believed Mugabe had said those things" is proof of this lack of certainty and the laxity of verification standards. It is disingenuous for the press to have separate ethical standards for different people, whatever their social or political standing or alleged blemishes and the two cases highlighted above should serve as a lesson that the press must always exercise impartiality consistent with Rawls's theory of ethical theory of "Justice as Fairness behind a veil of ignorance", whereby every citizen enjoys equal treatment "when they access the hypothetical social contract and when the principles of justice are created" (Runcheva, 2013, p.1) Kasoma concurs with the need for fairness and impartiality in journalism practice regardless of the circumstances when he states that:

... the harm that unfounded accusations against those in government can do to society and individuals who constitute it can be devastating. Even Africa's dirty politicians, as most of them are, deserve justice and fair play from media and should not be accused, tried and sentenced by the press of wrongs they have not committed. (Kasoma, 1996, p.101)

The lack of scepticism means that journalists have become "susceptible to partisan interests" (Price, 2015, p.8) thereby limiting their capacity to provide reliable information, particularly in conflict situations. Because of the fast pace of journalism, legacy journalism appears to be lagging behind the online media or citizen journalists who publish as events happen and operate outside the ethical constrains (and legal regimes) of traditional media. Because they allow online media to set the agenda, traditional journalists are forced to parrot the rumours and propaganda in online media rather than debunking them, thus contributing to "misinformation and scaremongering" (Price, 2015, p.8). In this case *The Daily News* and *New York Times* were presumptuous about the correctness of their sources and as a result suspended any form of scepticism. Yet traditional journalisms requires that journalists be sceptical of their sources whoever they are, and whatever they social standing is. Buttry corroborates this view when he asserts that:

The need for verification starts with the simple fact that many of our information sources are wrong. They may be lying maliciously or innocently passing along misinformation. They may have faulty memories or lack of context or understanding. They may be in harm's way and unable to provide everything they know, or unable to see the full picture of events as they unfold. Our job is not to parrot sources and the material they provide, but to challenge them triangulate what they provide with other credible sources and verify what is true, weeding from our work (before we publish, map or broadcast) what is false or not adequately verified. (Buttry, 2013, p.17)

By publishing their stories on the basis of shaky evidence, it means that the two newspapers were prepared to parrot their sources. Although the actual reasons for the publication of what turned out to be false stories are outside the purview of this chapter, it can be argued that in both cases reviewed in this chapter the journalists concerned failed to question seemingly authoritative sources, and as a result they fell prey to hoaxes. The anonymity of the Internet and the fact that the medium is host to unlimited information exacerbated the challenge to verify the information as they had to rely on second hand and third hand sources. As will be argued below, this reliance on second hand and third hand sources might further compromise legacy journalism's capacity to provide the citizenry with information to make informed decisions and democratic participation (Godler & Reich, 2015).

Intra-Media Agenda-Setting and Challenge of Retraction

Smith (cited in Nieves-Pizarrro, 2015) defines a retraction as "a public statement made about an earlier statement that withdraws, cancels, refutes, diametrically reserves the original statement or ceases and desists from publishing the original statement". The essence of a retraction is to correct or withdraw the offending story. Although both newspapers retracted their stories, millions of people had already read them and numerous other publications had picked up the stories for wider dissemination. For instance, and as mentioned earlier, the *Guardian* (UK)'s correspondent in Zimbabwe at the time, Andre Meldrum had published the story from the *Daily News* without verifying it and appeared in the Guardian's edition of 24 April 2002 (Chari, 2007). The millions of people who read the story might have believed it to be true, particularly given the fact that at the time there was of political violence in Zimbabwe. At the time of writing, the original story was still available online (see Excerpt 1),fourteen years after it was published. This is an affirmation that the Internet makes it easier to propagate falsehoods and rumours to a global audience, and once false or fake stories are published it is not guaranteed that the damaging stories can be retracted as was the case with the print media. Since false stories cannot easily be retracted this has far reaching ramifications on the global image of individuals and nations that are in dire need of Foreign Direct Investment (FDI) or are dependent on tourism.

It is trite to say that had it not been for the Internet it would not have been possible for other journalists to dispatch a story that had not been adequately verified, and in the case of Gentleman, it could no not have been possible for him to lift fake quotes from the Spectator C.O.K.E, the Kenyan satirical online that published the 'Mugabe' quotes. Because online stories are downloadable and can be shared among many people easily, they cannot be retracted. A retraction or recall of the damaging story cannot stop the propagation of false stories, thus giving credence to the adage that "A lie can travel halfway around the world while the truth is putting on its shoes". This means that in the digital era,journalistic inaccuracies have far reaching implications for both individual and national reputations since offending stories cannot be totally recalled due to the seamlessness of the Internet. The very architecture of the Internet negates the verification process yet it is verification which sets journalism apart from other forms of communication. Nieves-Pizarrro (2015) rightly asserts that it is verification which gives journalism credibility and believability and without it journalism's claims to truth-telling will be seriously jeopardised.

CONCLUSION

This chapter has discussed ethical pitfalls confronted by journalists in the age of the Internet with special attention on verification. The study used two cases to highlight how core ethical principles of journalism such verification are taking a back seat in the digital age. The chapter argues that the fast pace of journalism in the Internet age and the desire by journalists to publish real time negates core cannons of journalism such as verification and further predisposes journalists to the use of 'second hand' and 'third hand' news sources.

The anonymity of the Internet and the vast information it carriers makes it difficult for journalists to ascertain the authenticity of its sources or its veracity, thereby exposing journalists to a very dangerous ethical minefield. As has been argued in this chapter, the difficulty of verifying information online may force journalists to defer the responsibility of verifying information to third parties rather than witnesses, thereby outsourcing the credibility of their stories to outsiders. The increasing trend by of relying on second hand and third hand sources among journalists, instead of eye-witnesses means that journalists are outsourcing the credibility of their work. The chapter has also argued that the Internet makes it difficult for newspapers to retract inaccurate or false stories because of its seamless architecture which allows people in different parts of the world to download and share stories. Even where a newspaper deletes an inaccurate story, such a story continues to circulate through other websites or email, meaning that more people get exposed to this misinformation. This has serious implications in so far as it erodes the credibilityof the media, which in turn might negatively compromise the media's capacity to influence the deepening of democratic cultures globally.

The chapter concludes by hazarding that, although the Internet has contributed to journalistic sloppiness occasioned by its architecture and political economy by making fabrications more acute or difficult to detect, its real impact and the threats and risks it poses on journalism ethics remain fully unexplored. The two cases reviewed in this chapter help to open debate on the possible threats of the Internet on journalism ethics. Such a research agenda does not in any way pretend to be blind to the numerous positive roles that new communication technologies in general and the Internet plays in enhancing journalism ethics. In the final analysis, how the Internet shapes journalism will in large measure depend on the attitudes, the pre-dispositions and agendas of those who use it. The preponderance of journalistic manual guides on online verification fundamentals and "essential" online tools for journalists to minimize ethical risks in the digital era is not only testament of the self-correcting capabilities of technology, but also evidence that technology is as good as those who use it. Since this study sought to examine how the Internet predisposes journalists to ethical pitfalls, its inclination was illustrative rather than conclusive. Future studies could employ ethnographic methods examine ways in which the numerous Internet based tools can be utilised to enhance journalism ethics in order to bring broader insights and expand knowledge on the dialectic that the Internet brings to bear in journalism practice in general and journalism ethics in particular.

REFERENCES

Afrol. (2002). *Zimbabwe's Daily News' Editor Arrested*. Retrieved September 16, 2016 from http://afrol.com/News2002/zim043_nyarota_arrest.htm

Arant, D. (2000). *Online Media Ethics: A Survey of US Daily Newspaper Editors*. Paper Presented at the Association for Education in Journalism and Mass Communication Convention, Phoenix, AZ. Retrieved 7 August 2016 from http://facstaff.elon.edu/andersj/onlinesurvey.html

Banda, F. (2010). Negotiating Journalism Ethics in Zambia: Towards a 'Glocal' Ethics. In Media Ethics Beyond Borders: A Global Perspective (pp. 124-141). New York: Routledge.

Berger, G. (1996). *The Internet: A Goldmine for Editors and Journalists*. Paper Presented at the World Editors Forum, Washington, DC. Retrieved 7 August from http://guyberger.ru.ac.za/fulltext/Goldmine.htm

Berger, G. (Ed.). (2005). *Doing Digital Journalism: How Southern African Newspapers Are Using ICTs*. Grahamstown: Rhodes University.

Berkman, R. I., & Shumway, C. (2003). *Digital Dilemmas: Ethical Issues for Online Media Professionals*. London: Blackwell Publishing.

Brandtzaeg, P. B., Luders, M., Spangeberg, J., Rath-Wiggins, L., & Folstad, A. (2016). Emerging Journalistic Verification Practices Concerning Social Media. *Journalism Practice*, *10*(3), 323–342. doi:10.1080/17512786.2015.1020331

Brewer, D. (2011). *The Importance of Fact-Checking for Journalists*. Retrieved from 16 August 2016. http://www.mediahelpingmedia.org/training-resources/journalism-basics/640-fact-checking-separates-journalism-from-rumour-and-gossip

Bromley, D. B. (1990). Academic Contribution to Psychological Counselling: A Philosophy of Science for the Study of Individual Cases. *Counselling Psychology Quarterly*, *3*(3), 299–307. doi:10.1080/09515079008254261

Buttry, S. (2013). Verification Fundamentals: Rules to Live By. In *Verification Handbook: additional Materials to Verifying Digital Content for Emergency Coverage*. Retrieved 14 September 2016 from http://verificationhandbook.com/downloads/verification.handbook.pdf

Chari, T. (2007). Rethinking Ethical Issues in African Media. *African Identities*, *5*(1), 39–60. doi:10.1080/14725840701253704

Chari, T. (2009). Ethical Challenges Facing Zimbabwean Media in the Context of the Internet. *Global Media Journal*, *3*(1), 46–79.

Chari, T. (2013). New Communication Technologies and Journalism Ethics in Zimbabwe: Practices and Malpractices. *Online Journal of Communication and Media Technologies*, *3*(2), 112–136.

Christians, G. (2010). The Ethics of Universal Being. In Media Ethics Beyond Borders: A Global Perspective (pp. 6-23). New York: Routledge.

Couldry, N. (2010). Media Ethics: Towards a Framework for Media Producers and Media Consumers. In Media Ethics Beyond Borders: A Global Perspective (pp. 42-58). New York: Routledge.

Dombo, S. (2014). *Daily Struggles: Private Print Media, The State, and Democratic Governance in Zimbabwe in the Case of the African Daily News (1956-1964) and The Daily News (1999-2003)* (Unpublished PhD Thesis). School of Social Sciences, University of Kwazulu-Natal, Durban.

Encyclopaedia Britannica. (2015). *The New York Times*. Retrieved 12 September 2016, from https://global.britannica.com/topic/The-New-York-Times

Ess, C. (2009). *Digital Media Ethics*. Cambridge, UK: Polity Press.

Fourie, P. J. (2010). Moral Philosophy as the Foundation of Media Theory: Questioning African Ubuntuism as a Framework. In Media Ethics Beyond Borders: A Global Perspective (pp. 105-123). New York: Routledge.

Friend, C., & Singer, J. (2007). *Online Journalism Ethics: Traditions and Transitions*. Armonk, NY: E Sharpe.

Gaingos, C. J. (2008). *Towards a New Media Law in Independent Regulatory System* (Unpublished LLB Dissertation). University of Nambia. Retrieved 8 August 2016, from http://wwwisis.unam.na/theses/gaingos2008.pdf

Gebremedhim, S. (2010). Media Ethics in Ethiopia. In Media Ethics Beyond Borders: A Global Perspective (pp. 142-146). New York: Routledge.

Godler, Y., & Reich, Z. (2015). Journalistic Evidence: Cross-Verification as a Constituent of Mediated Knowledge. *Journalism*, 1–17.

IMediaEthics. (2015). *Robert Mugabe Didn't Say Kenyans Were Thieves: NY Times Published Fake Quote*. Retrieved 12 August 2016, from http://www.imediaethics.org/robert-mugabe-didnt-say-kenyans-were-thieves-nytimes-published-fake-quote/

IMPI Report, . (2014). *Information and Media Panel of Inquiry to Promote and Elevate the Standards of Media Practice in Zimbabwe (IMPI): Report of the Official Inquiry into the State of the Information and Media Industry in Zimbabwe*. Harare: Ministry of Information, Media and Broadcasting Services.

International Freedom of Expression Exchange Clearing House. (2003). *Protest over Journalist in Hiding as Harare Court Raps Media Law*. Retrieved 16 September 2016 from http://www.zimbabwesituation.com/old/may15_2003.html

Kasoma, F. (1996). The Foundations of African Ethics (Afriethics) and the Professional Practice of Journalism: The Case for a Society Centred Media Morality. *Africa Media Review*, *10*(3), 93–116.

Lasica, J. D. (1997). Preserving Ethics in a News Medium. *American Journalism Review*. Retrieved 7 August 2016, from http://www.jdlasica.com/1997/12/07/preserving-old-ethics-in-a-new-medium/

Lee, A. Y. L. (2012). Online News Media in the Web 2.0 Era: From Boundary Dissolution to Journalistic Transparency. *Chinese Journal of Communication*, *5*(2), 210–226. doi:10.1080/17544750.2012.664442

Lee, J. (2015). A Double-Edged Sword: The Effects of JournalistsSocial Media Activities on Audience Perceptions of Journalists and their News Products. *Journal of Computer-Mediated Communication*, *20*(3), 312–329. doi:10.1111/jcc4.12113

Mabweazara, H. M. (2010). New Technologies and Journalism Practice in Africa: Towards a Critical Sociological Approach. In The Citizen and Communication: Revisiting Traditional, New and Community Media Practices in Southern Africa. Claremont: Juta & Co Pvt Ltd.

Mabweazara, H. M. (2011). Newsmaking Practices and Professionalism in the Zimbabwean Press. *Journalism Practice*, *5*(1), 100–117. doi:10.1080/17512786.2010.493331

Mabweazara, M. H. (2010). *New Technologies and Print Journalism Practice in Zimbabwe: An Ethnographic Study* (Unpublished DPhil Thesis). School of Arts and Creative Industries, Edinburgh Napier University, Edinburgh, UK.

Mendoza, N. (2012). The Crisis of Global Journalism and the Freedom of the Press Foundation. *Aljazeera*. Retrieved 16 September 2016, from http://www.aljazeera.com/indepth/opinion/2012/12/2012122012051496867.html

Moyo, D. (2005). The 'Independent' Press and the Fight Democracy in Zimbabwe. A Critical Analysis of the Banned Daily News. *Westminster Papers in Communication and Culture, 2,* 109-128. http://doi.org/10.16997/wpcc.45

Moyo, D. (2007). Alternative Media Diasporas and the Mediation of the Zimbabwean Crisis. *Ecquid Novi: African Journalism Studies*, *28*(1&2), 81–105.

Moyo, D. (2009). Citizen Journalism and the Parallel Market of Information in Zimbabwes 2008 Election. *Journalism Studies*, *10*(4), 551–567. doi:10.1080/14616700902797291

Mudhai, O. F., Tettey, W., & Banda, F. (2009). *African Media and the Digital Public Sphere*. New York: Palgrave Macmillan. doi:10.1057/9780230621756

Newman, I., & Benz, C. (1998). *Qualitative Research Methodology: Exploring the Interactive Continuum*. Southern Illinois University Press.

News Wire. (2015). *Zimbabwean Police Launch 'Manhunt' for Journalist who Verified Fake Mugabe Quotes to the New York Times*. Retrieved from http://www.mashada.com/blogs/p/221702/zimbabwean-police-launch-manhunt-for-journalist-who-verified-fake-mugabe-quotes-to-the-new-york-time

Nieves-Pizarro, Y. (2015). *Corrections, Apologies and Retractions: Misinformation in Social Media News*. Retrieved 13 September 2016, from https://lagacetaboricua.wordpress.com/2015/05/21/corrections-apologies-and-retractions-misinformation-in-social-media-news/

Price, G. (2015). *Opportunities and Challenges for Journalism in the Digital age: Asian and European Perspectives*. London: The Royal Institute of International Affairs.

Runcheva, H. (2013). John Rawls: Justice as Fairness behind a Veil of Ignorance. *Iustinianus Primus Law Review*, *4*(2), 1–12.

Schifferes, S., & Newman, N. (2013). *Verifying News on the Social Web: Challenges and Prospects*. International World Wide Web Conference Committee. Retrieved 19 September 2016, from http://www2013.wwwconference.org/companion/p875.pdf

Shakuntala, R. (2010). Post-Colonial Theory and Global Media Ethics: A Theoretical Intervention. In Media Ethics Beyond Borders: A Global Perspective (pp. 59-73). New York: Routledge.

Silverman, C., & Perlman, M. (2013). *Verification Handbook: Additional Materials to Verifying Digital Content for Emergency Coverage*. Retrieved 14 September 2016, from http://verificationhandbook.com/downloads/verification.handbook.pdf.

The Chronicle. (2015). *Us Paper Says Sorry to President Mugabe*. Retrieved 12 November 2016, from http://www.chronicle.co.zw/us-paper-says-sorry-to-president-mugabe/

The Herald. (2014, November 14). NYTimes Scribe Apologises. *The Herald*.

The New York Times. (2004). *Ethical Journalism: A handbook of Values and Practice for the News and Editorial Department*. Retrieved 12 September 2016, from http://www.nytco.com/wp-content/uploads/NYT_Ethical_Journalism_0904-1.pdf

The Standard. (2015). *Police Hunt Journalist Over Mugabe Offensive Story*. Retrieved from http://www.thestandard.co.zw/2015/11/15/police-hunt-journalist-over-mugabe-offensive-story/

Ward, S. J. A. (2008). Global Journalism Ethics: Widening the Conceptual Base. Global Media Journal, 1(1), 137-149.

Ward, S. J. A. (2010). Ethics for the New Mainstream. In The New Journalist: Roles and Skills, and Critical Thinking (pp. 313-326). Toronto: Edmond Montgomery Publications.

Ward, S. J. A. (2010). *Global Journalism Ethics*. Montreal: McGill-Queen's University Press.

Ward, S. J. A. (2010). A Theory of Patriotism for Global Journalism. In Media Ethics Beyond Borders: A Global Perspective (pp. 42-58). New York: Routledge.

Ward, S. J. A. (2013). Media Ethics as Global. In S. J. A. Ward (Ed.), *Global Media Ethics: Problems and Perspectives*. West Sussex, UK: Wiley-Blackwell Publishers.

Ward, S. J. A. (n.d.). *Digital Media Ethics*. Retrieved 14 September 2016 from https://ethics.journalism.wisc.edu/resources/global-media-ethics/

Ward, S. J. A., & Wasserman, H. (2010). *Media Ethics: Beyond Borders: A Global Prospective*. New York: Taylor and Francis.

Watiri, S. (2015). *New York Times Journalist Forced to Apologise for Publishing Part of the Fake Mugabe Story That Triggered KOT's War Against Mugabe*. Retrieved 12 August 2016, from http://www.ghafla.co.ke/blogs/tv/4204-ny-tiumes-responds

Wood, M. (2013). *Social Media as Breaking –News Feed Worse, Faster*. Retrieved from13 September 2016.https://www.cnet.com/news/social-media-as-breaking-news-feed-worse-information-faster/

Yin, R. K. (2004). *Case Study Research Methods*. Unpublished Draft Paper. Retrieved 15 July 2016, from http://www.cosmoscorp.com/docs/aeradraft.pdf

Zainal, Z. (2007). Case Study as Research Method. *Journal Kemanusian bil*. Retrieved 12 August 2016 from http://eprints.utm.my/8221/3/ZaidahZainal2007_CaseStudyasaResearchMethod.pdf

Zucker, D. M. (2009). *How to do case Study Research*. School of Nursing Faculty Publication Series Paper 2. Retrieved 6 July 2016 from http://scholarworks.umass.edu/nursing_faculty_pubs/2

Chapter 3
To Lie or Not to Lie: Interrogating Codes of Conduct on Photo Ethics in the Era of Digital Technologies

Bevelyn Dube
University of Venda, South Africa

ABSTRACT

New digital technologies have radically transformed the face of journalism in general and photo journalism in particular. These new technologies have not only made it easy for photo journalists to obtain images and to transmit them quickly to newsrooms and consumers across the globe, but they have also provided limitless opportunities for photo manipulation to take place, thus raising questions about the authenticity of those images. This has led to some scholars calling for the rethinking of media ethics to address these ethical dilemmas. This chapter, therefore, examines the codes of conduct for journalists in ten southern African countries to ascertain whether they have responded to this ethical dilemma brought in by the new digital technologies and if so, whether these responses give adequate guidance to journalists when called upon to make ethical decisions while processing photographs. The concepts of truth, reality and accuracy are also interrogated in the chapter. Findings revealed that most of the codes which do not make reference to photo manipulation are outdated and that those which do, are not comprehensive enough to give guidance to photo journalists.

INTRODUCTION

New digital technologies, such as smart cell phones, Adobe Photoshop and Silicon Beach Software's Digital Darkroom, to mention a few, have radically transformed the face of photo journalism, raising concerns about their impact on the ethics of photo journalism. These digital technologies have not only made it easy for professional photo journalists to capture, process and transmit images within minutes to newsrooms all over the world, but they have also brought with them limitless opportunities to manipulate photos, for example, by moving objects from or within the frame, adding elements which did not exist before or putting together two frames to make one. This manipulation has, in some cases, resulted in the distortion of news, promotion of propaganda and also in individuals or organisations being harmed (see

DOI: 10.4018/978-1-5225-2095-5.ch003

Horner, 2015; Besark, 2006). The exponential increase in the number of photo manipulation scandals that continue to rock the world of photo journalism all over the world proves that this ethical dilemma is on the increase in the 21st century. The well-publicised *TIME* magazine's publication of the deliberately darkened face of OJ Simpson on their cover page is a case in point (Hofer & Swan, 2005).

Other notable examples include *Los Angeles Times* photographer, Brian Walski's splicing of two photographs of a group of British soldiers in Iraq to create one photograph (Bersak, 2006); the University of Wisconsin's digital insertion of the image of a black student in a crowd of white football fans to give the impression that the university respected diversity in its enrolment (Hofer & Swan, 2005); the Reuters journalist's manipulation of a photograph to increase smoke billowing from a building in Beirut, in order to create the impression that Israel's bombing of that city was worse than it really was (The Reuters Photo Scandal, 2006); and Egypt's state-run newspaper, Al-Ahram's doctoring of a photo of the Egyptian president Hosni Mubarak walking in front of the Israeli, US, Palestinian and Jordanian leaders, yet in the original he is walking behind the other leaders (BBC, 2010, September 15). In recent times, 2015, the ethical dilemma of photo manipulation was underscored at the World Press Photo competition in which several images were disqualified and a major prize revoked because of excessive manipulation, staging and misleading captions (The *New York Times,* October, 16, 2015).

The increase in the number of scandals related to photo manipulation have prompted some scholars to call for the rethinking and the reinvention of media ethics, in order to address the ethical challenges brought by new media technologies (Horner, 2015; Bersak, 2006). The ease and the stealth with which photo journalists are manipulating photographs prompted Gladney and Ehrlich (1996, p. 506) to suggest that photo manipulation should be placed in the 21st century list of "ethical pitfalls". Thus, this chapter analyses the journalistic codes of conduct of ten southern African countries in the era of digital technologies to ascertain whether they have taken cognisance of this new ethical dilemma and if so, what stipulations they have put in place to address it.

In my choice of the codes of conduct, I am cognisant of the fact that some scholars do not believe in the efficacy of codes of conduct in dealing with ethical challenges in general, and photo manipulation in particular (see, Housley, 2002). Aiex and Gottlieb (1999), for example, argue that codes of conduct take away professional journalists' ability to make difficult decisions, and instead make them passively obey the guidelines without asking why they should do so. In this chapter, however, I argue that codes of conduct are fundamental in addressing this dilemma. The online Business Dictionary defines codes of conduct as a set of guidelines issued by an organisation or professional body to its workers to help them do their duties in accordance with its primary values and ethical standards. Horner (2015) describes them as norms and rules which seek to determine how media practitioners should execute their duties.

Evidence abounds in literature which shows that many organisations, both within and outside the media, consider codes of conduct a vital element in maintaining the integrity of their organisations. For example, 17 empirical studies reviewed by Loe and Ding (2000) showed a positive relationship between ethical codes and behaviour. Harrington's (1996) study also found that the availability of a code of conduct in an organisation improved the judgements and intentions of some employees. Gonzalez (n.d.) argues that the accelerated pace at which the 21st century world is changing because of technological developments and globalisation requires ethical principles that would ensure "proper functioning of the economic, political and social network and, therefore, for the well-being and development of the potential of every world citizen".

According to Wilkins and Brennen (2004), codes of conduct were originally adopted by the media industry to, among others, gain public trust after the First World War. Some scholars argue that they are vital for ensuring that journalists are held to a high standard in the execution of their duties (Steele, 2003). White (2001) adds that codes of conduct strengthen journalists when making ethical decisions against unethical pressures both from within and from without the organisation. Sturges (2009) also argues that codes of conduct enable the profession to tell its members what they should or should not do when faced with an ethical dilemma and at the same time demonstrate to the audience that the profession gives good guidance to its members. Cranberg (2003, p. 13), for example, posits that "An institution that makes everybody's business its business has to be mindful of the standards by which its business is conducted". Thus, codes of conduct are fundamental because they give the media industry the aura of professionalism, which, in turn, makes it more respectable and trustworthy in the eyes of the public (Blanchard, 1998).

The vitality of codes in addressing photo manipulation is underlined by Steele and Black's (1999) study which revealed that half of the 33 US codes of conduct they studied prohibited photo manipulation. Lowrey (2003), in a study of 225 newspapers also discovered that the majority had formal codes of conduct to deal with issues of digital alteration of photographs, once again revealing that media organisations believe that codes of conduct are vital to the operations of their organisations.

In 2003, a year popularly referred to as a "benchmark year" for codes of conduct, many media organisations revisited their codes of conduct following the Jayson Blair scandal (Steele, 2003, p. 8). Jayson Blair, a young national reporter for *The New York Times,* was dismissed for fabricating and plagiarising stories. Several other journalists have been dismissed from their jobs for violating the codes of conduct of their organisations (Housley, 2002). Seglin (2001) posits that newspapers which fire journalists who violate their codes have strong codes of conduct which are meant to guide journalists when making ethical decisions.

So important are codes of conduct in addressing this ethical dilemma posed by new digital technologies on photo journalism that big media organisations, such as The National Press Photographers Association (NPPA) and the *Washington Post,* have put in clauses in their codes of conduct to guide photo journalists on what is considered ethical and unethical in the processing and dissemination of photographs. The NPPA code of conduct, for example, stipulates that "it is wrong to alter the content of a photograph in any way that deceives the public [...] altering the editorial content of a photograph, in any degree, is a breach of the ethical standards recognised by the NPPA" (Cited by Horner, 2015, p. 147). The *Washington Post* also prohibits any photographic manipulation which could mislead, confuse or misrepresent the accuracy of events, while *The New York Times* also prohibits the alteration of images and states that any image that is published should capture reality.

However, several scholars have made a case for the manipulation of photos provided the photographer is honest about it and informs the public of what has been done to the image (see Horner, 2015; *The New York Times,* October 16, 2015; Manning, 2005; Mullen, 1998). This argument resonates with that of the proponents of utilitarianism who argue that ethical decision making should be driven by the need to achieve greater good in society (Horner, 2015; Peck, 2013). Scholars who subscribe to utilitarianism, unlike deontologists, argue that decision makers should always take into account the consequences or outcomes of telling the truth (Peck, 2013). They argue that telling a lie or being conservative with the truth, if it results in good outcomes in society, is a positive ethical decision (Horner, 2015; Peck, 2013). This means that photo journalists will be within their rights to manipulate photographs if the aim is to achieve good outcomes. Codes of conduct of major news organisations such as the NPPA, the *Washington Post* and *The New York Times*, for example, stipulate that only traditional manipulation technics such as contrast adjustments and those aimed at improving clarity and accuracy can be used. They go on further to state that where manipulation of images is done, this should be made clear to the readers.

Thus, this study examined codes of ethics from ten southern African countries to ascertain how they have responded to the ethical tensions brought by new media technologies to the journalistic arena. Each code of conduct was analysed individually and then compared to the others. The following questions guided the analysis:

- How have the codes of conduct responded to the ethical dilemmas brought by new media technologies to the journalistic arena?
- Do the codes of conduct adequately address the ethical problems of photo manipulation?
- How do codes of conduct define truth and reality in photo journalism?

In the next section, I review relevant literature in order to locate this current study within the body of scholarship of ethics of photo manipulation in the era of digitisation. The concepts of truth and reality are also interrogated in this study to reveal the complexities involved in trying to define them in this era of digital technologies. A content analysis of the codes of conduct then follows, and the chapter ends with recommendations for future research and a conclusion.

BACKGROUND

It is important to note from the onset that the manipulation of images is not a new phenomenon; it is as old as photography itself (see Bersak, 2006). In the early years of photography, it was not uncommon for early pictures to be staged or to be composed from different elements or for elements to be removed from or added to the frame. According to Campbell (2014, p. 6):

Politicians had their heads placed on other people's bodies, absent individuals were inserted into portraits, political opponents were scrubbed from images after they fell out of favour, and damaging associations between individuals were made by splicing pictures together.

A good example is the iconic portrait of the US president, Abraham Lincoln, which is a composite of Lincoln's head and the body of the Southern politician, John Calhoun (Foreman, 2016). Stalin was also known to routinely air brush those members of his party who had fallen out of favour with him (Horner, 2015, p. 142).

In the early years of photography, media professionals were also not averse to the manipulation of photographs (see Bersak, 2006). Scholars argue that, because of technological limitations in the early years of photo journalism, photo manipulation was both desired and expected, in order to improve the quality of the image (see Bersak, 2006). In newspapers, photographs did not have the power to tell a story in their own right, but they were used to merely support or illustrate a story (Baradell, 2012). Thus, in the early years, pictures that were put in the newspapers were mostly artist's impressions of the event (Kobré, 2004). It was not unheard of for newspapers, such as the *Daily Graphic,* an evening New York City paper, to ask artists to create publishable drawings based on photographs of events because hand drawn pictures were preferred to those produced by photographic technology (Bersak, 2006).

It was also acceptable for photo journalists to create composographs (photographs created out of several shots). One of the most famous ones was the picture of an almost nude woman which the *Daily Graphics* put on their front page to re-enact a courtroom scene which they had not been able to capture.The woman was asked by her lawyer to strip for the benefit of the jurors to prove to them that her husband, who was suing for divorce on the grounds that she had concealed her ethnicity from him, was lying. The sensationalisation of the courtroom drama earned the newspaper a 500% rise in circulation figures and those who criticised the newspaper did not do so because of the manipulation of the photos, but did so because of the newspaper's placing of the picture of an almost nude woman on the front page (Baradell, 2012; Bersak, 2006).

According to Coyne, "before Photoshop, it was considered OK to change the images in a darkroom – burn, dodge, crop, print excessively dark to give a different mood. Or sandwich two negatives for a double exposure" (cited in Baradell, 2012, p. 14). So welcome was the practice of manipulating photographs that some legendary photographers of the 20th century, such as W. Eugene Smith, earned their fame by using these techniques in processing their photographs (Coyne cited in Baradell, 2012, p. 14).

Thus, the way photo manipulation was perceived by media professionals in the early history of photo journalism might leave one wandering whether fundamental journalistic principles of truth telling and the credibility of the journalism profession were of no consequence to them. It is the contention of this chapter that this would be a misreading of the situation. It is clear from the accounts of the early history of photography that media professionals did not deliberately set out to deceive people about the images they published; photographs were merely used as illustrations of the events (see Kobré, 2004). It could be argued that, even though images were manipulated by media professionals, this did not violate the principle of truth telling because photo journalists were largely honest about the fact that the images had been altered. They did not attempt to pass on manipulated pictures as real. Thus, questions of deception did not arise because it was understood that the photographs were an illustration of the events and not a "real" depiction of them.

This differs from the way manipulation of photographs is done in the 21st century. New digital technologies have brought with them the ability to alter a photograph in such a way that no one can detect that it has been altered. This is what is causing concern to both professionals and the public (Horner, 2015; Fahmy, Fosdick, & Johnson, 2005; Harris, 1991; Lester, 1991). Byron Scott (cited in Harris, 1991, p. 165) states that:

Not until this decade have we had the ability to edit[a photograph] in a way that no one could tell that it had been edited. We've had an imperfect ability to lie with photographs for almost as long as we've had the ability to lie with words. But pictures have always had a credibility that words have not. With the new technology, the question is no longer what can we do, but what ought we to do?

The increased number of photo manipulation scandals involving photographs which have been seamlessly altered using new technologies and passed on to the reading public as the truth illustrates the threat that these technologies are posing to the fundamental principles of journalism. Truth has become a casualty of these new media technologies and, consequently, the credibility of the journalism profession. A study by Greer and Gosen (2002) revealed that, in the 1990s, there was a drastic reduction of the public's confidence in the media because of the increased levels of photo manipulation.

Issues of truth and journalistic credibility are fundamental principles on which the foundations of the profession stand (Horner, 2015; Harris, 1991). Ford (1998) also concurs that telling the truth is a fundamental principle of journalism (Ford, 1998). According to photojournalist Nancy Ford:

The photojournalist must capture the truth [...]. This means the photographer must only photograph what has happened, when it happened and not recreate a situation because they didn't get there on time. They must not move things around on the scene of an event to make pictures look better. They must not alter their photographs on the computer or in the darkroom, like an ugly telephone pole out of a picture. The photojournalist must tell the truth, just like the reporter. (Ford, 1998)

This insistence that journalists should tell the truth echoes the tenets of deontology propounded by scholars such as Immanuel Kant (see Horner, 2015; Peck, 2013). Deontologists are of the view that human beings are bound by a moral duty to tell the truth whatever the outcomes; lying is considered intrinsically wrong (see Horner, 2015:124; Peck, 2013). They subscribe to the realist school of thought which argues that photographs are mere copies of reality and that they convey the sense of "being thereness" to the reader (Barthes, 1984). Realism resonates with the positivist beliefs which argue that the world is observable and that it is a given reality that exists independently from the human being and the human being's mind (Fourie, 2007).

Applied to photo journalism, this argument assumes that there is a reality out there which can be captured on camera and represented in picture form to the world as a reality of the phenomenon which was observed. For deontologists, there is *absolutely* no room to manipulate photographs, as doing so is tantamount to tampering with the truth. Any form of manipulation will be considered by deontologists as a violation of one's moral duty to society, and so would an attempt by a journalist not to publish the photograph. No matter how gruesome a photo is, deontologists would argue that it is the journalist's moral duty to tell the truth regardless of the consequences (see Reed and Bracaglia, 2013, p. 189). On the face of it, therefore, it could be argued that journalism as a profession subscribes to deontological values and norms since the fundamental principle of journalism is truth telling.

However, the ability of the photograph to capture reality has always been contested by constructivists who argue that the assumption that photographs can capture the truth is a fallacy. Constructivists argue that the photograph is a construct of the photographer from the time the picture is taken to the time it is processed and, thus, dismiss arguments that a photograph can capture reality (see Horner, 2015). Strauss (2011), for example, argues that "every photograph or digital image is manipulated, aesthetically and politically, when it is made and when it is distributed". A seasoned photographer cited in a blog hosted by *The New York Times* (February 2, 2015) had this to say about photographs as being truthful:

What is truth? Photography certainly isn't. Photography is artifice. We can underexpose and overexpose the same image, neither version is 'true' or 'untrue' – it is just a different interpretation of the world in front of us.

This, therefore, raises questions about what is meant by telling the truth when, in reality, the photograph's authenticity is open to challenge from the time the picture is captured on camera (see Price, 2015; Strauss, 2003; Barthes, 1980). Barthes (1980, p. 6), for example, describes the photograph as "always invisible" and that "it is not it that we see", but an imitation of something that once existed. Price (2015, p. 93) also concurs that "we have always known that photographs are malleable, contrived and slippery".

However, despite this contestation, Price notes that people have always "been prepared to believe them to be evidential and more 'real' than other kinds of images" (Price, 2015, p. 93; see Horner, 2015; see also Harris, 1991). Despite the fact that, historically, manipulation of images was rife in the photojournalism industry, publishers endowed images with evidentiary status, in order to "assert the nonpartisan, objective view offered by the fourth estate" (Shcwartz, 2003, p. 28). Sanders (2006) argues that people believe something is true when they see it with their own eyes, and, traditionally, pictures have always provided that kind of authority. Trust in the truth of photography was predicated upon the belief that there is a direct and traceable causal link between the image and the source (Warburton, 1998).

The advent of new media technologies and the ease with which photo journalists can now manipulate images has, however, changed people's perceptions of the veracity of photographs, thus threatening not only the major journalistic principle of truth telling, but the evidentiary authority which the photograph carries (Horner, 2015). It is, therefore, not surprising that the ability of these new technologies to manipulate an image in such a way that the change would be undetectable has eroded the trust the public had of the evidentiary status of the photograph (Horner, 2015; Greer & Gosen, 2002).

The situation is further complicated by the fact that digital cameras by their very nature make photo manipulation inevitable and unavoidable (Campbell, 2014). Campbell (2014), for example, argues that at almost every stage in the photographic process, "from capture and production to the publication and circulation" of images, there is potential for images to be manipulated (2014, p. 5). He complicates the debate on the manipulation of photos when he argues that digital technology, by its very nature, makes the capturing of the truth impossible. According to Connor (2012), traditionally, the camera was a picture-making device, which through the use of chemicals in the darkroom produced an original image which could be used as a yardstick to evaluate copies made from it. However, digital cameras merely collect data which are not fully formed, and only through computational techniques is the full image processed (Campbell, 2014; Connor, 2012). According to Farid (2009), "only one-third of the samples in a colour image are captured by the camera. The other two thirds are computed by the camera software – a process known as colour filter array…". Thus, Farid concludes that "two thirds of your pixels are fake".

What this means is that, whereas in the era of analogue, manipulation was done sorely by the photographer in the darkroom, in the modern age, the digital technology, itself, automatically manipulates images in the process of computing them. According to Campbell (2014, p. 5), the assumption that there is an in-camera image which can function as the authentic, is no longer sustainable in the digital era. He adds that there is no original colour image in computational digital photography. This, therefore, raises questions about how 21st century journalists are expected to produce photographs and still remain ethical journalists who adhere to the principles of truth telling.

Campbell's (2014) argument resonates with that of constructivists. The characteristic of digital technologies to compute images, thus, render mythical the whole argument by realists that a truthful rendition of an event can be captured by a camera. This new view of what manipulation is, has a bearing on the interpretation of truth by journalism professionals and calls for a redefinition of major concepts such as truth, reality and manipulation in the era of digital technologies. The next section describes the codes of conduct selected for the study and how they were selected.

SOUTHERN AFRICAN JOURNALISTIC CODES OF CONDUCT

Southern Africa, in this study, was used to refer to countries in the grouping called the Southern African Development Community (SADC). SADC is a regional block made up of 15 countries, namely Angola, Botswana, Democratic Republic of Congo (DRC), Lesotho, Madagascar, Malawi, Mauritius, Mozambique, Namibia, Seychelles, South Africa, Swaziland, Tanzania, Zambia and Zimbabwe. In spite of the fact that these countries have different political and media systems, SADC was chosen because the researcher is a resident of this region and also because this regional block of countries has signed several protocols which obligate member states to work together towards achieving common goals. For example, the countries have worked together to craft media policies for the sub-region as seen in the signing of the Windhoek Declaration and the media reform advocacy of national chapters of the Media Institute of Southern Africa (MISA) (Chuma & Moyo, 2010), as well as the 2009 SADC agreement to ensure that the regional block worked together towards completing digital migration by 2013 (Berger, 2010). Only ten codes of conduct were chosen because they were easily available online. The other five which were not included in this study were either not available online or were written in languages that I could not speak or write. The choice of the ten codes of conduct from the same sub-region, however, enabled me to come up with a comprehensive picture of how individual countries in the region in general and the whole region in particular have responded to the threat of digital technologies in the processing of photographs.

It is critical to note that southern African countries, amongst them, have several journalistic codes of conduct, some operating at national level and others at organisational level. For purposes of this study, only codes of conduct which focus on journalistic practice at national level were considered for the study. However, some countries such as South Africa, had several such codes, for example, the code of conduct of the Press Ombudsman and Appeal Panel, Code of Conduct for the South African Union of Journalists and the Code of Ethics and Conduct for South African Print and Online Media monitored by the Press Council of South Africa.

To ensure a balanced comparison of the codes, I selected only those codes of conduct which are applied and enforced by the Press Councils (or the equivalent) of the selected countries. This means that ten codes of conduct, one from each country, were selected for the study. Codes of conduct for broadcasting were not included in the study as focus of the study was on the print media. Codes from specific media organisations were also excluded from the study. The Media Council of Tanzania was unique in that, while Press Councils in the other nine countries used a single code to cover all groups of journalists, the Tanzanian Media Council developed a number of codes to cover different groups of journalists. For example, the Media Council developed separate codes of ethics for reporters, for media managers/editors, for Public Relations officers and Media Advertising agents, and for Press Photographers and Video Producers. For purposes of this study, the code of ethics for Press Photographers and Video Producers was chosen. Table 1 gives a summary of the Codes of Conduct per country, which were analysed in the study.

Content analysis was used to analyse the selected Codes of Conduct. How this was done is described in the next section of the chapter.

Table 1. Summary of codes of conduct analysed in this study

Country	Name of Code
Angola	Code of Ethics
Botswana	Code of Ethics of the Press Council of Botswana
DRC	Code of Conduct of the Congolese National Press Union
Malawi	Media Council of Malawi Code of Ethics and Professional conduct
Namibia	Code of Ethics for the Namibian Media
South Africa	Press Council Code of Ethics and Conduct for South African Print and Online Media
Swaziland	Code of Ethics of Swaziland National Association of Journalists (SNAJ)
Tanzania	Code of Ethical Practice for Media Photographers and Video
Zambia	Code of Ethics of the Media Council of Zambia
Zimbabwe	Code of Conduct for Zimbabwean Media Practitioners

CONTENT ANALYSIS OF THE CODES OF CONDUCT

Qualitative content analysis was used to analyse the codes of conduct to establish how they have responded to the ethical challenge of photo manipulation brought by new digital technologies. Hsieh and Shannon (2005, p. 1278) define qualitative content analysis as "a research method for the subjective interpretation of the content of text data through the systematic classification process of coding and identifying themes or patterns". Patton (2002, p. 453) adds that it is "any qualitative data reduction and sense-making effort that takes a volume of qualitative material and attempts to identify core consistencies and meanings". According to Wigston (2009, p. 4), qualitative content analysis differs from quantitative content analysis in that the former approach involves "no physical counting of data" but tends to be "more critical in nature and can be used when we need to penetrate the deeper layers of a message", while the latter "involves some form of counting, and applies the scientific method rigorously".

To critically evaluate the codes of conduct, I first sought to establish when the codes were adopted and whether this has any bearing on their response to photo manipulation. The analysis then searched for clauses within the codes which specifically addressed photographs in general and photo manipulation in particular. These were then subjected to an analysis to establish how the stipulations are worded and how comprehensive they are in giving guidance to photo journalists on how to deal with the ethical dilemma. Table 2 summarises the results of this analysis. The countries are listed in alphabetic order.

The findings show that all the codes of conduct were adopted in the 21st century though some are older than the others. The oldest were the codes of conduct from Angola, Botswana and the DRC, which were all adopted in 2004. The most up-to-date is the South African code of conduct which was revised in 2016. Zimbabwe's code of conduct is also new because it was revised in 2015. The other codes are also fairly current, for example, Malawi and Namibia adopted theirs in 2009, while Tanzania and Zambia revised theirs in 2010.

As shown in Table 2, in general, the older codes of conduct from Angola, Botswana and the DRC do not make reference to photo manipulation. However, it could be argued that although Angola does not make specific reference to photo manipulation, this is implied in Section 9 which states that journalists must not falsify or alter situations. This assumes that the term "journalists" in the code refers to all cat-

Table 2. Summary of the findings

Country	Year Code Adopted	Findings
Angola	2004	Does not say anything about photo manipulation but gives a blanket statement which states that journalists must not falsify or alter situations
Botswana	2004	Nothing on photo manipulation. Only gives guidance on when and how pictures involving children should be taken, as well as that pictures for publication should not dehumanise people
DRC	2004	Nothing on photo manipulation. But makes reference to not altering documents, and emphasis is put on not manipulating the content of spoken and written texts
Malawi	2009	Stipulates that photographers must strive for accuracy and that pictures must relate to the story
Namibia	2009	Nothing on photo manipulation. Photos for publication should not depict brutality, sadism, violence and that photographers should not use devious means to obtain photographs, except in the public interest
South Africa	2016	Responds to manipulation as follows "Pictures and or Videos or …. Shall not misrepresent or mislead nor be manipulated".
Swaziland	2005	Photographs should give an accurate picture of an event; Photo journalists should not manipulate the image to imply that a person is HIV positive
Tanzania	2010	Responds to manipulation as follows: "Lenses, filters polarisers and tricks like angling, superimposition, editing, touch up, computer and mechanical effects should not be used to alter the reality of an image"
Zambia	2010	Responds to photo manipulation as follows: "Pictures shall not misrepresent or mislead nor be manipulated to do so". Only fair methods to be used to obtain photos. Pornography shall not be published
Zimbabwe	2015	Nothing on manipulation. Gives guidance on when, how and under what circumstances children should be photographed

egories of journalists. Botswana only makes reference to pictures with regards to when and how pictures involving children should be taken, as well as that pictures for publication should not dehumanise people. The DRC code of conduct, though it makes reference to abstaining from altering documents or distorting and warping people's opinions, headlines or comments, does not make reference to the manipulation of photographs (Articles 5 and 9). Article 4 of the code appears to affirm the code's emphasis on spoken and written texts only when it stipulates that journalists should "accept full responsibility for any text (written and spoken) that is published with his/her byline…".

The absence of clauses to deal with photo manipulation in these codes of conduct raises questions about how a major 21st century ethical dilemma has been overlooked or ignored by these codes of conduct which are fundamental in guiding journalistic practice. One possible reason for this oversight in the codes is that most of these codes are outdated. They were drafted in the first decade of the 21st century when new media technologies had not yet made their presence felt in most southern African countries. Jensen (2003), for example, argues that Africa had the lowest use of Internet and information technologies in the first 10 years of the 21st century. This is affirmed by the NEPAD Council Department (cited in Esipisu & Kariithi, 2007), which argues that, in the first decade of the 21st century, the penetration of new media technologies in Africa was only 2%. The absence of ethical guidelines on photo manipulation in most of these codes could, thus be attributed to lack of penetration of the new media technologies at the time when most of these codes of conduct were drafted.

However, while one might argue that the age of the code could be a factor in explaining the absence of clauses to deal with photo manipulation, the analysis surprisingly showed that even newly revised codes such as that of Namibia and Zimbabwe are silent on the subject of photo manipulation. As shown in Table 2, Namibia's code of conduct was adopted in 2009, while Zimbabwe's was revised as recently as 2015. Both Namibia and Zimbabwe only make reference to photography to describe when, how and under what conditions photographs should be taken. Section 11.1 of the Namibian code of conduct, for example, stipulates that journalists, photographers and camera persons must not obtain or seek information through misrepresentation or deception, and also that photographic or video material should be obtained with the consent of the owner. The Namibian code further states that photos for publication should not depict brutality, sadism violence etc. and that photographers should not use devious means to obtain photographs except in the public interest. Zimbabwe also mentions photographs with reference to when, how and under what circumstances children should be photographed. Focus in the codes of both countries is more on how and under what circumstances one should obtain photographs and not on how these photographs, once obtained, should be processed and presented.

One could argue that both codes do cover photo journalism in their general stipulations. For example, the Namibian code of conduct states that "*Every* journalist shall strive to report news and events accurately, fairly and with balance" (emphasis mine). However, while it can be argued, academically, that the word "every" encompasses all kinds of journalists, including photo journalists, this statement does not show the urgency with which this increasingly threatening ethical dilemma should be treated. In the case of the Zimbabwe code of conduct, an opportunity was lost when the term "media practitioner" was defined at the beginning of the code of conduct. The code defines "media practitioner" as a reporter, editor, radio and television programmer and presenter employed in a media institution, a freelance reporter or columnist who is a stringer or writes for media institutions. Nowhere in this definition is a photographer mentioned. Including photo journalists in the definition would strengthen this definition and ensure that photo journalists are also embraced by the code's stipulations. Bolder and more prominent statements on photo manipulation are required to address this increasingly growing threat to the integrity of the journalism profession.

The findings in Table 2 also show that the codes of conduct from five countries, namely Malawi, South Africa, Swaziland, Tanzania and Zambia, have clauses which stipulate, though in different ways, that photo manipulationis unacceptable. The words used in the codes of South Africa, Tanzania and Zambia are more explicit and direct in their rejection of the practice of photo manipulation. The South African code of conduct, for example, states in Section 10.3 that "Pictures and/or videos or audio content shall not misrepresent or mislead nor be manipulated to do so". The Zambian code uses the same words when it states that pictures shall not misrepresent or mislead nor be manipulated to do so. The Tanzanian code's stipulations, though also rejecting photo manipulation, state this differently as follows: "lenses, filters, polarisers and tricks like angling, superimposition, editing, touch-up, computer (electronic) and mechanical effects should not be used to alter the reality of an image".

Even though the codes from Malawi and Swaziland do not use the words "altering" or "manipulation" with reference to photographs, they state that photographs should be presented accurately, implying that photographers should capture the event as is without manipulation. Malawi's code of conduct stipulates in Section 3.2 that photographers must strive for accuracy and that pictures must give an accurate picture of an event and not highlight a minor incident out of context. Swaziland's code of conduct also states that "photographs and telecasts should be given an accurate picture of an event not highlight an incident out of context" and that "Journalists, photographers and camera-persons shall be sensitive to the dangers of implying or placing a person in a situation that may imply HIV status" (Articles 18 section 2; Article 19.4 section 7, Swaziland Code).

Though expressed in different ways, all five codes underscore the need to tell the truth or to be objective and accurate in capturing the image. This is not surprising as truth seeking and verification of content are fundamental pillars of the journalistic enterprise (Foreman, 2016). Davies, for example, argues that telling the truth is fundamental to the practice of news reporting. In his words, "For journalists, the defining value is honesty – the attempt to tell the truth. That is our primary purpose. All that we do […] must flow from the single source of truth-telling" (Davies, 2009, p. 12).

While this is both desirable and expected because truth telling is a fundamental principle of the journalism profession, it is equally important to acknowledge that photographic truth is a complex notion. The Tanzanian code's stipulation, for example, that the reality of an image should not be altered is problematic because the concept of reality is contested. Several scholars argue that photographs have no ability to capture reality (Horner, 2015; Price, 2015; Strauss, 2011; Harris, 1991; Barthes, 1980). Batchen (1994), for example, argues that photographers inevitably manipulate every photo they make, meaning that even those photographs which are believed to depict the truth are in actual fact products of manipulation. According to Mullen (1998), arguing that photographs depict the truth is not correct; instead "what they actually depict are slices of life selected and framed by the photographer". Filo (cited in Manning, 2005) also argues that photographers are never objective because they choose what to photograph, the angle of the shot and also what to include or exclude in the frame. According to Filo, the photograph is a construct of the photographer, which is imbued with intent, bias, culture and the subjectivity of the photographer. Thus, when codes of conduct stipulate that manipulation of photographs is unethical and that photographers should be accurate in capturing the reality, one could argue that they are being simplistic about a much more complex process. The notions of photographic "reality", "truth" and "accuracy" should be redefined taking into consideration that these concepts are products of culture and the history of a people (see Mullen, 1998).

An online survey carried out by the Oxford University's Reuters Institute for the Study of Journalism and the World Press of the 5158 entrants who participated in the World Press competition in 2015, also revealed the complex nature of the concept of "truth". More than half of the 1549 photographers who participated in the survey said they sometimes staged photos, an unethical practice that is forbidden by all major wire services and newspapers in the USA (*The New York Times,* October 16, 2015). Some of the participants argued that staged photos can be real in the sense that the events actually happened (Lyon cited in *The New York Times*, October 16, 2015). Staging of photos takes place at the shooting stage and, according to Sim Chi Yin, a participant in the survey, this manipulation is difficultto detect or to prove. Others such as Liss (cited in *The New York Times,* October 16, 2015), are of the view that staged pictures can tell the truth better than an unstaged photograph. In his words, "I would respectfully submit that a directed picture can sometimes convey a greater truth about a subject than a candid picture".

All this reveals that the notions of truth and reality differ from person to person.Thus, merely stating that photos should convey the truth begs the question: Which truth? According to Mullen (1998), these concepts are dependent on culture, beliefs, history, understanding and human nature, meaning that what might be true in one context might not be true in another. One is here reminded of Kasoma's (1996) plea for Afriethics. While some of Kasoma's arguments are problematic, the society-centred ethics, which he advocates for in ethical decision making is important as it takes into consideration the culture and the history of that society. According to Kasoma, the major criterion for disseminating information should be the good that information would bring to society in the first instance. This resonates with Merril's (cited in Kasoma, 1996) submission that a media system should reflect the political philosophy in which it functions. It follows, therefore, that concepts of truth and reality should be defined from the perspective of that particular society and not from a Western perspective. It is critical, therefore, that drafters of codes of conduct should not appropriate definitions of truth and reality that are foreign to the audiences that they are serving.

A close analysis of all five codes which condemn photo manipulation reveals that they only promote deontological ethical ideals of telling the truth. This is commendable, but truth from whose perspective? There does not seem to be any room for utilitarian decision-making which would allow the photo journalist to manipulate a photograph for the greater good of the society, a central consideration in society centred ethics (see Kasoma, 1996). This is a major criticism that has been levelled against codes of conduct by some scholars who argue that they leave little or no room for grey areas (Steele, 2003). 'Adopt the ASNE code' (1993) states that ethical guidelines which leave little room for interpretation of the situation can do more harm than good.

This is a stance taken by some scholars such as Mullen (1998, p. 94) who argues that manipulation is often required to tell the truth. Manning (2005) also argues that some manipulation of photographs is necessary so as to improve the quality of the product. To that end, he argues that photo journalists should be given advice on what is acceptable manipulation. Swan (cited in Manning, 2005) considers acceptable manipulation to include "dodging, burning, color balancing, spotting and contrast adjustment to achieve accurate recording of an event or object". Some scholars argue that staged photographs, which are forbidden by many major media organisations, can tell the truth better than unstaged photographs (see *The New York Times,*October, 16, 2015). Horner (2015, p. 148-149) adds that manipulating an image can be appropriate if it is done for "benevolent motives".

One is reminded, here, of the South African newspaper, *Die Beeld,* which digitally covered the body of a learner, Richard King, who was knocked down by a taxi, as a sign of respect to the deceased and also so as not to offend the public (see Cass, 1998, p. 91). To publish the original photo, which showed the uncovered body of the learner, would have been truthful, but the picture might have caused the young boy's family untold pain and offended the reading public's sensibilities. A similar incident happened when the South African newspaper, *The Citizen,* doctored a picture which showed a burnt out minibus destroyed by a suicide bomb attack in Kabul, Afghanistan on 18 September 2012 (see *Mail & Guardian,* September 27, 2012). The Press Club of South Africa took exception to the newspaper's removal of images of the two bodies of South African nationals from the frame; the original photograph from *Agence France Press* showed the two bodies in the mangled wreck of the minibus.

However, where the two incidents differed is that *Die Beeld* made it clear through its caption that they had doctored the photograph in respect of the relatives of the learner and the public, while *The Citizen* was quiet about its action. The latter's actions raise serious ethical questions about the veracity of photographs to convey the truth. *Die Beeld's* action of alerting the readers that the photograph had been manipulated to spare the grieving family's feelings opens up possibilities of how newspapers can present manipulated images, in the event that doing do is in the interest of the public. Horner (2015:149) argues for example that "a reconstruction (or manipulation" may be legitimate if it is clearly referred to as such". In his view, if the viewer is not deceived into believing that the image they are seeing is authentic, then the producer has told the truth. Sim Chi Yin (*The New York Times,* October 16, 2015), concurs that, as long as the viewer is not misled about the nature of the photograph, there is no problem. In her view, the key to addressing the ethical problem of photo manipulation is to be honest and transparent about how one made the image. This view resonates with the recommendations made by the

1996 five-member committee appointed by the New York University's programme on 'Copyright and the New Technologies' that media organisations should institute a system of labelling for manipulated images (Horner, 2015:149). Wheeler also recommended ethical labelling for different types of images, a strategy adopted by some newspapers to indicate that an image has been manipulated (2002, p. 167; see also Horner, 2015:149).

A study done by Boyle (1992) also reveals that some professional journalists are of the view that readers should be informed when images have been manipulated. However, as Black, Steele and Barney (1995) observed in their study, some media professionals are averse to the idea of informing the audience that a picture has been manipulated. A study by Fosdick and Fahmy (2003) also revealed that some magazine editors were not keen to inform the public. It is the contention of this paper, however, that lessons should be drawn from the openness of the newspaper organisations in the early years of photography which did not try to pass on photographs as nothing other than illustrations of the events. Because of their candidness, the reading public did not doubt their intentions, nor did they treat the images in the newspapers with suspicion. In fact, despite the obvious manipulation of images, the public in the early years of photograph placed a high value on the evidentiary authority of images.

Thus, this paper argues that southern African codes of conduct should make provision for photo manipulation not only to help the photo journalists to deal with some ethically difficult situations, but to also earn the public's trust. Passing a doctored photograph as the real thing is to falsify the picture or to tell a lie, and this, consequently, will erode the reading public's confidence in the journalism profession. As Manning (2005) observes, "credibility is the main asset of any news organisation. Once compromised, this can be difficult to maintain, and once lost it is impossible to restore". A study carried out by Huang (2001) revealed that the public expected the media to let them know if a picture had been altered and that the degree of trust amongst readers increased. Based on his findings that awareness played a significant part in gaining the reading public's trust, Huang recommended that the media should strongly consider informing readers that an image has been manipulated. Codes of conduct for the *Washington Post* and *The New York Times,* for example, have adopted this stance because they make it clear that, while they do not approve of photo manipulation, where it happens, it must be made clear to the reader through use of captions and credits (Horner, 2015).

FUTURE RESEARCH DIRECTIONS

One of the major limitations of this study is that it focused only on national codes of conduct of selected southern African countries, and, even then, only one code per country was studied. Codes of conduct from individual media organisations were not interrogated in this paper. In South Africa, for example, media organisations such as the *Mail & Guardian, Sowetan, The Star,* to mention but a few, have in-house codes of conduct which control the manner in which journalists in those organisations operate. A similar situation prevails in media organisations of other southern African countries whose national codes of conduct were examined in this paper. This means that one cannot make conclusive judgements about the state of photo journalism in southern African countries based only on the findings of this study. Thus, to get a more comprehensive picture of photo journalism ethics in the age of digital technologies, it is vital that future studies focus on codes of conduct of media organisations within the selected countries. Such a study would give a more realistic picture of the state of photo journalism in individual countries in the region.

The literature review revealed a dearth of studies on photo manipulation in southern Africa and, because of that, the prevalence of photo manipulation in the region, as well as the voices of southern African photo journalists on the subject could not be ascertained. Most examples of photo manipulation in the era of digital technologies, in this study, are mostly from Western countries. There is, thus, a need to carry out research on how prevalent photo manipulation in the era of digital technologies is in southern Africa and also how photo journalists and the media organisations view the practice.

CONCLUSION

The chapter set out to examine the responses of codes of conduct of ten southern African countries to photo manipulation which has increased exponentially with the advent of new digital technologies. The chapter was guided by questions which sought to find out how the codes have responded to digital photo manipulation, whether their responses give adequate guidance to journalists when called upon to make ethical decisions while processing and disseminating photos, and what they perceive to be truth telling in photo journalism.

The findings show that most of the codes of conduct which did not have clauses to address this 21st century ethical dilemma were outdated and require revision. Codes from Angola, Botswana and the DRC were last revised in 2004, a time when digital technologies had not yet penetrated these countries in a significant way (see Esipisu & Kariithi, 2007). However, with the exponential rise in digital technologies in these countries (see Balancing Act Report, 2014), it is vital that the codes be revised to make them in line with the new developments in photo journalism and also to give photo journalists in those countries guidance on how to process and present images to the reading public.

However, it has to be noted that codes from countries such as Zimbabwe and Namibia, whose codes of conduct were revised as recent as 2015 and 2009 respectively, had no clauses which address the issue of photo manipulation. Further studies would need to be done to ascertain why such a major ethical problem is not given prominence in these codes of conduct.

Those codes of conduct which took into consideration the issue of photo manipulation, while they must be commended, did not go far enough to address this complex situation. More comprehensive guidelines on photo manipulation are required because it is a subject which has generated diverse views on what is acceptable and what is not (see *The New York Times*, October 16, 2015). Upholding the fundamental journalism principle of telling the truth is commendable because media organisations which do not adhere to the deontological principle of truth telling are in danger of losing their credibility and, once lost, it is not easy to regain it. However, literature also shows that there is a strong case to be made for utilitarian ethics in photo journalism, especially if the photo is manipulated for benevolent reasons (see Horner, 2015) and also provided the reading public is made aware of this manipulation. If the latter is done, then the principle of telling the truth would not have been violated and the media's credibility would not be under threat. It is when photographers try to pass on a doctored picture as real that deception sets in.

Besides, codes of conduct should also give guidelines to photo journalists on what truth, reality and accuracy entail in this era of digital technologies. This is in view of the fact that these are heavily contested terms which are open to a variety of interpretations. For example, some photographers and scholars argue that staged photos, which are forbidden by many media organisations, may be real, because the events actually happened, while others consider them false because the shooting of these pictures involved some manipulation (see *The New York Times,* October 16, 2015). Others, like the constructivists, argue that every photograph, whether staged or not, is a construct of the photographer and should, therefore, never be treated as real. There is also the argument that digital cameras, by their very nature, are manipulative devices. How then is a photographer expected to successfully navigate this minefield of diverse opinions in the absence of clear guidelines on how to process images? What is truth for one individual or group of people might not be so for another. Notions of truth and reality are not universal; they depend on culture, beliefs, history, understanding and human nature (see Mullen, 1998). This means that notions of truth and reality must be defined in the codes of conduct and not left wide open to a variety of interpretations. Thus codes of conduct should not just give photo journalists one line statements, such as those given by the codes of five countries which responded to the ethical dilemma of photo manipulation. Instead, they should be more comprehensive about what they consider to be manipulation, truth, reality and accuracy in this era of new technologies.

REFERENCES

Adopt the ASNE code. (1993). *Editor & Publisher, 126*(42), 6-7.

Aiex, N., & Gottlieb, S. (1999). *Issues in media ethics* (Report No. EDO-CS-99-07). Bloomington, IN: ERIC Clearinghouse on Reading, English and Communication. (ERIC Document Reproduction Service No. ED436015)

Balancing Act Report. (2014). *The sub-Saharan Africa Media Landscape – Then, Now and in the Future*. Retrieved February 12, 2016, from http://balancingact-africa.com/sites/balancingact-africa.com/files/products/1.%20SSA%20Media%20Landscape.pdf

Baradell, S. (2012). *Photojournalism, technology and ethics: What's right and wrong today*. Black Star Publishing Co. Retrieved February 14, 2016, from http://rising.blackstar.com/wp-content/uploads/2008/11/photoethics.pdf

Barthes, R. (1980). Camera Lucida. Reflections on photography (R. Howard, Trans.). New York: Hill and Wang.

Barthes, R. (1984). *Camera Lucida: Reflections on Photography*. London: Fontana.

Batchen, G. (1994). Phantasm: Digital imaging and the death of photography. *Aperture, 136*, 48.

BBC. (2010, September 15). *Egyptian newspaper under fire over altered photo*. Retrieved January 16, 2016, from http://www.bbc.com/news/wordl-middle-east-11313738

Berger, G. (2010). *Challenges and Perspectives of Digital Migration for African Media*. Grahamstown, South Africa: Highway Africa, Media Matrix.

Bersak, D. R. (2006). *Ethics in photojournalism: Past, Present and Future* (Masters dissertation). Massachusetts Institute of Technology. Retrieved January, 12, 2016, from http://web.mit.edu/drb/Public/PhotoThesis/

Black, J., Steele, B., & Barney, R. (1995). *Doing Ethics in Journalism* (2nd ed.). Boston: Allyn & Bacon.

Blanchard, M. A. (Ed.). (1998). *History of the Mass Media in the United States*. Chicago, IL: Fitzroy Dearborn Publishers.

Boyle, P. (1992). *Standards for photography's cutting edge*. Washington Journalism Review.

Business Dictionary. (n.d.). Retrieved February 20, 2016, from http://www.businessdictionary.com/definition/code-of-ethics.html

Campbell, D. (2014). *The Integrity of the Image. A World Press Photo Research Project*. Published by the World Press Photo Academy.

Cass, T. M. (1998). *A comparison of the views of South African and American photo journalists to the digital manipulation of news photographs* (Unpublished Masters dissertation). Rhodes University, South Africa.

Connor, K. (2012). *Photojournalism ethics on shifting technological ground*. Retrieved February 4, 2016, from http://www.fourandsix.com/blog/2012/2/13/photojournalism=ethics-on-shifting-technological-ground.html

Cranberg, G. (2003). No shortage of codes. *The American Editor*, *78*(6), 13.

Davies, N. (2009). *Flat Earth News*. London: Vintage.

Dunleavy, D. (2005). *Camera phones prevail: Citizen shutterbugs and the London bombings*. Retrieved February 22, 2016, from http://www.digitaljournalist.org/issue0507/dunleavy.html

Esipisu, I., & Kariithi, N. (2007). New media development in Africa. *Global Media Journal*, *1*(1), 21–63.

Fahmy, S., Fosdick, S.B. & Johnson, T.J. (2005). Is seeing believing? A survey of magazine professionals' practices and attitudes towards ethical standards for photographs. *Journal of Magazine and New Media Research,* 1-8.

Farid, H. (2009). Digital Imaging. *Encyclopedia of Perception*. Retrieved March 3, 2016, from http://www.cs.dartmouth.edu/farid/downloads/publications/digitalimaging09.pdf

Ford, N. L. (1998). *Photojournalism vs Journalism*. Retrieved March 14, 2016, from http://nlford.com/career/journalism.shtml>

Foreman, G. (2016). *The Ethical Journalist: Making Responsible Decisions in the Digital Age* (2nd ed.). West Sussex, UK: Wiley Blackwell.

Fosdick, S., & Fahmy, S. (2003). *Punctuation and Epistemic Honesty: Do Photos Need What Words Have?* Paper presented at the Association for Education in Journalism and Mass Communication Conference, Kansas City, MO.

Fourie, P. J. (Ed.). (2007). *Media Studies: Media History, Media and Society* (2nd ed.). Cape Town: Juta & Co.

Gladney, G., & Erlich, M. C. (1996). Cross-media response to digital manipulation of still and moving images. *Journal of Broadcasting & Electronic Media*, *40*(4), 496–508. doi:10.1080/08838159609364371

Gonzalez, F. (n.d.). *Values and Ethics for the 21st Century*. BBVA Foundation. Retrieved July 5, 2016, from http://www.bbvaopenmind.com

Greer, J. D., & Gosen, J. D. (2002). How much is too much? Assessing levels of digital alteration as factors in public perception of news credibility. *News Photographer*, *4*(10), 4–13.

Harrington, S. A. (1996). The effects of codes of ethics and personal denial of responsibility on computer abuse judgements and intentions. *Management Information Systems Quarterly*, *20*(3), 257–278. doi:10.2307/249656

Harris, C. R. (1991). Digitization and manipulation of news photographs. *Journal of Mass Media Ethics*, *6*(3), 164–174. doi:10.1207/s15327728jmme0603_4

Hofer, M., & Swan, K. O. (2005). Digital image manipulation: A compelling means to engage students in discussion of point of view and perspective. *Contemporary Issues in Technology & Teacher Education*, *5*(3/4), 290–299.

Horner, D. S. (2015). *Understanding Media Ethics*. London: SAGE.

Housley, E. E. (2002). *Evaluating the effectiveness of newspaper codes of ethics: A Star-Telegram case study* (Masters Dissertation). Texas Christian University. Retrieved June 28, 2016, from http://citeseerx.psu.edu/viewdoc/download?doi=10.1.1.582

Hsieh, H. F., & Shannon, S. E. (2005). Three approaches to qualitative content analysis. *Qualitative Health Research*, *15*(9), 1277–1288. doi:10.1177/1049732305276687 PMID:16204405

Huang, E. S. (2001). Readers perception of digital alteration in photojournalism. *Journalism Communication Monographs*, *3*(3), 149–182. doi:10.1177/152263790100300302

Jensen, M. (2003). *ICT in Africa: A Status Report*. Retrieved March 3, 2016, from https://www.itu.int/osg/spu/wsis-themes/.../jensen-itcs-africa.doc

Kasoma, F. (1996). The Foundations of African Ethics (Afriethics) and the professional Practice of Journalism: The case of society-centred media morality. *Africa Media Review*, *10*(3), 93–116.

Kobré, K. (2004). *Photojournalism: The Professionals' Approach*. Burlington, MA: Focal Press.

Le Kay, E., Pretorious, N., Rowles, P., Rusch, K., Scott, C., Taljaard, R., & Whitehead, A. (2003). *Digital Manipulation of Images. Group Report on Grocott's Mail*. Rhodes University.

Lester, P. M. (1991). *Photojournalism: An Ethical Approach*. Hillsdale, NJ: Erlbaum.

Loe, C., & Ding, C. G. (2000). A review of empirical studies assessing ethical decision making in business. *Journal of Business Ethics*, *25*(3), 185–204. doi:10.1023/A:1006083612239

Lowrey, W. (2003). Normative conflict in the newsroom: The case of digital photo manipulation. *Journal of Mass Media Ethics*, *18*(2), 123–142. doi:10.1207/S15327728JMME1802_05

Mail & Guardian. (2012, September 27). *Citizen fires photographer over doctored picture discussion*. Retrieved August 20, 2015, from http://mg.co.za/article/2012-09-27-citizen-fires-whistleblower-of-doctored-cover-photo

Manning, C. (2005). *Photo-Journalism ethics in the digital age*. Retrieved July 23, 2016, from http://www.newmediarepublic.com/articles/photoethics.pdf

Moyo, D., & Chuma, W. (Eds.). (2010). *Media Policy in a Changing Southern Africa: Critical Reflections on Media Reforms in the Global age*. Pretoria: UNISA Press.

Mullen, L. (1998). *Truth in photography: Perception, Myth and Reality in the Postmodern World* (Masters Dissertation). University of Florida. Retrieved July, 23, 2016, from http://etd.fcla.edu/UF/and0040/Leslie.pdf

Patton, M. Q. (2002). *Qualitative Research and Evaluation Methods*. Thousand Oaks, CA: SAGE.

Peck, L. A. (2013). Tools of ethical decision making. In L. A. Peck & G. S. Reel (Eds.), *Media Ethics at Work: True Stories from Young Professionals* (pp. 5–22). London: SAGE.

Price, D. (2015). Surveyors and surveyed: Photography out and about. In L. Wells (Ed.), *Photography: A Critical Introduction* (5th ed.; pp. 75–132). London: Routledge.

Reed, B. S., & Bracaglia, D. (2013). Hard questions, big backlash: The case of the train track death. In L. A. Peck & G. S. Reel (Eds.), *Media Ethics at Work: True Stories from Young Professionals* (pp. 189–201). London: SAGE.

Sanders, K. (2006). *Ethics and Journalism*. London: SAGE.

Schwartz, D. (2003). Professional oversight: Policing the credibility of photojournalism. In L. Gross, J. S. Katz, & J. Ruby (Eds.), *Image Ethics in the Digital Age* (pp. 27–51). Minneapolis, MN: University of Minnesota.

Seglin, J. (2001, December 17). *Codes of ethics: Why writing one is not enough*. Poynter Online. Retrieved July 18, 2016, from http://www.poynter.org/content/content_view.asp?id=4697

Steele, B. (2003). Genuinely torn. *The American Editor*, *78*(6), 8–9.

Steele, B., & Black, J. (1999). Can you improve your code of ethics? (or create a good one if you don't have one?). *American Editor*, *74*(2), 4.

Strauss, D. L. (2003). *Essays on Photography and Politics*. New York: Aperture.

Strauss, D. L. (2011). *Doctored photos: The art of the altered image*. Retrieved March 12, 2016, from http://time.com/3778075/doctored-photos-the-art-of-the-altered-image/

Sturges, P. (2009). Information ethics in the twenty first century. *Australian Academic & Research Libraries*, *40*(4), 241–251. doi:10.1080/00048623.2009.10721415

The National Press Photographers Code of Ethics. (n.d.). Retrieved August 18, 2015, from http://www.nppa.org/professional_development/business_practices/ethics.html

The New York Times. (2015). *Debating the Rules and Ethics of Digital Photojournalism*. Retrieved July 22, 2016, from http://lens.blogs.nytimes.com/2015/02/17/world-press-photo-manipulation-ethics-of-digital-photojournalism/?module=BlogPost-Title&version=Blog+Main&contentCollection=Mutlimedia&action=Click&pgtype=Blogs&region=Body&_r=2

The New York Times. (2015, October 16). *Staging, Manipulation and Truth in Photography*. Retrieved July, 23, 2016, from http://lens.blogs.nytimes.com/2015/10/16/staging-manipulation-ethics-photos/

The Reuters Photo Scandal. (2006). *A Taxonomy of Photo Fraud Committed by Reuters*. Retrieved August 20, 2015, from www.zombietime.com/reuters_photo_fraud/

The Washington Post Standard and Ethics. (n.d.). Retrieved August 25, 2015, from asne.org>Ethics

Warburton, N. (1998). Ethical photojournalism and the electronic darkroom. In M. Kieran (Ed.), *Media Ethics* (pp. 123–134). London: Routledge.

White, A. (2001). Setting standards. *Unesco Sources*, (134): 11.

Wigston, D. (2009). Qualitative content analysis. In P. J. Fourie (Ed.), *Media Studies: Media Content and Media Audiences* (Vol. 3, pp. 3–38). Cape Town: Juta.

Wilkins, L., & Brennen, B. (2004). Conflicted interests, contested terrain: Journalism ethics codes then and now. *Journalism Studies*, *5*(3), 297–309. doi:10.1080/1461670042000246061

KEY TERMS AND DEFINITIONS

Camera: A device which is used to capture images.

Deontology: The belief that the truth must always be told even if the outcomes of doing so bring pain to people.

Image: A depiction of something, for example a picture.

Manipulation: The act of changing the original form of something.

Photographs: An image or picture captured by a device.

Realist: Someone who believes that there is a tangible and observable reality out there in the world.

Utilitarian: The belief that an action is good if it helps the greatest number of people.

Chapter 4
Media-Invented Stories and Outright Lies a Threat to Journalism Ethics and Media Credibility

Agnes Lucy Lando
Daystar University, Kenya

ABSTRACT

Several authors have researched on diverse challenges affecting media practice in different parts of the world: the growing influence of bribery (Dirbaba, 2010), one-sided and distorted reporting (Mfumbusa, 2008), pornographic and oversexed content, an inclination to acceptance of the brown envelope (Kasoma, 2010; Skjerdal, 2010; White, 2011; Nwabueze, 2010), and the disconnect between media training and practice (Lando, 2013). But with ICT, contemporary challenges include sources of news. With the aid of modern technology, a story that has appeared in one media house or platform can be reproduce in another without the reproducing journalist citing the previous source, and without disclosing to audiences that the story being presented is not original. Further, some journalists have presented stories that only exist in their fantasy. All these are cases of media lies. This chapter examines select cases of media lies and the ethical and credibility threat they pose to journalism.

INTRODUCTION

On 23rd October 2014, the newspaper with the largest circulation in Kenya, also generally considered most credible, The Daily Nation, carried a unique photo story on the front page. The story indicated that a cow from Chepkeche in Uasin Gishu County was allowing two little lambs feed on her milk after the mother of the lambs wondered off in search of green pastures (Awiti, 2014). Noticing the unique fur on the lambs, a bizarre feature for lambs in that part of Kenya, readers quickly brought it to the attention of others that the newspaper had lifted the picture and caption from a website. The occurrence had actually taken place in New Zealand and not Kenya and the story had been reported on 21st June 2014 in New

DOI: 10.4018/978-1-5225-2095-5.ch004

Zealand (Bletchly, 2014). Whereas major parts of the story (the incidence) are correct, changing the location to Kenya and attributing the coverage to himself was a misconduct on the part of the journalist. The presented story is partly plagiarized and partly *cooked.*

This is not the only newspaper in Kenya that has *lifted* a story from a different source and presented it as their own. Other media practitioners have, for example, created a full story out of their imagination (Elbagir, 2013). Further, this is not a Kenyan problem, but a challenge that reputable media practitioners and media houses are involved in, worldwide. World famous news media, such as CNN, is an example where the media and media practitioners have created realities to portray what is not the case. This includes, but not limited to, generating non-existing content and presenting it as a factual occurrence. That is, media *creating* news and stories purely based on the imagination of the particular journalist. For instance, during the build up to the 2013 General Elections in Kenya, CNN carried an exclusive story that private armies/gang groups in Kenya were already being recruited and organizing themselves ready to fight. They referred to this as Post-Election Violence (PEV) in the making. The CNN story depicted Kenya as preparing for war ahead of the 3rd March 2013 General Elections (Elbagir, 2013). The video clip titled "Kenyans armed and ready to vote" was uploaded on the CNN website and broadcast a few days before the General Elections. The clip featured four people whose faces were beclouded carrying what the CNN reporter Nima Elbagir described as "guns fashioned from iron piping, home-made swords and bullets bought from the black-market". This was followed by a social media campaign by Kenyans with the #tag, someonetell CNN. Eventually CNN apologized.

Such kind of practice would be excused of the gutter press or citizen journalism whose practitioners have had little or no formal training at all on professional communication and media ethics. The questions that this practice raises are numerous, for example, why do trusted mainstream media choose to lie to their audiences? Surrounded by ICT world that is full of information that is just a click away, and thus tempting to google, copy and paste, how can media practitioners remain faithful to their special and unique profession and vocation? This is especially important because many persons still believe in the traditional print (newspapers) and electronic media (radio and TV) as credible news sources. When these present a view that is not accurate, what harm can they cause to the society? And to what extent do they taint the name/image of media practitioners, specifically those not involved in the practice? In this researcher's view, both plagiarized and cooked stories are media lies.

By examining select-cases of media lies, this chapter intends to highlight stories from the print and electronic media that have been presented by media houses as their own stories when the contrary is the case; or where a media practitioner has *cooked* up a story when that story does not actually exist. This reflection paper covers the malpractice of journalists – of fabricated and / or plagiarized stories.

Methodological Approach and Theory

This study employs content analysis where the author examines a number of stories that have been *cooked* by media practitioners and houses, or copied and pasted from varied sources, and the implication therein. Interpersonal deception theory helps explain why mainstream media tell lies on their stories. According to Littlejohn (1999, p. 146), the source attempts to manipulate a message so as to be untruthful, "which may cause them apprehension concerning their false communication being detected. Simultaneously, communication receivers try to unveil or detect the validity of that information, causing suspicion about whether or not the sender is being deceitful." The process usually starts off when a sender's expectations, goals, prior knowledge and skill set all combine and result in a communication that is true or not true. It is important to note that the communication is accompanied by an initial behavioral display. Deceptive messages are inclusive of the content itself and also the extra effort put in by the sender or even the strategic plan that the media house may use in an aim to make the story believable (Par Anders Granhag, 2015).

As technology becomes more and more of an intricate part of contemporary society it allows for information to travel quickly and more widely available. By this information being so widely available some ethical issues have come to light when it comes to proper credit received to the owners of these ideas. Interpersonal deception theory explains a sender's attempt to manipulate messages so as to be untruthful which may cause them apprehension concerning their false communication being detected.

According to this theory, receivers try to unveil or detect the validity of that information, causing suspicion about whether or not the sender is being deceitful. Deception in this theory is defined as an "intentional act in which senders knowingly transmit messages intended to foster a false belief or interpretation by the receiver" (Littlejohn, 1999, p. 147). Another set of authors, Buller & Burgoon (1998), explain that people often find themselves in situations where they make statements that are less than completely honest in order to avoid hurting or offending another person, to emphasize their best qualities, to avoid getting into a conflict, or to speed up or slow down a relationship. Weasley (2015) concurs, adding that reputable journalists and mainstream media may choose to lie to their audiences because of various reasons: First, high pressure from the working environment; second, high expectations from people around them, fear of not living up to what people expect from you); third, increased worry over ratings and; last, competition for jobs as more and more people are laid off.

These findings are in agreement with an earlier study (Lando, 2013) in which media practitioners admitted to being guided in their profession not by professionalism and ethics but by ratings, competition for by-lines and Advertisements. This reality is despite the fact that Journalism is centred on a set of essentially ethical concepts of, but not limited to, freedom, democracy, truth, objectivity and honesty. The journalists are therefore expected to have these in mind and maintain the quality of the information they put out to the world. As clearly presented by Christians, Fackler, McKee, Kreshel, & Woods (2009), actions of fabrications and plagiarism decrease a paper's integrity as a credible source of news. They note that:

The credibility of a newspaper is its most precious asset, and it depends almost entirely on the integrity of its reporters. When that integrity is questioned and found wanting, the wounds are grievous, and there is nothing to do but come clean with our readers, apologize to the Advisory Board of the Pulitzer Prizes, and begin immediately on the uphill task of regaining our credibility. (Maraniss, 1981, p. 37)

This scenario can further be explained by News Framing theory as described by Pinter and Willis (2016) who write that "when journalists frame an issue, they select some aspects of a perceived reality and make them more salient in a communicating text, in such a way as to promote a particular problem definition, causal interpretation, moral evaluation, and/or treatment recommendation for the item described" (p.. 92). This is especially true of *cooked* stories whose motive why they are told and how they are told is only known to that particular dishonest journalist.

SELECT CASES OF MEDIA LIES

The media are such a powerful force because a good percentage of people tend to trust them as their primary source of information. The media are also sources of reference. For instance, during the hearing of the 2007 Post-Election Violence case of Kenya at the International Criminal Court (ICC), the lawyers for the defence and prosecution utilized Kenyan Newspaper stories and video clips to argue their case. Yet as recent research has shown, the pressure is high for journalists on who is first to break the news, to come up with the most unique stories that will set their media house apart and make it stand out to attract a large audience and by extension, advertisers (Lando, 2013). On the flipside, in the rush to be the first, facts are not double-checked or are ignored, costing reporters their jobs and media their credibility. This is why David and Gordon (2011) argue that the success of new media attracts strong critical reaction, especially when they use questionable strategies to produce content to attract consumers.

In the next section here below, the author presents a number of cases from different parts of the world where media practitioners have simply lifted a story or a photo or a concept from the website or another media house and presented it as their own. This is plagiarism. Whereas the plagiarized story (whole or part) might be factually correct, the act (plagiarizing) is misconduct on the part of the journalist. This, in return, has impact on the manner in which the audiences view the profession and practitioners. Also being examined are examples of *cooked* stories. This is when a journalist comes up with a story that has not happened, but one originating out of his/her imagination, and presenting it as a news (not feature or fiction) story. These twelve (12) cases – plagiarized and *cooked* stories - enunciate the challenges on journalism ethics and media credibility.

Case 1: Felician Kabuga Story

In 2012, Kenyan Nation TV (NTV) aired a feature on Rwandan fugitive Felician Kabuga, entitled, *In the footsteps of Kabuga.* They showed a photo of a man whom they claimed to be Kabuga peacefully residing in a town in Kenya and freely going about his business. However, the photo in the story turned out to be of a Daniel Muthee Ngeera, who later sued the media house for defamation. Mr Daniel Muthee Ngeera, a 58-year-old man who retired from the civil service in 2000, said the photos published in the Daily Nation of 12/7/2012 and aired in an *NTV* investigative documentary, were of him taken in his timber workshop in Isiolo. The man was accompanied by his wife and children at a press conference organized by the police at Vigilance House, the police headquarters. Daniel claimed that He was born in Meru and he had never been to Rwanda and the furthest he had travelled was Kisumu, Moyale and Garissa in Kenya. That story brought Mr. Ngeera undue publicity and he was provided with two armed police officers to guard him and his family round the clock after he expressed fear that the news had exposed him to danger. Had NTV taken the time to approach Ngeera before publishing the story, he would have been able to clarify his identity and the journalist and media house saved themselves embarrassment.

Case 2: Baltimore Shooting

The Baltimore shooting is an example of a *cooked* story. On 4th May 2015 Michael Tobin, a reporter for Fox News, called in live at 2.45 pm on a 'into Fox News *The Real Story* show hosted by Gretchen

Carlson. Tobin claimed he had seen police officers chase after a man, as one police officer drew his weapon, shot at the escaping suspect who fell to the ground (Kirell, 2015; Farhi, 2015; Bellware, 2015; Parco, 2015). The video apparently showed the wounded man handcuffed, put on a stretcher and loaded into the ambulance as the police tried to secure the area using pepper spray. This gave the impression that another black man had been shot at, making the Baltimore community restless, causing unreasonable tension. The Baltimore Police Department saw the situation was getting out of hand and sent a message that there had been no shooting. Tobin noticed that and called back saying he had not witnessed the shooting, he only heard gunfire. Leland Vittert, another Fox News reporter, found out that while the man was being taken into custody his gun went off in his pockets, but no one was hurt. He was being taken to hospital as a precautionary measure (ibid).

Shep Smith, a Fox News anchor, was forced to make a formal apology from the network live on air and talk about the facts of the story.

Case 3: Fox 5 News – False Story on the iPhone 5

On 17th September 2012 during the late night news, Fox 5 news reported that the iPhone 5 would have a laser keyboard that would be able to project holographic images into thin air. The reporter covering the story, Lydia Curanaj was out in the streets interviewing people who had stayed on the line for days waiting to buy the iPhone 5 as soon as it was launched. In her report, the Fox 5 reporter included images showing a laser keyboard and holographic images being projected from the supposed iPhone 5. However, according to Michael Rose (2012), a blogger who appears regularly on Fox Business news to speak about apple products, the video clip showing the images of the iPhone 5 were from a one year old concept video done by Aatma studio. He explained that the concept video was a wishful thinking kind of video that predicts the kind of features a phone would have or even just an imagination of a creative person.

A few hours after the airing of the story, various people took to the internet to say that the features presented in the news story were actually fake and not exactly what should be expected in the real iPhone 5. Fox 5 news also later issued a clarification on the story admitting that their report had not been right and that the iPhone 5 would neither have a laser keyboard nor holographic projection of images.

Case 4: 'A Letter to My 20 Something Self'

On 3rd September 2012 famed Kenyan radio host Caroline Mutoko featured an article named 'A letter to my 20 something self' in her weekly column 'Mutoko on Monday' in The Star Newspaper. This was in the wake of the infamous Facebook group "Campus Divas for rich men" created by young female university students who referred to themselves as 'divas'. Their agenda was to provide a networking forum where the divas would arrange to provide sexual pleasures for rich men in exchange for money and an extravagant and elegant lifestyle in universities.

In the article Mutoko seemed to be taking on the role of an older sister, the letter was aimed at the young ladies who were in their twenties in an effort to avert them from following in the footsteps of the Campus Divas. Mutoko spoke in retrospect to her younger self giving life lessons that she had learned while growing up. The article was well received by the public and was seen as the voice of reason in the uproar that followed the launching of the scandalous Facebook page.

Following the popularity of the article, The Star Newspaper received many complaints that Mutoko had plagiarized the article from a feminist blog online. These accusations culminated when controversial blogger Robert Alai featured Mutoko's plagiarism on twitter by posting a link to Mutoko's article and a link to the original post in the 'Crunk Feminist Collective' blog. Mutoko had lifted the story from a 2011 internet post titled '20 Things I Want to Say to My Twenty-something Self'. The author of the post was Robin M Boylorn, an assistant professor at the University of Alabama in the US. Dr. Brittney Cooper of Rutgers University, a co-founder of the blog, sent a letter of complaint she had sent to The Star after being alerted to the problem by an email and a comment on the Crunk blog (WMEA, 2012). The original post had appeared on a blog called the Crunk Feminist Collective. The story was copied word for word save a few lines of commentary in brackets at the end of some of the phrases to localize it.

Even after the story went viral Mutoko did not cave to the calls for her to make an apology. "I will not apologize or respond to nonsense that tries to imply I may have borrowed something from the internet," she wrote. "I borrow from everything around me—cocktail parties I go to, baby showers, I borrow from drunkards, thieves, cab drivers and my housekeeper—I borrow from the lines of songs I listen to and tweets I read and even posts on Nicki Minaj's FB wall….I am no copycat—I am the original and I'm different and that's tough for some people to take" (WMEA, 2012). The Crunk Feminist Collective blog requested that The Star Newspaper either acknowledge the improper use of Boylorn's post in a retraction or that it take down the column. The newspaper did the latter and sent their apologies for the unattributed use of the blog's content.

Case 5: The Late Njenga Karume's Story

The late Njenga Karume was prematurely declared dead on NTV's social media platform while he was critically ill and admitted in hospital on 4th February 2012. This incident was referred to as "one of the biggest media goofs of the year" (Oyugi, 2012). Critics lashed out at the NTV;s social media wall terming the story "a serious offence of journalism". They pointed out to Journalists that they are not in a position to declare anyone dead, only medical professionals can, no matter how critical the person is (Luke, 2012). Njenga Karume died 20 days later.

Case 6: An Argentinian Teacher Suspended for Having Sex with Student

Several magazines in Argentina; Latin Times, Malaysian Digest, and Mirror carried a story of a teacher who reportedly had sex with a 16-year-old pupil who secretly took a video of the tryst. The various media reported that Lucita Sandoval, a 26-year-old teacher from the city of Santiago del Estero, in north-central Argentina, was facing disciplinary action over the video. It later emerged that the teacher in the video wasn't Sandoval, but an entirely different woman from the city of Corrientes. It was widely reported that Lucita Sandoval was filmed having sex with a student but the man in the video is actually in college and the woman in the footage is not Sandoval. A Journalist from Nuevo Diario, an alternative media,was able to track down the man in the video. It was also falsely reported the 'teacher' has several times faced disciplinary hearings over inappropriate relationships with pupils. The video was posted on a pornographic site in September 2014. Mystery still surrounds where the story emerged from, and why Sandoval was targeted in this way.

Case 7: Maureen Dowd's Plagiarized Paragraph

Maureen Dowd is a New York columnist who plagiarized a 43-word paragraph from a blog by Joshua Marshall (editor and chief impresario of the liberal blog Talking Points Memo) on 16th May 2009. Marshall protested that Dowd had lifted the paragraph word for word placing the evidence on his blog on 14th May 2009. Dowd's defense in an email to the Huffington Post claimed that she got the paragraph from a friend who must have read Marshall's blog and never informed her. This was however unbelievable because she plagiarized a whole forty three words with only a slight alteration.

Dowd's column was later fixed with an acknowledgement to Marshall's paragraph. The paragraph was serving as contribution to her column on the then vice president Dick Cheney's torture policies. The article was titled, "Cheney, master of pain".

Case 8: Fareed Zakaria's Plagiarized Story

Fareed Zachariah was suspended for lifting parts of a story from the New Yorker. The similarities were picked by a conservative watchdog news buster concerning an article did on gun control by Fareed and an article on the same by New York writer Jill Leopore in April 22nd. Leopore wrote; "As Adam Winkler, a constitutional-law scholar at U.C.L.A., demonstrates in a remarkably nuanced new book, "Gunfight: The Battle over the Right to Bear Arms in America," firearms have been regulated in the United States from the start. Laws banning the carrying of concealed weapons were passed in Kentucky and Louisiana in 1813, and other states soon followed: Indiana (1820), Tennessee and Virginia (1838), Alabama (1839), and Ohio (1859). Similar laws were passed in Texas, Florida, and Oklahoma. As the governor of Texas explained in 1893, the "mission of the concealed deadly weapon is murder. To check it is the duty of every self-respecting, law-abiding man." The Times and CNN later suspended Zachariah.

Case 9: The Kronen Zeitung (Krone) Newspaper Syria Photoshop

According to the Media Ethics News & Investigative Reports website, reporter Richard Wolf reported about an Austrian newspaper that apologized for publishing a doctored photograph of a family fleeing from a 'war-torn' Syria. Wolf, R. (2012) claim that Kronen Zeitung (Krone) is Austria's biggest selling newspaper. He wrote, "The Krone does boast a readership of 2.7 million, which in a country of just over eight million, backs the claim to it being one of the world's most successful tabloids."

On July 28, 2012, page four, the Krone published a photograph of a man carrying a child with a woman beside him, "as they hurry through what appears to be the bombed out ruins of the city. It was being used to illustrate a story on people fleeing the city as government forces clash with rebels" (Wolf, R. 2012). However, sharp-eyed bloggers at the social news website Reddit noticed that while the family image was genuine, the background had been photoshoped. The original photo was first published on the European Press photo Agency's website just two days before. "The original… shows an ordinary family walking along an undamaged street" wrote Wolf. "Austrian newspaper publisher Christoph Dichand apologized after Kronen Zeitung was caught using a faked dramatic photograph." A news site from Libya commented on the photograph, claiming that it was"… a blatant deception of the reader with Photoshop." (Wolf, R. 2012).

Case 10: Kenya Today.com Copy-Pastes Condom Story from China Daily.com

Kenya Today (kenyatoday.com) deceived Kenyans with a counterfeit condom story, picked directly from a story that ran in China. On 22nd April 2015, Shanghai Daily online,(shanghaidaily.com) published a story on a fake condom ring bust, by Shanghai police, where 3 million *Durex* & *Jissbon* counterfeits condoms were seized. Two days later, on 24th April 24, the Kenya Today published the same story claiming that Shanghai police officers had busted an operation manufacturing fake high-end condoms destined for the Kenyan market.

Case 11

On 28th April 2003 San Antonio Ex-Press News reporter Macarena Hernandez called the NY Times national reporter with concerns about similarities between an article in the NY Times and his own article in his paper. This resulted to inquiries and the NY Times discovered that the writer, Jason Blair, had plagiarized and cheated his way through dozens of stories. They discovered that he wrote about locations he never visited, ripped off quotes from other publications, and fabricated events that never took place. One such story was the beltway sniper attack story. It wasabout a series of coordinated shooting attacks that took about 3 weeks during the month of October 2002 in Maryland, Virginia and Washington DC resulting to the death of 10 people and 3 injured.His was a combination of plagiarism and fabrication.

"Correcting the Record" is a 7,239-word article that ran in the front page of the NY times on May 11, 2003. It shows evidence of witnesses and reports that unveiled the deception in Blair's work. The report outlines some of the 36 out of 73 articles he is believed to have misrepresented. His reason for plagiarism and fabrication was the fear of not meeting the expectation set for him by himself and others.

Case 12: Accident Caused by Pastor

On July 26th 2015, an accident occurred in Kiambu County, Kenya. The accident involved a range rover sport and a small Nissan March that was at the time being driven by Mr. Martin Mbugua who was with his wife Mrs. Mercy Njeri. Mercy died on the spot while Martin sustained serious injuries.Conflicting media reports emerged relating to the accident, who was driving the vehicle that killed Mercy Njeri, why the original driver of the range rover hurriedly left the crime scene, who helped them escape and why the details from the police seemed inconsistent.

The media rushed to conduct their own investigations but some of the details they gave were later found to have been false. In a follow up story published in the Daily Nation on 6th August 2015, titled "*Pastor denies driving crash vehicle amid reports he was treated in city*", a Daily Nation reporter wrote that "Investigators believe that after the accident, Pastor Ng'ang'a got out of the driver's seat and into another vehicle belonging to Pastor David Muriithi, the Senior Pastor of House of Grace Church in Lang'ata."

Pastor David Muriithi denied the allegations of involvement and immediately asked the Daily Nation and the Police to reveal the sources to clear his name. On 6th August through his Facebook page, the Pastor demanded an apology from the Nation newspaper. "Linking my name to this unfortunate incident has caused distress to me, my family and the House of Grace congregation. I, therefore, demand that the said statement be withdrawn and an apology issued failure to which I will seek legal redress."Two weeks after publishing the story, the Daily Nation finally apologized to Pastor Muriithi.

Audience's Reactions to the Stories

With such cases of plagiarism or *cooked* stories, the audience tends to get disappointed and slowly losing faith in the media; and the media thereby beginning to slowly lose credibility. The result could also be the audience seeking alternative sources of information, audience becoming suspicious of certain media outlets and practitioners or even audiences confronting news sources. This latter was the Kenya reaction to CNN *cooked* story on PEV preparation in Kenya. This phenomenon impacts negatively also on the true stories and honest sources. Regaining the trust of such an audience might be an uphill task because audiences will then consume stories with doubt and caution. This aspect has been very well captured by the Interpersonal Deception Theory. The stories also cause dissonance to the audience. Media are generally perceived as the watchdog of the society yet their plagiarized and *cooked* stories are doing the opposite, leaving the audience angry, trying to reconcile their beliefs in the fourth estate verses the behavior of the fourth estate. This is why it is now very common to find people shunning certain news sources, or double-checking a story with an alternative source. These adverse effects of audience loss of credibility on the source are very well captured and expressed by Christians et al (2009) who indicate that when a news source's integrity is questionable, the credibility restoration is almost irreparable.

SOLUTIONS AND RECOMMENDATIONS: DEVELOPING OWN ETHICAL BASE

There is growing need for adherence to journalism ethics as seen from the stories above. According to the Kenya Media Council Act (2007) on Accuracy and fairness "a person subject to this act shall write a fair accurate and unbiased story on matters of public interest." This was clearly contravened in all the 12 cases presented in this chapter. These cases show that media practitioners who are highly trained or otherwise, are all gullible to producing and presenting stories that violate the journalistic ethics and professional practice. It is therefore, in the researcher's view, not so much knowledge or exposure, but one's ethical base that can contribute to one's communication and journalism excellence while carrying out the duties. It is therefore imperative that media practitioners, in addition to their professional trainings, develop a personal work ethic that will guide them individually into making ethical decisions on their trade, whether alone or in the company of others. Further, development of such a code will enable the specific media practitioner to stand the pressures that come with ICT – such as the pressure to be the first to report, the pride of presenting the most bizarre story, and the pressure to have a story at all costs. Media lies essentially challenge the integrity of individuals. In examining how recommending how to deal with the issue of media lies, the author proposes media practitioners developing own ethical base. This will guide every practitioner in facing every scenario that presents itself. This could also include Day 2 journalism which is telling the same story to the same audience for the second time but on a different day, or to a different audience for the first time, but using a different approach. That is, Day2 journalism acknowledges that the story has already happened, but then brings in additional or new development on the same. Thus adding updates to the story, and hence making it appear new. Day 2 Journalism might try to contextualize things by getting an expert in the said field to tell more about it than what was reported the first time.

Hasan (2013, p. 174) describes Journalism as a "discipline of collecting, analyzing, verifying and presenting news regarding current events, trends, issues and people." From the 12 cases presented, it seems that *verifying* is the missing element in contemporary journalism. Could *verifying* have been removed from the definition or journalists just pay very little attention to it?

This might be due to the fact that upto now, in many countries, journalism is a profession that does not, unlike other professions such as teaching, nursing, medical or law; require specific specialized education, qualification, training or registration for one to practice. Journalism tends to be an open for all profession, embracing all and excluding none. In the larger Eastern Africa region, for example, some popular media practitioners found their way into the industry because of their good looks (for TV), good voice and ability to crack an ethnically-accented joke (for radio) or simply by blood relationship or some other association to certain individuals or groups in the business or political arena. Such non-professional qualifications would never admit anyone in the bar, bench or in the medical field.

Further, while we acknowledge that a number of countries now have Codes for Journalists through their various Media Councils, these are rarely enforced. This researcher thus is inclined to concluded that lack of collective ownership of the journalism profession is one major challenge leaving journalists on their own in terms of practice. It is in this regard therefore that this chapter proposes, to serious journalists, development of one's ethical base, in addition to the existing codes and laws, as a daily guide for one's journalistic practice. While it can be argued that development of an individual ethical base leaves the proposed solution open-ended and thus even open to abuse, the recommendation here is intended for individuals with already high personal integrity and with the intention to further develop oneself and hold oneself in high regard in the profession. This personal ethical base pushes the journalist to be driven by nothing but by values that build oneself and society while upholding the journalism profession to its intended level.

As Hasan (2013) posits, probably self-censorship could be a major contributor in developing one's ethical base. Self-censorship is "the act of censoring or classifying one's own work (blog, books, film or other means of expression), out of fear and a degree to the sensibilities of others without an authority directly pressuring one to do so" (p. 580). Whereas journalists are not forbidden to refer or copy from other sources, the best approach to avoid plagiarism is to give credit, and the best way to avoid *cooked* stories is to be honest with self and then with others. The Washington Post Writer's Group laments that occasionally reporters are caught not doing their work and not attributing it to the person who did it . "If somebody else writes it first, it's theirs. For people whose commodity is language, plagiarism is stealing, as much as taking someone else's tape recorder and selling it on the street" (Washington Post Writer's Group, 1990:345 – 346).

FUTURE RESEARCH DIRECTIONS

This chapter has focused on identifying cases of media lies from different contexts. However, the chapter did not succeed in finding those particular reporters to share what motivates them to *cook* or plagiarizing news stories. Therefore, a possible area for further research would be reaching out to the media practitioners who have *cooked* or plagiarized stories, and interview them on why they are involved in the practice. Another area of further study would be to listen to editors on the challenges journalism in the digital age is adding to their already full plate. This is because, when a journalist *cooks* or plagiarizes a story, the Editorial too bears the blame.

CONCLUSION

This chapter has presented media practitioners with the reality that media lies - be they plagiarized or *cooked* stories are very costly to the particular media house and journalist involved in the practice. The high cost comes in the fact that media lies have the potential to taint one's image, and the image of the particular media house. The chapter has also brought to the awareness of the media practitioners that audiences who consume their content have a certain level of intelligence and capability to cross-check factual (but plagiarized) or imaginary stories; hence exposing the fact that audiences are not *tabula rasa*. The chapter has, hopefully, persuaded those in the media industry to exercise professionalism, ethics and uphold their integrity. Media is one of the most powerful tools of communication today. It is unfortunate that some journalists, editors and media house create their own stories or copy word for word someone's work without citing or acknowledging them. It is within media ethics that media practitioners tell the truth because at times their word is final and the audience takes it as the 'gospel truth'. This is posing new challenges for the editors because they have to get involved in extra work of verification of all stories that they receive. Frequently running apologies do not augur well with any given media house or journalist. Media practitioners need to be truthful. They are tasked with informing and educating the general public and they must be honest with that *call* at all times.

REFERENCES

Awiti, J. (2014). *Mother Nature: Little Lambs seek unusual nourishment*. Nairobi: NMG.

Bellware, K. (2015). Fox News Host Shephard Smith Apologizes for Network's Baltimore Shooting Mistake. *Huffington Post*. Retrieved from: http://www.huffingtonpost.com/2015/05/04/shephard-smith-baltimoreapology_n_7208214.html-black-female-child-in-class-was-sued-twice/

Bletchly, R. (2014). *From surrogate dogs to adopted pigs, 26 animals that looked out for each other*. Retrieved from http://www.mirror.co.uk/news/world-news/surrogate-dogs-adopted-pigs-26-3731138

Buller, D. B., & Burgoon, J. K. (2005). *Interpersonal Deception Theory. In Readings in Persuasion, Social Influence, and Compliance Gaining*. Allyn & Bacon.

Christians, C. G., Fackler, M., McKee, K. B., Kreshel, P. J., & Woods, R. H. (2009). *Media Ethics: Cases and Moral Reasoning* (8th ed.). Allyn & Bacon.

Christians, C. G., Fackler, M., McKee, K. B., Kreshel, P. J., & Woods, R. H. (2009). *Media Ethics: Cases and moral reasoning*. Boston: Pearson Educarion, Inc.

Coverage [VIDEO]. (n.d.). Retrieved on 7th November 2015 from http://www.hngn.com/articles/89701/20150504/baltimore-shooting-shepard-smith-fox-news-apologize-for-false-account-coverage-video.htm

David, A., & Gordon, J. M. (2011). *Controversies in Media Ethics*. New York: Routledge.

Dirbaba, B. O. (2010). The growing influence of bribery in Ethiopian Journalism. *African Communication Research*, (1), 207-231.

Elbagir, N. (2013). *Kenyans armed and ready to vote*. Retrieved from http://www.digitaljournal.com/article/344615

Farhi, P. (2015). *Fox News erroneously reports that police in Baltimore shot man*. Retrieved from https://www.washingtonpost.com/lifestyle/style/as-it-turned-out-nobody-was-shot-fox

Hasan, S. (2013). *Mass Communication: Principles and Concepts* (2nd ed.). New Delhi: CBS Publishers and Distributors.

Huizhi, C. (2015). City police bust fake condom ring, seizing 3 million Durex, Jissbon counterfeits. *Shanghai Daily*. Retrieved from: http://www.shanghaidaily.com/metro/society/City-police-bust-fake-condom-ring-seizing-3-million-Durex-Jissbon-counterfeits/shdaily.shtml

Kasoma, T. (2010). Zambian PR Practitioners' perspective on 'brown envelopes' and freebies: working through the confusion. *African Communication Research,* (3), 451-474.

Ken. (2012, July 9). *Why Albert Gachiri Will Never Forgive Emmanuel Juma*. Retrieved from Nairobi Wire: http://nairobiwire.com/2012/07/Albert-Gachiri-Emmanuel-Juma-beef.html

Kennedy, D. (2009). Maureen Dowd's Lazy New York Times Column. *The Guardian*. Retrieved from: http://www.theguardian.com/commentisfree/cifamerica/2009/may/18/maureen-dowd-plagiarism-new-york-times

Kenya Today. (2015). Shocking: Chinese caught manufacturing three million fake condoms for Nairobi. *Kenya Today*. Retrieved from: http://www.kenya-today.com/news/shocking-chinese-caught-manufacturing-three-million-fake-condoms-for-nairobi

Kirell, A. (2015). Shep Smith apologizes for Fox reporter's erroneous 'shooting' account: 'we screwed up'. *Mediaite*.

Lando, A. L. (2013). Ethics in the Kenyan Media? Understanding the disconnect between the classroom and practice. *African Journal of Communication, 1*(1), 15–42.

Littlejohn, S. W. (1999). *Theories of human communication* (6th ed.). Belmont, CA: Wadsworth.

Luke, M. (2012, February 6). *Social media dilemma after NTV clips reporter off the screen*. Retrieved from Business Today: http://www.businesstoday.co.ke/news/2012/02/6/social-media-dilemma-after-ntv-clips-reporter-screen

Maraniss, D. A. (1981, April 16). *The hoax project*. Retrieved October 25, 2015, from jclass.umd.edu: http://jclass.umd.edu

Media Council Of Kenya. (2013). *Code of Conduct for the Practice of Journalism in Kenya*. Nairobi: Media Council.

Mfumbusa, B. (2008). Newsroom ethics in Africa: Quest for a normative framework. *African Communication Research,* (1), 139-157.

Mirkinson, J. (2012) Fareed Zakaria Suspended for Plaigiarism: Time Editor, CNN Host Apologizes for 'Terrible Mistake'. *Huffington Post*. Retrieved from http://www.huffingtonpost.com/2012/08/10/fareed-zakaria-plagiarism-new-yorkertime_n_1764954.html

Mutoko, C. (2012, September 13). Letter to my 20-something self. *The Star*, p. 28.

Noer, M. (2014). The Original Forbes Takedown of Stephen Glass. *Forbes*. Retrieved from: http://www.forbes.com/sites/michaelnoer/2014/11/12/read-the-original-forbes-takedown-of-stephen-glass/

Nwabueze, C. (2010). Brown envelopes and the need for ethical re-orientation: Perceptions of Nigerian Journalists. *African Communication Research,* (3), 497-520.

Oyugi, K. (2012, July 6). *Albert Gachiri Speaks Out on the Karume Saga and Whether He Really Was Fired from NTV*. Retrieved from Ghafla: http://www.ghafla.co.ke/news/tv/2711-albert-gachiri-speaks-out-on-the-karume-saga-and-whether-he-really-was-fired-from-ntv

Painter, C., & Willis, E. (2016). Flipping the Script: Newspaper Reporting of the Trayvon Martin Shooting. In Impact of Communication and the Media on Ethnic Conflict. IGI Global.

Par Anders Granhag, A. V. (2015). *Detecting deception*. Chichester, UK: Wiley Blackwell.

Plaisance, P. L. (2000). The Concept of Media Accountability Reconsidered. *Journal of Mass Media Ethics, 15*(4), 257–268. doi:10.1207/S15327728JMME1504_5

Review by Eokhardah. (2015). Role of Mesia in Our Society. *Review by Eokhardah.* Retrieved from: https://eokhardahreview.wordpress.com/2015/02/13

Rose, M. (2012, September). *Fox 5 New York gets suckered by iPhone 5 concept video*. Engadget.com

Rosin, H. (2014). Hello, My Name is Stephen Glass, and I'm Sorry. *New Republic*. Retrieved from: http://www.newrepublic.com/article/120145/stephen-glass-new-republic-scandal-still-haunts-his-law-career

Sawyer, S., & Tapia, A. (2005). The sociotechnical nature of mobile computing work: Evidence from a study of policing in the United States. *International Journal of Technology and Human Interaction, 1*(3), 1–14. doi:10.4018/jthi.2005070101

Scandalism. (2011, October 11). Retrieved from Scandalism: https://journalismscandals.wordpress.com/2011/10/

Schedule of the Media Council Act. (2013). Retrieved from www.mediacouncil.or.ke

Skjerdal, T. S. (2010). Research on brown envelope journalism in the African Media. *African Communication Research,* (3), 367-406.

SPJ. (2014). SPJ Code of Ethics. *SPJ.* Retrieved from: http://www.spj.org/ethicscode.asp

Washington Post Writer's Group Messages. (1990). *The Washington Post Media Companion*. Allyn & Bacon.

Weasley, M. (2015, February 5). *Daily Kos*. Retrieved October 27, 2015, from dailykos.com: http://www.dailykos.com/story/2015/02/05/1362540/

White, R. (2011). *Are Tanzanian journalists accepting bribes?*. Dar es Salaam: Media Council of Tanzania.

WMEA. (2012, September 19). *Mutoko On Monday: When Borrowing Goes Over The Line*. Retrieved from Wired Magazine - East Africa: https://web.facebook.com/Wired.EastAfrica/posts/480763305281214

Wolf, R. (2012). *Austrian Newspaper Apologizes for Fake Syria Photo*. Belmont, CA: Wadsworth.

KEY TERMS AND DEFINITIONS

Cooked Story: This term, as used in this study, refers to the tendency of media practitioners to come up with stories, which are neither true nor factual. These are from the imagination of the respective journalist.

Day 2 Journalism: A journalist telling the same story to the same audience for the second time, but on a different day, and using a different approach. Day 2 Journalism might try to contexualize a story by, for example, getting an expert in the said field to share more about it than what was reported the first time.

Framing: Skewing or angling a story.

Media Lies: Non-factual reporting of stories by media. This is where facts are either distorted or exaggerated. Further, the term refers to stories, whether factual or not, that have already been published elsewhere, but then a journalist re-submits them as new stories; with the particular journalist as the first/original authors. These are plagiarized stories. This term also refers to media concocted stories, those that do not exist or have not happened, but formulated in the mind of a particular journalist, who then proceeds to report it as an occurrence. The reporting could be in print, electronic or social media. So both plagiarized stories and / or those that are as a result of the journalist's fantasy are both media lies.

Personal Ethical Base: Each journalist developing a professional and ethical self-censorship device to guide his or her media work. This practice should be irrespective of whether or not an authority is watching them. This recommendation is intended for individuals with already high personal integrity and with the intention to develop one professionally.

Professional Ethics: Every profession has certain professional code of conducts within which the practitioners operate. These could be derived from various sources. However, in this chapter, the term professional ethics is used to refer to the society's expectations of the high moral level for the media to operate. The term further refers to someone who is qualified in Journalism so that his knowledge and training in the same can enable him know and apply the rules learnt. This can then bring rules and order in the practice, detailing who can and cannot enter the practice, and also put down the rules for inclusion, exclusion and striking off of an individual from the profession.

Select Cases: There are many such instances, but these few have been singled out for the indicated purpose.

Sources of News: Where the journalists obtain their news from. This could be from other media serving as sources, individuals or even an event.

Chapter 5
Ethical and Legal Challenges of Election Reporting in Nigeria:
A Study of Four General Elections, 1999-2011

Tayo Popoola
UNESCO Centre of Excellence in Journalism and Media Training, Nigeria

ABSTRACT

The probing thesis in this study is premised on investigating why the mass media which are globally regarded as the playing field of politics as well as the road upon which presidential campaign travels every four years could suddenly develop contours, leading to the game of politics being devoid of convivial and smooth playing in Nigeria, especially between 1999 and 2011. The study observes that hardly was there any election in the post-independent era in Nigeria that did not end in serious disputations, crisis, violence and bloodletting such that academics across disciplines declared that since independence on October 1, 1960, the electioneering process in Nigeria has been an experience of tears, blood and sorrow. The study evaluates media compliance to reportorial code which demands factual, accurate, balanced and fair reportage of electioneering stories. Using historical research method which relies on primary and secondary data collected from 150 media professionals consisting of 44 political editors, 10 line editors and 96 political reporters, the study, using power and conflict theories found out that non-compliance to ethical code of conduct for media professionals as well as legal rules governing the practice of journalism as one of the major factors responsible for publication or airing of provocative stories capable of engendering violence during elections. The study therefore suggested how the existing plural media system could be exploited to grow democracy, engender peace and promote national development as it's done in South Africa and other countries of the world.

DOI: 10.4018/978-1-5225-2095-5.ch005

INTRODUCTION AND BACKGROUND TO THE STUDY

This study focuses on ethical and legal challenges of election reporting in Nigeria, with specific reference to the four general elections conducted in Nigeria between 1999 and 2011. The study notes that crisis has become a regular characteristic feature of virtually all the post-independent elections in Nigeria to the extent that academics across disciplines have concluded that since independence on October 1, 1960, the electioneering process in Nigeria has been an experience of tears, blood and sorrow, (Ologbenla, 2003; Akinfeleye, 2004; Akinboye, 2009; Ogbeide, 2010; Olurode, 2011; & Fadakinte, 2014).

Thus far, hardly was there any election in the country that did not end in serious disputations, crisis, violence and at times, bloodletting. The study is curious about this development especially why the mass media which are globally regarded as the playing field of politics could be fingered as contributory agents of electoral violence.

Electoral violence has been a major threat to democratic consolidation in Nigeria. From the 1959 general elections which ushered in independence on October 1, 1960 to the first post-independent elections of 1964/65 during Nigeria's First Republic to the Second, Third and Fourth Republics till date, electoral violence has no doubt become a national malaise.

Thus far, hardly was there any organized election in the country in which tempers, fear and insecurity did not pervade the land with political tension at the highest level. Top pre-election stories in the media during electioneering periods are usually on the negative side. It is either some political aspirants have been killed, kidnapped, campaign rallies bombed or political thugs armed with charms and dangerous weapons attacked political opponents.

In a piece entitled: "History of political violence in Nigeria", Ali (2003:32) states that before the attainment of independence, reports of political violence have been with us. Those who were old enough at that time would remember the myriad of political violence that attended the general elections of 1964".

The defunct Western Region in Nigeria acquired the epithet – Wild Wild West due to violence which characterized the conduct of the October 1965 parliamentary election in the region. Prior to the election, Anifowose (1982: 206) observed that regional elections had taken place in 1951, 1956, and 1960 while Federal Elections were held in 1954, 1959 and 1964.

Quoting Mackintosh (1970), Anifowose (1982:201) described political parties in Nigeria as agencies for winning power but having taken hold of power at any level, they are reluctant to defend their position by argument and the creation of an electoral machinery.

Pre – voting utterances of political elites in the Region confirmed Mackintosh's declaration. Quoting the Premier of the Region, Chief S.L. Akintola through a press statement, Anifowose (1982:201) noted that Chief Akintola pointed out to his critics the fact that in the pervious fifteen years, no regional government had lost an election.

Anifowose contends further that during the campaigns which preceded the October 11 poll, the Premier, Chief Akintola and his Deputy, Chief Fani-Kayode were alleged to have boasted that whether the people voted for them or not, their party – the NNDP would be returned to power. The political tension in the region was so high before the day of election such that President Azikiwe as quoted by Anifowose (1982:207) warned that "the country was heading for troubles worse than the Congo". While describing politics in the region as a 'deadly' serious business, Anifowose further states that "the abuse, violence, bribery and viciousness of the election campaign were so outrageous". Ali (2003:32) further noted that "the general elections of 1979, those of 1983, 1993 and 1999 were not without bloodletting."

Onuoha (2004:38) on his part, identified composition of electoral commission as part of the root causes of electoral violence in Nigeria. He observed that from Nigeria's First Republic till date, the electoral body has never been independent. "Instead, incumbents are tempted to appoint their loyalists into the commission who will ensure their hold onto power". The implication is that they are always biased. Hence, Onuoha (2004:77) advocated for a truly independent electoral commission that is independent of any of the organs of government so as to avoid anything that could precipitate violence during elections.

CONCEPTUAL FRAMEWORK

Political Reporting

There is an inseparable relationship between democracy and political reporting. The relationship between the two concepts can be equated to the relationship between the 'snail' and its 'shell' in which the snail cannot move without the shell. Similarly, democracy cannot exist without communication. From the time of Walter Lippmann, the 20th century journalist who first drew attention to the power of the press to create pictures in peoples heads, the press has emerged as an indisputable ally in the democratic process, hence, Thomas Jefferson's declaration, cited in Akinfeleye (2011:13), that "were it left for me to decide whether we should have a government without the press, I would not hesitate a moment to choose the latter." Akinfeleye (2009:20) quoted another statesman, Kenneth Kaunda, a former President of Zambia as describing press as being "capable of making government, given the appropriate condition, would create condition for peace and promote development."

Various political communication scholars, notably Karl Deutsch, Richard Perloff and Idowu Sobowale captured this relationship vividly. To Deutsch (1963:35) "democracy is communication". He stresses that just as war could not be fought without communication, similarly, politics could not exist without communication. Sobowale (1999:38) equally states that the press can provide guidance and assurance in periods of critical events. They can arouse our awareness of crises of various descriptions, just as they can foster integration among diverse groups… They can also confer legitimacy and status."

Prior to 1999, the commencement date for this study, political reporting in Nigeria can be discussed under four headings, namely: The period after independence on October 1,1960 to January 15, 1966. This phase is officially known as Nigeria's First Republic.

The second phase is the era of military regime, January 15, 1966-1979 while the third phase is the period of Nigeria's Second Republic, October 1, 1979 - December 31,1983. The fourth phase is the period of another military regime, December 31, 1983 – May 29, 1999.

After independence, the third federal election was held in 1964. It was the first poll to be conducted by Nigerians without British supervision. The election laid the foundation for electoral crisis in Nigeria because the political class could not agree among themselves over who should rule at the centre and in the regions. The insecurity of lives and property in Western Region together with the acrimony and distrust generated by the 1964 and 1965 elections provided the excuse for the military to take-over government of Nigeria in January 1966. Thus, during the First Republic, the era of crusading journalism, fired by the objective of pursuing a common cause had gone down considerably as a result of division and self-interest among the nationalist political class. Nationalist leaders who were also leaders of leading political parties in the country then with few exceptions owned some of the newspapers in the country. Reflecting on the role of the press in the country after independence, Popoola (2003:94) quoted Omu, (1996) thus:

The feud between the West African Pilot and the Daily Service (in the 1940s), contributed to the regionalisation of inter-group tension and animosity which characterized political developments for a long time.

With the exception of the Preventive Detention Act of 1963, other national issues of the First Republic saw the press pursing interest of their political godfather.

Popoola (2003:94) quoted Omu (1996) once more,

The first few years of Independence saw little change in the political style of the newspapers. Indeed, the struggle for power among the politicians assumed a new fury and the competing party newspapers advertised their fanaticism. The Action Group crisis of 1962, the Census crisis of 1963/64 and the Federal Election of 1964 and its aftermath, the newspaper press provided a remarkable example of overzealous and irresponsible partisanship and recklessness.

In what looked like an attempt to rise to the occasion, the government of the First Republic enacted various laws in addition to the Seditious Offences Ordinance of 1909 and Newspapers Act Cap. 129 of 1958, to regulate journalism practice. The laws which are still in force till date are Seditious Meeting Act No. 48 of 1961, Defamation Act No. 66 of 1961.

Defamation (Amendment) Act No 1 of 1963 and Newspapers (Amendment) Act of 1964 which made it a criminal offence to publish any false statement.

Apart from the 1993 and 1999 presidential elections, two of the country's major tribes, Igbo of the South East and Yoruba of the South West hardly agree on political issues due to what Omu called "irresponsible partisanship and recklessness of the mass media". The seed of mistrust between the two tribes was sown through the press during the First Republic. For instance, during the 1964/65 Federal and Western Regional Elections, the press inflamed an already tensed political atmosphere by publishing inflammatory campaign speeches of politicians. One-time Premier of the Western Region, Chief S.L. Akintola, who disagreed with his leader, Chief Obafemi Awolowo, over political alliance with either the North or East said while justifying his preference for the North that:

While the Northerners have a good exchange of commodities in kolanuts and cows with Yoruba, the Ibo have nothing to offer the Yoruba except 'second hand clothing"

Such inflammatory statements disseminated through the press remain the major source of suspicion and unhealthy political relationship between the East and West till today. The period under review also witnessed the emergence of government owned newspapers whose interest was also at variance with privately owned newspapers. They include *The Morning Post* established by the Federal Government in 1961, the *Daily Sketch* established by Western Region in 1964, the *Eastern Outlook* established by Eastern Region in 1960, and *The New Nigerian* established by Northern Region in 1964.

With the arrival of government newspapers, the coffin of crusading journalism was seriously nailed. Quoting Alhaji Babatunde Jose, then Managing Director of *Daily Times* who believed that the press after independence needed to hold its fire, fight one battle at a time (against the British) and then face other problems after independence was quoted by Popoola (2003:95) saying:

I was absolutely convinced that in the years before independence, all our energies should be used to join politicians in getting rid of British rule. We should not be fighting British rule with one hand and discrediting the Nigerian Political leaders with another.

Political Violence

Conducting violence free and credible elections is a major problem confronting democratic growth in Africa. The phenomenal growth in election-related violence in African countries, especially in Cameroun, Ethiopia, Guinea, Guinea-Bissau, Kenya, Mali, Niger, Nigeria, Zimbabwe amongst others have attracted scholarly attention within and outside Africa.

While these African states, for various reasons, are finding it tough, Adele-Jinadu (2011:55) however states that countries like Botswana, Ghana, Mozambique, Sierra Leone, South Africa and Tanzania have recorded best practices and are regarded as success stories in electoral governance in Africa.

The current democratic dispensation which took off in 1999 in Nigeria has been fraught with violence. The most dramatic and worrisome aspect of the violence is that the degree of occurrence increases at every election across the country.

Umar, (2003:210) attributed the problem to politicians across the country who employed violence in the pursuit of their political interests. According to him:

The most worrisome behavior of our politicians is the manner they have intertwined politics with violence. They are not only ready to recruit and work with political thugs, but have come to accept thugs and violence as a 'legitimate' part of the political process.

Writing on electoral violence from the perspective of the North-East geo-political zone, Umar (2003:210) stated that "there is hardly any politician or political party in the zone that does not have a militia group or at least one person who has ties to thugs and has the capability to organize them (thugs) to attack, maim or assassinate a political rival or destroy political office in furtherance of political interest."

Irrespective of the geo-political zone in Nigeria where in politician resides, Umar (2003:210-211) argued that Nigerian politicians have the same attitude to politics. He stated that politicians in Nigeria do not believe in failure or losing an election or even the thought of it happening. They can only take responsibility of winning but not losing.

A major reason why politicians employ violence has been attributed to quest for power and the drive towards primitive accumulation of wealth (Ologbenla, 2003:80), Ogunsanwo, (1994:14) & Umar, (2003:210). As a result, Ogbeide (2010:43) declared that in Nigeria, "the political class is believed to be making it practically impossible to conduct free and fair elections." The attitude of the political class is largely responsible for such assertion. For instance, during the 2007 elections, there was a report concerning falsification of voters' register such that names of Bill Clinton, Mike Tyson were smuggled into the voters' register. In order for politicians in the North East geo-political zone of the country to achieve their selfish political goal, Umar, (2003:212) stated that politicians in the zone used the youths as cannon powder for the perpetration of violence in the zone in particular and the nation at large. "Politicians recruit them to serve as hit men, bodyguards and militia for the parties."

Mu'azu (2003:375) however, described violence as the raw material for the media to produce news. He argued that violence has a natural attraction to the media to improve sales. He noted that the attention that is given to violence by the media depends on how it unfolds. He stressed that as soon as violence is suppressed, media attention moves to other issues unless it recurs or takes on new dimensions.

A recent survey conducted by INEC and Friedrich Ebert Stiftung on voter apathy across the six geo-political zones of Nigeria after the 2011 elections revealed that in all regions, violence and insecurity were major reasons for apathy. The survey provided the under listed figures. In the North East where serious apprehension was nursed due to pre-election violence in certain areas in the zone, 61% felt that violence was a major reason for voter apathy. This however was much lower than the figures returned from the South South geo-political zone (86%) and South West (83%). Reflecting on the extent to which violence had become an endemic problem, the following figures were similarly returned from the other geo-political zones; North Central (60%), North West (86%) and South East (52%).

In other words, the degree of occurrence of electoral violence during the 2011 elections was highest in the South South zone, followed by North West, South West, North East, North Central and South East respectively, South East being the least.

STATEMENT OF THE PROBLEM

At present, Nigeria operates a combination of autonomous and ancillary media; a plural and indeed eclectic system where private, religious and state owned media organizations operate side by side disseminating information in the country. The autonomous media make their own rules of operation, set their own goals and decide their own content independent of government influence, at least in principle. The ancillary media, on the other hand, being owned, directed and controlled by the government, often operate as the mouthpiece of political parties in power, either at the state or federal level, with most state governors scrambling to own radio, television and newspaper houses.

Consequently, especially as observed during the elections covered by this study, there is serious encroachment on the editorial objectivity of the Nigerian media, projecting them as ignorant of the rules and ethics of their profession. The political class and other stakeholders have hijacked this anomaly to become partisan, and have abandoned constructionism, a concept which allows people to independently construct meanings from media messages, to the act of deliberately dissembling information, half-baked truths, outright falsehood and spurious data that can, when aired, engender political violence. Such political violence has grown exponentially from the one republic to the other, claiming lives and property, and disturbing public peace in Nigeria.

To worsen matter, the media regulatory agencies, especially, The Nigeria Press Council (NPC), the National Broadcasting Commission (NBC) and the Advertising Practitioners Council of Nigeria (APCON) which are statutorily empowered to compel compliance of media professionals to ethical code of practice were not forthcoming in checking the excesses of the media.

Therefore, securing compliance of media professionals to reportorial code of conduct in Nigeria, especially, during elections has been very problematic. From the first election in the post-independent era in 1964/65 till date, hardly was there any election in which the mass media were not blamed for instigating, fuelling or spreading electoral violence.

It is similarly worrisome that media professionals themselves know that it was improper to flagrantly violate the ethical code of conduct as well as the various rules governing the conduct of election as espoused in the *Electoral Act.* Yet, they continue their contemptuous disposition to the rules and ethics of journalism. Although, proprietorial interest has been identified as the main cause of such attitude, yet, due to the prevailing economic crunch in the country which has made the unemployment market to be saturated, media professionals found it difficult to resign from any medium where the proprietors dictate contrary to the ethics of journalism and laws of the land.

Based on this, the media continue to lose credibility as source of objective information, professionalism of journalists dwindle at alarming rate, democracy and good government are threatened and the political development of Nigeria is lumbering. The study then becomes curious on one hand about these problems, especially as it concerns how to promptly checkmate an evolving state of anomie and through that put the Nigerian democracy on track. On the other hand, the study is curious about the degree of media compliance to their professional codes of conduct as well as how such compliance or otherwise has over the years affected political communication towards engendering violence in the society, how the violence has affected the socio-political development of Nigeria, and how such effect can be prevented and controlled. These issues also raise the research questions that will be addressed in the study.

OBJECTIVES OF THE STUDY

The specific objectives for the study are:

1. To evaluate whether the Nigerian media complied with their reportorial code which demands factual, balanced and fair reportage of electioneering processes between 1999 and 2011.
2. To determine how compliance or noncompliance to the reportorial code has affected the relationship between political communication and political violence in Nigeria.
3. To highlight the effects of media generated political violence in the democratic and overall political development of the country.
4. To recommend policy measures that can be taken to prevent media generated political violence in Nigeria.

RESEARCH QUESTIONS

1. Did the Nigerian media comply with their reportorial code which demands factual, accurate, balanced and fair reportage of electioneering processes between 1999 and 2011?
2. How did the compliance or noncompliance to the reportorial code affect the relationship between political communication and political violence in Nigeria?
3. What are the effects of media generated political violence on the democratic and overall political development in Nigeria?
4. What policy measures can be taken to prevent media generated political violence in Nigeria?

METHODOLOGY

The study, even though a political communication perspective, falls within the sub-field of political history and political development in Nigeria. Hence, it adopts the historical method of analysis of the four general elections conducted in Nigeria between 1999 and 2011.

The population for the study consisted of the 57 print media establishments and 243 broadcast media i.e. 148 T.V and 95 radio stations in the country identified by Akinfeleye (2003:44-47) and Komolafe (2004:107-110 & 116- 121). The sample size for the study were 24 print media and 19 broadcast media establishments in Lagos, extracted from the population of 57 print media establishments in the country and 243 broadcast media identified by Akinfeleye (2003) and Komolafe (2004). The 24 print media represents 73 percent of the 33 Lagos based print media currently in circulation in the country. In all, the sample size consists of 150 media professionals i.e. 44 political editors, 10 line editors and 96 political reporters. The 19 broadcast media consists of eight TV stations out of 12 in the state i.e. 67% and 11 out of the 21 radio stations i.e. 52% operating in the state.

The study used oral/In-Depth Interview (IDI) method in gathering data from political reporters, political editors and line editors who are the respondents in this study. The interview lasted averagely 20 minutes per respondent.

An In-Depth Interview guide was drawn up to elicit comments from the respondents. According to Sobowale (2008:67), In-depth interview requires the researcher to arm himself with a number of questions which will help the interviewee to respond to the questions in a way that would elicit adequate information about the subject of interest to the researcher. "This information –gathering technique enables the researcher to probe deeper into the inner recesses of the interviewee… unlike in a survey when they are limited by response options or the need to paraphrase their views".

LITERATURE REVIEW

Violence has become a regular feature of post-independent elections in Nigeria. The degree of its occurrence increases at every election across the country.

A feature of most of the post-independent elections in Nigeria is that of political violence. Scholars, especially those in the field of political behavior and Sociology had at different times attempted to operationalize and adduce reasons for violence. (Ologbenla, (2003:80); Olurode, (1987:64); Mu'azu, (2003:375; Anifowose, (1982:3); Ugo, (2004:105), Hoijer (1996:54); among others). They articulated indecent human behavior such as rioting, arson, verbal and physical assaults, oppression, harassment, intimidation, murder etc as variants of violence.

In what could be described as prelude or background to this politics of desperation, Uche (1989:53) through his work entitled: *Mass Media People and Politics in Nigeria* contends that the demise of public confidence and trust in government owned media in Nigeria started during the first post-independent election of 1964 in the Western Region.

He noted that the election was very controversial with various contentious issues bothering on allegations of rigging throughout the region which were substantiated and proved beyond doubt. In spite of this, Uche (1989:53) asserts that "the NBC still went ahead to broadcast the results of the discredited election. This angered some people in the Region who reacted sharply by cutting off their rediffusion boxes which relayed the false election results.

In a related perspective, Anifowose (1982:220-221), writing on "switching of results" says in several cases during the election, the United Progressive Grand Alliance (UPGA) candidates were declared elected by the Returning Officer and accordingly issued certificates only to hear over the radio that their opponents were declared elected. He cited two prominent examples to buttress his assertion.

Unprofessional conduct of media personnel during the elections was therefore a major prelude to the outbreak of electoral violence in the region popularly known as *operation wet e*(operation wet it!)

Writing on the "history, consequences and solutions to political violence in Nigeria", Ali (2003:32-35) identified a number of causes of electoral violence in Nigeria. The causes ranged from: Intolerance, Unemployment and idleness of able bodied young men and women, complicity and partisanship of the security agents, government policy/displacement of youths, composition of electoral body, faithlessness of politicians in the different religions they professed, election rigging, tribalism and nepotism among others.

Similarly, Ogundiya (2003:63-65) identified poor electoral administration and lack of well – defined ideology as well as politics of ethnicity.

While stressing that electoral violence has rendered transition from civilian to civilian administration problematic, Ogundiya (2003: 59) further identified use of religion, ethnic sentiments, outright bribery, the power of incumbency, corruption, abuse of electoral processes as additional causes of electoral violence.

Ayeni – Akere (2003:79) on his part identified the do-or-die approach to politics as a major cause of electoral violence.

On the consequences/effects of political violence on the political development of Nigeria, Ali (2003: 63-65) noted that several people were dispatched to the grave beyond, bread winners were killed in the presence of their wives, just as the acts breed and nurtures insecurity.

A school of thought however asserts that the media can contribute to the escalation or de-escalation of violence due to the manner they gather, process or package and disseminate information to the public. Leading proponents of this school of thought are Denis McQuail and Ralph Akinfeleye.

While McQuail (1987:266) notes that "the media can provoke a riot, create a culture of rioting and provide lessons on how to riot, spread a disturbance from place to place," Akinfeleye (2004:106) on his part observes that:

By their very nature and practice of their craft, journalists can make or mar the society and the politicians they serve. They can lift politicians up and they can pull them down. They can protect or harm the politicians they serve. They can cause war without participating in it. They can also bring about peace, harmony and concord within the society they serve.

However, McQuail and Akinfeleye's assertion have been a major source of concern since early 19th century when US President, Mckinley was assassinated. Burleigh (2009:72-88) states that Mckinley was assassinated in 1901 by Leon Czolgosz. According to him:

Czolgosz approached Mckinley outside the Temple of Music, where he shot him at close range. One bullet was deflected by the president's breast bone, but the second went so deep into his abdomen that surgeons could not recover it. The president slowly bled to death. A search revealed that Czolgosz not only had a newspaper clipping in his pocket but that he had used the same 32-calibre lver Johnson revolver which had been used for the assassination of Prime Minister of Spain and King Umberto of Italy. (Burleigh, 2009:72-88)

A detailed news report or in-depth reportage of the assassination of the Prime Minister of Spain as well as King Umberto of Italy provided home lesson for the assailant of President Mckinley.

The media are seen as part of the problem in Nigeria, because of the way they either gather and report or the way some political programmes were structured. Political violence falls directly into the category of hard news stuff. In the words of Fedler et al (2005:503), hard news gives important "information immediately" while Dominick (1993:341) described it as "news of important public events such as crime, environment, science, international happenings, social conditions, and the economy among others."

A major reason why media and violence remain a major problem of media coverage of elections in Nigeria is that of partisanship. This in turn gives birth to ethical problem in which media professionals set aside the code of ethics for Nigerian journalists, put together by the Nigerian Press Organization (NPO).

Uwalaka (2000:1) captured this trend in the following words:

In Nigeria, public officers, often make ethical undertaking and claims they do not intend to discharge with diligence, honesty and integrity. To foster true peace and lasting stability, politics must be practiced according to a set of moral values and code of norms. Politics must be both value-driven and value dependent.

Article 96(1) of the Electoral Act (2010) states that "no candidate, person or group of persons shall directly or indirectly threaten any person with the use of force or violence during any political campaign in order to compel that person or any other person to support or refrain from supporting a political party or candidate."

In most of the Nigerian post-independent elections, this rule was hardly enforced. Maitambari (2011:80) for instance observed that during the 2007 elections, snatching and destruction of electoral materials was rampant. "Thugs and party agents, sometimes with officials snatch and/or destroy ballot boxes in the area in which they suspect their opponents have an advantage. In some other instances, stolen ballot boxes are presented to the electoral officials as genuine documents".

THEORETICAL FRAMEWORK

The theoretical underpinnings for this study are: The conflict theory and the power theory.

Electoral violence is a form of conflict and conflict is regarded as bread and butter of journalism. Owens-Ibie (2002:32) quoting Tehranian (1996) and *Media Development* (1996) described conflict as a bread and better of journalism. He stressed that "conflict sells, conflict is a source of sensation, the yellow press and other periodicals and the commercial driven… find raw material to remain in competition in the daily battle for market share and profits."

Lulofs and Cahn (2000:2) regarded conflict as a fact of life; they contended however that violence is not part of life. It is however worthy of note ironically that in Nigeria, conflict and violence are part of life and hallmark of the electoral process. Hardly was there any election in the post-independent Nigeria in which violence and conflict did not occur.

Lulofs and Cahn (2000:2) further stated that "we encounter it at home, at school, and at work". They similarly presented two perspectives of conflict. At one end, they described conflict "as a disruption of the normal workings of a system" while at the other end, conflict is presented "as a part of all relationships". The aspect of conflict that is of interest to this study is that aspect that disrupts the system during pre-election campaign, election days and post-election process.

From sociological perspective, Peil (1977:41) remarks that "from the beginning of the discipline, sociologists have been concerned with the problem of order in society." while noting that "societies are a tissue of conflicts and loyalties", Peil (1977:44) stressed that "friends at one level may be enemies at another…." Peil's perspective of the conflict theory is equally relevant in explaining election violence in Nigeria where top politicians are fond of cross-carpeting and changing party allegiance at the eve of many major elections.

The relevance of the power theory on the other hand as a supportive theory for this study is premised on the fact that power is very central to the problem which characterized the conduct of the various elections covered in the study.

A German sociologist, Max Weber described politics as "striving to share power or striving to influence the distribution of power either among states or among groups within a state (Isaak, 1981:20).

William Bluhm, a political scientist equally stated that "politics is a social process characterized by activity involving rivalry and co-operation in the exercise of power and culminating in the making of decisions for a group."

Implicit from the Weberian and Bluhm's declarations on politics is that 'power' is very central to the problem which characterized the conduct of the various elections in this study. Hence, Gauba (2003: 248) asserts that power is regarded as one of the central concepts of political science. "It is said that the concept of power holds the same status in the realm of Political Science as held by the concept of money in the realm of economics".

A similar assertion was made by Hague & Harrop (2004:12) who observe that:

Power is the currency of politics. Just as money permits the efficient flow of goods and services through an economy, so power enables collective decisions to be made and enforced. Without power, a government would be as useless as a car without an engine. Power is the tool that enables rulers to serve and exploit their subjects.

In a related development, Gauba (2003: 249) quoting Frederick Watkins (1934) observes that the proper scope of political science is not the study of the state or any of other specific institutional complex, but the investigation of all associations in so far as they can be shown to exemplify the problem of power.

The significance of power in discussing political phenomenon was brought out by traditional political thinkers such as Machiavelli, Thomas Hobbes, as well as contemporary writers like Max Weber, Catlin, Merriam, Lasswell, Kaplan, Watkins, Trietschke, Hans Morgenthau among others.

Equally central or strategic to this study is Alan Ball's (1987:20) submission on power. According to him,

The concept of political power is a key concept in the study of politics for if politics is the resolution of conflict, the distribution of power within a political community determines how the conflict is to be resolved, and whether the resolution is to be effectively observed by all parties.

The emergence of British press barons, especially Beaverbrook, Northchiffe and Rothernere in the 1920s and 1930s was largely informed by power drive. According to Negrine (1996:48):

The press barons- in particular, Beaverbrook who owned the Express and Rothermere who own the Mail had amassed their vast power through their industrial holdings and/or their ownership of newspapers... Both newspaper proprietors decided to use their newspapers to pursue a political philosophy and policy.

Since the colonial days, a strategic political power equation has emerged amongst the Nigerian political elites. It is premised on an assumption that to be a serious contender to any elective political office, you must own or have controlling shares in one or two influential mass media. Notable politicians in this context were Herbert Macaulay, Ernest Sesei Ikoli, Nnamdi Azikiwe, Obafemi Awolowo among others.

This trend continues in the post-independent era. *African Media Barometer* (2011:24) for instance, states that "a former governor of Lagos state own *TV Continental*, *Radio Continental* and *Adaba FM* as well as *The Nation* and *National Life* newspapers."

The publication further notes that former President Olusegun Obasanjo allegedly allocated himself, 5 to 10 radio and television broadcasting licenses before leaving office.

Lasswell (1951) cited in Isaak (1981:204) identified eight values that are sought in politics. They include: power, wealth, well-being, skill, enlightenment, affection, rectitude and respect.

However, going by the trend of politicking in Nigeria, two of the eight values, namely: power and wealth; tend to be the core motives behind the aggressive pursuit of political power by the political class in Nigeria. Hence, Ologbenla's (2003:50) assertion that "they seek to use state power to accumulate wealth in a primitive manner… and thus gaining access to power is a do-or-die affair."

ETHICAL AND LEGAL CHALLENGES OF ELECTION REPORTING IN NIGERIA

In the context of Merrill (1974:163), "ethics has to do with duty-duty to self and/or duty to others". The goal of this section of the paper therefore is to appraise how the media professionals who are the respondents in this study carry out this sacred duty first to themselves and then to the society.

In doing this, data from the field work were analyzed qualitatively in order that its outcome is understood, digested and invariably used in tackling the research questions.

While analyzing the data, different issues were treated under appropriate research questions.

RQ1: Did the Nigerian media comply with their reportorial code which demands factual, accurate, balanced and fair reportage of electioneering processes between 1999 and 2011?

Statistical information from the respondents to this question showed that the level of compliance was at its lowest level in 2011 (7percent) and also at its highest level in 1999 (87percnent). During the 2003 and 2007 elections, compliance level was 27 percent.

Various reasons were adduced by media professionals for this ugly trend. The reasons ranged from partisanship, poverty, poor working conditions, inadequate training, sensationalism, ownership interest, lack of discipline, laziness/failure to confirm reports, over reliance on on-line reports, poor implementation of code of ethics among others. Details are hereby presented.

Adebanwi (2014) of *The News magazine* contend that whatever ethical problem observed in the Nigerian media reportage of election news could be shifted to media owners. It was his view that "media owners are often biased and this shapes the kind of stories published in their newspapers". Nwabueze (2014) of *Hallmark* newspaper attributed the problem to partisanship on the part of Nigerian journalists.

Babalola (2014), the news editor of *PM News* on his part blamed the problem on environmental, social and monetary factors. A similar view was expressed through the *African Media Barometer, Nigeria* (2011:50) thus: "Journalists covering government institutions are careful not to lose their accreditation, which is a standard practice when an official gets uncomfortable with the reporting of a particular journalist. The fear of losing perks such as monthly stipends for covering state houses and the use of free facilities such as the telephone, fax and internet access for filing their stories also forces journalists to practice self-censorship.

Iwuga (2014), a political correspondent of *BusienssDay* however blamed such stories on inexperience as well as inadequate training of journalists. Iwuga's colleague at *The Nation's* newspaper, Ibrahim Shamsudeen (2011), blamed the development on what he called "the quest to sensationalize by a section of the media".

His counterpart at same medium, Odufowokan (2014) chiefly attributed the problem to ownership interest. Odufowokan's boss, Remi Adelowo, an Assistant editor on the political desk expressed a similar view. He said "pecuniary gains, coupled with the publishers political interest are responsible." The political editor of the newspaper, Sam Egburonu, (2014) in a direct and pungent manner says "media owners who are politicians often fail to separate their political interest from the fortunes of the media houses."

Ibe (2014), the General Manager, publications and chairman of Editorial Board of *Champion* newspaper argued that partisanship in terms of ownership of the papers, ethnic biases of the owners, monetization of the political process leading to compromise of journalists and media organization are responsible. Bayagbon (2014), a senior journalist with *Vanguard* newspapers in his contribution stated that logistical constraints of many media houses could be responsible. Williams (2014), the Deputy Editor of *Guardian* newspaper said "generally, poverty could be responsible". Aghedo (2014), a political correspondent of *Guardian newspaper* on his part identified poor implementation of the code of ethics for Nigerian journalists, put together by the Nigerian Guild of Editors as being responsible. The political editor of the newspaper, Samson Eze says lack of discipline among the regulatory agencies and media professionals are responsible.

Olumide (2014), a political correspondent with *The Guardian* newspaper identified inadequate background training of journalists as well as ethical problems as being responsible. The political editor of *ThisDay* newspapers, Vincent Obia (2014) similarly identified lack of adequate training on election coverage as being responsible. Odiboshi (2014), the political editor of *National Daily* blamed the problem on partisanship on the part of reporters and over-bearing influence of the publishers. Nwabueze (2014) of the *Hallmark* newspaper claimed "Nigerian factor is mainly responsible." Williams (2014), the deputy editor of *The Guardian* newspapers however disagreed saying we did our best to be ethical in all our news reports.

Adeogun (2014), political editor of *Ovation* magazine says a major problem responsible for inaccurate reporting could be attributed to lack of standard remuneration for media professionals. Ajala (2014), the political editor of *Celebrity magazine* averred that over bearing tendency of the political class to promote falsehood was the main reason. George (2014), of *Insider magazine* stated that a factor responsible for the publication or airing of such stories could be attributed to financial inducement and intimidation of journalists by politicians which in turn erode their fairness and objectivity in reporting. Onabanjo (2014), the political editor of *Tell magazine* was of the view that different perspectives of reporting an event could be responsible. "The fact remains that all over the world, reporters report events differently as they view it".

The broadcast journalists equally expressed similar view. Kunle Fasina (2014), a political correspondent of *Lagos State Television* (LTV) identified materialism as the major reason why journalists may not be ethical in their news reports. Chukwulue (2014), an *FRCN* political reporter asserts that the urge by journalists to meet some basic needs tend to make them dance to the tune of desperate politicians who are ready to induce them financially. Chukwulue's boss, Ogunbunmi (2014) however disagreed saying "interference by the ownership i.e. government, is responsible. FRCN controller of News, Fred Braimah (2014), revealed that the major factor responsible for publication of inaccurate stories was the high level of corruption in the society. He declared, "politicians would do anything to have their ways including influencing media reports" Adagun (2014), a former deputy Director of News department of *Radio Lagos/Eko FM* claims that "the much talked about Nigerian mentality, laziness, poverty and greed are main causes of publication of inaccurate stories which in turn could provoke violent reactions.

Fatonji (2014), a senior editorial member of staff of *Voice of Nigeria (VON)* opined that inadequate education of journalists was responsible. Another staff of VON, Umoh (2014), the head of the organization's newsroom stressed that poor monitoring by relevant regulatory bodies are responsible. A political reporter of NTA, Adebayo (2014) noted that influences of political parties and government are responsible. He stressed that this is due to the fact that both political parties and government would do anything to win elections. Ajao (2014), a political reporter of MITV similarly said the Nigerian media was not adequately protected from violence, hazards and other views.

Akpan (2014), the political editor of *Inspiration 93.5FM* opened a new chapter on the issue as he identified three factors as causes of the problem. He noted inexperience on the part of the affected journalists, failure to confirm news reports and above all, over dependence on on-line media reports. Takuro (2014), the news editor of Unilag 103.1FM offers similar reasons to those who identified ownership influence and corruption by politicians who try to influence journalists through their ill-gotten wealth. His colleague at same medium, Waheed (2014) identified ownership and tribal influences as well as gratifications. Enitan further reveals that working conditions are generally tough for Nigerian journalists and this has pushed many to trade their integrity in order to survive. "Corruption and the acceptance of tips in cash and in kind are rampant within the industry. Greed also pushes even well-paid journalists to demand and accept money from news sources with a clear understanding that in return, they will either promote the agenda or cover-up the wrongdoings of their benefactors. *African Media Barometer* (2011:52) offers a similar explanation.

"It is common practice for media houses to demand 'fuel' or transport money to cover news events. Unable to pay salaries, some media owners encourage journalists to extort money from news sources in lieu of salaries. The situation is that bad that a panelist summed it thus: "the Nigerian media is corrupt and its integrity is on trial". Just as some journalists in the print sector disagreed with the majority views, a similar scenario presents itself in the broadcast media. Asuquo (2014), the Bulletin editor of *Television Continental (TVC)* said "most of the media organizations impacted accurately and fairly during these elections". He identified TVC as one of the stations. "Regardless of political linings, TVC reporters were so balanced in their reportage during these elections". Another editor from the stable, Adeyeye (2014) expressed a similar view. He pointed out that most TV stations reported what they saw, TVC inclusive. According to him, "We aired accurate, balance and factual stories". He was however quick to add that "corruption can be a cause"

In a related development, a senior editorial member of staff of *Bond FM,* Lagos, Ejiro (2014) equally dismissed to notion that the media news report during the elections were full of inaccuracies and ethically biased. According to him, "the mass media did not violate any ethical code, rather, politicians were violent and openly rigged the elections".

RQ2: How did the compliance or noncompliance to the reportorial code affect the relationship between political reporting and political violence in Nigeria?

A number of reasons were given by the respondents concerning noncompliance to the provision in section 100 (2-5) of the *Electoral Act* (2010) which states that "state apparatus including the media shall not be employed to the advantage and disadvantage of any political party or candidate at any election, media time shall be allocated equally among the political parties or candidates at similar hours of the day. At any public electronic media, equal time shall be allotted to all political parties or candidates during prime times at similar hours each day, subject to the payment of appropriate fees. At any public print media, equal coverage and conspicuity shall be allotted to all political parties".

Omotosho (2010), editor of *The Nation* newspaper attributed this to the political interest of the owners. Emewu (2010), the deputy editor of *The Sun* on his part blamed the non-adherence to the law on lack of openness and probity within the system. Okereke (2010), of the NUJ however attributed the problem to the do-or-die attitude of Nigerian politicians. Adeyemo (2010), the Editorial Director of *Tell* magazine says the problem could be attributed to government censorship as well as partisanship on the part of senior members of staff of government-owned media.

Alakija (2010), the General Editor of *City People* magazine attributed the problem to fear of reprisal measures including sack from the management if opposing views are aired/published. All the sampled print editors however agreed that the law is appropriate and should be implemented to the letter.

From the broadcast respondents, Uzoka (2010), the Head of Business Desk of Silverbird TV says "with over 50 political parties and thousands of contestants, it is difficult to give equal access. The ownership factor is another factor". The News editor of Continental Broadcast Services, Malagu (2010) expressed a similar view. He contends that "as at 2007, Nigeria had 52 registered political parties as a result of which it would be difficult to comply with the rule. Furthermore, media ownership is another reason which obstruct compliance with that provision in the Electoral Act.

Onahaegte (2010), Manager of News & Current Affairs of NTA attributed the problem to the LTP policy at NTA (Let them pay). He said political parties and candidates can access airtime as long as they are willing to pay.

Chukwuelu, (2010), a supervisor of News at FRCN said FRCN as a rule abides by the law except that the political parties/candidates are usually not forthcoming. An Editor with Bond FM, Okichie (2010) says the law would be difficult to comply with by state-owned media as a result of funding. Onimole (2010) of *Top Radio* says, all the Government-owned media are being managed by political appointees and that they will end up favouring the interests of their bosses.

Junaid (2010), Manager News, LTV on his part says "the law is ineffective because journalists in government-owned media are loyal to the party in power for fear of not losing their jobs". Olanrewaju, (2010) Acting News Editor of Radio Unilag says "it is generally believed that government owned media should support the government in power and deliberately exclude the opposition. It is a moral issue". Hassan (2010), acting controller of programme of Eko FM says "most media organizations are now being forced into the market to source funds, government which pays the media men could use them for political purposes".

On what factors are responsible for government in power using state apparatus including the media to the disadvantage of opposition parties, the respondents equally responded differently. Bola Dan Abu (2010), Executive Editor of *Newswatch* magazine says state media are strictly controlled by state government and they cannot but support their pay masters."It is a game of survival first. That is why they didn't perform well". Dan Abu's counterpart at *Tell* magazine, Adeyemo (2010) contended that politicians in public office can go to any length in achieving their aim. He cited the example of Broadcasting Corporation of Oyo State (BCOS), Ibadan, where a former General Manager was redeployed because he gave air time to opposition parties.

Alakija (2010), the General Editor of City People magazine noted that virtually all the state-owned media in the country, including the NTA aired more contents on the ruling People's Democratic Party (PDP) to the detriment of other political parties. Omotoso (2010), Editor of the ***Nation*** newspaper equally described state-owned media as mouth pieces of their owners.

Uzoka (2010), Head of Business Desk of *Silverbird TV* identified a number of factors as being responsible. They include lack of independence, financial autonomy coupled with the fact that government in power appoints the Chief Executives of the organizations including board members.

Ladeinde (2010), supervisor, News & Current Affairs of *Degue Broadcast* Network (DBN') argued that media professionals in the employment of state owned media can't resist the quest by government to use the media to the disadvantage of opposition parties due to fear of losing their jobs or being intimidated by the government.

Onimole (2010), the Chief Operating Officer of *Top Radio* declared that "there is no human being who is not biased. He stated that "even the workers in state media cannot speak against the incumbent government and go free".

The contention of most of the respondents is that it would be an herculean task for government not to use state media apparatus to the detriment of opposition parties, especially against the backdrop of the fact that they appoint the Chief Executive, the Board members and pay their salaries.

RQ3: What are the effects of media generated political violence on the democratic and over all political development of Nigeria?

The first major effect of violence or threat of violence on the electoral system identified by some of the respondents centered on the security response by the state through the electoral Umpire, INEC

Adelowo (2014), an Assistant political editor of *The Nation* newspaper says once there is a threat or outbreak of violence, state response has always been in the direction of deployment of security personnel so as to promptly contain violence or prevent outbreak of electoral violence. "Depending on the magnitude of such security operatives, once the figure is intimidating, it could affect voters turn out as many electorates might be scared of coming out to vote.

Oboh (2014), the political editor of *Daily Independent* newspaper says "violence provides opportunity for men of the Nigeria police to do what they know how to do best, harassing, embarrassing and at times ridiculing voters under the guise of checking. He argued that within the pro-democracy groups and civil societies groups in Nigeria, the police are regarded as the worst human rights violators and abuser.

Babalola (2014), The News editors of *PM News* on his part says low voters turn out due to electoral violence could affect the credibility of electoral outcome as well as the legitimacy of those elected through such elections.

Fasina (2014), the political correspondent of *Lagos State Television (LTV)* argued that violence could easily provide the dominant political actors opportunity to subvert the peoples will. "It is a known fact that over the years, the police and other security agents usually work hand-in-hand to protect the interest of the party in power either at the state or federal level.

Chukwulue (2014), a political reporter of *Federal Radio Corporation of Nigeria* (FRCN) says the head of security forces in the country are usually overzealous in their handling of security arrangements for any election. "At times, they behave as if they are working for the government and not the people. He argued that such overzealousness on the part of security agents attracted the attention of the Nigerian press, especially during the 2003, 2007and 2011 elections.

Takuro (2014), the News editor of *Radio Unilag 103.1fm* opines that the major effect of violence on the electoral system is that it constitutes a major threat to the political rights of Nigerians to exercise their political rights during elections.

Takuro is also of the view that desperate politicians could easily ferment trouble during elections as a result of the low strength of the Nigeria police. The staff strength of the police is put at 350,000 while there are 120,000 polling units across the country which INEC is contemplating to increase. In other words, it is a situation of about three policemen per polling unit. This is grossly inadequate and should be addressed especially, against the backdrop of the fact that historically, thuggery has been established as one of the ways through which politicians can easily cause violence during elections.

Williams (2014), the deputy editor of *Guardian* newspapers listed major effects of violence on the electoral system as assassination of political opponents, snatching of voting materials, disruption of political campaign, abusive and various forms of violent attack on opponents, among others. Ibe (2014), the General Manager, publications and Chairman of Editorial Board of *Champion* newspapers said thus far, violence has brought unmitigated disasters upon the society just as it has made nonsense of the whole essence of democracy. He argued that just as Nigeria's former senate President, Ken Nnamani was quoted by the press, violence has made it is difficult for us to deepen democracy. Rather than improving, every succeeding election is worse than the previous one. Taking a cursory look at the magnitude of violence which characterized the conduct of 2003, 2007 and 2011 elections in Nigeria, Ibe argued that it is not only shameful but disgraceful that each election is worse than the previous when we should be talking of consolidating democracy.

RQ4: What policy measures can be taken to prevent media generated political violence in Nigeria?

The dos and don'ts of political reporting during elections in Nigeria can be situated within the context of Article 95(1&2), 96(1) and 101(1) of the *Electoral Act* (2010). Section 95 (i-ii) of the Act states that "No political campaign or slogan shall be tainted with abusive language directly or indirectly likely to injure religious, ethnic, tribal or sectional feelings. Abusive, intemperate, slanderous or hate language or insinuations or innuendoes designed or likely to provoke violent reaction or emotions shall not be employed or used in political campaigns.

Section 96(1) of the Act further states that 'no candidate, person or group of persons shall directly or indirectly threaten any person with the use of force or violence during any political campaign in order to compel that person or any other person to support or refrain from supporting a political party or candidate. Section 101(1) of the Act similarly states that "a print or electronic medium that broadcasts, publishes, advertises or circulates any material for the purpose of promoting or opposing a particular

Table 1.

Options	Media Classifications		Respondents' Ranking	
	Print Media	Broadcast Media	Print Media	Broadcast Media
Desirable	80	48	86	84
Not Desirable	10	9	11	16
Undecided	3	-	3	-
Total	93	57	100%	100%

political party or the election of a particular candidate over radio, TV, newspapers, magazines…24 hours preceding or on polling day is guilty of an offence under this Act.

Non adherence to these rules was largely responsible for the generation of political stories which engendered violence during the period covered by this study. Interesting enough, respondents who were interviewed for this study were divided on the desirability of the rules, especially, on prohibition of campaign 24 hours preceding an election. The table below shed more light on the position of the respondents on the issues.

Electoral Mobilization

The electoral mobilization table above has the objective of determining how desirable is the rule stopping electoral mobilization/campaign 24 hours before any election. It is quite interesting to note that while 86% of the 93 print respondents interviewed supported the provision in Article 101 of the *Electoral Act* (2010) which states electoral mobilization including advertisements shall stop 24 hours preceding every election, 11% said the law is unnecessary while 3 percent were undecided. However, 84 percent of the 57 Broadcast respondents said the rule is desirable while 16 percent said it is unnecessary.

It is instructive to add that in exercise of this provision, *Channels Tv* and *AIT* were sanctioned during the 2007 elections and were consequently fined N500,000 each while during the 2011 elections, *Zamfara radio* was fined N500,000 for airing unauthorized election results.

Those who supported the rule and consequently said it's desirable argued that at this critical moment during elections, all hands must be on deck to ensure there is peace and tranquility. It is also stated that there must be no undue advantage to any political party. Another reason adduced is that the provision will prevent advertisement which could unduly influence the opinion of the electorate. The need for fairness and equity was another reason being put forward to support the rule. Another contention is that it is a global rule. Bunmi Idowu (2010), Assist News Manager of NTA says" the law is necessary for the avoidance of slander or libel from rival parties as there is limited time to respond."

Among the reasons put forward by those who said the provision is unnecessary are the need to recognize the fact that many of the broadcast stations which violated the rule are privately owned which needed the money to survive. Okoye (2010), the News editor of *Radio Continental* said the provision is unnecessary because there is need for the political parties to woo the electorates until the last day of election. Uzoka (2010), Head of Business Desk of *Rhythm FM* also said the law is unnecessary. He asked rhetorically "what about the Bill Boards? What about the posters on the walls etc.? I strongly feel electoral mobilization in form advertisement should be allowed as long as it falls within acceptable content level".

CONCLUSION

The study established the contributory role of the mass media in electoral violence during the elections covered by this study.

A number of factors responsible for the publication or airing of stories which could precipitate violence were equally explored. The factors ranged from partisanship, poor working conditions, inadequate training, sensationalism, ownership interest, laziness/failure to confirm reports, over reliance on on-line reports, poor implementation of code of ethics among others.

The study established the current plural media system in the country under which private, public and religious owned media exist side-by-side as being exploited for selfish political reasons by the political class during elections. It was established during the study that such media behave as mouth-piece of the political parties in power either at the federal or state levels. The private owned media also operate according to the dictate of their owners.

These problems erode media professionalism especially during elections between 1999 and 2011. The study also established that recalcitrant posture of the Nigerian political elites to ethics of electioneering campaign as one of the critical factors responsible for publication or airing of stories capable of breeding violence and recommends measures to check-mate the ugly trend in the interest of healthy growth and development of Nigerian democracy.

The study examined ethical and legal challenges of election reporting in Nigeria from 1999-2011.

It noted that violence has become a characteristic feature of most of the post-independent elections in Nigeria such that hardly was there any election in the post-independent era in Nigeria that did not end in serious disputations, crisis, violence and blood letting to the extent that academics across disciplines concluded that since independence on October 1, 1960, the electioneering process in Nigeria has been an experience of tears, blood and sorrow. Just as the crow of the Cock is the harbinger of dawn, similarly, electioneering campaign and voting in Nigeria have become a magnetic pull for violence.

The mass media in Nigeria which are regarded as the playing field of politics or the road through which campaign travels every four years were identified as contributory agents.

Based on the above, the study therefore examined circumstances or factors behind such unprofessional conducts which negate journalist's creed and the code of ethics for media professionals in the country as put together by the *Nigerian Press council (NPC)* and the *Nigerian Guild of Editors*

The study examined the above problems through four research questions.

RQ1: Asked "Did the Nigerian media comply with their reportorial code which demands factual, accurate, balanced and fair reportage of electioneering processes between 1999 and 2011.

RQ2: Asked did compliance or non-compliance to the reportorial code affect the relationship between political communication and political violence in Nigeria?

RQ3: Asked what are the effects of media generated political violence in the democratic and overall political development in Nigeria?

RQ4: Asked what policy measures can be taken to prevent media generated political violence in Nigeria?

Using the conflict and power theory as the main theoretical pole, the study found out among others, that the plural media system in the country under which the press deplored irritancy against military rule and consequently published adversarial stories against its elongation now tend to be unmindful of the debilitating effect of unprofessionalism in their electoral reportorial stylistic devices as this constitutes a threat to healthy growth and sustenance of democracy in Nigeria.

The study further discovered that non-compliance to ethical code of conduct as one of the major factors responsible for publication or airing of provocative stories capable of engendering violence during elections.

The study similarly discovered that contemptuous disposition of the Nigerian political elites to ethics of electioneering campaign as espoused through the *Electoral Act* is a major factor responsible for electoral violence in Nigeria

RECOMMENDATIONS

In the light of the above, the study puts forward the following recommendations.

1. Faithful implementation of the various laws regarding the operations of the mass media during elections as clearly spelt out in the *Electoral Act (2010)*, especially, section 100 (2-5).
   This section states that state apparatus including the media shall not be employed to the advantage and disadvantage of any political party or candidates at any election. As could be seen through the study, the rule was never respected by the government-owned media during the elections covered by the study.
   Similarly, the law states that media time shall be allocated equally among the political parties or candidates at similar hours of the day. This rule, as discovered through the elections covered by this study was equally not observed.
   Furthermore, another aspect of the rule states that at any public print media, equal coverage and conspicuity shall be allotted to all political parties. The study also found out that this rule was not enforced. Therefore, there is need for rigorous enforcement of rules relating to the conduct of the mass media during elections while violations of the rules should be appropriately sanctioned.
2. **Enforcement of Code of Ethics:** *The Nigerian Press Council (NPC), the Guild of Editors, National Broadcasting Commission (NBC)* and other media regulatory agencies should similarly sanction erring media or media professionals who violate the code of ethics to prevent further dissemination of stories capable of generating violence.
3. *The Advertising Practitioners Council of Nigeria (APCON)* should also sanction any Global System of Mobile Communication (GSM) service providers who violate *Electoral Act 2010* rules barring political advertisements 24 hours to any election. During the elections covered by this study, especially in 2011, as established in the study, some political parties/candidates violated the rule as they disseminated political advertisements, few hours to elections.
4. **Strict Enforcement of *Electoral Act 2010*:** During some of the elections covered by this study, especially, in 2007 and 2011, the *Electoral Act* which stipulated heavy sanctions against any mass medium that aired unauthorized election results were sanctioned. *Zamfara Radio, Channels TV* and *AIT/Raypower* were cited as culprits in the study. However, government owned media which violated other sections of the same *Electoral Act* were not sanctioned. For equity, justice and fair play, electoral rules ought not to be implemented selectively.

5. Any member of the political class who henceforth violate ethics of electioneering campaign by using abusive, intemperate and slanderous or hate language should similarly be sanctioned according to the law of the land as espoused through the Electoral Act.
6. **Regulation of Future Political Advertisements:** The study recommends an inter-governmental-cum-departmental approach to regulate and prevent releasing of similar hate SMS/advertisements that were documented in the study so as to prevent any matter that could induce violence during future elections.
7. **Editorial Decision:** Part of the reasons given for publication or airing of stories capable of inducing electoral violence ranged from sensationalism, blowing things out of proportion or not paying attention to all sides of a controversy. These are issues requiring good editorial decision. The recommendation here is that under no condition must news report be released in a highly charged and tensed political atmosphere that may cause people resorting to violence.
8. **Political Reporting:** To broaden the knowledge of media writers, especially, the political reporters and political editors on election coverage, it is hereby recommended the need to teach political reporting as one of the specialized courses in all tertiary institutions offering journalism and mass communication in Nigeria.

REFERENCES

Adele-Jinadu, L. (2011). Comparative Analysis of Security Challenges of Elections in Nigeria. In L. Olurode & A. Jega (Eds.), *Security Challenges of Election Management in Nigeria*. Abuja: Independent National Electoral Commission.

African Media Barometer, Nigeria. (2011). Windhoek: Friedrick Ebert-Stiftung (FES).

Akinboye, S. O. (2009). Nigeria's 2007 General Elections: Global perceptions, concerns and responses. In L. Olurode, S. Akinboye, & R. Akinyemi (Eds.), *The crisis of political succession*. Lagos: Rebonik Publications Ltd.

Akinfeleye, R. A. (2003). *Fourth Estate of the Realm or Fourth Estate of the Wreck: Imperative of Social Responsibility of the Press*. Lagos: University of Lagos Press.

Akinfeleye, R. A. (2004). Mass Media Machine in Winning Elections, Electoral Violence and the damage the journalists can do. In A. Jinadu (Ed.), Crisis of democratization, development and electoral violence in Nigeria. Lagos: A special publication of Unilag Sociological Review.

Akinfeleye, R. A. (2011). *Essentials of Journalism: An introductory college text*. Lagos: Malthouse publishers.

Ali, Y. O. (2003). Keynote Address. In B. A. Olasupo (Ed.), *Electoral Violence in Nigeria: Issues and Perspectives*. Lagos: Friedrich Ebert Stiftung.

Anifowose, R. (1982). *Violence and Politics in Nigeria, Tiv and Yoruba Experience*. New York: Nok Publishers Int.

Ayeni-Akere, A. (2003). Electoral violence and the democratization project: The Nigerian experience. In B. A. Olasupo (Ed.), *Electoral Violence in Nigeria: Issues and Perspectives*. Lagos: Friedrich Ebert Stiftung.

Ball, A. (1987). *Modern Politics and Government*. London: Macmillan press.

Burleigh, M. (2009). *Blood and Rage, A cultural history of Terrorism*. London: Harper Perennial.

Deutsch, K. (1963). *The Nerves of Government*. New York: The Free Press.

Dominick, R. J. (1993). *The Dynamics of Mass Communication* (4th ed.). New York: McGraw-hill Inc.

Electoral Act. (2010). *With 2011 Amendments*. Abuja: Panaf press.

Fadakinte, M. M. (2014). Nigeria and Election Crises: Debating Causes. International Journal of Humanities and Social Science, 4(6), 74-96.

Fedler, F., Bender, R-J., Davenport, L., & Drager, W. M. (2005). Reporting for the media (8th ed.). New York: Oxford University Press.

Gauba, O. P. (2003). *An introduction to political theory*. New Delhi: Palgrave Macmillan India Ltd.

Haque, R., & Harrop, M. (2004). *Comparative Government & Politics* (6th ed.). New York: Palgrave Macmillan.

Hoijer, B. (1996). The Dilemmas of Documentary Violence in Television. The Nordic Review of Nordic Research on Media & Communication, 1(1), 50-62.

Isaak, C. A. (1981). *Scope and Methods of Political Science, an introduction to the Methodology of Political Inquiry*. The Dorsey press.

Komolafe, F. (2004). *Nigerian Journalists Directory*. Lagos: Friedrich Ebert Stiftung Stiftung.

Lulofs, R. S., & Cahn, D. D. (2000). *Conflict: From Theory to Action* (2nd ed.). Boston: Allyn and Bacon.

Maitambari, U. (2011). Emerging pattern of security challenges: some reflections on 1983 and 2007 elections. In L. Olurode & A. Jega (Eds.), *Security Challenges of Election Management in Nigeria*. Abuja Independent National Electoral Commission.

McQuail, D. (1987). *Mass Communication Theory* (3rd ed.). London: SAGE Publications ltd.

Merrill, J. C. (1974). *The Imperative of Freedom, A Philosophy of Journalistic Autonomy*. New York: Hastings House.

Mu'azu, A. (2003). Legal and Ethical Issues in Reporting Conflict. In U. A. Pate (Ed.), *Introduction to Conflict Reporting in Nigeria*. Lagos: Friedrich Ebert Stiftung.

Negrine, R. (1996). *Politics and the Mass Media in Britain* (2nd ed.). London: Routledge.

Ogbeide, M. M. (2010). A culture of failed elections: Revisiting democratic elections in Nigeria, 1959-2003. *Historia Actual Online*, *21*, 43–56.

Ogundiya, I. S. (2003). Electoral Violence and democratization project: The Nigerian Experience. In B. A. Olasupo (Ed.), *Electoral Violence in Nigeria: Issues and Perspectives*. Lagos: Fredrick Ebert Stiftung.

Ogunsanwo, A. (2003). Keynote Address. In 2003 General Elections and Democratic Consolidation in Nigeria. Lagos: Friedrich Ebert Stiftung.

Ologbenla, D. (2003). Political Instability, Conflict and the 2003 General Elections. In 2003 General Elections and Democratic Consolidation in Nigeria. Lagos: Firedrich Ebert Stiftung.

Olurode, L. (1987). *A Political Economy of Nigeria's 1983 Election*. Lagos: John West Publishers.

Olurode, L. (2011). Incumbency factors: Appropriation of state security resources and electoral governance in Nigeria. In L. Olurode & A. Jega (Eds.), *Security Challenges of Election Management in Nigeria*. Abuja: Independent National Electoral Commission.

Onuoha, B. (2004). The electoral machine: The Bureaucracy and the electoral process in the making of Nigeria's Fourth Republic. In L. Olurode & R. Anifowose (Eds.), *Issues in Nigeria's 1999 General Elections*. Lagos: John West Publications Ltd & Rebonick Publications Ltd.

Owens-Ibe, N. (2002). Socio-Cultural considerations in conflict reporting in Nigeria. In U. A. Pate (Ed.), *Introduction to Conflict Reporting in Nigeria*. Lagos: Friederich Ebert.

Peil, M. (1977). *Consensus and Conflict in African societies: An Introduction to sociology*. Edinburgh, UK: Longman Group Ltd.

Popoola, I. S. (2003). Role of mass media in a transitory troubled democracy. Babcock Journal of Management and Social Sciences, 2(1), 20.

Popoola, I. S. (2015). *Political Reporting and Electoral Violence in Nigeria, 1999 – 2011* (Ph.D Thesis). University of Lagos, Lagos Nigeria.

Sobowale, I. (1999). Nigerian Press coverage of national issues. In R. Akinfeleye, G. Omole, & O. Omang (Eds.), *Nigerian Mass Media and National Crises*. Lagos: Nigerian Press Council.

Sobowale, I. (2008). *Scientific Journalism*. Ago Iwoye: School of communication & Information science, Olabisi Onabanjo University, in conjunction with Idosa Konsult.

Uche, L. U. (1989). *Mass Media, People and Politics in Nigeria*. New Delhi: Concept Publishing Company.

Ugo, S. C. (2004). Electoral Malpractice and violence in 2003 Elections in Nigeria. *Unilag Journal of Politics*, *1*(1), 164–186.

Umar, M. M. (2003). The role of youths and politicians in political violence in North-East Nigeria. In B. O. Olasupo (Ed.), *Electoral Violence in Nigeria: Issues and Perspectives*. Lagos: Friedrich Ebert Stiftung.

Uwalaka, A E. (2000). *Ethics of Political Leadership*. Lagos: Techsarap Communications.

Chapter 6
Copying, Branding, and the Ethical Implications of Rights in Immaterial Cultural Goods

Ute M. Röschenthaler
Goethe University, Germany

ABSTRACT

Laws and regulations are important instruments for governing the relationships between people. In recent years, however, scholars have noted a growing judicialization, which concerns particularly immaterial cultural goods that are turned into intellectual and cultural properties. This chapter explores the implications of these regulations for the different actors involved, their moral responsibility and economic practices in the domains of branding and copying with examples of immaterial cultural goods from different African countries and from Austria. It argues that legal regulations that govern the use of immaterial cultural goods form part of the capitalist system. These regulations may be good for some and a hindrance for others. Piracy might damage the investments of an entrepreneur or artist in a brand or art work but might also help to secure the livelihood of other people and enhance the renown of products. Hence, it is important to analyze the perspectives and interests of individuals that are related to these economically important and ethically relevant activities.

INTRODUCTION

The evolution of media technology in the past decades has provided social actors with hitherto unknown opportunities to connect globally and exchange information, experiences and images, as well as to disseminate media contents and create software-based designs and products. The digital facilities of reproducing landscapes, architecture, people, objects, design patterns, or machines, have immensely increased the precision and speed with which images and information can be appropriated, processed, and commercialized. Marcus Boon called this "the infinite proliferation of copies in contemporary culture" (2011: 24). Digital media helps not only to create products and market them faster, but also to reach audiences across vast distances and diverse cultural identities. It also enlarges the opportunities for a countless number of individuals to access and appropriate goods, images, and information.

DOI: 10.4018/978-1-5225-2095-5.ch006

The opportunities that the widespread access to digital media offers have been praised as a form of democratization of immaterial cultural goods that makes these accessible for common use. But these opportunities also raise questions about the legitimacy of these uses, particularly when commercial interests are involved. Should everybody be allowed to glean immaterial goods as if from a playground or supermarket as it pleases them? Are images unclaimed goods that belong to everybody in the same way? Do they fall under intellectual property law or do they need protection in the name of humankind? What are the ethical or legal implications when, for example, investors measure and copy an entire village for commercial purposes? Under what conditions should a company be allowed pharmaceutical prospecting of plants on the land of indigenous communities and/or be able to use their local knowledge?

This chapter explores some of these questions and the challenges that legal institutions face when called to regulate issues of appropriation that have come up in growing numbers with the proliferation of digital media. I will argue that the digital media that have spurred, intensified, and accelerated these appropriations, play different roles depending on the purpose for which social actors use them. I will also show that legal and ethical evaluations also depend on who appropriated which good from whom and that these regulations are beneficial for some but not for others. Often divergent interests are at stake working to protect valuable goods for different reasons, among them the immaterial goods of local people, of private individuals or of companies who have invested in developing a product or a brand for commercialization. Some of these issues are regulated by law; others solely depend on ethical considerations. In some cases ethical and legal considerations merge but often they also contradict each other and narratives of justification are played out to convince the public to accept explanations as being in the interest of progress and development.

In order to illustrate these findings, I will compare and discuss four scenarios in which immaterial cultural goods are appropriated: first, the transformation of "traditional" art forms into media products by individual young artists; this example is based on extensive field research on cult associations and their artistic performances in south-west Cameroon between 1987 and 2008 (Röschenthaler 2011) and related scholarly literature on Mali and Algeria; second, the protection of local knowledge from commercial companies in Southern Africa; this example is taken from Jean and John Comaroff's work *Ethnicity Inc.* (2009); third, the copying of brand-names by small-scale pirates in Yaounde, based on field research on trade networks and entrepreneurship in Cameroon's capital between 2008 and 2014; and fourth, the virtual transfer of an entire village, the Austrian village of Hallstatt in 2011, by Chinese property investors, which has been widely discussed in newspaper articles online.

The chapter begins with a discussion of scholarly work on digital media and the conceptual and ethical premises of copying and appropriation. I will then elaborate the four examples to discuss legitimate and illegitimate ways of appropriation by different social actors, and end with a comparison of the critical issues that the examples unfolded and an examination of the ethical implications of copying. This approach demonstrates the importance of taking into account the perspectives and interests of the different actors involved and brings out the complexity that the study of digital media, the copying of immaterial cultural goods and property entails.

DIGITAL MEDIA, ETHICS, AND INTELLECTUAL PROPERTY RIGHTS

The rise of digital media from the 1980s onward, corresponding intellectual property rights and ethical questions concerning the appropriation, processing, and multiplication of immaterial goods including art forms, knowledge, brands, or architecture are closely interconnected. Roughly at the same time that digital media such as mobile phones, digital cameras, and the internet became accessible for larger parts of the population, an increasing judicialization of immaterial cultural goods took shape, followed by a growing piracy activity and consequently attempts to fight it. A brief look at some aspects of scholarly discussion of these issues reveals that this process entails contradictions and ethical concerns that are complex and challenging to solve.

Multiple Uses of Digital Media

Digital media require gadgets that are able to encode information in a format that can be transmitted over a computer network, including text, images, sound, and design. They make it much easier than analogue technologies to store, modify, and distribute information. Digital technology allows people to communicate and exchange information or images easily across the world and brings audiences from different parts of the world closer to each other even across language barriers (Federman, 2006).

Most scholarly literature on digital media has focused on the social aspects of digital media and the opportunities of global connectivity. Digital media has cultivated new forms of communication and established ways to articulate collective interests and life projects. Gabriella Coleman questions, however, that these media are actually able to produce widely "shared subjectivity" or a "life world that might characterize a vast population" (2010, p.490). In this context, the study of local actors' perspectives provides a powerful means to counterbalance generalizing imaginaries of the digital media producing global communities and the universality of the digital experience. Coleman (2010, p.489) advocates an approach that "provincializes digital media", a term that she borrows from Dipesh Chacrabarty (2000), and which highlights a focus on the actual concerns and perspectives of the different actors who use digital media in their daily lives.

The influence of digital (and other) media largely depends on the purpose for which they are used (Coombe, 1997). Some scholars have noted the hopes that are connected with digital media, as with independent media more generally, to become an instrument for enhancing democracy and civil society (Athique, 2013; Hydén, Leslie, & Ogundimo 2002), others found that media might be used to consolidate radical religious movements (Eisenlohr, 2011) or be implemented to serve contexts of violence and civil war (Gewald, 2004; Bräuchler, 2013), and, in the case of digital media, of cybercrime and surveillance (Atique, 2013). As the ownership of digital media offers users opportunities to actively participate in the creation of media products, governments are concerned to regulate the use and control of media and media content, of images and artistic creation, as social media challenge state power with ever new means (Gosh, 2013, pp.65-66). As digital media offer platforms and arenas for different interest groups to present themselves and their concerns and call for support, they opened the way for a dynamic field of media production and interaction, and revolutionized industries such as journalism, music production, advertising, and the reproduction of images. These opportunities have created numerous opportunities to make a living but also multiple challenges for dealing with intellectual property rights that need adaptation and are not well-prepared to cope with these new evolutions.

Increasing Judicialization

When the digital media began to proliferate, scholars began to note an increasing judicialization in all domains of life (Smiers, 1999). The ownership and use of immaterial cultural goods and artistic production became to an ever greater extent the object of legal regulations and commercial interests (Coombe, 1998; Cowan, 2006; Cowan et al. 2001). In the debates surrounding such ownership issues, intellectual property rights have become a key concept. Hence, intellectual property has moved from its formerly exclusive location within legal discourse into much wider public prominence (Hirsch & Strathern, 2004, p.3). Jean and John Comaroff attribute this shift to the prevalence of the neoliberal order (2000, 2009; see also Coombe 2003), which appears to favour the appropriation and control of artistic products by big companies that earn a fortune from the rights to immaterial property (Benthall, 1999; Smiers, 1999). As such ideologies are globally distributed through the media, Thomas and Nyamnjoh (2007: 14) wonder whether increasing privatization is the inevitable fate of a connected world (see also Röschenthaler & Diawara, 2016).

From the seventeenth century onward, intellectual property rights were created to encourage creative actors to make their inventions and creations available for circulation in the society. The law allowed publishers to produce books and later music, and entrepreneurs to manufacture patented commodities and disseminate them on the market. Specific laws would guarantee the inventor or creator a share from the profits that producers or entrepreneurs made with their creation. Such rights in intellectual property were conceptualized as exclusive rights of individuals, and therefore each work required an individual creator or inventor who was entitled to receive such a share. In actual practice, the cultural landscape, however, is by far more complex. Immaterial cultural goods in many cases cannot easily be attributed to one single individual as no art work is fully original (Gosh 2013, p.64; Röschenthaler & Diawara, 2016).

Taking into account these challenges, concepts such as cultural heritage and folklore have been created to preserve long-standing traditions in the name of humankind. They particularly focus on (immaterial) cultural goods that are not easily attributable to an individual but are rather ascribed to entire ethnic groups or communities. However, these "traditions", presumably preserved for generations, have been constantly transformed and altered by "their owners", particularly after they have been nominated as intangible cultural heritage (for an illustrative example see De Jong, 2007). Opportunities to claim ownership of such a "tradition" as cultural heritage has in many cases led to an increase in identity politics when communities took this as a welcome means to draw attention to their interests in the states they live in (Comaroff & Comaroff 2000; Geschiere 2009).

Increasing judicialization is often promoted with the moral argument that cultural heritage needs to be preserved in the name of humankind and inventors and artistic creators should receive a certain percentage from the profits that others make with their work. These arguments advance that exclusive property rights are the basis of development and commonwealth. However, at times they seem to be more in favour of entrepreneurs than of creators. Historically, this concept came up during the times of industrial revolution, when John Locke promoted his labour value theory, which postulates the idea that unclaimed land and unclaimed things should become the property of those who had invested their labour in its development and creation. John Locke did not mean the farmer who works his field but the entrepreneurs who needed land to set up plantations and factories and also a labour force that would help them produce the new consumer goods (Greenfield 2014). Actually, governments have an interest to control intellectual property circulation, receive taxes and promote investment. The same applies to immaterial cultural goods that are increasingly judicialized in a similar process under the intellectual property law, a process that Gosh calls "imperialist globalization" and that tends to empower big companies and media giants who work to prevent creative art (2013: 66).

The narrative of justification that accompanies this process plays with double standards. It claims that the artists should be rewarded for their creative work, but those who profit are usually the producers who have invested in the production, multiplication, and marketing. When governments launch the fight against pirates and counterfeiting, they do this in the name of the poor artists and inventors that were robbed of their due share from their creation, and pirates should be persecuted because they profited from work that they did not create themselves.

The appropriation of a small part of a musical piece can even provoke a lawsuit despite the fact that entire musical and literary genres depend on copying, mixing, transforming, and collage (Anon. 2005; McLeod & Kuenzli 2011; Mose 2016) and that all inventions and creations are based on a cultural legacy that has been elaborated and developed for generations (Gosh 2013; Röschenthaler & Diawara 2016). Similar multi-layered complexity occurs in oral literary practices, the very art of which may consist precisely in the citation, modification, blending, and variation of other literary works (Barber 1999). In anthropology, it is above all Karin Barber (2003) who has pointed out that all texts are made from other texts (oral or written), and always build upon existing ideas and interpretations (see also Barber 2007; Finnegan 2007: 137).

Piracy and Efforts to Fight It

Property rights jurisdiction faces immense difficulty to distinguish legitimate ownership from illegitimate piracy given the multifaceted interconnections and entangled genealogies of artistic creations. Notwithstanding, an entire intellectual property defence industry has emerged, especially in the domain of digital media and biotechnology (Johns 2010: 498), which seems to evaluate and treat small pirates often very differently from big pirates. McLeod and Kuenzli rightly note that "by threatening internet service providers and search engines, intellectual property can simply make you disappear if they do not like what you have to say. Such obliterations were much more difficult to accomplish in a non-digital world" (2011: 17).

Throughout the history of thought and culture, practices of copying, appropriation, and collage were widespread. People in different regions have at various times developed their own ideas of these practices and also found ways to regulate and negotiate the appropriation of immaterial cultural goods. In all cultures, historically and at present, goods of particular value are counterfeited for which there is a bustling market. In Egypt it was cults, in the Middle Ages relics, later art work and at present brand name products and software (Jones 1994). In south-west Cameroon it was cult associations for which the use rights and the knowledge of their functioning had to be obtained (Röschenthaler 2011).

The copying of immaterial goods is perceived to be a problematic practice when individuals (or governments) begin to complain about the alienation of what they consider their property. Kavita Phillip (2005) and Ravi Sundaram (2010) noted that piracy is the necessary twin of intellectual property laws. There is no theft without property, i.e. there is no plagiarism (Theisohn 2009) and no piracy (Johns 2009; Sundaram 2010) without rights in immaterial cultural goods and no fake without an original (Jones 1994; Sundaram 2010) without rights in immaterial cultural goods and no fake without an original (Jones 1994). In this context, McLeod and Kuenzli (2011: 12) who studied collage practices noticed that "courts and various culture industries treat similar activities across media very differently. This also shows that art and law don't mix (pun intended)." In Asian economies pirated brand name products have even merged with originals to such an extent that they can no longer be separated from each other (see for example Chang 2004). Arjun Gosh also observes that "in the digital world, the original and the copy are the same (2013: 65), which particularly complicates the ethical dimension of copying.

Judicial Contradictions and Ethical Concerns

As noted earlier, the fruits of the entire history of thought and cultural production are based on the creations of previous generations, individuals, and communities. Controversial issues about their ownership seem to arise only with the emergence of economic asymmetries that are not accompanied by acts of redistribution. As long as no one profited from artistic or inventive creations more than others, immaterial cultural goods have not become a question of exclusive property.

Author rights and copyrights were introduced as legal instruments to face the increased literary production following the invention of the printing press in an attempt to regulate the relationship between the author and the publisher (author's rights) as well as the relationship between publishers among themselves (copyright) (Gosh 2013). Legal regulations governing immaterial cultural goods were actually never able to face the complexities of cultural practices but remained imperfect means to secure economic interests.

Among scholars, no clear opinion prevails as to what extent goods should be subject to regulations. Some argue that creators have to be protected legally, whereas others advocate that entire musical styles are endangered by the same regulations and that individual cultural elements ought to be freely accessible in the creative commons. Norms, standards, and laws are confronted with each other in the form of unwritten rules that fall in the domain of ethical considerations, and the form of written laws that become meaningful through the interpretation of a judge. Whereas in the music industry lawyers interpret the law very restrictively, in the fashion sector it is much more difficult to find evidence that a design has actually been copied, depending to the extent to which colours and designs have been altered. Hence, the discussion about intellectual property is guided by moral arguments of whether law and judges follow ethical criteria of social well-being in their decisions or rather defend economic interests and political considerations.

INTELLECTUAL PROPERTY AND THE OWNERSHIP OF CULTURE

The more general observations noted so far will now be illustrated with several examples from Africa and one from Austria. Due to the liberalization of the markets and the media reforms of the 1980s and 1990s in most African countries, independent media, internet facilities, and affordable digital gadgets such as mobile phones, photo and video cameras, and computers imported from Asia have become widely accessible in urban as well as increasingly also in rural areas. During the same time frame in which these media began to proliferate, intellectual property rights with all their contradictions have become a prominent issue (Röschenthaler & Diawara 2016).

Media in Africa might be shaped by external conditions (Almouza 2005: 351) but important to study is how they are utilized by African actors in often very creative ways for various purposes. However, these usages often also create dissent, as there are different interests at stake in a community, when, for example, individual artists register their art work as their intellectual property at the expense of other social groups who previously were entitled to perform such art and who fear to lose their privileges or even their livelihood. In the next subsection I will briefly illustrate such conflicting situations with examples of art productions from different African countries. These examples have in common that a younger generation of artists performs and commercializes established art forms with the help of digital media to which they, according to intellectual property law, have acquired the exclusive authors' rights. In contrast, the older generation of artists is unable to profit from the law and the new technology.

Who Owns Music and Performance? Case Studies from Africa

The first example is a performance artist in south-west Cameroon. He performs dances and masquerades taken from local cult associations of his village, which his team films and enriches with urban accessories, dance styles, and rhythms. The artist registers the DVDs that he produces in the studio with the Cameroonian office of authors' rights before he sells them. When the cult association owners got to know about his project, they summoned him to the village court and accused him of copying insignia and masquerades, which he did not have the right to wear and perform. He managed to convince the village court that he did not make profit from using the cult association insignia and secret knowledge but that he was reviving and preserving traditional dances. In the end, he did not have to pay damage to the cult association owners. Cult associations have, however, the power to force people to do this when they feel that copiers unlawfully appropriated their performance, because, as the owners argued, they had invested money and goods in the acquisition of the rights to own the cult and therefore all those who wished to perform it, had to acquire these rights as well (Röschenthaler 2011, 2016). Hence the performance artist had to cope with both property regimes, the local regime of the cult association owners and the national intellectual property law.

Similar cases are known from other African countries; just that in these cases there is no local regime of rights in immaterial cultural goods that would enable the older generation to force copiers to pay damages to them. In Algeria, Jane Goodman studied the rich repertoire of songs that rural women consider their domain. For generations, the women preserved these songs by teaching them to their daughters. With the introduction of digital media and the awareness of authors' rights, however, young urban artists began to interpret these songs, register them under their names and sell the products as CDs or DVDs on the market. The elderly women did not actually lose money but felt that they would deserve a share of the revenues. The French intellectual property law (on which the Algerian law is based), however, does not consider such claims (Goodman 2005). Mamadou Diawara (2016) made similar observations in Mali where the playing of music and the recitation of praise songs is the privilege of certain families (*griots*). Young artists, often from non-*griot* families, have gradually appropriated these songs without taking the pain to receive training from *griots*. They also registered their work under their name and sold the product. The normal procedure would have been that young artists from *griot* families invested several years in training to learn the trade rightfully. For the *griot* families such trends are bitter, moreover as their privilege of singing and praising for a particular family has gradually diminished since colonial times and with this also their means of making a living.

Not only performance and singing experience such challenges, but also other art work. The Ghanaian *Kente* weavers and *Adinkra* cloth producers are a group of professional weavers who have for centuries specialized in producing woven cloth with characteristic design patterns that are easily recognizable as such. During the past decades, they noticed that the demand in original *Kente* and *Adinkra* cloths diminished and that Ghanaian migrants in urban centers and the American diaspora began to copy the designs and sell cloth and decorated tourist souvenirs made from cheaper imported Asian cloth. The weavers called upon the Ghanaian government to help them protect their designs from being copied and marketed by (mostly) their compatriots, but their query cannot be dealt with by intellectual property law that only concerns individual creation and not group ownership of generation-old designs. The state has not helped the weavers; it rather considers the designs a national cultural heritage (Boateng 2011).

In these examples, young artists use digital media to record and commercialize songs or designs that they have not created as such but only appropriated and interpreted. Their art is protected by intellectual property rights, which entitles them to receive a certain amount of revenues. It allows individuals to profit from the immaterial cultural legacy, which specific families, elderly women, certain social groups, or the state, claim as their heritage. This situation raises ethical concerns for which intellectual property law has no solution, as it is not meant to protect the immaterial rights of entire groups whose immaterial cultural goods have been commercialized. Hence, in actual practice various forms of group property exist that are neither exclusive property of individuals, of a community or ethnic group nor unclaimed property. These practices entail creativity, skills, and knowledge, some of which are kept secret and considered an asset, as is known from trade guilds in the European Middle Ages (Somers 1996).

Branding Identities and Securing Local Knowledge in Southern Africa

As international and national legal regulations have difficulties to cope with group and subgroup rights that are neither fully communal nor exclusively individual, the World Intellectual Property Organization (WIPO), which is responsible for the protection and preservation of folklore, has envisaged means to protect "communal goods" or "communal property". As the examples illustrate, however, immaterial cultural goods are often not communal property but form part of a more complex system of subgroup ownerships. Notably Michael Brown discussed ways of how such immaterial cultural goods could be protected, not as folklore but as intellectual property (1998, 2003) so that local communities could protect their knowledge and defend it against commercial interests that profited from selling products that were developed on the basis of other peoples' local knowledge. Jean and John Comaroff (2009) indeed investigated cases in which communities such as the Bafokeng kingdom in South Africa managed to register as an enterprise due to which they successfully won lawsuits to recuperate their ancestral land that had been taken from them by the Apartheid regime and profit from the natural resources on that land.

The San in Southern Africa also registered themselves as a company, a legal personality, and managed, with the help of a lawyer, to win a lawsuit against the pharmaceutical company Unilever, which intended to appropriate the knowledge of plants for commercialization without sharing the profits with them. The San were successful in protecting their local plant knowledge against commercial companies that had turned into biopirates. The project of the San was, however, a complicated venture. To begin with, the San people had to depict themselves for the first time in history as one group with a common interest, as they had to decide who belongs to this group and who not. They used this newly created ethnic identity as a cultural resource, which also added value to their cultural heritage and local knowledge. They forced Unilever to buy the patent and return them eight percent of the profits that the company made with the product that they developed on the basis of the San's knowledge of a plant, the Hoodia cactus. The company tried to argue that the San had not invested any money in the research and production of the plant, whereas – and this reminds of John Locke's support of investors – the company had invested its means to make the product marketable. However, it is far from clear whether the San have invested nothing in the knowledge that they have of local plants. In the end, the San won the case and received 30,000 dollars due to the moral injustices that the San had experienced since colonial times, as pointed out by the lawyer.

With the lawsuit, the San have not only gained control of their territory but also won the case with a moral claim that it would be more than just to make the San as a marginalized local group participate in the gains of the big company practicing biopiracy (Comaroff & Comaroff 2009). This success was backed by social media that created a global awareness of the San's project and their condition of life, as numerous internet sites document (see Comaroff & Comaroff 2009: 174-179). The successful lawsuit of the San is an example that illustrates how a lawyer found a pathway to create a legal personality that was recognizable by law and a judge advocated the moral claim of the local ethnic group against a large financially powerful company. The women in Algeria, the *griots* in Mali, the *Kente* and *Adinkra* producers and the cult association owners in the south-west of Cameroon have not found a way yet to protect their immaterial cultural goods against appropriation by commercial interests on an national or international level even though or because they have to negotiate with the youth from their own community.

Who Is the Pirate? Copying Music and Brand Name Products in Cameroon

Piracy, the twin of intellectual property rights (Sundaram 2010), gained in importance in African countries when individuals were able to purchase affordable digital media gadgets imported from Asia. Not only musicians utilize them to produce and multiply their products, but also various individuals who copy the work of artists in backyard home factories. Different scholarly discourses have emerged commenting upon these activities. Some insist that unregulated multiplication of artists' work democratizes its consumption and enhances the artists' fame whereas others argue that the music branch is dying down due to piracy and that artists, producers, and the state lose great amounts of money (Röschenthaler & Diawara 2016). These moral arguments illustrate that divergent interests are at stake that became prominent with the growing attention that is paid to intellectual property and that these regulations are beneficial for some but not for others.

The Cameroonian performance artist mentioned earlier acquired digital media to produce copies of his own DVDs for sale, but soon also his fans did the same. He explained that it is above all his own fans who acquire and distribute his DVDs as copies via mobile phones because for them it is almost a duty to do this, as they feel they have to increase the renown of their star. They also upload his art work to internet platforms such as YouTube so that the clips are accessible to a worldwide audience. His fans do not feel doing something wrong but rather help to grow his fame. Hence, the artist sells his new media products as quickly as possible to be faster than the pirates in order to face the growing amounts copying (Röschenthaler 2016).

On the one hand, the sale of the pirated products enhances the renown of artists as their work is far more widely disseminated than would be possible with the formal distribution of "originals" as most people would not be able to buy the originals and perhaps not even get to know about them. On the other hand, there is evidence that musicians and their producers cannot survive from their art if it is irregularly copied and distributed. In Cameroon, hardly any music producers can survive for longer periods of time (Tcheuyap 2016). Numerous examples from other countries are known as well, such as the Senegalese artist and entrepreneur Youssou Ndour who had to shut down his music production company in Dakar due to piracy (Wane 2016).

Pirates are more reluctant to copy the music of local artists and the brands of local merchants, however, than those of foreign artists and company owners. Sellers in the central market of Ouagadougou, for example, explained in 2012 that they would first try to sell the original DVDs of local artists, and not the copies, but that they did not see any ethical problem in copying and selling foreign music as these foreign musicians would not immediately face losses due to these sales, particularly as they did not know about it. This observation is also valid for brand name products. However, the sellers' argument does not only express solidarity with compatriots but also the fear that illegal copies of local products are more severely persecuted than foreign ones.

Different from copying music and videos which can be accomplished in back yard factories, the copying of brand name products requires larger amounts of capital that the small local pirates normally do not have. Copies of brand name products are ordered by local entrepreneurs from factories in China who are ready to produce cheap goods. Any entrepreneur with sufficient capital can create the design of a brand name that he wishes to order and send it to his supplier in China by email attachment, pay an advance, and a few weeks later the product arrives ready for sale, often with the complicity of customs officers (Röschenthaler 2016). These products include highly-valued brand names of hand bags, clothing, shoes, and also foods such as powdered milk, tomato paste, toothpaste, or tooth brushes of which about a dozen different brands are available in local markets. Some of these products are available in original quality as well as in different lower qualities. Some of these are almost exact doubles; others have incidental or intentional orthographical errors or slightly divergent designs. Due to these copies, the promise attached to the brand name and its package content no longer helps customers to trust its quality but the sign value of the brand name still functions to enhance the social standing of customers, at least at first sight.

Consumers might have difficulties to identify original and copy, but they can get an idea of the quality from the price and sellers readily explain that they have different qualities of a product in their shelves. A street vendor near the Central Market in Yaounde, for example, who sold a good twenty brands of tooth paste, batteries, mobile phones, and soaps in his mobile kiosk, explained that he had three different types of Colgate tooth brushes and Signal tooth paste. He stated that it was possible to know the difference by studying the price, package, orthographic errors, the colour of the paste, and its taste. Actually, most brand name products are available in three qualities: the expensive original, a less expensive copy of good quality and a cheap copy of less good quality. These choices cater to customers with different budgets. The customers tell the vendor how much they want to pay or which quality they wish to acquire. The street vendors obviously work together with one or several shops or warehouses behind the sidewalk. In case a customer asks for a different product or quality, the street vendor disappears for a few minutes to return with the desired product.

The products that are copied or "pirated" are products that are selling well. There are no pirated copies of products for which there is no demand (Jones 1984). In the economic domain, brand names were originally made to distinguish quality (Chang 2004) and add value to manufactured products guaranteeing their quality and singularity in comparison to other brands. In this function brands operate as media of exchange between companies and consumers (Foster 2008: 12). The value of brand name products is further enhanced by advertisement in the media. Hence, "value is based on the readiness of consumers to pay for the renown attached to the brand" (Foster 2008: 15) and many brands have accumulated considerable value due to the investments of their owners. Copying a brand name and selling the product divert the profits to another individual (the pirate) and in case the product content is of low quality, this significantly reduces the value of the brand, as rumours emerge and consumers quickly refrain from purchasing it.

Lawsuits about brand name products are still quite rare in African countries. This is due to several reasons. In Mali and Cameroon, for example, most of the lawsuits that have been explained to me by merchants or are documented by the *Organisation Africaine de la Propriété Intellectuelle* (OAPI) have been fought between local merchants. However, to be able to win a case, a merchant needs a certain standing and means. In Cameroon as well as in Mali, merchants strongly advocated for solidarity among fellow merchants and were ready to involve the court only to tell competitors a lesson. After the decision, they preferred to regulate the issue among themselves, saying the pirate was their compatriot and fellow merchant who was trying to survive, as other traders as well, and should not be forced to lose more capital than necessary. They preferred to destroy the pirated packages but allowed the pirate to sell the product itself without the added value of the brand, as soon as the pirate promised not to copy the products again. Merchants argued that the great number of factories in China would produce anything that African entrepreneurs would order, and so the solidarity could only come from one's own people and not from the foreigners.

The examples discussed so far entail the creation of art work and brand names in which digital media are an important tool for production, global distribution, and in many cases moral support. They also entail ethical dimensions of the copying of immaterial cultural goods that belong to compatriots. In the case of artists, copying products advertises and increases the renown of their owner even though it might reduce their revenues from originals and the income of producers and the brands' value. In spite of the attempts of international organizations and governments to promote the usefulness of intellectual property law, only few African entrepreneurs are able to successfully defend their immaterial property. The following example from a European country illustrates another dimension of the complexity of immaterial property and the ethical implications of copying.

CHINESE COPY AUSTRIAN VILLAGE: THE CASE OF HALLSTATT

Hallstatt is a small village in the Salzkammergut of Austria, a region that is known for its salt mining, which began 7000 years ago. The salt brought wealth and was widely exported to places as far as to the Orient (Hallstatt 3, May 26, 2012). The entire area, including Hallstatt, has been nominated as a cultural heritage site by the UNESCO in 1997.[1] Its houses are situated between mountains and a lake, and some are built on stilts on the shores. Due to its idyllic setting, Hallstatt has attracted numerous tourists, including many Asians, for the past decades. It is also the site where the South Korean soap "Spring Waltz" was shot (Hallstatt 6, October 24, 2014). Notwithstanding the opportunities tourism offers, many Hallstatt youths have migrated to other areas with more promising employment. In 1951, the village still counted 1422 inhabitants, while it was left with only 780 inhabitants in 2012. The scarcity of space and restrictions due to its cultural heritage status contributed to the youths' exodus as conservation prescriptions prevent the construction of new homes (Hallstatt 5, June 2, 2012).

The quiet routine of Hallstatt's daily life was interrupted when its inhabitants incidentally got to know from a Chinese tourist that Chinese entrepreneurs had copied their entire village in 2011, including not only all the houses, the street, the church, the marketplace with pond, angel's statues, restaurants, hotels with names, but also the lake with its boats and the mountains surrounding it. Chinese investors had measured the entire village one to one and constructed a second Hallstatt in China. This Hallstatt clone now forms part of the town of Boluo which is situated near the four million boom town Huizhou in Guangdong Province.

Digital media had enabled the Chinese investors to take photographs of every detail without attracting attention. The inhabitants of the original Hallstatt were perplexed that this had happened without their notice. They were also annoyed that they had not even been informed about the Chinese project. Since the day they discovered that the village was cloned, nothing has remained the same in the original Hallstatt. Newspapers began to comment on the issue.[2] One newspaper reported that the pastor of Hallstatt worried that the copying of the church would desacralize the house of God, and the owner of a shop complained that her brand name, which was her intellectual property now also served in China. People strongly felt that their identity was at stake (Hallstatt 4, June 2, 2012).

After a period of initial irritation, the mayor of Hallstatt decided to turn the vice into a virtue and began to advocate for the advantages that the cloning would bring. He insisted that the inhabitants should not worry about their identity but accept that their being copied had positive effects: it would enhance tourism and make the village more attractive as tourists would want to see the original, which would bring the blessings of money to the place. They should accept the brand of their village as an asset and understand that their village was so important that other people had even considered copying it.

The Hallstatt double – the newspapers talk of a clone – was created by the Chinese investor Minmetals Land Inc. They measured all the houses and shops, but historical accurateness did not seem to have mattered that much, as they envisaged an ideal European village with apartments and houses for sale to wealthy Chinese. Such Hallstatt clone houses are sold for the equivalent of between 300.000 and 600.000 Euros each. The villas of 400 square meters, however, did not sell as quickly as expected, at least in 2012 when the village was officially opened to the public (Hallstatt 3, 26 May 2012).

The Hallstatt clone was inaugurated on June 2, 2012. It had taken Minmetals only one year to raise the Hallstatt clone, including the creation of the lake and the mountains (Hallstatt 3, May 26, 2012). Meanwhile, the mayor of the Austrian Hallstatt had contacted the Chinese investors and been invited for the festivities. He came with his family, journalists, and an orchestra who performed in Austrian miners' uniforms. He also signed a contract promoting cultural exchange and a friendship agreement with the city of Huizhou. However, so far no Chinese delegation has ever visited the original Hallstatt. At the opening the mayor stated that he was proud that his village was copied in China. However, when the Austrians visited the clone, they discovered that the birth house of Mozart, which is originally in Salzburg was included (Hallstatt 2, February 1, 2012) as well as a red British phone cell, palm trees, gold fish in the pond at the market place and the restaurant Feinschmecker Treffpankt (sic) served sea food, which is not really an Austrian speciality. The church had become a gigantic luxury apartment complex (Hallstatt 3, May 26, 2012)

Since then, the number of tourists has indeed persistently increased. In 2015, 600.000 visitors were counted in Hallstatt. The increase of tourists divided the village into those who are happy making money with it, who include the mayor and the souvenir shop, hotel and restaurant owners, and those who suffer from it. These are the remaining inhabitants who are not involved in tourism and have to endure the masses of people invading the village street, taking photographs of everything, and even intrude into private property. Most tourists are interested in enjoying the idyllic Austrian landscape with the beautiful mountains and the lake, whereas meeting the real inhabitants and their problems is not their aim. Villagers feel like "living in an open air museum" (Hallstatt 7, October 24, 2014). These villagers created an association to fight mass tourism and the sale of Hallstatt. They are not against tourism as such but against the unregulated arrival of bus loads full of tourists who for fifty minutes invade the village, have a coffee, and buy souvenirs before they leave again. They would prefer tourists who come for several days, stay in the hotels, and enjoy the place in a more sustainable manner, which could also create more employment for the villagers. Tourists should have the time to visit the salt mining sites and the shrine with the painted skulls. But even the mayor who is promoting tourism in the village, stated that he does not wish for more copies of Hallstatt in the future, for example in the US or the Emirates (Hallstatt 5, June 2, 2012). One clone that advertises the original village was enough for him.

What, however, about the rights of the Hallstatt people in the originality of their village? The mayor had asked the UNESCO for a statement, but the heritage specialists did not find any contradictions in the fact that the Chinese had copied part of the site (Hallstatt 3, May 26, 2012). Constructing buildings from photographs seems to be legal, however, the owners should have been given the opportunity to grant permission that their homes were measured (Laylin 2011). Would it not still make sense to argue that the people of Hallstatt ought to participate in the profits that the Chinese investor is making, which derive from the aura of authenticity and the added value that the original houses convey to the cloned buildings? Hallstatt would then be able to receive revenues from the Chinese twice, once through the tourists who visit the authentic Hallstatt and then through an agreement with the investor to share with them the massive profit he makes with the added value and the authenticity of the property of Hallstatt's inhabitants. These shares would be divided among the villagers, so that also those who do not directly profit from tourism would be encouraged to accept that masses of people invade and traverse the place every day.

ETHICAL IMPLICATIONS OF BRANDING AND COPYING

Both the village of Hallstatt and the San's local knowledge are subject to the appropriation by commercial interests from abroad without supplying them with part of their profit at first. To be able to receive a share of the profits, the San agreed upon a unifying ethnic identity and registered this group as a legal body. With the help of a lawyer, the San were able to defend their interests and their rights in local knowledge, whereas the people of Hallstatt also had the feeling that part of their identity was taken away, but so far did not proceed to claim their immaterial assets, the Hallstatt brand, with legal means as their property.

Hallstatt could have claimed – at least in theory – a moral right of entitlement to a share of the profits the Chinese investment company makes in China with the clone of their village due to its aura of an idyllic site that is associated in the Chinese imagination with beauty and authenticity. Although Hallstatt's continuity is endangered as more and more people abandon the village, the people of Hallstatt did not consider such a claim a realistic opportunity as this might also disturb the flow of tourists coming to the place, according to some newspaper reports. In contrast, the San people – and many others in different parts of the world – were inspired by international organizations supported by communities in social media that encouraged them to raise claims to be protected as indigenous people and ask for compensation (Comaroff & Comaroff 2009). The argument that pharmaceutical companies would earn a lot of money with the San's local knowledge is indeed comparable to the profits that the Chinese make with the clone of Hallstatt, but one could also argue that tourism brings sufficient reward to some of its inhabitants.

From a legal perspective, copying entire villages does not seem to pose a judicial problem as the architects are no longer living nor often even known. That an entire village has been measured and copied might be unique, as some newspapers claim, however, architectural copying is very widespread. Copying Hallstatt belongs to a trend in China of rebuilding various parts of the world. There are copies of the Bavarian Anting near Shanghai, the Neuschwanstein Castle, the Tour d'Eiffel, and the Swiss town Interlaken in China, with a daily carnival manifestation (Hallstatt 1, June 17, 2011). There are more than 97 reproductions of Venice all over the world, from Asia to South America (Venice 2008).[3]

However, the Hallstatt clone also includes the brands of the shop owners that are registered as their own intellectual property. If Hallstatt would have had a Louis Vuitton company and these products were sold in the Hallstatt clone, the situation would probably be different. Hence, if copying of places is legally possible, one wonders why there is such a moral outrage about the copying of music and brand names, and even of companies profiting from the local knowledge of ethnic minorities.

At this point it is important to remember that the intellectual property rights as we know them today have been introduced at a certain historical time in specific cultural contexts and countries, with important variations. At first they only concerned authors' rights and publishers' rights (copyright). Only later, rights in music, brand names, and patents were added (see Röschenthaler & Diawara 2016). With increasing judicialization it is quite possible that sooner or later also the copying of entire architectural ensembles (not only individual buildings) will fall under such legal protection. The fact that huge profits can be made with the reproduction of architecture to which popular imaginaries of authenticity and originality are attached that have actually become the brand of these places and with which these places also advertise their uniqueness for tourism suggest a step in that direction. Claims to property rights in immaterial goods are proliferating despite the fact that, as shown in this chapter, creations of individuals and also groups always are built upon the achievements and the legacies of generations before them and continue to be in constant transformation.

Two moral claims are connected with intellectual property law. One is in favour of entrepreneurs and the other in favour of marginalized groups. As intellectual property law turns immaterial cultural goods into intellectual property for a limited time span for commercial exploitation, it is built upon the idiom of investment of labour and capital to justify ownership. Ownership is legitimized by the investment of creativity an artist or an entrepreneur has made in the production of a product and the creation of a brand, which justifies protecting his ventures. Intellectual property rights are normally supported by governments who take advantage from the opportunity to regulate immaterial cultural goods, support companies and draw taxes from regulation and law enforcement. Its popular narrative of justification is in support of poor artists who cannot survive when their art work is copied by ruthless pirates and it also argues that the government is losing huge amounts of money due to copying. As mentioned at the beginning of this chapter, however, the chasing of small pirates is often represented as being much more urgent than that of big companies, and it is far from evident that the sums proclaimed could indeed be rescued when piracy was successfully combated.

The second claim is in favour of ethnic minorities and other groups whose concerns are not well represented by the legal regulations. Their rights however are differently formulated as they are often seen as "traditional", delivered from generation to generation without changes, and their immaterial assets belonging to the entire ethnic group as a whole. As this chapter has shown, immaterial cultural goods rarely belong to an entire ethnic group. San had to form such a group first and have found a solution by registering as a company. This way, they not only successfully fought for a percentage of profits that companies gain from their local knowledge but also for the recovery of their land. For *Kente* and *Adinkra*, songs and dances from the community, or from the repertoire of specific families or cult associations, no solution has yet been found.

So far, the intellectual property law protects only individual interpreters who in this way profit as individuals from the rich heritage of their group. Group rights are difficult to protect with this law, whether it is their cultural heritage or their brands. Cultural heritage conventions and collective human rights address group rights but conceptualize the addressees of such rights in terms of entire ethnic groups, which, in many cases, would open up new opportunities to claim revenues for individuals who were formerly not involved in the production of the immaterial cultural goods. As with artistic creations, individuals or companies have to be acknowledged as creators of a brand, whose claims of ownership can then be defended in the case of illegal copying. The narrative of justification for registering brand name products promotes the same idea of investment for which in some cases their taxes are reduced and they receive protection from the state. But only those who have sufficient means are able to protect and defend their creations, brands, or local knowledge in court.

Depending on the advantages they see (or do not see) in this regulation, some governments are very active in persecuting piracy while others remain rather reluctant or become active only due to international pressure. In some cases, appropriation is not only seen as an economic but also a political issue. Since antiquity, the appropriation of cultural heritage is a political strategy to demonstrate dominance, when cults and architectural items were appropriated and placed in the political centre (Harrison 1992).

The examples from Cameroon and Mali have shown that entrepreneurs and artists consider piracy a bad thing which they think is an expression of lacking solidarity, mainly when it concerns the brands or art work of local entrepreneurs or artists. Indeed court cases about brand name products concern cases in which local merchants of a sector sue each other when they discover that one of them pirated their product. Actually, an entrepreneur, similar to a Big Man (see also Röschenthaler and Schulz 2015), will only be successful in court if he has enough money and standing in society. The examples also show that acceptable behaviour depends largely on the perspective. What some consider being free advertisement – when fans widely distribute art work or Chinese copy a village and thereby bring more tourists to the place – can be regarded as piracy by others. The divergent interpretations also corroborate the idea that only valuable things are pirated and that without intellectual property there would be no piracy and without a complainant who notices an act of piracy or plagiarism a case does not become a lawsuit.

CONCLUSION

The examples discussed in this chapter highlight the complexity and partly contradicting implications of copying immaterial cultural goods and property and the role of digital media in this process, which greatly facilitated the copying, the distribution of the materialized products and presentations on the web to gain global support for a project. The examples also show that legal concepts often do not fit social realities of people on the ground. It is most often not the entire ethnic group nor an individual that was entitled to claim a cultural good of high value as their property, be it the songs that formed part of gendered musical repertoires in Algeria, of groups of craft specialists in Mali or Ghana, or that people created a local regime of rights in immaterial cultural goods in south-west Cameroon. Advocacy of legal regulations, however, regards exclusive property as the only way to resolve issues of intellectual property. If not the property of individuals, immaterial cultural goods are envisaged to be the legacy of a community or ethnic group, in the case of a cultural heritage or folklore with the objective to preserving this legacy in the name of humankind. Therefore, the San in Southern Africa had to find another legal means to claim a pecuniary compensation when they managed to register their ethnic groups as a company that was then entitled to receive revenues from other companies in exchange for the use of their local knowledge.

The promotion of intellectual property rights and the moral claims that are associated with them form part of the process of judicialization that has increased in the same time frame as digital media and technologies have become popular. The proliferation of copies that the introduction of digital media technology has encouraged enables users to quickly distribute such copies across large distances and share them with many people. However, digital technology enables also entrepreneurs and pirates to order goods with Chinese companies who normally carry out orders without worrying whether their customers have the right to do so. With increasing measures of control the sophistication of copying has increased too so that piracy becomes the necessary consequence of global manufacture and distribution of goods to the extent that original and copy are no longer distinguishable.

Moreover, the chapter has explained the conflicting economic and moral interests of actors that become virulent when national legal and local regulations are concerned but also between societies with diverging ethical or legal standards. Digital technology enables the creation of marketable products in a short time, has increased the speed of their marketing and their physical distribution, from which both merchants who produce original products as well as producers of copied goods profit. The highly morally connoted concept of piracy and the ethical claims attached to it are not self-evident. They form part of a discourse of property claims with which capitalist exploitation is justified and that regulate the access to material and immaterial goods in the world. Depending on the context, they can be free for everybody, communally-owned, owned by an ethnic group, a social category, the ruling elite, or the state, or by an individual or a company. The concept of property and the different property practices have to be seen in their historical and cultural context as well as the moral or ethical claims attached to them. Ethical questions of "correct" ways of dealing with the issue therefore cannot be universal or fixed but have to be adapted with time and the evolution of the property concepts and practices by local actors.

REFERENCES

Alzouma, G. (2005). Myths of digital technology in Africa: Leapfrogging development? *Global Media and Communication*, *1*(3), 339–356. doi:10.1177/1742766505058128

Anon., (2005). Jazz has got copyright law and that ain't good. *Harvard Law Review*, *118*(6), 1940–1961.

Atique, A. (2013). *Digital Media and Society: An Introduction*. Cambridge, UK: Polity Press.

Barber, K. (1999). Quotation in the constitution of Yorùbá oral texts. *Research in African Literatures*, *30*(2), 17–41.

Barber, K. (2003). Text and performance in Africa. *Bulletin of the School of Oriental and African Studies. University of London. School of Oriental and African Studies*, *66*(3), 324–333. doi:10.1017/S0041977X03000223

Benthall, J. (1999). The critique of intellectual property. *Anthropology Today*, *15*(6), 1–3. doi:10.2307/2678352

Boateng, B. (2011). *The copyright thing doesn't work here: Adinkra and Kente cloth and intellectual property in Ghana*. Minneapolis, MN: University of Minnesota Press. doi:10.5749/minnesota/9780816670024.001.0001

Boon, M. (2011). Digital mana: on the source of the infinite proliferation of copies in contemporary culture. In K. McLoed & R. Kuenzli (Eds.), *Cutting Across Media: Appropriation Art, Interventionist Collage and Copyright Law* (pp. 24–37). Durham, NC: Duke University Press. doi:10.1215/9780822393214-002

Bräuchler, B. (2013). *Cyberidentities at War: The Moluccan Conflict on the Internet*. New York: Berghahn Books.

Brown, M. (1998). Can culture be copyrighted? *Current Anthropology*, *39*(2), 193–222. doi:10.1086/204721

Brown, M. (2003). *Who Owns Native Culture?* Cambridge, MA: Harvard University Press.

Bruneau, M. (2010). Diasporas, transnational spaces and communities. In R. Bauböck & T. Faist (Eds.), *Diaspora and transnationalism: concepts, theories and methods* (pp. 35–49). Amsterdam: Amsterdam University Press.

Chakrabarty, D. (2000). *Provincializing Europe: Postcolonial Thought and Historical Difference*. Princeton, NJ: Princeton University Press.

Chang, H.-H. (2004). Fake logos, fake theory, fake globalisation. *Inter-Asia Cultural Studies*, *5*(2), 222–236. doi:10.1080/1464937042000236720

Coleman, E. G. (2010). Ethnographic approaches to digital media. *Annual Review of Anthropology*, *39*(1), 487–505. doi:10.1146/annurev.anthro.012809.104945

Comaroff, J., & Comaroff, J. (2000). *Millenial Capitalism and the Culture of Noeliberalism*. Durham, NC: Duke University Press.

Comaroff, J., & Comaroff, J. (2009). *Ethnicity, Inc*. Chicago: Chicago University Press. doi:10.7208/chicago/9780226114736.001.0001

Coombe, R. (1997). The demonic place of the 'not there': Trademark rumors in the postindustrial imaginary. In A. Gupta & J. Ferguson (Eds.), *Culture – power – place: Explorations in critical anthropology* (pp. 249–274). doi:10.1215/9780822382089-011

Coombe, R. (1998). *The cultural life of intellectual properties: Authorship, appropriation, and the law*. Durham, NC: Duke University Press. doi:10.1215/9780822382492

Coombe, R. (2003). Fear, hope and longing for the future of authorship and a revitalized public domain in global regimes of intellectual property. *De Paul Law Review*, *52*, 1–15.

Cowan, J. (2006). Culture and Rights after *Culture and Rights*. *American Anthropologist*, *108*(1), 9–24. doi:10.1525/aa.2006.108.1.9

Cowan, J., Dembour, M.-B., & Wilson, R. (Eds.). (2001). *Culture and rights: Anthropological perspectives*. Cambridge, UK: Cambridge University Press. doi:10.1017/CBO9780511804687

De Jong, F. (2007). A masterpiece of masquerading: Contradictions of conservation in intangible heritage. In F. de Jong & M. Rowlands (Eds.), *Reclaiming heritage: Alternative imaginaries of memory in West Africa* (pp. 161–184). Walnut Creek: Left Coast Press.

Diawara, M. (2016). Breaking the contract? Handling intangible cultural goods among different generations in Mali. In U. Röschenthaler & M. Diawara (Eds.), Copyright Africa: How intellectual property, media and markets transform immaterial cultural goods. Canon Pyon: Sean Kingston.

Eisenlohr, P. (2011). The anthropology of media and the question of ethnic and religious pluralism. *Social Anthropology*, *19*(1), 40–55. doi:10.1111/j.1469-8676.2010.00136.x

Federman, M. (2006). *The cultural paradox of the global village*. Keynote Speech at McLuhan Programme in Culture and Technology, University of Toronto.

Finnegan, R. (2007). *The oral and beyond: Doing things with words in Africa*. Oxford, UK: James Currey & Chicago University Press.

Foster, R. (2008). Commodities, brands, love and kula. *Anthropological Theory*, *8*(1), 9–25. doi:10.1177/1463499607087492

Geschiere, P. (2009). *The perils of belonging: Autochthony, citizenship, and exclusion in Africa & Europe*. Chicago: The University of Chicago Press. doi:10.7208/chicago/9780226289663.001.0001

Gewald, J.-B. (2004). Global media and violence in Africa. In W. van Binsbergen & R. van Dijk (Eds.), *Situating globality: African agency in the appropriation of global culture* (pp. 90–106). Leiden: Brill.

Goodman, J. (2005). *Berber culture on the world stage: From village to video*. Bloomington, IN: Indiana University Press.

Gosh, A. (2013). Censorship through copyright: From print to digital media. *Social Scientist*, *41*(1-2), 41–58.

Greenfield, S. (2014). The English enlightenment and "the economy": How some men with a vision created the modern world and its problems. In D. Wood (Ed.), *Production, consumption, business and the economy: Structural ideals and moral realities* (pp. 1–28). Bingley: Emerald. doi:10.1108/S0190-128120140000034001

Hallstatt. (2011). *Kopierte Idylle: Hallstatt in China*. Retrieved January 12, 2016, from http://www.nachrichten.at/oberoesterreich/Kopierte-Idylle-Hallstatt-in-China;art4,651557

Hallstatt. (2012a). *Begutachtung der Hallstatt-Kopie*. Retrieved January 12, 2016, from http://ooe.orf.at/news/stories/2519297/

Hallstatt. (2012b). *Besuch bei der chinesischen Hallstattkopie*. Retrieved January 12, 2016, from http://www.nachrichten.at/oberoesterreich/Besuch-bei-der-chinesischen-Hallstattkopie;art4,893576

Hallstatt. (2012c). *Hallstatt-Double: China weiht nachgebautes Alpendorf ein*. Retrievend June 4, 2012, from http://www.spiegel.de

Hallstatt. (2012d). *Auch Huizhou hat jetzt ein Hallstatt. China-Kopie mit "Austrian Flair" feierlich eröffnet: Jetzt wird weiter abgekupfert*. Retrieved January 12, 2016, from http://www.oe24.at/welt/Auch-Huizhou-hat-jetzt-ein-Hallstatt/67825240)

Hallstatt. (2014a). *Bitte lächeln! Hallstatt im Fokus der Asiaten*. Retrieved January 12, 2016, from http://www.nachrichten.at/oberoesterreich/Bitte-laecheln-Hallstatt-im-Fokus-der-Asiaten;art4,1526204

Hallstatt. (2014b). *Die Karawanen sind furchtbar, aber Hallstatt lebt vom Tourismus*. Retrieved January 12, 2016, from http://www.nachrichten.at/oberoesterreich/Die-Karawanen-sind-furchtbar-aber-Hallstatt-lebt-vom-Tourismus;art4,1526556

Harrison, S. (1992). Ritual as intellectual property. *Man*, *27*(2), 225-244.

Hirsch, E., & Strathern, M. (Eds.). (2004). *Transactions and creations: Property debates and the stimulus in Melanesia*. New York: Berghahn.

Hydén, G., Leslie, M., & Ogundima, F. (Eds.), *(n.d.). Media and democracy in Africa.* New Brunswick, NJ: Transaction Publishers.

Johns, A. (2009). *Piracy: The intellectual property wars from Gutenberg to Gates.* Chicago: University of Chicago Press. doi:10.7208/chicago/9780226401201.001.0001

Jones, M. (1994). Why fakes? In S. Pearce (Ed.), *Interpreting objects and collections* (pp. 92–97). London: Routledge.

Laylin, T. (2011). *China plans to clone the entire village of Hallstatt, Austria.* Retrieved from www.inhabitat.com

McLeod, K., & Kuenzli, R. (Eds.). (2011). *Cutting across media: Appropriation art, interventionist collage and copyright law.* Durham, NC: Duke University Press. doi:10.1215/9780822393214

Mose, C. (2016). Covers, remixes and mash-ups: Locating African hip-hop in intellectual property rights discourse. In U. Röschenthaler & M. Diawara (Eds.), Copyright Africa: How intellectual property, media and markets transform immaterial cultural goods. Canon Pyon: Sean Kingston.

Phillip, K. (2005). What is a technological author? The pirate function and intellectual property. *Postcolonial Studies, 8*(2), 199–218. doi:10.1080/13688790500153596

Röschenthaler, U. (2011). *Purchasing culture: The dissemination of associations in the Cross River region of Cameroon and Nigeria.* Trenton, NJ: Africa World Press.

Röschenthaler, U. (2016). 'Be faster than the pirates': Copyright and the revival of 'traditional dances' in south-west Cameroon. In U. Röschenthaler & M. Diawara (Eds.), Copyright Africa: How intellectual property, media and markets transform immaterial cultural goods. Canon Pyon: Sean Kingston.

Röschenthaler, U. (2016). Good Quality or Low Price? Competition between Cameroonian and Chinese traders. *African East-Asian Affairs.* 1: 32-65.

Röschenthaler, U., & Diawara, M. (2016). African intellectual worlds in the making. In Copyright Africa: How intellectual property, media and markets transform immaterial cultural goods. Canon Pyon: Sean Kingston.

Röschenthaler, U., & Schulz, D. (2015). Introduction: Forging fortunes: New perspectives on entrepreneurial activities in Africa. In U. Röschenthaler & D. Schulz (Eds.), *Cultural Entrepreneurship in Africa* (pp. 1–15). London: Routledge.

Smiers, J. (1999). Copyrights: A choice of no choice for artists and Third World countries. *Iwalewa Forum, 3*, 5–38.

Somers, M. (1996). The "misteries" of property: Relationality, rural industrialization, and community in Chartist narratives of political rights. In J. Brewer & S. Staves (Eds.), *Early Modern Conceptions of Property* (pp. 62–90). London: Routledge.

Sundaram, R. (2010). *Pirate modernity: Dehli's media urbanism.* London: Routledge.

Tcheuyap, A. (2016). Music for everyone: The dynamics of piracy in Cameroon generations in Mali. In U. Röschenthaler & M. Diawara (Eds.), Copyright Africa: How intellectual property, media and markets transform immaterial cultural goods. Canon Pyon: Sean Kingston.

Theisohn, P. (2009). *Plagiat: Eine unoriginelle Literaturgeschichte*. Stuttgart: Alfred Kröner.

Thomas, P., & Nyamnjoh, F. (2007). Intellectual property challenges in Africa: Indigenous property systems and the fate of connected worlds. In I. Mazonde & P. Thomas (Eds.), *Indigenous knowledge systems and intellectual property in the twenty-first century: Perspectives from Southern Africa* (pp. 12–25). Dakar: CODESRIA.

Venice. (2008, January 12). *Nur das Original zählt. Venedig bleibt einzigartig*. Retrieved January 12, 2016, from http://www.n-tv.de/reise/Venedig-bleibt-einzigartig-article286891.html

Wane, I. (2016). Wrestling, the media and marketing: When folklore meets show business. In Copyright Africa: How intellectual property, media and markets transform immaterial cultural goods. Canon Pyon: Sean Kingston.

KEY TERMS AND DEFINITIONS

Branding: The marketing practice of creating a name, symbol or design that identifies and differentiates a product from other products.

Capitalism: An economic system based on the private ownership of the means of production and their operation for profit, with private property, wage labour and competitive markets as important elements; it is often associated with the exploitation of the poor.

Copying: An activity of reproducing an existing material or immaterial thing; the activity is relevant in discussions about intellectual property rights, which distinguishes between legitimate and illegitimate copying (piracy).

Hallstatt: A village that forms part of the region of Salzkammergut in Austria, which is a UNESCO cultural heritage site.

Immaterial Cultural Goods: The intangible aspects of artistic and knowledge production such as music, oral texts, performances, textile designs, literature and forms of local knowledge.

Intellectual Property Rights: A judicial concept that defines the relationship between people with respect to the immaterial aspects of cultural goods.

Judicialization: The process of making cultural elements subject of law.

Media: A means of social communication that enables human beings to reflect about their condition and provides space for the negotiation of different interest groups; the specific materiality of media suggests that the transmitted information is neutral, but their impact depends on the purpose for which they are used.

Piracy: Illegitimate copying, this concept has come up with the introduction and the increasing control of rights in intellectual property.

Property: A concept that does not refer to a thing but a relationship between people with respect to material or immaterial things.

Value: Monetary or material worth for which something can be exchanged or obtained; this worth is not inherent in things but is attributed by people to things, for example, a product can obtain added value through branding and advertisement.

ENDNOTES

1 The region was awarded the UNESCO world heritage title "historical and cultural landscape Hallstatt-Dachstein-Salzkammergut"; http://www.dachstein-salzkammergut.com/en/dachstein/dachstein-salzkammergut/unesco-world-heritage/ (accessed July 4, 2016).

2 The newspapers are mostly Austrian newspapers. Some German-speaking and international journals also commented on the issue. Many are available online (see especially the Austrian online news at www.nachrichten.at, in German language).

3 Cloning is different from the transfer of house styles and entire architectonic ensembles such as "China Towns" by migrants who create a new home in the style they know in other countries. Their motive is different in that they use it primarily for place making and identity creation, and not for commercialization (Bruneau 2010).

Chapter 7
Intellectual Property Rights and the Protection of Africa's Traditional Knowledge

Benjamin Enahoro Assay
Delta State Polytechnic – Ogwashi-Uku, Nigeria

ABSTRACT

This chapter examines the media, intellectual property rights and the protection of Africa's traditional knowledge in the digital age. It reviews literature on intellectual property, intellectual property rights, the various forms of intellectual property rights and the misappropriation and infringement on intellectual property rights, traditional knowledge, and media in digital age. The chapter provides perspectives on the issues and controversies on the non-protection of traditional knowledge within the existing frameworks of IP system and rules. It points out that the products of Africa's traditional knowledge are in dire need of protection against global competitors and therefore urges African governments to take advantage of the IP rules to negotiate with industrialized countries for the protection of their products. The chapter called for the enactment of tougher legislations to halt the menace of counterfeiting and digital piracy and deliberate use of the media to promote the products. It also made some recommendations that would help Africa defend its IP.

INTRODUCTION

Globalization, an economic phenomenon, resulting in trade and business, has made the task of properly handling intellectual property rights on the international scene a sine quan non. The protection and enforcement of intellectual property rights (IPRs) have therefore become a topical issue within the context of international law and trade in most developed and developing countries of the world.

In a general sense, intellectual property rights are property rights in something intangible that protect innovations and reward innovative activity (US Council for International Business, 1985, p. 3). IPRs comprise a bundle of rights focusing on the physical manifestations of intellectual activity in a field of human endeavour. Intellectual property rights are concerned with the expression of an idea for an

DOI: 10.4018/978-1-5225-2095-5.ch007

invention, the details of which have been worked out and which takes the form of a product or process that can be applied industrially (Kameri-Mbote, 2005, p. 1).

In the protection and enforcement of these rights, it is worrisome to note that there is a wide disparity in the level of progress recorded between the rest of the world and Africa. While the rest of the world have moved steps ahead in protecting what is known as the intangible value of its production, African governments are yet to take determined steps to secure IP rights for their countries' products; which are created through traditional knowledge; and therefore qualify as African brands.

African governments have over the years failed to vigorously pursue the enforcement of agreed IP rights and take full advantage of negotiated flexibilities in the emerging global rules on intellectual property. This largely explains why the rules of the World Trade Organization (WTO) and World Intellectual Property Organization (WIPO) and the laws in individual African countries on trade marks, patents and copyright have no practical effect on the continent. Amid the growing deliberate neglect of strict enforcement of IP rules, they have continued to encourage counterfeiting and piracy of products. Almost everything (electronics and softwares; shoes and perfumes; films and music; books, phones and watches) in the continent is pirated, and these pirated products keep the informal sector going but stymied the growth of most African countries economy.

The counterfeit trade is well organized and is booming as the producers of the real fakes are ever willing to copy the latest collections within days of their launching. The International Anti-counterfeiting Coalition estimates that the cross border trade in counterfeit products will have a value of $1.8trn in 2015. Youths in almost every African capital are deeply involved in the pirated goods business (Gappa, 2015, p. 24). Africans are the end users and the middlemen in the counterfeit trade. Aside from local music and DVDs, they are usually not the creators of the products.

In every society where they exist, the media serve as sources of information and ideas for the large number of people consuming their messages. They are central in the provision of ideas and images which people use to interpret and understand a great deal of their everyday experience. The provision of information and education through the media is essential to efforts to create awareness of intellectual property rights issues and their relation to socio-economic development.

The challenges the lack of protection and enforcement of IP rights pose to African economies is enormous, but this chapter carries an optimistic note that the continent stands a lot to benefit if it decides to strictly enforce national laws on copyright, patent and trademarks and defend its intellectual property.

This chapter thus examines the media, intellectual property rights and the protection of Africa's traditional knowledge in the digital age. The objectives of the discussion are as follows:

1. To draw the attention of governments, researchers, policymakers and businessmen to the myriads of challenges the lack of protection and enforcement of intellectual property rights poses to African economies.
2. Based on the policy of protecting locally made goods, to establish the fact that there is an urgent need to protect African brands which are products of traditional knowledge from global competitors.
3. To highlight the benefits to be derived by African countries by ensuring full protection and enforcement of IP rights as it relates to African brands.
4. To come out with recommendations on ways African countries can establish and defend their brands against global competitors.

BACKGROUND

Intellectual Property

In the last several decades, intellectual property has increasingly become a strong feature of international, regional trade arrangements and national legal instruments. From multilateral to regional trade relations, IP issues almost inevitably come to the fore as a critical issue to be considered in any deals that are struck (Kameri-Mbote, 2005, p. 1). No wonder it is now a huge resource for government and individuals even as the world goes digital.

The World Intellectual Property Organization (WIPO), a specialized agency of the United Nations saddled with the responsibility to promote the protection of IP defines it as "creations of the mind: inventions; literary and artistic works; and symbols, names and images used in commerce" (www.wipo.intpubdocswipo_pub_450). The inventions referred to here are particularly technological inventions that impact positively on human society. Intellectual property is also seen as the creations of the intellect for which a monopoly is assigned to designated owners by law. Pavlik and Mcintosh (2011, p. 446) refer to IP as ideas that have commercial value such as literary or artistic works, patents, software programs, business methods, and industrial processes, particularly in the form of copyright protection.

It can be inferred from the above definitions that intellectual property encompasses all those things which emanate from the exercise of human brain such as ideas, inventions, poems, designs, micro computers etc. As intangible aspects of human creation, once protected under the law, they become exclusive reserve of the owner of the ideas or inventor, and as a result, no one else can use them without the permission of the owner.

Intellectual Property Rights

The law that protects various aspects of intellectual property is known as intellectual property right. Intellectual property rights, according to World Trade Organization (WTO), "are the rights given to persons over the creations of their minds. They usually give the creator an exclusive right over the use of his/her creation for a certain period of time (https://www.wto.orgtrips_eintell_e). Intellectual property like other distinct branches of the law (Nwabachili, Nwabachili & Agu 2015, p. 68), have sources to which references are usually made and from which its growth and development derive. These sources are international and regional conventions and treaties administered by international and regional bodies or organizations. Some of them include Berne Convention, Paris Convention, Lisbon Agreement, Patent Cooperation Treaty, African Regional Industrial Property Organization (ARIPO), Organization Africaine de la Propriete Intellectuelle (OAPI), European Union Copyright Direction (EUCD), WIPO Copyright Treaty (WCT), WIPO Performances and Phonograms Treaty (WPPT), the agreement on Trade Related Aspects of Intellectual Property Rights (TRIPS) signed in 1994 and administered by the World Trade Organization (WTO). TRIPS seeks to strengthen legal protection for intellectual property around the world (Adekola & Eze, 2015, p. 57). There is the African Economic Community Treaty whose objective is to attain a state of integration for the free movement of goods and services in member West African countries as well as national laws for various countries.

Intellectual property rights (IPRs) cover a wide range of issues such as patents, trade and service marks, copyright, rights in performances, industrial designs, plant breeders' rights, utility models, appellations of origins or geographical origin, layout designs and typography, among others (Bambridge, 1999, Akhere, 2014, Babafemi, 2007, US Council for International Business, 1985). At this juncture, let us take a look at the various forms of intellectual property rights, their infringement, misappropriation and enforcement.

Forms of Intellectual Property Rights

Patents

A patent is a form of right granted to an inventor by the government, giving the owner the right to exclude others from making, using, selling, offering to sell, and importing an invention for a limited period of time (generally 20 years), in exchange for the public disclosure of the invention. An invention is a solution to a specific technological problem, which may be a product or a process and it must fulfill three main requirements of being new, not obvious and needs to be industrially applicable (WIPO, 2008, Simon, 2001). Akhere (2014, p. 115) avers that patents provide incentives to stimulate the growth of both knowledge and economy, which in turn boost the quality of human life in society.

The right to a patent (Babafemi, 2007, p. 389) is infringed if another person uses or sells a patented invention without permission from the patent holder. The scope of the patented invention or the extent of protection is defined in the claims of the granted patent. Many jurisdictions provide a safe harbour to use a patented invention for research. Pradip and Shannon (2004, p. 70) contend that the safe harbour does not exist in the US unless the research is done for purely philosophical purposes, or in order to gather data to prepare an application for regulatory approval of a drug. Patent infringement cases are generally handled under civil law (e.g., in the United States) but in several other jurisdictions such as Argentina, China, France, Japan, Russia, South Korea, (Matthew, 2008 cited in Akhere, 2014) points out that patent infringement is incorporated also in criminal law.

Copyright

A copyright gives the creator of an original work exclusive right to it, usually for a limited time. Copyright may apply to a wide range of creative, intellectual, or artistic forms, or works (Peter, 2007, WIPO, 2008). Ideas and information, systems or business methods are excluded from the list of subjects of copyrights protection, only the form or manner in which they are expressed are copyrighted (Akhere, 2014, Simon, 2001). Works covered by copyright include, but are not limited to novels, poems, plays, reference works, newspapers, advertisements, computer programmes, data bases, films, musical compositions, choreography; paintings, drawings, photographs, sculpture, architecture, maps and technical drawings (WIPO, 2008, Babafemi, 2007).

Copyright laws grant authors, artists and other creators protection for their literary and artistic creations, which are generally referred to as "works". Copyright law, as it affects e-business, according to Akhere (2014, p. 101), seeks to protect an owner's web site against infringers and to ensure that people's web pages do not infringe on others' copyrighted materials. The creators of works protected by copyright, and their heirs and successors, which are referred to as "right holders", have certain basic rights under copyright law. They hold the exclusive right to use or authorize others to use the work on agreed terms. The right holder(s) of a work can authorize or prohibit:

1. Its reproduction in all forms, including print form and sound recording;
2. Its public performance and communication to the public;
3. Its broadcasting;
4. Its translation into other languages; and
5. Its adaptation, such as from a novel to a screenplay for a film (WIPO, 2008, p. 19).

The benefits of protecting copyright and related rights in any human society cannot be overstated. Both form an essential component in the fostering of human creativity and innovation. Apart from giving authors, artists and creators incentives in the form of recognition and fair economic reward, it increases their activity and output, and also enhances their results. The existence and enforceability of these rights enable individuals and companies to willingly invest in the creation, development and worldwide dissemination of their works. This will in turn help them to increase access to and enhance the enjoyment of culture, knowledge and entertainment globally as well as stimulates societal development.

However, with the advancement of technological development, which has in turn, given rise to new ways of disseminating creative works through forms of communication such as satellite broadcasting, compact discs and DVDs, the field of copyright and related rights has expanded greatly. The widespread dissemination of works via the Internet has continued to raise pertinent questions concerning copyright and related rights in this newest global medium that is not regulated.

In response to this growing concern, two treaties: WIPO Copyright Treaty (WCT) and WIPO Performances and Phonograms Treaty (WPPT), also known as "Internet Treaties" aimed at preventing unauthorized access to and use of creative works on the Internet and administered by World Intellectual Property Organization (WIPO) have come to the rescue but the efforts of WIPO appear insufficient to permanently deal with the issue.

The infringement of copyright, manifests in the form of reproducing, distributing, displaying or performing a work, or to make derivative works, without permission from the copyright holder. This copyright holder could be a publisher or other business representing the creator or assigned by the work's creator. Panathiere (2005, p. 2) also refers to it as piracy. While copyright is created the moment a work is created, experts (Akhere, 2014, Babafemi, 2007) contend that the copyright holder can only get monetary damage if the owner registers the copyright. To enforce copyright, Correa (2009, p. 211) submits that the copyright holder must take the responsibility for the enforcement. It is in line with this position that the Anti-Counterfeiting Trade Agreement (ACTA) signed in May 2011 by the United States, Japan, Switzerland, and the European Union specifies that its parties add criminal activities, including incarceration and fines, for copyright and trademark infringement, and obligated the parties to active police for infringement (Bitton, 2012, Irina, 2011). This notwithstanding, there are limitations and exceptions to copyright, allowing for limited use of copyrighted works, which does not constitute infringement. Such exceptions are the doctrines of fair use and fair dealing.

Industrial Design Rights

An industrial design consists of the creation of a shape, configuration or composition of pattern or colour, or combination of pattern and colour in three-dimensional form containing aesthetic value. Cornish and Liewellyn (2003) cited by Babafemi (2007, p. 412) defines industrial designs as "primarily those elements incorporated into mass-produced products that aim to enhance their attractiveness by their appearance. Today when so many consumer products are technically very similar, designs become an important distinguishing factor …" An industrial design can be a two or three dimensional pattern used to produce a product, industrial commodity or handicraft.

The main objective of the law governing industrial design is to protect a design that is new or essentially better in some ways than what was created before. An industrial design right is of immense benefit to artists, lace designers and designers of other types of products such as ceramic and marble products, earthenware products, rug products, shoe products, plastic products, etc.

The right of a design owner is infringed if another person uses, sells or does anything to the design which he is precluded from doing without permission from the design owner. The proprietor of the design could enforce his right in a law court by seeking damages, injunction, accounts or otherwise as available to him.

Trademarks

A trademark is a distinctive sign that identifies certain goods or services produced or provided by an individual or a company (WIPO 2008, p. 8). The Lahan Act of 1976 quoted by Akhere (2014, p. 91) defines a trade mark as a name, symbol, word, device or other designations or a combination of designations that is distinctive of such a person's goods or services and that is used in a manner that identifies and distinguishes his from the goods or services of others. It is obvious from the above definitions that a trademark is a recognizable sign, design or expression which distinguishes products or services of a particular trade from the similar products or services of other traders. The said mark must be used or intended to be used in good faith in commerce to qualify as a trademark.

Trademarks are generally classified into five categories:

1. **Suggestive Trademarks:** These are suggestive of the quality of the goods and services trademarked.
2. **Arbitrary Trademarks:** Which are usually not related to the product but are there to merely remind the public of the trademark owner.
3. **Fanciful Trademarks:** These are also not particularly related to the product or service trademarked.
4. **Generic Trademarks:** These do not enjoy any protection because they hardly distinguish the products sought to be registered from other products for being too general.
5. **Descriptive Products:** Which generally are protected only if the owners can prove distinctiveness or have acquired a "secondary meaning" in the market place (Akhere, 2014, p. 92).

Trademark protection, according to WIPO (2006, p. 9), "ensures that the owners of marks have the exclusive right to use them to identify goods or services, or to authorize others to use them in return for payment. The period of protection varies, but a trademark can be renewed indefinitely upon payment of the corresponding fees …" While further elucidating the benefits of trademark protection worldwide, WIPO contends that it promotes initiative and enterprise by rewarding their owners with recognition and financial profit; hinders the efforts of unfair competitors such as counterfeiters, to use similar distinctive signs to market inferior or different products or services, and it enables people with skill and enterprise to produce and market goods and services in the fairest possible conditions, thereby facilitating international trade.

Infringement on trademark occurs when one party uses a trademark that is identical or confusingly similar to a trademark owned by another party, in relation to products or services which are identical or similar to the products or services of the other party. In many countries of the world, a trademark receives protection without registration, but registering a trademark provides strong legal advantages for enforcement. Trademark protection is legally enforced by courts that have the authority to stop trademark infringement in most countries. Infringement can be addressed by civil litigation and, in several jurisdictions under criminal law (Bitton, 2012, Irina, 2011).

Service Marks

Service marks are registrable logos, phrases, words, or other symbols, which distinguish the services of a company from those of others and therefore give legal protection to the owners of service marks. To confer ownership (Akhere, 2014, p. 92) on these marks the letters (SM) and/or ® are added as a suffix to the words, symbols, and logos constituting the service.

In some countries, including Nigeria, their laws do not provide for the registration of service marks as registrable marks are defined only in relation to use on goods. Service marks infringement takes place when one party uses a service mark party, in relation to services which are identical or similar to the services of the other party.

Trade Secrets

Trade secrets are secret information developed or owned by an establishment, which give the establishment some advantages, usually economic advantages over competitors or customers. Akhere (2014, p. 127) asserts that protecting trade secrets is completely different from protecting business methods through patenting. Trade secrets, according to him, offer more room for protection, because as the name suggests, the mere fact that any data are claimed to be trade secrets often automatically render those data amenable to trade secrets protection. Thus it is completely within the discretion of the owner of the information in question to determine what to categorize as trade secrets. Items like customers' lists and invoices could come under the category of trade secrets and therefore protectable, whereas they do not qualify for protection under the business method system of patenting. The enforcement of trade secrets laws lies with the federal government as well as state governments. Both have competent jurisdictions to promulgate laws concerning trade secrets.

Trade secret misappropriation is different from violations of other intellectual property laws, since by definition trade secrets are secret, while patents and registered copyrights and trademarks are publicly available. For example, in the United States, trade secrets are protected under state law, and states have nearly universally adopted the Uniform Trade Secrets A ct.The United States also has federal law in the form of the economic Espionage Act of 1996 (18 U.S.C. SS 1831-1839), which makes the theft or misappropriation of a trade secret a federal crime. This law contains two provisions criminalizing two sorts of activity. The first, 18 U.S.C. S 1931 (a), criminalizes the theft of trade secrets to benefit foreign powers. The second, 19 U.S.C.S 1932, criminalizes their theft for commercial or economic purposes. The statutory penalties are different for the two offenses. In commonwealth common law jurisdictions, confidentiality and trade secrets are regarded as an equitable right rather than a property right but penalties for theft are almost the same as the United States.

As secrecy is the underlying element of trade secrets, positive efforts are often made to keep trade secrets secret and confidential (Babafemi, 2007, p. 302). This is done through the execution of trade secrets agreements between businesses and their employees, non-disclosure agreements between businesses and customers, and contracts in restraint of trade between businesses and professional employees and partners. In addition non-solicitation agreements are also employed to prevent parties from luring away employees imbued with knowledge of a business' secrets. Trade secrets remain protectable until the owner fails to maintain the secret or some other party independently develops the like of it.

Trade Dress

Trade dress could be described as the look, packaging and feel of a product that is registered. Merges (2007, p. 29) defines it as legal term of art that generally refers to characteristics of the visual appearance of a product or its packaging (or even the design of a building) that signify the source of the product to consumers. For these elements (visual appearance or look, packaging and feel of the product) to constitute trade dress, they must be distinctive.

An infringement on trade dress occurs when a company or an organization uses the same trade dress and design that are distinctive to another company or organization without the permission of the original owner. The two key features of trade dress are distinctiveness and product fame. To sue for infringement on trade dress in countries where the law is in force, the owner of the company or organization whose trade dress was infringed upon must necessarily show that the trade dress and design of the product are distinctive and the product design must have acquired a secondary meaning, which makes the product famous in the eyes of the consuming public. This proof of distinctiveness of the product design and fame of the product in the eyes of the consuming public has made the registration of trade dress near impossible.

Appellation of Origin and Geographical Indication

An appellation of origin, according to WIPO (2008), is a special kind of geographical indication used on products that have a specific quality exclusively or essentially due to the geographical environment in which the products are produced. Geographical indication encompasses appellations of origin. Both (geographical indication and appellation of origin) are signs used on goods that have a specific geographical origin and possess qualities, a reputation or characteristics that are essentially attributable to that place of origin. A geographical indication guarantees to consumers that a product was produced in a certain place and has certain characteristics that are due to that place of production. It may be used by all producers who make products that share certain qualities in the place designated by a geographical indication.

The protection for geographical indication is done in accordance with national laws and under a broad range of concepts, such as laws against unfair competition, consumer protection laws, laws for the protection of certification marks or special laws for the production of geographical indications or appellations of origin (WIPO, 2008).

Infringement on GI can occur if unauthorized parties use geographical indications to mislead the public about the true origin of the product. Such persons can be sued. The court can apply sanctions ranging to injunctions preventing unauthorized use to the payment of damages and fines or, imprisonment in serious cases.

Objectives of Intellectual Property Law

Promotion of Progress

One of the key objectives of most intellectual property law (with the exception of trademarks) is to promote progress in society (US Constitution, Article 1, section 8, clause 8). By exchanging limited exclusive rights for disclosure of inventions and creative works, society and the patentee/copyright owner mutually benefit, and an incentive is created for inventors and authors to create and disclose their work. Some experts like Lemley (2015) have noted that the objective of legislators of intellectual property and those who support its implementation across the globe is absolute protection. They opined that if some intellectual property is desirable because it encourages innovation, more is better. The thinking among them is that creators will not have sufficient incentive to invent unless they are legally entitled to capture the full social value of their works. This absolute protection or full value view canvassed by the experts treats intellectual property as another type of "real" property, typically adopting its law and rhetoric. Other recent developments in intellectual property law, such as the America Invents Act, have stressed international harmonization to realize its maximum benefits. Of late, there has also been much debate over the desirability of using intellectual property rights to protect cultural heritage, including intangible one, as well as over risks of commodification derived from this possibility (Farah & Tremolada, 2014). This position has continued to generate intense debate in the legal field-till date.

Financial Incentive

The exclusive rights provided by intellectual property enable owners to benefit from the property they have created, provide a financial incentive for the creation of an investment in intellectual property, and, in case of patents, (Schroeder and Singer, 2009) pay associated research and development costs. Levine and Boldrin (2008) however dispute this justification.

The financial benefit that intellectual property rights provide is incontrovertible. For example, in 2013 the United States Patent and Trademark Office said the worth of intellectual property to the U.S. economy was more than US & 5 trillion and creates employment for an estimated 18 million American people. The value of intellectual property was considered similarly high in other developed nations, such as those in the European Union (Bollyky, 2015). In the United Kingdom, IP has become a recognized asset class for use in pension-led funding and other type of business finance. However, Brassell and Martin (2013, p. 15) revealed that "There are millions of intangible business assets in UK whose value is either not being leveraged at all, or only being leveraged inadvertently".

Economic Growth

The World Intellectual Property Organization (WIPO) treaty and several related international agreements underline that the protection of intellectual property rights is essential to maintaining economic growth worldwide. The WIPO Intellectual Property Handbook gives two reasons for intellectual property laws:

One is to give statutory expression to the moral and economic rights of creators in their creations and the rights of the public in access to those creations. The second is to promote, as a deliberate act of

Government policy, creativity and the dissemination and application of its results and to encourage fair trading which would contribute to economic and social development (2008, p. 3).

In line with the above, the Anti-Counterfeiting Trade Agreement states that "effective enforcement of intellectual property rights is critical to sustaining economic growth across all industries and globally (https://en.m.wikipedia.org/wiki/Anti-counterfeiting_Trade_Agreement). Economists have estimated that two-thirds of the value of large businesses in the United States can be traced to intangible assets (Shapiro & Pham, 2015). Intellectual property-intensive industries are estimated (Shapiro & Pham, 2007) to generate 72 percent more added value per employee than non-IP-intensive industries.

A joint research project of WIPO and the United Nation University measuring the impact of IP systems on six Asian countries found a positive correlation between the strengthening of the IP system and subsequent economic growth (WIPO, 2007). Economists (Greenhalgh & Rogers, 2010, pp. 32-34) have also shown that IP can be a disincentive to innovation when that innovation is drastic. IP makes excludable non-rival intellectual products that were previously non-excludable. This creates economic inefficiency as long as the monopoly is held. A disincentive to direct resources toward innovation can occur when monopoly profits are less than the overall welfare improvement to society. This situation can be seen as a market failure, and an issue of appropriability.

Morality

Article 27 of the Universal Declaration of Human Rights states that everyone has the right to the protection of the moral and material interests resulting from any scientific, literary or artistic production of which he is the author. Although the relationship between intellectual property and human rights appears to be complex (WIPO 2008), there are moral arguments for intellectual property.

The moral arguments that can be used to justify intellectual property are classified into three major areas. The first one is the personality theorists who believe that intellectual property is an extension of an individual. Next is the utilitarians who strongly believe that intellectual property stimulates social progress and pushes people to engage in further innovative activities that benefit society, and lastly is the Lockeans who argue that intellectual property is justified based on deservedness and hard work.

However, there are various moral justifications for private property which can be used to argue in favour of the morality of intellectual property. They dovetail into the following:

1. **Natural Rights/Justice Argument:** This argument is based on Locke's idea that a person has a natural right over the labour and/or products which is produced by his/her body. To appropriate these products is viewed as unjust. Although Locke never clearly stated that natural right applied to products of the mind (Bettig, 1996, pp. 19-20), it is possible to apply his argument to intellectual property rights, in which it would be unjust for people to misuse another's ideas (DeGeorge, n.d, pp. 415-416). Locke's argument for intellectual property is based upon the idea that labourers have the right to control that which they create. They argue that we own our bodies which are the labourers, this right of ownership extends to what we create. Thus, intellectual property ensures this right when it comes to production.
2. **Utilitarian-Pragmatic Argument:** According to this rationale, a society that protects private property is more effective and prosperous than societies that do not. DeGeorge (n.d p. 416) asserts that innovation and invention in 19th century America was attributed to the development of the pat-

ent system. By providing innovators with "durable and tangible return on their investment of time, labour and other resources", intellectual property rights seek to maximize social utility (Spinello, 2007, pp. 12-22). The presumption according to Spinello (2007) is that they promote public welfare by encouraging the creation, production and distribution of intellectual works. Utilitarians argue that without intellectual property there would be lack of incentive to produce new ideas. Systems of protection such as intellectual property optimize social utility.

3. **Personality Argument:** This argument is based on a quote from Hegel: "Every man has the right to turn his will upon a thing or make the thing an object of his will, that is to say, to set aside the mere thing and recreate it as his own" (DeGeorge, n.d. p. 417). European intellectual property law is shaped by this notion that ideas are an extension of oneself and of one's personality (DeGeorge, n.d p. 418). Personality theorists therefore argue that by being a creator of something one is inherently at risk and vulnerable for having their ideas and designs stolen and/or altered. Intellectual property protects these moral claims that have to do with personality.

In her argument in favour of the protection of intellectual property, Rand (1967) contends that IP is essentially a moral issue and the human mind is the source of wealth and survival, and as a result, all property at its base is intellectual property. Therefore, to violate IP constitutes an immoral act just like other property rights which ensures the survival of human society.

Traditional Knowledge

Several definitions of traditional knowledge (TK) exist, but no one is universally accepted. The International Council for Science (2002, p. 3) defines TK as,

... a cumulative body of knowledge, know-how, practices and representations maintained and developed by peoples with extended histories of interaction with the natural environment. These sophisticated sets of understandings, interpretations and meanings are part and parcel of a cultural complex that encompasses language, naming and classification systems, resource use practices, ritual, spirituality and worldview.

Similarly, the Bureau of Public Information (2005, p. 1) refers to traditional knowledge as the "cumulative and dynamic body of knowledge, know-how and representations possessed by peoples with long histories of interaction with their natural milieu. It is intimately tied to language, social relations, spirituality and world view, and is generally held collectively".

In the text on draft articles for TK protection, the WIPO IGC (2008) defines traditional knowledge as including "... know-how, skills, innovations, practices, teachings and learning of indigenous [peoples] and [local communities] that are dynamic and evolving, and that are intergenerational/and they are passed on from generation to generation, and which may subsist in codified, oral or other forms". It proposes further that TK "[... may be associated, in particular, with fields such as agricultural, environmental, healthcare and indigenous and traditional medical knowledge and medical knowledge, biodiversity, traditional lifestyles and natural resources and genetic resources, and know-how of traditional architectural and construction technologies]."

Elaborating a little more in conceptual terms, WIPO IGC (2008) describes TK as,

> *... referring in general to the content or substance of knowledge resulting from intellectual activity in a traditional context, and includes the knowledge, skills, innovations, practices and learning that form part of traditional knowledge systems, and knowledge embodying traditional lifestyles of indigenous and local communities, or contained in codified knowledge system passed between generations. It is not limited to any specific technical field, and may include agricultural, environmental and medicinal knowledge, and knowledge associated to genetic resources. (http://www.wipo.int/edocs/mdocs/tk/en/wipogrtkfic13/wipogrtkfic135brev.pdf)*

It is obvious from the foregoing that traditional knowledge can mean many things at the same time.

The Convention on Biological Diversity (CBD) approach to TK is based on three prongs of "knowledge, innovations and practices". Hence the CBD defines traditional knowledge as the "knowledge, innovations and practices of indigenous and local communities around the world. It is experience gained over centuries, transmitted orally from generation to generation, taking the form of stories, songs, proverbs, beliefs and culture, most often linked to agriculture, animal husbandry, fisheries, horticulture, forestry and nature in general". A noteworthy international benchmark on traditional knowledge is the 1992 Convention on Biological Diversity whose far-reaching Article 8(j) requires state parties to "respect, preserve and maintain knowledge, innovations and practices of indigenous and local communities embodying traditional lifestyles relevant for the conservation and sustainable use of biological diversity".

The CBD's perspective shows that traditional knowledge is vital for the conversation of plants and animals, their genetic diversity and for managing the local environment. It can make substantial contribution to sustainable development and allow for a sustainable future for all humans. TK is widely used by the aromatic, flavouring, food, cosmetic and health industries. The use of plant-based traditional medicine to identify and fast-track the development of modern medicines and drugs as well as cosmetic products is widely acknowledge across the world.

From the definitions of TK, it is useful to separate the elements of traditional knowledge into distinct, although related categories: an intangible (knowledge perse); a tangible (material products or material innovations themselves), and processes or procedures (expressed in the form of techniques or more sophisticated technologies that can be expressed in some form-orally, in writing, through representations or exemplification). Such an approach, as Muller (2013, p. 8) puts it, will help to focus protection efforts on more specific and some what better defined categories, rather than relying on interpretation of broad and general concepts.

Unarguably, these identified different categories of traditional knowledge are closely interrelated and can overlap. This interrelation and overlapping constitute the defining feature of TK. In trying to provide a clearer picture of this defining characteristics, Muller (2013, p. 8) explains that "a material product or innovation is the result of developing and using knowledge. It is the material support that expresses a knowledge application. The same is true in the case of a technique or technology that is based on knowledge and sometimes results also in a material product or innovation. Depending on the specific dimension or category of TK, a particular form of protection may be required or applicable".

A second feature of traditional knowledge relates to its development and how it responds and adapts to environmental, social, cultural and economic pressures and demands. Traditional knowledge is all but static. It is continuously subjected to social and environmental tests to prove its effectiveness and relevance over time. This feature contrasts with the commonly held belief that TK is 'traditional' simply because of the passing of time and its limited variations. There are indeed some very old, often religiously based expressions of TK, that have not suffered major changes over time, but these are mostly linked to cultural, spiritual and social traditions and ceremonies. Day-to-day adoption by indigenous peoples to continuously changing environments requires rapid responses and adjustments of TK-especially in its application (Posey & Dutfield, 1996, pp. 12-13, Johnson, 1992, pp. 7-8, Muller, 2013, p. 8).

The third feature of traditional knowledge is that it is generally the result of a collective, intergenerational effort because it involves in social context (i.e. communal) where social actors play different roles in creating, maintaining, applying, and adopting TK according to needs and circumstances (Johnson, 1992, p. 8). Traditional knowledge is viewed as part of a defined cultural, environmental, religious and social context in which different actors play different roles. The actors understand their roles as part of tradition and vigorously respect the established order. Traditional knowledge is managed through a complex social system of customs and rules (WIPO 2008). Outside of this context, Muller (2013, p. 9) notes that traditional knowledge simply dissipates and loses its special connotations and that the 'holistic' nature of TK is its most district feature.

The fourth defining feature of TK is that it is mostly shared between communities across countries of the world. It is only in very exceptional situations that TK is restricted to a single indigenous peoples group or community. But this is not to say that there is no distinct and geographically confined traditional knowledge. Some traditional knowledge is still maintained in secrecy (Many Shammans, healers and certain farmers in rural communities hoard TK that they have developed) and this has posed a continued and complex problem regarding the loss of TK since it is not being passed on to younger generations simply because these generations are not interested.

Arising from the restrictive nature of some TK cases, it appears that confined, confidential and very unique TK is the exception rather than the rule. Though it may be hard to quantify, there is agreement among experts that most TK is shared between communities in countries and even across geographical borders (Muller, 2013, p. 9, BPI, 2005, p. 1). This traditional knowledge, according to Laird (2002, p. 45), is shared consciously; and it inadvertently passes and flows to neighbouring communities, and even foreigners play a role in disseminating it more widely.

It is instructive to note that TK manifests itself in many different forms and 'packages' – sometimes as knowledge perse, but often as part of a process or in product. In this regard, indigenous people face an uphill task in trying to galvanize efforts globally to protect traditional knowledge especially in the area of determining the subject matter and potential right owners. The challenges indigenous people and communities face are complex because of the extreme diverse conceptions, traditions, practices and cultural frameworks that define them and their environment. Added to this is the fact that the western legal concepts that give force and shape to IP are considered inappropriate when applied to TK protection. Indigenous people and communities desire to be part of the whole and nothing less, and this should be clearly reflected in whatever framework to be devised. Most policy and legal frameworks recognize these problems but have failed to reflect this in content and form (Muller, 2013, p. 9).

MEDIA AND DIGITAL AGE

Mass Media

In most modern societies, the mass media are regarded as veritable instruments of information dissemination, mass mobilization and social control. It is one of the means through which the general public is educated and sensitized about important issues affecting the lives of the people. Hence, Pavlik and Mcintosh (2011, p. 4) observe that the media of mass communication are fundamental to an informed and educated public.

The mass media are tools or technologies that facilitate dissemination of information and entertainment to a vast number of consumers (Hasan, 2013, p. 640). They comprise radio, television, film, books, sound recordings, newspapers, magazines and the internet. The internet is the newest media industry. Of course these are not the only mass media that exist. For example, billboards and posters are some other forms of mass media. The ones mentioned earlier appear to have the largest audiences, employ the most people, and have the greatest impact. They are also the ones with which most of us are most familiar (Dominick, 2002, pp. 24-25).

As vehicles of mass communication, the mass media have a special place in our life today. Individually or collectively they serve the needs of various audiences who have specific preferences. While some audiences want entertainment, sports, news, films, plays, serials, dance, music, etc. Others may have greater interest in news and views, and may seek guidance to solve their socio-economic problems. Each medium of mass communication is powerful in its own right in serving people and each has gone through several stages of development due to pressure (political, social and economic) and competition from newer communication technology.

The mass media help in shaping public perceptions on a variety of important issues, both through the information that is dispensed through them, and through the interpretations they place upon this information (Lorimer and Scannell, 1994, p. 26). It is obvious that the mass media are a pervasive part of our lives. In many ways we are reliant and dependent upon regular contact with the mass media for information, opinion, entertainment, ideas and a range of other resources, which are deeply bound up with our continuing attempts to maintain as coherent sense of 'who' and 'where' we think we are. Despite the pervasiveness of mass media in our lives, Baran (2012, p. 17) avers that many of us are dissatisfied with or critical of the media industries' performance and much of the content provided. Nevertheless, the nature of socio-cultural and political experience in modern societies has been profoundly affected by the development of systems of mass communication. Without these systems of mass communication, it would be impossible for modern societies to flourish.

As strategic socialization agencies, the mass media play a large role in shaping modern culture by selecting and portraying a particular set of beliefs, values, and traditions (an entire way of life), as reality. That is, by portraying a certain interpretation of reality, the mass media shape reality to be more in line with that interpretation (Vipond, 2000, p. 88). The mass media also affect our buying habits and politics. The population relies on the mass media as the main source of information and the basis on which they form their opinions and voting decisions (Hasan, 2013, p. 101).

They provide images, interpretations and explanations of events occurring in the wider world. The mass media do not simply and neutrally provide information about that world, but actively encourage us to see and understand it in particular ways and in certain terms. With the ability of the media to impact our everyday lives, the media determine how people perceive social norms, values, and morals.

Social scientists and communication scholars have observed that the mass media can be used to effectively inform broad masses of people about a problem of public interest; they can inspire ideas and feelings, stimulate discussion and an exchange of ideas and assist informing or creating public awareness. Such scholars as Mansurov (1988, pp. 60-64) have identified several factors which determine the creation through the media of public awareness and the stimulation of public interest in certain issues. These include:

1. How the issue is presented in the media, especially the use of clear and accurate information and facts;
2. Periodical repetition and frequent reference;
3. The amount of the time and space devoted to the issue in the media; and
4. Presentation of adequate analytical pieces on the issue and information on its effect on society.

On both a long and short-term basis, the mass media can make substantial contributions to the process of creating public awareness, whether the aim of such efforts is to:

1. Bring about an increase in the information or knowledge of the public or target group about a specific issue;
2. To generate a change in their opinions or attitudes; or to motivate them to action; that is to change their behaviour and habits.

Digital Age

Obviously, we live in a technological driven world and recent technological developments in the communication sector now form an integral part of the changes in the way mass media are delivered and consume (Biagi, 2003, p. 21). Technology has changed the basic elements of communication as humans engage in this never ending activity (Baran, 2012, p. 17), but it does not relieve us of our obligation to use mass communication responsibly and wisely. Because of the profound impact of technology on communication, our current era is being referred to as digital age.

The digital age, also called information age, computer age or new media age is defined as the time period starting in the 1970s with the introduction of the personal computer with subsequent technology introduced providing the ability to transfer information freely and quickly (http://www.yourdictionary.com>digital-age). It is also seen as the present time when most information is in a digital form, especially when compared to the time when computers were not used (www.dictionary.cambridge.org?dictionary). The period referred to in human history is characterized by the shift from traditional industry that the industrial revolution brought industrialization, to an economy based on information computerization. The onset of the information age is associated with the digital revolution, just as the industrial revolution marked the onset of the industrial age (Castells, 1999), Hilbert, 2015). The information age is built around the idea that access to and control of information is the defining characteristics of this current era in human civilization which is tightly coupled with the advent of personal computers (http://www.searchcio.techtarget.comdefinitioninformationAge).

Undoubtedly, digital technologies have revolutionized communication in the modern world – a revolution that was totally absent in the analog days. Digital technologies refer to electronic tools, systems, devices and resources that generate, store or process data. These include social media, online games and applications, multimedia, productivity applications, cloud computing, interoperable systems and mobile devices.

The media have always been influenced by social developments and the rapid and remarkable developments in technology and global economics are today significantly altering lives, community, and established social institutions – including media (STI, 2013). Pavlik (2008, p. 283) notes that digital technologies have fundamentally altered the nature and function of media in our society, reinventing age–old practices of public communication and at times circumventing traditional media and challenging its privileged role as gatekeepers of news and entertainments.

In this digital age, information is seen as a key resource and commodity that should be quickly and widely disseminated especially through the use of computer technology. Some of the influences of digital technologies are potential improvements, whereas others pose new problems or expand old ones. The impact of digital and networking technology on the media industry globally cannot be overestimated.

MAIN FOCUS OF THE CHAPTER

Issues, Controversies, and Problems

Issues

Intellectual property is widely acknowledged as a huge resource for individuals and governments all over the world. Consequently, most governments especially in industrialized societies who recognize its value are taking advantage of available IP systems and rules to leverage on its benefits for the sustainable development of their respective countries as well as improve the economic wellbeing of their citizens who are creators and inventors of intellectual works.

However, in Africa, most countries have not been able to take advantage of the existing IP rules to protect the products of traditional knowledge, which are today regarded as African brands. Only few countries such as Ethiopia and South Africa have been able to do something different from the vast majority (over fifty countries in the continent). Leveraging on the economic opportunities provided by geographical indications (Gls), a new category of IP that World Trade Organization (WTO) recognizes as signifying a product's quality, the Ethiopian Intellectual Property Office (EIPO) has secured trademark registrations in more than 30 countries for its three most popular brands of fine coffee: Sidamo, Harar and Yirgacheffe. By insisting that distributors of the three products have to buy licences to sell them, EIPO has doubled coffee farmers' incomes in a short time and protects them in the long term. Through a deal with the European Union (EU), South Africa has won recognition for the rooibos trademark after an unsuccessful 2013 French attempt to trademark rooibos, a plant traditionally grown and used for tea in South Africa but does not enjoy a patent, trademark or GI in South Africa. The efforts of Ethiopia and South Africa symbolize the hope of Africa's fight for its intellectual property (IP) rights.

Another contentious issue that impinges on the protection and enforcement of intellectual property rights is digital theft or piracy. Most of the misappropriation, infringement on intellectual property takes place online and African countries appear helpless in dealing with the scourge. Infringers of intellectual property online use trademarks as domain names for websites which makes it difficult for consumers to find the trademark owners official website. They also use file-sharing software and other new devices to duplicate digital video discs involving copyright works especially music and movies.

Although some countries have responded to these developments by putting in place laws to deal with these problematic issues, the laws have been deemed to be controversial, thus sparking off claims and counter claims. While intellectual property owners claimed the laws failed to provide full protection against unauthorized use of their property, various consumer groups argued that the laws interfered with the public's rights to engage in free speech and may invade their privacy. These arguments not withstanding, digital theft still pose a major challenge to IP rights protection in Africa.

Controversies

For quite some years now, controversies have continued to trail the persistent call for the protection of Africa's traditional knowledge amid large scale counterfeiting and piracy, and its attendant effect on the continent's economy. Scholars such as Muller (2013, p. 2) in advancing arguments against non-protection of TK opine that classic IP instruments such as patents, plant breeder's rights, and copyrights are unsuitable to protect indigenous peoples' intellectual interests both for technical and ideological reasons. They argued that these IP instruments promote individual recognition (in contrast to collective aspects of indigenous peoples' livelihoods), grant monopoly, exclusionary rights, which affect the interests of other indigenous individuals and especially, groups; require specific identification of a creator or innovator (then again, impacting collective interests); result in high transaction costs (i.e. administrative processes, negotiation of licenses, legal fees, maintenance of right fees, etc.); and grant rights over creations and innovations, which need to have a pre-defined degree of creativeness and innovation. They posit that this is a few reasons why TK does not fit into IP protection frameworks and templates.

It is for the same reasons that the Trade Related Aspects of Intellectual Property Rights (TRIPS) was silent on TK and made no reference to the Convention on Biological Diversity (CBD). This might have prompted developing countries to squeal and refer to the Trips-CBD relationship as unsatisfactory. Twelve developing countries from Asia, Africa and Latin America protested the relationship by submitting two joint papers to the General Council of World Trade Organization (WTO) in October 1999 explaining the implementation issues they were seeking solutions to.

The two papers put forward several TRIPs-related proposals. One of the proposals argued that TRIPS is incompatible with the CBD and sought a clear understanding that patents inconsistent with Article 15 of the CBD, which vests the authority to determine access to genetic resources in national governments, should not be granted. Several other proposals were directed to Article 27.3(b) and the review of its substantive provisions. One of the proposals was that the subparagraph should be amended in light of the provisions of the CBD taking fully into account the conservation and sustainable use of biological diversity, and the protection of the rights and knowledge of indigenous and local communities (Dutfield, 2003, p. 15).

Traditional knowledge has since become controversial and an important element of the debate to protect or not to protect. A communication from Kenya on 6 August, 1999, on behalf of the African Group of Countries proposed to the WTO General Council that in the sentence on plant varieties protection in article 27.3(b) "a footnote should be inserted stating that any sui generis law for plant variety protection can provide for (inter alia): (i) the protection of the innovations of indigenous farming communities in developing countries, consistent with the Convention on Biological Diversity and the International Undertaking on Plant Genetic Resources".

In trying to resolve the controversies surrounding the protection of TK, some process have been made at the conceptual and legal levels through numerous proposal and instruments – the Nagoya Protocol on Access and Benefit sharing, Andea Community Legislation, the African Union Model Law and the African Regional Intellectual Property Organization (ARIPO) instrument. However, discussions regarding existing legal instruments, including the draft: international regime on TK protection under the auspices of the WIPO IGC, acknowledge that the issue of shared TK among communities and across national borders remains an area for which policy and legal solutions are still to be thought through and devised.

Despite the arguments which point to the fact that it is difficult to protect traditional knowledge under the existing IP system and protocols, the same cannot be said of the products of traditional knowledge in Africa which are begging for protection against global competitors. These products of TK could be found in each of the countries of the continent but some of them include: Marula oil (Namibia), Barakat cotton (Sudan), Shea Butter (Burkina Faso and Nigeria), Zambique cashew nuts (Mozambique), Mpingo and Grenadilla Blackwood (Tanzania), Bogolan Mudcloth (Mali), Kente cloth (Ghana), Korhogo cloth (Cote d Iboire), Maasi cloth and jewelry (Kenya) and Bati, cabretta and Selallie leather (Ethiopia).

Problems

The inability of African governments to secure IP rights for the continent's products of TK, and prevent counterfeiting and piracy of products poses serious threat to the economy of the individual countries, as well as creators and inventors of intellectual works who are denied proceeds from their hard work and this discourages them from engaging in further creative activities and inventions. For instance, it is estimated that the Nollywood industry in Nigeria loses about $300m every year to digital theft or piracy. Other African countries have their stories to tell regarding the twin evil of IP (counterfeiting and piracy).

The fight for Africa's IP rights is of critical importance for the continent's future. Unless African governments sustain the fight by taking determined steps to secure IP rights for their countries' products, flora and fauna, art and culture, the continent stands to lose billions of dollars every year as the rest of the world protects its intellectual property.

SOLUTIONS AND RECOMMENDATIONS

Solutions

As mentioned earlier in this work, counterfeiting and piracy, though keep the informal economy of most African countries going, retard the growth of the formal sector of African economies. Because the cyberspace is open and unregulated, all sort of unwholesome activities including piracy are perpetrated online. This no doubt poses a major challenge to the entire continent economy. There is therefore an urgent need for African governments to put in place tougher legislations to halt the menace and this should be carefully followed with strict enforcement.

It is lamentable that in spite of the availability of several IP rules that may likely impact positively on Africa's TK products, majority of the countries are reluctant to take advantage of the prevailing situation to negotiate for the protection of their products. To say that, the time has come for African governments to wake up from their slumber, and fight for the adequate protection of the continent's brands, is to state the obvious. The rest of Africa should take a cue from the example of Ethiopia and South Africa who despite the initial setbacks still forge ahead to secure trademark registrations for their indigenous products through negotiations.

The geographical indication (GI) approach involving Ethiopia and South Africa is something that other African Countries can learn from. It shows that the system of IP rights protection can adapt to the demands of its member governments. But to ensure its workability, African governments must vigorously enforce agreed IP rights and take full advantage of negotiated flexibilities in the emerging global rules on IP. Failure to take reform and enforcement of IP rules seriously could result in huge revenue lost that runs into tens of billions of dollars.

As governments in the continent take pragmatic steps to address the above, there would be need to launch a vigorous media campaign to promote and protect the African brands so as to improve the earnings of the producers and make substantial improvement in the economy of African countries. The media (traditional and online) could be used to promote the products of traditional knowledge which have been referred to as African brands. These products deserved to become global brands. African governments should as a matter of priority use the available media channels especially online media platforms because of its wide reach and appeal to market these products to the outside world and indigenous people. Lack of African governments commitment to promote these products in collaboration with their creators (individuals or communities) is partly responsible for the non-recognition of the brands locally and in the global market. In this digital age, where everything is done online, African countries cannot afford not to keep pace with modern development.

Recommendations

This chapter has clearly shown that there is a ray of hope for the continent only if the countries can stand up and fight for the protection of their intellectual property. For Africa to win the battle, it must do the following:

1. African countries must ensure that local copyright, trademark and patent laws and enforcement meet international standards. This will help to boost the power of African producers and artists to secure legal protection in their own (local) and international markets.
2. There is compelling need to take and commission inventories of intellectual property in the individual countries and show producers and distributors how licensing deals can protect the uniqueness of their work and increase its value in retail markets.
3. African countries should demand that products such as cocoa, palm oil, vanilla and blackwood, and others get the same level of protection through the World Trade Organization's (WTO) geographical indications scheme.
4. They should develop a common position with Asia and Latin American countries on the legal protection of the widest range of traditional knowledge at the WTO and accelerate negotiations.
5. They should use fully the technical assistance offered by experts at the World Intellectual Property Organization both to defend their producer's legal rights and to get access to the technology transfer now available under international treaties.

FUTURE RESEARCH DIRECTIONS

In the light of the ideas canvassed in this work in favour of the protection of TK products vis-à-vis the general focus of the book which has to do with media law, ethics, and policy in digital age, it is germane to point to a new direction that may likely form the nucleus of future research in the topic area. With few countries (Ethiopia and South Africa) taking up the gauntlet in securing trademark registrations for their products after a hard battle of negotiation with industrialized countries, more are likely to overcome the hurdles and become key players in the emerging global IP regime.

Using the Ethiopia and South Africa benchmark, there would be need to conduct research into the level of compliance with the enforcement of agreed IP rights and full implementation of national laws on copyright, patent, trademark in individual countries. The ability of the continent to defend its IP would depend largely on how individual countries are able to drive these issues and put them on the front burner as part of public policy, as well as strictly enforce and implement these laws, which have implications for the development of agro-allied business, pharmaceuticals etc. within the overall framework of making media laws work for the benefit of the society.

The fight for IP rights in Africa would require clever strategy and patent negotiations with organizations such as WTO, WIPO, ARIPO and OAPI to mention but a few. This struggle is of critical importance for Africa's future. Africa needs to innovate but the innovation must be backed by IP strategies in order to help African farmers and entrepreneurs market their distinctive products and improve their income. As stated earlier, there is going to be a paradigm shift from a state of being lukewarm to active participation. Therefore the participatory model which stressed the importance of cultural identity of local communities (which TK represent) and democratization and participation at all levels – international, national, local and individual becomes useful. Freire (1983) cited in Servaes (2004), refers to this as the right of all people to individually and collectively speak their word. The main actors here would be the government, media and citizens (individuals, consumer groups, local communities, civil society). Participation is necessary in order to share information, knowledge, trust, commitment and a right attitude in planning, enforcing and implementing the laws. As government put in place strategies to enforce and implement the aforementioned laws and the agreed IP rights, the media and citizens should monitor what is being done for the interest of the overall society.

CONCLUSION

It is crystal clear from the foregoing discussion that traditional knowledge can provide a huge resource base for countries in the African continent if properly harnessed. Although attempts to protect and secure IP rights for traditional knowledge and its products have been fraught with controversies that make the issue of TK protection an endless debate at the international arena, individual countries in Africa and the entire continent stand a lot to benefit from the current IP regime if they negotiate harder with industrialized countries to recognize their products and secure IP rights for them.

As they pursue this arduous task, individual countries should also endeavour to ensure strict enforcement of laws on copyright, patents, trademarks, plant breeders rights etc. as this would make them look serious in the eyes of the international community and become active players in the new IP regime. This should be followed by a deliberate public policy to discourage counterfeiting and piracy in the continent. The theft of intellectual property, including the one carried out on the Internet (digital piracy) is depriving government as well as creators of intellectual works revenue that runs into billions. Piracy also discourages owners of intellectual property from engaging in further creative activities.

The intangible value of Africa's production deserved to be protected from global competitors who appropriate these products because of the absence of a strong political will on the part of African governments to do the needful. Now is the time to act.

REFERENCES

Adekola, T.A., & Eze, S.C. (2015). Intellectual property rights in Nigeria: A critical examination of the activities of the Nigeria Copyright Commission. *Journal of Law, Policy and Globalization, 35.*

Akhere, J. I. (2014). *Cyber law: An introduction.* Charlotte, NC: Ehiose Publishers.

Babafemi, F. O. (2007). *Intellectual property: The law and practice of copyright, trademarks, patents and industrial designs in Nigeria.* Ibadan: Justinian Books Ltd.

Bambridge, D. (1991). *Intellectual property* (4th ed.). London: Financial Times Pitman Publishing.

Baran, S. J. (2012). *Introduction to mass communication: Media literacy and culture.* New York: McGraw-Hill.

Bettig, R. V. (1996). Critical perspectives on the history and philosophy of copyright. In R. V. Bettig (Ed.), *copyrighting culture: The political economy of intellectual property.* Bolder, CO: Westview Press.

Biagi, S. (2003). *Media impact: An introduction to mass media.* Thomson Wadsworth.

Bitton, M. (2012). Rethinking the anti-counterfeiting trade agreement's criminal copyright enforcement measures. *The Journal of Criminal Law & Criminology, 102*(1), 67–117.

Bollyky, T. (2013, April). *Why chemotherapy that costs $70,000 in the US costs $2,500 in India.* The Atlantic Group.

Brassell, K., & Martin, K. (2013). *Banking on IP?* Newport, UK: The Intellectual Property Office.

Bureau of Public Information. (2005). *Traditional knowledge.* Available at www.unesco.org/links

Castells, M. (1999). The information age. *Journal of Economy, Society and Couture, 1*(3).

Convention on Biological Diversity. (2010). *Traditional knowledge, innovation and practices.* Available at www.cbdint/traditional

Correa, C. M., & Li, X. (2009). *International property enforcement: International perspectives.* Cheltenham, UK: Edward Elgar Publishing.

DeGeorge, R. T. (n.d.). 14 Intellectual property rights. In G. B. George & L. B. Tom (Eds.), *The Oxford handbook of business ethics.* Oxford, UK: Oxford University Press.

Dominick, J. R. (2002). *The dynamics of mass communication.* Madison, WI: McGraw Hill.

Dutfield, G. (2003). *Protecting traditional knowledge and folklore.* Retrieved from http://www.ictsd.org/iprsonline

Farah, P.D., & Tremolada, R. (2014, March). Desirability of commodification of intangible cultural heritage: The unsatisfying role of intellectual property rights. *Transnational Dispute Management, 11*(2).

Greenhalgh, C., & Rogers, M. (2010). *The nature and role of intellectual property: Innovation, intellectual property and economic growth.* Princeton University Press.

Hasan, S. (2013). *Mass communication: Principles and concepts.* New Delhi: CBS Publishers and Distributors PVT Ltd.

Hilbert, M. (2015). *Digital Technology and social change.* Retrieved from https://www.canvas.instructure.com/courses1949415

International Council for Science. (2002). *Science and traditional knowledge: Report from the ICSU study group on science and traditional knowledge.* Retrieved from http://www.icsu.org/publications/reports-and-reviews/science-traditional-knowledge/science-traditional-knoweldge.pdf

Irina, D. M. (2011). The puzzle of criminal sanctions for intellectual property infringement. *Harvard Journal of Law & Technology, 24*(2), 469–518.

Johnson, M. (1992). Research on traditional environmental knowledge: Its development and its role. In M. Johnson (Ed.), *Lore: capturing traditional environmental knowledge.* Ottawa: IDRC.

Kameri-Mbote, P. (2005). *Intellectual Property Protection in Africa: An Assessment of the Status of Laws, research and policy analysis on intellectual property right in Kenya.* Retrieved from http://www.ielre.org/content/w0502.pdf

Laird, S. (Ed.). (2002). *Biodiversity and traditional knowledge, equitable partnerships in practice, people and plants conservation services. WWF, UNESCO, Royal Botanic Gardens Kew.* London: Earthscan Publications Ltd.

Lemley, M.A. (2015). *Property, intellectual property and free riding.* Available at heinonline.org

Levine, D., & Boldrin, M. (2008). *Against intellectual monopoly.* London: Cambridge University Press.

Lorimer, R., & Scannell, P. (1994). *Mass communication: A comparative introduction.* Manchester, UK: Manchester University Press Ltd.

Mansurov, V.A. (1988). *Mass media and public opinion: Problems of interaction.* Mass media and public opinion Tampere University, Department of Mass Communication Publication Series B, No. 24.

Merges, R. P., Menell, P. S., & Lemley, M. A. (2007). *Intellectual property in the new technological Age* (4th ed.). New York: Wolters Kluwer.

Muller, M. R. (2013). *Protecting shared traditional knowledge: Issues, challenges and options; ICTSD programme on innovation, Technology and intellectual property; issue paper No 39.* International Centre for Trade and Sustainable Development. Available at www.ictsd.org

Nwabachili, C.C., Nwabachili, C.O. & Agu, H.U. (2015). The challenges of enforcing intellectual property rights across the economic community of West African States: The Nigerian experience. *Journal of Law, Policy and Globalization, 34.*

Panathiere, D. (2005 July). The persistence of piracy: The consequences for creativity, for culture, and for sustainable development. *UNESCO e. Copyright Bulletin*.

Pavlik, J. V. (2008). *Media in the digital age*. New York: Columbia University Press.

Pavlik, J. V., & Micintosh, S. (2011). *Converging media: A new introduction to mass communication*. Oxford, UK: Oxford University Press.

Pena, D. G. (2005). *Mexican American and the Environment*. University of Arizona Press.

Peter, K. Y. (2007). *Intellectual property and information wealth: copyright and related rights*. Westport, CT: Greenwood Publishing Group.

Posey, D.A., & Dutfield, G. (1996). *Beyond intellectual property: Towards traditional resource rights for indigenous peoples and local communities*. Ottawa: International Development Research Centre.

Rand, A. (1967). *Capitalism: The unknown ideal* (2nd ed.). New York: Signet.

Servaes, J. (2004). Multiple perspectives on development communication. In C. C. Okigbo (Ed.), *Development and Communication in Africa*. Rowman & Littefield Publishers Inc.

Shapiro, R.J., & Pham, N.D. (2007). *Economic Effects of intellectual property-Intensive manufacturing in the United States*. Available at archieve.org

Social Trends Institute. (2013). *What society needs from media in the age of digital communication*. Retrieved from https://www.socialtrendsinstitute. org/experts-meetings/civil-society-needs-frommedia-in-the-age-of-digital-communication

Sprinello, R. A. (2007, January). Intellectual property rights. *Library Hi Tech*, *25*(1), 12–22. doi:10.1108/07378830710735821

US Council for Intellectual Business. (1985). *A new MTN: Priorities for intellectual property*. Available at www.uscib.org/

Vipond, M. (2000). *The mass media in Canada*. Lorimer and Company.

WIPO. (2007). *Measuring the economic impact of IP systems*. Retrieved from http://www.wipo.int/portal/en/news/2007/article0032html

WIPO. (2008). *Intellectual property Handbook: Policy, law and use*. Retrieved from http://www.wipo.int>pubdocs>wipo_pub_450pdf

WIPO IGC. (2008). *Protection of traditional knowledge: Draft gap analysis*. Revision 4. WIPO Doc. WIPO/GRTKF/IC/13/5/6b Rev. Retrieved from http://www.wipo.int/edocs/mdocs/tk/en/wipogrtufic13/wipogrtkfic135b

KEY TERMS AND DEFINITIONS

African Brands: Indigenous products produced in Africa through the use of traditional knowledge. These products are found in almost every country and need to be protected against global competitors.

Counterfeit: An imitation of the original product. Counterfeit products are seen everywhere in the African continent.

Convention: An agreement between nations.

Digital Piracy: The unauthorized copying of software using digital technology.

Enforcement: The act of compelling people to obey rules and regulations.

Globalization: The interconnectedness of people and places through the converging processes of economic, political and cultural change.

Global Competitors: The producers of foreign goods that compete with locally produced goods in the global market.

Piracy: The unauthorized use of patented work.

WIPO: The World Intellectual Property Organization is an international organization dedicated to helping ensure the rights of creators and owners of intellectual property are protected worldwide. It also ensures that inventors and authors are recognized and rewarded for their ingenuity.

WTO: The World Trade Organization deals with the global rules of trade between nations. Its main function is to ensure that trade flows as smoothly, predictably and freely as possible.

Chapter 8
Overcoming the Legal Challenges of News Reporting:
A Case Study of a Start-Up News Corporation

Jonathan Bishop
Centre for Research into Online Communities and E-Learning Systems, UK

ABSTRACT

When one thinks of barriers to setting up a news corporation, one might think in terms of the costs of machinery and staffing. This case study of a start-up news corporation called Crocels News shows that the biggest cost can be in resolving legal disputes, most significantly from news articles scrutinising public bodies and their staff. This chapter investigates the difficulties faced by Crocels News in providing news content. By considering the legal correspondence received, the chapter provides insights into some of the problems all news services are likely to experience if they do not have access to the huge legal budgets of the established news corporations. The findings are particularly worrying for emerging forms of news reporting, such as citizen journalism. The chapter therefore proposes changes in statute so that case law that protects free speech is more easily enforced.

INTRODUCTION

Information it is said is power. Being able to convey such information equally requires power. When one is seeking to start up a news service one has to bear in mind that those who have power will seek to use that power to censor any criticism of them. The question therefore one must ask is that how can a new news service keep its power to scrutinise those with power when those persons often have the money to threaten litigation and convince one's supply chain of information society service providers to interrupt services.

This chapter explores a case study of Crocels News, which started as project of The Crocels Press Limited in the United Kingdom, but has had to be transformed into a fully incorporated limited liability company in the United States – Crocels News, LLC – in order that it can continue to scrutinise public authorities, public figures and those in public office in the UK, as well as reporting US news.

DOI: 10.4018/978-1-5225-2095-5.ch008

BACKGROUND

Setting up any business is challenging, but in the case of a news corporation that will have content produced by journalists, a grasp of media law is an essential criterion (Shemberger, 2015). Understanding media law is essential to being able to conceptualise the interactions between the law, the media and society (Price, Verhulst, & Morgan, 2013).

Media Regulation in the Digital Age

The main barrier to entry for a news organisation has been the necessity to establish a reputation in order to sell printed editions of newspapers or broadcasts of news reports (Ihlström Eriksson & Kalling, 2007). This has somewhat changed in the digital age, where the existence of weblogs has made creating news websites that much simpler (St Clair, 2015). Some have argued this provides for greater pluralism in news content (Craufurd Smith, Tambini, & Morisi, 2012), whereas others have argued that barriers to entry for the news industry are actually a good thing (Lau & Wydick, 2014).

One of the problems for news providers of all levels is that many people will try all manners of ways to get content they disapprove of removed from a news website or other news service. This is often done through takedown notices, which can be letters or emails that claim a news service is infringing the legal rights of the sender or the sender's client (Blankfield & Stevenson, 2012). Takedown notices are often used to harass content providers into taking actions to remove content they are under no legal obligation to remove (Ashley, 2009). Some see them as a double-edged sword that can both protect actual rights but at the same time stifle free speech (Doctorow, 2008). A significant number of the examples of legal issues discussed in this chapter are relating to takedown notices, which seem to be an efficient way for those claiming their rights are infringed to try to get such claims dealt with efficiently.

Politics and Policy in the Digital Age

There is often significant criticism of the news industry that they exist not to report the news in an objective way but to influence public policy and change the behaviour of the public (Antilla, 2008; Schultz & Achtenhagen, 2013). The criticisms of the way the news media have such an impact on governments and public policy through framing debates is of concern to some (Bennett, 2004; Fleming-Rife & Proffitt, 2004). There has also been criticism that news media is used more as a means of entertainment than to actually provide information in an accurate and meaningful way (Morris & Forgette, 2007). Furthermore, some are concerned of the way that national news media tends to occupy a greater part of the public consumption of news that local sources (Snider, 2000).

What is clear about the case study in this chapter is that those in positions of power within governmental bodies and public services do not like the way that the news media can be used to hold them to account. Many members of the public see journalist produced news reports as having significant credibility, and so trying to censor such reports is something public officials wanting to avoid scrutiny would want to attempt to do. Such is the truth of things that legal cases such as Derbyshire County Council v Times Newspapers Limited have been necessary to establish that public bodies have no right to sue for defamation. This also needed to be confirmed following the introduction in England of the Localism Act 2011 which set out that public bodies should have the same rights as individuals, leading to councils wanting to use the Act to sue for defamation.

AN INVESTIGATION INTO LEGAL TECHNIQUES USED BY PUBLIC AUTHORITIES, PUBLIC OFFICIALS, AND PUBLIC FIGURES TO ATTEMPT TO CENSOR CRITICISM IN THE NEWS MEDIA

This section investigates a number of techniques used against Crocels News and its journalists to try to get content removed that relates to the activities of public authorities, their office holders, politicians or other public figures.

The Case

Crocels News, LLC is a news corporation registered in the state of Delaware in the United States of America that was founded in the city of Swansea in Wales in 2012. The company was for a short period based in the city of Brussels in Belgium, but related to the United States when became clear the hosting provider Crocels News used – Heart Internet – was not willing to honour the more favourable laws in Belgium in relation to copyright. Crocels News hosts a news column called "Campus Quorum," which reports education stories in West Wales and the South Wales Valleys and was previously published by Trinity Mirror Plc. Among the articles posted are those that relate to how students with disabilities are being treated by universities within West Wales and the South Wales Valleys. Another column called "Speaking Out," which was also previously published by Trinity Mirror Plc, reports on how other public bodies within West Wales and The South Wales Valleys behave towards their customers. The selection of Crocels News as a case study was due to it being a new entrant to the news and publishing industry and because of the legal difficulties it has had to navigate in light of the investigative journalism it carries out, including as a result of court reporting, the conducting of freedom of information requests and counter-trolling services on behalf of young people and those with disabilities, who have fallen the wrong side of decisions by public officials.

Participants

The participants in the study were those persons to which the articles on Crocels News related, their solicitors and the In-House Counsel of Crocels who responded to allegations put by those who did not like what was reported about them. Those who reported mistreatment by publications included students with disabilities and other people with mental health conditions. The public bodies to which their complaints concerned were a university, police service and public bodies responsible for student support, which was a local council and a government owned limited company.

Methodology

The methodology used was a case study based on forensic linguistics. A collection of take-down notices and other documents containing allegations that received by Crocels News were assembled and the allegations put from them were extracted. Commonalities between those allegations were identified and they have been reported in the results section under headers relating to those categories. A background to the case that resulted in each takedown notice is reported and how the law protects Crocels News from such allegations is also explained.

Results

This section provides the results of the analysis of the case study, which looks at vexatious complaints and takedown notices in addition to malicious allegations. Legal issues covered include defamation, copyright, civil harassment, criminal harassment, privacy and a combination of these.

Vexatious Complaints and "Take Down" Notices

Take-down notices are essentially letters or other form of communication are made by one person asking another to remove content from an information society service, such as a website containing their copyright content(Taylor, 2006). Take-down notices are a common occurrence by people who want content about them removed from the Internet(Fabos, Childers, & Golitsynskiy, 2015).

Defamation

Defamation complaints are among the most popular for those seeking to censor content. For much of the Internet's history under UK Law, the Defamation Act 1996 was in place. This Act meant that publishers, including website providers, had to ensure anything hosted on their website was free of defamation, else they could be personally liable for defamation. In the US, the Telecommunications Act 1996 took a different approach. It stated that publishers could not be liable, only the persons who authored the content were liable. In the United Kingdom under the Coalition Government of Liberal Democrats and Conservatives the Defamation Act 2013 was introduced, which provider for greater freedom of speech into the handling of defamation disputes. In the case of websites, sysops are given immunity if they provide the contact details of the person who posted the content. This somewhat brings the UK into line with the US by placing liability with the author and not the publisher – in the case of websites at least. The Defamation Act 2013 also introduces the concept of "serious harm." This means that someone alleging defamation has to be substantially affected by the published content in order for a defamation claim to be successful. Prior to the Defamation Act 2013 there was the case of McAlpine v Bercow. The case involved the wife of the speaker of the House of Commons, Sally Bercow, posting to Twitter, "Why is McAlpine trending? *innocent face*" Lord McAlpine had been falsely accused of child abuse, but the false claims were being perpetuated. The High Court was of the opinion at the time that the reference to "*innocent face*" carried the imputation of guilt by Lord McAlpine, which is how it was intended. However, had the Defamation Act 2013 been in place, it could have been quite a different case. The allegations against Lord McApline first surfaced in the 20th century, and the Defamation Act 2013 introduced the "single publication rule," which means that there is a limitation period of 1 year from the first publicaiton to bring litigation. This would have meant the incidents referred to by Sally Bercow would be beyond the limitaitons period and no action could be taken against her. The reason for this is that the new single publication rule protects those publications which are not substaintially different from the original publication. In the case of Sally Bercow, her message could not be understood without reference to the original allegations. Her message could not be considered to seriously harm Lord McApline more than the original allegations already had. On that basis, it is likely had the Defamation Act 2013 been in force at the time of her tweet that she would have won her case. The case law eminating from her claim may still have implications, however. Where a defamatory claim can be impuated from a posting, and it could cause serious harm and is within the one year limitation period, then a person could be liable for a defamatory statement.

Figure 1. A take-down notice from a public body alleging defamation

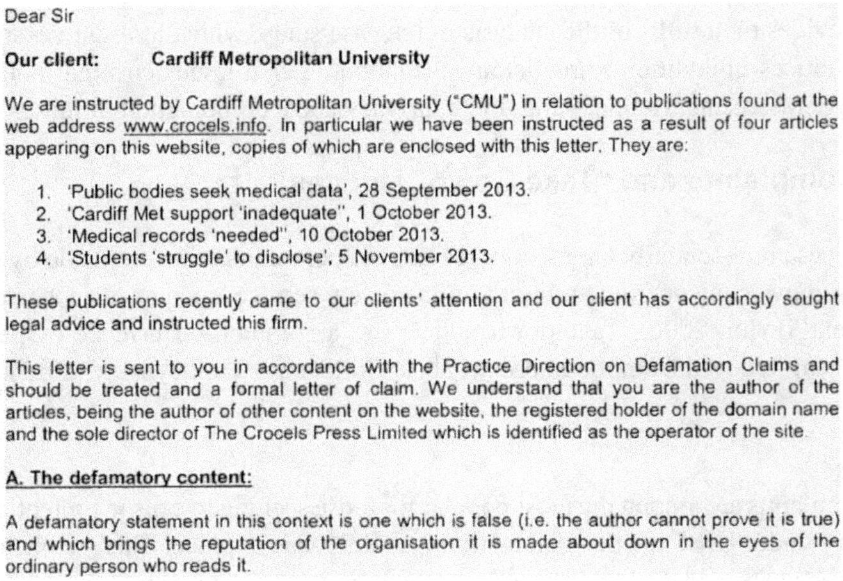

Dear Sir

Our client: **Cardiff Metropolitan University**

We are instructed by Cardiff Metropolitan University ("CMU") in relation to publications found at the web address www.crocels.info. In particular we have been instructed as a result of four articles appearing on this website, copies of which are enclosed with this letter. They are:

1. 'Public bodies seek medical data', 28 September 2013.
2. 'Cardiff Met support 'inadequate'', 1 October 2013.
3. 'Medical records 'needed'', 10 October 2013.
4. 'Students 'struggle' to disclose', 5 November 2013.

These publications recently came to our clients' attention and our client has accordingly sought legal advice and instructed this firm.

This letter is sent to you in accordance with the Practice Direction on Defamation Claims and should be treated and a formal letter of claim. We understand that you are the author of the articles, being the author of other content on the website, the registered holder of the domain name and the sole director of The Crocels Press Limited which is identified as the operator of the site.

A. The defamatory content:

A defamatory statement in this context is one which is false (i.e. the author cannot prove it is true) and which brings the reputation of the organisation it is made about down in the eyes of the ordinary person who reads it.

Figure 1 arose out of a case where a university in Cardiff took steps to exclude a disabled student from their university because they would not accept the support they had enjoyed from previous universities and which that university had originally accepted, to be prevented from being implemented.' The university concerned asked one student for their medical records as a condition of re-enrolment, which they said was in line with their policies. In other cases, a student felt unable to disclose their mental health condition, and another student with a visual impairment was not provided with a 'sighted guide.' Clearly the university did not want such facts made public and so they engaged a solicitors firm to serve a take-down notice.

If one considers the take-down notice in Figure 1, one can see how public authorities who do not like news content critical of them and their decision-making will try to make use of defamation law to their advantage. This notice was received prior to the Defamation Act 2013 coming into force. At this time Crocels News was part of The Crocels Press Limited. The letter is sent to the editor-in-chief of Crocels News, claiming that as the author of the articles and sole-director of The Crocels Press Limited that he is liable for the content. Under the Defamation Act 1996, both he as the author, and The Crocels Press Limited as the publisher would be liable, if the remarks were actually defamatory. The editor-in-chief refused to accept that the statements were defamatory, but because the host of the website – Eco Web Hosting and Heart Internet Ltd – were also liable, they suspended the website. The website was then temporarily hosted by Just Host's Green Web Hosting in the US, prior to being moved onto NearlyFreeSpeech.net. Subsequently, Crocels News was spun off as a US subsidiary of The Crocels Press Limited, namely Crocels News, LLC. This has made it more difficult for claims to be made against the hosting providers to shut down the services by proxy, as NearlyFreeSpeech.net's policy is to not do so without a court order. As it is protected by the Telecommunications Act 1996, there is no reason for it to do so.

Figure 2 shows a take-down notice from a public official whom it was alleged assaulted a member of the public when they were trying to access mental health services. In this case a man with a mental health condition was denied support from a member of the health service whom he had whilstleblown on

Figure 2. A take-down notice from a public official working for the police service

> The natural and ordinary meaning of these words is that our client is guilty of stripping and assaulting Mr Edwards as well as seriously unprofessional conduct, rudeness and intolerance, particularly in telling Mr Edwards to "*f**king wank over [his] Bible*".
>
> Clearly the allegation of assault is by far the most serious but, in placing this allegation in the context of the other allegations the article as a whole alleges that our client is a corrupt policeman. Such a meaning also implies that he is unfit to be a police officer, and that he should be prosecuted for committing criminal offences.
>
> The 16 November 2015 article *Police brutality victim in hunger strike victory* contains the following paragraph:
>
> > *A woman who fell victim to the attacks of a rogue police officer has had hope of a reprieve after her MP, Nia Griffiths, took up her case after she collapsed due to taking part in a hunger strike.*
>
> Your article later identifies our client as the 'rogue' police officer mentioned.
>
> This is a clear and unequivocal allegation that our client is guilty of attacking a woman and police brutality. In the following paragraph of your article the author underlines this allegation stating that:
>
> > *Yolande Rees-Hopkins is believed to be one of a number of people subject to violence from Dyfed-Powys police officer, PC Stuart Mann 553.*
>
> The natural and ordinary meaning of this article is that our client is guilty of using unjustified violence against a number of people including Ms Rees Hopkins. As with the earlier article such a meaning also infers that he is unfit to be a police officer, and that he should be prosecuted for committing criminal offences.

in the past and was then attacked, with the CCTV recorded of the incident of the disabled person being attacked by that member of staff and a police officer either failing to be recorded or being intentionally wiped. In another case another disabled person said they were attached by the same police officer. Clearly the police officer concerned would not want such information made public so alleged defamation.

In terms of the Defamation Act 2013, the publication of such information is protected as publishing allegations from two people who say they have had a similar experience with that police officer is in the public interest. The police station at which the police officer concerned is based has faced a string of allegations of maltreatment of members of the public to the point that the police watchdog, the Independent Police Complaints Commission have intervened following the spate of complaints. This shows how some people who might have taken part in a course of conduct can try to use the Defamation Acts to silence those whom might provide a basis for others who have experienced the same malpractice to feel confident enough to come forward.

Copyright and Defamation

Despite the Defamation Act 2013 being in force, that hasn't stopped public authorities trying it on to avoid criticism. Not only do they try it on with reference to defamation, but try to use other laws, such as in reference to copyright. References to copyright are a common way for who want to try it on to request content be removed (Taylor, 2006). In terms of copyright disputes, take-down notices are seen as an efficient way to make threats to unsuspecting providers of information society services (Romero, 2006).

The takedown notice in Figure 3 arose out of a decision maker at a student support service saying that a student with a mental health condition that developed following two periods of intensive programming was not entitled to help to overcome that impairment. The student concerned published their comments on a blog hosted by Crocels and the situation was reported on Crocels News also. The decision maker

Figure 3. A letter from a public body alleging defamation and copyright theft

We act on behalf of the Student Loans Company Limited ('SLC'), representing the interests of its employee, Nathan Lawler (the 'Employee').

It has been brought to the attention of the SLC that certain comments have been made on your websites which we understand are untrue and consider to be abusive and threatening in nature. In addition, we understand there has been an unauthorised use of the Employee's photograph.

The comments made on your websites at http://news.crocels.com and http://jonathanbishop.me.uk relate to our Employee's alleged conduct and competence. We consider these remarks to have the potential to lower the Employee's reputation in the eyes of the general public.

In particular, we consider the following comments to be defamatory:

http://news.crocels.com/news/8129/nathan-lawler-student-finance-wales-mental-health-support-not-within-definition/

"Student Finance Wales will not be providing support to computing students whose mental health conditions mean they require help with programming coursework, Assessing Coach, Nathan Lawler, has said.

Student Finance Wales has said that programming scribes – a computing equivalent of scribes used to aide people with dyslexia in exams – will not be funded by the scheme designed to help students with disabilities during the studies.

concerned complained the article defamed them and the use of the photograph from their social media account amounted to a breach of copyright.

Out of courtesy, reference to the decision-maker was removed from the Crocels News website, but because they were in public office and therefore in control of public funds, it was not deemed in the public interest to remove reference to them from the blog of the student, who was the customer that was adversely affected by the decision. Even though this was done, the public authority concerned still proceeded to try it on, by then claiming that the content was defamatory towards them instead of the decision maker.

Figure 4. Letter received following changing news article

We refer to our letter dated 9 February 2016. A copy of which is attached for ease of reference

We note that since this date further untrue and derogatory remarks have been made regarding the Student Loans Company and its employee, Nathan Lawler. These comments have been posted on various digital platforms including on a twitter feed, facebook page and at http://news.crocels.com/news/8129/student-finance-wales-mental-health-support-not-within-definition/ and http://jonathanbishop.me.uk/10475/unpluggedanduncut/nathanlawler/

If these comments are not removed by **5pm** on **Friday 26 February 2016** and/or in the event the Student Loans Company Limited or its employee receive anything further from you in this manner, SLC reserves the right to take such action as is necessary, without further recourse to yourself.

We shall reserve the right to rely on this letter in the event that legal proceedings become necessary.

We recommend that you seek independent legal advice on the terms of this letter.

Yours faithfully

For and on behalf of the Student Loans Company Limited

As can be seen from Figure 3, when the news article was changed to remove reference to the decision maker, this did not change the public authority's position. They then claimed that the article was defamatory of them. When one searches for this particular public body on Google there are only 245,000 results. For a public body with a revenue of $146,992,845, this is quite a low number of articles. Furthermore, there were only 26 blog posts in Google's blog search directory, of which most were blogs belonging to popular news services. This might make one wonder whether this public authority is routinely threatening legal action to those who are critical of them in any way, with only the mainstream media being able to fend off their legal claims.

When it became clear to the public authority that they were not going to get the content taken down through legal threats against Crocels News, and that Crocels News's web host, NearlyFreeSpeech.net, was not going to, they tried it on with the domain provider for Crocels News. In their letter to the company, Mesh Digital, they cited Article 14 of the E-Commerce Directive (2000/31/EC). This portion of the directive has been transposed into UK Law as Section 19 of the Electronic Commerce (EC Directive) Regulations 2002, which states:

Hosting. 19: Where an information society service is provided which consists of the storage of information provided by a recipient of the service, the service provider (if he otherwise would) shall not be liable for damages or for any other pecuniary remedy or for any criminal sanction as a result of that storage where— (a)the service provider— (i)does not have actual knowledge of unlawful activity or information and, where a claim for damages is made, is not aware of facts or circumstances from which it would have been apparent to the service provider that the activity or information was unlawful; or (ii)upon obtaining such knowledge or awareness, acts expeditiously to remove or to disable access to the information, and (b) the recipient of the service was not acting under the authority or the control of the service provider.

This only applies to web hosting providers, in this case NearlyFreeSpeech.net, but the public authority concerned tried it on with Mesh Digital, who lacked knowledge. This resulted in Crocels News sending

Figure 5. A take-down notice served on a domain provider

This email is to let you know that we have been contacted by the student loans company and they have requested that you take down posts that could be quite damaging to them.

The posts they would like removing are on the following URLS:

http://news.crocels.com/news/8129/nathan-lawler-student-finance-wales-mental-health-support-not-within-defination/
http://jonathanbishop.me.uk/category/publication-scheme/serious/injuries-lists/unfair-conduct/

The blogs within these pages are defamatory and have been requested to be removed under Article 14 of the E-commerce Directive (2000/31/EC)

Unfortunately, if the request hasn't been processed within the next 48 hours then the domains will need to be suspended.

Please respond back to this email once the posts have been removed.

Many Thanks,

a draft Part 8 Claim Form to Mesh Digital for the sum of £7,500 and an injunction on the basis that Section 19 of the Electronic Commerce (EC Directive) Regulations 2002 did not apply to them, because they as a domain provider were covered by Section 17 of those regulations, which state:

17.—(1) Where an information society service is provided which consists of the transmission in a communication network of information provided by a recipient of the service or the provision of access to a communication network, the service provider (if he otherwise would) shall not be liable for damages or for any other pecuniary remedy or for any criminal sanction as a result of that transmission where the service provider—(a) did not initiate the transmission; (b) did not select the receiver of the transmission; and (c) did not select or modify the information contained in the transmission. (2) The acts of transmission and of provision of access referred to in paragraph (1) include the automatic, intermediate and transient storage of the information transmitted where: (a) this takes place for the sole purpose of carrying out the transmission in the communication network, and (b) the information is not stored for any period longer than is reasonably necessary for the transmission.

The threat of legal action – which in the particulars of the draft claim referred to the fact that Section 19 of the Electronic Commerce (EC Directive) Regulations 2002 did not apply, but Section 17 did, resulted in Mesh Digital issuing the statement presented in Figure 6.

As can be seen from the email presented in Figure 6, Mesh Digital were highly apologetic and confirmed they would not be going ahead with any suspension of the domain. It begs the question of how many other domain providers had been forced to shut down domains that were highly critical of the public authority concerned.

Civil Harassment

Another avenue that public authorities will use to censor news services is to claim that the author of a news article is causing harassment to the decision maker being referred to in the news article. Figure 6

Figure 6. Response to threat of legal

Thanks for your patience.

We've spoken with our legal team and have looked into this matter further for you, they've since confirmed that we will not be going ahead with the suspension of any of your domain names, nor will there be any changes or downtime caused.

I can only apologise for the inconvenience and confusion in which this may have caused.

If you have any queries or questions then please do let us know.

Kind regards,

presents a letter from the legal firm Hugh James, whom it is assumed was funded by the public authority concerned, which claims that the conduct towards the decision maker amounted to harassment. In this case, news reports showed how the decision maker, who took leave to contest a public election where they made reference to their work for the public authority, were saying one thing to the public, but doing a different thing in reality.

As Figure 6 shows, the solicitors Hugh James are trying in on by claiming that the news articles concerned are causing anxiety to the decision maker, which they deem harassment. The decision maker had immediately prior to this stood in a UK Parliamentary election, and so one would expect that a couple of news articles would not faze them, suggesting their actual concern was to prevent lawful criticism of them.

Criminal Harassment

Another way in which public authorities or those in public office might try it on is through making complaints of criminal harassment. Research has established that policing teams are more likely to take action where the person complaining is a woman and the person being complained about is a man (Bishop, 2015). That was what happened in this case. The decision maker that was the subject of press scrutiny was a woman, and the journalist breaking the story was a man. This resulted in the police issuing what is called a 'police information notice,' which is the way the police tell someone their conduct is perceived as harassment by another person. The notice concerned is in Figure 7.

Figure 7. A take-down notice from a private solicitors firm alleging harassment

Dear Sir

Letter before Action in respect of your conduct towards Ms Karen Robson

Please note that we act as solicitors for Ms Karen Robson.

We have been instructed to advise Ms Robson in respect of the articles and postings that you have produced and/or published on the internet regarding her personally as well as her role as a member of the Disability Services Team at Cardiff Metropolitan University.

Be on notice that having reviewed these articles and web pages, we are satisfied that your conduct towards Ms Robson amounts to harassment as defined by the Protection from Harassment Act 1997. Hence we have advised Ms Robson that she does have a right to take civil proceedings against you in respect of your conduct.

If within the next 7 days you agree to undertake to remove all current postings relating to Karen Robson and further undertake not to post any further articles relating to her, it may be possible to avoid any further action in this respect. If you refuse to do so, we will issue county court proceedings against you in which Ms Robson will be entitled to recover damages for, (amongst other things), anxiety caused by your conduct as well as seeking injunctive relief to restrain your behaviour towards her. In addition to this, an order for legal costs will also be sought against you which in itself could amount to many thousands of pounds.

Do not ignore this letter.

Yours faithfully

Hugh James

Figure 8. A take-down notice from the police in the form of a 'police information notice'

Details of alleged conduct [specific actions that are cause for complaint]:
You have sent a letter to the home address of Karen Robson when all correspondence regarding your complaint should be sent to Rob Cummings at Cardiff Metropolitan University. You are not to contact Karen Robson directly and not send any items to her home address or post items relating to Karen Robson on the internet. Any concerns you have in relation to your grievance with the University must be sent via Rob Cummings.

The police have received an allegation of harassing behaviour against you.
Harassment is any behaviour which causes alarm or distress to someone else. Doing this on at least two occasions constitutes an offence.

At this stage, the police are not commenting on the truth of this allegation.

Instead, this letter is being provided to you in the spirit of crime prevention and to make you aware that *if* the kind of behaviour described were to continue, then you would be liable to arrest and prosecution.
You should also be aware that if further such behaviour resulted in prosecution then the behaviour complained of above could be referred to, or relied upon, in any subsequent proceedings.

This letter is neither a court order nor a criminal record, but will be kept by the police for the purposes of any future investigations and retained in accordance with national guidelines on the Management of Police Information.

Signature of recipient: Date: This is not an admission or acceptance of the allegation. You are signing to acknowledge that you are aware of the allegation and that you now understand what harassment and/or stalking are.	Officer Issuing [name, rank, collar no, station and contact number] PC 5169 S. EMERSON Pontypridd Witnessing Officer:

This copy is to be left with the person to whom it is being issued
Police Reference No: 6213 0107225

Figure 9. A take down notice alleging defamation, harassment and breach of privacy

Dear Mr Bishop

www.jonathanbishop.org.uk

I understand that you are the author / webmaster of the above website. As such you are responsible for the content posted by yourself and any contributors. I note your Website Terms and Conditions so understand your own protocols and "12 commandments of good practise".

Whilst the Council unreservedly supports freedom of speech and expression, it is most concerned regarding some of the website's posting on 25th February 2012, in terms of the comments made about a Council Officer and by implication the Council itself. The specific article can be accessed via the link below:

http://www.jonathanbishop.org.uk/2700/unplugged-and-uncut/how-karen-robson-uwic-cardiff-met-and-steve-evans-rct-student-support-make-me-feel-terrorised-like-a-muslim/

References to the Council officer 'making you feel terrorised like a Muslim' are defamatory and wholly inappropriate.

The Council is anxious to ensure that its Members and Officers should not be harassed, defamed or have their privacy breached in any unlawful way. Please would you therefore effectively police the content posted on your Website and remove those references (and any links or copies of that content posted on other websites), as they are clearly in breach of your own Website Codes of Conduct. This will ensure that recourse to legal remedies can be avoided.

Yours sincerely

L Gripton

Leigh Gripton
Director of Customer Care & ICT

Defamation, Harassment, and Privacy

Some public authorities will try it on with an even greater multitude of legal claims. In this section we look at a public authority who wanted one of its decision makers to escape public scrutiny by making reference to defamation, harassment and privacy. Figure 8 shows a takedown notice in the form of a police information notice where the police are claiming one of their service users deems content about them to amount to harassment. The complaint was a politician who worked as a clerk at a local university. When statements they made to the press in support of their election campaigns were re-reported with new information from the students affected by their decisions, they made a complaint to the police that it was harassment for those public statements they made when seeking election to be reused in a context that might discredit their claims during that election by referring to their behaviours in their professional life as a clerk that made decisions affecting students with disabilities.

As can be seen from Figure 8, this public authority claims that the way they made someone feel – like a Palestinian subject to abuse from the Netanyahu regime – was defamatory. The claim is quite non-sense. How can a public authority claim the way they made a member of the public feel is defamatory when that is how the member of the public felt? As can also be seen from Figure 8, the public authority claimed that by the member of the public saying how they were made to feel by the decision making, that the decision maker's privacy was being breached. It also claimed that the same decision maker was being harassed by the member of the public expressing how they felt. This shows the extent that public authorities will go to in order to avoid fair criticism.

Malicious Allegations and Treatment

In the case of one public figure and holder of public office, they went so far as to lie to their employer that the police had said something they did. This was then used against the Crocels News journalist concern in litigation and other official complaints procedures involving the police. When the occurrence happened, the journalist and their nearest relative complained to the Independent Police Complaint's Commission. Their response, shown in Figure 10.

Figure 10. Response from independent police complaints commission

However, this is explained by Ms Robson in her statement of 10 January 2014, whereby she states "any suggestion that Jonathan Bishop has had previous police contact was entirely an assumption" and "at no time has PC Davies disclosed any other police contact Jonathan Bishop may have had". Ms Robson goes on to say that the record made by Mr Doyle was a summary of their discussion and not a verbatim account. By signing it Ms Robson accepts accountability for the statement, and the repercussions for providing a false statement are considerable. I therefore consider that this statement carried added weight because of this and that it would be disproportionate to interview Mr Doyle as you suggest, as it is unlikely he could add any further weight to the matter as he was not there during the incident, and has already provided notes of the meeting between him and Ms Robson.

While I understand that it is your honest held belief that PC Davies disclosed inappropriate information, there is insufficient evidence to support the complaint. Not upheld is a suitable finding on this allegation.

Another way a public authority tried it on was to refuse freedom of information requests on the grounds of their 'commercial interests' and the fact that the journalist had made requests to them before, meaning their request could be considered "vexatious". This is evident from Figure 11. The use of claims a journalist requesting information is vexatious is commonly used to prevent the release of data that might be inconvenient for an organization (Lee, 2005).

In another incident a local councillor attempted to claim that news articles that attempted to discredit her as being a candidate able to represent local people – because she went to school in a different locality – resulted in a call to Crocels News from the police. Subsequently a complaint was made to the Public Service Ombudsman for Wales which established that the news content complained of would not

Figure 11. A communication from a public authority alleging request was "vexatious"

> In light of your subsequent comments when requesting an internal review and following discussion with our Student Services unit, I believe that our interpretation of your original request was different from the information you actually wanted. We now believe that what you might be referring to is the annual audit of the Assessment Centre which is undertaken against a quality assurance framework (QAF) by the accreditation body DSA-QAG. I do not find that there was any attempt to withhold information from you. It was merely an unfortunate misunderstanding.
>
> On the basis that this is what you are requesting, I confirm the University does hold this information. However, in accordance with Section 17 of the Freedom of Information Act 2000 this letter acts in full as a Refusal Notice.
>
> The exemption in respect of this specific request is Section 43 (Commercial Interests). In addition, taking into account previous requests you have made to this University, I am also applying Section 14 (Vexatious).

Figure 12. A response to a complaint about a local councillor involving the police in dispute about news content

> When considering your complaint about Councillor Mills' conduct in this context it appears to me also that the first stage is not met. For the reasons explained previously Councillor Mills' actions, as complained about, do not appear to breach the Code. I agree that her actions in contacting the Police to report her concerns about the comments you made would not amount to a breach of the Code. Councillor Mills clearly has the right as a private citizen to report matters of concern to the Police. Her election as a member does not, in my view, preclude her from exercising this right in circumstances where she considers that she is the victim of a crime. Further I am not persuaded that the evidence provided demonstrates that her actions were vexatious in nature.
>
> You are correct in your assertion and citation of relevant case law that as an elected member you are entitled to enhanced protection of your Article 10 right to the freedom of expression and in such circumstances your comments would not be considered to be a breach of the Code if you were bound by the Model Code as an elected member here in Wales. However it would not be appropriate for the Ombudsman to consider or comment on the application of this right to protection from complaints made to the Police, this would ultimately be a matter for the Police or Courts to interpret in the event that further action was taken.

have amounted to a breach of the local government code of conduct by the local councillor that was the benefactor of the news article. The letter received from the Ombudsman is in

Figure 12 shows that the Ombudsman was of the view that the content complained of was not of a nature that would amount to a breach of the code of conduct, but that the council had the right to go to the police even though there was an entitlement under the law to enhanced protection of free speech by politicians. It shows that the current system where police officials are required to investigate complaints, even if they would not lead to prosecutions for the reason that they are free speech could be considered an uncessary interference with the news media's right to publish content that might not be convenient for those public officials, public authorities or public figures.

Summary

As can be seen, public authorities will try it on in many different ways in order to prevent legitimate criticism and scrutiny of them from the press and others. These can involve take-down notices, where they claim content online is defamatory, breaching copyright, or amounts to harassment. They can also use other legal remedies at their disposal, including exemptions granted to them by the Freedom of Information Act 2000, and remedies from the police, such as issuing harassment warnings to journalist who are critical of them. Such a situation is worrying in a democracy so far from parliamentarians being concerned with placing additional restrictions on the press they should consider how public authorities should be more accountable to the public via the media, whether a huge global news corporation or a citizen journalist with legitimate concerns.

TOWARDS THE REFORM OF MEDIA REGULATION

The law on the scrutiny of public authorities should be quite clear. The case of Derbyshire County Council v Times Newspapers Ltd established that public authorities are not allowed to sue for defamation. However, as has been seen from this study, it does not stop them threatening to do so, in the apparent hope that they will be believed. This section sets out a proposal for key legal judgements to be codified into statue in order to ensure that the rights of politicians and the media to free speech and fair criticism are absolute.

The Creation of "Calver's Law"

Rhetoric from policing forces includes that they take every reported "crime" seriously. South Wales Police for instance responded to a freedom of information request into the use of 'police information notices' to that effect. As was discussed earlier, one of the journalists at Crocels News received such a notice when they published articles showing that a Conservative politician was claiming to be a disability champion to get into office, when their record that they wanted to be kept secret suggested otherwise. Most relevant to such a situation is the case of R (on the application of Calver) v The Adjudication Panel for Wales. This case found that politicians deserve and owe enhanced protection for their activities. It stated that politicians should not be able to bring claims of harassment against other politicians because they should have a "thicker skin." By the same token, a politician should be expected to be free from allegations of harassment if their actions relate to being a politician. Such rights should be afforded to journalists. A journalist should not face allegations of harassment for holding to account politicians or other public figures, as they are due enhanced protection through Calver. Calver's Law could therefore be seen to be the case that before initiating any action against someone for criticising the actions of others through either print or electronic communications, the law enforcement should establish whether the parties involved is a politician (or other public figure) and/or a journalist.

The Creation of "Chambers' Law"

Paul Chambers was the name of the person who appealed a conviction in what became known as the "Twitter joke trial." When Doncaster Robin Hood Airport was closed due to severe weather conditions, Paul Chambers posted to Twitter: "*Crap! Robin Hood airport is closed. You've got a week and a bit to get your shit together otherwise I'm blowing the airport sky high!!*" The message was discovered by staff a week later, but was not considered a credible threat. Chambers was subsequent subject to excessive treatment from the police, including his home and office being invaded by over-zealous anti-terror police. Chambers was convinced of sending a threatening communication under Section 127 of the Communications Act 2003. Chambers then appealed and the High Court sided with Chambers, pointing out that what he posted did not cause "apprehension" for the clear reason being that it lacked menace. Even though this judgement stands in relation to the Communications Act 2003, in laws such as the Protection from Harassment Act 1997, it needs to be applied also. At the time of writing the UK Government was consulting on the introduction of stalking prevention orders. With the existence of the Chambers judgement, and disparate injunctions in the Protection from Harassment Act and Family Law Act, it would make sense for the UK Government to consolidate the statutes and integrate protections like those in the Twitter joke trial, established by DPP v Chambers.

The Creation of "Collins's Law"

DPP v Collins was a case that established that even if a person from a given group did not receive a message, if they could be grossly offended by it then it is illegal. In theory, any person with a protected characteristic can be a victim of hate on grounds of that difference. In the Collins case, the defendant referred to non-White persons as "bloody foreigners" and even though they did not personally receive the messages because they were capable of being grossly offended by them, simply conveying the message was an offence within the meaning of Section 127 of the Communications Act 2003. Collins Law would therefore state that where a person has a protected characteristic that they will be protected from abuse relating to it on the Internet. The most obvious example is where a woman is sent a rape threat. Whilst it has been established that rape threats send by younger generations are meant in jest (Beech & Bishop, 2015), it is still the unfortunate case that the term "rape" is associated only with women, and used by trolls because they know mention of rape grossly offends women more than men(Bishop, 2014a; Bishop, 2014b). Collins's law would therefore be that anyone with a protected characteristic is protected from being abused online because of their protected characteristic.

The Creation of "Connolly's Law"

The case of DPP v Connolly [2007] EWHC 237 (Admin); [2008] 1 W.L.R. 276 involved a case where pro-life abortion campaigner, Veronica Connolly sent images of aborted foetuses to pharmacists with a political message. The images were deemed to be "obscene" and Connolly was convicted. The court found, however, that had Connolly sent the images and message to an abortion surgeon then the communications would be free speech. The reason for this is that the court said an abortion surgeon is used to being exposed to imagery of aborted foetuses and so it was a political message only. Pharmacists were not used to such messages, so they were obscene. Introducing a Connolly's Law could help journalists and news corporations. If one posts something highly critical of a politician, or one's reader's comments about them in no uncertain terms, then Connolly's Law would say that the politician should put up with it, because they would be expected in their profession to be exposed to abuse, as it is part of the job. In the case study above, where a politician had harassment proceedings brought against a Crocels News journalist, Connolly's Law would have protected them from allegations of harassment, as the politician concerned was more interested in censoring legitimate criticism, because they did not like the impact the truth was having on their political career.

IMPLICATIONS AND FUTURE RESEARCH DIRECTIONS

This chapter has looked at a case study of Crocels News to see the challenges it faced in establishing as a news service which scrutinised public bodies, especially those involved education. The case study has shown real examples of how public authorities, their employees, politicians and other public figures try to use the law to censor content they deem unfavourable. It has shown how a variety of agencies, such as the police, can conspire with public bodies and their staff to frighten journalists into removing content those persons would rather be kept offline. Future research should look at the extent to which practices affect other organisations. It might be that smaller news providers are targeted more, or simply that bigger news corporations having bigger budgets or departments to fend off vexatious claims against their journalists.

Discussion

When one thinks of barriers to setting up a news corporation, one might think in terms of the costs or machinery and staffing. This case study of a start-up news corporation called Crocels News shows that the biggest cost can be in resolving legal disputes, such as those that come perhaps surprisingly from providing content that is critical of public bodies. This chapter investigates the difficulties faced by Crocels News in providing news content that has resulted in it having to move its operations to, and incorporate within, the United States. Through considering the legal correspondence received, the chapter provides insights into some of the problems all news services are likely to experience if they do not have access to the huge legal budgets of the established news corporations.

The chapter found that public authorities will try it on in many different ways in order to prevent legitimate criticism and scrutiny of them from the press and others. These can invoice take-down notices, where they claim content online is defamatory, breaching copyright, or amounts to harassment. They can also use other legal remedies at their disposal, including exemptions granted to them by the Freedom of Information Act 2000, and remedies from the police, such as issuing harassment warnings to journalist who are critical of them. Such a situation is worrying in a democracy. After evaluating the cases of Calver v The Adjudication Panel for Wales, DPP v Chambers, DPP v Collins, DPP v Connolly and Derbyshire County Council v Times Newspapers Ltd, the chapter recommends that law on the scrutiny of public authorities should be made clearer. Public authorities are not allowed to sue for defamation. However, as has been seen from this study, it does not stop them threatening to do so, in the apparent hope that they will be believed. Equally, the fact that politicians, those in public office, and other public figures use the law to censor content should also be of concern.

REFERENCES

Antilla, L. (2008). Self-Censorship And Science: A Geographical Review Of Media Coverage Of Climate Tipping Points. *Public Understanding of Science (Bristol, England).*

Ashley, D. E. (2009). Public As Creator And Infringer: Copyright Law Applied To The Creators Of User-Generated Video Content. *The Fordham Intell. Prop. Media & Ent. LJ*, *20*, 563.

Beech, M., & Bishop, J. (2015). Cyber-Stalking Or Just Plain Talking?: Investigating The Linguistic Properties Of Rape-Threat Messages As Compulsive Behaviours. In J. Bishop (Ed.), *Psychological And Social Implications Surrounding Internet And Gaming Addiction* (pp. 111–137). Hershey, PA: IGI Global. doi:10.4018/978-1-4666-8595-6.ch007

Bennett, W. L. (2004). Gatekeeping And Press-Government Relations: A Multigated Model Of News Construction. In Handbook Of Political Communication Research, (pp. 283-314). Academic Press.

Bishop, J. (2014a). U R Bias Love: Using 'Bleasure' And 'Motif' As Forensic Linguistic Means To Annotate Twitter And Newsblog Comments For The Purpose Of Multimedia Forensics. *The 11th International Conference On Web Based Communities And Social Media.*

Bishop, J. (2014b). Youtube If You Want To, The Lady's Not For Blogging: Using 'Bleasures' And 'Motifs' To Support Multimedia Forensic Analyses Of Harassment By Social Media.*Oxford Cyber Harassment Research Symposium.*

Bishop, J. (2015). The Thin Blue Web - Police Crime Records Of Internet Trolling Show Chivalrous Attitudes That Can Be Resolved Through Transfer Of Powers. In P. E. Thomas, M. Srihari, & S. Kaur (Eds.), *Handbook Of Research On Cultural And Economic Impacts Of The Information Society*. Hershey, PA: IGI Global. doi:10.4018/978-1-4666-8598-7.ch004

Blankfield, S., & Stevenson, I. (2012). Towards A Digital Spine: The Technological Methods That UK And US Publishers Are Using To Tackle The Growing Challenge Of E-Book Piracy. *Publishing Research Quarterly*, *28*(2), 79–92. doi:10.1007/s12109-012-9265-4

Craufurd Smith, R., Tambini, D., & Morisi, D. (2012). *Regulating Media Plurality And Media Power In The 21st Century*. Academic Press.

Doctorow, C. (2008). Online Censorship Hurts Us All. *Meanjin*, *67*(3), 14.

Fabos, B., Childers, L. C., & Golitsynskiy, S. (2015). Digital Literacy, Public History, And FORTEPAN. *Media Education For A Digital Generation, 74*, 244.

Fleming-Rife, A., & Proffitt, J. M.Board of Education. (2004). The More Public School Reform Changes, The More It Stays The Same: A Framing Analysis Of The Newspaper Coverage Of Brown V. Board Of Education. *The Journal of Negro Education*, *73*(3), 239–254. doi:10.2307/4129609

Ihlström Eriksson, C., & Kalling, T. (2007). *Proposing A Business Model Framework For The E-Newspaper*. Paper Presented At The 15th European Conference On Information Systems (ECIS 2007), St Gallen, Switzerland.

Lau, M., & Wydick, B. (2014). Does New Information Technology Lower Media Quality? The Paradox Of Commercial Public Goods. *Journal of Industry, Competition and Trade*, *14*(2), 145–157. doi:10.1007/s10842-013-0157-x

Lee, R. M. (2005). The UK Freedom Of Information Act And Social Research. *International Journal of Social Research Methodology*, *8*(1), 1–18. doi:10.1080/13645570500046624

Morris, J. S., & Forgette, R. (2007). News Grazers, Television News, Political Knowledge, And Engagement. *The Harvard International Journal of Press/Politics*, *12*(1), 91–107. doi:10.1177/1081180X06297122

Price, M. E., Verhulst, S., & Morgan, L. (2013). *Routledge Handbook Of Media Law*. Routledge.

Romero, T. L. (2006). Internet Service Provider's Liability For Online Copyright Infringement: The US Approach. *Vniversitas,* (112), 193-214.

Schultz, C. J. P., & Achtenhagen, L. (2013). Discouraging Stereotypes? US Newspaper Coverage Of Ethnic Minority Entrepreneurs Before The Economic Downturn. *Journalism*, 1464884912473394.

Shemberger, M. (2015). Is The Sun Shining? A Qualitative Study On The Presence Of Sunshine Laws In The College And University Journalism Curriculum. *Journalism & Mass Communication Educator*.

Snider, J. H. (2000). Local TV News Archives As A Public Good. *The Harvard International Journal of Press/Politics*, *5*(2), 111–117. doi:10.1177/1081180X00005002010

St Clair, J. (2015). Doing It For Real: Designing Experiential Journalism Curricula That Prepare Students For The New And Uncertain World Of Journalism Work. *Coolabah*, *16*, 122–142.

Taylor, A. (2006). Publishing And Electronic Piracy. *Learned Publishing*, *19*(3), 168–174. doi:10.1087/095315106777877539

Chapter 9

Electoral Polling and Reporting in Africa:

Professional and Policy Implications for Media Practice and Political Communication in a Digital Age

Adebayo Fayoyin
United Nations Population Fund (UNFPA), South Africa

ABSTRACT

Opinion polling during elections plays a pivotal role in influencing the political and media agenda, and can potentially affect voting behaviour. However, evidence from various countries indicates that electoral polls have been characterised by contradictions and contentious debates which undermine their usefulness in democratic processes. The digital age has also led to a mushrooming of online polls, but some of them are of dubious quality. Thus, the chapter questions the continued use of electoral polls in multiparty politics in Africa. It argues that as a result of the inherent political and electoral volatility in many African countries, the utility of opinion polls need to be reconsidered. The paper recommends strategies for addressing the identified pitfalls, including increased professionalization of opinion polling, voter education on the limitations of pre-election polls and stronger appreciation of data journalism for media professionals. Stricter regulations, such as the embargo of election opinion polling may also be considered in different contexts.

INTRODUCTION

For over 80 years, opinion polling has been a major element of democratic polity and a source of data and information across the world. Polls are a permanent feature of democratic processes and are essential to policy making and public engagement on social issues globally (Esomar & Wapor, 2014; Lewis, 2001). As a component of survey research, opinion polls help to describe, understand, explain, analyse and predict the perceptions and behaviour of a population or its sample (Fayoyin & Ngwainmbi, 2015; Kou & Sobel, 2004).

DOI: 10.4018/978-1-5225-2095-5.ch009

Particularly, surveys conducted during elections in various countries are central to modern-day democratic practices and electoral strategy. According to Makulilo (2013) such polls are important for projecting voter intentions while to Ndati, Wambua, and Mogambi (2014) they help to measure the support of political parties and public perceptions on different issues. As Hillygus (2011, p. 965) argues, electoral surveys have three main uses in multiparty politics: to forecast the outcome of an election, to understand voter behaviour and to inform campaign strategies. Other writers have also highlighted the value of political polls in promoting political debates and public education (Jacobs & Shapiro, 2005; Patterson, 2005; Wright, Farrar, & Russell, 2013). Besides, polls can assist in expanding the political space of political elites (Ramshaw, 2014) and in some places serve as indications of the trajectory of future election (Wlezien, Jennings, Fisher, Ford, & Pickup, 2013). Also depending on the context, polls results can serve as a predictor of future electoral success (Zerback, Reinemann, & Nienierza, 2015).

Nevertheless, they are subject to varied controversies and contradictions. Holtz-Bacha (2012) opines that pre-election opinion polls have been misused in many countries and embroiled in public controversies. Among others, Jacobs and Shapiro (2005) and Makulilo (2013) have found that many pre-election surveys have failed in different countries, causing undesirable and contentious arguments among media, academia, politicians, and opinion leaders. From multiple case studies in sub Saharan Africa, Ramshaw (2014) concluded that election polls have accentuated acrimonious political temperaments and negatively impacted national political processes and outcomes. Additionally, the issue of reliability of elections polls has historically been raised in public opinion research. Dionne and Mann (2003) hypothesize that the odds that opinion polls about polls would end in unfavourable view of the pollster and their work is quite high. Overall, the failure of electoral polls in many countries has increased the army of sceptics on their use in our present-day political context (Holtz-Bacha, 2012).

Against this backdrop, the chapter examines the strengths and weaknesses of electoral polls in Africa and questions their continued use in multiparty elections. While recognizing that the culture of public opinion measurement is generally weak on the continent, (Church & Onyebuchi, 2012; Ramshaw, 2014), it establishes that political polls have become a major fixture of contemporary electoral dynamics. Thus, the chapter questions whether African countries should continue to utilise opinion polling as part of multiparty politics, despite its well-known failures. It argues that as a result of the inherent political and electoral volatility, African countries cannot afford the luxury of opinion polls which reinforce political cleavages and tribal politics endemic in some of the countries. The digital age, characterised by globalisation and democratisation of information has potentials for enhancing multiparty democracy and citizenship engagement. Yet, the Internet and social media platforms can be used for political disinformation and misinformation (Jessen, 2008; Lewandowsky, Ecker, Seifert, Schwarz, & Cook, 2012). Therefore, the chapter calls for measures to enhance the adherence of actors in the electoral polling business to ethical standards of public opinion research. It also proposes stricter regulation, including an embargo on pre-election surveys.

The chapter is organised into five main segments. First, a short introduction on the role of election surveys in different political contexts is outlined. Second, as a conceptual orientation, the chapter presents an overview of the literature on the function and dysfunction of political polling from a global perspective. This section also highlights important issues concerning the digital age and electoral polling. Third, brief case studies from four African countries – Malawi, Kenya, Nigeria, and Egypt - are presented to illuminate the performance of opinion polls on contemporary multiparty democracy. Fourth, it discusses key issues and their implications in media and political settings. Fifth, and finally, the chapter outlines specific recommendations to address the identified pitfalls. Future areas of research are also proposed.

Essentially, the chapter directly or indirectly explores a number of ethical, policy and legal concerns pertaining to media and opinion polls in a digital age as outlined as follows.

Ethical issues:

- The question of data manipulation in society,
- Disinformation and misinformation,
- Adherence to the ethics of election reporting.

Policy Issues:

- Normative principles of opinion research,
- Measures for polls reporting during elections,
- Effective management of online media in African society,
- The value of data in governance,
- Enhancing knowledge-based journalism in multi-party politics.

Legal Issues:

- Legal implication of the embargo of election polls,
- Right to publish and freedom of information during elections.

BACKGROUND: A GLOBAL PERSPECTIVE ON ELECTION OPINION POLLS

Opinion polling has been in existence for over 200 years, but modern and commercial polling are just over eight decades old (Lewis, 2001; Traugott, 2012). The practice of electoral polling started in the US between the 1930s -1940s and has become a fixture of multi-party politics across the world. Historically, opinion polling is linked to advances in mass communication and the first nationwide polls were conducted for newspapers in 1935 (Zetterberg, 2004). Since then opinion polls among the general public and polls during elections have been part of the democratic process. While the US has had great success in conducting electoral polls, the country has also experienced a series of monumental controversies which undermine the prospects and business of opinion polling. Examples of large-scale failures of electoral polls in the country include the wrong forecast of election results in the case of Landen and Roosevelt in 1936, Dewey and Truman in 1948, and the failure to forecast the landslide victory of Ronald Reagan in 1980. In addition, Barone (2015) cites recent examples in governorship elections in the country where polling results differed from the actual results.

Media experts and social scientists in the country have attempted to unravel the failure of political polls. From the index case that happened in 1948, Zetterberg (2004) identifies the root cause as inadequate appreciation of the historical context of voting, ineffective use of probability sampling, limiting polls to the 'situation of the day', and gaps between the theory and practice in public opinion research. Yet, after over 50 years since the first electoral polling disaster, similar reasons for failure of election polling are still bandied around. According to Barone (2015) the list has been modified and extended to include the complex nature of opinion polling, challenges with the methodology of data collection and faulty interpretation of results.

Nonetheless, an intriguing aspect to the performance of pre-election polls is that even when the polls are accurate, they might still 'come under fire'. Jacobs and Shapiro (2005) opine that despite the accuracy of the 2004 political polls, they were heavily scrutinised in the country while media filtering, misreading of the results and influence of campaign consultants led to unwarranted public debate of the polls. Overall, the polling business in the country has suffered several setbacks with immense impacts on its future (Wuthnow, 2015). And this trend is being replicated in other parts of the world.

In Canada, election opinion polling is considered as an important and indispensable feature of political campaigns. However, as Emery (1994) opines, a myriad of weaknesses affect the quality of polls in the country. These include the transient nature of public opinion, divergent knowledge and opinions on issues, response rate to polls questions, and voter turn-out. Similarly, after over two decades of opinion polling in the country, pre-elections polls are still judged to be unpredictable and incapable of producing consistent results at times. (CBCnews, 2015).

Most European countries have integrated electoral polling and public opinion surveys as part of their democratic processes. But they have equally experienced major highs and lows in the performance of political polls. In an analysis of election surveys in Portugal from 19991 to 2004, Magalhães (2005) refutes the criticism of purposeful manipulation of results by pollsters, but affirmed that large errors was the norm in European parliamentary elections. In the UK, electoral polls have had huge problems. Barone (2015) contends that over the years, 15 of the polls in the country ended up in the wrong direction from the actual result, which questions their value and fuel scepticism on their use. The 2015 parliamentary election, where electoral polls did not accurately predict the outcome of the election is another classic example of the failure of electoral polls (Clark, 2015; Cowling, 2015).

Examining the situation in Germany, Holtz-Bacha (2012) claims that opinion research is treated with ambiguity, especially because of well-known weaknesses relating to methodology, interpretation and error margin. Besides, electoral polling in Germany has been subjected to major disasters. According to the author, the saga with the election polls in 2005 led to the following scathing remark by one politician:

Pollsters should say goodbye to trying to influence politics by way of public opinion research, and politicians should not succumb to temptation to justify their decisions with the help of public opinion research. (Holtz-Bacha, 2012, p. 93)

Electoral polls have also had different levels of performance in different countries. In Australia,Mills and Tiffen (2012) maintain that political polls are yet to have serious challenges since their inception and have been useful in electoral participation and framing political campaigns messages. But in Taiwan, the lack of high quality polls is responsible for decreased trust in electoral polls (Willnat, Lo, & Aw, 2012). In a multi-country review covering Sri Lanka, Israel, Poland Argentina, Canada and Turkey, it was concluded that most of the polls came up with unreliable outcomes (BMI Research, 2015).

From the broad cursory review of the praxis of opinion polls and electoral polling in different settings, a few cross-cutting issues can be identified.

First, electoral polls and political outcomes are related, but the dynamics of the relationship is uncertain (Warren, 2001). Although pre-election opinion polls are presumed to be powerful in democratic processes and have been useful for educating the public, forecasting election direction and influencing voter behaviour, a seminal study by Donsbach (2001) which investigated the "bandwagon" and the "boomerang" effect of opinion polls concluded that pre-election polls are not as powerful as assumed.

This conclusion is validated by Church and Onyebuchi (2012) in their study of public perception of opinion polls in Nigeria.

Second, across the world, electoral opinion polls have been fraught with noteworthy controversies (Holtz-Bacha, 2012; Willnat et al., 2012). Some of the polls produced discordant results with the actual outcome of the election which fuelled significant attacks on them. Indeed, this weakness is widely acknowledged in public opinion research. For instance, the World Association of Public Opinion Research (WAPOR) holds that "the occasional polls which appear to be wrong gets extensive media coverage with a very negative impact on the image of opinion polls and surveys and opinion research in general" (Esomar & Wapor, 2014). But in reality, electoral polling and forecasting is a complex issue. Polling is not an exact science, hence the possibility that some of the results may end up with results at variance with the actual. Although the science of polling has inbuilt techniques to ensure acceptable levels of validity of the process and reliability of its results, in practice, many election polls come up with results that are out of sync with reality, which invariably undermine the value and usefulness of such polls in society (Best, 2001a, 2001b, 2004; Wuthnow, 2015).

Third, several administrative, policy and legal measures have been put in place in different political settings to regulate electoral polls. As an example, guidelines which clearly stipulate normative principles and processes to ensure the highest level of professional integrity of opinion polls and surveys are in place by the World Association of Public Opinion Research (Esomar & Wapor, 2014). On the other are administrative measures such as embargo or blackout of pre-election polls are also in existence. According to Chung (2012) at least 46% outof the countries had blackout periods in which elections could not be published. Admittedly, restrictions and blackout of electoral polls are not popular policy options as they are considered a violation of freedom of information (Donsbach, 2001; Smith, 2004). However, it is reasoned that the negative impact of electoral polls in some countries is responsible for such measures (Emery, 1994; Lago, Guinjoan, & Bermúdez, 2015).

Fourth, the mass media play a critical role in the conduct and communication of electoral polls. Historically, the invention of polling is linked to journalism (Zetterberg, 2004). The media serve both as independent parties in conducting their own polls and mass purveyors of the findings from polls. Media role in political polls is two-fold: to use the polls results as a reflection of the political temperature and also to shape public opinion and political environments based on their interests and affiliations (Lewis, 2001; Mills & Tiffen, 2012). This is consistent with findings from Strömbäck (2012) who argues that polls provide the news media with access to exclusive news, facilitate their control over information packaging, and help to frame politics as a strategic game. However, electoral polling is much more than interviewing and reporting. Also, the media sometimes add to the drama of electoral polls in many countries.

Digital Media, Elections, and Electoral Polls

The advent of digital technology has been recognised as critical to democratic development. Advancements in digital media and communications technology have generated considerable optimism on their role in achieving democratic development and political change. At a broader level, digital media enhance social and political connectedness (Christakis & Fowler, 2011) but they can also be used as instruments of social change interventions (Fayoyin, 2011). Pertaining to election processes, digital technology has great potential for election reporting, monitoring and for political engagement (Smyth, 2013). The unprecedented availability of digital devices and platforms is now being availed for elections (Smyth,

2013; Stegmaier & Norpoth, 2013) with pollsters increasing the useof social media and the Internet for election surveys.

But the digital age poses major challenges for electoral polling. Firstly, as recognized by the WAPOR, there is a risk of disseminating unreliable information through the Internet. Other studies attest to the possible use of the Internet as a source of misinformation and disinformation in society (Fayoyin & Ngwainmbi, 2015; Jessen, 2008; Lewandowsky et al., 2012). So, while the digital media offer diverse solutions for enhancing democratic processes, the risk of mass circulation of unreliable data from flawed polls is also very high. Secondly, the digital platforms have become a source of data collection for pre-election surveys. Globally, there are several websites devoted to pre-election polls and election forecasts. But online polling creates a methodological challenge which needs to be effectively managed. A major hypothesis for the conundrum of electoral polls in the 2015 UK election was poor online polling (Clark, 2015). Thus, while the digital age increases the opportunity for speedy polling of respondents, it poses additional ethical challenges for pollsters.

To sum up, electoral polls are a major element of contemporary democracy. Although the evidence on their direct impact in multiparty elections is inconclusive, they have become a vital part of electoral strategy and a major staple of the media. Essentially, critics perceive electoral polls as 'guess work' (Stegmaier & Norpoth, 2013) and an industry driven by 'headlines' (Wuthnow, 2015). Yet, its defenders asks: "who's afraid of election polls" (Donsbach, 2001; Esomar & Wapor, 2014). Furthermore, the digital age offers profound opportunities for electoral polling, yet they present monumental challenges as well. Here lies some of the contradictions that confront African countries in the use of electoral polls.

ELECTION OPINION POLLS IN AFRICA

The advent of multiparty politics in Africa has led to the proliferation of election opinion polls (Ramshaw, 2014). But as established by various authors, the use of opinion polls on the continent is a recent phenomenon. Of the practice of opinion research in Nigeria, Luke (2010) describes the experience as a smattering of public opinion polls while for Botswana, Molefe and Mguni (2000) submit that they are a recent practice in the country. Despite the weak culture of opinion research on the continent, the number of African countries integrating opinion polls into multiparty election processed has increased.

Besides, the African continent has in recent years experienced significant progress and transformation in its digital technology systems. For instance, internet penetration in Africa has been described as 'phenomenal' and the emergence of mobile technology is generally perceived as the 'second communications revolution'. Specifically, Uys (2009, p. 1) observes that "mobile phones made it possible for millions of Africans to make their first telephone calls ever". A recent report on the media landscape in sub-Saharan Africa concluded as follows:

Sub-Saharan Africa is the cockpit of change in terms of global divide and changing media use; in little over a decade, it has gone from being largely unconnected to the Internet to having millions using it. (Balancing Act, 2014, p. 10)

The ubiquity of social media and various online platforms in Africa creates significant opportunities for their use in pre-election polls. Against this background, this section presents four case studies from: Malawi, Kenya, Nigeria, and Egypt to illuminate the pattern of electoral polling and the challenges in their conduct and communication. The most recent elections in each country are used as the unit of analysis, but additional insights from previous pre-election polls are integrated where appropriate. Critical issues and implications from the case studies are discussed hereafter.

Malawi: A Parody of Opinion Polls

Election opinion polls are relatively new in Malawi. The country has a history of one-party rule and dictatorship which spanned generations. However, the introduction of multiparty elections encouraged the use of election opinion polls. The 2014 presidential election highlighted the use and misuse of political polls in the country. First, the polls were conducted by different organisations with different professional expertise in opinion research. The main pollsters during the election were: the European Intelligence Unit, the Africa Confidential, a consulting agency, Research Tech consultants, media organisations including Sunday Times and Nyasa Times, and the Africa Barometer, a regional political institution. While some of the organisations like the European Intelligence Unit and the Africa Barometer had significant competencies in polling research, this could not be said of some others. Specifically, many institutions and individuals questioned the credibility of Research Tech consultants as a pollster. A report by the Southern Africa Editors Forum after the election disproved the credibility of Research Tech consultant because their origin and track record as credible pollsters could not be established (M'ule, 2014).

Second, polling quality varied widely. For example, polls by the Times media group were based on responses from mobile phone text messages (SMS) of self-selected respondents through the website of the organisation. It also used ill-defined "weighted average votes" as the analytical framework. Even without a sophisticated knowledge of polling theory and methodology, the process adopted was methodologically flawed and could only produce questionable results. In a critique of the pre-election polls in the country, Dionne and Dulani (2014) concluded that most of the polls were drawn from non-representative samples and produced dubious outcomes.

Third, the polls presented conflicting conclusions on the outcome of the election. Most of them concluded that different candidates/parties would win the elections, which created significant division and contentious debates (Mtika, 2014). Inextricably linked to divergent electoral outcomes was different perceptions of the polls. Even polls results from the Africa Barometer considered as credible by some observers were judged as unreliable by others. In the final analysis, many politicians denounced findings from the opinion polls as "bogus" and "sponsored" (Mzale & Nyondo, 2014). Furthermore, the polls were decried for creating confusion, voter apathy and electoral manipulation in the electoral process. The overall performance of pre-election surveys prompted the electoral commission to the conclusion that some of the polls were conducted by individuals and institutions with "questionable credentials" who produce "questionable statistics" (Malawi Voice, 2013). But this wasn't the first time election polls created such controversy in the country. According to Dalitso (2012) the country had poor polls in 1999 and 2004, with serious political ramifications.

Kenya: A Harvest of Corrupt Pollsters

The emergence of public opinion in Kenya started with the introduction of multiparty politics in 1992. Although pockets of polls were conducted after the commencement of democratic elections, the watershed for public opinion polling in the country was during the various referenda which took place in the country (Ramshaw, 2014). However, opinion polling in the 2013 political election serves an archetypal performance of flawed political polling in the country. The polls have been variously described as "poll pollution" (Makulilo, 2013), "corrupt polls" (Njagi, 2013) and "suspicious polls" (Gathigah, 2013). Although most of them were conducted by leading pollsters with international reputation such as Infotrack, Synovate and Strategic Research, the credibility of the polls was significantly berated. Njagi (2013) opines that from the inside working of the research agencies, the opinion polling process was "simply a business", a euphemism for the manipulation of polls process. The author also suggested that normative standards of research protocols and processes were compromised.

Another assessment basically describes the behaviour of one of the polling organisations as that of a "weather forecaster," conducting four limited and unrepresentative polls in one week and projecting for the entire elections. (Makulilo, 2013, p. 1). In addition, the opinion polls were methodologically defective, leading several commentators to belie the polls for their unreliability and weaknesses. Cheeseman (2014) posits that polling methods were 'frequently misunderstood, overlooked or studiously ignored". Likewise, Makulilo (2013) identifies seven fundamental weaknesses in the polls such as sampling bias, problem with the design of the polls, poor contextual analysis, level of honesty of the responses, polls design, timing of polls, technical competence of pollsters, and response rate. In the end, the author concluded that the polls were problematic on several fronts which caused "overestimation or underestimation in projecting the electoral outcome" (p.26).

Findings from the polls also became a major staple for traditional and social media. Different interpretations were offered for the polls results based on the political affiliations. Although, Kenya has a law called The Publication of Electoral Opinion Polls Act of 2012 which guides the conduct and communication of poll results, its existence did not significantly affect the poor performance of the polls (Makulilo, 2013; Ndati et al., 2014; Ramshaw, 2014).

Finally, the polls were blamed, in part for the political crisis that took place after the election (Njagi, 2013; Ramshaw, 2014). A major lesson from the overall conduct of the elections was the effect of flawed polls. Wachira (2013, p. 1) opines:

One major lesson we have belatedly learned is that election opinion polls as they are done in Kenya today can be very misleading or even biased. They can create misplaced expectations that can trigger unnecessary tensions and even chaos. In future, we may need to write a few guidelines and regulations to enhance professionalism and credibility in opinion polls.

Nigeria: Many Polls, One Result, Yet...

Nigeria has a well-developed media structure and vibrant political context, but the culture of opinion polling is relatively new to the public sector. The weak culture of opinion polls in the country is validated by Church and Onyebuchi (2012) and Ramshaw (2014). Nonetheless, pre-election polls have been progressively introduced in Nigerian polity.

The 2015 election is a good case in point. It reinforces the thesis of 'polls frenzy'. According to Nda-Isaiah (2015), a minimum of 13 pollsters of varying expertise conducted different polls in the lead up to the election. These are broadly classified as media institutions, professional posters, bloggers, politicians, political parties and unclassified others. The number of pollsters and rapidity of polls also suggest that opinion polling became a critical political strategy, and many of the polls were conducted through various online and traditional methods. However, the countless number of citizen pollsters/

journalists disseminated the information on social and digital media (Smyth, 2013). A twitter poll was conducted by the former assistant to the President and widely reported in all media – mainstream, digital and trado-digital media. The unregulated approach to opinion polling raises serious questions on the methodological soundness and reliability of results of the electoral polls.

Second, the results from the polls became the subject of various political debates on different platforms. However, given that most of the polls were not conducted by professional pollsters and that the results could not be scientifically proven, this heightened the risk of misinformation and disinformation on the political development and dynamics.

An intriguing discovery is the uniform trajectory of polls results. Most of the polls forecast victory for the opposition which eventually happened. The surprising agreement in the outcome of the polls could not be attributed to the accuracy of the polls but to the political temperament which desired a political change. Still, the poll's results were subjected to different debates based on political affiliations.

The performance of pre-election survey has raised the need to improve pre-election polling in the country (Obia, 2014). Yet this call is not limited to the 2015 electoral polls but to the general practice of opinion polling in the country. From an analysis of the 2003-2011 election, (Ramshaw, 2014) describes the performance of electoral polling in the country as below expectation, a finding affirmed in Church and Onyebuchi (2012).

Egypt: Discordant Polls Results, Public Suspicion

The Arab Spring which saw the end of the Mubarak regime ushered in multiparty elections in the country. The 2012 election was a milestone in the history as it provided, for the first time, considerable space for political competition.

As expected, several polls were conducted during the elections by national and international institutions which basically reflect the 'horse race' in the country. But they ended up with discordant results of the outcome of the election. The Brookings Institute in the US undertook several polls in the lead up to the presidential election, which suggested that the candidate of the Muslim Brother Mohammed Morsi, might lose the election (Telhami, 2012). Conversely, finding from Pew Research also based in the US confirmed that the incumbent President would win the election. Several questions were raised on the validity of the findings, necessitating the publication of the overall procedure in the media. Even with the full disclosure of the methodology, online commentators suggested that the findings were not credible.

Additionally, government-owned newspapers produced polls which were in agreement with results from the Pew Research. But another poll by the Cabinet Information and Decision Support centre put all the candidates running 'neck to neck'. Such conflicting results increased the scepticism of the polls.

An important feature of the polls was pervasive public suspicion. The Middle East correspondent of the BBC captures public perception of the polls as follows: "Egyptians are naturally suspicious of these polls, believing the pollsters are simply getting the answers they want to hear" (Leyne, 2012).

ISSUES AND IMPLICATIONS

From the foregoing, a number of critical issues pertaining to electoral polling and reporting in Africa can be identified.

Polls Proliferation

Opinion polling has emerged as a major element of electoral dynamics in African politics. Although the number and types of opinion polls vary in different countries, there is no doubt that in many African countries, there is a movement toward integrating opinion polling as part of the electoral process and political culture. Even in other African countries not covered in the case studies, such as Uganda, Tanzania, and Zambia, electoral polls continue to be used to reflect the current political context and to frame the political outcomes. They have also been useful in exploring or explaining voter preferences and are important in forecasting election outcomes. While it is argued that this trend will continue in many African countries, it is also important to note that there is a trend toward limited desire for electoral polls in some countries. Mattes (2012) observed a trend toward limited supply and demand for electoral polls in South Africa attributed to the political system which does not encourage the political elite to know the opinion and preferences of the electorate. Therefore, in countries with similar political systems to South Africa, there might be a limited incentive to undertake electoral polls.

Polls Controversies

From the cases studies, pre-election opinion surveys have resulted in twisted arguments which affect their value and usefulness. Of the opinion polls in Kenya, Ndati et al. (2014) affirm that the political polls were flawed, and resulted in hostile debates in the country. Similarly, Makulilo (2013) maintains that in other African countries, including Zambia, Zimbabwe, Tanzania, and Zanzibar, findings from election opinion polls have been subjected to public disputes. Also, the Tanzania election of 2015 was characterised by many opinion polls which produced discordant results (Lyimo, 2015) and for Ghana, Sophism (2004) claims that polling results are sometimes misunderstood or taken as the final results of election. Overall, the author suggests that the potential for public misunderstanding of polls in the country is very high.

Polls Quality

One of the major findings is the quality of opinion polls. Clearly, many of the polls were undermined by a plethora of methodological and reporting weaknesses. In Nigeria, some polls were conducted by bloggers and citizen pollsters with dubious expertise in polling. Their reports also did not fully adhere to the 'gold standard' of conducting and communicating electoral polls. In Malawi, there were serious questions on the quality of the polls. Other methodological pitfalls from election surveys in Africa include presentation of data and how the findings are used to frame media, public and political agenda (Makulilo, 2013; Ramshaw, 2014). But as earlier noted with electoral polling in developed countries, even the use of sophisticated polling methods is no guarantee for consistent poll accuracy. Thus, the debate about the quality of polls may likely continue in both developed and developing countries.

Polls as Political Instruments

It is generally argued that the extant political structure and temperament affect the performance of opinion polling (Best, 2001a, 2001b). This indicates that any process connected with politics is open to manipulation of outcomes. Presumably, pre-election polls are expected to be 'scientific'. However, in practice, the use of polls in the various elections demonstrates that it is quite 'political'. African politics is characterised by political patronage, religious and ethnic politics, polarisation, competition for power, fractionalisation, and ethnicisation (Conroy-Krutz, 2013; Long & Gibson, 2015). As seen from the Kenya case study, electoral polls were compromised through "ethnicity, preference for a political candidate, political parties, political euphoria, personal beliefs and euphoria" (Ndati et al., 2014:267). Similarly, (Ramshaw, 2014) submits that survey researchers in transitional societies are also political actors, implying that polls could be used as part of political strategy for horse trading. To be clear, the variables that influence the generation and dissemination of polls data are beyond the science of opinion polling. Thus, sanitizing opinion polling in Africa as an important source of credible information and political education, cannot be done outside of the prevailing political determinants and structures.

Polls Regulation

Although Ndati et al. (2014) postulate that the most African countries do not have any laws regulating opinion polls, it is critical to observe that specific guidelines or processes are in place in many countries to ensure that pre-election surveys are well conducted. Kenya has a regulation on the conduct and the communication of pre-election opinion polls. Still, going by the experience from the 2013 election, it was poorly implemented. In Malawi, the electoral commission put in place orientation mechanisms to equip journalists to effectively report on electoral polls. But with some of the weaknesses manifested in their reports of the polls, such mechanisms did not achieve much result. Even in Nigeria, only a partial compliance to the standards of reporting electoral polls was observed, which raises an issue of ethical reporting during elections. Overall, the performance of some of the pollsters and media institutions point to weak adherence to professional and ethical standards in electoral polling and reporting.

Digital Media and Electoral Polls

From our case studies social media have become an indispensable tool for conducting and communicating electoral polls in African countries. In all the four countries, digital media were used to conduct and to disseminate polls results. Various digital solutions for electoral processes and political development have also been deployed in different countries. Nonetheless, the plethora of online platforms has resulted in an increased publication of online political polls of different qualities. It is argued that in an age of individual political activists without global gatekeepers for editorial control on what individuals can publish or post, there is a risk of mass circulation of un-vetted and unreliable information. As Fayoyin and Ngwainmbi (2015) argue, in the digital age data and statistics from questionable sources can be tweeted, vibered, whats-apped, or Face-booked within social networks without critical interrogation. Therefore, in view of the proliferation of online election polls, it is imperative to effectively manage and control the dissemination of results from flawed polls on the digital media. Ensuring the effective adherence to sound ethical guidance electoral polling and the communication of the results thus become a major challenge in a digital age.

SOLUTIONS AND RECOMMENDATIONS

Election opinion polls in African countries have now been integrated into multiparty politics in Africa. While they are useful in gauging the opinion of the public, in some cases they have been used as tools of political manipulation by politicians and campaigners. Likewise, their use has created challenges and implications for political misinformation and disinformation in the current digital age. The following solutions are proposed for addressing the pitfalls.

Enhanced Sophistication of Election Public Opinion Surveys

To enhance the value of electoral polls in Africa, it is critical to improve their quality. This can only take place when all the actors in the polling business adhere to the established ethical guidelines. Furthermore, based on the debacle of electoral polls in developed countries, it has become imperative to apply more sophisticated approaches to accommodate the multiple variables which affect electoral outcomes. This may include interrogating variables such as the predictable and unpredictable changes that affect party support (Fisher, 2015), examining the biases in forecasting elections (Rothschild, 2009), investigating gender dimension to election campaign (Walter, 2013), and testing the impact of age, experience and contextual determinants in electoral formation (Górecki, 2015) and many others. But given that even developed countries still grapple with the reliability of their polls, it is most unlikely that African countries will be able in the short run to overcome the challenges posed by the multidimensional variables that affect multiparty politics.

Media's Role in the Conduct and Communication of Electoral Polls

Admittedly, the mass media are intrinsically linked to the technology of opinion polling. But over the years it has taken a more scientific approach and requires sophisticated competencies in sound research methodologies which most of the poorly-resourced African media organizations cannot afford. Therefore, it is proposed that African media organizations get out of the business of opinion to avoid producing deficient and dubious polls. Journalism is one thing and scientific polling is another. It is most unlikely that our media institutions can produce reliable opinion polls without adequate support of professional researchers. Second, as purveyors of social data and information on elections and platforms for political campaigns, media professionals need to apply a critical mind-set in the use of pre-election polls. They need to ask questions that help to establish the soundness of polls before they publish their results. To do so effectively requires more exposure to data journalism principles. Also, additional editorial and gatekeeping functions are needed to ensure the dissemination and reporting of valid and sound opinion surveys. Courses in data journalism and knowledge-based reporting are needed to instil the culture of critical interrogation of social statistics and election related data without adequate support of professional researchers. Above all, data appreciation for media professionals should be mainstreamed in various courses and levels of communications education. This is to help media professionals effectively report political polls, and not turn them into certified social scientists who can design and implement large scale electoral polling programmes. Thus, both social and traditional media ought to exercise caution on the use of polls data, whether online or offline. The reporting of political polls ought to move beyond the headlines around the horse race to more knowledge-based journalism and communication.

Enhancing Public Education on Polls Data

A concerted public education on opinion polling and electoral polls in particular is necessary for proper utilisation by the public. Essentially, polls are a tool for measuring the pulse of the society on specific issues but such measurements changes with time and with social developments. In many cases, political campaigners and analysts have used polls data as a principle or even a holy testimony of election results. Educating the public in understanding the limited role of opinion in the political process is necessary. Yet, in view of the level of education of the majority of the population and public mobilisation strategies of the political elite, getting the public to recognise the limitation of opinion polls as part of electoral strategy is a major hurdle.

Regulating Pre-Election Opinion Polls

Stricter regulations and restrictions, including blackout of election opinion surveys in African countries should be considered. Although none of the four African countries that were investigated in the global study currently applies such embargoes, it is argued that African countries should avoid fuelling their fire of political and electoral volatility with the use of electoral polls, which at best is a guess work. Applying the aphorism 'no news is good news' it is submitted that within the context of multiparty democracy, 'no poll is good poll'.

RESEARCH DIRECTIONS

As electoral polls have different ramifications in the African political context, additional studies for better understanding of the merits and demerits of pre-election opinion surveys are needed. The following areas of future research are therefore suggested.

- Longitudinal investigations on the trends in opinion polling in various African countries would be critical to generate fresh perspectives on the value of political polls in Africa's democratic system and for evidence-informed policy options in addressing the pitfalls of election surveys. This should also include empirical innovative studies on polling accuracy.
- Comparative studies on how election opinion polls differ from other opinion polls in African countries is worth considering. Such studies will elaborate on the similarities and differences and the impact on society.
- The merits and demerits of polls embargo as a panacea for correcting the weaknesses of election surveys deserve more empirical attention. This should come up with models that can be adopted based on different country's political typologies.
- Finally, further empirical work is called for on the relationship between opinion polling, electoral surveys and political participation. While opinion polls have become part of the electoral strategy in African politics, it needs to be established whether such polls are instruments of genuine political participation or tools of political manipulation by the political elite. Moreover, investigation on how public opinion polling can help to change the political narrative from the voice of the political elites to the voice of the people for genuine citizenship engagement and political mobilisation is advocated.

CONCLUSION

The chapter sought to examine the function and dysfunction of election surveys on multiparty politics in Africa, using case studies from the most recent elections as the analytical framework. The chapter has demonstrated that there is no shortage of polls during elections in African countries. Election surveys have become a critical element of the contemporary electoral and democratic process and a staple for the media. Potentially, they help to reflect the society and shape voter action. Pollsters have been integrated into electoral activities of political parties. While evidence on the real effect of pre-election opinion polls is inconclusive, they are now a major fixture of multiparty politics on the continent. However, many of the polls have been steeped in controversies and have played negative roles in the political processes. The digital age has also led to a mushrooming of online polls, but some of them are of dubious quality. Thus, in its current configuration, juxtaposed with the existing political dynamics in Africa, electoral polls do not add any constructive value to the democratic process of African countries. However, to address the identified pitfalls, the chapter recommends increased professionalization of the conduct and communication of political polls, voter education on the role and stricter regulations of election opinion polls. But additional empirical investigations on the dynamics of opinion polling and democracy in Africa is advocated to further establish its added value and the most appropriate policy fit to rectify the attendant weaknesses.

REFERENCES

Act, B. (2014). *The Sub-Saharan African Media Landscape – Then, Now and in the Future*. Retrieved from http://www.balancingact-africa.com/sites/balancingact-africa.com/files/products/1.%20SSA%20Media%20Landscape.pdf.

Barone, M. (2015). Why Political Polls Are So Often Wrong. *The Wall Street Journal*. Retrieved from http://www.wsj.com/articles/why-political-polls-are-so-often-wrong-1447285797.

Best, J. (2001a). *Damned lies and statistics*. Berkeley, CA: Academic Press.

Best, J. (2001b). *Telling the truth about damned lies and statistics. The Chronicle Review*.

Best, J. (2004). *More damned lies and statistics: How numbers confuse public issues*. Univ of California Press.

CBCnews. (2015). *Canada election 2015: Online polling defended, while some still question reliability*. Retrieved from http://www.cbc.ca/news/politics/canada-election-2015-grenier-duffy-aug21-1.3200371.

Cheeseman, N. (2014). *Lies, damned lies, and opinion polls*. Retrieved from http://democracyinafrica.org/lies-damned-lies-opinion-polls.

Christakis, N. A., & Fowler, J. H. (2011). *Connected: the amazing power of social networks and how they shape our lives*. HarperPress London.

Chung, R. (2012). *The Freedom to Publish Opinion Poll Results. A worldwide update of 2012*. Academic Press.

Church, S. A., & Onyebuchi, C. A. (2012). Quantitative and Qualitative Analysis of Audience Perception of the Effects of Public Opinion Polls in Nigeria's Nascent Democracy. *International Journal of Humanities and Social Science*, *2*(15), 231–244.

Clark, T. (2015). New research suggests why general election polls were so inaccurate. *The Guardian*. Retrieved from http://www.theguardian.com/politics/2015/nov/13/new-research-general-election-polls-inaccurate.

Conroy-Krutz, J. (2013). Information and ethnic politics in Africa. *British Journal of Political Science*, *43*(02), 345–373.

Cowling, D. (2015). Election 2015: How the opinion polls got it wrong. *BBC News*. Retrieved from http://www.bbc.com/news/uk-politics-32751993.

Dalitso. (2012). *Examining Parody of Opinion Polls; Sticking to Ballot Power*. Retrieved from http://dalitsopublicforum.blogspot.co.za/2012/12/we-pride-in-joyce-banda-and-henry.html.

Dionne, & Dulani, B. (2014). On the eve of Malawi's election. *The Washington Post*. Retrieved from https://www.washingtonpost.com/news/monkey-cage/wp/2014/05/19/on-the-eve-of-malawis-election.

Dionne, & Mann, T. E. (2003). *Polling & Public Opinion: The good, the bad, and the ugly*. Retrieved from http://www.brookings.edu/research/articles/2003/06/summer-elections-mann.

Donsbach, W. (2001). *Who's afraid of election polls?: Normative and empirical arguments for the freedom of pre-election surveys*. Foundation for Information.

Emery, C. (1994). Public opinion polling in Canada. Canada. Library of Parliament. Research Branch: Library of Parliament, Research Branch.

Esomar, & Wapor. (2014). *Esomar/Wapor Guideline on Opinion Polls and Published Surveys*. Retrieved from http://www.esomar.org/uploads/public/knowledge-and-standards/codes-and-guidelines/ESOMAR-WAPOR-Guideline-on-Opinion-Polls-and-Published-Surveys-August-2014.docx.

Fayoyin, A. (2011). Promoting children's rights through the new media: The Nigerian experience. *Journal of Communication*, *2*(2), 57–65.

Fayoyin, A., & Ngwainmbi, E. (2015). Use and misuse of data in advocacy, media and opinion polls in Africa: Realities, challenges and opportunities. *Journal of Development and Communication Studies*, *3*(2), 528–545.

Fisher, S. D. (2015). Predictable and unpredictable changes in party support: A method for long-range daily election forecasting from opinion polls. *Journal of Elections, Public Opinion, and Parties*, *25*(2), 137–158. doi:10.1080/17457289.2014.952732

Gathigah, M. (2013). Kenya's Electoral Opinion Polling Marred by Suspicion. *Inter Press Service*. Retrieved from http://www.ipsnews.net/2013/02/kenyas-electoral-opinion-polling-marred-by-suspicion.

Górecki, M. A. (2015). Age, Experience and the Contextual Determinants of Turnout: A Deeper Look at the Process of Habit Formation in Electoral Participation. *Journal of Elections, Public Opinion, and Parties*, *25*(4), 425–443. doi:10.1080/17457289.2015.1028411

Hillygus, D. S. (2011). The evolution of election polling in the United States. *Public Opinion Quarterly, 75*(5), 962–981. doi:10.1093/poq/nfr054

Holtz-Bacha, C. (2012). *Opinion polls and the media in Germany: A productive but critical relationship. In Opinion Polls and the Media* (pp. 93–112). Springer. doi:10.1057/9780230374959_5

Jacobs, L. R., & Shapiro, R. Y. (2005). Polling politics, media, and election campaigns. *Public Opinion Quarterly, 69*(5), 635–641. doi:10.1093/poq/nfi068

Jessen, W. (2008). *YouTube as a Source of Health Misinformation*. Highlight Health Tech.

Kou, S. G., & Sobel, M. E. (2004). Forecasting the vote: A theoretical comparison of election markets and public opinion polls. *Political Analysis, 12*(3), 277–295. doi:10.1093/pan/mph019

Lago, I., Guinjoan, M., & Bermúdez, S. (2015). Regulating Disinformation Poll Embargo and Electoral Coordination. *Public Opinion Quarterly, 79*(4), 932–951. doi:10.1093/poq/nfv036

Lewandowsky, S., Ecker, U. K., Seifert, C. M., Schwarz, N., & Cook, J. (2012). Misinformation and its correction continued influence and successful debiasing. *Psychological Science in the Public Interest, 13*(3), 106–131. doi:10.1177/1529100612451018 PMID:26173286

Lewis, J. (2001). *Constructing public opinion: How political elites do what they like and why we seem to go along with it*. Columbia University Press.

Leyne, J. (2012). *Opinion polls give few clues to Egypt presidential election*. BBC News. Retrieved from http://www.bbc.com/news/world-middle-east-18110194.

Long, J. D., & Gibson, C. C. (2015). Evaluating the Roles of Ethnicity and Performance in African Elections Evidence from an Exit Poll in Kenya. *Political Research Quarterly*, 1065912915608946.

Luke, A. (2010). Possibilities of public opinion polls in politics and mass media in Nigeria. *Journal of Liberal Studies, 13*(1), 31–45.

Lyimo, K. (2015). Stratagem: Tanzanian election opinion polls a political Trojan horse. *The Citizen*. Retrieved from http://www.thecitizen.co.tz/oped/Tanzanian-election-opinion-polls-a-political-Trojan-horse/-/1840568/2897034/-/xafw78z/-/index.html.

M'ule, E. K. (2014). *Observation of Media Conduct during the 2014 Malawi Tripartite Elections*. Open Society Initiative in Southern Africa.

Magalhães, P. C. (2005). Pre-Election Polls in Portugal: Accuracy, Bias, and Sources of Error, 1991–2004. *International Journal of Public Opinion Research, 17*(4), 399–421. doi:10.1093/ijpor/edh078

Makulilo, A. B. (2013). Poll-'Pollution'?: The Politics of Numbers in the 2013 Elections in Kenya. *Poll-'Pollution*, 1-32.

Mattes, R. (2012). *Opinion polls and the media in South Africa. In Opinion Polls and the Media* (pp. 175–197). Springer. doi:10.1057/9780230374959_9

Mills, S., & Tiffen, R. (2012). *Opinion Polls and the Media in Australia. In Opinion Polls and the Media* (pp. 155–174). Springer. doi:10.1057/9780230374959_8

Molefe, W., & Mguni, B. (2000). Opinion polls in Botswana. *Botswana Journal of African Studies, 14*(1), 122–129.

Mtika, C. (2014). Malawi elections: Big four vie for power. *Mail & Guardian*. Retrieved from http://mg.co.za/article/2014-05-16-malawi-elections-big-four-vie-for-power.

Mzale, D., & Nyondo, E. (2014). MEC warns on opinion polls. *The Nation*. Retrieved from http://mwnation.com/mec-warns-on-opinion-polls

Nda-Isaiah, J. (2015). How Accurate Are Opinion Polls In Nigeria? *Leadership*. Retrieved from http://leadership.ng/news/423020/how-accurate-are-opinion-polls-in-nigeria.

Ndati, N., Wambua, P., & Mogambi, H. (2014). The Impact of Legislation on Electoral Opinion Polls in Kenya. *European Scientific Journal, 10*(34).

Njagi, D. (2013). What if Kenya's election violence points to corrupt pollsters? *The Africa Report*. Retrieved from http://www.theafricareport.com/News-Analysis/what-if-kenyas-election-violence-points-to-corrupt-pollsters.html.

Obia, V. (2014). Opinion Poll Politics in Elections. *THISDAY* Retrieved from http://www.thisdaylive.com/articles/opinion-poll-politics-in-elections/178268.

Patterson, T. E. (2005). Of polls, mountains US journalists and their use of election surveys. *Public Opinion Quarterly, 69*(5), 716–724. doi:10.1093/poq/nfi065

Ramshaw, G. (2014). *The power of perceptions: elites, opinion polling, and the quality of elections in sub-Saharan Africa*. University of Sussex.

Research, B. (2015). *Unreliability Of Opinion Polls Bringing More Political Surprises*. Retrieved from http://www.bmiresearch.com/blog/unreliability-of-opinion-polls-bringing-more-political-surprises.

Rothschild, D. (2009). Forecasting elections comparing prediction markets, polls, and their biases. *Public Opinion Quarterly, 73*(5), 895–916. doi:10.1093/poq/nfp082

Smith, T. W. (2004). Freedom to conduct public opinion polls around the world. *International Journal of Public Opinion Research, 16*(2), 215–223. doi:10.1093/ijpor/16.2.215

Smyth, T. N. (2013). *Social media, elections, and democracy in West Africa* (Unpublished PhD Thesis). Georgia Institute of Technology.

Sophism, Y. (2004). The Role Of Public Opinion Polls In Our Emerging Democracy. *GhanaWeb*. Retrieved from http://www.ghanaweb.com/GhanaHomePage/NewsArchive/The-Role-Of-Public-Opinion-Polls-In-Our-Emerging-Democracy-53816.

Stegmaier, M., & Norpoth, H. (2013). *Election forecasting*. Academic Press.

Strömbäck, J. (2012). *The media and their use of opinion polls: Reflecting and shaping public opinion. In Opinion Polls and the Media* (pp. 1–22). Springer. doi:10.1057/9780230374959_1

Telhami, S. (2012). *What Do Egyptians Want?* Brookings: Key Findings from the Egyptian Public Opinion Poll.

Traugott, M. (2012). *Methodological trends and controversies in the media's use of opinion polls. In Opinion Polls and the Media* (pp. 69–89). Springer.

Uys, P. (2009). Africa's second communications revolution. *Global-ICT, 2009*, 11.

Voice, M. (2013). *MEC cautions media on opinion polls. Some pollsters have questionable credentials, produce questionable statistics*. Malawi Voice.

Wachira, G. (2013). 10 lessons for Kenya from the 2013 General Election. *Business Daily*. Retrieved from http://www.businessdailyafrica.com/Opinion-and-Analysis/-/539548/1737838/-/py76ac/-/index.html.

Walter, A. S. (2013). Women on the battleground: Does gender condition the use of negative campaigning? *Journal of Elections, Public Opinion, and Parties, 23*(2), 154–176. doi:10.1080/17457289.2013.769107

Warren, K. F. (2001). *In defense of public opinion polling*. Westview Press.

Willnat, L., Lo, V.-h., & Aw, A. (2012). *The good, the bad and the ugly: Public opinion polling in Taiwan. In Opinion Polls and the Media* (pp. 198–222). Springer. doi:10.1057/9780230374959.0016

Wlezien, C., Jennings, W., Fisher, S., Ford, R., & Pickup, M. (2013). Polls and the Vote in Britain. *Political Studies, 61*(S1), 66–91. doi:10.1111/1467-9248.12008

Wright, M. J., Farrar, D. P., & Russell, D. F. (2013). Polling accuracy in a multiparty election. *International Journal of Public Opinion Research.*

Wuthnow, R. (2015). IN POLLS WE TRUST. *First Things (New York, N.Y.), 39*(255). Retrieved from http://www.abc.net.au/radionational/programs/theminefield/in-polls-we-trust3f/6654686

Zerback, T., Reinemann, C., & Nienierza, A. (2015). Whos Hot and Whos Not? Factors Influencing Public Perceptions of Current Party Popularity and Electoral Expectations. *The International Journal of Press/Politics, 20*(4), 458–477. doi:10.1177/1940161215596986

Zetterberg, H. L. (2004). *US Election 1948: The First Great Controversy about Polls, Media, and Social Science.* Paper presented at the WAPOR regional conference on Elections, News Media and Public Opinion, Pamplona, Spain.

Chapter 10
Digital Media in Uganda: Where Regulation and Freedom of Expression Contradictions Are Sharpest

Brian Semujju
Uganda Christian University, Uganda & Makerere University, Uganda

ABSTRACT

This chapter is an analysis of the law in the face of the growing digital media in Uganda. It begins with a summary of Uganda's digital media terrain which helps the chapter to raise an argument of numbers in relation to relevance and external pressure, as forces behind digital media regulation. The background introduces the gist of the chapter, which is the regulation of Uganda's media in the digital age. A recent court case in Uganda, in which a local singer was sentenced to one year in jail along with her video producer, who was convicted for producing a pornographic music video that was distributed online, inspires this chapter. Didi Mugisha pleaded guilty and became the first victim of the Anti-Pornography Act, which was signed into law in 2014. Beyond that court drama and the international fame it garnered are some serious concerns. First is the relationship between the bulk of Uganda's media laws and the existing producer/consumer digital platforms, and secondly are the broad implications the current state of affairs of that and similar laws has on the freedom of expression.

INTRODUCTION

The chapter therefore reviews the above landmark case in Uganda's digital content production and the Anti-Pornography Act (2014), which was used to charge the two artistes, to present the contradictions that are apparent between the application of the digital technology, which is premised on the freedom of expression argument, and the protection of other freedoms and rights. The Neo-liberal understanding of globalization technology and the Neo-Marxist counter-views are used to ground the analysis into global scholarship. Furthermore, international and regional instruments which protect free expression and their stand on both the limitations and the regulation of the same freedom are used to strengthen the argument.

Indecent and pornographic clauses are not new in Uganda's media law history. In fact government takes a pragmatic view on the issue, arguing that media should exercise their freedom with responsibility.

DOI: 10.4018/978-1-5225-2095-5.ch010

In 2004 for example, an FM radio station, Radio Simba, was fined $1,000 by the Broadcasting Council and ordered to make a public apology (BBC, 2004) for hosting homosexuals on a show, contrary to the Penal Code Act. Debates about freedom of expression and laws among traditional media have been around for quite some time. But the way media laws are designed in the face of digital media, how they relate with freedom of expression and the implications of that regulation for new media, has received little attention.

The other crucial issue that the chapter addresses, apart from attempting to cover the above gap, is whether or not media literacy extends to digital content producers. Article 19 of the Universal Declaration of Human Rights, assumes 'equal access to channels of communication' (Nassanga, 2009). After getting access, people should actively utilise the resource of information. Media literacy, or the "ability of individuals to analyze and evaluate media critically and to express themselves, producing social communication in a variety of forms"(Nassanga, 2009), has been advanced as an idea for media consumers mostly. What about the producers, especially the digital content producers, who may also act as the distributers? Using that background, issues of digital media literacy for local entertainment content producers, who are mesmerized by the free digital distribution channels, are highlighted in this chapter as well.

THE DIGITAL MEDIA FORM

The "digital revolution" is made important by the fact that it uses the web as a centre stage for voice, picture and text media that previously were mutually exclusive (Verweij, 2009, p. 75). That kind of convergence has been hailed for its production capacity that is massive, for its interactivity, for defying distance over time, and for its individualization of producers and consumers (McQuail, 2010). In the pre-digital era, the video described above would have to be through a major state/private TV/film company regulated by government. The new dawn of digital media has ushered in the "convergence of citizenship and journalism" (Berger, 2011, p. 708) and created possibilities for alternative content production such as the ones used to produce the music video that this chapter analyses.The advances in mobile phones are pushing the internet possibilities further by introducing a smartphone (Weiss, 2013) which has lessened the regular visits to internet cafes. Nevertheless, issues of the digital divide cannot be neglected when discussing the digital revolution especially in Africa, a region that remains the world's under-penetrated with subscriber growth standing at 12% (GSMA, 2015).

Regardless, "mobiles have been the platform for a uniquely massive and multidimensional enhancement of capabilities in developing countries" (Smith, Spence, & Rashid, 2011, p. 77) and "people turn to their mobile phones to get news and information and to be entertained" (Wei, 2008, p. 37). In Uganda specifically, there are 17 million people now having access to mobile phones (UCC, 2015). The number of people using smart phones in Uganda is not yet recorded but studies done on ICT and media in rural areas indicate that 1.6 percent use the phone to access the internet for various purposes (Semujju, 2013; 2016). The African internet picture is picking up too with one in five people using the internet (ITU, 2015). In Uganda, there are 6 million people with access to the internet (UCC, 2015) of the total population of 35 million people (UBOS, 2015). Mobile phones have been instrumental in promoting Uganda's digital revolution. In relation to this chapter, whether or not the current laws provide for content that is produced (and consumed) online using gadgets like the mobile phone, computer, and others, is crucial.

LOCATING THE PROBLEM IN THEORY: GLOBALISATION THEORIES

The internet is a global technology, one that is responsible for speeding up the process of globalisation in the area of media content, regulation and form. This creates necessity for this chapter to apply theories of globalisation to explain various understandings of digital media regulation. Regulation in the digital age can be theoretically explained using the globalisation theories of neo-liberalism, neo-Marxism and traditionalists theories (Servaes and Lie, 2003; Banda, 2006).

The neo-liberals include the content producers and consumers who see the internet as an invention that will help them to circumnavigate the authoritarian rule that puts undemocratic inscriptions on the enjoyment of fundamental rights. Due to the creation of "consumer-citizens" (Lemmens, 2015) or "prosumers" meaning producers who are also consumers (Rennie, 2007), the internet is a liberation tool against despotism or any despotic form of rule or, in this case, countries' communication commissions that go from regulation to control, draconian laws that criminalise the enjoyment of fundamental freedom (like the Anti-Pornography Act) and other government mechanisms. The technical aspects of digitalization and multimedia help to promote the pervasive and ubiquitous nature of the neoliberal interests (Kaul, 2011). However, despite the promise of globalisation to bypass the local political will, media policy-making is still influenced by national and political factors (Ndlela, 2007). In more progressive economies, content platforms like YouTube can be blocked as the 2009 case in China was (Antony and Thomas, 2010). As for the video that is discussed in Uganda's case, since the conviction of Mugisha and the imprisonment of Kansiime, the song that got them into trouble, is still on line. In the traditional media sense, if there was someone convicted, the radio or TV would be ordered to remove the content or risk being switched off. This happened to four radio stations in 2009 which were switched off-air for, as the government noted, 'hosting opposition' (Lumu, 2010).

On the other hand, the argument by the neo-Marxists is an argument of access at its least but inherent in it are the various economic, political and other interests (Banda, 2006). Issues like the digital divide come into play here. Out of the 35 million people in the country, although it is not known how many watched the video within the boundaries of Uganda, the video has 18,819 views. Even if one assumes that all these were Ugandans, it is not enough to say that the internet facilitates information access to Ugandans. The neo-Marxists therefore see no reason to be excited since the new media are just continuing to facilitate information access to people who can already afford to have information. On top of that, only those who understand computer knowledge and those who have a stable internet connection (or those who can pay for one) will be the only people to upload (or to comment on) information. In the end, they control both production and consumption processes and rather than liberating people, they enslave them (Verbeek, 2015; Lemmens, 2015). The digital revolution in addition, either introduces a new set of owners like the search engine giants or consolidates power to the previous owners like Rupert Murdoch who owns MySpace (Beckett, 2010). The majority are held hostage by those few people who happen to be those who have financial and literacy power. It is their information that millions and millions of people are consuming, which reinforces their domination.

The Traditionalists worry about the potential of "the new" or of globalisation to alter the status quo and disrupt the power of established order (Servaes and Lie, 2003; Banda, 2006). We would theoretically put the ideas behind the Anti-Pornography Act under the arguments raised by the traditionalists. The law could have been raised by people who thought it was necessary to preserve the cultural heritage or norms that relate to some music genre. Traditionally for example, among the Baganda, one of the 52 tribes in Uganda, when a couple bears twins, there should be a function thereafter where attendees hull obscenities to the couple while the couple fires back. In fact, the couple is expected to shout the most explicit of all the words. Normally, the function takes place in the absence of children and at night. Between random shouting of obscenities, there are pornographic songs that have even more vulgar lyrics, passed on from generation to another. It is the way things are done traditionally. The digital media, like the internet, gets this tradition out in the open without regard for children or the rules of engagement. Additionally, the traditionalists worry about the globalisation of culture (Kraidy, 2002), especially at their own cultures' expense. While the traditionalists may enjoy trans-border data flow, they worry about other influences of globalisation like cultural imperialism (Jan, 2009). However, instead of undermining cultures, globalisation technology and economics create ways for new media setting to emerge, although weak cultures might be eroded in the process (Wang, 2008).

UGANDA

To be able to contextualise the arguments presented in the coming part, the background of the country talked about in the chapter is important. Uganda is located in East Africa. It is the twenty-first poorest country globally (Global Finance, 2013), a factor that is crucial in understanding the realities talked about in this chapter. The World Bank (2014) notes that Uganda is a low-income country (LIC) with a gross domestic product (GDP) per capita of US$506 and an economy growing at the rate of 5.2 percent. While agriculture employs 66 percent of the working population, jobs advertised in the public service decreased from 80 percent in 2010 to 49 percent in 2011(UBOS, 2015). That put employment in civil service to 275,149 jobs in 2011.The country's population stands at 35.4 million people (UBOS, 2015). Forty nine percent of that population is below 14 years of age. Although life expectancy is 53 years, the infant mortality rate is 76 per 1,000 live births. The maternal mortality ratio stands at 438 deaths per 100,000 births (Ministry of Health Maternal and Perinatal Death Review Uganda, 2013). The literacy levels on the other hand stand at 79 percent for men and 66 percent for women (UBOS, 2015).

THE MEDIA LEGAL REGIME

Uganda has a constitution that was made in 1995. It provides for freedom of expression and freedom of the press in article 29 which states that

Every person shall have the right to-

1. Freedom of speech and expression, which shall include freedom of the press and other media.

The constitutional guarantee above is supported by two international agreements on freedom of expression: the Universal Declaration of Human Rights (UDHR) article 19, and the International Covenant on Civil and Political Rights (ICCPR) article 10. On top of these, several regional covenants like the Johannesburg Principles, the African Commission on Human and People's Rights, and others, reemphasise the need for free expression.

Regardless of such a group of guarantees, freedom of expression is not absolute and so there is a legitimate (constitutional) limitation to the freedom. Article 43 (1) states that:

... no person shall prejudice the fundamental or other human rights and freedoms of others or the public interest.

The limitation cannot block free expression unless under 'demonstrably justifiable' circumstances. This has been a challenge to the Ugandan government in relation to freedom of association where the police's blocking of demonstrations sparks off violence.

But to safeguard freedom of expression, the constitution, article 43(c) has a limitation on the above limitation which regulates how article 43 should work. The other article that is important in the constitution is article 2 which states that "the constitution is the supreme law of Uganda and shall have binding force on all authorities and persons throughout Uganda." Since there are laws outside the constitution that affect freedom of expression, article 2 helps to regulate their impact on freedom of expression. Some of the limitations are found in the two principle laws that govern the press and broadcasting sectors. For example, the Press and Journalist Act (1995), limits people from practicing journalism (Section 15) by demanding a university degree from reporters and editors. This section violates Article 29 above which grants free expression for all, if you consider the fact that media are just a conduit of expression. The Press and Journalist Act, which regulates print, was condemned right before it was signed into law, in 1992, when journalists met in a conference in Kampala and declared it (then bill) "ill conceived, superfluous, dictatorial, draconian, obnoxious, and that it curtailed freedom of expression" (Okello, 2009). There is also the Uganda Communications Commission Act (2013) designed for broadcasting and new media. However, the criminal provisions for media are found in several laws some of which include: the Penal Code Act (1950), the Anti-Terrorism Act (2002) and the Anti-Pornography Act (2014), which concerns this paper.

The Penal Code Act for example still maintains Section 37 (Publication of Information Prejudicial to National Security), Section 51 (Inciting Violence) and Section 100 (Contempt of Court). The Anti-Terrorism Act (2002) on the other hand was intended to spy on people the Government suspects of terrorism by tapping into their phone calls. Journalists have sometimes been accused of collaboration in that regard like former *Monitor* news editor Wanyama Wangah, and Andrew Mwenda, a journalist, who survived a jail sentence or death penalty under that law. While it blocks coverage of conflict and conflict resolutions, it also hampers media from covering stories of the opposition (Okello, 2009). The current digital revolution makes it necessary for the regulators to create laws for the digital life. Among such laws that were made with online content in mind is the Anti-Pornography Act (2014).

THE ANTI-PORNOGRAPHY ACT

The Anti-Pornography Act defines pornography as "*any representation, through publication, exhibition, cinematography, indecent show, information technology or by whatever means, of a person engaged in real or stimulated explicit sexual activities or any representation of the sexual parts of a person for primarily sexual excitement*". Additionally, the Act mentions the internet as a possible distribution channel of pornographic material. Among the ideas noted in this chapter will be whether by publishing pornographic material online, the content producers fit within the realm of freedom of expression or they are just ignorant of the current legal and policy trends relating to the platforms that they use.The gist of this law is the section that prohibits and another that states the consequences of the prohibited action. Section13 (1)states: *"A person shall not produce, traffic in, publish, broadcast, procure, import, export, sell or abet any form of pornography."* Section 13 (2)notes: *"A person who produces or participates in the production of, or traffics in, publishes, broadcasts, procures, imports, exports or in any way abets pornography, contrary to subsection (1) commits an offence and is liable, on conviction, to a fine not exceeding five hundred currency points or imprisonment not exceeding ten years or both."*

The first part of the Act interprets the terms used. The Act states that *"Internet-content-developer" means a person, individual or corporate, who produces and uploads or causes to be uploaded on the internet, any matter.* The Act also notes that "traffic" means to deal in or cause or permit or aid the provision or circulation of pornographic matter by way of trade or publishing or entertainment or programming or unrestricted internet access or any access or any other means or purpose. Section 17 too mentions "internet service providers".

THE LANDMARK CASE

On October 30, 2014, Jemimah Kansiime aka Panadol W'abasajja (stage name literally translating into Men's painkiller) and her manager Didi March Muchwa Mugisha, were arrested in Kampala and taken to court. The first defendant, Kansiime is a local singer while the second defendant, Mugisha, is an audio and video producer. The prosecution alleged that the two defendants trafficked and abetted pornography by making a pornographic music video called *Nkulinze* (Am waiting for you) and posting it on the internet, contrary to the anti-pornography law (Wesaka, 2014). If convicted, Kansiime faced 10 years in jail while Mugisha would go for four years. Mugisha pleaded guilty and apologised for his involvement, noting that he did not know that he was committing a crime. He was fined 10 currency points ($75) and released that day. Kansiime did not plead guilty and was remanded to prison pending another trial the following month. By entering a guilty plea, Mugisha was the first person to be convicted under the law that had been signed the same year.

There are two major implications of the above case on Uganda's media law scene: It implicitly exposes the relationship between the country's media laws and content producers while at the same time, it has implications on freedom of expression as guaranteed by the constitution. This chapter is concerned with whether or not the limitation on freedom of expression found in the above law (especially section 13) is consistent with article 43, which is the legitimate (constitutional) limitation on freedom of expression. The conditions set by the legitimate limitation on freedom of expression (article 43) are that "*...no person shall prejudice the fundamental or other human rights and freedoms of others or the public interest.*"

Posting a pornographic video does not prejudice the fundamental or other human rights. If anything, the act contributes to ways in which citizens can "seek, receive and impart" information, as protected by article 29 of the Ugandan constitution. However, it is in public interest to make sure that morals of different cultures are protected, alongside the protection of minors from accessing illicit sexual content (Edick, 1998), as the intention has been for countries that make laws to regulate indecent content (Saul, 2015). But inherent in the above good intentions is the freedom to enjoy or to produce content as a constitutional right. The above law protects children and family values at the expense of that constitutional right and this is done by banning the production and distribution of content which is the same as banning content itself.

The constitution (article 43c) still guides that public interest should not be used to allow *"Any limitation of the enjoyment of the rights and freedoms prescribed by this chapter beyond what is acceptable and demonstrably justifiable in a free and democratic society"*. There are two other problems created by article 43 (c) that the Anti-Pornography Act does not answer. One is of what is acceptable and what is not. The other is of whether or not the limitation in the act is not beyond what is "demonstrably justifiable". Putting a ban on content is to go "beyond what is acceptable" in relation to the principles of "free and democratic" life. It limits both the freedoms of personal and public expression (Sturges, 2006) and gives credence to the fact that most of the nation-states that created bills of rights after the end of the cold war with influence from liberalism have laws that are "mere window dressing" instead of protecting the rights they claim to protect (Keith, 2002, p. 112).

When the constitution was made, TVs, radios and newspapers dominated the media arena and any information through them would reach to millions. There was pornographic content then with measures to make sure that it did not make it on TV or radio at a time when children were supposed to be awake. Apart from culture and beliefs helping to create self-censorship in media where content with nudity lost support among certain age groups, such content was broadcast at a certain time of the night when children were in bed, for example after 10pm (Baliboola, 2015). Additionally, warnings were given before that content, which was mostly in western movies, was aired. Regardless, the TV station still chose a movie with less explicit sexual content or blacked out some scenes that were deemed to be excessively sexual as the conditions for licensing were (Otto, 2013). This is how the balance was reached between the fundamental right of expression and the protection of minors and morals.

For a law to be truly helpful, the conditions set in article 43 and 43c have to be met. But, we must also consider the view that the constitution was created to regulate freedom of expression as it was understood in 1995. More than 25 years later, a lot has changed, especially with the emergence of the internet. These new changes and challenges have to be met without foregoing the fundamental freedoms. The internet is a multimedia (Lehman-Wilzig and Cohen-Avigdor, 2004) global network of computers (Dominick, 1996). In such a complex global system that promotes global lifestyles, only a network as complex as the internet can help us claim our global positions (Qvortrup, 2006). Undemocratic interference in content distribution means denying Ugandans freedom of expression in the global village.

In other jurisdictions, for example in Europe and America, restrictions tend to allow a certain level of enjoyment based on an understanding that opportunities and risks go hand in hand (Livingstone, 2011). In the United States, pornography or obscenity as the court held in *Roth v. UnitedStates* (1957) is not a right protected by the law. However, the enjoyment is still provided for. In relation to pornography online, the 1996 Communications Decency Act stipulates that content distributers online should protect minors by " requiring use of a verified credit card, debit account, adult access code, or adult personal identification number" (Edick, 1998, p. 447). Under those restrictions, children who access the internet should never have access to indecent material. In the UK, the 2014 amendment of the Communications Act specifies certain actions within pornographic material that should never be acceptable for children's consumption like "strangulation, facesitting and fisting" (Saul, 2014), on top of including a rating sign on content that should not be watched by persons under 18 years.

OTHER CRITICAL ISSUES ARISING FROM THE CASE

The landmark case above also raises issues of media literacy on the side of the audience and the producers of media content in Uganda. Mugisha told the court that he did not know he was breaking the law, and yet the Penal Code Act (section 166), which was repealed by the coming of the new law, prohibited trafficking obscene publications. The Penal Code Act had been active way before Mugisha started his music journey. Being a music producer, he ought to know the law that regulates what he does. In an interview done for this chapter, Mugisha actually admitted that he advised the singer to make the video. He did not think even for a second that he would end up having trouble with the law. He also argued that "in a country that is still bound by cultural norms, the acceptability of certain things nude is still low compared to the West and this influences our ways of life, including laws" (D.M. Mugisha, personal communication, February 2, 2016).

The singer too was oblivious of the fact that she would be taken to court and even remanded for a video of herself dancing nude. According to Mugisha, the singer, Kansiime, is a sex worker and a friend, who too did not know about the legal implications of the video. Mugisha tended to mean by that statement that most sex workers in Uganda are girls who did not get a lot of education and even if some of them did get an education, without a special attention to the law, they would never know such details. What the court did not know (perhaps) is that Kansiime had not been singing for a long time. In fact Mugisha noted in the interview that Kansiime was not known in Uganda before the video. She was not a fulltime singer before the song in question. Mugisha, on the other hand, was a household name in Uganda's music production for having started off artists who are now superstars in the country, including one Eddy Kenzo, who recently won an American BET award.

Most importantly, the law criminalises speech and expression to an extent that artistes' creativity can be limited, which is a form of self-censorship. This is in addition to losing one's licence as Mugisha lost his. He survived going to jail, paid a fine but has no work because of the revocation of his licence. The law should have been designed in a way that someone pays a fine instead of both a fine and a prison as it states currently. Most importantly, speech and expression transgressions should be treated as a civil matter.

The media are known for their educational, informational and entertainment functions. The law provides for educational and informational purposes but does not do the same for entertainment. What about the adults who may want to watch pornography for entertainment? Should there be a special curved-off virtual space where such explicit content is enjoyed? What qualities should such a place have? Or most importantly, how could the law provide for such space? These questions are answered by the examples from the UK and US above where specific extremes are banned but not content in its entirety and provisions are made to limit children from accessing such content since the internet is a global medium. Internet service providers should make sure that they put the above procedures in place to comply with the law. Currently, by not providing for all those options, the law implies that watching a music video that is pornographic for entertainment is completely illegal.

CONCLUSION

This chapter made an analysis of Uganda's media laws in the digital era and revisited the Anti-Pornography Act that was enacted in 2014. The Chapter questioned the law's ability to respect freedom of expression, a right that is guaranteed by the Ugandan constitution, using some clauses that prohibit the distribution of pornography. In addition, the landmark case, in which the law was first applied where a music video producer and a singer were charged, is cited. The chapter concluded that by protecting both morality and the minors, the law takes away the right to free expression and this makes the law inconsistent with the legitimate limitation of freedom of expression. The chapter used examples of regulation of indecent material in other jurisdictions like the UK and the US to suggest that the best law could focus on prohibiting the excesses of adult content and also specify exactly the circumstances under which an adult person seeking such adult content for entertainment can access or make the same content. Some of the major challenges pointed at include lack of digital media literacy by the relevant stakeholders in Uganda, especially the content producers, and the fact that the current law against pornography creates self-censorship, something that stifles creativity.

REFERENCES

Antony, M. G., & Thomas, R. J. (2010). This is citizen journalism at its finest: YouTube and the public sphere in the Oscar Grant shooting incident. *New Media & Society*, *12*(8), 1280–1296. doi:10.1177/1461444810362492

Baliboola, I. N. (2015). *Church TV Runs An Erotic Dating TV Programme*. Retrieved from http://oops.ug/2015/06/02/church-tv-runs-an-erotic-dating-tv-programme/

BBC. (2004). *Fine for Ugandan radio gay show*. BBC News. Retrieved from http://news.bbc.co.uk/2/hi/africa/3712266.stm

Beckett, C. (2010). *Globalisation, the media and UK communities*. York, UK: Joseph Rowntree Foundation.

Berger, G. (2011). Empowering the youth as citizen journalists: A South African experience. *Journalism*, *12*(6), 708–726. doi:10.1177/1464884911405466

Dominick, J. (1996). *The Dynamics of Mass Communication*. McGraw-Hill.

Edick, D. A. (1998). Regulation of Pornography on the Internet in theUnited States and the United Kingdom: AComparative Analysis. *Boston College International and Comparative Law Review*, *21*, 437–460.

Ericsson Mobility Report. (2015). *On the pulse of the networked society*. Retrieved from http://www.ericsson.com/res/docs/2015/mobility-report/ericsson-mobility-report-nov-2015.pdf

Global Finance. (2013). *The Poorest Countries in the World*. Retrieved from http://www.gfmag.com/component/content/article/119-economic-data/12537-the-poorest-countries-in-the-world.html#axzz2u1qY1Raz

GSMA. (2015). *The mobile economy*. Retrieved from http://www.gsmamobileeconomy.com/GSMA_Global_Mobile_Economy_Report_2015.pdf

International Telecommunication Union. (2015). *ICT facts and figures*. Retrieved from http://www.itu.int/en/ITU-D/Statistics/Pages/facts/default.aspx

Jan, M. (2009). Globalization of Media: Key Issues and Dimensions. *European Journal of Scientific Research*, *29*, 66–75.

Kaul, V. (2011). Globalisation and Media. *Journal of Mass Communication and Journalism*, *1*(01), 1–8. doi:10.4172/2165-7912.1000105

Keith, L. C. (2002). Constitutional Provisions for Individual Human Rights (19771996): Are They More than Mere Window Dressing? *Political Research Quarterly*, *55*(1), 111–143. doi:10.1177/106591290205500105

Kraidy, M. (2002). Globalization of culture through the media. In J. R. Schement (Ed.), Encyclopedia of communication and information (pp. 359–363). New York, NY: Macmillan Reference USA. Retrieved from http://repository.upenn.edu/asc_papers/325

Lehman-Wilzig, S., & Cohen-Avigdor, N. (2004). The natural life cycle of new media evolution: Inter-media struggle for survival in the internet age. *New Media & Society*, *6*(6), 707–730. doi:10.1177/146144804042524

Lemmens, P. (2015). Social Autonomy and Heteronomy in the Age of ICT: The Digital Pharmakon and the (Dis) Empowerment of the General Intellect. *Foundations of Science*. doi:10.1007/s10699-015-9468-1

Livingstone, S., Haddon, L., Görzig, A., & Ólafsson, K. (2011). *EU Kids Online: final report 2011*. London: EU Kids Online Network.

Lumu, T. D. (2010, April 28). CBS Radio is set to reopen after eight months off-air, following President Museveni's change of heart, The Observer has Learnt. *The Observer*, p. 2.

Ministry of Health Maternal and Perinatal Death Review Uganda. (2013). *Why did they die? Reviewing the evidence to save tomorrow's mothers and babies*. Kampala: Ministry of Health.

Nassanga, L. G. (2009). An assessment of the changing community media parameters in East Africa. *African Journalism Studies*, *30*(1), 42–57. doi:10.3368/ajs.30.1.42

Ndlela, M. N. (2007). Broadcasting reforms in Southern Africa: Continuity and change in the era of globalization. *Westminster Papers in Communication and Culture*, *4*, 67–86.

Ojambo, H. O. (2008). *Reflections on Freedom of Expression in Uganda's Fledgling Democracy: Sedition, "Pornography" and Hate Speech*. HURIPEC Working Paper No. 18.

Okello, J. (2008). *Situation of Community Radio in Uganda*. Paper presented at the Our Media 7 conference, Accra, Ghana.

Otto, A. (2013). *Media Houses Warned on Pornography*. Retrieved from http://ugandaradionetwork.com/a/story.php?s=57490

Qvortrup, L. (2006). Understanding New Digital Media: Medium Theory or Complexity. *European Journal of Communication*, *21*(3), 345–356. doi:10.1177/0267323106066639

Saul, H. (2014). *UK porn legislation: What is now banned under new government laws*. Retrieved from http://www.independent.co.uk/news/uk/home-news/uk-porn-legislation-what-is-now-banned-under-new-government-laws-9898541.html

Semujju, B. (2013). ICT as an engine for community participation: An assessment of Ugandas community media. *International Journal of Information Communication Technologies and Human Development*, *5*(1), 20–36. doi:10.4018/jicthd.2013010102

Semujju, B. (2016). Introducing Community Audio Towers as an alternative to Community Radio in Uganda. *Journal of Alternative and Community Media, 1*, 141–153.

Servaes, J., & Lie, R. (2003). Media, globalisation and culture: Issues and trends. *Communicatio. South African Journal for Communication Theory and Research, 29*, 7–23.

Smith, M. L., Spence, R., & Rashid, A. T. (2011). Mobile Phones and Expanding Human Capabilities. *Information Technologies & International Development, 7*, 77–88.

Sturges, P. (2006). Limits to Freedom of Expression?Considerations arising from the Danish cartoons affair. *IFLA Journal, 32*(3), 181–188. doi:10.1177/0340035206070164

The World Bank. (2014). *Uganda Economic Review/Performance*. Retrieved from http://www.worldbank.org/en/country/uganda/overview

Uganda. (1950). The Penal Code Act 1950.

Uganda. (1995). The Constitution.

Uganda. (1995). The Press and Journalist Act 1995.

Uganda. (2002). Anti-Terrorism Act.

Uganda. (2014). The Anti-Pornography Act 2014.

Uganda Bureau of Statistics. (2015). *Statistical abstract*. Kampala: UBOS.

Uganda Communications Commission. (2015). *Status of the Communications Market*. Kampala: UCC.

Verbeek, P. (2015). The Struggle for Technology: Towards a Realistic Political Theory of Technology. *Foundations of Science*. doi:10.1007/s10699-015-9470-7

Verweij, P. (2009). Making Convergence Work in the Newsroom A Case Study of Convergence of Print, Radio, Television and Online Newsrooms at the African Media Matrix in South Africa During the National Arts Festival. *Convergence (London), 15*(1), 75–87. doi:10.1177/1354856508097020

Wang, D. (2008). Globalization of the Media: Does It Undermine National Cultures. *Intercultural Communication Studies, 17*, 203–211.

Wei, R. (2008). Motivations for using the mobile phone for mass communications and entertainment. *Telematics and Informatics, 25*(1), 36–46. doi:10.1016/j.tele.2006.03.001

Weiss, A. S. (2013). Exploring news apps and location-based services on the smartphone. *Journalism & Mass Communication Quarterly, 90*(3), 435–456. doi:10.1177/1077699013493788

Wesaka, A. (2014). *Local singer Kansiime further remanded to Luzira over porn song*. Retrieved from http://www.monitor.co.ug/News/National/Local-singer-Kansiime-further-remanded-to-Luzira-over-porn-song/-/688334/2521220/-/naixug/-/index.html

Chapter 11
Citizen Journalism on Facebook and the Challenges of Media Regulation in Zimbabwe:
Baba Jukwa

Collen Sabao
Stellenbosch University, South Africa & Midlands State University, Zimbabwe

Vimbai Rejoice Chingwaramusee
Midlands State University, Zimbabwe

ABSTRACT

The chapter discusses the rise of citizen journalism, examining the manners in which such form of journalistic practice impacts media regulatory frameworks and journalistic ethics in Zimbabwe, specifically looking at the Baba Jukwa Facebook wall. It discusses the nature of reporting in citizen journalism and the challenges these pose on media regulating laws and journalistic ethics. Over the last decade, social networking websites and other social forums have exploded in popularity in the whole world, Zimbabwe included. These social networking sites have become quite central as alternative news media, breaking stories before the mainstream official media does. The impact that such social networks have on contemporary society as public spheres - platforms for group social interactions and news outlets should not be undermined because of how they allow people to interact freely and to (re)construct their desired realities in the face of the gag of stringent media laws.

THE DIGITAL AGE AND THE RISE OF CITIZEN JOURNALISM

The chapter examines the manners in which citizen journalism impacts media regulatory frameworks in Zimbabwe, specifically looking at the Baba Jukwa wall as a case study. Through the analysis of the news 'breaking' and news 'reporting' culture on Facebook among Zimbabwean users, the chapter examines the language as well as images used in citizen journalism and the challenges these pose on media regulating laws and journalistic ethics. Over the last decade, social networking websites such as

DOI: 10.4018/978-1-5225-2095-5.ch011

Facebook, Twitter, MySpace, Belbo and other social forums such as the mobile phone based chat services like Whatsapp have exploded in popularity in the whole world, Zimbabwe included. The phenomenon of citizen journalism is not restricted to the internet alone as well as to the independent 'broadcast' of news via the internet. As Goode (2009) explains, 'citizen journalism is generally associated with the internet and yet does not begin and end online or even with digital-interactive media. Broadcast news, for example, sometimes feeds off and incorporates elements of citizen journalism: examples include eyewitness footage from cell phones, reporting of stories originally broken by citizen journalism initiatives on the web, or even guest reporter slots in which citizens front and participate in packaging an item for a television or radio newscast.' These social networking sites have also become quite central as alternative news media, breaking stories before the mainstream official media does. The impact that such social networks have on contemporary society as platforms for group social interactions and news outlets should not be undermined.

Social networking sites have become widespread and grown in popularity because they allow people to interact freely and to (re)construct and reveal their desired realities by proving an alternative space for the dissemination of 'news' in the face of the gag of stringent media laws and regulatory frameworks. For example, Subrahmanyam et al (2008) estimate that sites such as MySpace and Facebook have over 100 million users between them, many of them adolescents and emerging adults. The proposed study seeks to examine the constructions of alternative media on the social networking websites using a case study of Zimbabwe. The advent of web based networking sites however has meant that the questions of professional and ethical journalistic practices have to be (re)confronted and (re)interrogated. Of particular interest in proposed chapter is how this alternative digital public sphere has offered Zimbabweans 'an avenue to discuss a taboo subject in Zimbabwe without fear or being reprimanded by the secretive and authoritarian state. The 'taboo' in this context refers to issues that the state does not want discussed in public like the president's health, genocide, ZANU-PF factionalism or succession debate and state sponsored corruption just to mention but a few. The state has tabooed the genocide debates within Zimbabwe for national cohesion and ZANU-PF's political expediency. Most precisely, the article explores how the internet has challenged the elitist dominated domestic public sphere into a sphere where ordinary citizens interact among themselves and those in power' (Mpofu, nd). Such are the issues the Baba Jukwa wall largely reported on. Whereas the Baba Jukwa wall offered an alternative source of news, in many instances offering narratives parallel to official government controlled reports and making it possible for the proliferation of counter-hegemonic voices, the chapter seeks to explore how such uncontrolled and 'free' news outlets represent media regulatory challenges in Zimbabwe.

Observing that citizen journalists are people that are not trained professional newspersons, and usually present 'news' as the see them through the use of gadgets such as mobile phones and the internet with complete disregard of journalistic ethics and laws, the study here examines how the proliferation of such 'newspersons' present challenges for media regulation in Zimbabwe. Ruellan (2007: 2) for instance, observes in this regard that, '[s]ince 2005, the Internet has given rise to several novel initiatives concerning journalism designated by the generic term "citizen journalism". Underlying a set of heterogeneous systems, a unique principle can be observed: web users, who are not professional journalists, contribute directly to the production of the daily news. These practices raise a series of questions, one of which is the link, in the media and journalism, between professional and amateur practices.' For example there have been instances of nude pictures being posted on the internet as part of 'breaking news' by citizen journalists, who clearly lack a code and journalistic ethics. With regards to the ethical problems of citizen journalism, Carpenter (2007:532) argues that there has been animosity 'between those who consider themselves online citizen journalists and those who work as journalists for traditional news organizations. Citizen journalists are criticized for their propensity to feature entertainment articles with little background research, rather than informing the public on matters that benefit them as citizens. Many citizen journalists have not been trained to subscribe to the same standards (e.g., objectivity, thoroughness, fairness, accuracy) as journalists working for news organizations.' Until recently, the working routines and values of journalistic culture had remained highly stable for almost a century (Tuchman 2002; Schudson 2005), even after being declared in crisis (Dahlgren 1996; Blumler and Gurevitch 1996).

Traditionally, journalism has been attached to the institution of the media, based on the production of news by dedicated paid labour, the journalists. The term 'gatekeeper', used to describe a main task of journalists, indicates their claim to be the ones who decide what the public needs to know, as well as when and how such information should be provided. The gatekeeper role is maintained and enforced by professional routines and conventions that are said to guarantee the quality and neutrality of institutional journalism (Shoemaker 1991; Reese and Ballinger 2001). The impact of the Internet and other new information- and communication technologies on the profession of journalism should not be underestimated. The Internet is changing the profession of journalism in at least three ways: it has the potential to make the journalist as an intermediary force in democracy superfluous (Bardoel, 1996); it offers the media professional a vast array of resources and sheer endless technological possibilities to work with (Quinn, 1998; Pavlik, 1999); and it creates its own type of journalism on the Net: so-called *digital* or rather: *online* journalism (Singer, 1998; Deuze, 1999). The motivation to undertake such a study comes from observing the communicative potential of social networking sites to influence both change and development in society. We observe that these sites have the power to unite people with shared opinions and at times even diverse one to come together and discuss issues pertaining to their lives.

The choice of research is also motivated by the observation that social networking sites have by and large become a replacement of traditional news reporting channels. The chapter seeks to explore the manners in which the internet has become an alternative platform for Facebook users (and Zimbabweans to be precise) to exercise their right to freedom of expression given the historically recorded repressive media regulatory conditions in the country. Theoretically the chapter utilises the Digital Alternative Media Theory as well as Habermas' ambit of the public sphere. The proposed chapter explores, using the Baba Jukwa Facebook page, how the internet (and Facebook to be precise) has grown as a form of alternative media, reporting on and challenging the tabooed topics and issues in Zimbabwe. The chapter seeks to demonstrate that the proliferation of citizen journalism aided by the internet has made it possible for counter-hegemonic voices (Mitra, 2001) 'to upset the elite and politically dominated public spheres. The internet is credited for simultaneously enabling the user to exercise the right to freedom of expression through receiving and disseminating information, ideas and opinions visually or phonetically to large audiences at the lowest possible cost. Also, this evolution of technology has caused global dramatic changes in the field of journalism.'

The new information and communication technologies of the digital age are continuing to affect all spheres of life in late modern society but still there is ambiguity as to the extent to which they are enhancing democracy (Anderson and Cornfield 2003). Blumer and Gurevitch (2000), note that the traditional systems of political communication in western democracies are being destabilized by changes in late modern society. Banda (2011) considers the new information and communication technologies revolution as a stepping stone to improving democratic and developmental institutions on the African continent. This research examines how the new information and communication technologies in Zimbabwe have changed the political communication in the country. Many scholars look at how the new information and communication technologies have paved way for freedom of speech amongst citizens yet they fail to look at the ills of the so called freedom of speech. This research examines the chaos, inefficiency and unpredictability caused by the new information and communication technologies which has given a platform to untrained citizens to be journalists. This scenario presents challenges in media regulation because citizen 'journalists' are unregistered and cannot be monitored or controlled since they largely use nom de plumes. It becomes difficult to make them accountable for the stories, half-truths they 'report' as well for all violations of journalistic ethics.

The Baba Jukwa Phenomenon in Zimbabwe Politics and Media

Baba Jukwa, (Shona, loosely translated to 'Father of Jukwa') was a 'vigilante' Zimbabwean figure on the internet based social networking site, Facebook, who became popular for exposing corruption, plots and 'murders' in Zimbabwean politics, especially in the ZANU-PF political party, sometimes before they even occurred as well as other tabooed subjects. The case of Baba Jukwa can be imagined as the biggest case of citizen journalism in Zimbabwean history. Emerging just before the 2013 harmonised presidential and parliamentary elections, the Baba Jukwa Facebook wall was immensely popular amongst Zimbabweans seeking alternative news that counteracted the official narrative controlled by the ZANU Pf party due to its handle on the control of the flow of information in the country. Baba Jukwa was imagined as a 'mole' within ZANU-PF who was privy to, and published very classified and sensitive political material on his public page on Facebook. Presenting himself as a disenfranchised ZANU PF big wig, evinced a proclivity to reveal ZANU PF's well kept secrets and in the process work in unison with other progressive political actors to not only challenge but also topple the political party's 'despotic' hegemony. Several current and expelled ZANU-PF bigwigs have been speculated on to have been Baba Jukwa. 'The case of Baba Jukwa, a faceless Facebook character who emerged in March 2013, claiming to be a disaffected ZANU PF insider with "top", secrets about the internal workings of the party is very interesting in as far as it exposes how citizen journalism can cause despondency within the camp of those considered powerful' (Mujere & Mwatwara, 2015: 223). Many have speculated that Baba Jukwa, the faceless and shadowy character who exposed controversial issues and stories about high ranking ZANU PF and government officials by giving exposes of state violence, corruption and assassination plots, election rigging plots, could not have been one person but instead a group of individuals coordinating the writing of the leaks. His rise to fame can be largely credited on his 'valour' to speak about tabooed subjects in Zimbabwean politics such as factional wars within ZANU PF, the President's health the succession issue within ZANU PF as well as ZANU-PF plots to rig the 2013 harmonised Presidential and Parliamentary elections. The ZANU-PF leadership eventually embarked on a 'manhunt' to unmask Baba Jukwa, with the president himself allegedly offering a reward of US$300 000 to anyone who could identify him. The popularity of this figure can be attributed to the search for alternative media in the context of a country with stringent media regulatory laws. The proliferation of such news outlets like Baba Jukwa speaks volumes about the media environment in the country in which they occur. The case of Baba Jukwa thus 'epitomises the efficacy of citizen journalism' (Mujere & Mwatwara, 2015: 223).

Media(ted) News in Zimbabwe and the Rise of Alternative Digital Media

The popularity of use of social media as a form of citizen journalism in Zimbabwe, as is the case with many other nations, can largely be attributed to the need to counterbalance 'regulated' information flow controlled by a dominating non-democratic hegemony. In other words, such popularity arises from the need to challenge 'the elitist dominated domestic public sphere into a sphere where ordinary citizens interact among themselves and those in power.' (Mpofu, nd: 1). Up until around 2013, when the government seemed to ease up, the media regulatory framework in Zimbabwe has been regarded as one of the most draconian in the world, comparatively. Zimbabwean political evolutions from the year 2000, in which the then ruling political party, the Zimbabwe African National Patriotic Front (ZANU-PF), led by incumbent president Robert Gabriel Mugabe faced the strongest possible opposition ever to its traditionally 'one party state' hegemony from the Morgan Tsvangirai led Movement for Democratic Change (MDC) culminated in a serious gag on the media. Regarded as the fourth pillar of states, the power of the media in influencing public opinion, and by extension, political and social change must never be undermined. The high proliferation of a diversity of free speech and opinions is anathema to the sustenance of despotic political hegemonies. In the face of serious opposition, ZANU-PF realised that the control of the media was key to its continued survival. Stringent media regulating statutes such as the Access to Information and Protection of Privacy Act (AIPPA) and the Public Order and Security Act (POSA) we promulgated. Such laws, together with previously existing laws such as the Official Secrets Act (OSA) and the Broadcasting Services Act (BSA) made it nearly impossible for the freedom of expression to thrive. Unrestricted by the gags of such constraints imposed by such media laws, as well as the use of a nom de plume which did not require registration with the powers that be, Baba Jukwa provided a counter narrative to the ZANU PF government propaganda. In essence, the popularity and success of Baba Jukwa was chiefly due to the fact that it was nearly impossible during this period to register new newspapers and radio stations as the then ZANU-PF led government was bent on maintaining its grip on power by regulating the flow of information. In the face of this, there was a high rise in the births of web based 'newspapers' as a form of alternative digital media in Zimbabwe. Web based news publications such as www.newzimbabwe.com, www.myzimbabwe.com, www.zimonline.com and www.thezimbabwean.com among others represent such. Many Zimbabwean began looking up to these for more diverse reportage of news from and in Zimbabwe. The embracing of these digital web based alternative forms of news can be credited as having played a critical part in Zimbabweans' embrace of the 'new' trend of citizen or participatory journalism. Mujere and Mwatwara (2015: 216) opine in this regard that, '…Zimbabweans have reacted to the narrowing of the democratic space by resorting to subterranean methods. Thus…a narrow media in Zimbabwe incubated the rise of citizen journalism'.

It became more clear that the majority if Zimbabwean began to use the internet not only as consumers but rather as 'prosumers' of information. 'Their status as 'prosumers' gives them freedom, power and a voice to speak up to authority and generate content. The internet offers an alternative digital public sphere where ordinary citizens meet and discuss issues they would not ordinarily discuss in government controlled public spheres because regimes of control have made discussions of these taboo topics impossible. In addition, the fact that public media stifle vibrant debate that speaks against state programmes, means people will forever be in the dark. To circumvent this, the internet, as a forum for power, voice and self-expression, has made it possible for debate and tensions between the elite and ordinary people to be experienced in a typical Habermasian public sphere fashion online' (Mpofu, nd: 7).

So restricted was the free flow of information in Zimbabwe that several subjects, such as the President's health, ZANU-PF party politics and political processes such as corruption as well as the presidential succession and national political process such as elections were taboo to report on freely and 'objectively'. Instead, they could only be 'properly' reported on by the state controlled media (both broadcast and print). Because of the need for counter narratives from those of the 'despotic' ZANU PF government, there was need to (re)formulate new ways of dispersing information to the general public. 'A broad range of activities by the populace under the banner citizen journalism has also been deployed to counter the state metanarrative and of course in some cases to affirm it. Thus citizen journalism has played an important role in shaping political attitudes, altering the boundaries of political interaction and bringing into existence new methods and channels for resistance since the build up to the 2008 elections and 2013 elections' (Mujere & Mwatwara, 2015: 216).

Citizen Journalism as Alternative Media and Public Sphere

Citizen journalism has for some time been a very difficult phenomenon to define and ascribe parameters to. In other words, the definition of citizen journalism does not have completely settled boundaries (Lasica, 2003). Bowman & Willis (2003: 9) believe citizen journalism to be 'the act of a citizen, or group of citizens, playing an active role in the process of collecting, reporting, analysing and disseminating news and information. Citizen journalism refers to the concept of an active audience in a new dispensation in which journalism has evolved significantly to cater to an audience equipped with the ability to not only consume but also produce media content. Citizen journalism appears thus, to be about 'a set of practices that are embedded with the everyday lives of citizens' (Atton 2002:267). Citizen journalism seems to capture something of a countervailing ethos of ordinary person`s capacity to bear witness especially during a social or a political crisis (Allan 2009:18). Citizen journalism is redefining the whole essence of journalism. Technological innovation has indeed enhanced the work of citizen journalists the world over though contrary to popular belief the concept is not entirely new (Mutsvairo, 2012). Citizen journalism can largely be viewed as an outgrowth of the internet and new media, which have given the readers opportunities to contribute to news production, not as just readers but also producers. Social and technological forces are pushing the field of journalism to evolve, and as it moves forward, a re-evaluation of what journalism should look like is occurring (Gillmor, 2004; Merritt & McCombs, 2004).

Citizen journalism empowers the audience in such a way that they are no longer mere receivers but participants as they are platforms to debate issues released by the citizen journalist. Moyo (2011) notes that in Zimbabwe citizens are no longer helplessly bombarded with messages by mass media but instead are also actively producing news and initiating news flows among themselves (Moyo, 2011:10). The approach of professional journalism adopted on the coverage ensures the representation is clinical in its narration of the facts while simultaneously conveying both manifest and latent meanings that largely falls within the mainstream global framing (Chuma, 2005). Before the emergence of new media technologies so called deviants or dissidents had their grievances aired by foreign media organisations such as BBC; CNN; VOA (Chuma, 2005:3). 'The intent of this participation is to provide independent, reliable, accurate, wide-ranging and relevant information that a democracy requires'. Largely viewed as an outgrowth of the internet and new media, citizen journalism is argued to have provided the readership prospects of contributing to news production, not as just readers but also producers.' The concept itself has been defined in many ways and within different parameters. Goode (2009) opines that 'Citizen[ship] journalism' refers to a range of web-based practices whereby 'ordinary' users engage in journalistic practices. Citizen journalism includes practices such as current affairs-based blogging, photo and video sharing, and posting eyewitness commentary on current events. Sometimes the term is used quite broadly to include activities such as re-posting, linking, 'tagging' (labeling with keywords), rating, modifying or commenting upon news materials posted by other users or by professional news outlets, whereby citizens participate in the news process without necessarily acting as 'content creators'. Commenting on the advent of citizen journalism, Papacharissi (2009: i) opines that 'journalism is in the middle of sweeping changes in its relationships with the communities it serves, and the audiences for news and public affairs it seeks to address. Changes in technology have blurred the lines between professionals and citizens, partisan and objective bystanders, particularly in the emerging public zones of the blogosphere.'

According to Domingo et al (2008) "Participatory journalism seems to add another dimension that questions previous boundaries—and definitions—of professional journalism'. The borderline that separates professional journalists and their audience seems to be blurring (Bruns 2005; Jenkins 2006). Citizen journalism as referred to as 'Network journalism' 'might well change the relation between the journalists and their public in a fundamental way that affects the profession as a whole; its major characteristics as we have pointed out before seem to reflect clearly a shifting balance of power between information suppliers and users' (Bardoel et al). 'Journalism is carried out in specific institutional circumstances, within concrete organisational settings and under particular technological conditions. The advent of cyberspace will inevitably impact on the factors which shape how journalism gets done - and may well even colour how we define what journalism is' (Dahlgren, 1996: 60). Ruellan (2007: 3) observes 'that the expression 'citizen journalism' is problematic. It assigns too great a responsibility for certain media or individuals to bear and why them, and not others? Sometimes the term participatory journalism is used. This is a more neutral, operational expression. While it is less emotionally charged, it also reduces the phenomenon: users simply contribute to media output dominated by professional journalists, whereas certain sites … are completely managed by associate web users.'

The public choice of the digital media arises from the need by the populace to seek alternative truths from those relayed by the dominant elites. Burton (1990) contends that, the fact that news organizations set up an agenda of topics as well as ideological positions for reading them from that form, 'opposes the idea that news is somehow a collection of truthful events and facts from 'out there.' This view is also expressed by Fairclough (1995) who argues that media texts do not merely 'mirror realities' as is sometimes naively assumed, but 'they constitute versions of reality in ways which depend on the social positions, interests and objectives of those who produce them'. This shows the link between media representation and ideology. According to Baran (1998), '[n]ewspapers tell readers what is significant and meaningful through their placement of stories in and on their pages.' Hall cited in Griffin (1991) notes, in line with this observation, that the primary function of discourse is to make meaning and that meaning in influenced by the intentions of the person(s) who generate(s) it.

Hall, cited in Griffin (1991), contends that 'it is folly to divorce communication from the cultural context in which it is found and ignoring the realities of unequal power distribution in society'. Gramsci's concept of 'hegemony' expresses the link between the cultural aspects of social life and ideology. According to Fairclough (1995) 'hegemony' is a term used by Gramsci and others for describing power and struggles over power. He further maintains that 'hegemony' emphasizes forms of power which depend upon consent rather than coercion and is sustained ideologically. Burton (1990):261) argues in this context that, the media have the effect of 'endorsing the dominant ideology, the dominant view of power, relationships between groups in society, the dominant view of how thing are run.' Burton (1990) argues that the media is an important part of hegemony. He also maintains that media professionalism is tied up with the values that inform the organization such that in this sense professionalism becomes ideological. Fairclough's (1995) sentiments suggest that, hegemony is sustained in the common sense assumptions of everyday life. Burton (1990) reinforces this view by suggesting that, 'what hegemony does is to naturalise ideology itself, and all the values and beliefs built into ideology.'

The effect of the naturalisation of the dominant ideology is that it becomes invisible. This explains why people tend to believe what they hear from the media without questioning it. The media has the muscle to change the perception of the public on different issues. 'The media affect our beliefs, attitudes, values and behaviour directly or indirectly' (Burton 1990). Habermas' concept of 'the public sphere', while largely biased towards notions of democracy, is also fundamental in shedding light on this power of the media. What Habermas terms 'the bourgeois public sphere' consists of social spaces where individuals gather to discuss their common public affairs and to organize against arbitrary and oppressive forms of social and public power. The essential principle of the public sphere was open discussion by members of the public in order to reach a consensus on issues affecting them for the public good.

This 'public sphere' is contemporarily represented by the media since they remain the major arena facilitating maximum public participation and debates over key issues affecting the public. The media provide(s) evidence of political events, issues and activities, thereby enabling us to understand the operation of politics in our society and to work more constructively in that political process (Burton, 1990). The implications of this are that the media promote(s) participatory democracy. This view of the role of the media is consistent with what, according to White (1997) is the claim made by journalist themselves that the news report is 'an objective, neutral and impersonal mode of meaning making'. Burton (1990) opines, however, that the evidence given by the media on political events gives us the illusion of participating in the political process, but actually merely endorsing the authority of those who continue to run over our lives unquestioned. He goes on to argue that the media are capable of mobilising public opinion by raising issues that the public may not have thought of and they can also suggest a way of looking at those issues. As such, the media are capable of shaping public opinion about political events and issues. The goal of citizen journalism in this context is to challenge such hegemonic forms of media use by dominant classes.

The public sphere is understood as a assemblage of communicative spaces in society that authorize the circulation of information ; ideas ; debates ideally in an unfettered manner and also the formation of political will (Dahlgren 2005:148). The public space created by the internet offers an interactive media which serves to aid communicative links between citizens and the power holders of society (Dahlgren 2005:148). Habermas who coined the term public sphere defined it as an interactive space. Habermas`s imagination of the public sphere was very discriminatory since it excluded women; poor men and children. According to Habermas, the public sphere only accommodated elite men`s views. This research, however, utilising the works of Habermas and other scholars who have written about the public sphere, demonstrates how the internet has created a public sphere. The public sphere consists of three dimensions: structures; representation and interaction (Dahlgren 1995). The structural dimension directs our attention to classic democratic issues such as freedom of speech; access and the dynamic of inclusion and or exclusion (Dahlgren 2005). The structural dimension points to society`s political institutions which serve as a sort of "political ecology" for the media and set boundaries for the scenery of the information and forms of expression that circulate (Dahlgren 2005:149).

A society where democratic tendencies are weak does not give rise to healthy institutional structures for the public sphere which in turn means that the representational dimension will be inadequate (Dahlgren 2005:149). Therefore, in such a scenario the internet comes up to pave a way for citizen journalism which is more participatory and independent. The citizen participation is ignorant to media laws and ethics and there is no need for 'journalists' to have academic qualifications in journalism. This research examines the role of the citizen journalist in the 'new public sphere' and how the citizen journalism is a 'voice' and public sphere for the oppressed and repressed. Habermas and Dewey (1954) argue that a 'public' should be conceptualised as something other than just a media audience. Habermas and Dewey argue that publics exist in discursive interactional processes in the public sphere. The advent of the internet has taken a major historical step by ensuring that the public sphere goes online thus the public sphere becomes more accentuated (Lewis 2001).

The public sphere is a vital part of social organisation and it can be understood as a precondition for structuring society (Saxer, 2005: 24). This research argues that the Baba Jumwa Facebook wall made possible by the internet became a public sphere in Zimbabwe which gave and continues to a 'voice' to the citizens and allows for the proliferation of free and unrestricted speech. It has to be noted that as a public sphere, Baba Jukwa and others exponentially grew to be of central importance to the Zimbabwean citizenry as an alternative source of news. The Baba Jukwa wall, as public sphere became 'an open forum for communication' (Neidhardt, 1994: 7). The public sphere has a system of communication where issues and opinions are being gathered, processed and then passed on (Neidhardt, 1994:8). Habermas notes that the discursive model of public sphere sees a purpose of public sphere in rational decision making through public debate and learning processes which structure the basis for communication processes and rational decision making. Popular sovereignty is ensured by, public opinion which is the output of the public sphere (Habermas 1992:209).

The arena model identifies different arenas of public sphere which are formed by issues and opinions, observers and persons involved such as speakers, intermediaries and recipients actively participate in diverse arenas and levels of public sphere (Donges 2001:108). Theories on democracy view the public sphere as a precondition for providing information and therefore as a precondition to enable formulation of will (Dahl 2000:37). I will use the democracy views of the public sphere to see how the internet plays a role in liberating the voices of the subaltern on the blogosphere. This research incorporates the representative liberal and participatory liberal theory of the public sphere as ideal models were by the representative model tends to exhibit a strong emphasis on the elite (Rucht, 2002:295).

Zimbabwe's Media[ted] News, Media Laws, and the Digital Alternative Media

The media regulatory laws in Zimbabwe have made it nearly impossible to 'realistically' practice as a journalist, as long as one was not sympathetic to the ZANU-PF 'national' cause. For over a decade now, a period spanning from the heavily disputed 2000 harmonised plebiscite in which ZANU-PF faced the hugest opposition ever in the history of the Zimbabwean nation state, the Zimbabwean media platform has been largely characterised by severely stringent media regulatory laws that made it nearly impossible for other players outside government controlled media to effectively and realistically participate. Realising the 'damage' that the power of the privately owned press such as *The Daily News* and *The Daily Mirror* had inflicted on its 'one party' political hegemony, the ZANU-PF led government embarked on an exercise to tighten media regulatory laws on Zimbabwe, in the process nipping off all the chances of private players coming into the play. Led by then Minister of Information and Publicity, Professor Jonathan Moyo, the ZANU-PF government promulgated into law some of the most draconian laws in the country, laws that equalled a serious gag on the freedom of expression and the free flow of information through conducive operating environment for the media. The passing of AIPPA and POSA witnessed severe restrictions on the operations of the privately owned media. The laws made it a near impossibility to register their publications as well as journalists. Moyo (2006: 81) commenting on this condition an show it help birth the rise of reliance on digital alternative media in Zimbabwe opines that,

Restricted democratic space has spawned a multiplicity of alternative public spheres that enable groups and individuals to continue to participate and engage in the wider debate on the mutating crisis gripping the country since the turn of the century...the diaspora are creatively exploiting new media to resist state propaganda churned out through the mainstream media.

Zimbabwe`s political arena has been a site of contestation with citizens having little or no freedom of speech due to fear of repression from the Central Intelligence Organisation; Police and the army. For example many citizens fear expressing their views because they fear the wrath of the Central Intelligence Organisation which is believed to have silenced political activists suspected of being anti the establishment and have schemed against people who were against the Mugabe led regime. Likewise the mass media is also controlled by the draconian laws such as AIPPA and BSA thus they cannot air their views freely. In this case the internet has plays a pivotal role in exposing the evils of the government, with citizens playing the role of the journalist. The internet has become a space for the citizens to air their views. Zimbabwe has seen the emergence of many political commentators using pseudonyms for example Mai Jukwa and Baba Jukwa on Facebook. Social media is a virtual public sphere created by alternative media. It can also be conceived of as a counter hegemonic tool which seeks to challenge or question political and cultural control of the masses by the elite but also demystify the ruling elite`s social engineering that is usually projected as natural and common sense by the mainstream media.

In an environment that does not promote media plurality and the proliferation of free speech and critical thinking such as the Zimbabwean environment of recent years, Mpofu (nd) envisions the internet and by extension citizen journalism as some extension of Habermas' public sphere. Habermas (1989: 73-74) defines such a public sphere as,

[A] realm of our social life in which something approaching public opinion can be formed. Access is guaranteed to all citizens... with the guarantee of freedom of assembly and association and the freedom to express and publish their opinions—about matters of general interest.

The policing of the media in Zimbabwe through all repressive means including the Central Intelligence Organisation (CIO), the Zimbabwe Republic Police (ZRP) and often times the military itself has resulted in a high proliferation of online news media aided by the internet. An important observation is that from the nascence of alternative digital media practices in Zimbabwe, most journalists on these web based news media have been able to communicate and report on issues and matters they would not normally do in Zimbabwean media houses. Also, we notice that most of them were journalists based in the country and reporting in most instances under *nom de plumes* who saw the internet as a means to report on these issues freely and without fear. In other words, in the Zimbabwean context,

The internet is credited for simultaneously enabling the user to exercise the right to freedom of expression through receiving and disseminating information, ideas and opinions visually or phonetically to large audiences at the lowest possible cost. Also, this evolution of technology has caused global dramatic changes in the field of journalism. Of particular interest...is how this alternative digital public sphere offers Zimbabweans an avenue to discuss a taboo subject in Zimbabwe without fear or being reprimanded by the secretive and authoritarian state. The 'taboo' in this context refers to issues that the state does not want discussed in public like the president's health, genocide, Zanu-Pf factionalism or succession debate and state sponsored corruption... (Mpofu, nd: 1)

It is within this context that we observe that the power of social media as citizen journalism cannot be underestimated. The contributions that bloggers and social media actors such as Baba Jukwa have made as an alternative form of news must never be overlooked. New media technologies, in this digital age, and in Zimbabwe in particular, have influenced political changes. The new media technologies have influenced social and political change in Zimbabwe by the use of social media platforms. Social media in its various forms has drawn international attention to Zimbabwe during the most intense period of the Zimbabwe crisis up to 2008 (Mhiripiri and Mutsvairo, 2013). Mhiripiri and Mutsvairo (2013) argue that social media activism in Zimbabwe can also be credited for contributing to the formation of the 2009 – 2013 political dispensation of a Government of National Unity (GNU) between ZANU PF and the two factions of the opposition political party, the Movement for Democratic Change (MDC). The increased use of the new communication technologies has helped to publicize extra-legal activities and human rights abuses often blamed on Robert Mugabe, ZANU-PF, affiliated militia groups and the security forces which led to diplomatic intervention (Mhiripiri and Mutsvairo, 2013).

Within the Zimbabwean context, citizen journalism especially in social media, the likes of Baba Jukwa, has become alternate space and practice were the civic virtues and freedoms of ordinary people in authoritarian regimes find expression (Moyo, 2014). Citizen journalism practices imply a paradigm shift from citizen as just political membership based on a codification of rights and responsibilities to citizen as discursive, deliberative, dialogic and transformative space and identity (Moyo, 2014). Citizen Journalism recasts citizen as a practice of freedom and a medium of communication that allows ordinary people to tell their stories (Moyo, 2014). According to Mutsvairo (2012), conventional media in Zimbabwe is still sceptical about the prospects of embedding the works of the citizen journalists into mainstream packages. Mutsvairo, notes that in as much as they operate on their own, citizen journalists have thrived further underscoring the perceived democratic value of citizen journalism. Mutsvairo, notes that the emergence of new media technologies has led to participatory journalism.

Baba Jukwa, Journalistic Ethics, and the Implications of Media Regulation in Zimbabwe

Observing the contributions that Baba Jukwa as citizen journalism has made towards the realisation of the freedom of expression ideal in 'democracies', it is imperative that one assess the ethical issues and regulatory problems such forms of 'journalism' present. Citizen journalists, the infamous Baba Jukwa included, have been and will continue to be criticised for lacking transparency especially by choosing to remain anonymous when they publish or broadcast their work (Mutsvairo, 2012). Citizen journalists often do not have by lines and therefore they are criticised for lack of credibility as it becomes difficult for anyone to be made accountable for any forms of ethical violations such as the 'reporting' of 'half-truths', biases and a refrains from one of journalism's canons of 'objectivity'. One must not deny the need for a proper regulation of the flow of information, the need for accountability and transparency. However, as Mutsvairo (2012) argues, Zimbabwean mass media has often been associated with no by lines as journalists fear victimisation. Bowman and Willis (2003:7) coined the term participatory journalism as an act of citizens playing a pivotal role in the process of collecting; reporting; analysing and disseminating news.

While indeed '...it is impossible to ignore the dominance of an emerging new form of journalism characterized by rapid reporting, interminable interactivity and ubiquitous multimedia content sharing and customization. Indeed, digital technologies have had a profound effect on the way news content is perceived, produced, shared and analysed...Produced in a matter of seconds, news can be shared instantly across the world, with the supremacy of citizen-inspired content becoming an overriding feature of contemporary news production' (Mutsvairo, 2015: 1), it would be folly to ignore the regulatory imperative. Gerry L. Dickert, editor of the *Silsbee Bee*, quoted in Lewis, Kaufhold & Lasorsa (2010: 8) and commenting on citizen journalism as a phenomenon opined that the newspaper's editors and reporters 'have to control the content.... We have a good idea of what's newsworthy based on our experience.... When you have people who are not professional journalists they don't have a grasp of the ethics involved.... You risk diluting the news to hearsay and gossip.... If you (a journalist) and I do a story, we talk to at least three sources. When we print something, we know it's as close to the truth as possible (but) when you have a citizen who has a gripe about the police department, that's going to be as much opinion as fact. It affects the credibility of your organization.'

Of course one needs to also acknowledge the reasons for the need for secrecy and anonymity in citizen made necessary by the conditions that propagate its rise. Because citizen journalism in the Zimbabwean context arose from the need to provide counter narratives to the propagandistic nature of the state controlled media, and the need for anonymity arising from the desire to protect themselves from repressive state apparatus one could understand them. An example would be how the ZANU PF government so much desired to identify the individual behind the Baba Jukwa wall. The Robert Gabriel Mugabe led government went as far as offering a US$300 000.00 reward to anyone able to expose Baba Jukwa. This then signals how much of the 'truth' Baba Jukwa was revealing and how far the ZANU PF government would go to 'hide' such 'truths'. It also gives one an idea of how powerful citizen journalism really is and how justified citizen journalists are in remaining anonymous.

However, be that as it may, one cannot overlook the ethical and legal violations that citizen journalists make. Much of the ethical violations are largely of 'objectivity'. Most of what constitutes citizen journalism is largely opinionated. While commonly referred to as citizen 'journalists', it not clear whether such people are indeed journalists. Due to the opinionated nature of content produced by citizens (Nah and Chung, 2009), citizen journalism cannot be considered "journalism". Keen (2007) opines that citizen and professional journalists cannot work hand in hand because the former does not leverage ethical issues such as neutrality and objectivity, which form the foundation of the latter's reporting. Since they do not adhere to accuracy, independence or autonomy, fairness, transparency, professional responsibility and objectivity (Kovach and Rosenstiel, 2001), citizen journalists cannot be classified as "journalists" (Mutsvairo, 2015: 3). Citing Carr *et al.* (2014), Mutsvairo (2015: 4) argues that citizen journalism while certainly having its own problems, it evidently provides a powerful opposing narrative to traditional journalism. New research has also shown that, with professional journalism fast losing its credibility, citizen journalism has gained momentum

Brown (2005) draws a clear distinction between citizen and professional journalists, suggesting that while trained journalists are obliged to respect some journalistic principles such as accuracy and fact-checking, citizen journalists do not have specific ethical standards guiding their conduct. With this distinction in mind, one can appreciate why citizen journalism has been subjected to intense scrutiny over ethical concerns. (Mutsvairo, 2015: 4). A key characteristic of citizen journalism, depending on geographical location, could, as already confirmed by Brown (2005), be the absence of journalistic ethics. That means, for instance, that news can be instantaneously produced and distributed, with no facts checked or verified. While some bloggers may willingly verify some of the news they publish, fact-checking is not a prerequisite for entering the largely self-regulating blogging world. The problem is, when facts are not properly and carefully checked, empowering readers with truthful and accurate information becomes an impracticable task. 'Participatory media production in general and the notion of user-generated news in particular present philosophical and technical challenges to the professional logic of journalism. This is especially true as reporters and editors take on and operate within their role as gatekeepers for public knowledge' (Lewis, Kaufhold & Lasorsa, 2010: 5-6). Davis McAuley, editor of the *Bastrop Advertiser*, quoted in Lewis, Kaufhold & Lasorsa (2010: 8), provides a good concluding remark to citizen journalism and the need for regulation when he said of citizen journalism, 'It does not make any sense. News is meant to be reported professionally, not through some random citizen.... Journalism is a profession and it cannot be done by anyone.' While offering a very pertinent service as alternative media and a public sphere, the regulation of information flow is pivotal to the sustenance of journalistic ethics. It is quite unfortunate that such a control mechanism in Zimbabwe through the security forces and with regards to Baba Jukwa seems to be driven more by political will and not ethical considerations. Just a discord between the need for professional journalistic conduct and political will continue to haunt and torment professional journalistic practices in Zimbabwe.

REFERENCES

Alasuutari, P. (Ed.). (1999). *Rethinking the media audience*. Los Angeles, CA: Sage Publications Ltd.

Bardoel, J., & Deuze, M. (2001). Network Journalism: Converging Competences of Media Professionals and Professionalism. *Australian Journalism Review*, *23*(2), 91–103.

Carpenter, S. (2010). A study of content diversity in online citizen journalism and online newspaper articles. *New Media & Society*, *12*(12), 1064–1084. doi:10.1177/1461444809348772

Dahl, R. (2000). *On democracy*. New Haven, CT: Yale University Press.

Dahlgren, P. (1996). Media logic in cyberspace: repositioning journalism and its publics. *Javnost/The Public*, *3*, 59-72.

Dahlgren, P. (2000). Media citizens and civic culture. In M. Gurevitch & J. Curran (Eds.), *Mass Media and society* (3rd ed.). London: Edward Arnold.

Dahlgren, P. (2000). The Internet and the democratisation of civic culture. *Political Communication*, *17*(4), 335–340. doi:10.1080/10584600050178933

Dahlgren, P. (2005). *Internet, public spheres and political communication*. London: Routledge.

Goode, L. (2009). Social news, citizen journalism and democracy. *New Media & Society*, *11*(11), 1287–1305. doi:10.1177/1461444809341393

Habermas, J. (1989). *The structural transformation of the public sphere: an inquiry into a category of bourgeois society*. Cambridge, MA: MIT Press.

Kohn, M. (2000). Language, power and persuasion: Towards a critique of deliberative democracy. *Constellations (Oxford, England)*, *7*(3), 408–429. doi:10.1111/1467-8675.00197

Kozinets, R. (2009). *Netnography: Doing Ethnographic research online*. Los Angeles, CA: Sage Publications Ltd.

Lessig, L. (1999). *Code and other laws of cyberspace*. New York: Basic books.

Lessig, L. (2001). *The future of ideas: The fate of the commons in a connected world*. New York: Random House.

Lewis, S. C., Kaufhold, K., & Lasorsa, D. L. (2010). Thinking about citizen journalism: The philosophical and practical challenges of user-generated content for community newspapers. *Journalism Practice*, *4*(2), 163–179. doi:10.1080/14616700903156919

Masunungure, E. V. (2006). Nation Building, State Building and Power Configuration in Zimbabwe. *Conflict Trends Magazine*, (1), 1-10.

Mhiripiri, N. A., & Mutsvairo, B. (2013). Social Media, New ICTs and the Challenges Facing the Zimbabwe Democratic Process. In New Media Influence on Social and Political Change in Africa (pp. 402-421). Hershey, PA: IGI Global.

Mitra, A. (2001). Marginal Voices in Cyberspace. *New Media & Society*, *3*(1), 29–48. doi:10.1177/1461444801003001003

Moyo, D. (2010). *The New Media as Monitors of Democracy. Mobile Phones and Zimbabwe's 2008 Election*. Paper presented at the Conference on Election Processes, Liberation Movements and Democratic Change in Africa, Organised by IESE and CMI, Maputo.

Mpofu, S. (n.d.). *The power of citizen journalism in Zimbabwe*. Unpublished Manuscript.

Mujere, J., & Mwatwara, W. (2015). Citizen Journalism and National Politics in Zimbabwe: The Case of the 2008 and 2013 Elections. In Participatory Politics and Citizen Journalism in a Networked Africa: A Connected Continent (pp. 215 – 228). London: Palgrave, Macmillan.

Mutsvairo, B. (2015). Recapturing Citizen Journalism: Processes and Patterns Citizen Journalism and National Politics in Zimbabwe: The Case of the 2008 and 2013 Elections. In Participatory Politics and Citizen Journalism in a Networked Africa: A Connected Continent (pp. 1 – 15). London: Palgrave, Macmillan.

Papacharissi, Z. (2009). Introduction. In Journalism and Citizenship: New Agendas in Communication. Routledge.

Rosen, J. (2008). A Most Useful Definition of Citizen Journalism. *PressThink*. Retrieved from http://journalism.nyu.edu/pubzone/weblogs/pressthink/2008/07/14/a_most_useful

Wilhelm, A. (2000). *Democracy in the digital age*. London: Routledge.

Chapter 12
Naming Crime Suspects in the News:
"Seek Truth and Report It" vs. "Minimizing Harm"

Robin Blom
Ball State University, USA

ABSTRACT

Whereas some news outlets fully identify crime suspects with name, age, address, and other personal details, other news outlets refuse to fully identify any crime suspect—or even people who have been convicted for a crime. News media from a variety of countries have accused and fully identified people of being responsible for crimes, although those persons turned out to be innocent. Yet, when someone types the names of those people in online search engines, for many, stories containing the accusations will turn up at the top of the search results. This chapter examines the positive and negative aspects from those practices by examining journalistic routines in a variety of countries, such as the United States, Nigeria, and The Netherlands. This analysis demonstrates that important ethical imperatives—often represented in ethics codes of professional journalism organizations—can be contradictory in these decision-making processes. Journalists need to weigh whether they would like to "seek truth and report it" or "minimize harm" when describing crime suspects.

INTRODUCTION

It is not a question whether someone got caught with meth or another controlled substance, but rather who it is this time. Readers of many local newspapers in the Midwest of the United States are used to receiving reports about drug busts in their communities. At times it almost seems to be a daily occurrence:

Three people were arrested on a variety of felony charges after a methamphetamine lab was discovered in their South Side home.

As common with these types of stories, thereporters dutifully add the names of the arrestees. The report would look like something like this if it would make the next day's newspaper:

DOI: 10.4018/978-1-5225-2095-5.ch012

John Johnson, 36, and Pete Peterson, 32, were arrested at their home, at 747 E. Sixth Ave., after city police went there about 12:30 a.m. Thursday. Also found at the house were Jane Jones, 33, 4100 N. Keller St., and three children, ranging in age from 3 to 12.

And, as a bonus, the readers usually get to see the mug shots of the suspects that were taken at the police station or county jail after the arrest. Or, if someone from the newspaper staff rushed in soon enough, some pictures snapped at the scene could be part of the publication as well. It is common practice for thousands of media outlets around the world (and not just in the United States) to release such types of information in local crime stories—from rural weeklies to daily newspapers in large metro areas, as well as broadcast stations, blogs, and other types of citizen journalism outlets of all sizes.

Regardless of whether the three suspects from the example above are eventually convicted or not, a simple Google or Bing query—even many years later—for John, Pete, and Jane will most likely pull up their arrest story at, or near, the top of the search results. That could lead to big problems for all three down the road. Potential employers or graduate school admission officers would, perhaps, be less inclined to invite them for an interview. Banks may not provide them mortgages or loans to start a business. And their children could become isolated when other parents in the neighborhood don't want their offspring to play at a house where there are potentially illegal substances lying around—even when charges are dropped soon after the arrest.

In this case, it would have been better if they were Johan, Peter, and Sjaan—while living in The Netherlands—when they were arrested. Or Jon, Pétr, and Janna in Sweden. Because then their identities and pictures would likely not have appeared in a local daily right away after their arrest. Johan or Jon would have been "a 32-year-old resident" or the "32-year-old J." The identity would likely not be fully revealed at all, or only after conviction.

These reporting routines have been developed over a long time by journalists within their industries and could lead to the adoption of a "gold standard" of journalistic practices in individual media companies. In many cases (regardless of country), the "rules" on naming suspects is taught in journalism schools and in newsrooms as "the way we do things in our profession" without much thought about whether it is the best practice in *all* situations. As Fullerton and Patterson (2013) pointed out, "the most profound differences in press practices with respect to crime coverage result from ritualised, largely unexamined habits and from voluntary ethics policies – not from laws and formal regulation" (p. 124). Importantly, the authors also found that reporters have little knowledge about practices of colleagues and ethical codes in other countries. This probably applies to many journalists all over the planet.

It is certainly warranted to have larger discussions within media industries around the world as the digitalization of news could have large repercussions for many people who have digital footprints that they would like to—but can't—erase. Scientists warned about the influence of computers on people's daily life decades before the Internet became a household utility (see: Westin & Baker, 1972). Nowadays, social media messages float around the Twitterverse and other online repositories even when they are removed within minutes by their creators. Automatic Web crawlers or human Internet users have already captured and stored those virtual blips for eternity.

That becomes problematic when someone wants to forget some events from the past. "Since the beginning of time, for us humans, forgetting has been the norm and remembering the exception. Because of digital technology and global networks, however, this balance has shifted" (Mayer-Schönberger, 2011, p. 2). Social forgetfulness, the opportunity for a fresh start because no one can remember someone's particular history, is disappearing—as frustrating it may be for some (Blanchette& Johnson, 2002; Bannon, 2006). A criminal past or the accusation of being responsible for a crime may be a simple Internet search away to be known by others: "[o]ur pasts are becoming etched like a tattoo into our digital skins" (Lasica, 1998).

This chapter will discuss approaches to naming suspects during several stages of the judicial process in a variety of countries to establish a large range of practices and rationales for each of those routines, including Norway and the United Kingdom, among others. How are those practices around the world taking into account the threats to the presumption of innocence? What about the public right to know? Should there be a right to forget? And how are the potential negative experiences of victims taken into account? The answers of those questions provide an overview of how reporters and editors struggle with the classic battle between *seek truth and report it* and *minimizing harm*, as depicted in the Society of Professional Journalists' Code of Ethics, and with similar wording in many other ethics codes around the world. Moreover, the choices may also be influenced by local laws and regulations that lead to double standards within the coverage of some news organizations.

The goal is to provide the readers an overview of journalistic practices on naming suspects and the potential consequences of adopting one over the other in particular circumstances. In a period of time that people's history can easily be traced online, it is important that those re-evaluations take place to make sure that journalists inform the public about crime in their communication and also minimize harm for those involved, especially people not responsible for a crime. This analysis starts with an overview of the influence of organizational socializations journalistic routines and practices, in particular on news source selection and ethical decision-making. This will lead to a recommendation that there is a need for a more pragmatic approach in which journalists take into account the context of each case and all of its stakeholders (see: Husselbee, 1994).

Routines in the Newsroom

News production is a construction of themes and details to build stories that are gathered through routine practices that journalists have adopted on an ongoing basis (Strentz, 1989). This includes a high degree of consensus on storytelling and the way how to report news (Bennett, Gressett, & Halton, 1985). Routines are patterned, repeated practices or methods that people, such as news media workers, use to do their jobs. They are necessary to produce news efficiently. Without routines, journalists could not decide efficiently what to put into the news report and what issues and events must be left out (Brown, Bybee, Wearden, & Straughan, 1987).

Routines provide "regularity and manageability in a job that is inherently unmanageable" (Shoemaker, 1991, p.50). If reporters would not be able to cope with unexpected events, "news organizations, as rational enterprises, would flounder and fail" (Tuchman, 1973, p.111). Repeated practices save time in finishing a news piece and makes it easier to cope with deadlines set by news media organizations to get their message out on a set time on a daily basis or throughout a day(Niven, 2005). This also makes the news process cheaper (Sigal, 1986).

Routinization does not happen automatically when a person enrolls in an undergraduate journalism program or joins a news media organization. This happens over time by learning norms and values of an industry or work field. The journalistic routines are reinforced in the newsroom on a daily basis; they are often unwritten rules followed by the majority of, if not all, members of a news outlet (Sigal, 1973). This process is called organizational socialization. Some studies, such as Breed's (1955) analysis of social control in the newsroom, show how reporters and editors are socialized to ascertain policies within organizations and work fields (also see: Bennett, Gressett, & Halton, 1985).

Taking into account societal forces on the norms, values, and beliefs of journalists, it still appears that individuals have much room to decide what ends up in the newspaper and what does not. Many journalism and mass communication professionals and scholars – and also the public – think that the personal views and beliefs influence the news selection process (Gaziano, 1987; Domke, Watts, Shah, & Pan, 1999; Lichtenberg, 2000; Lee, 2005).

Yet on the other hand, Reese (1991) argued that individuals are also "constrained in their power by structures beyond their immediate control" (p. 310). As a result of hundreds of years of organizational socialization within the field of journalism, newsmakers share criteria for news selection (Fishman, 1980).

Grossman and Kumar (1981) provided anecdotal evidence for organizational socialization in their book about reporting practices of White House correspondents. "[A]lthough newly arrived White House officials and reporters alike in the post-Watergate era may think of themselves as free agents, they variably follow the routines dictated by the needs of the organizations they work for" (p. 14). Each journalist tries to fulfill the organization's expectations bounded by the constraints placed by the outlet. Consequently, newly assigned reporters attempt to "follow the same routines as the reporters who preceded them to the White House" (p.14).

Especially the logistical and organizational limits affect what individuals within news media can do in providing news accounts to the public (Reese, 1991). Shoemaker (1991), therefore, proposed to examine "the extent to which the individual is merely carrying out a set of routine procedures" (p.49).

Cassidy (2006) compared the results of a content analysis of news articles by several news outlets and a survey of the reporters at those organizations, he found that factors on the routine level (peers on staff, supervisors, journalistic training, news sources, priorities of prestige publications, local competing news media, and wire service budgets) seemed to have more influence on what makes the news than individual demographics (e.g. age, educational history, racial/ethnic make-up, and political ideology).

Manning (2001) indicated that by looking at the journalistic routines used within one news organization, the news outcome could be predicted because of their adopted routines, but also warned that this view is too simplistic as a description of the effects of daily routines at news outlets on the news outcome. She maintained that it underemphasizes the extent to which individual characteristics, values, beliefs, and opinion make a significant difference.

There are indications that individual-level influence still is at work at news media organizations. This is not surprising considering the many individuals involved in the newsmaking process; within news media organizations, several kinds of conflicts influence the news outcome: conflicts between business and professional norms, between partisan and ideological factions, and between neutral and participant news values (Ettema, Whitney, &Wackman, 1987).Of course, the extent to which individuals can shape the news output is likely to differ by news organization and even by individual reporter or editor.

News Sources

Journalists need to make important decisions for each story about which sources to include. This selection procedure is also heavily routinized to turn events and issues into story as efficiently as possible. Journalists are often not able to witness events for themselves – they rely on stories of others (Berkowitz & Beach, 1993). "Even when the journalist is in the position to observe an event directly, he remains reluctant to offer interpretations of his own, preferring instead to rely on his news sources. For the reporter, in short, most news is not what has happened, but what someone says has happened or will happen" (Sigal, 1973). Or as Gans (1980) put it, journalists "don't deal in facts, but in attributed opinions" (p.130). Even in cases when these attributed opinions are lies, "journalists can suggest that they have done so but only if they find other sources who allow themselves to be quoted to that effect" (Gans, 2003, p.47).

Journalists cannot take forever to complete stories; news holes need to be filled with their copy, and therefore, reports often need to be finalized before the next deadline (Bennett, 2005). As Sigal (1986) suggested, "Reporters need sources who can provide information on a regular and timely basis; they are not free to roam or probe at will" (p.16). To get a certain number of articles in the next day's newspaper, journalists need to receive lots of information in a short period of time in order to make the deadline (Hallin, Manoff, & Weddle, 1993). A steady flow of news is necessary. Journalists must make the "spontaneous predictable" and anticipate where newsworthy events develop (Bennett, 2005, p.166).

The choice of sources is an important force shaping the news. It is a decision of what information, like defining decision-making options, is included and which are excluded (Brown, Bybee, Wearden, & Straughan, 1987). In such way, sources are "primary definers" (McLeod, Kosicki, & McLeod, 2002, p. 244) of what happened, and thereby determine how that story is told (Kasoma & Maier, 2005). Sources try to influence what information gets out in the symbolic arena by managing what facts and opinions are discussed in public (Gans, 1980). Reporters, therefore, turn to people who provide information that can be used for news output on a regular basis. For instance, government agencies provide a "high volume of professionally produced, ready-to-report news matters" (Bennett, Gressett, & Halton, 1985, p. 50).

In many occasions, those who report on public affairs turn to bureaucrats, politicians, and other authorities. Journalists do this to hold (elected) officials accountable (the news media's watchdog function in society), but they are also easily accessible to provide information (Gandy, 1982; Hallin, Manoff, & Weddle, 1993).

Entman and Gross (2008) pointed out that this is often the case for news about criminal cases. Consequently, it is often slanted in favor of the prosecution, because there is often no credible source that voices a competing frame. "[U]nlike in coverage of policy debates over, say, social security, abortion, or the environment, there is no institutionalized political-party system to provide a more-or-less automatic two-sided debate among credible elites that journalists can reflect in their coverage" (p. 95).

Attorneys could provide a counterargument to accusations by the prosecutor, but public comments may not always be in the best interest for a defendant. Furthermore, the authors argued, pretrial reporting "tends generally to treat the presumption of innocence as a formality, largely limited to using the word allege" (p. 95).

Verifying Facts

Journalists always deal with the issue that some facts are verifiable in theory but not verifiable in practice (Tuchman, 1978). When a prosecutor "alleges" that a person has committed a crime, there is often not enough time to check out claims by sources to publish an article on the same day. Or worse, on many occasions, verifiable facts are just not readily available at all. This leads reporters to an alternative approach: reporting the truth-claims of sources. And because journalists often lack time to verify statements, this could deny them the opportunity to include multiple sides of stories and to find out if those claims are true *before* the next deadline, or when they are coping with real-time coverage (see: Deuze, 2004; García-Avilés, 2014). As a result, reporters can indicate only that something happened (or is happening); journalists most likely will focus on what has happened rather than addressing questions on why something happened, or to provide a broader context (Perloff, 1998).

Journalists have little time to reflect on whether they have gotten at the truth when they turn in an assignment. And after all, in many instances they have been clearly wrong. For example, Sen. Joseph McCarthy was able to get his accusations in the news columns and broadcasts of U.S. news media during the anti-Communism era, even while many of them were found to be false. Furthermore, some reporters themselves thought McCarthy claims were false, but put the allegations in their news reports anyhow because they kept holding onto some newsroom routine practices, providing face-value coverage of important political figures (Bayley, 1981; Oshinsky, 1983; Hacket, 1984). Kovach and Rosenstiel (2001) illustrated this idea with a speech of Defense Secretary Robert McNamara on the war in Vietnam. His assertions were eventually found out not to be true, and the press "did not get at the truth of what he knew" (p. 37).

This contradicts the recommendations of the Hutchins Commission (1947), which warned—almost seven decades ago—about dangers of publishing accounts that are "factually correct but substantially untrue" (p. 219) By just reporting the facts - in this case: what a speaker claims - the distribution of lies cannot automatically be avoided. According to Rupar (2006), this shows that journalism is not just a matter of portraying ''facts as they are," but also a "matter of assembling truth beneath and around 'facts as they are told''' (p. 128). Even when the claims are truthful, it still could be doubtful the picture drawn by the politician is a complete picture of the whole story.

Ethical Decision-Making

Journalists have important roles in society. As gatekeepers and story framers, there is a tremendous opportunity to inform fellow citizens about vital issues and events about success and failure in creating just societies. This task comes with immense responsibilities. Journalists can hurt people's feelings in news coverage and they need to make sound moral judgements in choosing the story elements and descriptions to be informative without unnecessarily offending or defaming certain individuals or groups.

Moral judgment is defined as "the process of choosing between right and wrong based upon what one finds important and is used to define the quality of reasons used by people making ethical choices" (Meader, Knight, Coleman, & Wilkins, 2015, p. 235). Those decisions between right and wrong (or good and bad) are made based on the values that a person or a group (united by a code of ethics) applies in such ethical choices. Values are "conceptions of the desirable that guide the way (people) select actions, evaluate people and events, and explain their actions and evaluations" (Schwartz, 1999, p. 24).

Ethical decisions can be difficult to take because they usually involve balancing positive and negative consequences for many stakeholders (Bugeja, 2008). This is particularly true "whenever two or more duties would lead to different decisions" (Christians, 2007, p. 122).

Although the foundation of many ethics philosophies do not change, the applications of the philosophies may take different meanings and lead to a new set of consequences within rapid changing social environments that are spurred by new communication forms and other technological innovations. Those developments lead to new questions about human rights in this Digital Age (Mathiesen, 2014) and the role of journalism in shaping those protections. As Christians and colleague (1991) pointed out, "Open news remains our national glory in a complicated world, and expectations of journalistic performance are higher than ever before" (p. 29).

Journalists likely have been exposed to at least some ethics training through their education and professional careers. Many journalism undergraduate programs have included media ethics education in their (core) curricula, either as a stand-alone course or in combination with media law. This exposes aspiring journalists to philosophies in ethical reasoning and case studies to explore the consequences of ethical decision-making in real life. And many (student) news outlets have adopted ethics codes from professional organizations, such as the Society of Professional Journalists (SPJ), which has adopted four sub-headers to explain the duties in covering news: (1) Seek truth and report it; (2) Minimize harm; (3) Act independently; and (4) Be accountable and transparent.

Codes of ethics provide journalists with some helpful guidance, yet they do not provide templates for adequate responses for each ethical dilemma. It is still up to the journalists to balance the interest of all stakeholders. "Journalistic codes of ethics seldom offer precise, bright-line rules that define problematic situations.... The flexible language of these codes leads to varied interpretations and a resultant lack of consensus on their meaning and application" (Morant, 2005, pp. 613-614). For instance, the code of ethics of the Nigerian Press Council (2016) proposes that publishing information about an individual is justified if a crime is being exposed, yet in many cases it is not sure that a suspect has committed an alleged crime. And the Press Council (2016) of South Africa points out that the right of privacy may only be overridden by the public interest and that the facts need to be true or substantially true. But, again, that may be hard to establish early in a crime investigation when suspects are interviewed and arrested.

Thus, codes of ethics do not provide guidance for a one size-fits-all solution when it comes to naming crime suspects in news coverage. In fact, using the SPJ codes as an example, the imperative of "seeking truth and report it" seems to challenge the imperative of "minimizing harm," according to Steele, Black, and Barney (1998).Thus, journalists need to balance on a case-by-case basis whether invading someone's privacy, or the extent to which someone's privacy is being invaded, is "necessary in order to permit others access to information needed to make equally important choices in their lives" (Etzioni, 1999, p. 23) or prevents harm to others. However, there is a variety of cases in which harm was done to the people's whose privacy was invaded by presenting them—mistakenly—as crime perpetrators. Despite many good intentions by journalists to adhere to journalists codes of ethics as much as they can, this does not prevent them from identifying the wrong people in crime cases. Consequently, such news coverage has haunted these false positives for many years after publications identified them as suspects of horrific crimes.

The False Positives

One of the most famous cases, because of the widespread—global—coverage, involves the person who was accused of planting a backpack with three pipe bombs at a park in Atlanta during the 1996 Summer Olympics that killed one person and injured 111 others. He was initially considered a hero for alerting the police when he discovered the explosives, which led to a large-scale evacuation that saved many lives. Yet, soon after, he was considered the prime suspect in the case. This led to large scrutiny by law enforcement, as well as the world media that followed him and his family around—even though he was just a "person of interest." Jewell has never been charged or indicted of any crime.

The news media played a vital role in continuous dissemination of information that made the person suspect, yet without any valid evidence (and, in hindsight, there was none). Alicia C. Shephard (1994), a senior writer for the *American Journalism Review*, wrote that "some restraint [by the news media] would have helped" in this particular case, because the finger pointing started before anyone was arrested, charged or indicted. In an unusual act, the U.S. attorney's office wrote a letter to the man's lawyers exonerating him: "This is to advise you that based on the evidence developed to date, your client [...] is not considered a target of the federal criminal investigation into the bombing on July 27, 1996, at Centennial Olympic Park in Atlanta. Barring any newly discovered evidence, this status will not change. I am hopeful that [...] will provide further cooperation as a witness in the investigation."

Another famous case, a decade later, involved several athletes from the Duke University lacrosse team. They were falsely accused of raping a student from another local university. Because the alleged victim was African-American and the students Caucasian, the case was framed as a potential hate-crime as well. Entman and Gross (2008) concluded that the press coverage of this case was not always one-sided and unfavorable to the students, yet the "early phase was also less balanced andexhibited a slant toward the prosecution" (p. 124).

Those early stories—filled with accusations against the players—are still easy to retrieve online. Peltz (2008) did a Google search and nine of first ten links were to stories in which it was not mentioned that the players were innocent. This could have large implications later on in life of these men, the author argued:

Imagine you are a harried hiring coordinator working for Big X Corporation. Before you sits a stack of 600 resumes, and your job today is to winnow the field by eliminating persons of dubious character. Your tool is Google ...[they] will probably not get the benefit of careful reading and follow-up searches concerning their charges. (p. 718)

The players were exonerated more than a year after they were accused. Their innocence was declared in a letter from the Attorney's Office of North Carolina, similar to Jewell. It is very rare the suspects receive a written account of their innocence in a case. Usually, charges are dropped or during a court case it is determined that there is not enough evidence to pronounce someone guilty. That is not the same as a declaration of innocence. Therefore, in many cases where there is no DNA evidence available to prove someone's innocence or other aspects of a case—in the public's eye—there is still the possibility that the suspects did commit the crime.

That is exactly what happened to another person who was accused of a crime he didn't commit:

[T]he libel actions have by no means addressed all the damage done to my personal and professional reputation, which I spent over 30 years building. ... I doubt the damage done can ever be repaired. Had I not been retired, I think the effect on my career would have been catastrophic. (see: Cathcart, 2011)

In another example, a man accused of raping a teenager, the struggle was worse. He spent ten years fighting to clear his name after he was not indicated by a grand jury and even won a defamation suit against his accusers. According to Reza (2005), "he had first taken a leave of absence and then left his job as a state prosecutor, undergone therapy, suffered daily threats and taunts from members of the public (to him and to his school-aged daughter), and endured constant attention from the media" (p. 771).

These cases are not overly rare, because a large percentage of state felony cases are dismissed after arrest in major urban centers, from 10 percent for driving-related offenses to 40 percent for assault cases. Similar numbers are found in federal cases, where prosecutors do not prosecute about one-third of the suspects for violent crimes. This pertains to many ten-thousands of people who were arrested but not prosecuted (Reza, 2005).

The Case for Naming Crime Suspects

The "assumptions about the value of names remain widely accepted, if not unchallenged, in U.S. practice" (Vultee, 2010). This is the case in other countries as well, such as the United Kingdom. This assumption is fueled by the desire for the press to be part of the broader marketplace of ideas, in which competing claims are assessed for their value. When it comes to information, it is assumed that "truth naturally overcomes falsehood when they are allowed to compete—[which] was used continually during the eighteenth century as a justification for freedom of expression" (Smith, 1988, p. 31).

In other words, according to Meyers (1993), the journalist's job is to gather and report all the details and "let the readers or viewers decide." The author also pointed out that such an interpretation of reporting practices "also divorces the journalist from her role as a moral agent, accountable to others" (p. 142). That is a deliberate approach from many news organizations in the United States and United Kingdom that value informing the public more than any other stakeholders, including the people accused of crime (Fullerton & Patterson, 2013).

This is noticeable for news outlets that run so-called mug shot websites, where all profile photos released by police in their distribution area, automatically, are placed online with all personal information of the arrestees and a description of the crime they are accused of by the police. For instance, mugshots and other personal information are directly published on the Tampa Bay Times website as soon as the police releases the information in the newspaper's four prime distribution counties (Hillsborough, Pasco, Pinellas, and Manatee). The images and the other information (name, photograph, booking ID, height, weight, age, gender, eye color, birth date, booking date and booking charge) remain searchable on the website for 60 days from the booking date. Several other newspapers have similar additions to their news sections, such as the *Chattanooga Times Free* Press. The pages are visited by thousands each day, which allow the outlets to sell lucrative advertising space to accompany the mugshots.

The *Tampa Bay Tribune* mugshot website has a disclaimer on its front page in which it states that the information mirrors open county sheriff's Web sites in the Tampa Bay area. Additionally, it acknowledges that the people appearing on the Website have not been convicted and are presumed innocent. "Do not rely on this site to determine any person's actual criminal record." The mugshots are removed from the Website after 60 days, yet that does not happen with all crime-related news coverage. However, the newspaper cannot prevent others from copying the crime reports and those stories may still float around the World Wide Web after being removed from the newspaper website.

Such openness about all the facts, including the names of suspects, may help victims of crime to step forward, if they have not done out of fear of repercussions by the perpetrator, concern of being stigmatized as a victim, or fearing to not be believed. In fact, a newspaper with all the details of a case could lead to criminals ending behind bars. A simple explanation that someone is investigated for sexual misconduct could lead to a breakthrough in multiple cases.

- **Arizona (Little Rock):** A Catholic priest was placed on administrative leave while police investigate allegations of sexual misconduct with a minor. The Rev. [John Doe], 53, wasn't charged with any crime.

This Associated Press local wire story about this man (his name was mentioned in full in the original report printed in the San Francisco Chronicle in the Fall of 2002), even emphasizing that he is not charged or arrested. It is only mentioned that the Douglas Police Department investigates him for misconduct of a minor. Further there is a short history about his work as a priest, but there is not any evidence attributed in the story that supports the allegations.

Yet, in similar cases, victims filed police reports after discovering that they were not alone. In the case of actor Bill Crosby (who at this point has not been convicted), dozens of women accused him of sexual assault after a few others had spoken out in public and made news headlines nationally and internationally. Lawyers of victims of British publicity agent Max Clifford praised the value of naming suspects of sexual crimes. After two women came forward, dozens of others did as well (Saunderson, 2014).

The Case against Naming Crime Suspects

In several West and North European countries the majority of daily newspapers do not publish full names of most suspects, such as in Norway, although the names would likely be published when an armed criminal is on the run. Names are usually published by almost all newspapers after people are formally charged and their cases go to trial (Bowers, 2013).

In Sweden, the full name may appear in crime coverage, but only after a person has been convicted by the courts. That would not even be the case in The Netherlands, except for a rare occasion. For instance, some media organizations provided the full name of the murderer of Pim Fortuyn, a popular politician who was killed a few days before the 2002 parliament elections; other outlets still used the killer's first name and initials for years, instead.

In an extraordinary case, one Dutch daily newspaper published not only the name of a convicted pedophile, but also his address (something that was unheard of in the Dutch press). This led to a mob scene outside of the apartment of the man with people demanding the pedophile to move out of town. This case was a source for heavy debate within the Dutch journalism industry and the newspaper's chief editor has publicly apologized for publishing the address. The newspaper also paid him 750 euro as compensation.

Whether you are a suspect or convict, in The Netherlands, the face is also rarely recognizable on a picture that accompanies a crime story. In a small amount of court stories, an artist impression of the scene may include a drawing of the suspect. But those impressions are more in the style of a caricature rather than a Rembrandt with all the fine details of facial expressions. The ability to recognize a specific person is small; and there is anecdotal evidence that suspects, judges, and prosecutors do not even recognize themselves in some of those drawings. Instead of drawings, some news outlets would publish a picture of a suspect or convict, yet would place a black box over the eyes of the suspect, which makes it much harder to recognize the person—even if you would pass the person in the street the next day. (Interestingly, this practice has been considered sensational in some of the ethics policies of daily newspapers, although that did not stop their reporters and editors from using pictures with some facial parts covered by the black box.)

There are many media outlets around the world that question the benefit for their audiences to know all personal details about a suspect, and whether they should do more to minimize harm to people that may later turn out to be innocent. For instance, more than 250 people have been exonerated in the United States while they were on death row, because DNA evidence dismissed them from involvement of the crime they were convicted for. When those people were named in newspaper reports before, during, and after the trial means they were falsely accused of brutal crimes.

Whether it's an old-fashioned news report or a modern online database, the main question remains the same: Are the people mentioned guilty of committing the crimes they are accused of? The main imperative of journalism is to tell the truth, but right after an arrest that is almost always impossible to say with limited access to evidence. Not all "facts" are checked and double-checked by the Justice Department at that point. Furthermore, not all "facts" are checked and double-checked by the journalists. That goes against the "most commonly repeated adage in U.S. criminal justice is the presumption of innocence: defendants are deemed innocent until proven guilty" (Baradaran, 2011, p. 723) and "Likewise in England, comments in the media about a person's guilt were criticized when the individual had not yet been found guilty (p. 735).

Reporters never know for sure what turns and twists a specific crime story will take during the course of a long judicial process. As James Carey (2002) explained, "premature scoops" could be "nothing more than gossip and sensationalism" (p. 80). That is the reason for why a growing number of U.S. college newspapers (e.g., University of Connecticut and Miami University) have decided to omit names from their daily police blotter if there is no need to identify a person to avoid additional harm to the community. The editors decide in individual cases whether identification is necessary.

Reza (2005) also questioned the necessity of naming suspects in many instances, because the majority of people who read the story will never will have any contact with that person. According to Solove (2007), "facts of the story may be of legitimate concern to the public, but the identification of the people involved might not further the story's purpose" (p. 133). Some journalists argue that publicity is not part of a court sentence and as Tor Mørseth, managing editor of Bergens Tidende (BT), told Bowers (2013), "identification of a person in media is an added burden, and we have taken a stand that we will not identify for this reason" (p. 80).

Rehabilitation: The Right to Be Forgotten

Related to that argument, an important reason for not naming convicted criminals (and thus as well in the stage when they were suspects) is the ability to rehabilitate after fulfilling their sentence. Full disclosure of all private facts could limit opportunities to make a living and support a family. That is less likely when a person is fully identified in news coverage. Other people may be less inclined to interact with someone they know has a criminal past (Fullerton & Patterson, 2013).

It has been advocated numerous times that courts should recognize a right to be forgotten. In that sense, citizens should have the right to have information deleted after a certain time, the right to have a "clean slate," and the right to be connected only to present information (Koops, 2011; McNealy, 2012).

The highest European court decided in 2014 that people have a right to have links removed from search websites, such as Google and Yahoo!, when the links connect Internet users to information that is deemed irrelevant or outdated. Hundreds of thousands of links and ten thousands of web pages have been removed since, although sometimes only for searches conducted in EU territory and not necessarily from other areas on the planet. However, media companies do not have to automatically honor all requests when it is assessed that there is a public interest in providing access to contended pages. Lower European courts have supported media companies in several of such cases.

It was not a surprise that the European Union would establish a right that would allow people to keep some sort of control of private information when there would not be an outweighing public interest in the information. Spanish courts have been supportive of the right to be forgotten argument and also French courts have long acknowledged the concept of *oubli*, or oblivion, that gives individuals the control of their past and future (Rosen, 2012; Ambrose &Ausloos, 2013).

The European approach is in direct conflict with protections found in the First Amendment of the United States, but that does not mean that that private information is automatically public (see: Warren

& Brandeis, 1890). The right of privacy is protected in many instances and limits news media somewhat in how and what to report in certain cases, although courts have refrained from clearly defining newsworthiness and its relation to privacy laws. And there is no overhauling legal framework that helps convicted criminals in their rehabilitation efforts by shielding them from press coverage.

Ironically, providing someone a second chance is regarded as a noble act in countries where the press predominantly is providing all details about crime suspects. Comeback stories are considered heroic and have often been glorified in many countries. Yet, for criminals such opportunity is made much harder with non-stop press coverage to take advantage of a new chance, whereas many criminals and innocent suspects would want nothing more. As Bannon (2006) explained, "Who has not experienced the liberating feeling of throwing off the baggage of the past and beginning afresh to confront the world? In a sense acts of pardon, amnesty, Catholic absolution in confession, are all mechanisms by which people can bury the past and begin anew" (p. 10).

Such pleas only count for juvenile crime suspects and convicts in many countries. This is even the case in the United States, although there is no consensus among journalists on such practice either. Reporters are more hesitant to fully identify juvenile suspects, in particular when they are not tried as an adult. Once rehabilitated, the child-turned-adult can petition the judge to destroy his record in certain cases for "its rationale - protecting juvenile offenders from attention that would stigmatize them and hinder their integration into society" (Reza, 2005, p. 785). Yet, as Howard Snyder, of the National Center for Juvenile Justice in Pittsburgh, explained in Hancock's (1998) article, "you can't expunge a newspaper article. Not now. Not ten years down the road." (p. 18-19).

But others disagree that juvenile criminals should be unnamed in news coverage: "No, naming a juvenile offender is not a breach of ethics. Not naming one would be, because it leave a hole in the story and could put the public at risk" (Kolb, 2011, p. 74). Many other journalists agree with this assessment and lean toward publishing all names of suspects, regardless of age. Many news managers at Ohio newspapers and television stations were often revealing the identity of juvenile suspects. (About 15 percent revealed the names in almost all instances.) The managers based their decision on the severity of the crime, age of the suspect, the distance of the crime to the distribution area of their news stories, and whether other news outlets had revealed the identity. The way the competition was covering the story also played a role (Hanson, 2004).

Imperfect Solutions

Whereas the European court decisions in favor of the right to be forgotten withholds media companies from disseminating certain news items after it has been published when it is deemed irrelevant or outdated, others have argued that is not enough. In the United Kingdom there have been repeated calls to make it a crime to publicly name a suspect in any police inquiry (Peachey, 2015). Some go even as far as arguing that U.S. courts should allow prior restraint on a narrowly tailored range of pre-trial information to avoid unfair trials, which also would mean that information about the suspect would not be discussed publicly until the first verdict of guilt or innocence by the courts (See: Phillipson, 2008).

Those calls for limiting press freedom are usually placed in context in which the media industry is capitalizing "on the public's insatiable hunger for sensations" to increase its profits (Mitrou, 2012, p. 4). In similar vein, Beale (2006) argued that "media content is shaped by economic and marketing considerations that frequently override traditional journalistic criteria for newsworthiness" (p. 398). Fullerton and Patterson (2013) pointed out that the 'tell-all-and-then-some' style of crime coverage is adopted by British media to "routinely probe an accused person's private life in search of villainous elements to explain alleged wickedness—but also to entertain" (p. 116).

Some of those criticisms may be correct in certain cases, but many journalists are in the business to inform audiences about the problems and successes in their communities—not the profit status of their employers. What may be lacking is a dialogue with those audiences about *how* the news is covered. Some news outlets have addressed this by appointing an ombudsperson to explain decisions made in the newsroom and answer questions from readers, listeners, or viewers in regards to such choices. But also other members of newsrooms have addressed concerns or comments to establish a better understanding of the public.

For instance, Scott Sherman (2010), a crime and court editor of the *Salt Lake Tribune*, explained in an article how the newspaper tended to deal with the question whether to name individual crime suspects:

The Tribune's decision to name or not name a person accused of a crime is never about protecting them from public scrutiny. We aim to inform our readers about events in their communities, but we also recognize the enormous responsibility we bear to be fair to those whose guilt or innocence will be decided by judge or jury.

Sherman went on to explain that covering news is "more than simply retelling the events –it requires thoughtful evaluation about what we cover and how we cover it." Furthermore, Sherman assumed that not many readers "will care to read follow-up stories on hearings, motions and ultimately a sentence for such a crime." Thus, the newspaper wanted to select only those stories that most important for public scrutiny to allow identification for the accused. Reporters would follow the case throughout the court system when it has been decided to use the name in early coverage.

This is to avoid that people are not only named when they are accused of committing a crime, but also when it turns out that those accusations were not correct. This would be especially damaging for a person when all Web searches would provide articles when he or she was suspect, but not when innocence have been proven or, otherwise, there was not enough evidence for a conviction. For instance, Shephard (1994) reported a case of a 15-year-old girl who allegedly had suffocated her half-sister. A local daily newspaper printed her name when she was convicted by the trial court, but did not name her when the conviction was overturned. Consequently, her name could come up in a Web search for being convicted of murder, while none of the stories that clear her from any liability could show up in during the same search using her name.

Several scholars have pointed out that these false positive findings—the identification of innocent people as suspects—must be debated in journalism more thorough to get a more pragmatic approach in naming suspects. For instance, Hodges (1994) maintained that "[i]n reporting on criminal behavior we should report all aspects of the criminal's private life that might help to understand the criminal and his or her acts," but not for sake of being complete. (p. 208).

Fullerton and Patterson (2013) pointed to a framework developed by Lennart Weibull, a senior researcher at the SOM Institute and professor in the Department of Journalism, Media and Communication at Gothenburg University. When a suspect is a private person without public function and the crime involves a private event, then journalists should refrain from publishing the name. On the flip side, when a crime case involves a public person at a public event, it is warranted to publish the name.

Yet, it becomes a more difficult decision when it involves a private citizen in a public event, or vice versa. Furthermore, the framework does not take into account the type of event or the impact for the public (e.g., news audiences may want more information about a serial killer targeting random people in a community than when there was a targeted, stand-alone murder, as disturbing that may be). The framework does also not take into account any concerns about rehabilitation either—even for public officials. For instance, Hodges (1994) argued that information about public officials only should be published "if their private activity might reasonable have a significant effect on their official performance" (p. 205).

Husselbee (1994) argued that "the journalist must be able to distinguish between a right to knowledge and a curious interest in knowing" (p. 145). The author advocated for a case-by-case evaluation that forces journalists to (1) evaluate what elements of a story the public need to know; (2) examine whether the story could effectively inform the public without personal information, or what would be the least amount of personal information that would be required to achieve the goal of informing the public; (3) determine the research procedure to verify the accuracy of information related to a case; (4) develop strategies to minimize harm to stakeholders; and (5) determine whether, and if so how, the decisions related to revealing private information will be communicated to the audience along with the news report(s).

In other words, there must be an important public purpose to know, meaning that news outlets should not automatically publish the names of all suspects, nor refuse to publish any. As journalistic routines and practices have been shaped through decades of organizational socialization it may take a while until newsrooms are willing to adopt a case-by-case approach. But internal newsroom discussions and broader debates within media industries can only be effective when discussants are aware of the wide range of policies, with all their pros and cons, to determine the fine lines on what details to report in crime news. Only then could media professionals find solutions to minimize or eliminate the number of false positives: stories about innocent people being linked to horrific crimes.

REFERENCES

Ambrose, M. L., & Ausloos, J. (2013). The right to be forgotten across the pond. *Journal of Information Policy*, *3*, 1–23. doi:10.5325/jinfopoli.3.2013.0001

Bannon, L. J. (2006). Forgetting as a feature, not a bug: The duality of memory and implications for ubiquitous computing. *CoDesign*, *2*(1), 3–15. doi:10.1080/15710880600608230

Baughman, S. B. (2011). Restoring the presumption of innocence. *Ohio State Law Journal*, *72*, 724–776.

Bayley, E. (1981). *Joe McCarthy and the Press*. Madison, WI: University of Wisconsin Press.

Beale, S. S. (2006). The news media's influence on criminal justice policy: How market-driven news promotes punitiveness. *William and Mary Law Review*, *48*, 397–481.

Bennett, S. C. (2012). The "right to be forgotten": Reconciling EU and US perspectives. *Berkeley Journal of International Law*, *30*, 161–195.

Bennett, W. (2005). *News: The politics of illusion* (5th ed.). New York: Pearson Longman.

Bennett, W., Gressett, L., & Halton, W. (1985). Repairing the news: A case study of the news paradigm. *Journal of Communication*, *35*(2), 50–68. doi:10.1111/j.1460-2466.1985.tb02233.x

Berkowitz, D., & Beach, D. (1993). News sources and news context: The effect of routine news, conflict and proximity. *The Journalism Quarterly*, *70*(1), 4–12. doi:10.1177/107769909307000102

Blanchette, J.-F., & Johnson, D. G. (2002). Data retention and the panoptic society: The social benefits of forgetfulness. *The Information Society: An International Journal, 18*(1), 33–45. doi:10.1080/01972240252818216

Bowers, J. O. (2013). *American and Norwegian press' approaches to identification of criminal suspects or arrestees: The public's right to know versus the private citizen's right to privacy, reputation, and presumption of innocence* (Unpublished master's thesis). University of Oregon.

Breed, W. (1955). Social control in the newsroom: A functional analysis. *Social Forces, 33*(4), 326–335. doi:10.2307/2573002

Brown, J., Bybee, C., Wearden, S., & Murdock Straughan, D. (1987). Invisible power: Newspaper news sources and the limits of diversity. *The Journalism Quarterly, 64*(1), 45–54. doi:10.1177/107769908706400106

Bugeja, M. (2008). *Living ethics: Across media platforms*. New York, NY: Oxford University Press.

Carey, J. (2002, Spring). What does "good work" in journalism look like? *Nieman Reports*, 79-81.

Cassidy, W. (2006). Gatekeeping similar for online, print journalists. *Newspaper Research Journal, 27*, 6–23.

Cathcart, B. (2011, October 8). The ordeal of Christopher Jefferies. *Financial Times Magazine*. Retrieved from http://www.ft.com/cms/s/2/22eac290-eee2-11e0-959a-00144feab49a.html

Christians, C. G. (2007). Utilitarianism in media ethics and its discontents. *Journal of Mass Media Ethics, 22*(2-3), 113–131. doi:10.1080/08900520701315640

Christians, C. G., Rotzoll, K. B., & Fackler, M. (1991). *Media ethics: Cases & moral reasoning* (3rd ed.). New York, NY: Longman.

Deuze, M. (2004). What is multimedia journalism? *Journalism Studies, 5*(2), 139–152. doi:10.1080/1461670042000211131

Domke, D., Watts, M., Shah, D., & Pan, D. (1999). The politics of Conservative Elites and the Liberal Media argument. *Journal of Communication, 49*(4), 35–58. doi:10.1111/j.1460-2466.1999.tb02816.x

Entman, R. M., & Gross, K. A. (2008). Race to judgment: Stereotyping media and criminal defendants. *Law and Contemporary Problems, 71*, 93–133.

Ettema, J., Whitney, D., & Wackman, D. (1987, 1997). Professional mass communicators. In D. Berkowitz (Ed.), Social meanings of news. Thousand Oaks, CA: SAGE Publications.

Etzioni, A. (1999). *The limits of privacy*. New York: Basic Books.

Fishman, M. (1980). *Manufacturing the news*. Austin, TX: University of Texas Press.

Fullerton, R. S., & Patterson, M. J. (2013). Crime news and privacy: Comparing crime reporting in Sweden, the Netherlands, and the United Kingdom. In J. Petley (Ed.), *Media and public shaming: Drawing the boundaries of disclosure*. New York: I. B. Tauris & Co.

Gandy, O. (1982). *Beyond agenda setting: information subsidies and public policy*. Norwood, NJ: Ablex Publishing.

Gans, H. (1980). *Deciding what's news: A study of CBS Evening News, NBC Nightly News, Newsweek, and Time*. New York: Random House.

Gans, H. (2003). *Democracy and the news*. New York: Oxford University Press.

García-Avilés, J. A. (2014). Online newsrooms as communities of practice: Exploring digital journalists applied ethics. *Journal of Mass Media Ethics*, *29*(4), 258–272. doi:10.1080/08900523.2014.946600

Gaziano, C. (1987). News people's ideology and the credibility debate. *Newspaper Research Journal*, *9*, 1–18.

Grossman, M., & Joynt Kumar, M. (1981). *Portraying the President: The White House and the News Media*. Baltimore, MD: John Hopkins University Press.

Hackett, R. (1984). Decline of a paradigm? Bias and objectivity in news media studies. *Critical Studies in Mass Communication*, *1*(3), 329–359. doi:10.1080/15295038409360036

Hallin, D., Manoff, R., & Weddle, J. (1993). Sourcing patterns of national security reporters. *The Journalism Quarterly*, *70*(4), 753–766. doi:10.1177/107769909307000402

Hancock, L. (1998, July/August). Naming kid criminals. *Columbia Journalism Review*, 18–19.

Hanson, G. (2004). Identifying juvenile crime suspects: A survey of Ohio TV stations, newspapers. *Newspaper Research Journal*, *25*, 121–125.

Hodges, L. (1994). The journalist and privacy. *Journal of Mass Media Ethics*, *9*(4), 197–212. doi:10.1207/s15327728jmme0904_1

Husselbee, L. P. (1994). Respecting privacy in an information society: A journalists dilemma. *Journal of Mass Media Ethics*, *9*(3), 145–156. doi:10.1207/s15327728jmme0903_3

Hutchins Commission. (1947, 2004). "The Requirements," from Afree and responsible press. In J. Durham Peters & P. Simonson (Eds.), *Mass Communication and American Social Thought: Key texts, 1919-1968*. Lanham, MD: Rowman & Littlefield Publishers.

Kasoma, T., & Maier, S. (2005). *Information as good as its source: Source diversity and accuracy at nine daily U.S. newspapers*. Paper presented at the meeting of the International Communication Association, New York, NY.

Kolb, J. J. (2011, June). Coming of age: Naming juvenile criminal suspects shouldn't pose an ethical quandary. *Editor & Publisher,* 30.

Koops, B.-J. (2011). Forgetting footprints, shunning shadows. A critical analysis of the "right to be forgotten" in big data practice. *Scripted*, *8*, 229–256.

Kovach, B., & Rosenstiel, T. (2001). *The elements of journalism: What newspeople should know and the public should expect*. New York: Three Rivers Press.

Lasica, J. D. (1998). The Net never forgets. *Salon.* Retrieved from http://www.salon.com/1998/11/25/feature_253/

Lee, T. (2005). The liberal media myth revisited: An examination of factors influencing perceptions of media bias. *Journal of Broadcasting & Electronic Media*, *49*(1), 43–64. doi:10.1207/s15506878jobem4901_4

Lichtenberg, J. (2000). In defence of objectivity revisited. In J. Curran & M. Gurevitch (Eds.), *Mass Media & Society* (3rd ed.; pp. 225–242). London: Arnold.

Manning, P. (2001). *News and news sources: A critical introduction*. Thousand Oaks, CA: SAGE Publication.

Mathiesen, K. (2014). Human rights for the digital age. *Journal of Mass Media Ethics*, *29*(1), 2–18. doi:10.1080/08900523.2014.863124

Mayer-Schönberger, V. (2011). *Delete: The virtue of forgetting in the digital age*. Princeton, NJ: Princeton University Press.

McLeod, D., Kosicki, G., & McLeod, J. (2002). Resurveying the boundaries of political communication effects. In J. Bryant & D. Zillman (Eds.), *Media effects: Advances in theory and research*. Mahwah, NJ: Lawrence Erlbaum.

McNealy, J. E. (2012). The emerging conflict between newsworthiness and the right to be forgotten. *Northern Kentucky Law Review*, *39*, 119–135.

Meader, A., Knight, L., Coleman, R., & Wilkins, L. (2015). Ethics in the digital age: A comparison of the effects of moving images and photographs on moral judgment. *Journal of Mass Media Ethics*, *30*(4), 234–251. doi:10.1080/23736992.2015.1083403

Meyers, C. (1993). Justifying journalistic harms: Right to know vs. interest in knowing. *Journal of Mass Media Ethics*, *8*(3), 133–146. doi:10.1207/s15327728jmme0803_1

Mitrou, L., & Karyda, M. (2012). EU's data protection reform and the right to be forgotten: A legal response to a technological challenge?*5th International Conference of Information Law and Ethics*.

Morant, B. D. (2005). The endemic reality of media ethics and self-restraint. *Notre Dame Journal of Law, Ethics & Public Policy*, *19*, 595–636.

Nigerian Press Council. (2016). *Code of ethics*. Retrieved fromwww.prescouncil.gov.ng/?page_id=281

Niven, D. (2005). An economic theory on political journalism. *Journalism & Mass Communication Quarterly*, *52*(2), 247–263. doi:10.1177/107769900508200202

Oshinsky, D. (1983). *A conspiracy so immense: The world of Joe McCarthy*. New York: The Free Press.

Peachey, P. (2015, October 17). Hogan-Howe backs law against naming suspects in sex inquiries. *The Independent*, 20.

Peltz-Steele, R. J. (2008). Fifteen minutes of infamy: Privileged reporting and the problem of perpetual harm. *Ohio Northern University Law Review*, *34*, 717–754.

Perloff, R. (1998). *Politics, Press, and Public in America*. Mahwah, NJ: Lawrence Erlbaum.

Phillipson, G. (2008). Trial by media: The betrayal of the First Amendment's purpose. *Law and Contemporary Problems*, *71*, 15–29.

Press Council. (2016). *Code of ethics and conduct for South African print and online media.* Retrieved fromwww.presscouncil.org.za/ContentPage?code=PRESSCODE

Rachels, J. (1984). Why privacy is important. In F. Schoeman (Ed.), *Philosophical dimensions of privacy* (pp. 290–299). Cambridge, UK: Cambridge University Press. doi:10.1017/CBO9780511625138.013

Reza, S. (2005). Privacy and the criminal arrestee or suspect: In search of a right, in need of a rule. *Maryland Law Review (Baltimore, Md.)*, *64*, 755–874.

Rosen, J. (2012). The right to be forgotten. *Stanford Law Review*, *64*, 88–92.

Rupar, V. (2006). How did you find that out? Transparency of the newsgathering process and the meaning of news. *Journalism Studies*, *7*(1), 127–143. doi:10.1080/14616700500450426

Saunderson, D. (2014, April 30). Clifford case 'shows value of naming suspects'. *The Times*, 17.

Schwartz, S. (1992). *Universals in the content and structure of values: Theory and empirical tests in 20 countries*. New York, NY: Academic Press.

Shephard, A. C. (1994). Identifying juvenile suspects. *American Journalism Review*, 14.

Sherman, S. (2010, August 20). Reporters follow clear policy in naming suspects, victims in crime stories. *The Salt Lake Tribune*.

Shoemaker, P. (1991). *Gatekeeping*. Newbury Park, CA: Sage Publications.

Shoemaker, P., & Reese, S. (1996). *Mediating the message: Theories of influences on mass media content*. New York: Longman.

Sigal, L. (1973). *Reporters and officials: The organization and politics of newsmaking*. Lexington: D.C. Heath.

Sigal, L. (1986). Sources make the news. In R. Manoff & M. Schudson (Eds.), *Reading the news: A pantheon guide to popular culture* (pp. 9–37). New York: Pantheon Books.

Smith, J. A. (1988). *Printers and press freedom: The ideology of early American journalism*. New York: Oxford University Press.

Solove, D. J. (2007). *The future of reputation: Gossip, rumor, and privacy on the Internet*. New Haven, CT: Yale University Press.

Steele, B., Black, J., & Barney, R. D. (1998). *Doing ethics in journalism: A handbook with case studies* (3rd ed.). Boston, MA: Allyn & Bacon.

Strentz, H. (1989). *News reporters and news sources: Accomplices in shaping and misshaping the news* (2nd ed.). Ames, IA: Iowa State University Press.

Tuchman, G. (1973). Making news by doing work: Routinizing the unexpected. *American Journal of Sociology*, *79*(1), 110–131. doi:10.1086/225510

Tuchman, G. (1978). Introduction: The symbolic annihilation of women by the mass media. In G. Tuchman, A. Kaplan Daniels, & J. Benét (Eds.), *Heart and home: Images of women in the mass media*. New York: Oxford University Press.

Vultee, F. (2010). Credibility as a strategic ritual: The Times, the interrogator, and the duty of naming. *Journal of Mass Media Ethics*, *25*(1), 3–18. doi:10.1080/08900521003621975

Warren, S., & Brandeis, L. (1890). The right to privacy. *Harvard Law Review*, *14*(5), 193–220. doi:10.2307/1321160

Westin, A. F., & Baker, M. A. (1972). *Databanks in a free society: Computers, record-keeping, and privacy*. New York: Quadrangle Books.

Chapter 13
Boko Haram Insurgency in Cameroon:
Role of Mass Media in Conflict Management

Afu Isaiah Kunock
University of Yaounde I, Cameroon

ABSTRACT

Cameroon has recently become a target of deadly attacks including shootings, kidnappings and suicide bombings by the Islamic insurgent group Boko Haram. Cognizant of the fact that Cameroon has not experienced anything like this since independence, the Cameroon mass media is challenged as to how to appropriately report this insurgency in a manner that will result in conflict containment and management rather than escalation. The researcher set to examine the role of the media in managing this armed conflict through the critical analysis of documents as well as interviews and observations from the theoretical perspective of framing. Framing by the media has been a very effective strategy in managing the conflict by mobilizing the national population against the sect while maintaining calm and lessening panic and anxiety. This effort by Cameroon media is highly commended although more still needs to be done.

INTRODUCTION

Africa in the last decade has witnessed a sharp surge in insurgent attacks from groups like Al Shabab and more recently Boko Haram that has resulted in countless deaths, displacements and untold human suffering. Cameroon, the 'island of peace' in the Central African sub-region has since 2014 been the object of deadly attacks by the Northern Nigerian indigenous islamist sect Boko Haram. Although Northern Nigeria is no stranger to such deadly attacks such as shootings, suicide bombings, kidnappings, and the burning down of houses and property that frequently target innocent citizens in public spaces such as markets, bus stations, places of worship and media, this phenomenon is relatively new in Cameroon - a country that is highly reputed for the peaceful resolution of the conflict over the ownership of Bakassi

DOI: 10.4018/978-1-5225-2095-5.ch013

peninsular with Nigeria. Since May 2014, Cameroon has suffered an unprecedented wave of deadly assaults and shootings by the gunmen of this sect. These killings were presumably heightened after Cameroon's head of state publicly declared war on Boko Haram at a summit in France that brought together heads of state of the Central African Region with the aim of seeking ways to battle out the sect.

Cognizant of the fact that Cameroon has not experienced anything like this since independence, the Cameroon mass media is challenged as to how to appropriately report this insurgency in a manner that will result in conflict containment and management rather than escalation. Against this backdrop there is need for skilled and professional reporting with the observation of ethical norms that will hearten the nation to face this than throw it into greater panic. Given that media reporting of such conflicts can sometimes throw populations into deeper fears as a result of over reporting or spark a backlash from the terrorists as in the case of some Nigerian journalists that were killed by Boko Haram for their supposed bias (Ekwueme & Obayi, 2012), moderation is required. The reporting of the damages and human casualties by the mass media both national and international tends to cast a spell of fear that grips the entire nation. In the face of this assailing crisis, the role of the mass media cannot be undermined in either exacerbating or containing and resolving the conflict.

The following questions therefore arise; what role does the mass media play in the fight against Boko Haram in Cameroon, and how does framing of media messages shape the present perception of the crisis? It is along these lines that the researcher set to examine the role of the Cameroon mass media in the handling of this armed conflict through the critical analysis of documents as well as interviews and observations.

The researcher will begin by presenting terrorism and the mass media, theoretical framework for the analysis of the study, Cameroon media vis-a-vis Boko Haram reporting, anti-terrorism law and the media, role of media in conflict management, government's response, national population's response and finally conclusion.

Terrorism and the Mass Media

The terrorists and mass media both enjoy a symbiotic relationship in which terrorists seem to need the media more. It is in this light that Brian Jenkins (1975) asserts that "terrorist attacks are often carefully choreographed to attract the attention of the electronic media and the international press. The hostages themselves often mean nothing to the terrorists". Walter Laqueur (1977) holds up Jenkins' observation by postulating that "terrorists have learned that the media are of paramount importance in their campaigns and that the terrorist act by itself is next to nothing, whereas publicity is all". This fits well with a widely quoted statement of Margaret Thatcher, a former prime minister of Great Britain which says "publicity is the oxygen of terrorism" (Muller et al. 2003; Vieira, 1991). This affirmation is factual in that terrorism is often aimed at the audience and not at the actual victims. This might inform the reason why terrorists desperately seek media attention following the popular adage that "if it does not bleed, it does not lead". Terrorists take advantage of the media's insatiable hunger for dramatic, sensational, unusual, and alarming human interest stories to gain cheap and wide-spread publicity for their actions. The mass media on the other hand usually tend to thrive in crisis reportage as it significantly increases viewership, listenership and readership – ad patronage and hence respond to terrorist attacks with undisguised zeal and enthusiasm (Ekwueme & Obayi, 2012). Putting it in another way, terrorism is theatre and the news media, for their part, are seen as unable to resist the chance of a good story, so they obligingly provide extensive coverage of terrorist bombings, hijacks, kidnapping and assassinations (Schlesinger et al, 1983).

The media in turn are remunerated for broadcasting terrorism in that they energize their competition for audience size and circulation – and thus for all-important advertising, (Nacos, 2006). By so doing, the media often help spread the propaganda message of terrorists. This in turn directly achieves one of the prime objectives of these terrorists-the quest for publicity, power and fame. For this reason, terrorists have to be continually innovative to stay relevant. The desire for media attention may also help explain some characteristics of the "new" terrorism, which is characterized by more victims, the indiscriminate targeting of civilians, and frequent use of suicide tactics (Hoffman, 2006).

Cameroon often commended as an 'island of peace' and stability in a turbulent region has not been invulnerable to the threat of terrorism but has become the object of several terrorist attacks, most recently the Boko Haram insurgency. Vulnerability to terrorist threats has steadily risen from roughly 28 major terrorist incidents which occurred in Cameroon between 1970 and 2011, and 13 major terrorist attacks between 2011 and November 2013 (Ewi, 2013) to more than a hundred between 2014 and 2015 (Cameroon radio television [CRTV], 2015). Moreover, the number of suicide bomb attacks on Cameroonian soil targeting civilians in public places is steadily on the rise. Due to the fact that the military are overpowering the sect, the terrorists have resorted to unconventional methods like suicide bombs to keep pace with gaining publicity, which unfortunately the media cannot resist also. Ewi adds that the drivers of terrorism in Cameroon may be found in the country's complex historical, geostrategic, religious and socio-economic dynamics which though has never been a source of conflict, but does provide a setting conducive to the exploitation of certain groups and religions. With a population of over 21 million people and more that 250 ethnic groups, the country is comprised of very diverse peoples. This diversity also exists in relation to religion, with the population consisting of roughly 40% Christians, 30% Muslims and 30% espousing traditional beliefs. The media has the potential to exploit gaps in diversity positively by actively engaging in journalism geared towards national unity. The role of the media therefore becomes very crucial in forging bonds of national cohesion that will empower the state to remain united in the fight against terrorism and insurgency.

THEORETICAL FRAMEWORK

This study is built on the framing theory of the mass media. The theoretical perspective developed in this study suggests that terrorist events are commonly understood through news frames that simplify, prioritize and structure the narrative flow of events (Goffman, 1974; Entman, 1993). According to Entman (1993), framing essentially involves selection and salience. He further explains that in order to frame, certain aspects of a perceived reality are selected and made more significant in a communicating text with the aim of endorsing a particular problem definition, interpretation, and moral evaluation for the event described. Although Entman views framing as a 'scattered conceptualization' with previous studies lacking clear conceptual definitions and relying on context-specific, rather than generally applicable operationalisations, Brosius and Epps (1995) agree with Entman by further positing that framing is not a clearly explicated but generally applicable concept. McCombs et al (1997) suggested that agenda-setting and framing are related, with framing being an extension of agenda-setting. They described the impact of the salience of the characteristics of media coverage on audiences' interpretation of news stories as second level agenda-setting. While purporting that the entire study of mass communications is based on the premise that the media have significant effects (p. 327), McQuail (1994) described the present era of the history of research on media effects from the early 1980's onwards as characterized by "social constructivism" where the media have both strong and limited effects. To him, media have a strong impact in "constructing social reality by framing images of reality… in a predictable and patterned way" (p. 331) and on the other hand limited effects by an interaction between the mass media and recipients. The theory of framing therefore suggests that the way a news item is presented determines the way it is interpreted by the audience (Scheufele & Tewksbury, 2007) and consequently the decisions and choices made. Scholars (Zaller, 1992; Kahneman & Tversky, 1984; Iyengar, 1991) agree that though cognitively active, people are often not well-informed on most matters of socio-political significance; hence framing weighs in heavily and indeed influences their reaction to communications.

To understand the news coverage of terrorism in Cameroon, this study theorizes that the Boko Haram insurgency denotes a critical shift in the predominant 'news frame' used by Cameroon for understanding issues of national security, altering perceptions of peace and threats of national unity. I argue that the narratives used in reporting the activities of this islamist sect have been carefully tailored to boost national unity, minimize panic and the escalation of conflict. The government is the main source of information in the country on the ongoing war with Boko Haram and feeds the public with what it deems necessary. Private press often report information gotten from official sources coupled with the difficulty of direct coverage. Even journalists working for the government must take the cover of the military in order to get firsthand information and therefore see things from a government/military perspective. Thus the government maintains a tight grip on the information collected and determines what to disseminate. Significant developments on the progress of the war are made public by the government spokesperson through news conferences, thus the frames used for reporting are determined by the government. This work seeks to understand how the process of communication, particularly the role of the news media, contributes towards the frames used for understanding national security issues, and the conflict with Boko Haram. Evidence provided by the Ministry of Defense indicates that Cameroon is under threats of insurgents infiltrating through the porous borders on the North-Western front with Nigeria and Eastern front with Central Africa Republic. The core of the matter is in how journalists use news frames representing patterns of selection and emphasis to deliver a coherent interpretation and evaluation of events that guarantee national interest. Members of the press rely on conventional frames set up by the government to make meaning and order of complex events by slotting news items into familiar categories. Conventional news frames of terrorism are important because they furnish consistent, predictable, simple and powerful narratives that are embedded in the social construction of reality (Norris et al, 2003). Explaining these developments requires an understanding of perceptions of terrorist threats, and, in particular, the role of the news media in this process.

George Lakoff (2004) asserts that "the elements of the communication frame include: a message, an audience, a messenger, a medium, images, a context, and especially, higher-level moral and conceptual frames". A frame therefore refers to the way reporters organize and present the events, and how audiences interpret what they are provided. According to Nyamnjoh (2005), the media in many ways are a reflection of the society in which they operate. Pudephatt (2006) supports Nyamnjoh by noting that the range of communication outlets and media enable a society to view representations of itself and are inevitably actors in its conflicts. Media are therefore a recognized part of the society (Kuusik, 2010). To use anthropological terms, every media exists in a socio-cultural context, and given that culture is an assembly of solutions put together to resolve people's problems, the Cameroon media becomes a part of this cultural element used to resolve problems related to the conflict with Boko Haram. The media is perceived as a partner in the fight against Boko Haram and management of conflict. News content and images presented to the audience especially those highlighting gains made by "our brave soldiers" and heavy losses inflicted on the enemy in terms of number of assailants killed or captured and ammunitions seized or number of suicide bombs neutralized as well as support received from other nations become very important in defining how the Cameroonian public perceives and deals with the threat posed by the sect. This theory is relevant to this study because the mass media can contribute immensely in the containment and ultimately, the defeat of the sect in the way they frame news stories on the sect and its activities. Although framing could be used to explain the role of the mass media in managing the conflict with Boko Haram in Cameroon, the theory also has its limitation as the search for truth is one of man's natural rights. Man is no longer perceived of as a dependent being to be led and directed by framing, but rather as a rational being able to discern between truth and falsehood, and better and worse when faced with conflicting evidence and alternative choices. Truth is no longer considered as the property of the government especially with the emergence of social media. This might explain why in some news items presented framing does not determine the way it is interpreted, decisions taken and choices made. Audiences question the truth and reality of some of these news items.

CAMEROON MEDIA VIS-À-VIS BOKO HARAM REPORTING

Reporting on terrorism presents a number of dilemmas and paradoxes to journalists whose responsibility is to inform the public objectively, fairly and accurately (Adesina, 2009). Faced with the threat of Boko Haram, the Cameroon media is confronted with the enormous challenge of learning and practicing the kind of reporting that does not result in further escalation, but rather containment and resolution given the novelty of the menace. Cameroon has a rich media landscape constituting several televisions, radios and the print media, public as well as private, as elaborated below:

In the print media sub-sector, close to a thousand news papers enjoy a legal existence with over 600 hundred of them sparingly making their regular appearances, while over a hundred is claiming to respect their stated periodicity including seven dailies. Major privately-owned French or English-speaking newspapers are distinguished by their hardline editorial policies which are sometimes very critical of the government. It is worth recalling that over 150 private commercial radio stations are operating under administrative tolerance. This is the same with over 20 Television channels offering a diversified range of programmes to Cameroonians through their various approaches of processing information. The ongoing switch over to the digital process will bring fresh impetus in this potentially rich sub-sector. With the support of international partners such as UNESCO, the government has encouraged the establishment of community radio stations in different regions of the country. These local radio stations (over fifty), have enriched the national media landscape and do reach not only remote locations but also the out-of-school populations. (Cameroon Tribune, May 3rd 2016:57)

In addition to the above mentioned media is the "new" social media that is becoming prevalent in the country through the phenomenal growth of the internet and the facilities it offers, providing a platform for the dissemination of information not just by media professionals but also by people who do not master the rules and ethics of the journalistic profession. This poses a real challenge to the government as they often have to hold news conferences to clarify the public of sensitive information that might have gone viral on social media to maintain and promote a particular definition and interpretation of events. Social networks are a great opportunity for the development of press-related professions, especially with regard to broadcasting but they can also be a threat to social cohesion if they continue to be used as tools for disseminating unverified information.

The environment under which media operate in Cameroon is complicated by political, cultural and economic ramifications. Many governments exercise rigid control of the media over the diffusion of news and the licensing of those permitted to exercise the profession (Sean, 1980), and Cameroon is not an exception. The government still maintains a heavy hand of control over media organs both public and private by ensuring that all news is edited by the designated authorities before release to the public. Mindful of the bilingual nature of the country stemming from its historical past of two colonial masters where some entities of the smaller part remain disgruntled that the terms of the reunification were not fully respected, and the over 250 ethnic groups with different cultural backgrounds within her boarders, the media is often used as an instrument to consolidate this national unity that sometimes seems threatened, and strengthen the sovereignty of the party in power. This is not an easy task as there are those who seek opportunities to use diversity as a source of conflict because of perceptions of discrimination and underlying feelings of disadvantage just because they come of a particular part of the country. Economically, the practice of journalism remains an uphill task especially for the private media who are limited by finances and lack of state-of-the-art news gathering equipment and oftentimes have to depend on government sources for information.

As a result of the unexpected spill over of conflict which has now grown in to a regional crisis due to failure of the Nigerian government to contain the sect and its activities, Adesina (2009) argues that the media in the course of executing the noble task of meeting the public's need of information especially in the face of such danger, often though indirectly paradoxically meet the primary objectives of the terrorist sect which is to create fear and a psychological effect on the public. In surmounting this challenge, the Cameroon media including national and local televisions, radios and news papers have slipped into the comfortable shoes of using conventional narratives and frames supported by the government. In other words, the state works through the media to protect its institutions and foster its interests by providing frames, official definitions and perspectives of terrorism which are adopted by the media. These stereotypical projections by media serve the purpose of delimiting the public ideology of terrorism and terrorists which directly influence the cognitive and affective feelings of the public. These stereotypes, resulting from the framing of terrorism, are intended at maintaining sharp boundary definitions of who are clearly within and who are clearly beyond the boundary of acceptability, us and they, insiders and outsiders illustrated as the strategy of splitting by Hall (1997). This is done using evaluative language and labels of terrorists that leaves little or no room for resolution. Some of the labels refer to the sect and its activities as barbaric, inhumane, ruthless and senseless killers, enemies of peace and national unity, faceless terrorists operating in the dark. Such language clearly defines and draws a dividing line between the state and its opponents thus constructing a version of reality about terrorism to the public.

Tunman (2003) notes that in reporting terrorism "media prime our discourse and preconception of and about terrorism, by their symbols and narratives, their interpretations and depiction of terrorism". The media frame our attitudes, cognitive and affective feelings towards the terrorists in the narrative ways they report terrorism. In this regard, Cameroon media outlets do not seek to differ much from international news agencies. News concerning Boko Haram activities characterized by horrible statistics of the dead, injured, displaced, suffering and casualties inflicted on innocent civilians is reeled out to the public. The language used is aimed at creating feelings of anger and hate towards the so-called terrorists.

However, there seems to be some degree of distrust of national media by the public in that they believe the government is keeping much information away from them as they say nothing about who the terrorists are and what they want. Interestingly, the private owned media seem to be toeing the same line as the government media. The public seems to be in the dark of what this war about Boko Haram really is except for the fact that they have been labeled as faceless terrorists. Journalism that is aimed only at labeling and dehumanizing the enemy does not promote an atmosphere of peace-building, conflict management and resolution but rather gives more time for the fighting parties to prolong the war. Labeling by the government might as well serve to obscure "certain truths and realities" from the public.

ANTI-TERRORISM LAW AND THE MEDIA

With the upsurge of acts of terrorism along Cameroon's porous borders, the upper and lower houses of parliament passed the anti-terrorism bill in December 2014 defining acts of terrorism perpetrated by individuals or groups and their corresponding sanctions. This bill drew criticism from opposition parties and civil society organizations within the country as well as without like the international freedom of the press advocacy group Reporters Without Borders who called on the President of the Republic not to promulgate this bill into law because it has "provisions that would have a disastrous impact on freedom of information if implemented in a heavy-handed manner" (Reporters Without Borders, Dec. 18 2014). A member of the leading opposition party expressed the fear that "the government could use the law to suppress dissent and control the media. As now written, the new law would require journalists to submit stories for government approval before publication". Another leading opposition figure commented that "this anti-terrorism law is manifestly against the fundamental liberties and rights of the Cameroonian people …" These calls were however ignored and the bill was promulgated into law by the President of the republic. The government defended her position on this law by saying that all this was done to protect the entire social bedrock of the State and her core values of peace, unity, stability and national solidarity, as well as her citizens and institutions, describing all those opposing it as ill-intentioned (Cameroon Tribune, Dec.9 2014). Of particular interest was the point of disproportionate sanctions raised in the following excerpt.

The Cameroonian authorities recently stepped up pressure on the media and the anti-terrorism law could make it even harder for journalists to operate. Its problems include an extremely vague definition of terrorism, disproportionate penalties and provision for only military courts to try terrorism cases... The law seems to have been drafted ignoring the recommendations of many international conventions that make it possible to reconcile combating terrorism with respect for freedoms. It expresses a series of intentions and means, without ever relating them to a clear definition of terrorism.... This is the case with journalists, for whom "defending terrorism" in spoken or written word is punishable by 15 to 20 years in prison and/or a fine of 25 million to 50 million CFA francs (28,000 to 76,000 Euros)....The decision to give military courts exclusive jurisdiction is also worrying because the use of military courts to try civilians should be the exception, not the rule. Furthermore, the defense minister has the power to appoint and assign military judges, which raises questions about their independence vis-à-vis the government. (Reporters Without Borders, Dec.18 2014)

Reporters are occasionally harassed or detained by security forces while attempting to cover sensitive stories as the case with some journalists in connection with the new anti-terrorism law. Media outlets however continue to operate under the constant threat of prosecution or regulatory sanctions, leading many journalists, particularly in the broadcast media, to self-censor. The government spokesperson, Minister of communication often reiterates that media professionals must abide by the rules governing the media profession with the obligation to cross-check information prior to release, comply with information presentation techniques and professional ethics, and the duty to keep an eye on the societal environment in order to each time ask oneself whether all good information is publishable (Cameroon Tribune, May 3 2016:57). Reporting on terrorism in Cameroon remains a sensitive issue and is largely dominated by the government.

ROLE OF MEDIA IN CONFLICT MANAGEMENT

The media constitute a space in which the conflicts of a society can be articulated and are inevitably themselves actors in that conflict, meanwhile combatants in a conflict will usually relate to each other either on the battlefield or through the way they are represented in the media (Pudephatt, 2006). In modern day conflicts, the latter may often be more important to them than the former. The mass media often plays a key role in today's fight against terror the world over. Basically, the media role can take two different and opposed forms. In as much as the media can play a crucial role in provoking and escalating conflicts, it equally has enough potential to contribute effectively to conflict resolution and reconciliation. As far as the history of violent conflicts is concerned, Rwanda continues to occupy an outstanding position in how the Rwandan media actively helped in the instigation of genocide. Since independence, Radio Rwanda had been the main source of information until the late 1980's when political struggles started about the possibility of opposition parties to get coverage of their opinions (Forges, 2002, P. 236-55). Radio Rwanda became the place of several power struggles from 1990 up to the genocide in 1994. In 1992, Radio Rwanda spurred attacks on Tutsis and members of the opposition for the first time (Article 19, 1996, P 53). Following an outcry from the opposition and international donors, a coalition was formed between the opposition and the ruling party resulting in the evolution of the Radio Rwanda which became less biased with fewer inflammatory programmes between 1990 and 1992 (Bonde, n.d.). Bonde further adds Radio Mille Collines, the first private owned media set up in 1993 mainly by some members of the ruling party actively incited genocide unchecked by spreading false rumours, stereotypes, and hate speech and also presented individual persons as opponents of the regime that resulted in the Rwandan genocide.

In the case of Nigeria, Ahmad (2015) points out that the Nigerian media in some instances has been accused of worsening crisis through biased, unfair and irresponsible coverage and reporting coupled with subjectivity and sensationalism thus undermining the contributions of the media in conflict management and resolution. Okali (2011) in Hamid and Baba (2014) unveils in his study that the Nigerian media have not done well in discharging their surveillance role, particularly in the Boko Haram crisis.

In the case of Cameroon and the war against Boko Haram unlike Rwanda and Nigeria, the state media is the main source of information in the country with the widest coverage in addition to numerous private owned media on the on-going war with Boko Haram have been very instrumental in galvanizing the support of the entire Cameroonian peoples the defense forces as part of war efforts. In addition, both the ruling party and the opposition for the first time despite their deep differences took a common stand in publicly condemning the sect and its activities, viewing it as a common enemy to the nation. Private owned media have fallen in line with the state controlled media in airing and echoing messages of national unity and boosting the strength of the defense forces. Either the media takes an active part in the conflict and has responsibility for increased violence, or stays independent and out of the conflict, thereby contributing to the resolution of conflict and alleviation of violence (Puddephatt, 2006).

Internal conflicts often tend to have a history and background of mishandled grievances but this does not come up in the news. When the tensions escalate into armed conflicts, then come the international media to report the violence and violations of human rights, and then disappear subsequently in the post conflict phase. National media are usually better placed to report internal conflicts as they have a clear understanding of the historical undertone and are likely able to relate to both parties in their own terms and not as foreign detectors. Local media have a huge potential for mediating conflict resolution because they are accepted and seen as part of the society and can be very effective in preventing full-blown conflict in the pre-conflict phase.

The mass media and journalism can be of great assistance in conflict management and peace building. According to Galtung (1998) in Eytan (2009), Kirthi (2014) and Kuusik (2015) a measure of peace-building is enhanced peace journalism which gives room for both parties in a conflict to be heard by uncovering the root of the grievances as well goals of each side, giving room for social dialogue and new horizons for lasting win-win solutions while making sure to humanize all victims of the conflict. In this case, journalists do not try to exploit the loss and suffering but make sure that the reporting is balanced. Kuusik (2010) and Kirthi (2015) further emphasize that peace-building is a process that starts from knowledge in understanding what has happened and why, then understanding the social ethos in which actors are operating so that the best possible solution can be identified in which the local community will own and identify with it because an external solution often remains a mere imposition that does not succeed. Often, only national or local media are better placed to undertake such pains-taking peace-building process. A suggested framework used by peace-building media can employ different strategies such as conflict-sensitive and peace journalism, peace-promoting entertainment media, media regulation to prevent incitement of violence, but also peace-promoting citizen media (Himelfarb et al., 2008). Unlike national media, international media can attract worldwide attention in case of a crisis or a conflict, though the number of conflicts that get attention is small. Unfortunately, they are most often attracted to the violent phase of conflicts and provide reports that project the conflict arena with the visible or tangible effects of war and soon disappear after the violent phase of the conflict. While international media has the most important potential influence in conflicts in the violent phase, national media are most effective for long-term, sustainable conflict management in pre- and post conflict phases. The Cameroon media could actively pursue this noble task of peace-building journalism and conflict management as part of the larger effort required for long term sustainable peace plan. Up to this point, the Cameroon media should be commended for their peace-building effort.

GOVERNMENT RESPONSE

The response of the Cameroon government has been multidirectional and largely effectual. At the initial stage, the President of Cameroon declared war against the group and vowed to eradicate it. Consequently new military and Gendarmerie posts were created in the affected region and qualified military personnel appointed to head them. In addition, more military personnel were deployed to the region all in a bid to combat the group. The government has worked hard to negotiate and ensure the release of foreign and national hostages taken by the islamist sect, a highly commendable effort at home and abroad. In all this, the government has spared no effort to continually assure the population through press releases by the government spokesman, the minister of communication, that all is been done to keep them safe. In the same vein, the country's military might has been frequently showcased through display of weapons, songs and messages through the media to assure the population of security but also as signals to the sect of their strength. Media practitioners have consistently been told and even trained on how to report the activities of the group without instilling fear and panic into the population. Another important effort to ward off the threat posed by the terrorist group and step up security measures nationwide following the recent wave of sporadic suicide attacks along some border villages in the affected areas include the printing and distribution of flyers by the police to the public.

The flyers distributed nationwide contained practical guides on how citizens have to be security conscious, easily detect threats such as keeping clear of all abandoned luggage as well as informing the police of any cases of suspicion through the toll free number 1500. The production of these practical guides is the handiwork of the communication and public relations unit of the General Delegation of National security working to inform the society regarding behaviours to adopt at public places such as markets, travel agencies, public places and other hot spots that attract crowds urging them as well to remain hyper vigilant, observant and attentive to happenings around them. Citizens were equally called upon to desist from hastily opening their doors to people claiming to be pastors, hawkers and cable TV technicians. The police through the flyers equally urged Cameroonians to scrupulously respect the security measures put in place by government and collaborate with the forces of law and order by always carrying their identification documents and present them whenever the need arises. Authorities operating travel agencies were also called upon to ensure that the passengers' names are entered in the vehicle's manifesto. (Hot News, August 24 2015: 4)

The use of flyers by the police is a government attempt to use the print media not just to inform and educate all segments of the population of the imminent threat posed by the insurgency but also as a rallying point to involve citizens in the fight against it. All these moves by the government make headlines of various media actors for days. Media practitioners skillfully reframe these news items in terms of gain in order to bolster the strength and image of the nation. This corroborates the recommendation of the rules for reporting terrorism by governments and press (Jamieson & Seligman, 2002) following the September 11 attacks in America. News headlines and news papers have as caption gains made against the enemy framed in terms of number of assailants killed and ammunition seized or destroyed. Government casualties are not readily reported and even when it is done, the report is quite brief and not often rebroadcasted as much as those of the sect. Thus gains are projected and magnified in contrast to losses incurred. The exact number of government soldiers killed is hardly broadcasted on the national media compared to the enemy casualties. This represents Entman's views on framing involving salience and emphasis in which issues of importance such as victory, superiority, and a strong national defense are emphasized through repeated broadcasting. Consequently, the public is fed with positive information that instills calm and courage, while diminishing panic and the notion that threat posed by the terrorists will be dealt with effectively and efficiently.

NATIONAL POPULATION'S RESPONSE

This section portrays solidarity marches, role of churches and national council of Imams, financial and material contributions, and the role of political parties in the fight against Boko Haram as a response by the Cameroonian public to the conflict.

Solidarity Marches

The national population is greatly mobilized behind the president of the republic and the armed forces in the fight against the group and its activities. This unflinching support has been variously expressed through various patriotic marches organized all over the country as well as monetary and material donations. These solidarity marches were particularly heightened during the preparations for the national youth day and national day celebrations in February and May respectively. The youth and national days are very important days for the country and such events surrounding these days are very symbolic, sending strong messages to all Cameroonians. Inspiration for these patriotic marches could partly have been drawn from the famous solidarity march in Paris in protest of the Charlie Hebdo attack featuring many heads of state and high profile personalities from around the world in January 2015. Featuring in these patriotic marches are people from all walks of life and all age groups ranging from young school children to civil society organizations and political parties bearing messages of support to the head of state in the fight against Boko Haram. Figure 1 is an example of a solidarity march against Boko Haram that took place in Fako, Buea, the South-West regional capital of Cameroon led by high ranking administrative authorities.

One informant had this to say "I came out to show solidarity with my brothers and sisters in the Far North of Cameroon who are suffering from the onslaughts of the Boko Haram insurgents, and also to show to the military that we are one, we are together. We may not have guns to join them but they should

Figure 1. Fako population rally against Boko Haram
Cameroon Journal, 18/ 3/ 2015.

know that we have them at heart". Another informant said "we are praying for our army, we are supporting them. I am convinced that coming out like this, they will be galvanized." Still another informant said "You never know the importance of peace until it is disturbed, so seeing our children, our brothers, our parents giving their lives up there in the Far North for our sake, it is very important to come out to show our support to them".

Another great solidarity march took place in Yaoundé, capital city of Cameroon on February 28 2015. This march was distinctively characterized by the holding of the national flag, banners and placards with messages condemning the terrorist sect and its activities such as "Great patriotic march for our brothers and sisters in the Far North, for our brave soldiers, for a united Cameroon, this February 28 at 8am at the May 20 Avenue" as shown in Figure 2. Other placards carried messages like "Train me to fight Boko Haram" as shown in Figure 2 and still another "I will kill Boko Haram".

Others had signs like "I am the Cameroon army, I would not lose Fotokol", "I am the Cameroon army, I will not lose the Far North region", "Je Suis L'Armée Camerounais" and many others standing with the military in this fight against insurgency. Each time such a march occurred, it will be given the widest possible and most prolonged exposure by various media outlets on their news headlines and front pages of news papers. Images of such moments form the caption of news papers as well as make headlines of local television reports. Contrary to the general notion that media have a huge craving for reporting terrorist attacks to gain a wide audience and popularity, local media in Cameroon rather seek to create a strong impact by spreading messages that enforce national unity and speak out against the islamist sect and its activities in a predictable patterned way in order to create a version of social reality as illustrated by McQuail (1994), that falls in line with government agenda. In this way, the media play an important role in promoting peace, defusing tensions, easing anxiety within the population and managing the conflict. Figure 3 shows the media focusing more on events and symbols of national unity as in the great patriotic march of February 28 2015 in Yaoundé.

Figure 2. Great patriotic march in support of soldiers fighting Boko Haram in Yaounde CRTV 28/ 2/2015.

Figure 3. Great patriotic march in support of soldiers fighting Boko Haram in Yaounde CRTV 28/ 2/2015.

Role of Churches and National Council of Imams

Christian and Muslim leaders on their part have been very instrumental in mobilizing their faithful to handle the matter spiritually by seeking God's intervention through prayers. Christian leaders on their part have been standing with the nation to quell the enemy spiritually through prayers by calling on Almighty God to intervene. Throughout the country, various churches do organize fasting and prayers and preach openly against the evils perpetrated by this sect. Christians are called upon to remain steadfast and have faith in God, trusting that He will conquer the enemy. In praying, God is invoked as the Lord of Hosts and Jehovah Nissi, fighter of all battles. At the heart of inter-religious events frequently organized all over the national territory is the prominent role of women. A woman informant had this to say, "God is the mighty man in battle. There is no battle that He cannot win. He has never losed a battle and therefore the battle against Boko Haram is in His hands. We pray that He should use our military men in the Far North to grant us victory. He should grant the military wisdom, strength and protection, and set confusion in the camp of Boko Haram". Women cognizant of the fact that they always the hardest hit in conflicts enjoined their fellow women to come together as mothers and sisters to decry any actions contrary to peace and wellbeing of mankind and cry out genuinely to God to heal, forgive and restore Cameroon. A glaring example is the Christian women in Bamenda, North West region of Cameroon who organized a solidarity march in which they had to march in from various junctions throughout the town carrying placards to converge at the city centre where the interfaith event was held. Placards carried messages such as "Evil can never triumph over good, Boko Haram must bow in Jesus name! We invoke God to heal our land Cameroon". This event was an inter-religious service organized by the Women's Interfaith Ad hoc committee to pray for peace, unity, security and good health in Cameroon. In Yaoundé, Cameroon's capital city, similar events have been organized by women in which they come on national media to sensitize and call on women to cry out to God for His intervention. Because of the extensive media coverage, many women feel intricately involved in this fight supporting in their own individual ways.

On the other hand, because the terrorists are perceived to be muslim, muslim authorities have frequently used the media to deny and reject them as true followers of Islam. The media is often used to slam and denigrate the barbaric and inhumane treatment inflicted on fellow muslims and human beings by the sect. An Imam made this statement "Boko Haram activities like killing, destruction and kidnapping do not reflect and do not represent the Islamic faith. On the contrary, these are heartless people who do not care about Allah and his people. They will certainly suffer the wrath of Allah and will not go unpunished. Muslims should denounce such evil doctrines". Several times, the national council of Imams has sent out educative messages through the mass media calling on muslim faithful to denounce false doctrines, reject violence and practices that do not reflect Islam. They have been particularly vocal in also warning their faithful against ambulant preachers filtering in from outside the country with radical messages aimed at inciting young ones to embrace terror as a means of claiming their rights. Moreover, muslim clerics have been called for peaceful cohabitation of muslims and non-muslims. In all this the mass media have been active and helpful in conveying these messages to the wider public. This goes a long way in shaping opinions and swinging the views of the society from violence and notoriety to peace and national unity. The voice of Imams is particularly important at this critical moment because faithful tend to reckon with their religious leaders. This is equally important in preventing especially the young ones from being carried away by radical fundamentalist ideologies. It is important to recall that this war against Boko Haram is largely an ideological war in which winning the hearts and minds of the people is crucial in winning the war. Moreover, peace, national unity and nation-building messages from Imams are of crucial importance given that we live at a time when the world is suffering from terrorist attacks all over in which some perpetrators are incited and radicalized through the social media networks.

The youth and students of all levels on their part have not been left out in this fight. All over the national territory, they have been visibly conspicuous through their solidarity marches with powerful messages of encouragement and gratitude to the armed forces who are sacrificing their lives to protect the nation. Such actions were applauded by the hierarchy and given the widest publicity by media as an appeal to all youth to stand up with our armed forces as they battle out the sect. These actions serve as a clarion call to all strata of society that none is left out in the eradication of this evil. As the president of the republic Paul Biya has often said "terrorism is a global menace that requires a global response" and so none has been left out in this fight.

Financial and Material Contributions

Financial and material contributions have been an essential part of war efforts as the Cameroonian public has been very generous in their support to the army fighting Boko Haram not just in word but in deed. Through a fundraising program called the 'National solidarity Chain' initiated by Cameroon's Minister of Trade following a call by the head of state to support the armed forces fighting at the war front, 2.1 billion FCFA (€3.2 million), hundreds of tons of food stuff like rice, milk, sardines, vegetable oil, and other basic commodities have already been collected within a few months to support the troops, said the CRTV. It worth noting that these gifts were contributed by Cameroonians of all walks of life from peasant farmers to big commercial companies. The media have been very prominent at the various fundraisings organized all over the national territory to keep Cameroonians updated and serve as motivation to those who are still drawing their feet. The media played an important role in making Cameroonians to own the war and fight it with their resources however small. In this wise, a strong bond of national unity has been forged among the different regions of the country causing even dominant opposition communities to lay down their differences and fight the war as one man. The head of state and his wife have been very conspicuous in donating important consignments of food stuff and basic commodities to assist soldiers as well as war victims and refugees alongside messages of encouragement and congratulations to the Defense and Security Forces for their ceaseless efforts to stop the atrocities caused by Boko Haram on our compatriots as shown in Figure 4.

At the heart of these gestures is the media framing and projecting Cameroon as a nation united in condemning and rejecting the barbaric actions of the insurgents. The media has been the instrument used by government to rally the national population behind the president of the republic, seen as the most important statesman leading the fight against Boko Haram in the capacity of the commander in chief of the armed forces. The national response against this insurgency has been skillfully magnified to obscure existing and potentially volatile differences among different sections of the country by the national media, mostly backed and censored by the government. However, this fight and the present gains have been highly politicized and projected by the media as the efforts and fruits of the President and his ruling CPDM (Cameroon People's Democratic Movement) party and not as the concerted efforts of Cameroonians irrespective of political and social differences. The media should be praised for their efforts to promote peace and national unity through framing by laying emphasis on gains made by the security forces and magnifying positive actions of citizens of good will as well as the entire nation in the fight against Boko Haram and minimizing the use of words that might lead to escalation and national disintegration.

Role of Political Parties

The CPDM ruling party and all other political parties seem to have some common ground that peace is primordial for political parties to freely exercise their political activities. It is for this reason that various political parties have acted in rallied support to the armed forces by mobilizing their militants to decry the activities of the terrorist sect. The main opposition party in Cameroon, the Social Democratic Front

Figure 4. Paul and Chantal Biya at the forefront of support to the armed forces
www.prc.cm/news/1233-April 2015.

(SDF), has been part of the war effort by donating money, food stuff, and paying visits to wounded soldiers as well as communing with the victims of Boko Haram. In other press releases, the party has consistently condemned the activities of the terrorist sect while commending the efforts of soldiers at the war front to encourage them as they fight for the security of the entire nation.

Other opposition political parties like the Cameroon People's Party (CPP) and Cameroon's Democratic Union (CDU) have followed suit in various denunciations against the islamist terrorist group that have been multiplying attacks in Cameroon's Far-North region. In separate press releases issued following recent attacks in Far North region, the party leaders reaffirmed their support to President Paul Biya and the defense forces in the fight against the sect. In the course of extending consolatory messages to the victims and families of fallen heroes, the opposition political parties urged the government to review its strategies and mobilize available resources nationally and internationally to intensify the fight against Boko Haram. Both opposition parties equally saluted Cameroon's armed forces that have countered many attacks leading to the killing of assailants and release of hostages. The media has been highly solicited at these rallies in a bid give the events the widest publicity, but also to magnify the efforts of the opposition parties in the fight against Boko Haram. The ruling party celebrated 33 years in power and several speeches were made to rally the nation under the theme "all behind President Paul Biya for the final assault against Boko Haram securing the enabling environment for the future contingencies". The CPDM celebrated 30 years of existence and 33 years of President Biya's accession to power in 2015. Activities to celebrate the anniversaries were marked by messages of support to President Paul Biya for spearheading the fight against Boko Haram. From North to South and from East to West, the message was clear, bar the way to Boko Haram. The media continue to urge the different political parties to come together as one to fight against terrorism and the common enemy despite their different political ideologies.

CONCLUSION

Cameroon popularly called the 'island of peace' in the central African subregion has recently become the target of several attacks by the Nigerian indigenous sect Boko Haram. Through the mass media, the government uses frames to construct a version of social reality that they want Cameroonians to adopt by what they see and hear about the war with Boko Haram. In selecting issues that are considered salient, they seek to paint the picture of a strong nation with a strong leadership and unbeatable national defense force capable of dealing with warding off any threat posed by terrorists while maintaining national unity and integrity. Since the beginning of the Boko Haram assault, the government has given it utmost importance and used it to shift attention away from other burning national issues. Although the media was used to galvanize the support of the entire nation morally, materially and financially, gains made have been credited to the President and his ruling party.

Framing and censorship in this light have been a very effective strategy in managing the conflict with Boko Haram by maintaining calm and lessening anxiety within the national population. In this regard, the media has been the single most influential actor in bringing together Cameroonians of all strata and walks of life to own the war against Boko Haram and stand united as a nation, together with the armed forces to fight the common enemy through patriotic marches, financial and material donations. The effort by Cameroon media is highly commended although more still needs to be done. The Cameroon mass media has a great potential and critical role to play in shaping the outcome of this conflict. If this potential is properly and positively harnessed, then, the high road to lasting peace would have been chosen. The media can do this effectively by stripping the terrorists of their oxygen support, the publicity essential for their survival and proliferation by restraining itself from the insatiable craving of constantly putting the terrorists and their activities in the spotlight.

REFERENCES

Adesina, L. A. (2009). The Role of the Media in Reporting Terrorism: A Personal Viewpoint. *Journal of Communication and Media Research, 1*(1).

Ahmad, M. A. (2015). Communication and Conflict in Nigeria: What Role for the Media? *Global Advanced Research Journal of Educational Research and Review*, *4*(8), 154–160.

Article XIX (1996) Broadcasting Genocide – Censorship, Propaganda & State-Sponsored Violence in Rwanda 1990-1994.

Bonde, B.N. (n.d.). *Mass Media and Journalism on the Edge in Violent Conflicts - Media Freedom or Social Responsibility*. Academic Press.

Brosius, H. B., & Eps, P. (1995). Prototyping through key events: News selection in the case of violence against aliens and asylum seekers in Germany. *European Journal of Communication*, *10*(10), 391–412. doi:10.1177/0267323195010003005

Cameroon Radio Television. (2015). *News on the fight against Boko Haram*. Author.

Cameroon Tribune. (2014). *Anti-terrorism Bill: Gov't Give Clarifications*. Retrieved from www.cameroon-tribune.cm

Cameroon Tribune. (2015). *The fight against Boko Haram continuous*. N.0.10992/7191

Cameroon Tribune. (2016). *Our country has realized the value of information*. N.0.11087/7286

CRTV. (2015). *Fighting Boko Haram: A unity march in the agenda*. CRTV.

Ekwueme, A. C. & Obayi, P. M. (2012). Boko Haram Assault on Nigeria: Towards Effective Mass Media Response. *New Media and Mass Communication,* (5).

Entman, R. B. (1993). Framing: Toward clarification of a fractured paradigm. *Journal of Communication*, *43*(4), 51–58. doi:10.1111/j.1460-2466.1993.tb01304.x

Ewi, M. (2013). *Terrorism and the threat radical Islam poses to Cameroon*. ISS Today.

Eytan, G. (2009). Media and Conflict Resolution: A Framework for Analysis. *Marquette Law, 93*(87).

Forges, A. D. (2002). *Silencing the Voices of Hate in Rwanda.* In M. E. Price & M. Thompson (Eds.), *Forging Peace* (pp. 236–258). Edinburgh, UK: Edinburgh University Press.

Galtung, J. (1998). *High Road, Low Road: Charting the Course for Peace Journalism*. 7 TRACK TWO 7.

Goffman, E. (1974). *Frame analysis*. Boston: New England University Press.

Hall, S. (1997). Representation: Cultural Representations and Signifying Practices. London, Thousand Oakes. *Sage (Atlanta, Ga.)*, 257–261.

Hamid, A. M., & Baba, I. M. (2014). Resolving Nigeria's 'Boko Haram' Insurgence: What Role for the Media?. *The International Conference on Communication and Media*. Elsevier Ltd. doi:10.1016/j.sbspro.2014.10.249

Himelfarb, S., & Chabalowski, M. (2008). *Media, Conflict Prevention and Peacebuilding: Mapping the Edges.* United States Institute for Peace. Retrieved from http://www.usip.org/resources/media-conflict-prevention-and-peacebuilding-mapping-edges

Hoffman, B. (2006). *Inside terrorism (rev. and exp. ed.).* New York: Columbia University Press.

Hot News (2015). *Fight against insecurity: Police Force sensitizes citizens, distributes practical guides.* N° 062/RDDJ/J06/BASC. No 224 of 24/8/2015.

Iyengar, S. (1991). *Is anyone responsible?* Chicago: University of Chicago Press. doi:10.7208/chicago/9780226388533.001.0001

Jenkins, B. (1975). *International Terrorism.* Los Angeles, CA: Crescent Publication.

Kahneman, D., & Tversky, A. (1984). Choice, values, and frames. *The American Psychologist, 39*(4), 341–350. doi:10.1037/0003-066X.39.4.341

Kirthi, J. (2014). Peace journalism and Boko Haram. *Media and Journalism in Peace Work.*

Kottak, P. (2002). Anthropology: The exploration of human diversity. New York: Academic Press.

Kuusik, N. (2010). The Role of the Media in Peace Building, Conflict Management, and Prevention. *E-International Relations.*

Lakoff, G. (2004). *Don't think of an elephant: know your values and frame the debate.* Chelsea Green.

Laqueur, W. (1977). *Terrorism.* London: Weidenfield and Nicolson.

McCombs, M., Shaw, D. L., & Weaver, D. (1997). *Communication and Democracy: Exploring the intellectual Frontiers in agenda-setting theory.* Mahwah, NJ: Erlbaum.

McQuail, D. (1994). *Mass communication theory: an introduction* (3rd ed.). Thousand Oaks, CA: Sage.

Ministry of Communication. (1994). *Proceedings of the National Forum on CommunicationYaoundé.* Cameroon: National Printing Press.

Muller, E. R., Spaaij, R. F. J., & Ruitenberg, A. G. W. (2003). *Trends in Terrorism. Alphen aan de Rijn.* Kluwer.

Nacos, B. L. (2006). *Terrorism/Counterterrorism and Media in the Age of Global Communication.* United Nations University Global Seminar Second Shimame-Yamaguchi Session, Terrorism—A Global Challenge.

Norris, P., Kern, M., & Just, M. (2003). Framing terrorism. In P. Norris, M. Kern, & M. Just (Eds.), *Framing Terrorism: The News Media, the Government and the Public.* New York: Routledge.

Nyamnjoh, F. (2005). Africa's media: Democracy and the politics of belonging. ZED Press.

Presidency of the Republic of Cameroon. (2015). Retrieved from https://www.prc.cm/en/news/1233-support-of-the-armed-forces-paul-and-chantal-biya-at-the-forefront.April

Puddephatt, A. (2006). *Voices of war: Conflict and the role of the media*. International Media Support.

Reporters Without Borders. (2014, Dec. 18). *Disproportionate Penalties for Media in Cameroon's Anti-Terrorism Law*. Author.

Scheufele, D., & Tewksbury, D. (2007). Framing, agenda setting, and priming: The evolution of three media effects models. *Journal of Communication*, (57): 9–20.

Schlesinger, P. (1983). *Televising Terrorism: Political Violence in Popular Culture*. London: Comedia Publishing Company.

Sean, M. (1980). *Many Voices, One World*. Ibadan: Nigeria and UNESCO Press, Paris.

Tunman, J. S. (2003). *Communicating Terror: The Rhetorical Dimensions of Terrorism*. London: Sage.

Vieira, J. D. (1991). Terrorism at the BBC: The IRA on British television. In Media coverage of terrorism, methods of diffusion. London: Sage Publications.

Zaller, J. (1992). *The nature and origins of mass opinion*. New York: Cambridge University Press. doi:10.1017/CBO9780511818691

KEY TERMS AND DEFINITIONS

Boko Haram: A Northern Nigerian indigenous Islamist sect that is largely responsible for mass killings, abductions, suicide bomb attacks and kidnapping of local and foreign hostages mainly in Nigeria and neighbouring countries like Cameroon, Chad and Niger in a bid to establish an ISLAMIC caliphate in Northern Nigeria.

Cameroon: A country in the Central Africa subregion sharing a long porous border with Nigeria currently facing insurgency from the Nigerian islamist sect Boko Haram in its Far North region.

Conflict Management: All measures taken to limit the negative effects of war by preventing further violence while seeking to completely stop the violence and resolve the problems that provoked the violence in the first place.

Escalation: The process by which a conflict situation becomes more serious or worse over time with the result of more negative effects of war.

Insurgency: The use of force by Boko Haram, an organized group to over a constituted government through acts of violence and terrorism to impose and propagate their religious ideals.

Mass Media: Means of communication and sources of information such as television, radio, news papers, magazines, and the internet.

Terrorism: The use of violence and intimidation people in their area of operation by Boko Haram to achieve its political aims.

Chapter 14
Deferring Citizens' "Right to Know" in an Information Age:
The Information Deficit in Namibia

William Edward Heuva
North West University – Mafikeng, South Africa

ABSTRACT

Namibia is one of the emerging democracies that have not yet enacted the Access to Information legislation. While the country has guaranteed freedom of expression and media in its constitution, it has not provided for Access to Information as a constitutional right. This chapter seeks to examine Namibia's reluctance to adopt an Access to Information legislation. It interrogates views that locate the omission of this fundamental human right in the country's constitutional (legal) and policy frameworks. It underscores the failure by Namibia to reverse the information black-out suffered under the Apartheid dispensation. The chapter starts with a theoretical/philosophical rationale for the right to know to elicit an understanding of this discourse and its relevance to emerging democracies, such as Namibia. It then examines attempts by state and civil society to introduce the legislation in the country. Predicted on praxis, the chapter in conclusion provides some suggestions that may help resolving the impasse in adopting the Access to Information legislation in the county.

It is our considered view that the Freedom of Information Act will not only buttress the Bill of Rights but will critically enhance good governance, as it will bring the actions by both public and private bodies under closer scrutiny. This, we believe, can only enhance the quality of our democracy. Democracy by its nature is an open process driven by its citizens. And an informed citizenry will make for better interlocutors. It is for these reasons that we view Freedom of Information Act not as a stick to beat the Government with but as a centre piece in the armoury of an accountable government. (Tsudao Gurirab, 2012)

DOI: 10.4018/978-1-5225-2095-5.ch014

INTRODUCTION

African governments have enacted two pieces of legislation during the last few years: one authorising them to intercept their citizens' communication 'lawfully' and the other seeking to empowercitizens with the righttoaccess information held by public and private bodies. Namibia ranksamong the noticeable few that have delayed adoptingan Access to Information (Freedom of Information Act) law, while it is one of the early states to legislate a legal instrument that seeks to 'lawfully' intercept citizen's information (Heuva, 2012).

Interestingly, Namibia which ranked among the first African nations to convert to 'neo-liberalism'at its independence from South Africa in 1990had been reluctant to embraceone of the core tenets of liberalism, notably the principle of the right to information forits citizens.The country adopted a liberal constitution, hailed as one of the best in Africa at the time of its adoption. The constitution embraces most of the basic human rights and freedoms. As a result, Namibia was seen in the 1990s as a beacon of hope among the post new dispensation African countries due to its liberal constitution. In 1991 shortly after Namibia's independence, the United Nations Educational, Scientific and Cultural Organisation (UNESCO) opted to hold its conference on the promotion of a free, independent and pluralistic media in Africa, in Windhoek, the country's capital city. The subsequent Windhoek Declaration culminated in the inauguration of the World Press Freedom Day (3 May) by the United Nations (UN) General Assembly.

Furthermore, the country enjoys an impeccable human rights record, and its media ranks among the most free in Africa and the world.Economically, Namibiahasalso been doing relatively well. The country has been rated as one of the best performing economies in Africaby major global economic institutions, including the United Nations Development Programme (UNDP), World Bank and the International Monetary Fund (IMF) in recent years. The country's former president, Hifikepunye Pohamba, (2005-2015) received the 2015Mo Ibrahim Award in good governance in Africa.But despite all these accolades the country had been reluctant, for the past quarter of a century since its independence from Apartheid colonialism, to adopt a legislation that allows citizens access to information.

The foot-dragging has meant that the state became less open in its operations, earning it the title of one of the "most secretive states" in southern Africa (Media Institute of Southern Africa [MISA], 2010, p.53). Initsrecent reports on the level of openness and secretiveness of governments and public institutions insouthern Africa, MISA notes on Namibia that "secrecy still remains entrenched in Namibia's government and public institutions" (Media Institute of Southern Africa [MISA], 2010). The 2010 MISA study, which was a follow up to the one done the previous years, revisited the openness of the Namibian government and its institutions. It targeted nine public institutions and measured their openness against international best practice and the right to information principles (Media Institute of Southern Africa [MISA], 2010). While acknowledging 'progress' made in terms of openness compared to the previous year (2009) the report notes that Namibia still has a long way to go before achieving openness and transparency in its government and institutions. The MISA report adds:

The current landscape for requesting public information feels like the futile attempt of shooting in the dark with near none chances of hitting the target. Without procedures of how the public can access information, silence is the tool being used to deny the public information as most written requests are literally ignored and go unanswered despite having officials designated to handle public information requests. (Media Institute of Southern Africa [MISA], 2010 p.10)

It is generally acknowledged that the citizens' needto access information is based on the principle of the 'right to know', which is further based on the right of direct access to public information, including direct access to state information. This 'right to access information' is not limited to the media (practitioners), but it is a right of the broader society (Sénécal, 1995, p.12). While the concept freedom of expression traditionally focuses strongly on the media practitioners and professionals, the 'right to information', in contrast, favours the interests of the receivers of information. The result is that this right (to information) demands "a legal framework other than that being built around the principles of the freedom of expression" (Sénécal, 1995, p.14).

The principle of the right to know compels democratic governments to provide information on request by the public (citizens). Governments possess vast amounts of information, which they gather as well as generate. Furthermore, governments exercise control over this information in terms of state secrets, national interests and certain privileges. In addition, governments use various measures to control this information, including:

... losing, hiding, or destroying information, foot-dragging in response to requests for information, and evasiveness in answering questions, on occasion government officials have resorted to lying. The flow of information is also not only controlled by such withholding techniques, but by ... 'leaks' and 'background reports'. (Sénécal, 1995, p.113)

The notion of the 'right to know' and the 'free-flow of information' are premised on the strong links that connect communication to democracy (O'Neil, 1998, p.1). For a society to function effectively its citizens have to be enlightened in order to become knowledgeable about crucial issues affecting them and their society. Thus information must flow relatively freely.However, at the bottom of all this, is the need for citizens to have a right to information, which is a basic human right, as we shall see below.

This chapter seeks to document the right of access to information discourse in Namibia. It examines attempts and shortcomings with regard to the adoption of the right of access to information. More particularly the chapter interrogates the government long delay in the implementation of the access to information law, and the reasons for the delay. It also examines the factors that compelled the government to ultimately decide to introduce the draft freedom of information legislation. The chapter further discusses efforts as well as the shortcomings of civil society in its campaign to promote the adoption of the right to information law in the country. It starts with a theoretical/philosophical rationale for the right to access information to elicit an understanding of this discourse and its relevance to emerging democracies, such as Namibia. Finally the chapter highlights important features of the proposed freedom of information Bill and the draft revised information policy of the country, which the government released for public input almost 17 years later after Cabinet took a decision to enact the right to know legislation.

Theoretical Understanding of the 'Right to Know'

Proponents of the right to information (RTI) discourse have maintained that this freedom (of information) is a basic human right (Mendel, 2008).Human rights are the rights that people have because they are human beings. They are the "norms that help to protect all people everywhere from severe political, legal and social abuses" (Stanford Encyclopaedia of Philosophy, 2005, p.14). There are core concepts, everywhere, which define the idea of human rights, notably:

Human rights are the rights that one has simply because one is human. They are universal and equal. Human rights are inalienable. They may be suspended, rightly or wrongly, at various places and times, but the idea of inherent rights cannot be taken away. One can no more lose these rights than one can stop being a human being. (US Government, n.d.)

Rights are "entitlements (not) to perform certain actions, or (not) to be in certain states; or entitlements that others (not) perform certain actions or (not) certain states". Most rights "entitle" their holders to freedom in some sense" (Stanford Encyclopaedia of Philosophy, 2005, p.21). Holders of the rights are free in one or more ways. There are "active incidents", which entitle right holders the *freedom to* act in certain ways; and the "passive incidents", which protect holders of the right the *freedom from* undesirable actions or states" (Stanford Encyclopaedia of Philosophy, 2005, p14, emphasis in original).

The idea of human rights is drawn from works of early philosophers among them Immanuel Kant (1724-1804) and John Locke (1632 – 1704). Other important sources of human rights are Bills of Rights such as the *Magna Carta* (1215), the *English Bill of Rights* (1689), the *French Declaration of the Rights of Man and the Citizen* (1789), the *Jefferson's Declaration of Independence* (1776) and the *Bill of Rights of the United States* (1791) (Ivester, 1977). In recent times human rights are inscribed in international (and regional protocols), including, Article 19 of the Universal Declaration of Human Rights; Article (2) of the International Covenant on Civil and Political Rights; Article 9 (2) of the African Charter on Human an Peoples' Rights; Article 13 (1) of the American Convention on Human Rights and Article 10 (1) of the European Convention on Human Rights.

John Locke (1632–1704) and Immanuel Kant (1724-1804) arecredited for having contributed to the concept of human rights. Their work informed the American and French political documents (Bills of Rights). John Locke's understanding of human beings'as "natural rights" (rights of life and liberty and estate) in a "pre-political state of nature" made an immense contribution to the liberal political philosophy, in terms of the conception of individual rights and limited government (Forde, n.d.). This (liberal) tradition is founded on individual rights, private property and the limited government. John Locke has argued that people form societies, while societies set up governments that are responsible for protecting peoples' "natural rights". The government, according to him, must be seen as a "social contract" between the rulers and the citizens. The citizens are only obliged to show allegiance to the government if it protects their rights. Thus, the government can only be legitimate if it honours and protects the citizens' rights. Moreover, these rights may even have precedence over the interests of the government (see Sabine and Thorson, 1973, pp.478-499; Forde, n.d.).

Furthermore, David Michel Ivester (1977) tells us that the liberal democratic (political) systemis predictedon a self-governing people and not on two (separate) groups: the rulers and the ruled, like in an authoritarian system. People assume the authority to exercise control while at the same time they are subject to control. In such a situation the government is established and maintained by consent of the people, while it has independent powers to compel the people to obey the laws (Ivester, 1977). In reference to the American political system, he (Ivester, 1977) notes that this is a "two-fold system, which "... firstly the government must be designed as a self-regulating system; second, the people, apart from the government, must exercise their inalienable power to oversee and discipline the government". Thus, this system is based on the concept of a "balance of power", which does not entrust "absolute power to no one". In addition, the people in this system are sovereign, and exercise their inherent power to make and unmake governments". Thus, people delegate some powers to government, while reserving all remaining rights and powers. This explains the liberal concept of a 'limited government' (Ivester, 1977).

In this political arrangement the people retain the right to know what the government is doing with the (limited) powers allocated to it by the citizens. The right to know is very critical for citizens because knowing governmental affairs provides an enormous potential for "counteracting the power" that the government enjoys as a result of its possession and control of information (Ivester, 1977, pp.112-114). The word 'to know' is very critical in this regard. To know, means to be "cognizant of, to be acquainted with, or to have a concept of in the mind" (Webster's Third International Dictionary 1252, P. Gove Ed. 1971 as cited in Ivester, 1977, pp.109-110). David Michel Ivester notes that the concepts of freedom of speech, freedom of information, the right to receive information, the right to gather information, and the right of access to government information "are all related to, and part of, the right to know, but it is the desired end 'to know' that is important". For him:

Only with knowledge can the people truly have a will to which the government can be accountable. The right to know, like all enduring constitutional principles, cannot be defined as if it were only a word in a dictionary. It must be allowed to grow and evolve with the circumstances. Perhaps at one time the right to receive information from an unrestrained was adequate; in a more complex society the right to know may impose upon government an affirmative duty actively to inform the public in the absence of prior requests for information. (Ivester, 1977, p.110)

In addition, David M. Ivester (1977) proposes three "political foundations" on which the concept 'right to know' can be explained. The first, relates to governance in democratic states. He argues that democratic governance demands leaders to be responsible and responsive to the will of the people. However, for the will of the people to have "validity" and for them to function as a "rationale electorate' they need to have "adequate knowledge of what their government is doing". Thus, without such knowledge the citizen cannot participate effectively in governmental processes or hold their government accountable for its actions (pp.115-116).

The second foundation relates to the nature and structure of self-governing systems. David Mitchel Ivester maintains that sovereign people have an inherent right to know what their government is doing. This right to know "is implicit in the inalienable power of the people to make and unmake governments. Drawing from John Locke's insights, he maintains that this right is never forfeited to the government, but remainsone of the "constitutionally protected un-enumerated rights retained by the people" (p.117).

The third draws from theories of popular sovereignty and government by impact. In terms of this idea the concept of the right to know is recognised as a corollary to the government's limited power to withhold information sovereignly and it would be irrational for the government to deny citizens information without which power may be abused (p. 118).

In democracies, the free flow of information is critical, since citizens must have access to information to make informed decisions, while those who make decisions (policies and laws) must also have access to information upon which to base their decisions (p. 109). Finally, David Mitchell Ivester reminds us that the right to know encompasses the right to receive information from "willing sources, to gather information from willing or neutral sources and to acquire information from a perhaps unwilling governmental source". Despite this, he emphasises that the 'right to know' is not absolute, as it is sometimes limited by the need to further compelling national interest (Ivester, 1977).

Having established the theoretical/philosophical rationale for the right to information, in the section below we will examine the emerging 'paradigm shift' in the discourse of the right to know.

Shifting Focus: From Human Rights to Economic/Commercial Rights

There is an apparent shift being experienced around the focus on the right to information discourse. Increasingly, the focus of this discourse is predicted on the need to combat corruption in public life and slightly away from issues of governance and democratic participation of citizens in their governments. This is despite the fact that the right to information initially emerged as a liberal policy based on liberal political ideals. More concern is being placed on 'corruption' in the public and private lives in the commercial arena and relatively less attention is paid on non-commercial imperatives in the political and social lives of the people. It is because of this shift that the attention of many African states is currently on the establishment of 'anti-corruption' bodies and less on thecreation of the human rights commissionsand other similar institutions to promote citizens' right-to-know. Little isdone to advance and consolidate citizens' participation in the democratic life of their nations. To this effect, African governments have been eager to establish the so-called anti-corruption commissions that are set to stem the tide of corruption while relegatinghuman rights issues to the back door.

Powerful donor agencies, countries and international and regional financial institutions have promoted the adoption of anti-corruption regime (measures) on poor and vulnerable developing nations. Multilateral agreements and conventions have also played a role in the adoption of the anti-corruption instruments. In terms of Africa, the following agreements have been crucial to many African states: Article 9 of the African Union Convention on Preventing and Combating Corruption and Article 10 (a) of the United Nations Convention against Corruption. Namibia is a signatory to both these agreements that oblige a country to adopt access legislation as a tool to fight corruption (Mohan, 2012).

Interestingly, the Pan African Conference on Access to Information (PACAI) Declaration signed in Cape Town in September 2011 supports the idea of Access to Information as a tool to fight corruption. Article 11 of this Declaration's "Application of Principles" states:

By contributing to openness and accountability, Access to Information can be a useful tool in anti-corruption efforts. Besides ensuring that Access to Information legislation is effectively implemented, governments have a duty to guarantee a broader legal and international framework conducive to preventing and combating corruption. (cited in Mohan, 2012, p.9)

In the midst of this development the dominant discourse around this shift has tended to maintain that the move has broadened the focus of Access to Information beyond narrow political issues to touch on economic and social questions. African nations seem to have been converted to this new gospel. For instance, there is said to have been "growing consensus in a number of African countries" that Access to Information is critical to stem corruption (Mohan, 2012 p.9). There might be a grain of truth in this as the majority of countries that have adopted Access to Information legislation during the last two decades were those that experienced waves of corruption (Roberts 2010 as cited in Mohan2012). Karen Mohan (2012, p.11) in this regard argues:

It is clear that Access to Information not only affects the right to freedom of expression, but also affects Namibia's economic growth, its promotion of democratic principles, the socio-economic rights of the citizens, as well as the fight against corruption amongst many others.

The commercial imperative in this development is advanced by the anti-corruption group among them, Transparency International. Foreign investors, international financial institutions and donor communities have been the prime proponents of the anti-corruption agenda. Shekhar Singh (n.d.), for instance, maintains that multilateral donor agencies have been credited with pursuing governments, more especially in the developing world, to set up transparency regimes. This was given as a condition attached to the sanctions of loans and aid. Thus, only those nations with transparent governance can be recipient of donor funding and loans from Western financial institutions. It is because of the insistence of funding organisations on transparency that this concept became the dominant one at the turn of this century. To this effect, the concept "transparency" was named the "word of the year" by the Webster's Dictionary in 2003 (Singh, n.d.).

Despite the popularity of the anti-corruption discourse, we are reminded that the right to information is much broader than anti-corruption issues. For instance, the Commonwealth Human Rights Initiative (CHRI) on the right to information maintains that the "key tool for the public at large is to participate directly in the democratic processes of their government and hold public bodies and their functionaries accountable to their actions" (CHRI, 2007, p.2).

An examination of the right of access to information in Namibia cannot be attempted without examining the country's policy and legal frameworks. The section below therefore seeks to locate the discussion on the freedom of information legislation within the policy and legal architecture of the country.

Namibia Information Policy Provision

The origin of Namibia's liberal constitution must be traced back to the 'negotiated political settlement' (Bauer, 2001) that ushered in the independence of the country. This process was sealed as a 'package' containing 'constitutional principles', which set the contours within which the country's constitution would be drafted and within which the country's major institutions would be established or be transformed (Saunders, 2001). These guidelines informed the constitution of the country and subsequently major economic and public policies, including the country's information policies. The constitutional principles were proposed by the Five Western members (USA, UK, Canada, Germany and France) of the UN Security Council that since 1978 assumed the responsibility to solve the protracted question of Namibia's independence. The guidelines recommended the adoption of a liberal political system, based on multiparty democracy, adherence to the rule of law, the separation of powers among the legislature, executive and judiciary, the adoption of the *Bill of Fundamental Rights*, the adoption of a free market economy and the protection of private property.

The most important of these constitutional provisions relevant to this chapter is the *Bill of Rights* covered in Article 21 of the Constitution that conforms to the liberal tradition. The *Bill of Rights* guarantees fundamental freedoms of which Sub-Article (1) (a) provides for freedom of speech and expression, including freedom of the press and other media (Republic of Namibia, 1990, p.13). Recognising that freedom of expression or freedom of media is not absolute, the *Bill of Rights* provides parameters within which these freedoms should be exercised. Set out in Sub-Article (2), these parameters comprise issues necessary in a democratic society. For instance, interests of the sovereignty and integrity of Namibia, national security, public order, decency or morality, or in relation to contempt of court, defamation or incitement of an offence" (Republic of Namibia, 1990, p.14).

Namibia's first information policy, adopted in 1991, draws from these liberal notions in its attempts to lay down the basic principles and norms of the entire information/communication sector. It defines the freedoms, roles and functions of this sector, by clarifying critical questions of freedom of expression, press freedom, access to information, free-flow of information, media ownership and control, infrastructure expansion, among others (Heuva, 2010). In addition, this policy acknowledges key elements of freedom of expression including the right to access information, especially information on public affairs. However, two shortcomings must be noted here. Firstly, the policy was not backed by legal instruments to facilitate its implementation, and thereby rendered it toothless. Secondly, and most importantly, the definition of Access to Information in this policy points to information that the government wants the citizens to know and not necessarily information that the citizens want (Heuva, 2010, pp.74-77).

The country's first information policy was revised in 2007 for the first time. The revised policy provides renewed commitment to the freedom of information and goes a step further in calling for the constitutional right to information (MISA, 2010; Mohan, 2012). However, the Commonwealth Human Rights Initiative (CHRI) in its comments on this policy maintains that the revised policy, like its predecessor, still places emphasis on the "dissemination of information that the government believes the people should know" (CHRI, 2007, p.3). In addition, the CHRI argues that the revised policy is more of a media policy and proposes that an "additional policy document be drafted that would address the right to information as a separate issue in its own right. It suggests that it sets out clearly identified roles, strategies and timelines for the drafting and implementation of the Freedom of Information or Right to Information Bill" (CHRI, 2007, p.2).

The CHRI further notes that while the revised policy makes reference to "proactive disclosure" it does not make this aspect its critical feature. It maintains that the notion of proactive disclosure is more than what governments decide to make available to the citizen, as it entails the provision of "specific categories of information public institutions must make known to the people without waiting for it being asked for" (CHRI, 2007).

In this regard, the CHRI recommends that concepts of "access to information" or "freedom of information", in the revised policy, be replaced with the "right to information". This would arguably "ensure that implementing bodies are clear that access to information is not a discretionary gift granted to the people by a benevolent government, but rather it is an internationally mandated obligation on the Government, which must implement the corresponding right" (CHRI, 2007, p.4).

The CHRI further advises government that the right to know legislation should be informed by principles that go beyond issues of combating corruption. It urges the government to consult a wide range of civil society organisations (including media, human rights formations) in the process of drafting the right to information legislation. In fact, the CHRI calls for a 'participatory law-making process, which would allow the emerging legislation to be "owned" by both the government and the public/citizens' (CHRI, 2007, p.5).

The government did not only take nine years before reacting on these recommendations, but when it eventually responded or acted on them, it did so selectively. It ignored some while accepting others. Nevertheless, the government produced a draft right to know legislation and then released this for consultation with 'stakeholders'. There was no consultation process prior to the drafting of the legislation, while the post-drafting consultation process was confined to a small group of 'stakeholders'. Some critics argued that the consultation process should have started earlier and that it should had been open to the general public and not only the so-called 'stakeholders' (see The Namibian, 2016, p.11).When this author requested a copy of the draft legislation during the week of the 'consultations' with 'stakeholders', he was told by a Director in the Ministry of Information and Communication Technology (the sponsor of the legislation), that he would be provided with the copy of the draft legislation *only* after the workshop at which the consultation took place. However, this author has not received the copy of this legislation by the time he finished drafting this chapter (31 July 2016).

Having examined Namibia's policy and regulatory (legal) framework in which attempts at the right to information were made, we now proceed to review the statues of information in colonial Namibia, which the new policies and legislation sought to change.

A Legacy of Colonial 'Information Black-Out'

The Apartheid state was secretive and did not entertain the notion of the right to know. Instead information flow was restricted and controlled. The state ensured that a host of legal instruments inhibited freedom of expression and the free flow of information. These laws imposed severe restrictions directly on the gathering, production and dissemination of information (Louw, 1993), and indirectly through self-censorship on the part of the media organisations (Oosthuizen, 1989, p.45). In this context the Namibian media during the colonial time, operated within a legal environment deliberately aimed at curtailing and controlling freedom of expression and free access to gathering and dissemination of information (Mulongeni, 1998 cited in Heuva, 2010, p.78). The initial information policy sought to redress this situation. As indicated above, this policy embraced the notion of free-flow of information to eliminate the 'information blackout' created by the Apartheid government's restrictions imposed on the gathering, production and dissemination of information. Despite this noble objective the policy did very little to address this situation in concrete terms, as indicated above.

It is instructive to note some of the Apartheid's legal instruments that adversely affected the access to and free flow of information in both South Africa and Namibia. Sections 3, 4, and 5 (2) of the Protection of Information Act, 1982 (Act 84 of 1982), for example, restricted media practitioners from gathering and disseminating information freely by prohibiting the dissemination of what was regarded as classified information related to security matters and thus restricting access to crucial information by citizens (Stuart 1990, 150). The Defence Act of 1957 (Act 44 of 1957), the Police Act of 1958 (Act 7 of 1958), the Prison Act of 1959 (Act 8 of 1959), and the Internal Security Act of 1982 (Act 74 of 1982) also prevented the media to report freely on matters relating to the coercive 'state apparatuses' – the army, police and prisons, without obtaining prior permission to do so from these coercive state apparatuses first (Herbstein, 1985 cited in Heuva, 2010, p.78).

In addition, the Defence and the Protection of Information Acts controlled the free flow of information between the 'war zone' and the outside world (Herbstein 1985 cited in Heuva, 1993, p.96). As a result the northern part of Namibia, dubbed the "operational area", where Swapo waged "low intensity" guerrilla warfare, became a no-go area for media practitioners during the years (between 1966 and 1989) of the armed liberation struggle for freedom. Any information obtained in northern Namibia had to be cleared with the defence and other security apparatuses before it could be disseminated (Heuva, 2010, pp.77-78).

As noted, censorship was another impediment to the realisation of the twin issues of access to and free-flow of information. The Publications Act, 1974 (Act 42 of 1974) for instance forced the media into self-censorship. Specifically, Section 47 (2) of this Act prohibited the publication of material that was deemed to be either indecent or obscene or offensive or harmful to public morals; or blasphemous or offensive to religious convictions and feelings (ibid.).

The legislation also prohibited the publication of materials that would bring a section of South Africans (and South West Africans) into ridicule or contempt; harmful to race relations and prejudicial to safety of the state. Given the above-mentioned strict criteria, a number of media organisations in both colonial Namibia and in Apartheid South Africa, resorted to self-censorship (ibid.).

The restrictive environment sketched above made it difficult, if not impossible, for the free flow of information and for access to public information. With the media gagged and the state operating in secrecy, there were no spaces open that could flourish as vital and critical platforms for freedom of expression. The result was a denial of citizens' basic right to access information and thereby, undermining any possibility for a democratic culture to take root in colonial Namibia.

While the post-independence government initially sought to change this restrictive media environment it was caught in some contradictions related to the realisation of the ideals of the 'right to know' and the 'free flow of information'. These contradictions include among others: the failure by the new government to adopt the right to information instruments and also the failure to speedily repeal and/or amend all apartheid laws as well as the government's tendency to adopt similar restrictive laws. While the failure to adopt the right to access information legal framework will be outlined later (below) in the chapter I would like to highlight a few pieces of legislation that are still on the Namibian statutes that are seen by civil society organisations to have continued pre-empting the free-flow of information and preventing the adoption of the right to information law.

The United Nations Security Council Resolution 435 that ushered independence to the country made provision for the repeal of discriminatory and repressive Apartheid laws. Other similar laws were left to be repealed by the new government. However, Article 140, Paragraph (1) of the Namibian Constitution insists that "all laws which were in force immediately before the date of independence shall remain in force until repealed or amended by an Act of Parliament or until they are declared unconstitutional by a competent court" (Republic of Namibia 1990, 79). However, despite this constitutional provision a host of Apartheid laws have remained on the statues for a number of years after independence. Among the remnants of the colonial period that have had direct impact on the discourses of the 'right to know' and 'free-flow of information' was the Protection of Information Act, 1982 (Act 84 of 1982). Section 4 of the Act prohibits public servants from disclosing government-related information. The objective of the Section is to safeguard national security by protecting state secrets. However, civil society activists have argued that Section 4 impedes access to information as it provides "excessive wide-ranging limits on access to official information" (Kandjii, 2004, p.57).

Another Apartheid legislation that continues constraining the free flow of information in post-colonial Namibia is the Criminal Procedure Act, 1977 (Act 51 of 1977). Although some of the provisions of this Act were amended by the Criminal Procedure Amendment Act, 2003 (Act 24 of 2003), Section 205 was not amended. This Section gives powers to judges and magistrates to compel any person (including journalists) to reveal sources of their information, at the request of the public prosecutors. It could thus undermine the journalistic practice of maintaining the confidentiality of sources and have a negative impact on the right to access information (Heuva, 2010, pp.80-82).

As hinted earlier, some post-independence laws adopted by the new government had inclinations of curtailing freedom of expression as well. Of particular importance to the right to access information is the Defence Act of 2002 (Act 1 of 2002), which is generally modelled on the Apartheid Defence Act of 1957(Act 44 of 1957). Section 46 (1) of the 2002 Act creates punishable offences for the disturbance, interruption, contempt, ridicule and disrepute of military courts, while Section 54 (1) prohibits any person from publishing or broadcasting any information seen to endanger national security or the safety of defence force members. Sub-paragraph (3) of this Section makes it an offence to disclose any secret or confidential information relating to the defence force (ibid.).

Also, attempts were made in 1996 and 1997 by Namibian lawmakers to curb freedom of expression by proposing restrictive provisions into the draft Powers, Privileges and Immunities Bill (1996/1997) (Staby, 1997). These provisions not only sought to compel citizens, including journalists, to reveal sources of their information to parliamentary standing committees, but also to prohibit journalists from interviewing parliamentarians on matters that still needed to be tabled in Parliament. However, lawmakers were forced to withdraw these provisions from the Bill because of pressure from civil society organisations (*The Namibian*, 22 September 1997, p.3).

In addition to the laws just mentioned, Karen Mohan (2012, p.7) provides a list of other restrictive legal instruments in Namibia that in her opinion interfere with both the freedom of expression and the right to information. These are laws that need to be repealed or amended to pave the way for the enactment of the freedom of information legislation:

1. Namibian Broadcasting Act 1991 (Sections 4(2) and 5 interfere with broadcasting independence).
2. Public Service Act 1997 (Article 25) prohibits civil servants from releasing information without prior permission).
3. Namibia Central Intelligence Service Act (overboard limitations).
4. Namibia Film Commission Act 2010 (secrecy provisions).
5. Defence Act 2002 (Article 54 stretches limitations far beyond the boundaries of permissible restrictions on Access to Information with regards to state security).
6. Communications Act (Part 6 provides for interception and monitoring of citizens 'private' communication).
7. Research, Science and Technology Act of 2004 (requires any individual or group intending conducting research to seek permission from the government-appointed National Commission of Research, Science and Technology, and thus stifles freedom of expression and access to information).

As can be seen from this discussion, the Namibian government has not successfully addressed impediments to the free-flow and access to information in the post-independence era. While it has tried to abolish restrictive legislation to ensure free flow of information, it has at the same time relied on some old laws as indicated above. However, and as we shall see below, the government in June 2016 produced a draft access to information document (Bill) to the surprise of many and invited 'stakeholders' for consultations on this document. Before addressing aspects of this draft legislation and the dynamics that forced its introduction, let us first examine earlier attempts and shortcomings experienced with attempts to introduce an access to information legislation in the country.

Namibia's Attempts at the Right to Information

Namibia's first attempts at Access to Information legislation happened in 1998, about eight years after the independence of the country and relatively earlier than the subsequent flood of attempts by African states experienced at the start of the new millennium on the African continent. But despite this relatively early attempt (by African standards) it was only about 18 years later that the government produced a draft access to information legislation and a draft revised information policy for discussion with stakeholders. Many African governments that started the process much later than Namibia already adopted their freedom of information legislation by the time Namibia produced its first draft legislation. These nations include among others South Africa (2000), Angola (2002), Zimbabwe (2002), Uganda (2005),

Ethiopia (2008), Liberia (2010), Guinea-Conakry (2010), Tunisia (2011), Niger (2011), Nigeria (2011) and Rwanda (2013) to mentioned but a few (IDRC Communications, 2012, p.2).

In 1998 the government hosted a consultative conference with stakeholders where it announced the decision to adopt a freedom of information legislation. A year later (in 1999) Cabinet at its 4th ordinary session in March 1999 decided that the Freedom of Information Act should be passed and constitutional amendments be made to facilitate this process (Republic of Namibia, 1999). Following from this decision the Office of the Prime Minister together with other government offices and ministries including the Office of the Attorney General and the MICT, initiated exploratory work with regard to the drafting of the Freedom of Information Bill (Elliott, 2008). It took another four years before government could comment again on its initiative. This happened in August 2012 at a conference organised by a local pressure group, Action Coalition Group (ACTION), consisting of media advocacy and civil society organisations united in their attempts to force the government to adopt the freedom of information legislation.

By the end of 2015 the country obtained a mere one point rating by the MISA for its lack of progress in implementing the Pan African Conference on Access to Information (PACAI) resolution calling for the enactment of the freedom of information legislation across Africa (MISA, 2015). This is not an indication that the country has been slow in the process of implementing the legislation, but an indication that the country has not even started the process. However, despite the reluctance in implementing its own Cabinet decision of 1999, the Namibian government is on record to have acceded (and or ratified) numerous conventions that contain provisions of right to access information. Thus, the country had been therefore under obligation to ensure compliance with them. Four of these conventions are instructive here:

1. Universal Declaration of Human Rights (UDHR) of which Article 19 states:

Everyone has the right to freedom of opinion and expression; this right includes freedom to hold opinions without interference and to seek, receive and impart information and ideas through any media and regardless of frontiers. (as cited in Louw, 2004, p.6)

2. International Convent of Human and Peoples' Rights (ICCPR), Article 19 (2), reads:

Everyone shall have the right to freedom of expression, this right shall include freedom to seek, receive and impart information and ideas of all kinds, regardless of frontiers, either orally, in writing or in print, in the form of art, or through any other media of his choice. (Louw, 2004, p.8)

3. African Charter on Human and Peoples' Rights of which Articles 9 (2) provides that:

... every individual shall have the right to express and disseminate his opinions within the law. (Louw, 2004, p.9)

4. The Declaration of Principles on Freedom of Expression in Africa provides Access to Information in Article IV, which states:

... public bodies hold information not for themselves but as custodians of the public good and everyone has a right to access information, subject only to clearly defined rules established by law. (African Commission on Human and Peoples' Rights, 2002, p.2)

The Declaration further provides principles in terms of which the right toaccess information would be guaranteed in law.

This is a contradiction the state has faced and it can be ascribed to a lack of political will of those holding political office. In the section below we will examine another contradiction experienced in terms of the direction adopted to address the question of the right to access information.

Anti-Corruption Agenda

The quest for access to information can be understood from two interlocking directions: as a good governance tool and an important anti-corruption tool. Due to a number of factors (some discussed in this chapter) the government's focus on the right to information shifted from good governance and human rights, to one of pre-occupation with the rooting out of corruption – a concern with material issues. What is interesting and sometimes ignored by critics of the Namibian government is the fact that at its 1998 consultative meeting the government spelt out clearly the two directions it intends to undertake with regard to the right to information, notably: one of an anti-corruption legislation and the other the Freedom of Information legislation (Elliott, 2008). However, while the government presented both directions, it could only move on one – the anti-corruption route. Thus, the anti-corruption initiative took more precedence compared to the human right perspective in this respect. The state managed to set and control the policy agenda, including the practical implementation of it. It shifted the focus of policy to the anti-corruption rationale and civil society was not bold enough to advance human right imperatives of the right to access information.

The declaration by Namibia's post-independence second president, Hifikepunye Pohamba, to root out corruption in public and private sectors, after taking office on the 21st March 2005, gave more impetus to the anti-corruption drive. The government enacted the Anti-Corruption Act in 2005 and subsequently appointed the Director and the Deputy Director to head the Anti-Corruption Commission. Nevertheless, the institution of the Anti-Corruption Commission rekindled hopes for the adoption of the freedom of information legislation as after its inauguration the Commission immediately became vocal on the adoption of a legislation that would protect whistle-blowers. While the media waited for the legislation with abated breaths, this did not happen.

It can be seen that it was an easier option for the government to enact an anti-corruption legislation and establish the Anti-Corruption Commission. Being so, one is tempted to ask why not the enactment of the Access to Information Act and the establishment of an Access to Information Commission or Commissioner? Why would a government opt for an anti-corruption direction and ignore an equally important aspect such as human rights? It is not difficult to establish why the government opted for the anti-corruption route. A casual glance reveals that African governments find it easier to rush to economic issues than political ones. Economic issues such as corruption do not only scare investors, but prevent governments from accessing loans, grants and other financial and economic resources from the powerful Western nations and institutions. But African governments survive on politics, even if they have bad human rights records, as some African governments can testify.

Namibia's concentration on anti-corruption issues while snubbing human rights must be seen in this broader context. Despite the African state's preoccupation with anti-corruption ('economic') issues to the detriment of human rights ('political') issues, the emerging perspectives are geared towards the balancing of these two imperatives. Below efforts by civil society on promoting the right to information in Namibia are examined.

Attempts by the Civil Society

The civil society in general was passive with its activities confined to media events, such as press statements and media conferences at which mere calls were made for the introduction of the Access to Information legislation. While some civil society organisations participated in earlier 'consultations' with government on freedom of information, these 'consultations' were dominated by the state and thus the direction moved towards concerns of anti-corruption and the protection of whistleblowers. There was no concerted effort by civil society organisations to rally the citizens around the issue of right to information. While the media was the most active part of civil society organisations campaigning for the right to access information, its concerns were more informed by the desire to have the right of whistleblowers recognised and legislated (protected) by the state, for obvious reasons for the media.

It was only after the Pan African Conference on Access to Information (PACAI) conference in Cape Town in September 2011 that some Namibian civil society organisations set up an umbrella body called ACTION (Access to Information Namibia) and kick-started an 18-month campaign for the introduction of the freedom of information legislation. This move came as a result of the PACAI conference recommendation to set up pressure groups in each country and to campaign for the introduction of the freedom of information legislation. But in Namibia this campaign remained confined to the media and failed to make any impact on the broader society, the beneficiary of the right to information.

The campaign also started almost after a full year following the Cape Town conference. Its launch was an occasion characterised by hosting prominent South African media and human rights personalities, who were invited to present their views of the issues related to media and human rights in Namibia. There were no concrete activities aimed at mobilising the broader society. Thus, very few ordinary people were involved in these media events and conferences where foreign 'experts' were invited to talk on experiences in their respective countries.

Finally it must be re-emphasised that civil society organisations in general have not been effective in mobilising the citizens to rally behind the right to information. The fact that this issue has not reached the national agenda is testimony to this, and this can only blamed on civil society. It is perhaps not wrong to argue that many civil society groupings had very little impact on the question of the right to information. Freedom of information is an issue that has enormous impact on the entire society. It is a societal or national issue and should not be confined to small groups of people whom some members may not be well informed about the impact of such issues on the broader society.

Failure to take the right to information to a national level has resulted in the undermining of this issue by the state. It has created a loophole exploited by the state in undermining both the issues and those behind it. The state could not have ignored this issue for long had the people (the citizens) mobilised themselves and unitedly supported the idea. The state dismissed this question as an issue promoted by 'foreign interests', while moving to implement the anti-corruption one, which is equally promoted by foreign governments and financial institutions.

Shortcomings of Both State and Civil Society

To understand the shortcomings, the reader is invited to look at observations made by two prominent agents of the Namibian civil society. One is a renowned academic and public intellectual, Prof André du Pisani, and the second is an esteemed independent but liberal research entity, the Institute of Public

Policy Research (IPPR). Du Pisani (2007, p.10) has on a number of occasions lamented the Namibian civil society's "failure to turn freedom of expression and access to information issues into national issues". The IPPR in its 2014 report on investment has blamed the government for a lack of political will to "achieve certain goals". It argues that the failure of the government to implement adopted policies, is its "perennial problem" (2014, p.7). These two issues are, in our opinion, at the core of the delay in the adoption of the Access to Information legislation, and not the lack of constitutional or legislative measures as was popularly claimed. Thus, the delay and failure to implement the Access to Information legislation must be ascribed to both the state's lack of political will on the one hand, and the civil society inactiveness and failure to place the right to access to information on the national agenda, on the other hand.

Popular perceptions have it that the lack of Access to Information law in Namibia should be attributed to the lack of a constitutional provision for access to information. For instance, Karen Mohan (2012) in her study on the need for an Access to Information law in Namibia, commissioned by the IPPR, under its Anti-Corruption Programme in 2012, concludes that the failure for adoption of Access to Information was due to the lack of constitutional provision. While claiming that there were a number of factors limiting the adoption of such legislation in Namibia, she only identifies one – "current legislative framework". This, she argues was not "conducive to facilitating the right of citizens to access information by virtue of the fact that there is currently no Access to Information law in place in the country". She goes on to explain that while the constitution of the country guarantees "freedom of expression", it does not provide for the right to access information (ibid. p.1).

This explanation does not help us much. Laws are made by people, and that is why parliamentarians are elected. Perhaps we need to explore further why those elected are not doing what they have been elected to do. This may bring us closer to the reason why amendments have not yet been made to facilitate the enactment of the Access to Information legislation. The attitude of those elected and appointed to ensure the implementation of government policies and the enactment of laws need to be examined, if we need to understand why government has not implemented some of its human rights related policies, including its 1999 decision to enact the freedom of information legislation. However, the political leaders have been on record for denying accusations of lack of commitment to implement this long-delayed decision.

It is perhaps suitable to examine the views of a senior government official, who at one time was entrusted with the portfolio of the Minister of Information and Communications Technology. As a person entrusted with the functions of producing and disseminating government information, and also government's chief spokesperson, the MICT minister was at that time the right person to express government views on the enactment of the freedom of information legislation. In response to an accusation that government was dragging its feet on the implementation of Access to Information legislation, former minister, Joél Kaapanda, in a statement, read on his behalf by the chief administrator of his ministry, at the opening of the conference launching the ACTION campaign, dismissed these accusations. In response Kaapanda is quoted as having said:

Access to Information goes hand in hand with some major administrative arrangements, which must facilitate legislative access. Having an Act on Access to Information is not enough to ensure public access to information... Proper filing and retrieval systems have to be in place to ensure that requested information can be found and availed. In order to facilitate legislation on Access to Information, the Office of the Prime Minister has embarked on an electronic documentation and records management system in all ministries, government-owned offices and state-owned institutions... This project is at an advanced stage, and several government-owned institutions are already using the system to ensure better information and management retrieval...However, until such a time that the Namibian Government is convinced that the accompanying administrative processes are in place, it will not just jump into legislating Access to Information, just for the sake of having a legislation on its books. (New Era, 2012, p.3)

The comments of the minister are focused on what is called the supply side of the freedom of information legislation. Reading through Joél Kaapanda's comments one sees a similarity in arguments raised in debates in the House of Commons (United Kingdom) at the same time, on the reform of Freedom of Information Act (FOIA). Members of the House of Commons lamented that debates on the reform of FOIA were focusing on the "demand side of the FOIA", while neglecting the "supply side issues". Among the Conservative benches were demands for a more focus on matters of record management and the archiving of information rather than on questions of demand for information. Kaapanda advanced the same rationale as the Conservative members of the UK House of Commons in his speech.

It is perhaps interesting to note that the same Kaapanda in 2009 rushed the adoption of the Communications Act (2009) that contains a clause which authorises the interception of citizen's private communication by the state and its agencies through parliament, despite civil society's objections and a National Council Standing Committee having taken in further comments from the public including media institutions. This law was further passed without having 'administrative arrangements' and 'facilities' in place. It came into force without even the 'interception centres' in place, not to speak of regulations that had not been finalised even a couple of years after its adoption. If the government was serious with the adoption of the Freedom of Information legislation, it could have followed the same procedures as it did with the adoption of the Communications Act (2009), by adopting the legislation first and then working on the structures and agencies (institutions) needed by the Act. Or did the former minister not want to repeat that same disastrous experience?

As indicated, the delay in implementing the Access to Information legislation in Namibia is primarily due to a lack of political will from the side of government and the failure of civil society to register the issue on a national agenda and to mobilise society around it. The delay was not about the lack of information on what to do or how to go about doing it. There had been numerous sources available on how to draft the Access to Information legislation. There were even model legislations. Namibia did not need to re-invent the wheel as the cliché goes. The following sources had been available and could have been consulted in when drafting such legislation:

The Public's Right To Know: Principles on Freedom of Information Legislation" (or ARTICLE 19 Principles) published by ARTICLE 19 in 1999. Also "A Model Freedom of Information Law" published by ARTICLE 19 in 2001. In addition there are the "UN Standards", which detail the standards to which freedom of information legislation should conform, and which is contained in the UN Special Rapporteur on Freedom of Opinion and Expression's Annual Report of 2000 (see Mendel, 2008). In "Freedom of Information: A Comparative Legal Survey". Others include the 2002 Recommendation of the Committee of Ministers of the Council of Europe (COE Recommendations). These recommendations according to Toby Mendel are critical since they contain a list of "legitimate aims which might justify exceptions to the right of access" (Mendel, 2008). Others include the Commonwealth Principles adopted by the Commonwealth Law Ministers in 1999 and the Declaration of Principles on Freedom of Expression in African, adopted in 2002 (Mendel, 2008).

Eventual 'Adoption' of the Right to Know Legislation

A combination of factors have fast-tracked the finalisation of the right to know legislation in Namibia. Most importantly, the appointment of Namibia to the Chair of the General Council of UNESCO during 2015/ 2016 period and the ministerial targets and deadlines of the Namibia's Harambee Prosperity Plan have played a critical role in the production and release of the draft right to know legislation in Namibia.

The appointment of Namibia to the chair of UNESCO's highest decision making body at the start of the country's fourth administration headed by President Hage Geingob has hasten the adoption of the right to information legislation. The country was placed in a dilemma. Chairing a decision making organ of an organisation that is in charge of the global communication and information sector, and which is at the same time the driving force behind critical human rights including the right of access to information, Namibia had no choice but to embrace and implement all UNESCO's programmes and projects. Occupying such a crucial position (temporary though) Namibia had to be "exemplary in leading the global crusade for an informed citizenry, which should enjoy access to information" according to the country's deputy minister of Information and Communication Technology (Simataaas cited in Tjihenuna, 2016:1). Thus, Namibia was under the obligation to embrace and also lead by example in living-out UNESCO agreements and programmes. To many right to know activists, the nomination of Namibia to the chair of UNESCO's General Council was a blessing in disguise.

Another contributing factor to the hasty adoption of the freedom of information draft legislation has been the Harambee Prosperity Plan (HPP) of the Hage Geingob Administration (see Tjihenuna, 2016). The HPP has been described as an "ambitious plan" that seeks to achieve specific objectives (targets) over a set period (*The Southern Times*, 2016, 1). It is built on five pillars of (i) effective governance and service delivery(ii) economic advancement (iii) social progression (iv)infrastructure development, and (v) international relations and cooperation (Republic of Namibia, 2016: .i) The Plan places access to information at the centre of the delivery of public services. The latter together accountability and transparency are prominent features of this Plan. However, the Plan placed more emphasis on aspects of corruption and the prevention thereof in the public and private lives. It does not directly address issues of citizen's democratic participation in their government. The Plan's "Access to Public Information" strategy is explained as:

To ensure that our citizens have access to relevant Government information, the MICT will develop a Plan for aligning the functions of the Public Relations and Liaison Officers to their core functions of information dissemination before end of June2016. In addition, permissible access to information by the public must also be included in the Plan. (Republic of Namibia, 2016c, p18)

However, an important aspect of the Plan that might have contributed to the release of the right to know legislation is in terms of implementation of government decisions. Under the Plan governments ministries are allocated targets and deadlines for reaching these targets. The urgency to meet some of its targets has forced the Ministry of Information and Communication Technology to finalise the access to information legislation and the review of the information policy. This is the context in which the MICT had rushed the draft freedom of information legislation and the revised information policy. The rush to release these documents has resulted in the lack of proper public consultation prior to the drafting of these documents as well as the poor preparation and presentation of the documents.

Features of the Draft Revised Information Policy and the Right to Know Bill

Both the draft revised information policy and the draft freedom of information legislation touch on crucial aspects of information that are relevant to the freedom of information discourse. Briefly the revised information policy that was released for public consultation in June 2016 acknowledges citizens' right to information and subscribes to the principle of maximum disclosure (Republic of Namibia, 2016a, p.7). The policy fills important gabs that were not included in the first post-independence policy or the 2007 revised policy. The revised policy, while not neglecting the traditional information sector, it also places emphasis on what it calls the "rapid development and convergence of technologies" in the contemporary information and communication sector (Republic of Namibia, 2016a, p.6).

Most importantly the 2016 revised policy covers all aspects of the information and communication technologies and the so-called new media. Drawing from the Ministry's (of Information and Communication Technology) mission statement, the revised policy notes that while Namibia's first Information Policy (1991) defined the role and place of the information sector in the country,

... the emergence of new ways of communication as well as the developments in the Information and Communication Technologies demands new ways of thinking and realignment to new modes of delivering information. This necessitate the revision of the Information Policy (1991) in order to fill-up gaps for new technologies in the process of addressing the information demands in this modern contemporary society. (Republic of Namibia, 2016a, p.4)

Section of 7.4 (Access to Information) of the revised Information Policy addresses the question of right to information of the citizens, and it is therefore very important to this chapter. This section links access to information to the consolidation of democracy and to the stimulation of development in the country. It notes that access to information "allows citizens to gain knowledge and to make informed decisions about participating in the governmental and governmental processes in the country" (Republic of Namibia, 2016a, p.10).

Recalling the 1999 Cabinet decision that first recognises the people's right to information, the revised policy proposes strategies to implement this decision. Some of the proposed policy strategies are to:

1. Draft an access to information legislation,
2. Provide mechanism for the disclosure of information, and the monitoring of freedom of information to ensure that the public is granted access to information as required,
3. Amend Constitution of the country to safeguard access to information
4. Revise of existing laws that militate against access to information and the free press,
5. Draw up an Action Plan to implement the Information Policy with technical assistance from UNESCOs *Information for All* programme (Republic of Namibia, 2016a, pp.10-11).

The draft freedom of information legislation (Bill) on the other hand provides Namibian citizens and permanent residents the right of access to "any record under the control of a government institution or any private body that may assist in the exercise or protection of any right" (Republic of Namibia, 2016b, p.3). The Bill further provides for the responsibilities of both the government and private institutions in terms of the provision of information. It also obliges the Minister of Information to proactive compile on annual basis a list of organisations and type of information they produce/contain. The Bill also provides for various types of requests, issues of access to information and records and exemptions to access. On the institutional framework, the Bill provides for the Office of the Information Commissioner, under Sections 54 to 58, who will be responsible for all aspects of access to information. The Commissioner will be appointed by the President of the country on the recommendation of a Parliamentary standing committee (Republic of Namibia, 2016b, p.35).

As just indicated the Bill introduces an Act that will provides "for the members of the public to access information under the control of public/government authorities or any private body that may assist in the exercise or protection of any right" (Republic of Namibia, 2016b, p.2). As such it does provide of broader legal issues and institutional framework of the legislation. It does not provide much more than that. What are crucial in any piece of legislation are the regulations. The latter places flesh to the bare legal bones. Unless, the regulations are completed and released for public attention, we will not be able to establish effectiveness of the right to know legislation in Namibia. Thus, it is still early to make a fair judgement onthis piece of legislation at this point in time. More public scrutiny and critical research are needed to analyse and critique both documents.

CONCLUSION AND THE WAY FORWARD

The chapter has argued that the long delay before the adoption of the right to know information can be ascribed to the lack of political will by the government and the failure of civil society to seize the policy vacuum created by the state and thereby mobilise society behind the right to know as a basic human right. The government preferred the combat of corruption in public life while downplaying a critical human right, the right to know, which is important for the consolidation of democracy in an emerging young nation, such as Namibia. While the civil society organisations was aware of the nature and scope of the problem, notably the lack of political will by the state to make the necessary constitutional amendment that would pave the way for the enactment of the right to know law, they did not much to pressurise the government into action.

Being a human right issue the right to know needed to be placed on the national agenda. It should have been elevated to a national debate in which every section of society: workers, students, youths, religious and political groupings and everybody could participate. In this way the demand would have become a national one, broadened beyond the narrow confines of media right groupings. The more the issue could have been discussed and debated the more people would have been enlisted for the demand of right to know. Generally, it is at this point that a national issue reaches the level of "political agenda" (see Bardoel and Van Cuilenburg 2009, p.105). Unfortunately, the Namibian right to know policy debate (discourse) did not follow this rationale. After years of delays and lapses from the state and civil society, the government parachuted draft legislation, forced by a combination of dynamics.

However, the release of the draft revised Information Policy and Right to Know Bill does not mean the end of the campaign for freedom of access to information. Citizens still need to be informed and educated on their right to know and how to ago about obtaining information they need in terms of the proposed legislation. In the meantime, these preliminary documents need proper scrutiny, consultation and consensus from all sectors of society and not only from the so-called 'stakeholders'. Both documents highlight issues society need to debate and agree upon. They need not be rushed through because government ministries and departments want to meet deadlines in terms of the HPP. Skimming through these documents shows that there are still more work to be done. Moreover, there is still the important function of constructing the necessary regulations to ensure the practical implementation of both the revised policy and the Bill. It is hoped that citizens would be consulted during the process of drafting the regulations, and not only 'consulted' on the already drafted rules.

REFERENCES

African Commission on Human and Peoples Rights. (2002). *Declaration of Principles on Freedom of Expression in Africa.A dopted in Banjul, The Gambia, from 17th to 23rd October 2002*. Retrieved from http://www.daneprairie.com

Bardoel, J., & Cuilenburg, J. (2008). The Nature of Media and Communications Policy. In P.J. Fourie (Ed.), Media Studies: Policy, Management and Media Representation. Cape Town: Juta & Co. Ltd.

Bauer, G. (2001, March). Namibia in the First Decade of Independence: How Democratic? *Journal of Southern African Studies*, *27*(1), 33–55. doi:10.1080/03057070120029491

Burns, Y. (2001). *Communications Law*. Durban: Butterworths.

Commonwealth Human Rights Initiative (CHRI). (2007). *Analysis of the Government of the Republic of Namibia: Revised Information Policy, 2006*. New Delhi: CHRI.

Du Pisani, A. (2007, September 10). Power and Democratic Space. *Die Republikein*, 10-11.

Elliott, G. D. (2008). *Statement on Provisional Policy Framework on the Development of Access to Information Legislation for Namibia Office of the Prime Minister 18 August 2008 Administrative Justice Conference, Windhoek*. Unpublished Paper.

Forde, S. (n.d.). *John Locke and the Natural Law and Natural Rights Tradition*. University of North Texas. Retrieved from http://www.nlnrac.org

Gramsci, A. (1971). *Selections from Prison Notebooks* (Q. Hoare & G. Nowell-Smith, Trans. & Eds.). London: Lawrence and Wishart.

Hall, S. (1980). Encoding and Decoding. In S. Hall et al. (Eds.), *Culture, Media and Language*. London: Hutchison.

Heuva, W. E. (1993). Resistance in Print: The Nationalist Press during the Liberation Struggle. Ecquid Novi, 14(1), 94-104.

Heuva, W. E. (2010). *Transforming communication in a changing milieu: Challenges and contradictions of reform in Namibia*. Köln, Germany: LAP Lambert Academic Publishers AG & Co. KG.

Heuva, W. E. (2012). State invasion of privacy in the ICT surveillance legislation: The case of Namibia. *Africa Communication Research*, *5*(3), 261–282.

IDRC Communications. (2012). *Access to information gains ground in Africa*. Retrieved from http://www.idrc.ca/EN/Programs/Science_and_Innovation/Information_and_Network

Institute for Public Policy Research (IPPR). (2014). *Easing the Way for Investment in Namibia.* IPPR Research Report.

Ivester, D. M. (1977). Constitutional Right to Know. *Hastings Constitutional Law Quarterly*, *4*(Winter), 109–163.

Kandjii, K. (2004). Namibia. In R. Louw (Ed.), *Undue Restriction: Laws impacting on media freedomin the SADC*. Windhoek: Media Institute of Southern Africa.

Karuaihe-Upi, N. (2011). *Government Secrecy in an Information Age: 2011 Report on the most open and secretive government institutions in Namibia*. Windhoek: Media Institute of Southern Africa.

Louw, R. (1993). Foreword. In P. E. Louw (Ed.), *South African Media Policy: Debates of the 1990s*. Bellville: Anthroppos. doi:10.1075/hl.20.1.01for

Louw, R. (2004). *Undue Restrictions. Laws impacting on media freedom in the SADC*. Windhoek: UNESCO.

Media Institute of Southern Africa. (2010). *A Report on Open & Secretive Public Institutions in Southern Africa*. Windhoek: MISA.

Media Institute of Southern Africa. (2015). *A Report on Open & Secretive Public Institutions in Southern Africa*. Windhoek: MISA.

Mendel, T. (2008). *Freedom of Information: A Comparative Legal Survey* (2nd ed.). Paris: UNESCO.

Ministry of Information and Broadcasting. (1991). *Namibia's Information Policy*. Author.

Ministry of Information and Broadcasting. (2006). *Draft Revised Information and Communication Policy*. Author.

Mohan, K. (2012). Sunlight is the best disinfectant: Why Namibia needs Access to Information. Windhoek: Institute for Public Policy Research, Paper 11.

New Era. (2012). *Namibia: Kaapanda on Access to Information Legislation*. Retrieved from http://allafrica.com/stories/201208230745.html

O'Neil, P. H. (Ed.). (1998). Communicating Democracy. The Media and Political Transitions. London: Lynne Rienner Publishers.

Oosthuizen, L. M. (1989). *Media policy and ethics*. Cape Town: Juta& Co., Ltd.

Republic of Namibia. (1990). Constitution of the Republic of Namibia, 1990 (Act 1 of 1990).

Republic of Namibia. (1991). Namibian Broadcasting Act, 1991 (Act 9 of 1991). Government Gazette, 223.

Republic of Namibia. (1992a, March). New Era Publication Corporation Act, 1992 (Act 1, 1992). *Government Gazette, 377*, 24.

Republic of Namibia. (1992b). Namibia Press Agency Act, 1992 (Act 3 of 1992). Government Gazette, 382.

Republic of Namibia. (1992c). Namibian Communications Commission Act, 1992 (Act 4 of 1992). Government Gazette, 384.

Republic of Namibia. (1997). Namibia Central Intelligence Service Act, 1997 (No 10 of 1997). Government Gazette of the Republic of Namibia, 1699.

Republic of Namibia. (1999, March 2). Press Release.

Republic of Namibia. (2000). Film Commission Act, 2000 (Act 6 of 2000). Government Gazette, 2749.

Republic of Namibia. (2002a). Film Commission Act, 2000 (Act 6 of 2000). Government Gazette, 2322.

Republic of Namibia. (2002b). Defence Act, 2002 (Act 1 of 2002). Government Gazette, 2749.

Republic of Namibia. (2003). Criminal Procedure Amendment Act, 2003 (Act 24 of 2003). Government Gazette, 3123.

Republic of Namibia. (2004). Research, Science and Technology Act (Act 23 of 2004).

Republic of Namibia. (2009). Communications Act, 2009 (No 8 of 2009). Government Gazette of the Republic of Namibia, 4378.

Republic of Namibia. (2016a). Draft Revised National Information Policy, March 2016.

Republic of Namibia. (2016b). Draft Access to Information Bill, April 2016.

Republic of Namibia. (2016c). Harambee Prosperity Plan 2016/17 – 2019/20. Namibian Government's Action Plan towards Prosperity for All, April 2016.

Republic of South Africa. (1957). Defence Act of 1957 (Act 44 of 1957).

Republic of South Africa. (1958). Police Act of 1958 (Act 7 of 1958).

Republic of South Africa. (1959). Prison Act of 1959 (Act 8 of 1959).

Republic of South Africa. (1974). Publications Act of 1974 (Act 42 of 1974).

Republic of South Africa. (1977). Criminal Procedure Act of 1977 (Act 51 of 1977).

Republic of South Africa. (1982). Internal Security Act of 1982 (Act 74 of 1982).

Republic of South Africa. (1982). Protection of Information Act, 1982 (Act 84 of 1982).

Sabine, G. H., & Thorson, T. L. (1973). *A History of Political Thought* (4th ed.). Hinsdale, IL: Dryden Press.

Saunders, C. (2001). From Apartheid to Democracy in Namibia and South Africa: Some Comparisons. Discussion Paper, No. 10. In *Transition in Southern Africa: Comparative Aspects*. Nordic Africa Institute.

Sénécal, M. (1995). Democratisation of the Media: Liberty, Right and Privilege. In B. Tankha (Ed.), *Communications and Democracy: Ensuring Plurality*. Penang: Southbound.

Singh, S. D. (n.d.). *The Genesis and Evolution of the Right to Information in India*. Unpublished Paper.

Staby, J. (1997, September 24). Muzzled off: Motion to curb press freedom. Windhoek Advertiser.

Stanford Encyclopaedia of Philosophy. (2005). *Human Rights*. Retrieved from http://plato.standord.edu/entries/rights -human/

The Namibian. (1997, September 22). MPs urged to reject law 'which is set to suffocate democracy …'". *The Namibian.*

The Namibian. (2016, June 17). Editorial: Right to Privacy does not equate to Secrecy. *The Namibian*, p. 11.

The Southern Times. (2016, April 12). Harambee Prosperity Plan ... a guide in Namibia's quest to be Africa's competitive economy by 2020. *The Namibian.*

Tjihenuna, T. (2016, June 14). Hold us accountable. *The Namibian.*

University of Namibia. (2008). *Service Delivery Survey Report for the Ministry of Information and Broadcasting*. Multi-Disciplinary Research Centre.

US Government. (n.d.). *Human Rights in Brief.* Bureau of International Information Programmes, US Department of State. Retrieved from http://www.america.gov/

Chapter 15
Rethinking Information Privacy in a "Connected" World

Ufuoma Akpojivi
University of the Witwatersrand, South Africa

ABSTRACT

The emergence and usage of Information Communication Technologies (ICTs) by states, institutions and individuals has challenged and created a shift in the normative idea of privacy from rights to solitude. Consequently, this chapter sought to ascertain if emerging democracies and economies such as South Africa and Nigeria have privacy frameworks that adequately guarantee and protect the privacy of their citizens in this globalized era. Using policy analysis, this chapter argues that although the privacy provisions in South Africa are comprehensive, the privacy framework fails to address the privacy leak associated with the usage of these ICTs. Whereas, in Nigeria, it was observed that the privacy framework is inadequate as there are no specific privacy provisions, thus the assertion that Nigerians have no privacy in this globalized era of connectivity.

INTRODUCTION

There is no doubt we are living in a global village facilitated by the connectivity of people across the globe with the help of the internet, and this has facilitated the constant sharing and receiving of information amongst individuals and across borders. The African continent is tapping into this connectivity through information communication technologies (ICTs) and smart mobile devices that have helped in bridging the gap in information flow between the global north and south. Consequently, the ever-increasing embrace of ICTs and smart mobile devices in the continent has empowered vast majority of the public to participate in societal discourses (Schmidt and Cohen, 2010). Schmidt and Cohen (2010) while extending this thought, further held that the rise and usage of these information communication technologies across the globe has made us all connected or live in an 'interconnected estate'. In this 'interconnected' estate, ordinary citizens who were once disempowered are now empowered as they can easily access information and participate in both socio-economic and political discourses. However, despite the euphoria of this connected space and the numerous benefits accruable to the development

DOI: 10.4018/978-1-5225-2095-5.ch015

of societies, Assange (2014) warned that there is a serious concern over privacy issues as multinational corporations like Google, nation states, and individuals could easily invade the privacy of others.

For this reason, the issue of privacy has become a salient and controversial debate in this 21st century. Many political, economic and social factors have made the dichotomy between private and public space slim or difficult to distinguish. Politically, many governments with assistance from multinational corporations such as Google, Yahoo, Bing etc. have started monitoring the activities of their citizens online in order to ensure that national security and public lives are not compromised. This process entails the collation and storage of individuals' data (see Assange, 2014). For instance, the United States and United Kingdom run a mass surveillance program. According to them, the 'fight against terrorism' justifies this invasion of privacy. Furthermore, in this global information and competitive business age, many businesses thrive on the collation of personal information through mechanisms of loyalty programmes, mobile advertisement, and client history tracing as a means of improving business activities (see Akpojivi, 2014; Akpojivi & Bevan-Dye,2015). For example, Amazon has publicly acknowledged that they collect and gather consumer information every time they search for products online, and they use consumer search history for recommending products to consumers. Not only does this confirm that Amazon develops a profile for each consumer (Hochhauser, 2000), they could also pass these profiles or data to other associates who could use them for economic purposes. Likewise, socially, millions of people are always disclosing and sharing information with their friends and loved ones via new media platforms (Bevan-Dye & Akpojivi, 2015). For example, in 2014, "Facebook recorded an average of 864 million daily active users, an estimated 300 million photographs uploaded per day and 4.75 billion pieces of content shared per day" (see Bevan-Dye & Akpojivi 2016). Consequently, it can be reasoned that information sharing on Social Networking Sites (SNS) has become a ubiquitous part of many individuals' lives in our contemporary society (Gross & Acquisti, 2005).

It is therefore established that the privacy within this connected world is problematic and difficult to enforce. This is more worrisome in emerging democracies like South Africa and Nigeria that are regarded as the fastest growing economies in Africa, as they are currently witnessing a rapid integration of information communication technologies in all spheres of society, and so constantly shifting the boundaries of privacy. In addition, there is a growing concern that the mass media or digital media in the form of citizen journalism could easily breach or invade the privacy of individuals in their attempt to broadcast news and meet the ever increasing demand for breaking or soft news by the public. Pretschner, Hilty and Basin (2006) while buttressing the above point, further held that the great potentials of these information technologies in this connected world has made privacy and regulation of these tools a significant debate for emerging democracies. More so, social critics and scholars are concerned that African countries are lagging behind in terms of keeping and meeting international standards in ensuring and promoting privacy of their respective citizens. These concerns are evident in the fact that African countries have recently started to think about the need to protect the privacy of their citizens through the formulation of policies. For instance, South Africa formulated policies such as the privacy provis'ons in the 1996 Constitution, Electronic Communications and Transaction Act 2002, Consumer Protection Act 2009. Likewise, the Nigerian government formulated and implemented the 1999 constitution, cybercrimes prohibition, prevention Act 2015, National Action Plan for the Promotion and Protection of Human Rights in Nigeria 2006, and Nigeria: Personal Information and Data Protection Bill 2013. This chapter therefore seeks to examine the adequacy and applicability of privacy from the policy perspectives of both South Africa and Nigeria in this era of interconnectivity.

This is particularly relevant because there is an increasing difficulty in differentiating a private space from the public space in this interconnected world, and this has posed serious challenges to the normative concept of privacy. For instance, in 2015, the president and vice president of the Student Representative Councils at University of Witwatersrand and University of Cape Town respectively were reprimanded for what they disclosed on their Facebook accounts. Some scholars and social critics however argued they should not have been reprimanded as their disclosure on Facebook was on their private space. The obvious question then is how can the privacy of citizens be protected, and how can privacy leaks be managed in this era of connectivity and information driven age?

This study aims to ascertain how privacy is conceptualized in this era of connected space in both South Africa and Nigeria, determine the rationale behind such conceptualization, and ascertain if there are common patterns in such conceptualizations between both countries. It will also attempt to ascertain if the many privacy provisions in both countries are adequate to guarantee and protect the privacy of the public, and if there is need to rethink privacy in order to achieve a balance between protection of individual rights and the state/institutions' freedom to use such information for national security.

In order to achieve the set aims, the following research questions are posed:

- Are there provisions for privacy protection within South African and Nigerian policies?
- How is privacy conceptualized in the various policy documents in South Africa and Nigeria?
- Are the provisions for privacy protection within the policy documents adequate in today's information driven society?

What Is Privacy?

There is no universally acceptable definition of privacy as any definition is subject to debate. any definition it is subjected to a huge debate. According to Nwauche (2007), the word privacy is a legal term and this to a large extent can be attributed to the numerous controversy associated with any definition. Likewise, Smith, Milberg and Burke (1996) while substantiating further argue that the multidimensional features of privacy has made it to mean different things to different people. For instance, it is generally perceived in society that the quest for privacy means the desire to hide certain information from the public (see Stamatellos, 2007, pp. 36) i.e. if one does not have anything to hide there will be no need to protect certain information about themselves being in the public domain. This idea has influenced the way scholars approach the concept of privacy, hence the multi-perspective from which privacy is conceptualized.

However, the principal idea of privacy as a vital fundamental human right cuts across most definitions in law, psychology and sociology fields (The Yale Law Journal, 1981), hence making it one of the fundamental dimensions of privacy. Weinstein, while buttressing this argument held that "human rights are a complex but yet a fundamental aspect of all human society….as they represent each individual's claim to dignity of person and fair treatment" (1983, pp.171). The need to protect human rights has been promoted at supra-international, international and national organizations as it constitutes the very foundation of human existence[1]. Privacy is considered as one aspect of human rights that should be protected and respected, as its importance to the human dignity cannot be "fairly or accurately ranked on the relative scale" (The Yale Law Journal, 1981, pp.337). To Goodwin (1991), privacy is a fundamental human right which should be respected. Collier (1995) equates privacy to other fundamental human rights i.e. speech, association, life etc. According to Collier, "privacy is a value which underpins human dignity and other key values like freedom of association and freedom of speech" (1995, pp.5). This idea of human rights makes privacy a natural human right, hence the legalistic notion that has influenced the policy framework of most countries. For instance, in the United States, the Fourth Amendment of the constitution states that "the right of the people to be secure in their persons, houses, papers, and effects against unreasonable searches and seizures shall not be violated, no warrants shall be issued, but upon probable cause, supported by oath or affirmation, and particularly describing the place to be searched, the persons or things to be seized". Similarly, in the United Kingdom, there are provisions within the human rights bill to protect the privacy of the citizens. For example the human rights bill protects to a reasonable degree the rights of the citizen to communicate privately, and an individual's right to private or family life is guaranteed so long as his activities are not contrary to the law (Human Rights Act, 1998; see also Barendt & Hitchens, 2000).

This perspective of privacy as a human right has two attributes that are central to its conceptualization. These two attributes are "the ability to keep personal information unknown to others and to keep one's self separate from interaction with others" (Yale Law Journal, 1981, pp. 329). In other words, individuals have the right devoid of intrusion or invasion, and to determine the usage, control and access of personal data. These attributes have always influenced the codification of privacy within legislatures. Prosser (1960) while extending this thought posited that the rights notion of privacy as codified in most legislatures encompass four vital elements i.e. intrusion (the personal life of an individual should not be invaded), disclosure (public disclosure of personal details without approval), false lights (the presentation of false information about individuals in public) and the use of personal details without permission. These elements have generally been used by societies and courts in the determination of privacy cases. Consequently, re-enforcing the normative idea of non-intrusion to the concept of privacy coined by Brandeis and Warren (1890). However, this idea of privacy is being challenged in this global connected world. For example, a proposed security bill in the United kingdom would require technological companies to "keep records for 12 months, detailing when emails were sent and to whom, or when people connected to social media sites such as Facebook", and security operatives would be able to see the online activities of everyone (Ford, 2015, pp. 2). This therefore challenges the normative idea of non-intrusion that is codified in the definition of privacy already discussed.

This brings about the idea that the right notion of privacy codified in most constitutions does not necessarily suggest the right to exclusion or the right to be left alone, as such conceptualization is myopic, seeing that no one can live in isolation in a society and with the emergence of smart technologies this will be difficult to enforce. Therefore, Roos (2012) argues that there is need to broaden the legalistic perspective of privacy from inclusiveness to encompass wider concepts as the idea of inclusiveness is too simplistic. According to Goodwin (1991) the legalistic perspective of privacy should entail the right of individuals to control unwanted information about themselves in the public domain instead of the right of exclusion i.e. left alone. This idea recognises the fact that although individuals cannot live in isolation because of numerous political factors (state surveillance), economic (giving out of information becoming a perquisites in order to have business transactions and services) (see Solove, 2004), and social factors (constant sharing and disclosing of information on social networking sites), they should be aware, and be able to control and manage the usage of their information (Dworkin, 1961).

This notion of awareness and control lay the philosophical perspective from which some scholars conceptualize privacy. As earlier stated, one cannot live in exclusion or devoid of invasion as contained in the legalistic codification of privacy. However, this raises the issue of control and the degree to which individuals should be allowed to control the access and usage of information about themselves (Westin 1967 cited in Roos, 2012, pp. 378). This has become increasingly important as the rise of the new media technologies coupled with increasing state surveillance programs (Assange, 2014) have challenged the philosophical idea of privacy. There is always the tendency for individuals to control information about themselves in the public domain and their inability to control such personal information raises privacy concerns which will invariably influence their notion of privacy (Fusilier and Hoyer 1980 cited in Culnan, 1993). According to Culnan and Armstrong (1999), people generally want to know why their information is being collected, its expected uses, the steps that will be taken to protect its confidentiality, integrity and quality, and the consequences associated with such information collection.

Nevertheless, the idea of control is relative because the ability to exercise control over the collection and usage of personal information is dependent on political, social or cultural factors which vary from context to context (Johnson 1989 cited in ibid). According to Culnan (1993), empirical studies have suggested that privacy issues are linked to cultural values as society determines the degree to which individuals can control information about themselves. Rule (2004) while buttressing the above position, argued that everyone is not entitled to the right of controlling their personal details, and even when they enjoy such entitlements, they do not actually live a private life because society dictates such entitlement(s) and how it is implemented. Taylor (2002) held that, throughout history countries have monitored or policed the activities of citizens, and with the emergence of new information communication technologies citizens have lost the power of living a private life into a public life despite the fact that privacy provisions are made to protect them. This is in accordance with Mill's argument that, because individuals live in society, society morally has jurisdiction over their affairs and conducts, thus the complexity in controlling personal information in the hands of others (1869 {1974}). This is more relevant in the 21st century when states are struggling and dealing with global terrorism. The collection and monitoring of individual information is seen as a key tool in tackling global terrorism (Solove, 2004; Taylor, 2002)

This idea that society has moral jurisdiction over the affairs and activities of individuals raises another fundamental aspect of privacy i.e. ethical perspective and the balance between individual's rights to privacy and society's moral jurisdiction to ensure the safety of all, and societal development. Societies have increasingly different roles including safety, economic growth, political and cultural development, which they must play at different times. In the process of carrying out these roles, the privacy of individuals may be breached or individuals may have to forgo some of their privacy, hence the question of how ethical is it for institutions within society to pry into the activities of individuals without their knowledge. This question is salient as the revelations from Assange and Snowden highlight how nation states could abuse their powers in the process of carrying out their moral jurisdictions, by simply generating digital dossier of the public, which doesn't necessarily help in the fight against terrorism. Some British spy officials while extending this thought further held that due to the massive nature of individual data collected, security services might overlook valuable intelligence in the process, hence defeating the end goal of national security (BBC, 2016). According to Solove (2001), it is unethical for individual's data to be used by institutions or states whether for national security or not without the permission of the individual. This idea from Solove challenges the collection and usage of individual's information without prior knowledge, literally meaning that it is unethical for states or institutions to surveil or monitor individual activities. However, Phelps, Nowak and Ferrell (2000) argued that the practice of institutions collecting and using individual's data without prior notice or information is not unethical as these data are being used to provide valuable service for the development of both the individual and society. This notion re-enforces Mill's argument that society has jurisdiction over the activities of individuals in society. Therefore, establishing the 'slippery notion' of privacy due to its complexities (Yilma and Birhanu, 2013), and the challenges in conceptualizing privacy in this connected world.

Privacy Framework in South Africa and Nigeria

As earlier stated, South Africa and Nigeria are regarded as the leading economies in Africa hence the need to examine the privacy framework in these emerging democracies and economies cannot be overemphasized. Also, Information communication technologies has played a germane role in the socio-economic and political developments of both countries. According to Zongo (2001, pp.4) information communication technologies are "formidable tool to better address the various developmental issues in a rapid and cost effective manner", as these technologies are regarded as the "driving force of development" (McQuail, 1997, pp. 128).

Consequently, both countries have embraced and integrated ICTs into the socio-economic, political and cultural developments. For instance, Nigeria is alleged to have the "biggest and fastest telecommunications market in Africa and has huge potential for information technology (IT) market growth" (Kusamotu, 2007, pp. 149). Odufuwa (2012) while extending this thought held that the penetration rate of information technologies has significantly increased, as 62% of Nigerians use their mobile devices to access internet and this is outside people making use of fixed household internet. Similarly, in South Africa, the telecommunication industry is witnessing a dynamic growth and this is evident in the embedment of information communication technology in all spheres (economic, social and political). Gillwald, Moyo and Stork (2012) in their study of information technologies usage in South Africa posit that there is a significant increase in the number of households with internet usage. According to them, 71% of South Africans access the internet with their mobile devices. Therefore, it can be argued that the explosion of mobile/internet penetration in both countries has not only empowered once marginalized group of people but has re-defined the concept of privacy due to their connectivity trend and 'disruptive' nature (AFP, 2015 cited in Guardian Newspaper, 2015). Hence, there is need to examine policy framework surrounding privacy in both countries, and if the policy framework is adequate in this connected world that has blurred the boundaries of privacy.

Therefore, this section shall identify and explore the underlying reason(s) for the various policy provisions on privacy, and the rationale for such conceptualization of privacy within the policy framework. To this end, it is important to give a brief synopsis of the major legislations in South Africa and Nigeria that discuss information privacy or privacy as a whole.

Privacy in South Africa and Nigeria: From the Policy Perspective

The conceptual problem of defining privacy allows for different legal systems across the world and how to resolve privacy issues (Wacks, 1979). Privacy is contained in various provisions since apartheid in South Africa. According to Roos, privacy was first recognized in South African case law in 1950 (2012, pp. 376), and with time it was broadly covered in most legislatures. Therefore, this section will discuss the relevant policy documents with privacy provisions.

Constitution of the Republic of South Africa No. 108 of 1996

This constitution was largely influenced by the past history of the country as is vividly captured in the preamble of the constitution which states that "we, the people of South Africa recognize the injustices of the past…adopt this constitution as the supreme law of the Republic so as to heal the divisions of the past and establish a society based on democratic values, social justice and fundamental human rights" (1996 constitution). Consequently, the constitution was built around protecting the rights of the citizens and according every citizen dignity and equality (Section 1, 1996 Constitution).

The constitution adequately protects the privacy of citizens. Section 14 of the 1996 constitution states that "everyone has the right to privacy, which includes the rights not to have (a) their person or home searched, (b) their property searched, (c) their possessions seized or (d) the privacy of their communication infringed", hence making privacy a fundamental human right. This provision is similar to the privacy laws of other developed countries, like the United States Fourth Amendment. It can therefore be argued that apart from being influenced by the country's antecedent, the privacy provision in South Africa, was to a large extent drafted to meet or conform to international standards like the Organization for Economic Cooperation and Development(OECD) guidelines of privacy. These include personal information use, secondary use of personal information, and protection of information (Park, 2008). Although, this provision within the constitution deals mainly with privacy in general, Section 14 (d) which protects personal communication can be linked to information privacy. This is because the issue of information privacy arises when personal information and communication are infringed upon (see Goodwin, 1991).

Electronic Communications and Transactions Act 2002 of South Africa

This Act came into effect on July 31, 2002 when it was assented to by the president. As stated in the Act, its purpose is to "provide for human resource development in electronic transactions, to prevent abuse of information systems, to encourage the use of e-government services and to provide for matters connected therewith" (Electronic Communications and Transactions Act, 2002). Apart from acting as a framework for regulating electronic transactions, this act also deals with protecting the information privacy of citizens.

The need to protect trade or electronic transactions from criminal elements necessitated the formulation of the Act and its framework was influenced by international practices. As Heisenberg and Fandel (2004) put it, "the trans-Atlantic regulatory asymmetry which resulted from the strict European Union data directive sensitized the United State to develop a regional standard that can preempt the incompatibility of national rules" (cited in Park, 2008, pp. 58). This impacted on other countries including South Africa who had to formulate the Electronic Communication and Transaction Act 2002 in order not to be left behind in this global drive, hence the policy initiation was basically for economic reasons (Park, 2008).

Section 10 (2) of the Act also states that electronic transactions policy should be in line with "international best practices and conform with the laws and guidelines of other jurisdictions and international bodies" (Electronic Communication and Transaction Act, 2002). In relation to privacy, the Act protects the citizens from unwanted communication or direct marketing from traders. According to Section 45 (1A) of the Act, the consumer has the option to leave any mailing list, while Section 45 (4) makes it an offence for an individual to send unsolicited commercial messages or communication to someone who had opted out from such program (Electronic Communication and Transaction Act, 2002). The Act also calls on all data controllers to tell consumers why their data are being collected, i.e. for what purpose. It also states that they must not use the data for any other purpose without the written permission of the consumer (Section 51 (3 and 4). Likewise, consumer data must not be transmitted to a third party, unless it is required by law (Section 51 (6)). Aggrieved individuals can lodge complaints with the Consumer Affairs Committee who are required to investigate and resolve issues (Electronic Communication and Transaction Act, 2002). From the above, it can be argued that the ideologies behind the Act were influenced by international standards and that the Act deals mainly with information privacy of citizens.

Consumer Protection Act 2008 of South Africa

Just like the Electronic Communications and Transaction Act 2002, the Consumer Protection Act (CPA), No. 68 of 2008 was promulgated to protect the economic activities of consumers and give them some level of privacy. In the preamble of the Act, it is stated that "the Act seeks to promote and protect the economic interests of consumers…" (CPA 2008). In order to achieve the set objective of the Act, nine (9) principles framed in line with the South Africa Bill of Rights were adopted. They include rights of privacy, rights of equality, right to choose, right to disclose information, right to fair marketing, right to fair and honest dealing, right to fair values and product safety, right to fair trading terms and conditions and right to accountability. Although, it can be argued that the Act deals mainly with marketing activities and regulating business activities to ensure that they are in accordance with international standards, the theme of information privacy clearly stands out and is one of the principles in the Act.

According to the Section 11 (1) of the Act, every citizen has the right to privacy which include the right to "(a) refuse to accept (b) require another person to discontinue or (c) in the case of an approach other than in person, to pre-emptively block, any approach or communication to that person, if the approach or communication is primarily for the purpose of direct marketing" (CPA, 2008). From the above provision, the citizens have the right to protect and stop their personal information from indiscriminate use by organizations. This is further supported in Section 11 (2) that states that "to facilitate the realization of each consumer's right to privacy, and to enable consumers to efficiently protect themselves against the activities contemplated in Subsection (1), a person who has been approached for the purpose of direct marketing may demand during or within a reasonable time after that communication that the person responsible for initiating the communication desist from initiating any further communication". From the CPA, it can be argued that privacy within the context of the Act involves the rights of citizens or consumers to be aware of what their personal details are being used for by business organization and the right and or ability to stop business organizations from using their details if displeased with their approach.

Protection of Personal Information Act 2013

This is one of the key privacy policy document in South Africa. According to the Act, it seeks to protect how public and private institutions process individuals' personal data and to lay the requirements for the usage of personal data (Protection of Personal Information Act, 2013, pp. 2). According to the Act the interconnectivity of societies in this era of information society which facilitates the free flow of information necessitated the promulgation of the Act.

A lucid review of the Act indicates that the concept of privacy was framed along constitutional provisions and consumer protection Act 2008 of exclusion and right to be aware of data usage. Consequently, the purpose of the Act includes "give effect to the constitutional right to privacy, by safeguarding personal information when processed by responsible party, subject to justifiable limitations that aimed at balancing the right to privacy against other rights, particularly the right of access to information, and protecting important interests, including the free flow of information within the Republic and across international borders, regulate the manner in which personal information may be processed by establishing conditions, in harmony with international standards that prescribe minimum threshold requirements for the lawful processing of personal information remedies to protect their personal information from processing that is not in accordance with this Act" (Protection of Personal Information Act, 2013, pp. 16).

Therefore, it can be argued that the protection of personal information act 2013 was framed along international standards that covers the collection and usage of personal information from within the country and outside the country, and mechanisms in place that should be followed when collecting and using personal data. For instance, Section 21 (2) states that "the operator must notify the responsible party immediately where there are reasonable grounds to believe that the personal information of a data subject has been accessed or acquired by any unauthorized person" (Protection of Personal Information Act, 2013, pp. 34).

The 1999 Constitution of the Federal Republic of Nigeria

The constitution established the democratic principles in Nigeria after 29 years of authoritarian military rule (Akpojivi, 2014). Although the validity of the constitution has been questioned by numerous scholars and social critics because of the idea that it was promulgated without the public interest (Aguda, 2007). However, despite the numerous criticisms, the constitution was the first document to guarantee privacy to every Nigerian. According to Section 37 of the constitution "the privacy of citizens, their homes, correspondence, telephone conversation and telegraphic communications is hereby guaranteed and protected". It can be argued that this provision places privacy as a fundamental human right and built around the Western normative idea of privacy as already highlighted in the constitution of the United States of America and the British bill of rights. Nevertheless, it can be argued that this provision is too simplistic and vague in this age of interconnectivity as such provision does not recognize the changing dynamics of the societies, communications and businesses.

Cybercrimes Prohibition Prevention Act 2015 of Nigeria

This policy document provides for a unified regulatory framework in the prevention, prosecution and punishment of cybercrimes in Nigeria. This was necessary following the increase in cybercrime also known as 419[2] which is associated with Nigeria. Therefore, the Act aims to "ensures the protection of critical national information infrastructure, and promotes cybersecurity and the protection of computer systems and networks, electronic communications, data and computer programs, intellectual property and privacy rights" (Cybercrimes prohibition prevention Act, 2015).

Although the general objective of the Act is to prevent financial crimes and protect the individuals from fraudulent financial activities, it also provided for individual rights to privacy as Section 38 (5) states that "anyone exercising any function under this section shall have due regard to the individual's right to privacy under the constitution of the Federal Republic of Nigeria, 1999 and shall take appropriate measures to safeguard the confidentiality of the data retained, processes or retrieved for the purpose of law enforcement". From the above, it can be argued that the concept of privacy is vaguely defined as privacy is linked to the constitutional provision. Privacy within the framework of the constitution and this act is vague as there are no specific contextualization outside privacy to exclusion, and confidentiality when government or state institutions are making use of individual data. This is more worrisome because in this connected world the boundaries of privacy have been shifted from the normative views captured in both documents. For instance, there is no mechanism within the framework of the Act to ensure confidentiality and the concept of confidentiality can easily be contested in this era surveillance and need for national security.

National Action Plan for the Promotion and Protection of Human Rights in Nigeria 2006

This policy document was formulated to promote the socio-cultural, political and economic rights of Nigerians. This document was largely influenced by international and national forces. According to the National Act Plan for the promotion and protection of Human Rights in Nigeria, the policy document is a response to "the recommendation of the Vienna Declaration and Programme of Action adopted at the World conference on Human Rights in Vienna Austria in 1993 that requested that each state consider the desirability of drawing up a national action plan identifying steps whereby the state would improve the protection and promotion of human rights" (2006, pp. 4). Similarly, the historical antecedent of Nigeria that recognizes freedom of speech, association, privacy to enjoy property and right to family and kin influenced the framing of this policy document (ibid).

Consequently, the central objective of the policy document is to promote and protect the fundamental human rights of all Nigerians. To this end, the policy recognizes privacy as a fundamental human right. According to the policy, everyone has the privacy not to have his/her "home searched, property searched, possession seized, and privacy of their communications infringed" (ibid, pp. 24). However, it should be noted that this conceptualization of privacy is tied to the constitutional provision of privacy as this provision contained in this policy document is similar to the privacy provision contained in the 1999 constitution.

According to the policy framework, the need to protect the human right of privacy of every Nigerian is tied to Nigeria's international obligations such as the Article 12 of the Universal Declaration of Human Rights and Article 14 of the African Charter on Human Rights. Nevertheless, it should be noted that Nigeria is a signatory to the Universal Declaration of Human Rights and the African Charter on Human Rights, an obvious reason to have this provision. Despite this privacy provision which is framed along the constitutional provisions, there are legal limitations to the exercise of privacy which according to the policy document is tied to the penal code, criminal code, criminal procedure act amongst others (ibid, pp. 24). The above legal documents that limit the privacy of individuals are mainly concerned with criminal activities, thus it can be posited that the privacy of individuals in Nigeria are only withdrawn when there is a criminal case against an individual.

Nigeria: Personal Information and Data Protection Bill 2013

This bill is currently not passed into law. The importance of this bill to the privacy debate in Nigeria cannot be over-emphasized. The bill emanated as a result of the government's desire to protect the personal and sensitive data of Nigerians in this era of new, mobile, smart technologies which could easily be used to breach the privacy of others consequently making privacy a fundamental human right. Although the bill has not been passed into law, the bill is needed to help address the issues of organizations gleaning sensitive personal information of others using these new technologies that has shifted and challenged the concept of privacy.

Also, the bill will help prevent institutions whether public or private and multinationals organizations operating in Nigeria from disclosing or selling individual data to third parties, who could likewise transfer such data from the boundaries of Nigeria, therefore posing a threat to national security. However, the numerous issues which the bill has raised has consequently affected the inability of the government to pass it into law. According to Article 19 (2013), the inability of the proposed bill to meet international standard in the protection of the citizen's privacy coupled with its poorly drafted nature has led to a serious debate over the bill. According to Article 19 while extending this thought further stated that the bill should be redrafted in order to allow for effective implementation and understanding by the public. In addition, they requested that the bill should cover all government institutions instead of just the private institutions so as to make the bill holistic (ibid).

From Policy Ambition to Realization: A Discussion

It can be observed that the various policies examined have approached privacy from a certain perspective which cuts across both countries. This perspective to a large extent shaped the context and framework of privacy in both countries. It should be noted that although there is significant difference in both countries' frameworks i.e. in South Africa the privacy provisions are specific (which will be elaborated upon later), whereas in Nigeria there are no specific provisions as the policy provisions are vaguely constructed.

Nevertheless, privacy is constructed from the perspective of freedom and control of personal information which is the dominant approach in the conceptualization of privacy as previously discussed. According to Neethling (2005) the South African courts see privacy from the perspective of freedom of the citizens to control information about themselves and how such information is used, as anything outside of these constitutes breach of privacy (cited in Roos, 2012, pp. 395). Likewise, in Nigeria, the right to private life is considered a fundamental human right and this has influenced the constitutional interpretation of privacy. Therefore, it is important to examine this perspective and its applicability in this connected world.

Freedom to Withdraw Information

This is the most common way privacy was conceptualized in most of the examined policy documents in South Africa. For instance, the South African 1996 Constitution gives citizens the right of solitude i.e. privacy to home, communication and correspondence, which is the dominant approach in the conceptualization of privacy (see Brandeis and Warren, 1890). In addition, Section 45 (1a and b) of the Electronic Communications and Transactions Act, 2002 and Section 11(1 and 2) of the Consumer Protection Act 2008 extended this privacy by giving citizens the freedom to withdraw from any marketing activities using their personal information.

The question arising from these provisions is whether citizen's privacy is holistically protected in this connected sphere. From the policies earlier reviewed it can be argued that the citizens general right to privacy i.e. not having his/her communication, property searched has been adequately protected in the constitution. Likewise, privacy to economic activities as business organizations or data controllers requires that consumers be informed on what their personal data are used for and if it will be used for other purposes. According to Section 51 (4) of the Electronic Communications and Transactions Act 2002, "data controller may not use the personal information for any other purpose than the disclosed purpose without the express written permission of the data subject unless he or she is permitted or required to do so by law". Likewise, Section 51(6) charged the data controller not to reveal or disclose personal information collected to third parties. These provisions do not only empower the citizens to be well informed about their data usage but also to withdraw from any activities that might infringe on their privacy as contained in Section 11 (2) of the Consumer Protection Act 2008. Therefore, it can be argued that the privacy framework in South Africa accords the 'human dignity concept' (Nwauche, 2007) to every South African by protecting them from intrusion, and public disclosure of personal information through the various control mechanisms outlined in the policy documents.

However, the question that remains is whether governmental and other relevant agencies follow the policy framework i.e. do they protect citizen's data from unauthorized access, use citizen's data for other purposes without notifying them, especially in this era where information could easily be shared. More so, the above policies did not address the issue of privacy leaks associated with online platforms. The example of the president and vice president of the Student Representative Councils at University of Witwatersrand and University of Cape Town respectively that were reprimanded for what they disclosed on their Facebook accounts further buttresses this fact. To what extent does this constitute a breach of privacy. Also, to what extent is the practice of employers searching and looking at the online activities of potential employees, ethical or a breach of privacy (see Beven-Dye and Akpojivi, 2015). Can the constitutional provision to right of solitude or data protection be applicable to citizen's online activities? This is one aspect of privacy that has not been addressed in the policy framework, and is also a dominant area that has consistently shifted the boundaries of privacy and created tension to the interpretation and applicability to the normative concept of privacy in society. Although Section 14 (c) of the protection of personal information Act 2013 calls for the protection of individual online identifier, this is not comprehensive to address the above examples, hence creating tension over when a private space becomes public in society.

In Nigeria, privacy was conceptualized from the idea of freedom and to withdraw information from the public domain as contained in the examined policy documents. For example, Section 37 of the constitution protects the privacy of citizen's property and communication. This is the dominant approach that has influenced all other policy documents and privacy framework in the country. However, it should be noted that the privacy framework in Nigeria is not holistic like that of South Africa that addresses different aspects of citizen's privacy. The framework in Nigeria are general and draws heavily from the constitutional provision which to a large extent is problematic because of its vagueness. Consequently, Nwauche (2007), held that it might be easy to say that there are no privacy provisions in Nigeria.

Kusamotu (2007, pp. 152) while buttressing this fact further held that "Nigeria does not have specific privacy laws, but guarantees the right to privacy in the constitution". However, the constitutional provision of privacy as contained in Section 37 of the 1999 constitution is to a large extent incomprehensive in nature. Nwauche (2007) while extending this thought further held that the constitution did not define the concept of privacy but vaguely states that one has the right to solitude. This is further reflected in the fact that privacy is conceptualized as a fundamental human right in all the other policy documents such as national action plan for the promotion and protection of human rights 2006, without a detailed mechanism on how this human right of privacy can be actualized and enforced apart from a vague provision contained in Section 46 of the constitution. According to Section 46 subsection (1) of the constitution, anyone who feels his fundamental rights have been breached may apply to the High Court to seek redress. This provision although provides framework for citizens to address breach of privacy, however, access to the Nigerian courts is problematic due to the expensive nature of the judiciary system in Nigeria.

Furthermore, the question arising from these provisions is the extent to which the privacy of Nigerians is protected since there are no comprehensive privacy framework. This is of concern in this era of connectivity because the personal information of these subscribers could easily be shared, used without their knowledge, especially as Nigeria has the largest telecommunication market in Africa (Kusamotu, 2007, pp. 149). There is no doubt that this is already the case in Nigeria, as the proposed personal information and data protection bill 2013 that would to a large extent helped in addressing data sharing facilitated by new media technologies, and establish relevant mechanisms in place to protect privacy is yet to be passed into law. This is more worrisome considering the fact that there are no privacy provisions in the national telecommunication policy of 2000 to help protect the privacy of citizen's online activities. Therefore, it can be argued that privacy framework in Nigeria is not adequate to protect the privacy needs of Nigerians.

Digital Media and Privacy in South Africa and Nigeria: The Unanswered Question

Although the focus of this chapter is on privacy framework and their adequacies in the information driven age, there is need to briefly discuss how media organizations in South Africa and Nigeria are capitalizing on this privacy leak of differentiating between private and public space in their practices.

There is no doubt that the emergence of information communication technologies has revolutionized journalism practices in both countries, further raising the question of privacy in an interconnected world. Goode (2009) stated that new media technologies and social media platforms such as Facebook, Twitter and Instagram amongst others have made people not professionally trained as journalists to be citizen journalists who publish whatever they can access. Similarly, Franklin (2013) stated that Facebook and Twitter have become sources of news to people and some media organizations. Consequently, Nicola (2011) in his study titled "tweet first verify later" held that the ethical dimensions of journalism are being breached. This gives room for privacy concerns as individual's photos, videos and blogs are now used by journalists both in main stream media and digital media for gossips, and soft news.

This practice is becoming rampant both in South Africa and Nigeria as some media organizations now derive their news story from individual posts on Facebook or tweets from Twitter. For instance, on July 2016, most media houses in South Africa published series of selfies of a lady called Lindokuhle Dlamini being kissed by President Jacob Zuma, accusing him of being a sugar daddy to the 18 years old lady. While this can be regarded as an invasion of privacy of the personal life of the president and invasion of the lady's private space "Facebook", on the other hand this could be seen as an act of whistleblowing i.e. exposing the immoral activity of the president. Similarly, in Nigeria most digital journalists do make use of Facebook or Twitter as their source of news. For example, Linda Ikeji, a well-known blogger in Nigeria makes use of social media platforms as sources of news. In the same way, some newspapers cull news stories from social networking sites. Therefore, the need ascertains if this practice is ethical because of the serious privacy concerns i.e. uplifting personal post or disclosure for public consumption.

This practice can be regarded as unethical because of the risk and implications involved in the usage of such personal information, as such information were derived and used without the consent of the individual involved. Solove (2004) argued that the usage of such easily available data do pose a profound effect on the lives of the individuals involved. Furthermore, this practice questions the notion of news,

news gathering processes and the ethics of journalism as it further shifts the boundaries of privacy and the ethical principles governing news as reflected in most press code of conduct. While some social critics might argue that the culling of news from individual posts does not constitute a breach of privacy or question journalism code of ethics because social media are sometimes regarded as public space, this practice however has re-enforced the debate of privacy leaks and the need to rethink privacy in this information driven age due to the difficulty in establishing the dichotomy between private space from public space in an interconnected world.

CONCLUSION

The boundaries and normative idea of privacy is constantly changing in this era of interconnectivity where information sharing and gathering in the public domain is easy. This information sharing and gathering facilitated by information communication technologies used by individuals, business organizations and government institutions will inevitably breach the citizen's privacy despite the claims that such information gathering are essential in providing relevant services and protecting lives and properties. Neal and Morgan (2000) summed this privacy challenges in our contemporary societies by positing that privacy becomes an issue when citizens' data are used without the prior knowledge of the citizens or when such data are used for other purposes, hence the need to ascertain whether the policy provisions of South Africa and Nigeria are adequate in protecting the privacy needs of their citizens.

In this study, it was established that the concept of privacy is extensively covered within South African legislations as the various policy documents provide for the freedom of citizens. These include freedom to a life of privacy, freedom to control the usage of their personal data (i.e. what and how their personal data is used), which are all in accordance with international standards and requirements. However, it was revealed that the policy framework did not address the privacy of citizens' online activities, thus the applicability of the available privacy framework in addressing online privacy issues will be problematic. This is further compounded by the idea of leak in the privacy policy framework i.e. to what extent can an individual's private space (e.g. online space or social networking sites) become a public sphere. Will it be possible for an individual to enforce his/her privacy in his private space in this era of surveillance? These are some of the issues not addressed by the available privacy framework in South Africa. Consequently, the white paper on telecommunication and the protection of personal information act should be amended to address this privacy leak and protect citizen's online activities.

In Nigeria, on the other hand, the privacy provision is inadequate due to the incomprehensive nature of the policy framework. While the privacy provisions call for the freedom of citizens to privacy, there are no mechanisms in place to enforce and protect this privacy. This can be attributed to the fact that there are no specific privacy provisions in Nigeria, thus the notion that Nigerians have no privacy (Nwauche, 2007). Furthermore, although there were attempts to formulate policies that will meet international standards, for example the personal information and data protection bill of 2013, inherent loopholes in the policy document has prevented the bill from being passed into law. Therefore, there is need for policymakers in Nigeria to formulate specific privacy laws in order to address the incomprehensive nature of the already existing provisions. These laws must go beyond stating the provisions for privacy but also establish a viable mechanism for enforcing privacy. In addition, the national telecommunication policy of 2000 should be amended to provide for citizens' privacy online and also address any privacy leak that might arise i.e. protect the public and private spaces of the citizens.

REFERENCES

AFP. (2015, September 15). Mobile Phones Driving User Growth in Africa: Facebook. *The Guardian*. Retrieved from http://www.ngrguardiannews.com/2015/09/mobile-phone-driving-user-growth-in-africa-facebook/

Aguda, O. (2007). *The need for a National Conference*. Retrieved from http://www.hg.org

Akpojivi, U. (2014). Democratizing the Media in the New Democracies of Ghana and Nigeria: Challenges and Prospects. *Ecquid Novi: African Journalism Studies*, *35*(3), 87–105.

Akpojivi, U., & Bevan-Dye, A. (2015). Mobile Advertisements and Information Privacy Perception Amongst South African Generation Y Students. *Telematics and Informatics*, *32*(1), 1–10. doi:10.1016/j.tele.2014.08.001

Article 19. (2013). *Nigeria: Personal Information and Data Protection Bill* [Data File]. Retrieved from http://www.article19.org/data/files/medialibrary/3683/Nigeria-Personal-Information-and-Data-Protection-Bill.pdf

Assange, J. (2014). *When Google Met WikiLeaks*. New York: O/R Books.

Barendt, E., & Hitchens, L. (2000). *Media Law Cases and Materials*. Harlow: Pearson Education Limited.

BBC. (2016, June 7). *'Leaked Report' Reveals Mass Data Fears*. Retrieved from www.bbc.com/news/technology-36469351

Bevan-Dye, A., & Akpojivi, U. (2015). South African Generation Students' Self-Disclosure on Facebook. *South African Journal of Psychology. Suid-Afrikaanse Tydskrif vir Sielkunde*. doi:10.1177/0081246315602645

Brandeis, L., & Warren, S. (1890). The Right to Privacy. *Harvard Law Review*, *4*(5), 193–220. doi:10.2307/1321160

Collier, G. (1995). Information Privacy. *Information Management & Computer Security*, *3*(1), 41–45. doi:10.1108/09685229510792979

Culnan, M. (1993). How did they get my Name? An Exploratory Investigation of Consumer Attitudes towards Secondary Information Use. *Management Information Systems Quarterly*, *17*(3), 341–363. doi:10.2307/249775

Culnan, M., & Armstrong, P. (1999). Information Privacy Concerns, Procedural Fairness and Impersonal Trust: An Empirical Investigation. *Organization Science*, *10*(1), 104–115. doi:10.1287/orsc.10.1.104

Dinev, T., & Hart, P. (2006). Privacy Concerns and Levels of Information Exchange AnEmpirical Investigation of Intended E-Services Use. *E-Service Journal*, *4*(3), 25–60. doi:10.2979/ESJ.2006.4.3.25

Dworkin, G. (1961). Privacy and the Press. *The Modern Law Review*, *24*(1), 185–189.

Facebook. (2014). *Newsroom*. Retrieved from http://newsroom.fb.com/company-info/

Federal Government of Nigeria. (1999). *1999 Constitution of the Federal Republic of Nigeria*. Lagos: Federal Government Press.

Federal Government of Nigeria. (2015). *Cybercrimes Prohibition Prevention Act 2015*. Lagos: Federal Government Press.

Federal Republic of Nigeria. (2006). *National Action Plan for the Promotion and Protection of Human Rights in Nigeria 2006*. Lagos: Federal Government Press.

Ford, R. (2015, November 2). Judges will Get Veto in Attempt to Salvage Snooper's Charter. *The Times*, pp. 1A, 2A.

Franklin, B. (2013). Editorial. *Digital Journalism*, *1*(1), 1–5. doi:10.1080/21670811.2012.740264

Gillwald, A., Moyo, M., & Stork, C. (2012). *Understanding What is Happening in ICT in South Africa: A Supply-and-Demand-Side Analysis of the ICT Sector*. Cape Town: ResearchICTAfrica.net

Goode, L. (2009). Social News, Citizen Journalism and Democracy. *New Media & Society*, *11*(8), 1–19. doi:10.1177/1461444809341393

Goodwin, C. (1991). Privacy: Recognition of a Consumer Right. *Journal of Public Policy & Marketing*, *10*(1), 149–166.

Gross, R., & Acquisti, A. (2005). Information revelation and privacy in online social networking. In S. De Capitani di Vimercati & R. Dingledine (Eds.), *Privacy issues in practice: 2005 ACM Workshop on Privacy in the Electronic Society* (pp. 71–80). New York: ACM Press.

Hochhauser, M. (2000). *Why I Stopped Shopping at Amazon.com: A Reading Expert Sound Off*. Retrieved from http://www.privacyrights.org/print/ar/amazon.htm

Journal, Y. L. (1981). Protecting Privacy Under the Fourth Amendment. *The Yale Law Journal*, *9*(2), 313–343.

Kusamotu, A. (2007). Privacy Law and Technology in Nigeria: The Legal Framework will not meet the Test of Adequacy as Mandated by Article 25 of European Union Directive 95/46. *Information & Communications Technology Law*, *16*(2), 149–159. doi:10.1080/13600830701597616

McQuail, D. (1997). *Audience Analysis*. London: Sage Publications Inc.

Mill, S. (1869). *On Liberty* (4th ed.). London: Longman.

Neal, D., & Morgan, N. (2000). Our Data, Our Selves. *The Wilson Quarterly*, *24*(4), 51–57.

Nicola, B. (2011). *Tweet First Verify Later*. Retrieved from reutersinstitute.politics.ox.ac.uk

Nwauche, E. (2007). The Right to Privacy in Nigeria. *CALS Review of Nigerian Law and Practice*, *1*(1), 62–90.

Odufuwa, F. (2012). *Understanding What is Happening in ICT in Nigeria: A Supply-and-Demand-Side Analysis of the ICT Sector*. Cape Town: ResearchICTAfrica.net.

Park, J. (2008). Privacy Regime, Culture and User Practices in the Cyber-Marketplace. *Information, 10*(2), 57–74.

Phelps, J., Nowak, G., & Ferrell, E. (2000). Privacy Concerns and Consumer Willingness to Provide Personal Information. *Journal of Public Policy & Marketing, 19*(1), 27–41. doi:10.1509/jppm.19.1.27.16941

Pretschner, A., Hilty, M., & Basin, D. (2006). Distributed Usage Control. *Communications of the ACM, 49*(9), 39–44. doi:10.1145/1151030.1151053

Prosser, W. (1960). Privacy. *California Law Review, 48*(3), 383–423. doi:10.2307/3478805

Republic of South Africa. (1996). Constitution of the Republic of South Africa No.108 of 1996. Cape Town: Author.

Republic of South Africa. (2002). Cape Town: Electronic Communications and Transaction Act.

Republic of South Africa. (2009). Consumer Protection Act No. 68. Cape Town: Author.

Republic of South Africa. (2013). Protection of Personal Information Act 2013 No 4. Cape Town: Author.

Roos, A. (2012). Privacy in the Facebook Era: A South African Legal Perspective. *The South African Law Journal, 129*(2), 375–402.

Rule, J. (2004). Toward Strong Privacy: Values, Markets, Mechanisms and Institutions. *University of Toronto Law Journal, 54*(2), 183–225. doi:10.1353/tlj.2004.0008

Schmidt, E., & Cohen, J. (2010). The Digital Disruption. *Foreign Affairs*.

Smith, J., Milberg, S., & Burke, S. (1996). Information Privacy: Measuring IndividualsConcerns about Organizational Practices. *Management Information Systems Quarterly, 20*(2), 167–196. doi:10.2307/249477

Solove, D. (2001). Privacy and Power: Computer Databases and Metaphors for Information Privacy. *Stanford Law Review, 53*(6), 1393–1462. doi:10.2307/1229546

Solove, D. (2004). *The Digital Person: Technology and Privacy in the Digital Age*. New York: New York University Press.

Stamatellos, G. (2007). *Computer Ethics A Global Perspective*. Burlington: Jones & Bartlett Learning, LLC.

Taylor, N. (2002). State Surveillance and the Right to Privacy. *Surveillance & Society, 1*(1), 66–85.

United Kingdom Human Rights Act (1998). (n.d.). Retrieved from www.justice.gov.uk/human-rights

Wack, R. (1979). The Rights of privacy by John H.F. Shattuck 1977, The Law of Privacy inSouth Africa by David Jan Mcquoldmason 1978 Review. *The Modern Law Review, 42*(5), 587–608.

Weinsten, W. (1983). Human Rights and Development in Africa: Dilemmas and Options. *Daedalus, 112*(4), 171–196.

Yilma, M., & Birhanu, A. (2013). Safeguards of Right to Privacy in Ethiopia: A Critique of Laws and Practices. *Journal of Ethiopian Law, 26*(1), 94–152.

Zongo, G. (2001). *ICTs for Development in Africa.* Retrieved from http://www.unssc.org/web1/programmes/glnp

ENDNOTES

1 The United Nations and other organisations have the protection of human rights as their fundamental principle and goal.

2 419 is a scam that was named after the section of the Nigerian criminal code that punish those involved in fraudulent financial activities.

Compilation of References

Act, B. (2014). *The Sub-Saharan African Media Landscape – Then, Now and in the Future*. Retrieved from http://www.balancingact-africa.com/sites/balancingact-africa.com/files/products/1.%20SSA%20Media%20Landscape.pdf.

Adam, G. S. (2009). Freedom of Expression and the democratic liberal tradition. In The Handbook of Mass Media Ethics. New York: Routledge.

Adekola, T.A., & Eze, S.C. (2015). Intellectual property rights in Nigeria: A critical examination of the activities of the Nigeria Copyright Commission. *Journal of Law, Policy and Globalization, 35*.

Adele-Jinadu, L. (2011). Comparative Analysis of Security Challenges of Elections in Nigeria. In L. Olurode & A. Jega (Eds.), *Security Challenges of Election Management in Nigeria*. Abuja: Independent National Electoral Commission.

Adesina, L. A. (2009). The Role of the Media in Reporting Terrorism: A Personal Viewpoint. *Journal of Communication and Media Research, 1*(1).

Adopt the ASNE code. (1993). *Editor & Publisher, 126*(42), 6-7.

AFP. (2015, September 15). Mobile Phones Driving User Growth in Africa: Facebook. *The Guardian*. Retrieved from http://www.ngrguardiannews.com/2015/09/mobile-phone-driving-user-growth-in-africa-facebook/

African Commission on Human and Peoples Rights. (2002). *Declaration of Principles on Freedom of Expression in Africa.A dopted in Banjul, The Gambia, from 17th to 23rd October 2002*. Retrieved from http://www.daneprairie.com

African Media Barometer, Nigeria. (2011). Windhoek: Friedrick Ebert-Stiftung (FES).

Afrol. (2002). *Zimbabwe's Daily News' Editor Arrested*. Retrieved September 16, 2016 from http://afrol.com/News2002/zim043_nyarota_arrest.htm

Aguda, O. (2007). *The need for a National Conference*. Retrieved from http://www.hg.org

Ahmad, M. A. (2015). Communication and Conflict in Nigeria: What Role for the Media? *Global Advanced Research Journal of Educational Research and Review, 4*(8), 154–160.

Aiex, N., & Gottlieb, S. (1999). *Issues in media ethics* (Report No. EDO-CS-99-07). Bloomington, IN: ERIC Clearinghouse on Reading, English and Communication. (ERIC Document Reproduction Service No. ED436015)

Akhere, J. I. (2014). *Cyber law: An introduction*. Charlotte, NC: Ehiose Publishers.

Akinboye, S. O. (2009). Nigeria's 2007 General Elections: Global perceptions, concerns and responses. In L. Olurode, S. Akinboye, & R. Akinyemi (Eds.), *The crisis of political succession*. Lagos: Rebonik Publications Ltd.

Akinfeleye, R. A. (2004). Mass Media Machine in Winning Elections, Electoral Violence and the damage the journalists can do. In A. Jinadu (Ed.), Crisis of democratization, development and electoral violence in Nigeria. Lagos: A special publication of Unilag Sociological Review.

Akinfeleye, R. A. (2003). *Fourth Estate of the Realm or Fourth Estate of the Wreck: Imperative of Social Responsibility of the Press*. Lagos: University of Lagos Press.

Akinfeleye, R. A. (2011). *Essentials of Journalism: An introductory college text*. Lagos: Malthouse publishers.

Akpojivi, U. (2014). Democratizing the Media in the New Democracies of Ghana and Nigeria: Challenges and Prospects. *Ecquid Novi: African Journalism Studies*, *35*(3), 87–105.

Akpojivi, U., & Bevan-Dye, A. (2015). Mobile Advertisements and Information Privacy Perception Amongst South African Generation Y Students. *Telematics and Informatics*, *32*(1), 1–10. doi:10.1016/j.tele.2014.08.001

Alasuutari, P. (Ed.). (1999). *Rethinking the media audience*. Los Angeles, CA: Sage Publications Ltd.

Ali, Y. O. (2003). Keynote Address. In B. A. Olasupo (Ed.), *Electoral Violence in Nigeria: Issues and Perspectives*. Lagos: Friedrich Ebert Stiftung.

Alzouma, G. (2005). Myths of digital technology in Africa: Leapfrogging development? *Global Media and Communication*, *1*(3), 339–356. doi:10.1177/1742766505058128

Ambrose, M. L., & Ausloos, J. (2013). The right to be forgotten across the pond. *Journal of Information Policy*, *3*, 1–23. doi:10.5325/jinfopoli.3.2013.0001

Anifowose, R. (1982). *Violence and Politics in Nigeria, Tiv and Yoruba Experience*. New York: Nok Publishers Int.

Anon., (2005). Jazz has got copyright law and that ain't good. *Harvard Law Review*, *118*(6), 1940–1961.

Antilla, L. (2008). Self-Censorship And Science: A Geographical Review Of Media Coverage Of Climate Tipping Points. *Public Understanding of Science (Bristol, England)*.

Antony, M. G., & Thomas, R. J. (2010). This is citizen journalism at its finest: YouTube and the public sphere in the Oscar Grant shooting incident. *New Media & Society*, *12*(8), 1280–1296. doi:10.1177/1461444810362492

Arant, D. (2000). *Online Media Ethics: A Survey of US Daily Newspaper Editors*. Paper Presented at the Association for Education in Journalism and Mass Communication Convention, Phoenix, AZ. Retrieved 7 August 2016 from http://facstaff.elon.edu/andersj/onlinesurvey.html

Article 19. (2013). *Nigeria: Personal Information and Data Protection Bill* [Data File]. Retrieved from http://www.article19.org/data/files/medialibrary/3683/Nigeria-Personal-Information-and-Data-Protection-Bill.pdf

Article XIX (1996) Broadcasting Genocide – Censorship, Propaganda & State-Sponsored Violence in Rwanda 1990-1994.

Ashley, D. E. (2009). Public As Creator And Infringer: Copyright Law Applied To The Creators Of User-Generated Video Content. *The Fordham Intell. Prop. Media & Ent. LJ*, *20*, 563.

Assange, J. (2014). *When Google Met WikiLeaks*. New York: O/R Books.

Atique, A. (2013). *Digital Media and Society: An Introduction*. Cambridge, UK: Polity Press.

Awiti, J. (2014). *Mother Nature: Little Lambs seek unusual nourishment*. Nairobi: NMG.

Ayeni-Akere, A. (2003). Electoral violence and the democratization project: The Nigerian experience. In B. A. Olasupo (Ed.), *Electoral Violence in Nigeria: Issues and Perspectives*. Lagos: Friedrich Ebert Stiftung.

Babafemi, F. O. (2007). *Intellectual property: The law and practice of copyright, trademarks, patents and industrial designs in Nigeria*. Ibadan: Justinian Books Ltd.

Balancing Act Report. (2014). *The sub-Saharan Africa Media Landscape – Then, Now and in the Future*. Retrieved February 12, 2016, from http://balancingact-africa.com/sites/balancingact-africa.com/files/products/1.%20SSA%20Media%20Landscape.pdf

Baliboola, I. N. (2015). *Church TV Runs An Erotic Dating TV Programme*. Retrieved from http://oops.ug/2015/06/02/church-tv-runs-an-erotic-dating-tv-programme/

Ball, A. (1987). *Modern Politics and Government*. London: Macmillan press.

Bambridge, D. (1991). *Intellectual property* (4th ed.). London: Financial Times Pitman Publishing.

Banda, F. (2010). Negotiating Journalism Ethics in Zambia: Towards a 'Glocal' Ethics. In Media Ethics Beyond Borders: A Global Perspective (pp. 124-141). New York: Routledge.

Bannon, L. J. (2006). Forgetting as a feature, not a bug: The duality of memory and implications for ubiquitous computing. *CoDesign*, *2*(1), 3–15. doi:10.1080/15710880600608230

Baradell, S. (2012). *Photojournalism, technology and ethics: What's right and wrong today*. Black Star Publishing Co. Retrieved February 14, 2016, from http://rising.blackstar.com/wp-content/uploads/2008/11/photoethics.pdf

Baran, S. J. (2012). *Introduction to mass communication: Media literacy and culture*. New York: McGraw-Hill.

Barber, K. (1999). Quotation in the constitution of Yorùbá oral texts. *Research in African Literatures*, *30*(2), 17–41.

Barber, K. (2003). Text and performance in Africa. *Bulletin of the School of Oriental and African Studies. University of London. School of Oriental and African Studies*, *66*(3), 324–333. doi:10.1017/S0041977X03000223

Bardoel, J., & Cuilenburg, J. (2008). The Nature of Media and Communications Policy. In P.J. Fourie (Ed.), Media Studies: Policy, Management and Media Representation. Cape Town: Juta & Co. Ltd.

Bardoel, J., & Deuze, M. (2001). Network Journalism: Converging Competences of Media Professionals and Professionalism. *Australian Journalism Review*, *23*(2), 91–103.

Barendt, E., & Hitchens, L. (2000). *Media Law Cases and Materials*. Harlow: Pearson Education Limited.

Barone, M. (2015). Why Political Polls Are So Often Wrong. *The Wall Street Journal*. Retrieved from http://www.wsj.com/articles/why-political-polls-are-so-often-wrong-1447285797.

Barthes, R. (1980). Camera Lucida. Reflections on photography (R. Howard, Trans.). New York: Hill and Wang.

Barthes, R. (1984). *Camera Lucida: Reflections on Photography*. London: Fontana.

Batchen, G. (1994). Phantasm: Digital imaging and the death of photography. *Aperture*, *136*, 48.

Bauer, G. (2001, March). Namibia in the First Decade of Independence: How Democratic? *Journal of Southern African Studies*, *27*(1), 33–55. doi:10.1080/03057070120029491

Baughman, S. B. (2011). Restoring the presumption of innocence. *Ohio State Law Journal*, *72*, 724–776.

Bayley, E. (1981). *Joe McCarthy and the Press*. Madison, WI: University of Wisconsin Press.

BBC. (2004). *Fine for Ugandan radio gay show*. BBC News. Retrieved from http://news.bbc.co.uk/2/hi/africa/3712266.stm

BBC. (2010, September 15). *Egyptian newspaper under fire over altered photo*. Retrieved January 16, 2016, from http://www.bbc.com/news/wordl-middle-east-11313738

BBC. (2016, June 7). *'Leaked Report' Reveals Mass Data Fears*. Retrieved from www.bbc.com/news/technology-36469351

Beale, S. S. (2006). The news media's influence on criminal justice policy: How market-driven news promotes punitiveness. *William and Mary Law Review*, *48*, 397–481.

Beckett, C. (2010). *Globalisation, the media and UK communities*. York, UK: Joseph Rowntree Foundation.

Beech, M., & Bishop, J. (2015). Cyber-Stalking Or Just Plain Talking?: Investigating The Linguistic Properties Of Rape-Threat Messages As Compulsive Behaviours. In J. Bishop (Ed.), *Psychological And Social Implications Surrounding Internet And Gaming Addiction* (pp. 111–137). Hershey, PA: IGI Global. doi:10.4018/978-1-4666-8595-6.ch007

Bellware, K. (2015). Fox News Host Shephard Smith Apologizes for Network's Baltimore Shooting Mistake. *Huffington Post*. Retrieved from: http://www.huffingtonpost.com/2015/05/04/shephard-smith-baltimoreapology_n_7208214.html-black-female-child-in-class-was-sued-twice/

Bennett, W. L. (2004). Gatekeeping And Press-Government Relations: A Multigated Model Of News Construction. In Handbook Of Political Communication Research, (pp. 283-314). Academic Press.

Bennett, S. C. (2012). The "right to be forgotten": Reconciling EU and US perspectives. *Berkeley Journal of International Law*, *30*, 161–195.

Bennett, W. (2005). *News: The politics of illusion* (5th ed.). New York: Pearson Longman.

Bennett, W., Gressett, L., & Halton, W. (1985). Repairing the news: A case study of the news paradigm. *Journal of Communication*, *35*(2), 50–68. doi:10.1111/j.1460-2466.1985.tb02233.x

Benthall, J. (1999). The critique of intellectual property. *Anthropology Today*, *15*(6), 1–3. doi:10.2307/2678352

Berger, G. (1996). *The Internet: A Goldmine for Editors and Journalists*. Paper Presented at the World Editors Forum, Washington, DC. Retrieved 7 August from http://guyberger.ru.ac.za/fulltext/Goldmine.htm

Berger, G. (2010). *Challenges and Perspectives of Digital Migration for African Media*. Grahamstown, South Africa: Highway Africa, Media Matrix.

Berger, G. (2011). Empowering the youth as citizen journalists: A South African experience. *Journalism*, *12*(6), 708–726. doi:10.1177/1464884911405466

Berger, G. (Ed.). (2005). *Doing Digital Journalism: How Southern African Newspapers Are Using ICTs*. Grahamstown: Rhodes University.

Berkman, R. I., & Shumway, C. (2003). *Digital Dilemmas: Ethical Issues for Online Media Professionals*. London: Blackwell Publishing.

Berkowitz, D., & Beach, D. (1993). News sources and news context: The effect of routine news, conflict and proximity. *The Journalism Quarterly*, *70*(1), 4–12. doi:10.1177/107769909307000102

Bersak, D. R. (2006). *Ethics in photojournalism: Past, Present and Future* (Masters dissertation). Massachusetts Institute of Technology. Retrieved January, 12, 2016, from http://web.mit.edu/drb/Public/PhotoThesis/

Best, J. (2001a). *Damned lies and statistics*. Berkeley, CA: Academic Press.

Best, J. (2001b). *Telling the truth about damned lies and statistics. The Chronicle Review*.

Best, J. (2004). *More damned lies and statistics: How numbers confuse public issues*. Univ of California Press.

Bettig, R. V. (1996). Critical perspectives on the history and philosophy of copyright. In R. V. Bettig (Ed.), *copyrighting culture: The political economy of intellectual property*. Bolder, CO: Westview Press.

Bevan-Dye, A., & Akpojivi, U. (2015). South African Generation Students' Self-Disclosure on Facebook. *South African Journal of Psychology. Suid-Afrikaanse Tydskrif vir Sielkunde*. doi:10.1177/0081246315602645

Beyene, Z. (2011). Media use and abuse in Ethiopia. In R. S. Fortner & P. M. Fackler (Eds.), The Handbook of Global Communications and Media Ethics. Oxford, UK: Wiley-Blackwell.

Biagi, S. (2003). *Media impact: An introduction to mass media*. Thomson Wadsworth.

Bishop, J. (2014a). U R Bias Love: Using 'Bleasure' And 'Motif' As Forensic Linguistic Means To Annotate Twitter And Newsblog Comments For The Purpose Of Multimedia Forensics. *The 11th International Conference On Web Based Communities And Social Media*.

Bishop, J. (2014b). Youtube If You Want To, The Lady's Not For Blogging: Using 'Bleasures' And 'Motifs' To Support Multimedia Forensic Analyses Of Harassment By Social Media.*Oxford Cyber Harassment Research Symposium*.

Bishop, J. (2015). The Thin Blue Web - Police Crime Records Of Internet Trolling Show Chivalrous Attitudes That Can Be Resolved Through Transfer Of Powers. In P. E. Thomas, M. Srihari, & S. Kaur (Eds.), *Handbook Of Research On Cultural And Economic Impacts Of The Information Society*. Hershey, PA: IGI Global. doi:10.4018/978-1-4666-8598-7.ch004

Bitton, M. (2012). Rethinking the anti-counterfeiting trade agreement's criminal copyright enforcement measures. *The Journal of Criminal Law & Criminology*, *102*(1), 67–117.

Black, J., Steele, B., & Barney, R. (1995). *Doing Ethics in Journalism* (2nd ed.). Boston: Allyn & Bacon.

Blanchard, M. A. (Ed.). (1998). *History of the Mass Media in the United States*. Chicago, IL: Fitzroy Dearborn Publishers.

Blanchette, J.-F., & Johnson, D. G. (2002). Data retention and the panoptic society: The social benefits of forgetfulness. *The Information Society: An International Journal*, *18*(1), 33–45. doi:10.1080/01972240252818216

Blankfield, S., & Stevenson, I. (2012). Towards A Digital Spine: The Technological Methods That UK And US Publishers Are Using To Tackle The Growing Challenge Of E-Book Piracy. *Publishing Research Quarterly*, *28*(2), 79–92. doi:10.1007/s12109-012-9265-4

Bletchly, R. (2014). *From surrogate dogs to adopted pigs, 26 animals that looked out for each other*. Retrieved from http://www.mirror.co.uk/news/world-news/surrogate-dogs-adopted-pigs-26-3731138

Bloy, D. (2007). *Media Law*. London: Sage.

Boateng, B. (2011). *The copyright thing doesn't work here: Adinkra and Kente cloth and intellectual property in Ghana*. Minneapolis, MN: University of Minnesota Press. doi:10.5749/minnesota/9780816670024.001.0001

Bollyky, T. (2013, April). *Why chemotherapy that costs $70,000 in the US costs $2,500 in India*. The Atlantic Group.

Bonde, B.N. (n.d.). *Mass Media and Journalism on the Edge in Violent Conflicts - Media Freedom or Social Responsibility*. Academic Press.

Boon, M. (2011). Digital mana: on the source of the infinite proliferation of copies in contemporary culture. In K. McLoed & R. Kuenzli (Eds.), *Cutting Across Media: Appropriation Art, Interventionist Collage and Copyright Law* (pp. 24–37). Durham, NC: Duke University Press. doi:10.1215/9780822393214-002

Bowers, J. O. (2013). *American and Norwegian press' approaches to identification of criminal suspects or arrestees: The public's right to know versus the private citizen's right to privacy, reputation, and presumption of innocence* (Unpublished master's thesis). University of Oregon.

Boyle, P. (1992). *Standards for photography's cutting edge*. Washington Journalism Review.

Brandtzaeg, P. B., Luders, M., Spangeberg, J., Rath-Wiggins, L., & Folstad, A. (2016). Emerging Journalistic Verification Practices Concerning Social Media. *Journalism Practice*, *10*(3), 323–342. doi:10.1080/17512786.2015.1020331

Brassell, K., & Martin, K. (2013). *Banking on IP?* Newport, UK: The Intellectual Property Office.

Bräuchler, B. (2013). *Cyberidentities at War: The Moluccan Conflict on the Internet*. New York: Berghahn Books.

Breed, W. (1955). Social control in the newsroom: A functional analysis. *Social Forces*, *33*(4), 326–335. doi:10.2307/2573002

Brewer, D. (2011). *The Importance of Fact-Checking for Journalists*. Retrieved from 16 August 2016.http://www.mediahelpingmedia.org/training-resources/journalism-basics/640-fact-checking-separates-journalism-from-rumour-and-gossip

Bromley, D. B. (1990). Academic Contribution to Psychological Counselling: A Philosophy of Science for the Study of Individual Cases. *Counselling Psychology Quarterly*, *3*(3), 299–307. doi:10.1080/09515079008254261

Brosius, H. B., & Eps, P. (1995). Prototyping through key events: News selection in the case of violence against aliens and asylum seekers in Germany. *European Journal of Communication*, *10*(10), 391–412. doi:10.1177/0267323195010003005

Brown, J., Bybee, C., Wearden, S., & Murdock Straughan, D. (1987). Invisible power: Newspaper news sources and the limits of diversity. *The Journalism Quarterly*, *64*(1), 45–54. doi:10.1177/107769908706400106

Brown, M. (1998). Can culture be copyrighted? *Current Anthropology*, *39*(2), 193–222. doi:10.1086/204721

Brown, M. (2003). *Who Owns Native Culture?* Cambridge, MA: Harvard University Press.

Bruneau, M. (2010). Diasporas, transnational spaces and communities. In R. Bauböck & T. Faist (Eds.), *Diaspora and transnationalism: concepts, theories and methods* (pp. 35–49). Amsterdam: Amsterdam University Press.

Bugeja, M. (2008). *Living ethics: Across media platforms*. New York, NY: Oxford University Press.

Buller, D. B., & Burgoon, J. K. (2005). *Interpersonal Deception Theory. In Readings in Persuasion, Social Influence, and Compliance Gaining*. Allyn & Bacon.

Bureau of International Information Program. (2010). *Media Law: Handbook Series*. New York: United States Department of State.

Bureau of Public Information. (2005). *Traditional knowledge*. Available at www.unesco.org/links

Burleigh, M. (2009). *Blood and Rage, A cultural history of Terrorism*. London: Harper Perennial.

Burns, Y. (2001). *Communications Law*. Durban: Butterworths.

Business Dictionary. (n.d.). Retrieved February 20, 2016, from http://www.businessdictionary.com/definition/code-of-ethics.html

Buttry, S. (2013). Verification Fundamentals: Rules to Live By. In *Verification Handbook: additional Materials to Verifying Digital Content for Emergency Coverage*. Retrieved 14 September 2016 from http://verificationhandbook.com/downloads/verification.handbook.pdf

Cameroon Radio Television. (2015). *News on the fight against Boko Haram*. Author.

Cameroon Tribune. (2015). *The fight against Boko Haram continuous.* N.0.10992/7191

Cameroon Tribune. (2016). *Our country has realized the value of information.* N.0.11087/7286

Campbell, D. (2014). *The Integrity of the Image. A World Press Photo Research Project.* Published by the World Press Photo Academy.

Carey, J. (2002, Spring). What does "good work" in journalism look like? *Nieman Reports*, 79-81.

Carpenter, S. (2010). A study of content diversity in online citizen journalism and online newspaper articles. *New Media & Society*, *12*(12), 1064–1084. doi:10.1177/1461444809348772

Cass, T. M. (1998). *A comparison of the views of South African and American photo journalists to the digital manipulation of news photographs* (Unpublished Masters dissertation). Rhodes University, South Africa.

Cassidy, W. (2006). Gatekeeping similar for online, print journalists. *Newspaper Research Journal*, *27*, 6–23.

Castells, M. (1999). The information age. *Journal of Economy, Society and Couture*, *1*(3).

Cathcart, B. (2011, October 8). The ordeal of Christopher Jefferies. *Financial Times Magazine*. Retrieved from http://www.ft.com/cms/s/2/22eac290-eee2-11e0-959a-00144feab49a.html

CBCnews. (2015). *Canada election 2015: Online polling defended, while some still question reliability.* Retrieved from http://www.cbc.ca/news/politics/canada-election-2015-grenier-duffy-aug21-1.3200371.

Chakrabarty, D. (2000). *Provincializing Europe: Postcolonial Thought and Historical Difference.* Princeton, NJ: Princeton University Press.

Chang, H.-H. (2004). Fake logos, fake theory, fake globalisation. *Inter-Asia Cultural Studies*, *5*(2), 222–236. doi:10.1080/1464937042000236720

Chari, T. (2013). How new media technologies are impacting ethical practices: Perceptions of Zimbabwean journalists. *International Journal on Media and Communications*, *1*(1), 66-74.

Chari, T. (2007). Rethinking Ethical Issues in African Media. *African Identities*, *5*(1), 39–60. doi:10.1080/14725840701253704

Chari, T. (2009). Ethical Challenges Facing Zimbabwean Media in the Context of the Internet. *Global Media Journal*, *3*(1), 46–79.

Chari, T. (2013). New Communication Technologies and Journalism Ethics in Zimbabwe: Practices and Malpractices. *Online Journal of Communication and Media Technologies*, *3*(2), 112–136.

Cheeseman, N. (2014). *Lies, damned lies, and opinion polls.* Retrieved from http://democracyinafrica.org/lies-damned-lies-opinion-polls.

Chiumbu, S. (2010). Media, alternativism and power: The political economy of community media in South Africa. In N. Hyde-Clarke (Ed.), The Citizen in Communication (pp. 115–137). Claremont, South Africa: Juta.

Christakis, N. A., & Fowler, J. H. (2011). *Connected: the amazing power of social networks and how they shape our lives.* HarperPress London.

Christians, G. (2010). The Ethics of Universal Being. In Media Ethics Beyond Borders: A Global Perspective (pp. 6-23). New York: Routledge.

Christians, C. G. (2007). Utilitarianism in media ethics and its discontents. *Journal of Mass Media Ethics*, *22*(2-3), 113–131. doi:10.1080/08900520701315640

Christians, C. G., Fackler, M., McKee, K. B., Kreshel, P. J., & Woods, R. H. (2009). *Media Ethics: Cases and Moral Reasoning* (8th ed.). Allyn & Bacon.

Christians, C. G., Fackler, M., McKee, K. B., Kreshel, P. J., & Woods, R. H. (2009). *Media Ethics: Cases and moral reasoning*. Boston: Pearson Educarion, Inc.

Christians, C. G., Rotzoll, K. B., & Fackler, M. (1991). *Media ethics: Cases & moral reasoning* (3rd ed.). New York, NY: Longman.

Chung, R. (2012). *The Freedom to Publish Opinion Poll Results. A worldwide update of 2012*. Academic Press.

Church, S. A., & Onyebuchi, C. A. (2012). Quantitative and Qualitative Analysis of Audience Perception of the Effects of Public Opinion Polls in Nigeria's Nascent Democracy. *International Journal of Humanities and Social Science*, *2*(15), 231–244.

Clark, T. (2015). New research suggests why general election polls were so inaccurate. *The Guardian*. Retrieved from http://www.theguardian.com/politics/2015/nov/13/new-research-general-election-polls-inaccurate.

Coleman, E. G. (2010). Ethnographic approaches to digital media. *Annual Review of Anthropology*, *39*(1), 487–505. doi:10.1146/annurev.anthro.012809.104945

Collier, G. (1995). Information Privacy. *Information Management & Computer Security*, *3*(1), 41–45. doi:10.1108/09685229510792979

Comaroff, J., & Comaroff, J. (2000). *Millenial Capitalism and the Culture of Noeliberalism*. Durham, NC: Duke University Press.

Comaroff, J., & Comaroff, J. (2009). *Ethnicity, Inc*. Chicago: Chicago University Press. doi:10.7208/chicago/9780226114736.001.0001

Commonwealth Human Rights Initiative (CHRI). (2007). *Analysis of the Government of the Republic of Namibia: Revised Information Policy, 2006*. New Delhi: CHRI.

Connor, K. (2012). *Photojournalism ethics on shifting technological ground*. Retrieved February 4, 2016, from http://www.fourandsix.com/blog/2012/2/13/photojournalism=ethics-on-shifting-technological-ground.html

Conroy-Krutz, J. (2013). Information and ethnic politics in Africa. *British Journal of Political Science*, *43*(02), 345–373.

Convention on Biological Diversity. (2010). *Traditional knowledge, innovation and practices*. Available at www.cbdint/traditional

Coombe, R. (1997). The demonic place of the 'not there': Trademark rumors in the postindustrial imaginary. In A. Gupta & J. Ferguson (Eds.), *Culture – power – place: Explorations in critical anthropology* (pp. 249–274). doi:10.1215/9780822382089-011

Coombe, R. (1998). *The cultural life of intellectual properties: Authorship, appropriation, and the law*. Durham, NC: Duke University Press. doi:10.1215/9780822382492

Coombe, R. (2003). Fear, hope and longing for the future of authorship and a revitalized public domain in global regimes of intellectual property. *De Paul Law Review*, *52*, 1–15.

Correa, C. M., & Li, X. (2009). *International property enforcement: International perspectives*. Cheltenham, UK: Edward Elgar Publishing.

Couldry, N. (2010). Media Ethics: Towards a Framework for Media Producers and Media Consumers. In Media Ethics Beyond Borders: A Global Perspective (pp. 42-58). New York: Routledge.

Coverage [VIDEO]. (n.d.). Retrieved on 7th November 2015 from http://www.hngn.com/articles/89701/20150504/baltimore-shooting-shepard-smith-fox-news-apologize-for-false-account-coverage-video.htm

Cowan, J. (2006). Culture and Rights after *Culture and Rights. American Anthropologist, 108*(1), 9–24. doi:10.1525/aa.2006.108.1.9

Cowan, J., Dembour, M.-B., & Wilson, R. (Eds.). (2001). *Culture and rights: Anthropological perspectives*. Cambridge, UK: Cambridge University Press. doi:10.1017/CBO9780511804687

Cowling, D. (2015). Election 2015: How the opinion polls got it wrong. *BBC News*. Retrieved from http://www.bbc.com/news/uk-politics-32751993.

Cranberg, G. (2003). No shortage of codes. *The American Editor, 78*(6), 13.

Craufurd Smith, R., Tambini, D., & Morisi, D. (2012). *Regulating Media Plurality And Media Power In The 21st Century*. Academic Press.

Creech, K. (2007). *Electronic media law and regulation*. London: Focal Press.

Crone, T. (2002). *Law and the Media*. Oxford, UK: Focal Press.

CRTV. (2015). *Fighting Boko Haram: A unity march in the agenda*. CRTV.

Culnan, M. (1993). How did they get my Name? An Exploratory Investigation of Consumer Attitudes towards Secondary Information Use. *Management Information Systems Quarterly, 17*(3), 341–363. doi:10.2307/249775

Culnan, M., & Armstrong, P. (1999). Information Privacy Concerns, Procedural Fairness and Impersonal Trust: An Empirical Investigation. *Organization Science, 10*(1), 104–115. doi:10.1287/orsc.10.1.104

Dahlgren, P. (1996). Media logic in cyberspace: repositioning journalism and its publics. *Javnost/The Public, 3*, 59-72.

Dahlgren, P. (2000). Media citizens and civic culture. In M. Gurevitch & J. Curran (Eds.), *Mass Media and society* (3rd ed.). London: Edward Arnold.

Dahlgren, P. (2000). The Internet and the democratisation of civic culture. *Political Communication, 17*(4), 335–340. doi:10.1080/10584600050178933

Dahlgren, P. (2005). *Internet, public spheres and political communication*. London: Routledge.

Dahl, R. (2000). *On democracy*. New Haven, CT: Yale University Press.

Dalitso. (2012). *Examining Parody of Opinion Polls; Sticking to Ballot Power*. Retrieved from http://dalitsopublicforum.blogspot.co.za/2012/12/we-pride-in-joyce-banda-and-henry.html.

David, A., & Gordon, J. M. (2011). *Controversies in Media Ethics*. New York: Routledge.

Davies, N. (2009). *Flat Earth News*. London: Vintage.

De Jong, F. (2007). A masterpiece of masquerading: Contradictions of conservation in intangible heritage. In F. de Jong & M. Rowlands (Eds.), *Reclaiming heritage: Alternative imaginaries of memory in West Africa* (pp. 161–184). Walnut Creek: Left Coast Press.

DeGeorge, R. T. (n.d.). 14 Intellectual property rights. In G. B. George & L. B. Tom (Eds.), *The Oxford handbook of business ethics*. Oxford, UK: Oxford University Press.

Deutsch, K. (1963). *The Nerves of Government*. New York: The Free Press.

Deuze, M. (2004). What is multimedia journalism? *Journalism Studies*, *5*(2), 139–152. doi:10.1080/1461670042000211131

Diawara, M. (2016). Breaking the contract? Handling intangible cultural goods among different generations in Mali. In U. Röschenthaler & M. Diawara (Eds.), Copyright Africa: How intellectual property, media and markets transform immaterial cultural goods. Canon Pyon: Sean Kingston.

Dinev, T., & Hart, P. (2006). Privacy Concerns and Levels of Information Exchange AnEmpirical Investigation of Intended E-Services Use. *E-Service Journal*, *4*(3), 25–60. doi:10.2979/ESJ.2006.4.3.25

Dionne, & Dulani, B. (2014). On the eve of Malawi's election. *The Washington Post*. Retrieved from https://www.washingtonpost.com/news/monkey-cage/wp/2014/05/19/on-the-eve-of-malawis-election.

Dionne, & Mann, T. E. (2003). *Polling & Public Opinion: The good, the bad, and the ugly*. Retrieved from http://www.brookings.edu/research/articles/2003/06/summer-elections-mann.

Dirbaba, B. O. (2010). The growing influence of bribery in Ethiopian Journalism. *African Communication Research*, (1), 207-231.

Doctorow, C. (2008). Online Censorship Hurts Us All. *Meanjin*, *67*(3), 14.

Dombo, S. (2014). *Daily Struggles: Private Print Media, The State, and Democratic Governance in Zimbabwe in the Case of the African Daily News (1956-1964) and The Daily News (1999-2003)* (Unpublished PhD Thesis). School of Social Sciences, University of Kwazulu-Natal, Durban.

Dominick, J. R. (2002). *The dynamics of mass communication*. Madison, WI: McGraw Hill.

Dominick, R. J. (1993). *The Dynamics of Mass Communication* (4th ed.). New York: McGraw-hill Inc.

Domke, D., Watts, M., Shah, D., & Pan, D. (1999). The politics of Conservative Elites and the Liberal Media argument. *Journal of Communication*, *49*(4), 35–58. doi:10.1111/j.1460-2466.1999.tb02816.x

Donsbach, W. (2001). *Who's afraid of election polls?: Normative and empirical arguments for the freedom of pre-election surveys*. Foundation for Information.

Du Pisani, A. (2007, September 10). Power and Democratic Space. *Die Republikein*, 10-11.

Dunleavy, D. (2005). *Camera phones prevail: Citizen shutterbugs and the London bombings*. Retrieved February 22, 2016, from http://www.digitaljournalist.org/issue0507/dunleavy.html

Dutfield, G. (2003). *Protecting traditional knowledge and folklore*. Retrieved from http://www.ictsd.org/iprsonline

Dworkin, G. (1961). Privacy and the Press. *The Modern Law Review*, *24*(1), 185–189.

Edick, D. A. (1998). Regulation of Pornography on the Internet in theUnited States and the United Kingdom: AComparative Analysis. *Boston College International and Comparative Law Review*, *21*, 437–460.

Eisenlohr, P. (2011). The anthropology of media and the question of ethnic and religious pluralism. *Social Anthropology*, *19*(1), 40–55. doi:10.1111/j.1469-8676.2010.00136.x

Ekwueme, A. C. & Obayi, P. M. (2012). Boko Haram Assault on Nigeria: Towards Effective Mass Media Response. *New Media and Mass Communication*, (5).

Elbagir, N. (2013). *Kenyans armed and ready to vote*. Retrieved from http://www.digitaljournal.com/article/344615

Electoral Act. (2010). *With 2011 Amendments*. Abuja: Panaf press.

Elliott, G. D. (2008). *Statement on Provisional Policy Framework on the Development of Access to Information Legislation for Namibia Office of the Prime Minister 18 August 2008 Administrative Justice Conference, Windhoek*. Unpublished Paper.

Emery, C. (1994). Public opinion polling in Canada. Canada. Library of Parliament. Research Branch: Library of Parliament, Research Branch.

Encyclopaedia Britannica. (2015). *The New York Times*. Retrieved 12 September 2016, from https://global.britannica.com/topic/The-New-York-Times

Entman, R. B. (1993). Framing: Toward clarification of a fractured paradigm. *Journal of Communication*, *43*(4), 51–58. doi:10.1111/j.1460-2466.1993.tb01304.x

Entman, R. M., & Gross, K. A. (2008). Race to judgment: Stereotyping media and criminal defendants. *Law and Contemporary Problems*, *71*, 93–133.

Ericsson Mobility Report. (2015). *On the pulse of the networked society*. Retrieved from http://www.ericsson.com/res/docs/2015/mobility-report/ericsson-mobility-report-nov-2015.pdf

Esipisu, I., & Kariithi, N. (2007). New media development in Africa. *Global Media Journal*, *1*(1), 21–63.

Esomar, & Wapor. (2014). *Esomar/Wapor Guideline on Opinion Polls and Published Surveys*. Retrieved from http://www.esomar.org/uploads/public/knowledge-and-standards/codes-and-guidelines/ESOMAR-WAPOR-Guideline-on-Opinion-Polls-and-Published-Surveys-August-2014.docx.

Ess, C. (2009). *Digital Media Ethics*. Cambridge, UK: Polity Press.

Ettema, J., Whitney, D., & Wackman, D. (1987, 1997). Professional mass communicators. In D. Berkowitz (Ed.), Social meanings of news. Thousand Oaks, CA: SAGE Publications.

Etzioni, A. (1999). *The limits of privacy*. New York: Basic Books.

Ewi, M. (2013). *Terrorism and the threat radical Islam poses to Cameroon*. ISS Today.

Eytan, G. (2009). Media and Conflict Resolution: A Framework for Analysis. *Marquette Law, 93*(87).

Fabos, B., Childers, L. C., & Golitsynskiy, S. (2015). Digital Literacy, Public History, And FORTEPAN. *Media Education For A Digital Generation, 74*, 244.

Facebook. (2014). *Newsroom*. Retrieved from http://newsroom.fb.com/company-info/

Fackler, P. M., Obonyo, L., Terpstra, M., & Okaalet, E. (2011). Media and post election violence in Kenya. In R. S. Fortner & P. M. Fackler (Eds.),The Handbook of Global Communications and Media Ethics. Oxford, UK: Wiley-Blackwell.

Fadakinte, M. M. (2014). Nigeria and Election Crises: Debating Causes. International Journal of Humanities and Social Science, 4(6), 74-96.

Fahmy, S., Fosdick, S.B. & Johnson, T.J. (2005). Is seeing believing? A survey of magazine professionals' practices and attitudes towards ethical standards for photographs. *Journal of Magazine and New Media Research,* 1-8.

Farah, P.D., & Tremolada, R. (2014, March). Desirability of commodification of intangible cultural heritage: The unsatisfying role of intellectual property rights. *Transnational Dispute Management, 11*(2).

Farhi, P. (2015). *Fox News erroneously reports that police in Baltimore shot man.* Retrieved from https://www.washingtonpost.com/lifestyle/style/as-it-turned-out-nobody-was-shot-fox

Farid, H. (2009). Digital Imaging. *Encyclopedia of Perception*. Retrieved March 3, 2016, from http://www.cs.dartmouth.edu/farid/downloads/publications/digitalimaging09.pdf

Fayoyin, A. (2011). Promoting children's rights through the new media: The Nigerian experience. *Journal of Communication*, *2*(2), 57–65.

Fayoyin, A., & Ngwainmbi, E. (2015). Use and misuse of data in advocacy, media and opinion polls in Africa: Realities, challenges and opportunities. *Journal of Development and Communication Studies*, *3*(2), 528–545.

Federal Government of Nigeria. (1999). *1999 Constitution of the Federal Republic of Nigeria*. Lagos: Federal Government Press.

Federal Government of Nigeria. (2015). *Cybercrimes Prohibition Prevention Act 2015*. Lagos: Federal Government Press.

Federal Republic of Nigeria. (2006). *National Action Plan for the Promotion and Protection of Human Rights in Nigeria 2006*. Lagos: Federal Government Press.

Federman, M. (2006). *The cultural paradox of the global village*. Keynote Speech at McLuhan Programme in Culture and Technology, University of Toronto.

Fedler, F., Bender, R-J., Davenport, L., & Drager, W. M. (2005). Reporting for the media (8th ed.). New York: Oxford University Press.

Feltoe, G. (2002). *A Guide to Media Law in Zimbabwe*. Harare: Legal Resources Foundation. Retrieved from http://www.kubatana.net/docs/resour/021101mediaguide_ gf.pdf

Feltoe, G. (2002). *A Guide to Press Law in Zimbabwe*. Harare: Legal Resources Foundation.

Finnegan, R. (2007). *The oral and beyond: Doing things with words in Africa*. Oxford, UK: James Currey & Chicago University Press.

Fisher, S. D. (2015). Predictable and unpredictable changes in party support: A method for long-range daily election forecasting from opinion polls. *Journal of Elections, Public Opinion, and Parties*, *25*(2), 137–158. doi:10.1080/17457289.2014.952732

Fishman, M. (1980). *Manufacturing the news*. Austin, TX: University of Texas Press.

Fleming-Rife, A., & Proffitt, J. M.Board of Education. (2004). The More Public School Reform Changes, The More It Stays The Same: A Framing Analysis Of The Newspaper Coverage Of Brown V. Board Of Education. *The Journal of Negro Education*, *73*(3), 239–254. doi:10.2307/4129609

Fletcher, J. F. (1966). *Situation Ethics: the New Morality*. Philadelphia: Westminster Press.

Ford, N. L. (1998). *Photojournalism vs Journalism*. Retrieved March 14, 2016, from http://nlford.com/career/journalism.shtml>

Ford, R. (2015, November 2). Judges will Get Veto in Attempt to Salvage Snooper's Charter. *The Times*, pp. 1A, 2A.

Forde, S. (n.d.). *John Locke and the Natural Law and Natural Rights Tradition*. University of North Texas. Retrieved from http://www.nlnrac.org

Foreman, G. (2016). *The Ethical Journalist: Making Responsible Decisions in the Digital Age* (2nd ed.). West Sussex, UK: Wiley Blackwell.

Forges, A. D. (2002). *Silencing the Voices of Hate in Rwanda.* In M. E. Price & M. Thompson (Eds.), *Forging Peace* (pp. 236–258). Edinburgh, UK: Edinburgh University Press.

Fosdick, S., & Fahmy, S. (2003). *Punctuation and Epistemic Honesty: Do Photos Need What Words Have?* Paper presented at the Association for Education in Journalism and Mass Communication Conference, Kansas City, MO.

Foster, R. (2008). Commodities, brands, love and kula. *Anthropological Theory*, *8*(1), 9–25. doi:10.1177/1463499607087492

Foster, S. (2003). *Human Rights & Civil Liberties*. London: Pearson.

Fourie, P. J. (2010). Moral Philosophy as the Foundation of Media Theory: Questioning African Ubuntuism as a Framework. In Media Ethics Beyond Borders: A Global Perspective (pp. 105-123). New York: Routledge.

Fourie, P. J. (Ed.). (2007). *Media Studies: Media History, Media and Society* (2nd ed.). Cape Town: Juta & Co.

Franklin, B. (2013). Editorial. *Digital Journalism*, *1*(1), 1–5. doi:10.1080/21670811.2012.740264

Friend, C., & Singer, J. (2007). *Online Journalism Ethics: Traditions and Transitions*. Armonk, NY: E Sharpe.

Fullerton, R. S., & Patterson, M. J. (2013). Crime news and privacy: Comparing crime reporting in Sweden, the Netherlands, and the United Kingdom. In J. Petley (Ed.), *Media and public shaming: Drawing the boundaries of disclosure*. New York: I. B. Tauris & Co.

Gaingos, C. J. (2008). *Towards a New Media Law in Independent Regulatory System* (Unpublished LLB Dissertation). University of Nambia. Retrieved 8 August 2016, from http://wwwisis.unam.na/theses/gaingos2008.pdf

Galtung, J. (1998). *High Road, Low Road: Charting the Course for Peace Journalism*. 7 TRACK TWO 7.

Gandy, O. (1982). *Beyond agenda setting: information subsidies and public policy*. Norwood, NJ: Ablex Publishing.

Gans, H. (1980). *Deciding what's news: A study of CBS Evening News, NBC Nightly News, Newsweek, and Time*. New York: Random House.

Gans, H. (2003). *Democracy and the news*. New York: Oxford University Press.

García-Avilés, J. A. (2014). Online newsrooms as communities of practice: Exploring digital journalists applied ethics. *Journal of Mass Media Ethics*, *29*(4), 258–272. doi:10.1080/08900523.2014.946600

Gathigah, M. (2013). Kenya's Electoral Opinion Polling Marred by Suspicion. *Inter Press Service*. Retrieved from http://www.ipsnews.net/2013/02/kenyas-electoral-opinion-polling-marred-by-suspicion.

Gauba, O. P. (2003). *An introduction to political theory*. New Delhi: Palgrave Macmillan India Ltd.

Gaziano, C. (1987). News people's ideology and the credibility debate. *Newspaper Research Journal*, *9*, 1–18.

Gebremedhim, S. (2010). Media Ethics in Ethiopia. In Media Ethics Beyond Borders: A Global Perspective (pp. 142-146). New York: Routledge.

Geschiere, P. (2009). *The perils of belonging: Autochthony, citizenship, and exclusion in Africa & Europe*. Chicago: The University of Chicago Press. doi:10.7208/chicago/9780226289663.001.0001

Gewald, J.-B. (2004). Global media and violence in Africa. In W. van Binsbergen & R. van Dijk (Eds.), *Situating globality: African agency in the appropriation of global culture* (pp. 90–106). Leiden: Brill.

Gillwald, A., Moyo, M., & Stork, C. (2012). *Understanding What is Happening in ICT in South Africa: A Supply-and-Demand-Side Analysis of the ICT Sector*. Cape Town: ResearchICTAfrica.net

Gladney, G., & Erlich, M. C. (1996). Cross-media response to digital manipulation of still and moving images. *Journal of Broadcasting & Electronic Media*, *40*(4), 496–508. doi:10.1080/08838159609364371

Global Finance. (2013). *The Poorest Countries in the World*. Retrieved from http://www.gfmag.com/component/content/article/119-economic-data/12537-the-poorest-countries-in-the-world.html#axzz2u1qY1Raz

Godler, Y., & Reich, Z. (2015). Journalistic Evidence: Cross-Verification as a Constituent of Mediated Knowledge. *Journalism*, 1–17.

Goffman, E. (1974). *Frame analysis*. Boston: New England University Press.

Gonzalez, F. (n.d.). *Values and Ethics for the 21st Century*. BBVA Foundation. Retrieved July 5, 2016, from http://www.bbvaopenmind.com

Goode, L. (2009). Social news, citizen journalism and democracy. *New Media & Society*, *11*(11), 1287–1305. doi:10.1177/1461444809341393

Goodman, J. (2005). *Berber culture on the world stage: From village to video*. Bloomington, IN: Indiana University Press.

Goodwin, C. (1991). Privacy: Recognition of a Consumer Right. *Journal of Public Policy & Marketing*, *10*(1), 149–166.

Górecki, M. A. (2015). Age, Experience and the Contextual Determinants of Turnout: A Deeper Look at the Process of Habit Formation in Electoral Participation. *Journal of Elections, Public Opinion, and Parties*, *25*(4), 425–443. doi:10.1080/17457289.2015.1028411

Gosh, A. (2013). Censorship through copyright: From print to digital media. *Social Scientist*, *41*(1-2), 41–58.

Gramsci, A. (1971). *Selections from Prison Notebooks* (Q. Hoare & G. Nowell-Smith, Trans. & Eds.). London: Lawrence and Wishart.

Greenfield, S. (2014). The English enlightenment and "the economy": How some men with a vision created the modern world and its problems. In D. Wood (Ed.), *Production, consumption, business and the economy: Structural ideals and moral realities* (pp. 1–28). Bingley: Emerald. doi:10.1108/S0190-128120140000034001

Greenhalgh, C., & Rogers, M. (2010). *The nature and role of intellectual property: Innovation, intellectual property and economic growth*. Princeton University Press.

Greer, J. D., & Gosen, J. D. (2002). How much is too much? Assessing levels of digital alteration as factors in public perception of news credibility. *News Photographer*, *4*(10), 4–13.

Gross, R., & Acquisti, A. (2005). Information revelation and privacy in online social networking. In S. De Capitani di Vimercati & R. Dingledine (Eds.), *Privacy issues in practice: 2005 ACM Workshop on Privacy in the Electronic Society* (pp. 71–80). New York: ACM Press.

Grossman, M., & Joynt Kumar, M. (1981). *Portraying the President: The White House and the News Media*. Baltimore, MD: John Hopkins University Press.

GSMA. (2015). *The mobile economy*. Retrieved from http://www.gsmamobileeconomy.com/GSMA_Global_Mobile_Economy_Report_2015.pdf

Guchera, C. (2016). African journalists must do more to protect themselves online. *International Journalists' Network*. Retrieved from http://ijnet.org/en/blog/african-journalists-must-do-more-protect-themselves-online

Habassi, H. (2016). *New Media, New Rules: The impact of internet defamation and Press freedom in Tanzania* (Doctoral thesis). St Augustine University of Tanzania.

Habermas, J. (1989). *The structural transformation of the public sphere: an inquiry into a category of bourgeois society*. Cambridge, MA: MIT Press.

Hackett, R. (1984). Decline of a paradigm? Bias and objectivity in news media studies. *Critical Studies in Mass Communication, 1*(3), 329–359. doi:10.1080/15295038409360036

Hallin, D., Manoff, R., & Weddle, J. (1993). Sourcing patterns of national security reporters. *The Journalism Quarterly, 70*(4), 753–766. doi:10.1177/107769909307000402

Hall, S. (1980). Encoding and Decoding. In S. Hall et al. (Eds.), *Culture, Media and Language*. London: Hutchison.

Hall, S. (1997). Representation: Cultural Representations and Signifying Practices. London, Thousand Oakes. *Sage (Atlanta, Ga.)*, 257–261.

Hallstatt. (2011). *Kopierte Idylle: Hallstatt in China*. Retrieved January 12, 2016, from http://www.nachrichten.at/oberoesterreich/Kopierte-Idylle-Hallstatt-in-China;art4,651557

Hallstatt. (2012a). *Begutachtung der Hallstatt-Kopie*. Retrieved January 12, 2016, from http://ooe.orf.at/news/stories/2519297/

Hallstatt. (2012b). *Besuch bei der chinesischen Hallstattkopie*. Retrieved January 12, 2016, from http://www.nachrichten.at/oberoesterreich/Besuch-bei-der-chinesischen-Hallstattkopie;art4,893576

Hallstatt. (2012c). *Hallstatt-Double: China weiht nachgebautes Alpendorf ein*. Retrievend June 4, 2012, from http://www.spiegel.de

Hallstatt. (2012d). *Auch Huizhou hat jetzt ein Hallstatt. China-Kopie mit "Austrian Flair" feierlich eröffnet: Jetzt wird weiter abgekupfert*. Retrieved January 12, 2016, from http://www.oe24.at/welt/Auch-Huizhou-hat-jetzt-ein-Hallstatt/67825240)

Hallstatt. (2014a). *Bitte lächeln! Hallstatt im Fokus der Asiaten*. Retrieved January 12, 2016, from http://www.nachrichten.at/oberoesterreich/Bitte-laecheln-Hallstatt-im-Fokus-der-Asiaten;art4,1526204

Hallstatt. (2014b). *Die Karawanen sind furchtbar, aber Hallstatt lebt vom Tourismus*. Retrieved January 12, 2016, from http://www.nachrichten.at/oberoesterreich/Die-Karawanen-sind-furchtbar-aber-Hallstatt-lebt-vom-Tourismus;art4,1526556

Hamid, A. M., & Baba, I. M. (2014). Resolving Nigeria's 'Boko Haram' Insurgence: What Role for the Media?. *The International Conference on Communication and Media*. Elsevier Ltd. doi:10.1016/j.sbspro.2014.10.249

Hancock, L. (1998, July/August). Naming kid criminals. *Columbia Journalism Review*, 18–19.

Hanson, G. (2004). Identifying juvenile crime suspects: A survey of Ohio TV stations, newspapers. *Newspaper Research Journal, 25*, 121–125.

Haque, R., & Harrop, M. (2004). *Comparative Government & Politics* (6th ed.). New York: Palgrave Macmillan.

Harrington, S. A. (1996). The effects of codes of ethics and personal denial of responsibility on computer abuse judgements and intentions. *Management Information Systems Quarterly, 20*(3), 257–278. doi:10.2307/249656

Harris, C. R. (1991). Digitization and manipulation of news photographs. *Journal of Mass Media Ethics, 6*(3), 164–174. doi:10.1207/s15327728jmme0603_4

Harrison, S. (1992). Ritual as intellectual property. *Man, 27*(2), 225-244.

Hasan, S. (2013). *Mass Communication: Principles and Concepts* (2nd ed.). New Delhi: CBS Publishers and Distributors.

Hasan, S. (2013). *Mass communication: Principles and concepts*. New Delhi: CBS Publishers and Distributors PVT Ltd.

Heuva, W. E. (1993). Resistance in Print: The Nationalist Press during the Liberation Struggle. Ecquid Novi, 14(1), 94-104.

Heuva, W. E. (2010). *Transforming communication in a changing milieu: Challenges and contradictions of reform in Namibia*. Köln, Germany: LAP Lambert Academic Publishers AG & Co. KG.

Heuva, W. E. (2012). State invasion of privacy in the ICT surveillance legislation: The case of Namibia. *Africa Communication Research*, *5*(3), 261–282.

Hilbert, M. (2015). *Digital Technology and social change*. Retrieved from https://www.canvas.instructure.com/courses1949415

Hillygus, D. S. (2011). The evolution of election polling in the United States. *Public Opinion Quarterly*, *75*(5), 962–981. doi:10.1093/poq/nfr054

Himelfarb, S., & Chabalowski, M. (2008). *Media, Conflict Prevention and Peacebuilding: Mapping the Edges*. United States Institute for Peace. Retrieved from http://www.usip.org/resources/media-conflict-prevention-and-peacebuilding-mapping-edges

Hirsch, E., & Strathern, M. (Eds.). (2004). *Transactions and creations: Property debates and the stimulus in Melanesia*. New York: Berghahn.

Hochhauser, M. (2000). *Why I Stopped Shopping at Amazon.com: A Reading Expert Sound Off*. Retrieved from http://www.privacyrights.org/print/ar/amazon.htm

Hodges, L. (1994). The journalist and privacy. *Journal of Mass Media Ethics*, *9*(4), 197–212. doi:10.1207/s15327728jmme0904_1

Hofer, M., & Swan, K. O. (2005). Digital image manipulation: A compelling means to engage students in discussion of point of view and perspective. *Contemporary Issues in Technology & Teacher Education*, *5*(3/4), 290–299.

Hoffman, B. (2006). *Inside terrorism (rev. and exp. ed.)*. New York: Columbia University Press.

Hoijer, B. (1996). The Dilemmas of Documentary Violence in Television. The Nordic Review of Nordic Research on Media & Communication, 1(1), 50-62.

Holtz-Bacha, C. (2012). *Opinion polls and the media in Germany: A productive but critical relationship. In Opinion Polls and the Media* (pp. 93–112). Springer. doi:10.1057/9780230374959_5

Horner, D. S. (2015). *Understanding Media Ethics*. London: SAGE.

Hot News (2015). *Fight against insecurity: Police Force sensitizes citizens, distributes practical guides.* N° 062/RDDJ/J06/BASC. No 224 of 24/8/2015.

Housley, E. E. (2002). *Evaluating the effectiveness of newspaper codes of ethics: A Star-Telegram case study* (Masters Dissertation). Texas Christian University. Retrieved June 28, 2016, from http://citeseerx.psu.edu/viewdoc/download?doi=10.1.1.582

Hsieh, H. F., & Shannon, S. E. (2005). Three approaches to qualitative content analysis. *Qualitative Health Research*, *15*(9), 1277–1288. doi:10.1177/1049732305276687 PMID:16204405

Huang, E. S. (2001). Readers perception of digital alteration in photojournalism. *Journalism Communication Monographs*, *3*(3), 149–182. doi:10.1177/152263790100300302

Huizhi, C. (2015). City police bust fake condom ring, seizing 3 million Durex, Jissbon counterfeits. *Shanghai Daily.* Retrieved from: http://www.shanghaidaily.com/metro/society/City-police-bust-fake-condom-ring-seizing-3-million-Durex-Jissbon-counterfeits/shdaily.shtml

Husselbee, L. P. (1994). Respecting privacy in an information society: A journalists dilemma. *Journal of Mass Media Ethics*, *9*(3), 145–156. doi:10.1207/s15327728jmme0903_3

Hutchins Commission. (1947, 2004). "The Requirements," from Afree and responsible press. In J. Durham Peters & P. Simonson (Eds.), *Mass Communication and American Social Thought: Key texts, 1919-1968.* Lanham, MD: Rowman & Littlefield Publishers.

Hyde-Clarke, N. (2010). *The Citizen in Communication*. Claremont, CA: Juta.

Hydén, G., Leslie, M., & Ogundima, F. (Eds.), *(n.d.). Media and democracy in Africa*. New Brunswick, NJ: Transaction Publishers.

IDRC Communications. (2012). *Access to information gains ground in Africa*. Retrieved from http://www.idrc.ca/EN/Programs/Science_and_Innovation/Information_and_Network

Ihlström Eriksson, C., & Kalling, T. (2007). *Proposing A Business Model Framework For The E-Newspaper*. Paper Presented At The 15th European Conference On Information Systems (ECIS 2007), St Gallen, Switzerland.

IMediaEthics. (2015). *Robert Mugabe Didn't Say Kenyans Were Thieves: NY Times Published Fake Quote*. Retrieved 12 August 2016, from http://www.imediaethics.org/robert-mugabe-didnt-say-kenyans-were-thieves-nytimes-published-fake-quote/

IMPI Report, . (2014). *Information and Media Panel of Inquiry to Promote and Elevate the Standards of Media Practice in Zimbabwe (IMPI): Report of the Official Inquiry into the State of the Information and Media Industry in Zimbabwe.* Harare: Ministry of Information, Media and Broadcasting Services.

Institute for Public Policy Research (IPPR). (2014). *Easing the Way for Investment in Namibia.* IPPR Research Report.

International Council for Science. (2002). *Science and traditional knowledge: Report from the ICSU study group on science and traditional knowledge.* Retrieved from http://www.icsu.org/publications/reports-and-reviews/science-traditional-knowledge/science-traditional-knoweldge.pdf

International Freedom of Expression Exchange Clearing House. (2003). *Protest over Journalist in Hiding as Harare Court Raps Media Law*. Retrieved 16 September 2016 from http://www.zimbabwesituation.com/old/may15_2003.html

International Telecommunication Union. (2015). *ICT facts and figures*. Retrieved from http://www.itu.int/en/ITU-D/Statistics/Pages/facts/default.aspx

Irina, D. M. (2011). The puzzle of criminal sanctions for intellectual property infringement. *Harvard Journal of Law & Technology*, *24*(2), 469–518.

Isaak, C. A. (1981). *Scope and Methods of Political Science, an introduction to the Methodology of Political Inquiry.* The Dorsey press.

Ivester, D. M. (1977). Constitutional Right to Know. *Hastings Constitutional Law Quarterly*, *4*(Winter), 109–163.

Iyengar, S. (1991). *Is anyone responsible?* Chicago: University of Chicago Press. doi:10.7208/chicago/9780226388533.001.0001

Jacobs, L. R., & Shapiro, R. Y. (2005). Polling politics, media, and election campaigns. *Public Opinion Quarterly*, *69*(5), 635–641. doi:10.1093/poq/nfi068

Jan, M. (2009). Globalization of Media: Key Issues and Dimensions. *European Journal of Scientific Research, 29*, 66–75.

Jenkins, B. (1975). *International Terrorism*. Los Angeles, CA: Crescent Publication.

Jensen, M. (2003). *ICT in Africa: A Status Report*. Retrieved March 3, 2016, from https://www.itu.int/osg/spu/wsis-themes/.../jensen-itcs-africa.doc

Jessen, W. (2008). *YouTube as a Source of Health Misinformation*. Highlight Health Tech.

Johns, A. (2009). *Piracy: The intellectual property wars from Gutenberg to Gates*. Chicago: University of Chicago Press. doi:10.7208/chicago/9780226401201.001.0001

Johnson, M. (1992). Research on traditional environmental knowledge: Its development and its role. In M. Johnson (Ed.), *Lore: capturing traditional environmental knowledge*. Ottawa: IDRC.

Jones, M. (1994). Why fakes? In S. Pearce (Ed.), *Interpreting objects and collections* (pp. 92–97). London: Routledge.

Journal, Y. L. (1981). Protecting Privacy Under the Fourth Amendment. *The Yale Law Journal*, *9*(2), 313–343.

Kahneman, D., & Tversky, A. (1984). Choice, values, and frames. *The American Psychologist*, *39*(4), 341–350. doi:10.1037/0003-066X.39.4.341

Kameri-Mbote, P. (2005). *Intellectual Property Protection in Africa: An Assessment of the Status of Laws, research and policy analysis on intellectual property right in Kenya*. Retrieved from http://www.ielre.org/content/w0502.pdf

Kandjii, K. (2004). Namibia. In R. Louw (Ed.), *Undue Restriction: Laws impacting on media freedomin the SADC*. Windhoek: Media Institute of Southern Africa.

Karuaihe-Upi, N. (2011). *Government Secrecy in an Information Age: 2011 Report on the most open and secretive government institutions in Namibia*. Windhoek: Media Institute of Southern Africa.

Kasoma, T. (2010). Zambian PR Practitioners' perspective on 'brown envelopes' and freebies: working through the confusion. *African Communication Research,* (3), 451-474.

Kasoma, T., & Maier, S. (2005). *Information as good as its source: Source diversity and accuracy at nine daily U.S. newspapers*. Paper presented at the meeting of the International Communication Association, New York, NY.

Kasoma, F. (1996). The Foundations of African Ethics (Afriethics) and the Professional Practice of Journalism: The Case for a Society Centred Media Morality. *Africa Media Review*, *10*(3), 93–116.

Kasoma, F. (1996). The Foundations of African Ethics (Afriethics) and the professional Practice of Journalism: The case of society-centred media morality. *Africa Media Review*, *10*(3), 93–116.

Kaul, V. (2011). Globalisation and Media. *Journal of Mass Communication and Journalism*, *1*(01), 1–8. doi:10.4172/2165-7912.1000105

Keith, L. C. (2002). Constitutional Provisions for Individual Human Rights (19771996): Are They More than Mere Window Dressing? *Political Research Quarterly*, *55*(1), 111–143. doi:10.1177/106591290205500105

Ken. (2012, July 9). *Why Albert Gachiri Will Never Forgive Emmanuel Juma*. Retrieved from Nairobi Wire: http://nairobiwire.com/2012/07/Albert-Gachiri-Emmanuel-Juma-beef.html

Kennedy, D. (2009). Maureen Dowd's Lazy New York Times Column. *The Guardian.* Retrieved from: http://www.theguardian.com/commentisfree/cifamerica/2009/may/18/maureen-dowd-plagiarism-new-york-times

Kenya Today. (2015). Shocking: Chinese caught manufacturing three million fake condoms for Nairobi. *Kenya Today.* Retrieved from: http://www.kenya-today.com/news/shocking-chinese-caught-manufacturing-three-million-fake-condoms-for-nairobi

Kirell, A. (2015). Shep Smith apologizes for Fox reporter's erroneous 'shooting' account: 'we screwed up'. *Mediaite.*

Kirthi, J. (2014). Peace journalism and Boko Haram. *Media and Journalism in Peace Work.*

Kobré, K. (2004). *Photojournalism: The Professionals' Approach.* Burlington, MA: Focal Press.

Kohn, M. (2000). Language, power and persuasion: Towards a critique of deliberative democracy. *Constellations (Oxford, England), 7*(3), 408–429. doi:10.1111/1467-8675.00197

Kolb, J. J. (2011, June). Coming of age: Naming juvenile criminal suspects shouldn't pose an ethical quandary. *Editor & Publisher,* 30.

Komolafe, F. (2004). *Nigerian Journalists Directory.* Lagos: Friedrich Ebert Stiftung Stiftung.

Koops, B.-J. (2011). Forgetting footprints, shunning shadows. A critical analysis of the "right to be forgotten" in big data practice. *Scripted, 8,* 229–256.

Kottak, P. (2002). Anthropology: The exploration of human diversity. New York: Academic Press.

Kou, S. G., & Sobel, M. E. (2004). Forecasting the vote: A theoretical comparison of election markets and public opinion polls. *Political Analysis, 12*(3), 277–295. doi:10.1093/pan/mph019

Kovach, B., & Rosenstiel, T. (2001). *The elements of journalism: What newspeople should know and the public should expect.* New York: Three Rivers Press.

Kozinets, R. (2009). *Netnography: Doing Ethnographic research online.* Los Angeles, CA: Sage Publications Ltd.

Kraidy, M. (2002). Globalization of culture through the media. In J. R. Schement (Ed.), Encyclopedia of communication and information (pp. 359–363). New York, NY: Macmillan Reference USA. Retrieved from http://repository.upenn.edu/asc_papers/325

Kusamotu, A. (2007). Privacy Law and Technology in Nigeria: The Legal Framework will not meet the Test of Adequacy as Mandated by Article 25 of European Union Directive 95/46. *Information & Communications Technology Law, 16*(2), 149–159. doi:10.1080/13600830701597616

Kuusik, N. (2010). The Role of the Media in Peace Building, Conflict Management, and Prevention. *E-International Relations.*

Lago, I., Guinjoan, M., & Bermúdez, S. (2015). Regulating Disinformation Poll Embargo and Electoral Coordination. *Public Opinion Quarterly, 79*(4), 932–951. doi:10.1093/poq/nfv036

Laird, S. (Ed.). (2002). *Biodiversity and traditional knowledge, equitable partnerships in practice, people and plants conservation services. WWF, UNESCO, Royal Botanic Gardens Kew.* London: Earthscan Publications Ltd.

Lakoff, G. (2004). *Don't think of an elephant: know your values and frame the debate.* Chelsea Green.

Lando, A. L. (2013). Ethics in the Kenyan Media? Understanding the disconnect between the classroom and practice. *African Journal of Communication, 1*(1), 15–42.

Laqueur, W. (1977). *Terrorism.* London: Weidenfield and Nicolson.

Lasica, J. D. (1997) Preserving Old Ethics in a New Medium. *American Journalism Review*. Retrieved from http://ajrarchive.org/article_printable.asp?id=1787

Lasica, J. D. (1997). Preserving Ethics in a News Medium. *American Journalism Review*. Retrieved 7 August 2016, from http://www.jdlasica.com/1997/12/07/preserving-old-ethics-in-a-new-medium/

Lasica, J. D. (1998). The Net never forgets. *Salon*. Retrieved from http://www.salon.com/1998/11/25/feature_253/

Lau, M., & Wydick, B. (2014). Does New Information Technology Lower Media Quality? The Paradox Of Commercial Public Goods. *Journal of Industry, Competition and Trade*, *14*(2), 145–157. doi:10.1007/s10842-013-0157-x

Laylin, T. (2011). *China plans to clone the entire village of Hallstatt, Austria*. Retrieved from www.inhabitat.com

Le Kay, E., Pretorious, N., Rowles, P., Rusch, K., Scott, C., Taljaard, R., & Whitehead, A. (2003). *Digital Manipulation of Images. Group Report on Grocott's Mail*. Rhodes University.

Lee, A. Y. L. (2012). Online News Media in the Web 2.0 Era: From Boundary Dissolution to Journalistic Transparency. *Chinese Journal of Communication*, *5*(2), 210–226. doi:10.1080/17544750.2012.664442

Lee, J. (2015). A Double-Edged Sword: The Effects of JournalistsSocial Media Activities on Audience Perceptions of Journalists and their News Products. *Journal of Computer-Mediated Communication*, *20*(3), 312–329. doi:10.1111/jcc4.12113

Lee, R. M. (2005). The UK Freedom Of Information Act And Social Research. *International Journal of Social Research Methodology*, *8*(1), 1–18. doi:10.1080/13645570500046624

Lee, T. (2005). The liberal media myth revisited: An examination of factors influencing perceptions of media bias. *Journal of Broadcasting & Electronic Media*, *49*(1), 43–64. doi:10.1207/s15506878jobem4901_4

Lehman-Wilzig, S., & Cohen-Avigdor, N. (2004). The natural life cycle of new media evolution: Inter-media struggle for survival in the internet age. *New Media & Society*, *6*(6), 707–730. doi:10.1177/146144804042524

Lemley, M.A. (2015). *Property, intellectual property and free riding*. Available at heinonline.org

Lemmens, P. (2015). Social Autonomy and Heteronomy in the Age of ICT: The Digital Pharmakon and the (Dis) Empowerment of the General Intellect. *Foundations of Science*. doi:10.1007/s10699-015-9468-1

Lessig, L. (1999). *Code and other laws of cyberspace*. New York: Basic books.

Lessig, L. (2001). *The future of ideas: The fate of the commons in a connected world*. New York: Random House.

Lester, P. M. (1991). *Photojournalism: An Ethical Approach*. Hillsdale, NJ: Erlbaum.

Levine, D., & Boldrin, M. (2008). *Against intellectual monopoly*. London: Cambridge University Press.

Lewandowsky, S., Ecker, U. K., Seifert, C. M., Schwarz, N., & Cook, J. (2012). Misinformation and its correction continued influence and successful debiasing. *Psychological Science in the Public Interest*, *13*(3), 106–131. doi:10.1177/1529100612451018 PMID:26173286

Lewis, J. (2001). *Constructing public opinion: How political elites do what they like and why we seem to go along with it*. Columbia University Press.

Lewis, S. C., Kaufhold, K., & Lasorsa, D. L. (2010). Thinking about citizen journalism: The philosophical and practical challenges of user-generated content for community newspapers. *Journalism Practice*, *4*(2), 163–179. doi:10.1080/14616700903156919

Leyne, J. (2012). *Opinion polls give few clues to Egypt presidential election*. BBC News. Retrieved from http://www.bbc.com/news/world-middle-east-18110194.

Lichtenberg, J. (2000). In defence of objectivity revisited. In J. Curran & M. Gurevitch (Eds.), *Mass Media & Society* (3rd ed.; pp. 225–242). London: Arnold.

Littlejohn, S. W. (1999). *Theories of human communication* (6th ed.). Belmont, CA: Wadsworth.

Livingstone, S., Haddon, L., Görzig, A., & Ólafsson, K. (2011). *EU Kids Online: final report 2011*. London: EU Kids Online Network.

Loe, C., & Ding, C. G. (2000). A review of empirical studies assessing ethical decision making in business. *Journal of Business Ethics*, *25*(3), 185–204. doi:10.1023/A:1006083612239

Long, J. D., & Gibson, C. C. (2015). Evaluating the Roles of Ethnicity and Performance in African Elections Evidence from an Exit Poll in Kenya. *Political Research Quarterly*, 1065912915608946.

Lorimer, R., & Scannell, P. (1994). *Mass communication: A comparative introduction*. Manchester, UK: Manchester University Press Ltd.

Louw, R. (1993). Foreword. In P. E. Louw (Ed.), *South African Media Policy: Debates of the 1990s*. Bellville: Anthroppos. doi:10.1075/hl.20.1.01for

Louw, R. (2004). *Undue Restrictions. Laws impacting on media freedom in the SADC*. Windhoek: UNESCO.

Lowenthal, T. (2015). Surveillance forces journalists to think and act like spies. *Committee to Protect Journalists*. Retrieved from https://cpj.org/2015/04/attacks-on-the-press-surveillance-forces-journalists-to-think-act-like-spies.php

Lowrey, W. (2003). Normative conflict in the newsroom: The case of digital photo manipulation. *Journal of Mass Media Ethics*, *18*(2), 123–142. doi:10.1207/S15327728JMME1802_05

Luke, M. (2012, February 6). *Social media dilemma after NTV clips reporter off the screen*. Retrieved from Business Today: http://www.businesstoday.co.ke/news/2012/02/6/social-media-dilemma-after-ntv-clips-reporter-screen

Luke, A. (2010). Possibilities of public opinion polls in politics and mass media in Nigeria. *Journal of Liberal Studies*, *13*(1), 31–45.

Lulofs, R. S., & Cahn, D. D. (2000). *Conflict: From Theory to Action* (2nd ed.). Boston: Allyn and Bacon.

Lumu, T. D. (2010, April 28). CBS Radio is set to reopen after eight months off-air, following President Museveni's change of heart, The Observer has Learnt. *The Observer*, p. 2.

Lyimo, K. (2015). Stratagem: Tanzanian election opinion polls a political Trojan horse. *The Citizen*. Retrieved from http://www.thecitizen.co.tz/oped/Tanzanian-election-opinion-polls-a-political-Trojan-horse/-/1840568/2897034/-/xafw78z/-/index.html.

M'ule, E. K. (2014). *Observation of Media Conduct during the 2014 Malawi Tripartite Elections*. Open Society Initiative in Southern Africa.

Mabweazara, H. M. (2010). New Technologies and Journalism Practice in Africa: Towards a Critical Sociological Approach. In The Citizen and Communication: Revisiting Traditional, New and Community Media Practices in Southern Africa. Claremont: Juta & Co Pvt Ltd.

Mabweazara, M. H. (2010). *New Technologies and Print Journalism Practice in Zimbabwe: An Ethnographic Study* (Unpublished DPhil Thesis). School of Arts and Creative Industries, Edinburgh Napier University, Edinburgh, UK.

Mabweazara, H. M. (2011). Newsmaking Practices and Professionalism in the Zimbabwean Press. *Journalism Practice, 5*(1), 100–117. doi:10.1080/17512786.2010.493331

Magalhães, P. C. (2005). Pre-Election Polls in Portugal: Accuracy, Bias, and Sources of Error, 1991–2004. *International Journal of Public Opinion Research, 17*(4), 399–421. doi:10.1093/ijpor/edh078

Mail & Guardian. (2012, September 27). *Citizen fires photographer over doctored picture discussion*. Retrieved August 20, 2015, from http://mg.co.za/article/2012-09-27-citizen-fires-whistleblower-of-doctored-cover-photo

Maitambari, U. (2011). Emerging pattern of security challenges: some reflections on 1983 and 2007 elections. In L. Olurode & A. Jega (Eds.), *Security Challenges of Election Management in Nigeria*. Abuja Independent National Electoral Commission.

Makulilo, A. B. (2013). Poll-'Pollution'?: The Politics of Numbers in the 2013 Elections in Kenya. *Poll-'Pollution*, 1-32.

Manning, C. (2005). *Photo-Journalism ethics in the digital age*. Retrieved July 23, 2016, from http://www.newmediarepublic.com/articles/photoethics.pdf

Manning, P. (2001). *News and news sources: A critical introduction*. Thousand Oaks, CA: SAGE Publication.

Mansurov, V.A. (1988). *Mass media and public opinion: Problems of interaction*. Mass media and public opinion Tampere University, Department of Mass Communication Publication Series B, No. 24.

Maraniss, D. A. (1981, April 16). *The hoax project*. Retrieved October 25, 2015, from jclass.umd.edu: http://jclass.umd.edu

Masunungure, E. V. (2006). Nation Building, State Building and Power Configuration in Zimbabwe. *Conflict Trends Magazine*, (1), 1-10.

Mathiesen, K. (2014). Human rights for the digital age. *Journal of Mass Media Ethics, 29*(1), 2–18. doi:10.1080/08900523.2014.863124

Mattes, R. (2012). *Opinion polls and the media in South Africa. In Opinion Polls and the Media* (pp. 175–197). Springer. doi:10.1057/9780230374959_9

Mayer-Schönberger, V. (2011). *Delete: The virtue of forgetting in the digital age*. Princeton, NJ: Princeton University Press.

McCombs, M., Shaw, D. L., & Weaver, D. (1997). *Communication and Democracy: Exploring the intellectual Frontiers in agenda-setting theory*. Mahwah, NJ: Erlbaum.

McLeod, D., Kosicki, G., & McLeod, J. (2002). Resurveying the boundaries of political communication effects. In J. Bryant & D. Zillman (Eds.), *Media effects: Advances in theory and research*. Mahwah, NJ: Lawrence Erlbaum.

McLeod, K., & Kuenzli, R. (Eds.). (2011). *Cutting across media: Appropriation art, interventionist collage and copyright law*. Durham, NC: Duke University Press. doi:10.1215/9780822393214

McNealy, J. E. (2012). The emerging conflict between newsworthiness and the right to be forgotten. *Northern Kentucky Law Review, 39*, 119–135.

McQuail, D. (1987). *Mass Communication Theory* (3rd ed.). London: SAGE Publications ltd.

McQuail, D. (1994). *Mass communication theory: an introduction* (3rd ed.). Thousand Oaks, CA: Sage.

McQuail, D. (1997). *Audience Analysis*. London: Sage Publications Inc.

Meader, A., Knight, L., Coleman, R., & Wilkins, L. (2015). Ethics in the digital age: A comparison of the effects of moving images and photographs on moral judgment. *Journal of Mass Media Ethics*, *30*(4), 234–251. doi:10.1080/23736992.2015.1083403

Media Council Of Kenya. (2013). *Code of Conduct for the Practice of Journalism in Kenya*. Nairobi: Media Council.

Media Institute of Southern Africa. (2010). *A Report on Open & Secretive Public Institutions in Southern Africa*. Windhoek: MISA.

Mendel, T. (2008). *Freedom of Information: A Comparative Legal Survey* (2nd ed.). Paris: UNESCO.

Mendoza, N. (2012). The Crisis of Global Journalism and the Freedom of the Press Foundation. *Aljazeera*. Retrieved 16 September 2016, from http://www.aljazeera.com/indepth/opinion/2012/12/2012122012051496867.html

Merges, R. P., Menell, P. S., & Lemley, M. A. (2007). *Intellectual property in the new technological Age* (4th ed.). New York: Wolters Kluwer.

Merrill, J. C. (1974). *The Imperative of Freedom, A Philosophy of Journalistic Autonomy*. New York: Hastings House.

Meyers, C. (1993). Justifying journalistic harms: Right to know vs. interest in knowing. *Journal of Mass Media Ethics*, *8*(3), 133–146. doi:10.1207/s15327728jmme0803_1

Mfumbusa, B. (2008). Newsroom ethics in Africa: Quest for a normative framework. *African Communication Research*, (1), 139-157.

Mhiripiri, N. A., & Mutsvairo, B. (2013). Social Media, New ICTs and the Challenges Facing the Zimbabwe Democratic Process. In New Media Influence on Social and Political Change in Africa (pp. 402-421). Hershey, PA: IGI Global.

Mhiripiri, N. A., & Mutsvairo, B. (2013). Social Media, New ICTs and the Challenges Facing the Zimbabwe Democratic Process. In New Media Influence on Social and Political Change in Africa (pp. 402-421). IGI Global.

Mhiripiri, N. A. (2013). Alternative Dispute Resolution (ADR) Systems in the Zimbabwean Media Industry and the Debate On Self-regulation. *Journal of African Media Studies*, *5*(3), 313–336. doi:10.1386/jams.5.3.313_1

Mhiripiri, N. A. (2015). Narratives of the Zimbabwe Crisis, National Sovereignty and Human and Media Rights Violations. In S. Adejumobi (Ed.), *National Democratic Reforms in Africa: Changes and Challenges*. New York: Palgrave MacMillan. doi:10.1057/9781137518828_6

Mill, J. S. (1967). *Essays on Government, Jurisprudence, Liberty of the Press, and the Law of Nations*. New York: Academic Press. (Original work published 1825)

Mill, J. S. (2006). *On Liberty and the Subjection of Women* (A. Ryan, Ed.). London: Academic Press. (Original work published 1859)

Mill, S. (1869). *On Liberty* (4th ed.). London: Longman.

Mills, S., & Tiffen, R. (2012). *Opinion Polls and the Media in Australia. In Opinion Polls and the Media* (pp. 155–174). Springer. doi:10.1057/9780230374959_8

Ministry of Communication. (1994). *Proceedings of the National Forum on CommunicationYaoundé*. National Printing Press.

Ministry of Health Maternal and Perinatal Death Review Uganda. (2013). *Why did they die? Reviewing the evidence to save tomorrow's mothers and babies*. Kampala: Ministry of Health.

Ministry of Information and Broadcasting. (1991). *Namibia's Information Policy*. Author.

Ministry of Information and Broadcasting. (2006). *Draft Revised Information and Communication Policy*. Author.

Mirkinson, J. (2012) Fareed Zakaria Suspended for Plaigiarism: Time Editor, CNN Host Apologizes for 'Terrible Mistake'. *Huffington Post.* Retrieved from http://www.huffingtonpost.com/2012/08/10/fareed-zakaria-plagiarism-new-yorkertime_n_1764954.html

Mitra, A. (2001). Marginal Voices in Cyberspace. *New Media & Society*, *3*(1), 29–48. doi:10.1177/1461444801003001003

Mitrou, L., & Karyda, M. (2012). EU's data protection reform and the right to be forgotten: A legal response to a technological challenge?*5th International Conference of Information Law and Ethics*.

Mohan, K. (2012). Sunlight is the best disinfectant: Why Namibia needs Access to Information. Windhoek: Institute for Public Policy Research, Paper 11.

Molefe, W., & Mguni, B. (2000). Opinion polls in Botswana. *Botswana Journal of African Studies*, *14*(1), 122–129.

Morant, B. D. (2005). The endemic reality of media ethics and self-restraint. *Notre Dame Journal of Law, Ethics & Public Policy*, *19*, 595–636.

Morris, J. S., & Forgette, R. (2007). News Grazers, Television News, Political Knowledge, And Engagement. *The Harvard International Journal of Press/Politics*, *12*(1), 91–107. doi:10.1177/1081180X06297122

Mose, C. (2016). Covers, remixes and mash-ups: Locating African hip-hop in intellectual property rights discourse. In U. Röschenthaler & M. Diawara (Eds.), Copyright Africa: How intellectual property, media and markets transform immaterial cultural goods. Canon Pyon: Sean Kingston.

Moyo, D. (2005). The 'Independent' Press and the Fight Democracy in Zimbabwe. A Critical Analysis of the Banned Daily News. *Westminster Papers in Communication and Culture, 2,* 109-128. http://doi.org/10.16997/wpcc.45

Moyo, D. (2010). *The New Media as Monitors of Democracy. Mobile Phones and Zimbabwe's 2008 Election.* Paper presented at the Conference on Election Processes, Liberation Movements and Democratic Change in Africa, Organised by IESE and CMI, Maputo.

Moyo, D. (2007). Alternative Media Diasporas and the Mediation of the Zimbabwean Crisis. *Ecquid Novi: African Journalism Studies*, *28*(1&2), 81–105.

Moyo, D. (2009). Citizen Journalism and the Parallel Market of Information in Zimbabwes 2008 Election. *Journalism Studies*, *10*(4), 551–567. doi:10.1080/14616700902797291

Moyo, D., & Chuma, W. (Eds.). (2010). *Media Policy in a Changing Southern Africa: Critical Reflections on Media Reforms in the Global age*. Pretoria: UNISA Press.

Moyo, L. (2015). Digital age as ethical maze: Citizen journalism ethics during crises in Zimbabwe and South Africa. *African. Journalism Studies*, *36*(4), 125–144. doi:10.1080/23743670.2015.1119494

Mpofu, S. (n.d.). *The power of citizen journalism in Zimbabwe*. Unpublished Manuscript.

Mtika, C. (2014). Malawi elections: Big four vie for power. *Mail & Guardian*. Retrieved from http://mg.co.za/article/2014-05-16-malawi-elections-big-four-vie-for-power.

Mu'azu, A. (2003). Legal and Ethical Issues in Reporting Conflict. In U. A. Pate (Ed.), *Introduction to Conflict Reporting in Nigeria*. Lagos: Friedrich Ebert Stiftung.

Mudhai, O. F., Tettey, W., & Banda, F. (2009). *African Media and the Digital Public Sphere*. New York: Palgrave Macmillan. doi:10.1057/9780230621756

Mujere, J., & Mwatwara, W. (2015). Citizen Journalism and National Politics in Zimbabwe: The Case of the 2008 and 2013 Elections. In Participatory Politics and Citizen Journalism in a Networked Africa: A Connected Continent (pp. 215 – 228). London: Palgrave, Macmillan.

Mullen, L. (1998). *Truth in photography: Perception, Myth and Reality in the Postmodern World* (Masters Dissertation). University of Florida. Retrieved July, 23, 2016, from http://etd.fcla.edu/UF/and0040/Leslie.pdf

Muller, M. R. (2013). *Protecting shared traditional knowledge: Issues, challenges and options; ICTSD programme on innovation, Technology and intellectual property; issue paper No 39*. International Centre for Trade and Sustainable Development. Available at www.ictsd.org

Muller, E. R., Spaaij, R. F. J., & Ruitenberg, A. G. W. (2003). *Trends in Terrorism. Alphen aan de Rijn*. Kluwer.

Mutoko, C. (2012, September 13). Letter to my 20-something self. *The Star*, p. 28.

Mutsvairo, B. (2015). Recapturing Citizen Journalism: Processes and Patterns Citizen Journalism and National Politics in Zimbabwe: The Case of the 2008 and 2013 Elections. In Participatory Politics and Citizen Journalism in a Networked Africa: A Connected Continent (pp. 1 – 15). London: Palgrave, Macmillan.

Mzale, D., & Nyondo, E. (2014). MEC warns on opinion polls. *The Nation*. Retrieved from http://mwnation.com/mec-warns-on-opinion-polls

Nacos, B. L. (2006). *Terrorism/Counterterrorism and Media in the Age of Global Communication*. United Nations University Global Seminar Second Shimame-Yamaguchi Session, Terrorism—A Global Challenge.

Nassanga, L. G. (2009). An assessment of the changing community media parameters in East Africa. *African Journalism Studies*, *30*(1), 42–57. doi:10.3368/ajs.30.1.42

Nda-Isaiah, J. (2015). How Accurate Are Opinion Polls In Nigeria? *Leadership*. Retrieved from http://leadership.ng/news/423020/how-accurate-are-opinion-polls-in-nigeria.

Ndati, N., Wambua, P., & Mogambi, H. (2014). The Impact of Legislation on Electoral Opinion Polls in Kenya. *European Scientific Journal, 10*(34).

Ndlela, M. N. (2007). Broadcasting reforms in Southern Africa: Continuity and change in the era of globalization. *Westminster Papers in Communication and Culture*, *4*, 67–86.

Neal, D., & Morgan, N. (2000). Our Data, Our Selves. *The Wilson Quarterly*, *24*(4), 51–57.

Negrine, R. (1996). *Politics and the Mass Media in Britain* (2nd ed.). London: Routledge.

New Era. (2012). *Namibia: Kaapanda on Access to Information Legislation*. Retrieved from http://allafrica.com/stories/201208230745.html

Newman, I., & Benz, C. (1998). *Qualitative Research Methodology: Exploring the Interactive Continuum*. Southern Illinois University Press.

News Wire. (2015). *Zimbabwean Police Launch 'Manhunt' for Journalist who Verified Fake Mugabe Quotes to the New York Times*. Retrieved from http://www.mashada.com/blogs/p/221702/zimbabwean-police-launch-manhunt-for-journalist-who-verified-fake-mugabe-quotes-to-the-new-york-time

Nicola, B. (2011). *Tweet First Verify Later*. Retrieved from reutersinstitute.politics.ox.ac.uk

Nieves-Pizarro, Y. (2015). *Corrections, Apologies and Retractions: Misinformation in Social Media News*. Retrieved 13 September 2016, from https://lagacetaboricua.wordpress.com/2015/05/21/corrections-apologies-and-retractions-misinformation-in-social-media-news/

Nigerian Press Council. (2016). *Code of ethics*. Retrieved fromwww.prescouncil.gov.ng/?page_id=281

Niven, D. (2005). An economic theory on political journalism. *Journalism & Mass Communication Quarterly*, *52*(2), 247–263. doi:10.1177/107769900508200202

Njagi, D. (2013). What if Kenya's election violence points to corrupt pollsters? *The Africa Report*. Retrieved from http://www.theafricareport.com/News-Analysis/what-if-kenyas-election-violence-points-to-corrupt-pollsters.html.

Noer, M. (2014). The Original Forbes Takedown of Stephen Glass. *Forbes*. Retrieved from: http://www.forbes.com/sites/michaelnoer/2014/11/12/read-the-original-forbes-takedown-of-stephen-glass/

Norris, P., Kern, M., & Just, M. (2003). Framing terrorism. In P. Norris, M. Kern, & M. Just (Eds.), *Framing Terrorism: The News Media, the Government and the Public*. New York: Routledge.

Nwabachili, C.C., Nwabachili, C.O. & Agu, H.U. (2015). The challenges of enforcing intellectual property rights across the economic community of West African States: The Nigerian experience. *Journal of Law, Policy and Globalization, 34*.

Nwabueze, C. (2010). Brown envelopes and the need for ethical re-orientation: Perceptions of Nigerian Journalists. *African Communication Research,* (3), 497-520.

Nwauche, E. (2007). The Right to Privacy in Nigeria. *CALS Review of Nigerian Law and Practice*, *1*(1), 62–90.

Nyamnjoh, F. (2005). Africa's media: Democracy and the politics of belonging. ZED Press.

O'Neil, P. H. (Ed.). (1998). Communicating Democracy. The Media and Political Transitions. London: Lynne Rienner Publishers.

Obia, V. (2014). Opinion Poll Politics in Elections. *THISDAY* Retrieved from http://www.thisdaylive.com/articles/opinion-poll-politics-in-elections/178268.

Odufuwa, F. (2012). *Understanding What is Happening in ICT in Nigeria: A Supply-and-Demand-Side Analysis of the ICT Sector*. Cape Town: ResearchICTAfrica.net.

Ogbeide, M. M. (2010). A culture of failed elections: Revisiting democratic elections in Nigeria, 1959-2003. *Historia Actual Online*, *21*, 43–56.

Ogundiya, I. S. (2003). Electoral Violence and democratization project: The Nigerian Experience. In B. A. Olasupo (Ed.), *Electoral Violence in Nigeria: Issues and Perspectives*. Lagos: Fredrick Ebert Stiftung.

Ogunsanwo, A. (2003). Keynote Address. In 2003 General Elections and Democratic Consolidation in Nigeria. Lagos: Friedrich Ebert Stiftung.

Ojambo, H. O. (2008). *Reflections on Freedom of Expression in Uganda's Fledgling Democracy: Sedition, "Pornography" and Hate Speech*. HURIPEC Working Paper No. 18.

Okello, J. (2008). *Situation of Community Radio in Uganda*. Paper presented at the Our Media 7 conference, Accra, Ghana.

Ologbenla, D. (2003). Political Instability, Conflict and the 2003 General Elections. In 2003 General Elections and Democratic Consolidation in Nigeria. Lagos: Firedrich Ebert Stiftung.

Olurode, L. (1987). *A Political Economy of Nigeria's 1983 Election*. Lagos: John West Publishers.

Olurode, L. (2011). Incumbency factors: Appropriation of state security resources and electoral governance in Nigeria. In L. Olurode & A. Jega (Eds.), *Security Challenges of Election Management in Nigeria*. Abuja: Independent National Electoral Commission.

Onuoha, B. (2004). The electoral machine: The Bureaucracy and the electoral process in the making of Nigeria's Fourth Republic. In L. Olurode & R. Anifowose (Eds.), *Issues in Nigeria's 1999 General Elections*. Lagos: John West Publications Ltd & Rebonick Publications Ltd.

Oosthuizen, L. M. (1989). *Media policy and ethics*. Cape Town: Juta& Co., Ltd.

Oshinsky, D. (1983). *A conspiracy so immense: The world of Joe McCarthy*. New York: The Free Press.

Otto, A. (2013). *Media Houses Warned on Pornography*. Retrieved from http://ugandaradionetwork.com/a/story.php?s=57490

Owens-Ibe, N. (2002). Socio-Cultural considerations in conflict reporting in Nigeria. In U. A. Pate (Ed.), *Introduction to Conflict Reporting in Nigeria*. Lagos: Friederich Ebert.

Oyugi, K. (2012, July 6). *Albert Gachiri Speaks Out on the Karume Saga and Whether He Really Was Fired from NTV*. Retrieved from Ghafla: http://www.ghafla.co.ke/news/tv/2711-albert-gachiri-speaks-out-on-the-karume-saga-and-whether-he-really-was-fired-from-ntv

Packard, A. (2010). *Digital Media Law*. New York: McGraw-Hill. doi:10.1002/9781444318197

Painter, C., & Willis, E. (2016). Flipping the Script: Newspaper Reporting of the Trayvon Martin Shooting. In Impact of Communication and the Media on Ethnic Conflict. IGI Global.

Panathiere, D. (2005 July). The persistence of piracy: The consequences for creativity, for culture, and for sustainable development. *UNESCO e. Copyright Bulletin*.

Papacharissi, Z. (2009). Introduction. In Journalism and Citizenship: New Agendas in Communication. Routledge.

Par Anders Granhag, A. V. (2015). *Detecting deception*. Chichester, UK: Wiley Blackwell.

Park, J. (2008). Privacy Regime, Culture and User Practices in the Cyber-Marketplace. *Information*, *10*(2), 57–74.

Patterson, T. E. (2005). Of polls, mountains US journalists and their use of election surveys. *Public Opinion Quarterly*, *69*(5), 716–724. doi:10.1093/poq/nfi065

Patton, M. Q. (2002). *Qualitative Research and Evaluation Methods*. Thousand Oaks, CA: SAGE.

Pavlik, J. V. (2008). *Media in the digital age*. New York: Columbia University Press.

Pavlik, J. V., & Micintosh, S. (2011). *Converging media: A new introduction to mass communication*. Oxford, UK: Oxford University Press.

Peachey, P. (2015, October 17). Hogan-Howe backs law against naming suspects in sex inquiries. *The Independent*, 20.

Peck, L. A. (2013). Tools of ethical decision making. In L. A. Peck & G. S. Reel (Eds.), *Media Ethics at Work: True Stories from Young Professionals* (pp. 5–22). London: SAGE.

Peil, M. (1977). *Consensus and Conflict in African societies: An Introduction to sociology*. Edinburgh, UK: Longman Group Ltd.

Peltz-Steele, R. J. (2008). Fifteen minutes of infamy: Privileged reporting and the problem of perpetual harm. *Ohio Northern University Law Review*, *34*, 717–754.

Pena, D. G. (2005). *Mexican American and the Environment.* University of Arizona Press.

Perloff, R. (1998). *Politics, Press, and Public in America*. Mahwah, NJ: Lawrence Erlbaum.

Peter, K. Y. (2007). *Intellectual property and information wealth: copyright and related rights.* Westport, CT: Greenwood Publishing Group.

Phelps, J., Nowak, G., & Ferrell, E. (2000). Privacy Concerns and Consumer Willingness to Provide Personal Information. *Journal of Public Policy & Marketing*, *19*(1), 27–41. doi:10.1509/jppm.19.1.27.16941

Phillip, K. (2005). What is a technological author? The pirate function and intellectual property. *Postcolonial Studies*, *8*(2), 199–218. doi:10.1080/13688790500153596

Phillipson, G. (2008). Trial by media: The betrayal of the First Amendment's purpose. *Law and Contemporary Problems*, *71*, 15–29.

Plaisance, P. L. (2000). The Concept of Media Accountability Reconsidered. *Journal of Mass Media Ethics*, *15*(4), 257–268. doi:10.1207/S15327728JMME1504_5

Popoola, I. S. (2003). Role of mass media in a transitory troubled democracy. Babcock Journal of Management and Social Sciences, 2(1), 20.

Popoola, I. S. (2015). *Political Reporting and Electoral Violence in Nigeria, 1999 – 2011* (Ph.D Thesis). University of Lagos, Lagos Nigeria.

Posey, D.A., & Dutfield, G. (1996). *Beyond intellectual property: Towards traditional resource rights for indigenous peoples and local communities.* Ottawa: International Development Research Centre.

Presidency of the Republic of Cameroon. (2015). Retrieved from https://www.prc.cm/en/news/1233-support-of-the-armed-forces-paul-and-chantal-biya-at-the-forefront.April

Press Council. (2016). *Code of ethics and conduct for South African print and online media.* Retrieved fromwww.presscouncil.org.za/ContentPage?code=PRESSCODE

Pretschner, A., Hilty, M., & Basin, D. (2006). Distributed Usage Control. *Communications of the ACM*, *49*(9), 39–44. doi:10.1145/1151030.1151053

Price, D. (2015). Surveyors and surveyed: Photography out and about. In L. Wells (Ed.), *Photography: A Critical Introduction* (5th ed.; pp. 75–132). London: Routledge.

Price, G. (2015). *Opportunities and Challenges for Journalism in the Digital age: Asian and European Perspectives.* London: The Royal Institute of International Affairs.

Price, M. E., Verhulst, S., & Morgan, L. (2013). *Routledge Handbook Of Media Law*. Routledge.

Prosser, W. (1960). Privacy. *California Law Review*, *48*(3), 383–423. doi:10.2307/3478805

Puddephatt, A. (2006). *Voices of war: Conflict and the role of the media*. International Media Support.

Qvortrup, L. (2006). Understanding New Digital Media: Medium Theory or Complexity. *European Journal of Communication*, *21*(3), 345–356. doi:10.1177/0267323106066639

Rachels, J. (1984). Why privacy is important. In F. Schoeman (Ed.), *Philosophical dimensions of privacy* (pp. 290–299). Cambridge, UK: Cambridge University Press. doi:10.1017/CBO9780511625138.013

Ramshaw, G. (2014). *The power of perceptions: elites, opinion polling, and the quality of elections in sub-Saharan Africa*. University of Sussex.

Rand, A. (1967). *Capitalism: The unknown ideal* (2nd ed.). New York: Signet.

Reed, B. S., & Bracaglia, D. (2013). Hard questions, big backlash: The case of the train track death. In L. A. Peck & G. S. Reel (Eds.), *Media Ethics at Work: True Stories from Young Professionals* (pp. 189–201). London: SAGE.

Reporters Without Borders. (2014, Dec. 18). *Disproportionate Penalties for Media in Cameroon's Anti-Terrorism Law*. Author.

Republic of Namibia. (1990). Constitution of the Republic of Namibia, 1990 (Act 1 of 1990).

Republic of Namibia. (1991). Namibian Broadcasting Act, 1991 (Act 9 of 1991). Government Gazette, 223.

Republic of Namibia. (1992a, March). New Era Publication Corporation Act, 1992 (Act 1, 1992). *Government Gazette, 377*, 24.

Republic of Namibia. (1992b). Namibia Press Agency Act, 1992 (Act 3 of 1992). Government Gazette, 382.

Republic of Namibia. (1992c). Namibian Communications Commission Act, 1992 (Act 4 of 1992). Government Gazette, 384.

Republic of Namibia. (1997). Namibia Central Intelligence Service Act, 1997 (No 10 of 1997). Government Gazette of the Republic of Namibia, 1699.

Republic of Namibia. (1999, March 2). Press Release.

Republic of Namibia. (2000). Film Commission Act, 2000 (Act 6 of 2000). Government Gazette, 2749.

Republic of Namibia. (2002a). Film Commission Act, 2000 (Act 6 of 2000). Government Gazette, 2322.

Republic of Namibia. (2002b). Defence Act, 2002 (Act 1 of 2002). Government Gazette, 2749.

Republic of Namibia. (2003). Criminal Procedure Amendment Act, 2003 (Act 24 of 2003). Government Gazette, 3123.

Republic of Namibia. (2004). Research, Science and Technology Act (Act 23 of 2004).

Republic of Namibia. (2009). Communications Act, 2009 (No 8 of 2009). Government Gazette of the Republic of Namibia, 4378.

Republic of Namibia. (2016a). Draft Revised National Information Policy, March 2016.

Republic of Namibia. (2016b). Draft Access to Information Bill, April 2016.

Republic of Namibia. (2016c). Harambee Prosperity Plan 2016/17 – 2019/20. Namibian Government's Action Plan towards Prosperity for All, April 2016.

Republic of South Africa. (1957). Defence Act of 1957 (Act 44 of 1957).

Republic of South Africa. (1958). Police Act of 1958 (Act 7 of 1958).

Republic of South Africa. (1959). Prison Act of 1959 (Act 8 of 1959).

Republic of South Africa. (1974). Publications Act of 1974 (Act 42 of 1974).

Republic of South Africa. (1977). Criminal Procedure Act of 1977 (Act 51 of 1977).

Republic of South Africa. (1982). Internal Security Act of 1982 (Act 74 of 1982).

Republic of South Africa. (1982). Protection of Information Act, 1982 (Act 84 of 1982).

Republic of South Africa. (1996). Constitution of the Republic of South Africa No.108 of 1996. Cape Town: Author.

Republic of South Africa. (2002). Cape Town: Electronic Communications and Transaction Act.

Republic of South Africa. (2009). Consumer Protection Act No. 68. Cape Town: Author.

Republic of South Africa. (2013). Protection of Personal Information Act 2013 No 4. Cape Town: Author.

Research, B. (2015). *Unreliability Of Opinion Polls Bringing More Political Surprises*. Retrieved from http://www.bmiresearch.com/blog/unreliability-of-opinion-polls-bringing-more-political-surprises.

Review by Eokhardah. (2015). Role of Mesia in Our Society. *Review by Eokhardah*. Retrieved from: https://eokhardahreview.wordpress.com/2015/02/13

Reza, S. (2005). Privacy and the criminal arrestee or suspect: In search of a right, in need of a rule. *Maryland Law Review (Baltimore, Md.)*, *64*, 755–874.

Romero, T. L. (2006). Internet Service Provider's Liability For Online Copyright Infringement: The US Approach. *Vniversitas,* (112), 193-214.

Roos, A. (2012). Privacy in the Facebook Era: A South African Legal Perspective. *The South African Law Journal*, *129*(2), 375–402.

Röschenthaler, U. (2016). 'Be faster than the pirates': Copyright and the revival of 'traditional dances' in south-west Cameroon. In U. Röschenthaler & M. Diawara (Eds.), Copyright Africa: How intellectual property, media and markets transform immaterial cultural goods. Canon Pyon: Sean Kingston.

Röschenthaler, U. (2016). Good Quality or Low Price? Competition between Cameroonian and Chinese traders. *African East-Asian Affairs*. 1: 32-65.

Röschenthaler, U., & Diawara, M. (2016). African intellectual worlds in the making. In Copyright Africa: How intellectual property, media and markets transform immaterial cultural goods. Canon Pyon: Sean Kingston.

Röschenthaler, U. (2011). *Purchasing culture: The dissemination of associations in the Cross River region of Cameroon and Nigeria*. Trenton, NJ: Africa World Press.

Röschenthaler, U., & Schulz, D. (2015). Introduction: Forging fortunes: New perspectives on entrepreneurial activities in Africa. In U. Röschenthaler & D. Schulz (Eds.), *Cultural Entrepreneurship in Africa* (pp. 1–15). London: Routledge.

Rose, M. (2012, September). *Fox 5 New York gets suckered by iPhone 5 concept video*. Engadget.com

Rosen, J. (2008). A Most Useful Definition of Citizen Journalism. *PressThink*. Retrieved from http://journalism.nyu.edu/pubzone/weblogs/pressthink/2008/07/14/a_most_useful

Rosen, J. (2012). The right to be forgotten. *Stanford Law Review*, *64*, 88–92.

Rosin, H. (2014). Hello, My Name is Stephen Glass, and I'm Sorry. *New Republic*. Retrieved from: http://www.newrepublic.com/article/120145/stephen-glass-new-republic-scandal-still-haunts-his-law-career

Rothschild, D. (2009). Forecasting elections comparing prediction markets, polls, and their biases. *Public Opinion Quarterly*, *73*(5), 895–916. doi:10.1093/poq/nfp082

Rule, J. (2004). Toward Strong Privacy: Values, Markets, Mechanisms and Institutions. *University of Toronto Law Journal, 54*(2), 183–225. doi:10.1353/tlj.2004.0008

Runcheva, H. (2013). John Rawls: Justice as Fairness behind a Veil of Ignorance. *Iustinianus Primus Law Review, 4*(2), 1–12.

Rupar, V. (2006). How did you find that out? Transparency of the newsgathering process and the meaning of news. *Journalism Studies, 7*(1), 127–143. doi:10.1080/14616700500450426

Sabine, G. H., & Thorson, T. L. (1973). *A History of Political Thought* (4th ed.). Hinsdale, IL: Dryden Press.

Sanders, K. (2006). *Ethics and Journalism*. London: SAGE.

Saul, H. (2014). *UK porn legislation: What is now banned under new government laws.* Retrieved from http://www.independent.co.uk/news/uk/home-news/uk-porn-legislation-what-is-now-banned-under-new-government-laws-9898541.html

Saunders, C. (2001). From Apartheid to Democracy in Namibia and South Africa: Some Comparisons. Discussion Paper, No. 10. In *Transition in Southern Africa: Comparative Aspects*. Nordic Africa Institute.

Saunderson, D. (2014, April 30). Clifford case 'shows value of naming suspects'. *The Times*, 17.

Sawyer, S., & Tapia, A. (2005). The sociotechnical nature of mobile computing work: Evidence from a study of policing in the United States. *International Journal of Technology and Human Interaction, 1*(3), 1–14. doi:10.4018/jthi.2005070101

Scandalism. (2011, October 11). Retrieved from Scandalism: https://journalismscandals.wordpress.com/2011/10/

Schedule of the Media Council Act. (2013). Retrieved from www.mediacouncil.or.ke

Scheufele, D., & Tewksbury, D. (2007). Framing, agenda setting, and priming: The evolution of three media effects models. *Journal of Communication*, (57): 9–20.

Schifferes, S., & Newman, N. (2013). *Verifying News on the Social Web: Challenges and Prospects.* International World Wide Web Conference Committee. Retrieved 19 September 2016, from http://www2013.wwwconference.org/companion/p875.pdf

Schlesinger, P. (1983). *Televising Terrorism: Political Violence in Popular Culture*. London: Comedia Publishing Company.

Schmidt, E., & Cohen, J. (2010). The Digital Disruption. *Foreign Affairs*.

Schultz, C. J. P., & Achtenhagen, L. (2013). Discouraging Stereotypes? US Newspaper Coverage Of Ethnic Minority Entrepreneurs Before The Economic Downturn. *Journalism*, 1464884912473394.

Schwartz, D. (2003). Professional oversight: Policing the credibility of photojournalism. In L. Gross, J. S. Katz, & J. Ruby (Eds.), *Image Ethics in the Digital Age* (pp. 27–51). Minneapolis, MN: University of Minnesota.

Schwartz, S. (1992). *Universals in the content and structure of values: Theory and empirical tests in 20 countries*. New York, NY: Academic Press.

Sean, M. (1980). *Many Voices, One World*. Ibadan: Nigeria and UNESCO Press, Paris.

Seglin, J. (2001, December 17). *Codes of ethics: Why writing one is not enough.* Poynter Online. Retrieved July 18, 2016, from http://www.poynter.org/content/content_view.asp?id=4697

Semujju, B. (2013). ICT as an engine for community participation: An assessment of Ugandas community media. *International Journal of Information Communication Technologies and Human Development, 5*(1), 20–36. doi:10.4018/jicthd.2013010102

Semujju, B. (2016). Introducing Community Audio Towers as an alternative to Community Radio in Uganda. *Journal of Alternative and Community Media, 1*, 141–153.

Sénécal, M. (1995). Democratisation of the Media: Liberty, Right and Privilege. In B. Tankha (Ed.), *Communications and Democracy: Ensuring Plurality*. Penang: Southbound.

Servaes, J. (2004). Multiple perspectives on development communication. In C. C. Okigbo (Ed.), *Development and Communication in Africa.* Rowman & Littefield Publishers Inc.

Servaes, J., & Lie, R. (2003). Media, globalisation and culture: Issues and trends. *Communicatio. South African Journal for Communication Theory and Research, 29*, 7–23.

Shakuntala, R. (2010). Post-Colonial Theory and Global Media Ethics: A Theoretical Intervention. In Media Ethics Beyond Borders: A Global Perspective (pp. 59-73). New York: Routledge.

Shapiro, R.J., & Pham, N.D. (2007). *Economic Effects of intellectual property-Intensive manufacturing in the United States*. Available at archieve.org

Shemberger, M. (2015). Is The Sun Shining? A Qualitative Study On The Presence Of Sunshine Laws In The College And University Journalism Curriculum. *Journalism & Mass Communication Educator.*

Shephard, A. C. (1994). Identifying juvenile suspects. *American Journalism Review*, 14.

Sherman, S. (2010, August 20). Reporters follow clear policy in naming suspects, victims in crime stories. *The Salt Lake Tribune*.

Shoemaker, P. (1991). *Gatekeeping*. Newbury Park, CA: Sage Publications.

Shoemaker, P., & Reese, S. (1996). *Mediating the message: Theories of influences on mass media content*. New York: Longman.

Sigal, L. (1973). *Reporters and officials: The organization and politics of newsmaking*. Lexington: D.C. Heath.

Sigal, L. (1986). Sources make the news. In R. Manoff & M. Schudson (Eds.), *Reading the news: A pantheon guide to popular culture* (pp. 9–37). New York: Pantheon Books.

Silverman, C., & Perlman, M. (2013). *Verification Handbook: Additional Materials to Verifying Digital Content for Emergency Coverage*. Retrieved 14 September 2016, from http://verificationhandbook.com/downloads/verification.handbook.pdf.

Singh, S. D. (n.d.). *The Genesis and Evolution of the Right to Information in India*. Unpublished Paper.

Skjerdal, T. S. (2010). Research on brown envelope journalism in the African Media. *African Communication Research,* (3), 367-406.

Smiers, J. (1999). Copyrights: A choice of no choice for artists and Third World countries. *Iwalewa Forum, 3*, 5–38.

Smith, J. A. (1988). *Printers and press freedom: The ideology of early American journalism.* New York: Oxford University Press.

Smith, J., Milberg, S., & Burke, S. (1996). Information Privacy: Measuring IndividualsConcerns about Organizational Practices. *Management Information Systems Quarterly, 20*(2), 167–196. doi:10.2307/249477

Smith, M. L., Spence, R., & Rashid, A. T. (2011). Mobile Phones and Expanding Human Capabilities. *Information Technologies & International Development, 7*, 77–88.

Smith, T. W. (2004). Freedom to conduct public opinion polls around the world. *International Journal of Public Opinion Research, 16*(2), 215–223. doi:10.1093/ijpor/16.2.215

Smyth, T. N. (2013). *Social media, elections, and democracy in West Africa* (Unpublished PhD Thesis). Georgia Institute of Technology.

Snider, J. H. (2000). Local TV News Archives As A Public Good. *The Harvard International Journal of Press/Politics, 5*(2), 111–117. doi:10.1177/1081180X00005002010

Sobowale, I. (2008). *Scientific Journalism.* Ago Iwoye: School of communication & Information science, Olabisi Onabanjo University, in conjunction with Idosa Konsult.

Sobowale, I. (1999). Nigerian Press coverage of national issues. In R. Akinfeleye, G. Omole, & O. Omang (Eds.), *Nigerian Mass Media and National Crises*. Lagos: Nigerian Press Council.

Social Trends Institute. (2013). *What society needs from media in the age of digital communication.* Retrieved from https://www.socialtrendsinstitute. org/experts-meetings/civil-society-needs-frommedia-in-the-age-of-digital-communication

Solove, D. (2001). Privacy and Power: Computer Databases and Metaphors for Information Privacy. *Stanford Law Review, 53*(6), 1393–1462. doi:10.2307/1229546

Solove, D. (2004). *The Digital Person: Technology and Privacy in the Digital Age*. New York: New York University Press.

Solove, D. J. (2007). *The future of reputation: Gossip, rumor, and privacy on the Internet*. New Haven, CT: Yale University Press.

Somers, M. (1996). The "misteries" of property: Relationality, rural industrialization, and community in Chartist narratives of political rights. In J. Brewer & S. Staves (Eds.), *Early Modern Conceptions of Property* (pp. 62–90). London: Routledge.

Sophism, Y. (2004). The Role Of Public Opinion Polls In Our Emerging Democracy. *GhanaWeb*. Retrieved from http://www.ghanaweb.com/GhanaHomePage/NewsArchive/The-Role-Of-Public-Opinion-Polls-In-Our-Emerging-Democracy-53816.

SPJ. (2014). SPJ Code of Ethics. *SPJ.* Retrieved from: http://www.spj.org/ethicscode.asp

Sprinello, R. A. (2007, January). Intellectual property rights. *Library Hi Tech, 25*(1), 12–22. doi:10.1108/07378830710735821

St Clair, J. (2015). Doing It For Real: Designing Experiential Journalism Curricula That Prepare Students For The New And Uncertain World Of Journalism Work. *Coolabah, 16*, 122–142.

Staby, J. (1997, September 24). Muzzled off: Motion to curb press freedom. Windhoek Advertiser.

Stamatellos, G. (2007). *Computer Ethics A Global Perspective*. Burlington: Jones & Bartlett Learning, LLC.

Stanford Encyclopaedia of Philosophy. (2005). *Human Rights*. Retrieved from http://plato.standord.edu/entries/rights -human/

Steele, B. (2003). Genuinely torn. *The American Editor, 78*(6), 8–9.

Steele, B., & Black, J. (1999). Can you improve your code of ethics? (or create a good one if you don't have one?). *American Editor, 74*(2), 4.

Steele, B., Black, J., & Barney, R. D. (1998). *Doing ethics in journalism: A handbook with case studies* (3rd ed.). Boston, MA: Allyn & Bacon.

Stegmaier, M., & Norpoth, H. (2013). *Election forecasting*. Academic Press.

Strauss, D. L. (2011). *Doctored photos: The art of the altered image*. Retrieved March 12, 2016, from http://time.com/3778075/doctored-photos-the-art-of-the-altered-image/

Strauss, D. L. (2003). *Essays on Photography and Politics*. New York: Aperture.

Strentz, H. (1989). *News reporters and news sources: Accomplices in shaping and misshaping the news* (2nd ed.). Ames, IA: Iowa State University Press.

Strömbäck, J. (2012). *The media and their use of opinion polls: Reflecting and shaping public opinion. In Opinion Polls and the Media* (pp. 1–22). Springer. doi:10.1057/9780230374959_1

Sturges, P. (2006). Limits to Freedom of Expression?Considerations arising from the Danish cartoons affair. *IFLA Journal*, *32*(3), 181–188. doi:10.1177/0340035206070164

Sturges, P. (2009). Information ethics in the twenty first century. *Australian Academic & Research Libraries*, *40*(4), 241–251. doi:10.1080/00048623.2009.10721415

Sundaram, R. (2010). *Pirate modernity: Dehli's media urbanism*. London: Routledge.

Taylor, A. (2006). Publishing And Electronic Piracy. *Learned Publishing*, *19*(3), 168–174. doi:10.1087/095315106777877539

Taylor, N. (2002). State Surveillance and the Right to Privacy. *Surveillance & Society*, *1*(1), 66–85.

Tcheuyap, A. (2016). Music for everyone: The dynamics of piracy in Cameroon generations in Mali. In U. Röschenthaler & M. Diawara (Eds.), Copyright Africa: How intellectual property, media and markets transform immaterial cultural goods. Canon Pyon: Sean Kingston.

Telhami, S. (2012). *What Do Egyptians Want?* Brookings: Key Findings from the Egyptian Public Opinion Poll.

The Chronicle. (2015). *Us Paper Says Sorry to President Mugabe*. Retrieved 12 November 2016, from http://www.chronicle.co.zw/us-paper-says-sorry-to-president-mugabe/

The Herald. (2014, November 14). NYTimes Scribe Apologises. *The Herald.*

The Namibian. (1997, September 22). MPs urged to reject law 'which is set to suffocate democracy …'". *The Namibian.*

The Namibian. (2016, June 17). Editorial: Right to Privacy does not equate to Secrecy. *The Namibian*, p. 11.

The National Press Photographers Code of Ethics. (n.d.). Retrieved August 18, 2015, from http://www.nppa.org/professional_development/business_practices/ethics.html

The New York Times. (2004). *Ethical Journalism: A handbook of Values and Practice for the News and Editorial Department.* Retrieved 12 September 2016, from http://www.nytco.com/wp-content/uploads/NYT_Ethical_Journalism_0904-1.pdf

The New York Times. (2015). *Debating the Rules and Ethics of Digital Photojournalism*. Retrieved July 22, 2016, from http://lens.blogs.nytimes.com/2015/02/17/world-press-photo-manipulation-ethics-of-digital-photojournalism/?module=BlogPost-Title&version=Blog+Main&contentCollection=Mutlimedia&action=Click&pgtype=Blogs&region=Body&_r=2

The New York Times. (2015, October 16). *Staging, Manipulation and Truth in Photography*. Retrieved July, 23, 2016, from http://lens.blogs.nytimes.com/2015/10/16/staging-manipulation-ethics-photos/

The Reuters Photo Scandal. (2006). *A Taxonomy of Photo Fraud Committed by Reuters*. Retrieved August 20, 2015, from www.zombietime.com/reuters_photo_fraud/

The Southern Times. (2016, April 12). Harambee Prosperity Plan ... a guide in Namibia's quest to be Africa's competitive economy by 2020. *The Namibian.*

The Standard. (2015). *Police Hunt Journalist Over Mugabe Offensive Story*. Retrieved from http://www.thestandard.co.zw/2015/11/15/police-hunt-journalist-over-mugabe-offensive-story/

The Washington Post Standard and Ethics. (n.d.). Retrieved August 25, 2015, from asne.org>Ethics

The World Bank. (2014). *Uganda Economic Review/Performance*. Retrieved from http://www.worldbank.org/en/country/uganda/overview

Theisohn, P. (2009). *Plagiat: Eine unoriginelle Literaturgeschichte*. Stuttgart: Alfred Kröner.

Thomas, P., & Nyamnjoh, F. (2007). Intellectual property challenges in Africa: Indigenous property systems and the fate of connected worlds. In I. Mazonde & P. Thomas (Eds.), *Indigenous knowledge systems and intellectual property in the twenty-first century: Perspectives from Southern Africa* (pp. 12–25). Dakar: CODESRIA.

Tjihenuna, T. (2016, June 14). Hold us accountable. *The Namibian.*

Traugott, M. (2012). *Methodological trends and controversies in the media's use of opinion polls. In Opinion Polls and the Media* (pp. 69–89). Springer.

Tribune, C. (2014). *Anti-terrorism Bill: Gov't Give Clarifications*. Retrieved from www.cameroon-tribune.cm

Tuchman, G. (1973). Making news by doing work: Routinizing the unexpected. *American Journal of Sociology*, *79*(1), 110–131. doi:10.1086/225510

Tuchman, G. (1978). Introduction: The symbolic annihilation of women by the mass media. In G. Tuchman, A. Kaplan Daniels, & J. Benét (Eds.), *Heart and home: Images of women in the mass media*. New York: Oxford University Press.

Tunman, J. S. (2003). *Communicating Terror: The Rhetorical Dimensions of Terrorism*. London: Sage.

Uche, L. U. (1989). *Mass Media, People and Politics in Nigeria*. New Delhi: Concept Publishing Company.

Uganda Bureau of Statistics. (2015). *Statistical abstract*. Kampala: UBOS.

Uganda Communications Commission. (2015). *Status of the Communications Market*. Kampala: UCC.

Uganda. (1950). The Penal Code Act 1950.

Uganda. (1995). The Constitution.

Uganda. (1995). The Press and Journalist Act 1995.

Uganda. (2002). Anti-Terrorism Act.

Uganda. (2014). The Anti-Pornography Act 2014.

Ugo, S. C. (2004). Electoral Malpractice and violence in 2003 Elections in Nigeria. *Unilag Journal of Politics*, *1*(1), 164–186.

Umar, M. M. (2003). The role of youths and politicians in political violence in North-East Nigeria. In B. O. Olasupo (Ed.), *Electoral Violence in Nigeria: Issues and Perspectives*. Lagos: Friedrich Ebert Stiftung.

United Kingdom Human Rights Act (1998). (n.d.). Retrieved from www.justice.gov.uk/human-rights

University of Namibia. (2008). *Service Delivery Survey Report for the Ministry of Information and Broadcasting*. Multi-Disciplinary Research Centre.

Upson, S. (2016). WikiLeaks has morphed from journalism hotshot to malware hub. *BackChannel*. Retrieved from https://backchannel.com/wikileaks-has-morphed-from-journalism-hotshot-to-malware-hub-1bdd68cc560#.fz4qcvnk6

US Council for Intellectual Business. (1985). *A new MTN: Priorities for intellectual property*. Available at www.uscib.org/

US Government. (n.d.). *Human Rights in Brief*. Bureau of International Information Programmes, US Department of State. Retrieved from http://www.america.gov/

Uwalaka, A E. (2000). *Ethics of Political Leadership*. Lagos: Techsarap Communications.

Uys, P. (2009). Africa's second communications revolution. *Global-ICT*, *2009*, 11.

Venice. (2008, January 12). *Nur das Original zählt. Venedig bleibt einzigartig*. Retrieved January 12, 2016, from http://www.n-tv.de/reise/Venedig-bleibt-einzigartig-article286891.html

Verbeek, P. (2015). The Struggle for Technology: Towards a Realistic Political Theory of Technology. *Foundations of Science*. doi:10.1007/s10699-015-9470-7

Verweij, P. (2009). Making Convergence Work in the Newsroom A Case Study of Convergence of Print, Radio, Television and Online Newsrooms at the African Media Matrix in South Africa During the National Arts Festival. *Convergence (London)*, *15*(1), 75–87. doi:10.1177/1354856508097020

Vieira, J. D. (1991). Terrorism at the BBC: The IRA on British television. In Media coverage of terrorism, methods of diffusion. London: Sage Publications.

Vipond, M. (2000). *The mass media in Canada*. Lorimer and Company.

Voice, M. (2013). *MEC cautions media on opinion polls. Some pollsters have questionable credentials, produce questionable statistics*. Malawi Voice.

Vultee, F. (2010). Credibility as a strategic ritual: The Times, the interrogator, and the duty of naming. *Journal of Mass Media Ethics*, *25*(1), 3–18. doi:10.1080/08900521003621975

Wachira, G. (2013). 10 lessons for Kenya from the 2013 General Election. *Business Daily*. Retrieved from http://www.businessdailyafrica.com/Opinion-and-Analysis/-/539548/1737838/-/py76ac/-/index.html.

Wack, R. (1979). The Rights of privacy by John H.F. Shattuck 1977, The Law of Privacy inSouth Africa by David Jan Mcquoldmason 1978 Review. *The Modern Law Review*, *42*(5), 587–608.

Walter, A. S. (2013). Women on the battleground: Does gender condition the use of negative campaigning? *Journal of Elections, Public Opinion, and Parties*, *23*(2), 154–176. doi:10.1080/17457289.2013.769107

Wane, I. (2016). Wrestling, the media and marketing: When folklore meets show business. In Copyright Africa: How intellectual property, media and markets transform immaterial cultural goods. Canon Pyon: Sean Kingston.

Wang, D. (2008). Globalization of the Media: Does It Undermine National Cultures. *Intercultural Communication Studies*, *17*, 203–211.

Warburton, N. (1998). Ethical photojournalism and the electronic darkroom. In M. Kieran (Ed.), *Media Ethics* (pp. 123–134). London: Routledge.

Ward, S. J. A. (2008). Global Journalism Ethics: Widening the Conceptual Base. Global Media Journal, 1(1), 137-149.

Ward, S. J. A. (2010). A Theory of Patriotism for Global Journalism. In Media Ethics Beyond Borders: A Global Perspective (pp. 42-58). New York: Routledge.

Ward, S. J. A. (2010). Ethics for the New Mainstream. In The New Journalist: Roles and Skills, and Critical Thinking (pp. 313-326). Toronto: Edmond Montgomery Publications.

Ward, S. J. A. (n.d.). *Digital Media Ethics*. Retrieved 14 September 2016 from https://ethics.journalism.wisc.edu/resources/global-media-ethics/

Ward, S. J. A. (2010). *Global Journalism Ethics*. Montreal: McGill-Queen's University Press.

Ward, S. J. A. (2013). Media Ethics as Global. In S. J. A. Ward (Ed.), *Global Media Ethics: Problems and Perspectives*. West Sussex, UK: Wiley-Blackwell Publishers.

Ward, S. J. A., & Wasserman, H. (2010). *Media Ethics: Beyond Borders: A Global Prospective*. New York: Taylor and Francis.

Warren, K. F. (2001). *In defense of public opinion polling*. Westview Press.

Warren, S., & Brandeis, L. (1890). The right to privacy. *Harvard Law Review*, *14*(5), 193–220. doi:10.2307/1321160

Washington Post Writer's Group Messages. (1990). *The Washington Post Media Companion*. Allyn & Bacon.

Watiri, S. (2015). *New York Times Journalist Forced to Apologise for Publishing Part of the Fake Mugabe Story That Triggered KOT's War Against Mugabe*. Retrieved 12 August 2016, from http://www.ghafla.co.ke/blogs/tv/4204-ny-tiumes-responds

Weasley, M. (2015, February 5). *Daily Kos*. Retrieved October 27, 2015, from dailykos.com: http://www.dailykos.com/story/2015/02/05/1362540/

Weinsten, W. (1983). Human Rights and Development in Africa: Dilemmas and Options. *Daedalus*, *112*(4), 171–196.

Wei, R. (2008). Motivations for using the mobile phone for mass communications and entertainment. *Telematics and Informatics*, *25*(1), 36–46. doi:10.1016/j.tele.2006.03.001

Weiss, A. S. (2013). Exploring news apps and location-based services on the smartphone. *Journalism & Mass Communication Quarterly*, *90*(3), 435–456. doi:10.1177/1077699013493788

Wesaka, A. (2014). *Local singer Kansiime further remanded to Luzira over porn song*. Retrieved from http://www.monitor.co.ug/News/National/Local-singer-Kansiime-further-remanded-to-Luzira-over-porn-song/-/688334/2521220/-/naixug/-/index.html

Westin, A. F., & Baker, M. A. (1972). *Databanks in a free society: Computers, record-keeping, and privacy*. New York: Quadrangle Books.

White, A. (2001). Setting standards. *Unesco Sources*, (134): 11.

White, R. (2011). *Are Tanzanian journalists accepting bribes?*. Dar es Salaam: Media Council of Tanzania.

Wigston, D. (2009). Qualitative content analysis. In P. J. Fourie (Ed.), *Media Studies: Media Content and Media Audiences* (Vol. 3, pp. 3–38). Cape Town: Juta.

Wilhelm, A. (2000). *Democracy in the digital age*. London: Routledge.

Wilkins, L., & Brennen, B. (2004). Conflicted interests, contested terrain: Journalism ethics codes then and now. *Journalism Studies*, *5*(3), 297–309. doi:10.1080/1461670042000246061

Wilkins, L., & Christians, C. (Eds.). (2008). *The Handbook of Mass Media Ethics*. New York: Routledge.

Willnat, L., Lo, V.-h., & Aw, A. (2012). *The good, the bad and the ugly: Public opinion polling in Taiwan. In Opinion Polls and the Media* (pp. 198–222). Springer. doi:10.1057/9780230374959.0016

WIPO IGC. (2008). *Protection of traditional knowledge: Draft gap analysis*. Revision 4. WIPO Doc. WIPO/GRTKF/IC/13/5/6b Rev. Retrieved from http://www.wipo.int/edocs/mdocs/tk/en/wipogrtufic13/wipogrtkfic135b

WIPO. (2007). *Measuring the economic impact of IP systems*. Retrieved from http://www.wipo.int/portal/en/news/2007/article0032html

WIPO. (2008). *Intellectual property Handbook: Policy, law and use*. Retrieved from http://www.wipo.int>pubdocs>wipo_pub_450pdf

Wlezien, C., Jennings, W., Fisher, S., Ford, R., & Pickup, M. (2013). Polls and the Vote in Britain. *Political Studies*, *61*(S1), 66–91. doi:10.1111/1467-9248.12008

WMEA. (2012, September 19). *Mutoko On Monday: When Borrowing Goes Over The Line*. Retrieved from Wired Magazine - East Africa: https://web.facebook.com/Wired.EastAfrica/posts/480763305281214

Wolf, R. (2012). *Austrian Newspaper Apologizes for Fake Syria Photo*. Belmont, CA: Wadsworth.

Wood, M. (2013). *Social Media as Breaking –News Feed Worse, Faster*. Retrieved from13 September 2016.https://www.cnet.com/news/social-media-as-breaking-news-feed-worse-information-faster/

Wright, M. J., Farrar, D. P., & Russell, D. F. (2013). Polling accuracy in a multiparty election. *International Journal of Public Opinion Research.*

Wuthnow, R. (2015). IN POLLS WE TRUST. *First Things (New York, N.Y.)*, *39*(255). Retrieved from http://www.abc.net.au/radionational/programs/theminefield/in-polls-we-trust3f/6654686

Yilma, M., & Birhanu, A. (2013). Safeguards of Right to Privacy in Ethiopia: A Critique of Laws and Practices. *Journal of Ethiopian Law*, *26*(1), 94–152.

Yin, R. K. (2004). *Case Study Research Methods*. Unpublished Draft Paper. Retrieved 15 July 2016, from http://www.cosmoscorp.com/docs/aeradraft.pdf

Zainal, Z. (2007). Case Study as Research Method. *Journal Kemanusian bil*. Retrieved 12 August 2016 from http://eprints.utm.my/8221/3/ZaidahZainal2007_CaseStudyasaResearchMethod.pdf

Zaller, J. (1992). *The nature and origins of mass opinion*. New York: Cambridge University Press. doi:10.1017/CBO9780511818691

Zerback, T., Reinemann, C., & Nienierza, A. (2015). Whos Hot and Whos Not? Factors Influencing Public Perceptions of Current Party Popularity and Electoral Expectations. *The International Journal of Press/Politics*, *20*(4), 458–477. doi:10.1177/1940161215596986

Zetterberg, H. L. (2004). *US Election 1948: The First Great Controversy about Polls, Media, and Social Science*. Paper presented at the WAPOR regional conference on Elections, News Media and Public Opinion, Pamplona, Spain.

Zongo, G. (2001). *ICTs for Development in Africa*. Retrieved from http://www.unssc.org/web1/programmes/glnp

Zucker, D. M. (2009). *How to do case Study Research*. School of Nursing Faculty Publication Series Paper 2. Retrieved 6 July 2016 from http://scholarworks.umass.edu/nursing_faculty_pubs/2

About the Contributors

Nhamo Anthony Mhiripiri is an Associate Professor in the department of Media and Society Studies at the Midlands State University (MSU), Zimbabwe and a Visiting Lecturer at St Augustine University, Tanzania. He has also lectured at the Centre for Communication and Media Studies at the University of KwaZulu-Natal, and the Zimbabwe Open University. He was founding Acting Dean of the Faculty of Arts and Social Sciences at MSU. He has also done consultancy work for various media organisations. He studied English and History, and Masters degree in Communications and Media Studies at the University of Zimbabwe, before doing doctoral and postdoctoral studies in Media and Cultural Studies with the University of KwaZulu-Natal, Durban. He has a wide range of interests in media and cultural studies, and is a widely published scholar. He has co-edited African Football, Identity Politics and Global Media Narratives: The legacy of the FIFA 2010 World Cup . He was a member of the Information and Media Panel of Inquiry (IMPI) appointed by the Zimbabwe government. In 2015 he was nominated and interviewed to be a member of the Zimbabwe Media Commission.

Tendai Chari is a Lecturer at the University of Venda, South Africa. He holds a PhD from Wits University, South Africa. Previously, he lectured at the University of Zimbabwe (where he was Coordinator of the Media Programme in the English Department) Zimbabwe Open University (ZOU), National University of Science and Technology (NUST) (Zimbabwe) and Fort Hare University (South Africa). He is widely published in the field of Media Studies and specializes in political communication, media ethics, and new media and politics. His publications have appeared in the journal of African Media Studies, African Identities, Communicatio: South African Journal for Communication Theory and Research, Ecquid Novi: Journal of African Media Studies and the Journal on Media and Communications. He co-edited the book African Football, Identity Politics and Global Media Narratives: The Legacy of the FIFA 2010 World Cup. He served as the Chairman of the Zimbabwe Television (ZTV) a Board Member of the Zimbabwe Broadcast Holdings (ZBH) as well as a Member of the Media Commission (MIC) in Zimbabwe.

* * *

Ufuoma Akpojivi is a senior lecturer in the Media Studies Department, University of the Witwatersrand, South Africa. He holds a PhD and an M.A. in Communications Studies from the University of Leeds United Kingdom, and a B.A. in Mass Communication from Delta State University, Nigeria. His research interests cut across but are not limited to media policy, new media and citizens' participation, citizenship, political economy of the media, public relations, advertising, marketing, journalism ethics and practices from the global south amongst others.

Benjamin Assay teaches mass communication at Delta State Polytechnic, Ogwashi-Uku, Nigeria. He holds BA and MA degrees in mass communication from Delta State University, Abraka and University of Nigeria, Nsukka respectively. Currently he is a doctoral candidate of mass communication, Benue State University, Makurdi, Nigeria. He has published articles in scholarly journals and contributed chapters in several books. His research interests are in information and communication technology and national development, international communication and comparative media studies, media, democracy and good governance, population communication and health communication, and public relations and advertising. He is a member of several professional bodies, including African Council for Communication Education (ACCE) Nigeria chapter, Advertising Practitioners Council of Nigeria (APCON), Association of Communication Scholars and Professionals of Nigeria (ACSPN), Nigeria Institute of Public Relations (NIPR) Association for Promoting Nigerian Languages and Culture (APNILAC), National Association for Research Development (NARD), among others.

Jonathan Bishop is an information technology executive, researcher and writer. He founded the Centre for Research into Online Communities and E-Learning Systems in 2005, now part of the Crocels Community Media Group. Jonathan's research and development work generally falls within human-computer interaction. He has over 75 publications in this area, including on Internet trolling, cyber-stalking, gamification, cyberlaw, multimedia forensics, Classroom 2.0 and Digital Teens. In addition to his BSc(Hons) in Multimedia Studies and various postgraduate degrees, including in law, economics and computing, Jonathan serves in local government as a councillor, and has been a school governor and contested numerous elections, including to the UK Parliament. He is a fellow of numerous learned bodies, including BCS, CILIP, the InstAM, the RAI, the RSS and the RSA. Jonathan has won prizes for his literary skills and been a finalist in national and local competitions for his environmental, community and equality work, which often form part of action research studies. In his spare time Jonathan enjoys listening to music, swimming and chess.

Robin Blom is an Assistant Professor of journalism and graduate studies director at Ball State University where he teaches news reporting, business journalism, media theory, and media law courses. He earned degrees from the Hogeschool van Utrecht, The Netherlands (B.A., 2004), Point Park University (M.A., 2007), and Michigan State University (Ph.D., 2013). Robin has been a reporter for several regional and national daily newspapers in The Netherlands. His research interests include news media perceptions, memory and cognition, misinformation, and journalism education. This has led to publications in edited books and several journals, such as *American Behavioral Scientist, Journalism and Mass Communication Educator,* and the *International Journal of Interactive Communication Systems and Technologies.*

Jacqueline Chikakano is a Legal Programme Officer with the Media Institute of Southern Africa -Zimbabwe Chapter. She graduated with an LLB (Hons) degree from the University of Zimbabwe. She also holds a qualification in Broadcasting Policy and Regulatory Trends from the University of Witwatersrand. She has also worked as a Magistrate and later as a Legal Officer for the Zimbabwe Women Lawyers Association. She was a Coordinator of the African Platform on Access to Information. In 2014 she was a member of the Zimbabwe government appointed Information and Media Panel of Inquiry (IMPI) where she served as Committee Chairperson for the IMPI Thematic Committee on Media Law Reform and Access to Information.

Bevelyn Dube is a Senior Lecturer in the Department of Communication and Applied Language Studies at the University of Venda in South Africa where she teaches Media Economics, Mass Media Theory and Mass Communication Research Methodology. She holds a DPhil (Journalism) from Stellenbosch University in South Africa and an MA in English from the University of Zimbabwe. Her research interests are in journalism education, media law and ethics and mass media theory.

William Heuva is affiliated to the North West University in South Africa, where is the Head of Sub-School of Communication at the Mafikeng Campus. He holds BA, BA (Hons) and MA in Journalism and Media Studies (Rhodes University) and a PhD in Cultural and Media Studies (UKZN). He is the author of *Media and Resistance Politics: The Alternative Press in Namibia, 1960-1990*. Basel: P. Schlettwein Publishing (2001) and *Transforming Communication in a Changing Milieu: Challenges and Contradictions of Reform in Namibia*. LAP Lambert Academic Publishing (2010).

Adebayo Fayoyin is an expert in political advocacy, communication for development and corporate communications. He has over 20 years of professional experience in various communication capacities in development agencies including USAID, UNICEF and UNFPA. He currently serves as the regional communications adviser for UNFPA East and Southern Africa providing oversight and technical assistance in strategic communication. He has also held full-time and honorary faculty positions in communication institutions in Nigeria, Kenya and South Africa. He holds a PhD in communication and language arts from the University of Ibadan, Nigeria.

Afu Isaiah Kunock is a Lecturer in the Department of Anthropology of the University of Yaounde I, Cameroon. He obtained his PhD from the University of Yaounde I in 2014 for a dissertation on media and migration among the Moghamo people in the North-west Region of Cameroon. Among his research areas are internal and international migration, media, and development in Cameroon.

Agnes Lucy Lando is a PhD holder in Social Communication from the Pontifical Gregorian University, Rome; Associate Professor of Communication and Media Studies; and member of Ethics Review Board at Daystar University. She is the 2013 co-recipient of the George Gerbner Excellence Award; and consults for academic, governmental and NGOs. In addition to being External Examiner, adjunct professor and consultant for a number of Universities in Eastern Africa, Lando is also the founder and Patroness of Master Communicators Welfare Association (MCWA). In 2013, she successfully convened the 3rd East African Communication Association Conference (EACA) (Nairobi). Lando makes history as the first African to be elected to the Board of the prestigious International Communication Association (ICA) as Board Member-at-Large. Further, she successfully convened the first ICA Africa Regional Conference in Nairobi in October 2016. She has authored over 25 scholarly articles, books, book chapters, monographs; and academic papers. In addition, Lando has edited chapters in various peer reviewed books, and is also a reviewer for a number scholarly journals.

Ibitayo Popoola, a Political Communication scholar teaches at the World Bank Centre of Excellence in Multi-Media & Cinematography, UNESCO Centre of Excellence in Journalism and Media Training in Africa, Department of Mass Communication, University of Lagos. He holds amongst others, a first degree in Political Science, Second Class Upper Division, PGD & M.Sc in Mass Communication, M.Sc in Political Science as well as Ph.D degree in Political Science. He has published widely in reputable local and foreign journals including several chapter contributions in textbooks. Amongst places he has published are: USA, Great Britain, India, United Arab Emirate (UAE), South Africa, Kenya, Botswana, Namibia, and Ghana. He is the author of the following textbooks: *Introduction to Government (2001), GSM as a Tool for News Reporting in Nigeria (2003), Public Relations, Advertising and Promotions (2009), Specialized Reporting, A Global Trend in Media Training Vol.1 (2012), Specialized Reporting, A Global Trend in Media Training Vol. 2 (2013)* and many more.

Ute Röschenthaler is Professor of Social and Cultural Anthropology at the Johannes Gutenberg University Mainz. She is scientific collaborator in the Cluster of Excellence "The Formation of Normative Orders" and in the project "Africa's Asian Options" at the Goethe University Frankfurt. Among her research specialities are cultural mobility, cult associations, intellectual property, media and networks between Africa and Asia. Her most recent publications include *Copyright Africa: How Intellectual Property, Media and Markets Transform Immaterial Cultural Goods*, edited with Mamadou Diawara (Sean Kingston Publishing 2016), *Cultural Entrepreneurship in Africa*, edited with Dorothea Schulz (London: Routledge, 2016) and "Dressed in Photographs: Between Uniformization, Self-enhancement and the Promotion of Stars and Leaders in Bamako" (*Africa* 85, 2015, 4).

Collen Sabao is an American Council of Learned Societies' (ACLS) African Humanities Programme (AHP) Postdoctoral Fellow of Linguistics in the African Languages Department at Stellenbosch University, South Africa, and a Senior Lecturer of Pure and Applied linguistics in the Department of English and Communication at Midlands State University, Zimbabwe.

Brian Semujju lectures at Uganda Christian University and Makerere University. He is also a PhD candidate at the Centre for Communication and Media Studies, University of KwaZulu-Natal (South Africa). Currently, Brian is working on projects in the field of communication theory, climate change and development communication. Brian has reviewed articles for the *Journal of African Media Studies* and the *Journal of Community Informatics*. His publications have appeared in journals like: *Feminist Media Studies, International Communication Gazette, Journal of African Media Studies,* and the *International Journal of Information Communication Technologies and Human Development.*

Index

G

H

I

J

M

N

P

www.ingramcontent.com/pod-product-compliance
Lightning Source LLC
LaVergne TN
LVHW060418300926
849162LV00006B/1459